DOCUMENTS AND READINGS
in the
HISTORY OF EUROPE
SINCE 1918

Documents and Readings in the History of Europe Since 1918

By
WALTER CONSUELO LANGSAM, Ph.D.
UNION COLLEGE

With the Assistance of
JAMES MICHAEL EAGAN, Ph.D.
COLLEGE OF NEW ROCHELLE

J. B. LIPPINCOTT COMPANY
CHICAGO   PHILADELPHIA   NEW YORK

To
Eaton and Geoffrey

FOREWORD

This volume aims at providing, in convenient form, the exact texts of some of the most important documents and illustrative reading materials relevant to the general course on the history of Europe since 1918. The collection therefore includes treaties, pacts, conventions, constitutions, laws, court decisions, manifestoes, proclamations, party programs, authoritative narrative descriptions, speeches, examples of propaganda, and other items thought to be of interest and value in any serious study of the major developments in post-World War Europe. It is hoped that the teacher and student, in large colleges and small (and, for that matter, the intelligent general reader), may here find the basic "sources" essential to an accurate understanding of the recent background of current happenings.

The fundamental arrangement within chapters is chronological and topical, paralleling the organization adopted in the editor's *The World since 1914*. The introductory remarks preceding each item are intended to supply additional information not always easy of access, explain the origin and importance of the document, or indicate the reason for its inclusion in the series. Normally, the spelling forms of the original reference have been adhered to. Because of the limitation of space, some of the longer items have been reproduced in extract rather than in full. Resulting omissions are indicated by appropriate symbols: four dots (. . . .) indicate the omission of the remainder of a paragraph or an article; five dots (. . . . .) indicate the omission of one or more entire paragraphs or articles. Occasionally, in order to call the attention of the reader to alternative sources, similar items, such as treaties, are quoted from varying types of sources.

W. C. L.

Schenectady, N. Y.

CONTENTS

CHAPTER 2:   THE LEAGUE OF NATIONS

CHAPTER 4: SECURITY AND ARMAMENTS

CHAPTER 6: FRANCE

CHAPTER 9: GREAT GERMANY

CHAPTER 10: THE SOVIET UNION

xvi

DOCUMENTS AND READINGS
in the
HISTORY OF EUROPE
SINCE 1918

CHAPTER 1

THE PARIS PEACE SETTLEMENT

1. THE CHOICE OF A CONFERENCE CITY [1]

The selection of Paris as host to the peace conference after the World War had far-reaching consequences. The factors determining this choice were well summarized by Dr. George B. Noble, a member of the American Commission to Negotiate Peace.

The selection of Paris as the center of peace negotiations at the close of the World War had an important bearing on subsequent conference events. A number of cities had been under consideration by the Entente leaders for the honor of being host to the Peace Conference: London, Brussels, The Hague, Geneva and Lausanne as well as Versailles, or Paris. President Wilson at first favored Lausanne or Geneva, and Lloyd George agreed with Colonel House that the Conference should not be held on French soil, but rather in a neutral environment, preferably Geneva; while Orlando of Italy, promised to favor the American choice.

The French, however, were not to be casually brushed aside. Did not her sufferings entitle France to this honor? Was it not the Hall of Mirrors, in Versailles, in which the German Empire had been proclaimed in 1871? Where, unless in Berlin itself, could the collapse of the Bismarckian dream be more fittingly celebrated? When the matter was discussed between Clemenceau, Lloyd George and Colonel House, on October 29 [1918], the French Premier was determined that the peace should be consummated at Versailles. There was little public discussion of this subject, but the French point of view was shrewdly presented in the semi-official *Temps* (Nov. 3), in what was probably an inspired leader. "The city chosen as the seat of the Congress should be chosen because of its sacrifices, its heroism and martyrdom, or because of its

---

[1] From G. B. Noble, *Policies and Opinions at Paris, 1919. Wilsonian Diplomacy, the Versailles Peace, and French Public Opinion*, New York, 1935, pp. 1-3. By permission of The Macmillan Company, publishers.

3

history, and of past events which lend meaning and significance to those of today." Brussels might have been chosen for "noble and just reasons." Nevertheless, the choice should fall upon Versailles, said the *Temps,* not only because France had "borne the heaviest and bloodiest share of the war," but also for the reason that since Versailles had been "the cradle of the German Empire," it ought also to be "its grave." Mr. Wilson yielded, doubtless as a friendly gesture to France, and on November 8 cabled his acceptance of Versailles to Colonel House.

In actual fact, Paris, with its superior accommodations, became the center of deliberations between the Allied and Associated Powers, though the treaty was finally signed in the Hall of Mirrors at Versailles.

The choice of Paris meant that the French people, who had so vital a stake in the peace settlement, were to furnish "the atmosphere wherein the Peace Conference decisions" were to be taken. This was important because of the peculiar degree to which, in France, more than in any other great country, the driving force of opinion is concentrated in the nation's chief city, from which a multiplicity of newspapers and other instrumentalities dominate the national scene. The Conference was thus peculiarly exposed to the winds of French opinion, the significance of which was heightened by the fact that President Wilson and Premier Clemenceau often found themselves in almost fatal disagreement over major peace policies.

The decision was subsequently the source of regrets in Anglo-American quarters. Colonel House later confessed that it would have been better to locate the Conference elsewhere, away from the "intrigues of Paris"; and Seymour wrote: "We were hampered by the atmosphere of Paris. . . . Everyone was afraid of being called a pro-German." Mr. Wilson's threat in early February to have the Conference moved from Paris was indicative of his subsequent feelings, and Lloyd George, during the turbulent days of late March, bitterly remarked to the Council of Ten that the atmosphere of Paris was becoming intolerable.

卍 卍 卍

2. A BUSY DAY FOR PRESIDENT WILSON AT THE PARIS PEACE CONFERENCE [2]

The leading delegates at the Paris Peace Conference found it necessary to keep time-consuming engagements with many officials of more or less importance and with numerous representatives of semi-official and private organizations. Herewith is reproduced President Wilson's schedule for April 17, 1919—a fairly busy day.

11:00 A.M. Dr. Wellington Koo, to present the Chinese Delegation to the Peace Conference.

11:10 A.M. Marquis de Vogué and a delegation of seven others, representing the *Congrès Français,* to present their view as to the disposition of the left bank of the Rhine.

11:30 A.M. Assyrian and Chaldean Delegation, with a message from the Assyrian-Chaldean nation.

11:45 A.M. Dalmatian Delegation, to present to the President the result of the plebiscite of that part of Dalmatia occupied by Italians.

Noon M. Bucquet, Chargé d'Affaires of San Marino, to convey the action of the Grand Council of San Marino, conferring on the President Honorary Citizenship in the Republic of San Marino.

12:10 P.M. M. Colonder, Swiss Minister of Foreign Affairs.

12:20 P.M. Miss Rose Schneiderman and Miss Mary Anderson, delegates of the National Women's Trade-Union League of the United States.

12:30 P.M. The Patriarch of Constantinople, the head of the Orthodox Eastern Church.

12:45 P.M. Essad Pasha, delegate of Albania, to present the claims of Albania.

1:00 P.M. M. M. L. Coromilas, Greek Minister at Rome, to pay his respects.

Luncheon Mr. Newton D. Baker, Secretary of War.

4:00 P.M. Mr. Herbert Hoover.

4:15 P.M. M. Bratianu, of the Rumanian Delegation.

[2] *The Daily Mail,* Paris Edition, April 18, 1919. Quoted in E. J. Dillon, *The Inside Story of the Peace Conference,* Harper & Brothers, New York, 1920, p. 111n.

4:30 P.M.   Dr. Alfonso Costa, former Portuguese Minister, Portuguese
             Delegate to the Peace Conference.
4:45 P.M.   M. Boghos Nubar Pasha, president of the Armenian Na-
             tional Delegation, accompanied by M. A. Aharoman and
             Professor A. Der Hagopian, of Robert College.
5:15 P.M.   M. Pashich, of the Serbian Delegation.
5:30 P.M.   Mr. Frank Walsh, of the Irish-American Delegation.

3. AN AMERICAN DELEGATE'S CRITICISM OF THE METHODS OF
                 THE PEACE CONFERENCE [3]

*To their dismay, the Central Powers were excluded from the deliberations
of the Paris Peace Conference. Their governments recalled that President
Wilson in a speech of January 22, 1917, before the United States Senate, had
extolled the virtues of a negotiated over an imposed peace and had argued
that the only durable peace was a "peace between equals," a "peace without
victory"; but now the victors were of a different mind. The responsibility for
and consequences of this action were ably commented upon by Professor
James T. Shotwell, a member of the American Delegation.*

It is not too much to say that the Peace Conference never met. The
Conference of Paris was a meeting of the enemies of the Central Powers,
which dictated treaties for each of the ex-enemy States and hardly listened at all to their protests against the conditions imposed upon them.
To the post-war generation in every country this fact seems now almost
as incredible as it did to the leaders of liberal Germany at the time.
They had dared to hope that a peace based upon the Wilsonian program
would offer the new German Republic an opportunity to co-operate to
the full in building the structure of a world community. Instead, they
were not only rebuffed in their efforts to negotiate but the members of
their Delegation suffered the personal humiliation of ostracism in their
retreat at the Hôtel des Réservoirs at Versailles. For this treatment the
French Government was immediately responsible. But the responsibility rests as well upon a war-worn public opinion in England and America, benumbed by suffering and exhausted by both the effort of the war
and the long strain of overwrought emotions. There was no wide move-

[3] From J. T. Shotwell, *At the Paris Peace Conference*, New York, 1937, pp. 41-44. By
permission of The Macmillan Company, publishers.

ment of opinion against the treatment of the ex-enemy Delegations, only ineffectual protests from quarters that were, rightly or wrongly, suspected of pro-German sympathies. In the United States, the opponents of Wilson attacked his conduct of negotiations on other grounds. . . .

A dictated peace was accepted by all who had lost confidence in Germany's good faith, and that included the great majority of Americans as well as of the English and of the French. If, as Clausewitz phrased it, war was the continuation of policy, diplomacy was, as far as the conflicting aims of the contestants were concerned, the continuation or summation of war. Military leaders were afraid that what was gained on the battlefields would be lost at the council table, and both the "Khaki Election" in Great Britain and the attitude of the French Chamber showed that these apprehensions were widely shared. The debates in the American Congress, while upon the whole maintaining the high note of disinterestedness in material gains, showed no lack of stern purpose to carry through the "Great Crusade" to its appointed goal—that of democracy triumphant without a doubt, and so recognized in Berlin. . . .

Whether the peace was to be dictated or not, it was necessary for the Allied and Associated Powers to work together and to accept a common program. The winter months showed how difficult this was and what rifts might easily disrupt their forces. The discontent of Italy and the breach between China and Japan, which had such a strong reaction in Washington, were but indications of what might happen more generally. . . . It was chiefly to prevent the delegations of the Central Powers from exploiting this situation that they were kept so carefully isolated from the Conference to which they had supposed that they were invited. Conscious of how French diplomacy itself had divided the Allies opposed to it in the Congress of Vienna, the Quai d'Orsay saw to it that no German Talleyrand would have access to the counsels of the Allied and Associated Powers. Held off like prisoners from even social contact with former friends, the delegations of Germany and Austria and Hungary were held in strictest quarantine and under police supervision in their separate quarters in Versailles and St. Germain. When the real treaty-making should have begun, in the exchange of views over the detailed proposal of the draft treaty, the task was declared ended, and the signature of Germany was procured by the threat of an occupation of Berlin; the Allied armies were moved out beyond the bridge-heads of the Rhine, and were ready at a moment's notice to force the issue. There was nothing for Germany to do but accept. Nevertheless the German protests even under these circumstances did bring a certain measure of alleviation, enough to show how much more could have been attained had there been a fair chance at negotiation.

* * * * *

But the faulty organization of the Preliminary Peace Conference . . . had left its traces on the text. When the Treaty was finally put together it was evident to any fair-minded person that it was more than any country should be asked to bear, although—in spite of their critics— the majority at least of those who drafted its clauses were fair-minded men, as fair-minded and as liberal as could be found anywhere. But it had not been put together in time. The fault lay not so much in this or that single section of the Treaty, for in most cases these sections contained provisions that were not without justification and were not merely the embodiment of vindictive and arbitrary power over a helpless victim. What was wrong with the Peace Treaty was that, when all the sacrifices were added together, the whole was greater than the sum of the parts. It was impossible to accept because impossible to fulfill on the part of the citizens of the conquered nations and still maintain a decent standard of living. Since Germany had to take the Treaty as a whole, it, therefore, had every right to regard the cumulation of injury as vitiating all parts. Yet, had there been a negotiated peace, much of the Treaty would still have been kept.

The failure to see all this at the time was directly due to the fact that the organs of the Conference, as they finally developed, were never properly articulated with each other or with the directing heads. Covering so vast a field, which included almost all the conditions of life of all Europe and of much of the colonial world outside, the treaty was prepared in more than a dozen different commissions, each working at its own task and each task large enough for a full-sized treaty of its own: territorial questions, economics, conditions of trade, the safeguards of minorities and nationalities, and all the problems arising from the devastation of the war and the menace of its recurrence. It was only when these separate sections were finally put together that the makers of the different parts of the Treaty became aware of the nature of the whole document; and that was not until the Germans had been already summoned to Versailles.

4. A "SCENARIO OF THE PEACE CONFERENCE" [4]

"The appalling dispersal of energy which was the actual key-note of the Paris Conference" was well depicted in this selection from the pen of Harold Nicolson, a member of the British Delegation.

It is not easy, when using the silent machinery of printed words, to reproduce the double stress of turmoil and time-pressure which in Paris constituted the main obstruction to calm thinking or planned procedure. One writes the sentence: "It was a period of unremitting strain." The sedative notes of such a sentence, as applied to the scurrying cacophony of the Peace Conference, forces one to smile. Only through the medium of a sound film could any accurate impression, that sense of riot in a parrot house, be conveyed.

Were I to sketch such a scenario of my own impressions, the result would be something as follows. As a recurrent undertone throughout would run the rumble of Time's winged chariot: incessantly reiterant would come the motif of this time-pressure—newspapers screaming in headlines against the Dawdlers of Paris, the clamour for demobilisation, "Get the Boys back," the starving millions of Central Europe, the slouching queues of prisoners still behind their barbed wire, the flames of communism flaring, now from Munich, and now from Buda Pesth. Through this recurrent grumble and rumble of the time-motif would pierce the sharper discordances of other sounds: the machine-gun rattle of a million typewriters, the incessant shrilling of telephones, the clatter of motor bicycles, the drone of aeroplanes, the cold voices of interpreters, "le délégué des États-Unis constate qu'il ne peut se ranger . . ." the blare of trumpets, the thunder of guns saluting at the Invalides, the rustling of files, a woman in a black woollen shawl singing "Madelon" in front of a café, the crackle of Rolls Royces upon the gravel of sumptuous courtyards, and throughout the sound of footsteps hurrying now upon the parquet of some gallery, now upon the stone stairway of some Ministry, and now muffled on the heavy Aubusson of some overheated saloon.

[4] H. Nicolson, *Peacemaking 1919. Being Reminiscences of the Paris Peace Conference,* Houghton Mifflin Company, Boston, 1933, pp. 152-156. (*Note:* These pages have been copied in their entirety; the dots do not represent omissions.) Now published by Harcourt, Brace and Company, Inc.; reprinted with their permission.

These sound-motifs would be accompanied by a rapid projection of disjointed pictures. The tired and contemptuous eyelids of Clemenceau, the black button-boots of Woodrow Wilson, the rotund and jovial gestures of Mr. Lloyd George's hands, the infinite languor of Mr. Balfour slowly uncrossing his knees, a succession of secretaries and experts bending forward with maps, Foch striding stockily with Weygand hurrying behind. The silver chains of the huissiers at the Quai d'Orsay. Such portraits would be interspersed with files, agenda papers, resolutions, *procès verbaux* and *communiqués*. These would succeed each other with extreme rapidity, and from time to time would have to be synchronised and superimposed. "The Plenipotentiaries of the United States of America, of the British Empire, of France, of Italy and of Japan, of the one part . . . It is resolved that subject to the approval of the Houses of Congress the President of the United States of America accepts on behalf of the United States . . . Si cette frontière était prise en considération, il serait nécessaire de faire la correction indiquée en bleu. Autrement le chemin de fer vers Kaschau serait coupé . . . These coupons will be accepted in settlement of the table d'hôte meals of the hotel, the whole ticket is to be given up at dinner. . . . M. Venizelos told me last night that he had concluded his agreement with Italy in the following terms: (1) Italy will support Greek claims in Northern Epirus. . . . From the point where the western boundary of the area leaves the Drave in a northerly direction as far as the point about one kilometre to the east of Rosegg (Saint Michael). The course of the Drave downstream. Thence in a north-easterly direction and as far as the western extremity of the Wörthersee, south of Vlelden. A line to be fixed on the ground. The median line of that lake. Thence eastwards to its confluence with the river Glan. The course of the Glanfurt downstream. . . . (1) Audition de M. Dmosky. (2) Rapport de la Commission Interalliée de Teschen. (3) Le rapatriement des troupes du Général Haller. (4) Rapport de M. Hoover. (5) Prisonniers de guerre. (6) Répartition de la marine marchande allemande. . . . From the coming into force of the present Treaty the High Contracting Parties shall renew, in so far as concerns them, and under the reserves indicated in the second paragraph of the present Article, the conventions and arrangements signed at Berne on October 14, 1890, September 20, 1893, July 16, 1895, June 16, 1898, and September 19, 1906, regarding the transportation of goods by rail. If within five years of the coming into force of the present Treaty . . . Le traité concernant l'entrée de la

Bavière dans la Confédération de l'Allemagne du Nord, conclu à Versailles le 23 novembre 1870, contient, dans les articles 7 et 8 du protocole final, des dispositions toujours en vigueur, reconnaissant. . . . A meeting of the British Empire Delegation will be held on Tuesday the 14th instant at the Villa Majestic at 11.30 a.m. . . . Dr. Nansen came to see me this morning. He represents the urgent necessity of inducing the Supreme Council . . . An entertainment will be held on Saturday next at 9.30 p.m. in the Ball Room of the Hotel Majestic in aid of the Dockland Settlement. Miss Ruth Draper has kindly consented to give us two of her well-known character sketches. Tickets may be obtained from the hall-porter—Le Baron Sonnino estimait qu'il y avait lieu d'établir une distinction entre les représentants des Soviets et ceux des autres Gouvernements. Les Alliés combattaient les bolcheviks et les considéraient comme des ennemis. Il n'en était pas de même en ce qui concernait les Finlandais, les Lettons. . . . Telegram from Vienna. Count Karolyi has resigned and according to telephone message received by Mr. Coolidge this morning from his representative at Buda Pesth communist government has been formed under leadership of Bela Kun. Fate of Allied Mission uncertain. . . . Wir wissen dass die Gewalt der deutschen Waffen gebrochen ist. Wir kennen die Macht des Hasses, die uns hier entgegentritt, und wir haben die leidenschaftliche Förderung gehört, dass die Sieger uns zugleich als Ueberwundene zahlen lassen und als Schuldige bestraffen sollen. . . ."

A rapid succession of such captions, accompanied by the whole scale of sound which I have indicated, would furnish a clearer picture of the atmosphere of the Peace Conference than any chronological record in terms of the printed word. Could colour, scent and touch be added, the picture would be almost complete. The dominant note is black and white, heavy black suits, white cuffs and paper: it is relieved by blue and khaki: the only other colours would be the scarlet damask of the Quai d'Orsay curtains, green baize, pink blotting pads, and the innumerable gilt of little chairs. For smells you would have petrol, typewriting ribbons, French polish, central heating, and a touch of violet hair-wash. The tactile motifs would be tracing paper, silk, the leather handle of a weighted pouch of papers, the foot-feel of very thick carpets alternating with parquet flooring, the stretch of muscle caused by leaning constantly over very large maps, the brittle feel of a cane chair-seat which has been occupied for hours.

And behind it all the ache of exhaustion and despair.

5. THE TREATY OF VERSAILLES, JUNE 28, 1919 *(Extracts)* [5]

The Treaty of Versailles was signed in the Hall of Mirrors on June 28, 1919, the fifth anniversary of the assassination of Archduke Francis Ferdinand. Ratifications between the Allies and Germany were exchanged in Paris on January 10, 1920. The document—about two hundred pages long—comprised fifteen parts, including four hundred and forty articles and almost a score of annexes.

PART I.

THE COVENANT OF THE LEAGUE OF NATIONS. [6]

. . . . .

PART II.

BOUNDARIES OF GERMANY.

. . . . .

PART III.

POLITICAL CLAUSES FOR EUROPE.

. . . . .

SECTION III.

LEFT BANK OF THE RHINE.

ARTICLE 42.

Germany is forbidden to maintain or construct any fortifications either on the left bank of the Rhine or on the right bank to the west of a line drawn 50 kilometres to the East of the Rhine.

ARTICLE 43.

In the area defined above the maintenance and the assembly of armed forces, either permanently or temporarily, and military manœuvres of any kind, as well as the upkeep of all permanent works for mobilization, are in the same way forbidden.

---

[5] United States, 66th Congress, 1st Session, Senate Document No. 49, *Treaty of Peace with Germany,* Government Printing Office, Washington, 1919.
[6] For the twenty-six articles which comprise this part of the treaty, see Doc. No. 14.—*Ed.*

ARTICLE 44.

In case Germany violates in any manner whatever the provisions of Articles 42 and 43, she shall be regarded as committing a hostile act against the powers signatory of the present Treaty and as calculated to disturb the peace of the world.

SECTION IV.

SAAR BASIN.

ARTICLE 45.

As compensation for the destruction of the coal mines in the north of France and as part payment towards the total reparation due from Germany for the damage resulting from the war, Germany cedes to France in full and absolute possession, with exclusive rights of exploitation, unencumbered and free from all debts and charges of any kind, the coal mines situated in the Saar Basin. . . .

. . . . .

ARTICLE 49.

Germany renounces in favour of the League of Nations, in the capacity of trustee, the government of the territory defined above.

At the end of fifteen years from the coming into force of the present Treaty the inhabitants of the said territory shall be called upon to indicate the sovereignty under which they desire to be placed.

. . . . .

ANNEX.

. . . . .

CHAPTER I.

CESSION AND EXPLOITATION OF MINING PROPERTY.

1.

From the date of the coming into force of the present Treaty, all the deposits of coal situated within the Saar Basin as defined in Article 48 of the said Treaty, become the complete and absolute property of the French State.

The French State will have the right of working or not working the said mines, or of transferring to a third party the right of working them, without having to obtain any previous authorisation or to fulfil any formalities.

The French State may always require that the German mining laws and regulations referred to below shall be applied in order to ensure the determination of its rights.

. . . . .

5.

The value of the property thus ceded to the French State will be determined by the Reparation Commission referred to in Article 233 of Part VIII (Reparation) of the present Treaty.

This value shall be credited to Germany in part payment of the amount due for reparation.

It will be for Germany to indemnify the proprietors or parties concerned, whoever they may be.

. . . . .

14.

The French State shall always have the right of establishing and maintaining, as incidental to the mines, primary or technical schools for its employees and their children, and of causing instruction therein to be given in the French language, in accordance with such curriculum and by such teachers as it may select.

It shall also have the right to establish and maintain hospitals, dispensaries, workmen's houses and gardens and other charitable and social institutions.

. . . . .

CHAPTER II.

GOVERNMENT OF THE TERRITORY OF THE SAAR BASIN.

16.

The Government of the territory of the Saar Basin shall be entrusted to a Commission representing the League of Nations. This Commission shall sit in the territory of the Saar Basin.

17.

The Governing Commission provided for by paragraph 16 shall consist of five members chosen by the Council of the League of Nations, and will include one citizen of France, one native inhabitant of the Saar Basin, not a citizen of France, and three members belonging to three countries other than France or Germany.

The members of the Governing Commission shall be appointed for one year and may be re-appointed. They can be removed by the Council of the League of Nations, which will provide for their replacement.

The members of the Governing Commission will be entitled to a salary which will be fixed by the Council of the League of Nations, and charged on the local revenues.

. . . . .

28.

Under the control of the Governing Commission the inhabitants will retain their local assemblies, their religious liberties, their schools and their language.

The right of voting will not be exercised for any assemblies other than the local assemblies, and will belong to every inhabitant over the age of twenty years, without distinction of sex.

. . . . .

CHAPTER III.

PLEBISCITE.

34.

At the termination of a period of fifteen years from the coming into force of the present Treaty, the population of the territory of the Saar Basin will be called upon to indicate their desires in the following manner:

A vote will take place by communes or districts, on the three following alternatives: (*a*) maintenance of the régime established by the present Treaty and by this Annex; (*b*) union with France; (*c*) union with Germany.

All persons without distinction of sex, more than twenty years old at the date of the voting, resident in the territory at the date of the signature of the present Treaty, will have the right to vote.

The other conditions, methods and the date of the voting shall be fixed by the Council of the League of Nations in such a way as to secure the freedom, secrecy and trustworthiness of the voting.

. . . . .

36.

If the League of Nations decides in favour of the union of the whole or part of the territory of the Saar Basin with Germany, France's rights of ownership in the mines situated in such part of the territory will be repurchased by Germany in their entirety at a price payable in gold. The price to be paid will be fixed by three experts, one nominated by Germany, one by France, and one, who shall be neither a Frenchman nor a German, by the Council of the League of Nations; the decision of the experts will be given by a majority.

The obligation of Germany to make such payment shall be taken into account by the Reparation Commission, and for the purpose of this payment, Germany may create a prior charge upon her assets or revenues upon such detailed terms as shall be agreed to by the Reparation Commission.

If, nevertheless, Germany after a period of one year from the date on which the payment becomes due shall not have effected the said payment, the Reparation Commission shall do so in accordance with such instructions as may be given by the League of Nations, and, if necessary, by liquidating that part of the mines which is in question.

. . . . .

SECTION VI.

AUSTRIA.

ARTICLE 80.

Germany acknowledges and will respect strictly the independence of Austria, within the frontiers which may be fixed in a Treaty between that State and the Principal Allied and Associated Powers; she agrees that this independence shall be inalienable, except with the consent of the Council of the League of Nations.

SECTION VII.

CZECHO-SLOVAK STATE.

ARTICLE 81.

Germany, in conformity with the action already taken by the Allied and Associated Powers, recognizes the complete independence of the

Czecho-Slovak State which will include the autonomous territory of the Ruthenians to the south of the Carpathians. Germany hereby recognizes the frontiers of this State as determined by the Principal Allied and Associated Powers and the other interested States.

. . . . .

ARTICLE 84.

German nationals habitually resident in any of the territories recognized as forming part of the Czecho-Slovak State will obtain Czecho-Slovak nationality *ipso facto* and lose their German nationality.

. . . . .

SECTION VIII.

POLAND.

. . . . .

ARTICLE 89.

Poland undertakes to accord freedom of transit to persons, goods, vessels, carriages, wagons and mails in transit between East Prussia and the rest of Germany over Polish territory, including territorial waters, and to treat them at least as favourably as the persons, goods, vessels, carriages, wagons and mails respectively of Polish or of any other more favoured nationality, origin, importation, starting point, or ownership as regards facilities, restrictions and all other matters.

Goods in transit shall be exempt from all customs or other similar duties.

Freedom of transit will extend to telegraphic and telephonic services under the conditions laid down by the conventions referred to in Article 98.

. . . . .

ARTICLE 93.

Poland accepts and agrees to embody in a Treaty with the Principal Allied and Associated Powers such provisions as may be deemed necessary by the said Powers to protect the interests of inhabitants of Poland who differ from the majority of the population in race, language or religion.

Poland further accepts and agrees to embody in a Treaty with the said Powers such provisions as they may deem necessary to protect freedom of transit and equitable treatment of the commerce of other nations.

. . . . .

SECTION X.

MEMEL.

ARTICLE 99.

Germany renounces in favour of the Principal Allied and Associated Powers all rights and title over the territories included between the Baltic, the north-eastern frontier of East Prussia as defined in Article 28 of Part II (Boundaries of Germany) of the present Treaty and the former frontier between Germany and Russia.

Germany undertakes to accept the settlement made by the Principal Allied and Associated Powers in regard to these territories, particularly in so far as concerns the nationality of the inhabitants.

SECTION XI.

FREE CITY OF DANZIG.

. . . . .

ARTICLE 102.

The Principal Allied and Associated Powers undertake to establish the town of Danzig, together with the rest of the territory described in Article 100, as a Free City. It will be placed under the protection of the League of Nations.

ARTICLE 103.

A constitution for the Free City of Danzig shall be drawn up by the duly appointed representatives of the Free City in agreement with a High Commissioner to be appointed by the League of Nations. This constitution shall be placed under the guarantee of the League of Nations.

The High Commissioner will also be entrusted with the duty of dealing in the first instance with all differences arising between Poland and the Free City of Danzig in regard to this Treaty or any arrangements or agreements made thereunder.

The High Commissioner shall reside at Danzig.

ARTICLE 104.

The Principal Allied and Associated Powers undertake to negotiate a Treaty between the Polish Government and the Free City of Danzig, which shall come into force at the same time as the establishment of the said Free City, with the following objects:

(1) To effect the inclusion of the Free City of Danzig within the Polish Customs frontiers, and to establish a free area in the port;

(2) To ensure to Poland without any restriction the free use and service of all waterways, docks, basins, wharves and other works within the territory of the Free City necessary for Polish imports and exports;

(3) To ensure to Poland the control and administration of the Vistula and of the whole railway system within the Free City, except such street and other railways as serve primarily the needs of the Free City, and of postal, telegraphic and telephonic communication between Poland and the port of Danzig;

(4) To ensure to Poland the right to develop and improve the waterways, docks, basins, wharves, railways and other works and means of communication mentioned in this Article, as well as to lease or purchase through appropriate processes such land and other property as may be necessary for these purposes;

(5) To provide against any discrimination within the Free City of Danzig to the detriment of citizens of Poland and other persons of Polish origin or speech;

(6) To provide that the Polish Government shall undertake the conduct of the foreign relations of the Free City of Danzig as well as the diplomatic protection of citizens of that city when abroad.

. . . . .

SECTION XII.

SCHLESWIG.

Article 109.

The frontier between Germany and Denmark shall be fixed in conformity with the wishes of the population. . . .

. . . . .

PART IV.

GERMAN RIGHTS AND INTERESTS OUTSIDE GERMANY.

. . . . .

SECTION I.

GERMAN COLONIES.

Article 119.

Germany renounces in favour of the Principal Allied and Associated Powers all her rights and titles over her oversea possessions.

. . . . .

SECTION II.

CHINA.

ARTICLE 128.

Germany renounces in favour of China all benefits and privileges resulting from the provisions of the final Protocol signed at Peking on September 7, 1901, and from all annexes, notes and documents supplementary thereto. She likewise renounces in favour of China any claim to indemnities accruing thereunder subsequent to March 14, 1917.

· · · · ·

ARTICLE 131.

Germany undertakes to restore to China within twelve months from the coming into force of the present Treaty all the astronomical instruments which her troops in 1900-1901 carried away from China, and to defray all expenses which may be incurred in effecting such restoration, including the expenses of dismounting, packing, transporting, insurance and installation in Peking.

ARTICLE 132.

Germany agrees to the abrogation of the leases from the Chinese Government under which the German Concessions at Hankow and Tientsin are now held.

China, restored to the full exercise of her sovereign rights in the above areas, declares her intention of opening them to international residence and trade. She further declares that the abrogation of the leases under which these concessions are now held shall not affect the property rights of nationals of Allied and Associated Powers who are holders of lots in these concessions.

· · · · ·

SECTION VIII.

SHANTUNG.

ARTICLE 156.

Germany renounces, in favour of Japan, all her rights, title and privileges—particularly those concerning the territory of Kiaochow, railways, mines and submarine cables—which she acquired in virtue of the Treaty concluded by her with China on March 6, 1898, and of all other arrangements relative to the Province of Shantung.

All German rights in the Tsingtao-Tsinanfu Railway, including its branch lines, together with its subsidiary property of all kinds, stations, shops, fixed and rolling stock, mines, plant and material for the exploitation of the mines, are and remain acquired by Japan, together with all rights and privileges attaching thereto.

The German State submarine cables from Tsingtao to Shanghai and from Tsingtao to Chefoo, with all the rights, privileges and properties attaching thereto, are similarly acquired by Japan, free and clear of all charges and encumbrances.

. . . . .

PART V.

MILITARY, NAVAL AND AIR CLAUSES.

In order to render possible the initiation of a general limitation of the armaments of all nations, Germany undertakes strictly to observe the military, naval and air clauses which follow.

SECTION I.

MILITARY CLAUSES.

CHAPTER I.

EFFECTIVES AND CADRES OF THE GERMAN ARMY.

ARTICLE 159.

The German military forces shall be demobilised and reduced as prescribed hereinafter.

ARTICLE 160.

(1) By a date which must not be later than March 31, 1920, the German Army must not comprise more than seven divisions of infantry and three divisions of cavalry.

After that date the total number of effectives in the Army of the States constituting Germany must not exceed one hundred thousand men, including officers and establishments of depots. The Army shall be devoted exclusively to the maintenance of order within the territory and to the control of the frontiers.

The total effective strength of officers, including the personnel of staffs, whatever their composition, must not exceed four thousand.

. . . . .

(3) . . . . The Great German General Staff and all similar organisations shall be dissolved and may not be reconstituted in any form.

•   •   •   •   •

CHAPTER II.

ARMAMENT, MUNITIONS AND MATERIAL.

•   •   •   •   •

ARTICLE 168.

The manufacture of arms, munitions, or any war material, shall only be carried out in factories or works the location of which shall be communicated to and approved by the Governments of the Principal Allied and Associated Powers, and the number of which they retain the right to restrict.

Within three months from the coming into force of the present Treaty, all other establishments for the manufacture, preparation, storage or design of arms, munitions, or any war material whatever shall be closed down. The same applies to all arsenals except those used as depots for the authorised stocks of munitions. Within the same period the personnel of these arsenals will be dismissed.

•   •   •   •   •

ARTICLE 170.

Importation into Germany of arms, munitions and war material of every kind shall be strictly prohibited.

The same applies to the manufacture for, and export to, foreign countries of arms, munitions and war material of every kind.

ARTICLE 171.

The use of asphyxiating, poisonous or other gases and all analogous liquids, materials or devices being prohibited, their manufacture and importation are strictly forbidden in Germany.

The same applies to materials specially intended for the manufacture, storage and use of the said products or devices.

The manufacture and the importation into Germany of armoured cars, tanks and all similar constructions suitable for use in war are also prohibited.

•   •   •   •   •

CHAPTER III.
RECRUITING AND MILITARY TRAINING.

ARTICLE 173.

Universal compulsory military service shall be abolished in Germany. The German Army may only be constituted and recruited by means of voluntary enlistment.

ARTICLE 174.

The period of enlistment for non-commissioned officers and privates must be twelve consecutive years.

The number of men discharged for any reason before the expiration of their term of enlistment must not exceed in any year five per cent. of the total effectives fixed by the second sub-paragraph of paragraph (1) of Article 160 of the present Treaty.

· · · · ·

CHAPTER IV.

FORTIFICATIONS.

ARTICLE 180.

All fortified works, fortresses and field works situated in German territory to the west of a line drawn fifty kilometres to the east of the Rhine shall be disarmed and dismantled.

Within a period of two months from the coming into force of the present Treaty such of the above fortified works, fortresses and field works as are situated in territory not occupied by Allied and Associated troops shall be disarmed, and within a further period of four months they shall be dismantled. Those which are situated in territory occupied by Allied and Associated troops shall be disarmed and dismantled within such periods as may be fixed by the Allied High Command.

The construction of any new fortification, whatever its nature and importance, is forbidden in the zone referred to in the first paragraph above.

The system of fortified works of the southern and eastern frontiers of Germany shall be maintained in its existing state.

· · · · ·

SECTION II.

NAVAL CLAUSES.

ARTICLE 181.

After the expiration of a period of two months from the coming into force of the present Treaty the German naval forces in commission must not exceed:

    6 battleships of the *Deutschland* or *Lothringen* type,
    6 light cruisers,
    12 destroyers,
    12 torpedo boats,

or an equal number of ships constructed to replace them as provided in Article 190.

No submarines are to be included.

All other warships, except where there is provision to the contrary in the present Treaty, must be placed in reserve or devoted to commercial purposes.

    . . . . .

ARTICLE 183.

After the expiration of a period of two months from the coming into force of the present Treaty the total personnel of the German Navy, including the manning of the fleet, coast defences, signal stations, administration and other land services, must not exceed fifteen thousand, including officers and men of all grades and corps.

The total strength of officers and warrant officers must not exceed fifteen hundred.

Within two months from the coming into force of the present Treaty the personnel in excess of the above strength shall be demobilised.

No naval or military corps or reserve force in connection with the Navy may be organised in Germany without being included in the above strength.

    . . . . .

ARTICLE 191.

The construction or acquisition of any submarine, even for commercial purposes, shall be forbidden in Germany.

    . . . . .

SECTION III.

AIR CLAUSES.

ARTICLE 198.

The armed forces of Germany must not include any military or naval air forces.

Germany may, during a period not extending beyond October 1, 1919, maintain a maximum number of one hundred seaplanes or flying boats, which shall be exclusively employed in searching for submarine mines, shall be furnished with the necessary equipment for this purpose, and shall in no case carry arms, munitions or bombs of any nature whatever.

In addition to the engines installed in the seaplanes or flying boats above mentioned, one spare engine may be provided for each engine of each of these craft.

No dirigible shall be kept.

. . . . .

SECTION IV.

INTER-ALLIED COMMISSIONS OF CONTROL.

ARTICLE 203.

All the military, naval and air clauses contained in the present Treaty, for the execution of which a time-limit is prescribed, shall be executed by Germany under the control of Inter-Allied Commissions specially appointed for this purpose by the Principal Allied and Associated Powers.

. . . . .

ARTICLE 207.

The upkeep and cost of the Commissions of Control and the expenses involved by their work shall be borne by Germany.

. . . . .

PART VI.

PRISONERS OF WAR AND GRAVES.

. . . . .

PART VII.

PENALTIES.

ARTICLE 227.

The Allied and Associated Powers publicly arraign William II of Hohenzollern, formerly German Emperor, for a supreme offence against international morality and the sanctity of treaties.

A special tribunal will be constituted to try the accused, thereby assuring him the guarantees essential to the right of defence. It will be composed of five judges, one appointed by each of the following Powers: namely, the United States of America, Great Britain, France, Italy and Japan.

In its decision the tribunal will be guided by the highest motives of international policy, with a view to vindicating the solemn obligations of international undertakings and the validity of international morality. It will be its duty to fix the punishment which it considers should be imposed.

The Allied and Associated Powers will address a request to the Government of the Netherlands for the surrender to them of the ex-Emperor in order that he may be put on trial.

ARTICLE 228.

The German Government recognizes the right of the Allied and Associated Powers to bring before military tribunals persons accused of having committed acts in violation of the laws and customs of war. Such persons shall, if found guilty, be sentenced to punishments laid down by law. This provision will apply notwithstanding any proceedings or prosecution before a tribunal in Germany or in the territory of her allies.

The German Government shall hand over to the Allied and Associated Powers, or to such one of them as shall so request, all persons accused of having committed an act in violation of the laws and customs of war, who are specified either by name or by the rank, office or employment which they held under the German authorities.

· · · · ·

PART VIII.

REPARATION.

SECTION I.

GENERAL PROVISIONS.

ARTICLE 231.

The Allied and Associated Governments affirm and Germany accepts the responsibility of Germany and her allies for causing all the loss and damage to which the Allied and Associated Governments and their nationals have been subjected as a consequence of the war imposed upon them by the aggression of Germany and her allies.

ARTICLE 232.

The Allied and Associated Governments recognize that the resources of Germany are not adequate, after taking into account permanent diminutions of such resources which will result from other provisions of the present Treaty, to make complete reparation for all such loss and damage.

The Allied and Associated Governments, however, require, and Germany undertakes, that she will make compensation for all damage done to the civilian population of the Allied and Associated Powers and to their property during the period of the belligerency of each as an Allied or Associated Power against Germany by such aggression by land, by sea and from the air, and in general all damage as defined in Annex I hereto.

In accordance with Germany's pledges, already given, as to complete restoration for Belgium, Germany undertakes, in addition to the compensation for damage elsewhere in this Part provided for, as a consequence of the violation of the Treaty of 1839, to make reimbursement of all sums which Belgium has borrowed from the Allied and Associated Governments up to November 11, 1918, together with interest at the rate of five per cent. (5%) per annum on such sums. This amount shall be determined by the Reparation Commission, and the German Government undertakes thereupon forthwith to make a special issue of bearer bonds to an equivalent amount payable in marks gold, on May 1, 1926, or, at the option of the German Government, on the 1st of May in any year up to 1926. Subject to the foregoing, the form of such bonds shall be determined by the Reparation Commission. Such bonds shall be handed over to the Reparation Commission, which has authority to take and acknowledge receipt thereof on behalf of Belgium.

*   *   *   *   *

ANNEX I.

Compensation may be claimed from Germany under Article 232 above in respect of the total damage under the following categories:

(1) Damage to injured persons and to surviving dependents by personal injury to or death of civilians caused by acts of war, including bombardments or other attacks on land, on sea, or from the air, and all the direct consequences thereof, and of all operations of war by the two groups of belligerents wherever arising.

(2) Damage caused by Germany or her allies to civilian victims of acts of cruelty, violence or maltreatment (including injuries to life or health as a consequence of imprisonment, deportation, internment or evacuation, of exposure at sea or of being forced to labour), wherever arising, and to the surviving dependents of such victims.

(3) Damage caused by Germany or her allies in their own territory or in occupied or invaded territory to civilian victims of all acts injurious to health or capacity to work, or to honour, as well as to the surviving dependents of such victims.

(4) Damage caused by any kind of maltreatment of prisoners of war.

(5) As damage caused to the peoples of the Allied and Associated Powers, all pensions and compensation in the nature of pensions to naval and military victims of war (including members of the air force), whether mutilated, wounded, sick or invalided, and to the dependents of such victims, the amount due to the Allied and Associated Governments being calculated for each of them as being the capitalised cost of such pensions and compensation at the date of the coming into force of the present Treaty on the basis of the scales in force in France at such date.

(6) The cost of assistance by the Government of the Allied and Associated Powers to prisoners of war and to their families and dependents.

(7) Allowances by the Governments of the Allied and Associated Powers to the families and dependents of mobilised persons or persons serving with the forces, the amount due to them for each calendar year in which hostilities occurred being calculated for each Government on the basis of the average scale for such payments in force in France during that year.

(8) Damage caused to civilians by being forced by Germany or her allies to labour without just remuneration.

(9) Damage in respect of all property wherever situated belonging to any of the Allied or Associated States or their nationals, with the

exception of naval and military works or materials, which has been carried off, seized, injured or destroyed by the acts of Germany or her allies on land, on sea or from the air, or damage directly in consequence of hostilities or of any operations of war.

(10) Damage in the form of levies, fines and other similar exactions imposed by Germany or her allies upon the civilian population.

ANNEX II.

. . . . .

18.

The measures which the Allied and Associated Powers shall have the right to take, in case of voluntary default by Germany, and which Germany agrees not to regard as acts of war, may include economic and financial prohibitions and reprisals and in general such other measures as the respective Governments may determine to be necessary in the circumstances.

. . . . . .

ANNEX IV.

. . . . .

6.

As an immediate advance on account of the animals referred to in paragraph 2 (*a*) above, Germany undertakes to deliver in equal monthly instalments in the three months following the coming into force of the present Treaty the following quantities of live stock:

(1) *To the French Government.*

500 stallions (3 to 7 years);
30,000 fillies and mares (18 months to 7 years),
       type: Ardennais, Boulonnais or Belgian;
2,000 bulls (18 months to 3 years);
90,000 milch cows (2 to 6 years);
1,000 rams;
100,000 sheep;
10,000 goats.

(2) *To the Belgian Government.*

200 stallions (3 to 7 years), large Belgian type;

> 5,000 mares (3 to 7 years), large Belgian type;
> 5,000 fillies (18 months to 3 years), large Bel-
>   gian type;
> 2,000 bulls (18 months to 3 years);
> 50,000 milch cows (2 to 6 years);
> 40,000 heifers;
> 200   rams;
> 20,000 sheep;
> 15,000 sows.

The animals delivered shall be of average health and condition.

To the extent that animals so delivered cannot be identified as animals taken away or seized, the value of such animals shall be credited against the reparation obligations of Germany in accordance with paragraph 5 of this Annex.

. . . . . .

SECTION II.

SPECIAL PROVISIONS.

ARTICLE 245.

Within six months after the coming into force of the present Treaty the German Government must restore to the French Government the trophies, archives, historical souvenirs or works of art carried away from France by the German authorities in the course of the war of 1870-1871 and during this last war, in accordance with a list which will be communicated to it by the French Government; particularly the French flags taken in the course of the war of 1870-1871 and all the political papers taken by the German authorities on October 10, 1870, at the chateau of Cerçay, near Brunoy (Seine-et-Oise) belonging at the time to Mr. Rouher, formerly Minister of State.

ARTICLE 246.

Within six months from the coming into force of the present Treaty, Germany will restore to His Majesty the King of the Hedjaz the original Koran of the Caliph Othman, which was removed from Medina by the Turkish authorities and is stated to have been presented to the ex-Emperor William II.

Within the same period Germany will hand over to his Britannic Majesty's Government the skull of the Sultan Mkwawa which was removed from the Protectorate of German East Africa and taken to Germany.

The delivery of the articles above referred to will be effected in such place and in such conditions as may be laid down by the Governments to which they are to be restored.

. . . . .

PART IX.

FINANCIAL CLAUSES.

ARTICLE 248.

Subject to such exceptions as the Reparation Commission may approve, a first charge upon all the assets and revenues of the German Empire and its constituent States shall be the cost of reparation and all other costs arising under the present Treaty or any treaties or agreements supplementary thereto or under arrangements concluded between Germany and the Allied and Associated Powers during the Armistice or its extensions.

Up to May 1, 1921, the German Government shall not export or dispose of, and shall forbid the export or disposal of, gold without the previous approval of the Allied and Associated Powers acting through the Reparation Commission.

ARTICLE 249.

There shall be paid by the German Government the total cost of all armies of the Allied and Associated Governments in occupied German territory from the date of the signature of the Armistice of November 11, 1918, . . .

. . . . .

PART X.

ECONOMIC CLAUSES.

. . . . .

PART XI.

AERIAL NAVIGATION.

. . . . .

PART XII.

PORTS, WATERWAYS AND RAILWAYS.

. . . . .

SECTION II.

NAVIGATION.

. . . . .

CHAPTER III.

CLAUSES RELATING TO THE ELBE, THE ODER, THE NIEMEN
(RUSSSTROM-MEMEL-NIEMEN) AND THE DANUBE.

(I) *General Clauses.*

ARTICLE 331.

The following rivers are declared international:

the Elbe (*Labe*) from its confluence with the Vltava (*Moldau*), and the Vltava (*Moldau*) from Prague; the Oder (*Odra*) from its confluence with the Oppa; the Niemen (*Russstrom-Memel-Niemen*) from Grodno; the Danube from Ulm;

and all navigable parts of these river systems which naturally provide more than one State with access to the sea, with or without transhipment from one vessel to another; together with lateral canals and channels constructed either to duplicate or to improve naturally navigable sections of the specified river systems, or to connect two naturally navigable sections of the same river.

The same shall apply to the Rhine-Danube navigable waterway, should such a waterway be constructed under the conditions laid down in Article 353.

ARTICLE 332.

On the waterways declared to be international in the preceding Article, the nationals, property and flags of all Powers shall be treated on a footing of perfect equality, no distinction being made to the detriment of the nationals, property or flag of any Power between them and the nationals, property or flag of the riparian State itself or of the most favoured nation.

Nevertheless, German vessels shall not be entitled to carry passengers or goods by regular services between the ports of any Allied or Associated Power, without special authority from such Power.

. . . . .

PART XIII.

LABOUR. [7]

. . . . .

_____
[7] For the articles which comprise this part of the treaty, see Doc. No. 17.—*Ed.*

PART XIV

GUARANTEES.

SECTION I.

WESTERN EUROPE.

ARTICLE 428.

As a guarantee for the execution of the present Treaty by Germany, the German territory situated to the west of the Rhine, together with the bridgeheads, will be occupied by Allied and Associated troops for a period of fifteen years from the coming into force of the present Treaty.

ARTICLE 429.

If the conditions of the present Treaty are faithfully carried out by Germany, the occupation referred to in Article 428 will be successively restricted as follows:

(1) At the expiration of five years there will be evacuated: the bridgehead of Cologne and the territories north of a line running along the Ruhr, then along the railway Jülich, Duren, Euskirchen, Rheinbach, thence along the road Rheinbach to Sinzig, and reaching the Rhine at the confluence with the Ahr; the roads, railways and places mentioned above being excluded from the area evacuated.

(2) At the expiration of ten years there will be evacuated: the bridgehead of Coblenz and the territories north of a line to be drawn from the intersection between the frontiers of Belgium, Germany and Holland, running about from 4 kilometres south of Aix-la-Chapelle, then to and following the crest of Forst Gemünd, then east of the railway of the Urft Valley, then along Blankenheim, Valdorf, Dreis, Ulmen to and following the Moselle from Bremm to Nehren, then passing by Kappel and Simmern, then following the ridge of the heights between Simmern and the Rhine and reaching this river at Bacharach; all the places, valleys, roads and railways mentioned above being excluded from the area evacuated.

(3) At the expiration of fifteen years there will be evacuated: the bridgehead of Mainz, the bridgehead of Kehl and the remainder of the German territory under occupation.

If at that date the guarantees against unprovoked aggression by Germany are not considered sufficient by the Allied and Associated Governments, the evacuation of the occupying troops may be delayed to the extent regarded as necessary for the purpose of obtaining the required guarantees.

ARTICLE 430.

In case either during the occupation or after the expiration of the fifteen years referred to above the Reparation Commission finds that Germany refuses to observe the whole or part of her obligations under the present Treaty with regard to reparation, the whole or part of the areas specified in Article 429 will be re-occupied immediately by the Allied and Associated forces.

ARTICLE 431.

If before the expiration of the period of fifteen years Germany complies with all the undertakings resulting from the present Treaty, the occupying forces will be withdrawn immediately.

. . . . .

PART XV.

MISCELLANEOUS PROVISIONS.

. . . . .

ARTICLE 437.

The High Contracting Parties agree that, in the absence of a subsequent agreement to the contrary, the Chairman of any Commission established by the present Treaty shall in the event of an equality of votes be entitled to a second vote.

6. THE TREATY OF SAINT-GERMAIN-EN-LAYE,
SEPTEMBER 10, 1919 *(Extracts)* [8]

In addition to the Treaty of Versailles, four other treaties were drawn up by the conference, with Austria (Saint-Germain-en-Laye), Hungary (Trianon), Bulgaria (Neuilly), and Turkey (Sèvres). Collectively these five treaties were called the Peace of Paris. Many of the articles in the treaties with the smaller states were directly copied or adapted from the Versailles clauses. The Treaty of Saint-Germain-en-Laye comprised 381 articles. It was signed on September 10, 1919, and ratifications were exchanged in Paris on July 16, 1920.

[8] United States, 66th Congress, 1st Session, Senate Document No. 92, *Treaty of Peace between the Principal Allied and Associated Powers and Austria,* Government Printing Office, Washington, 1919.

. . . . .

ARTICLE 63.

Austria undertakes to assure full and complete protection of life and liberty to all inhabitants of Austria without distinction of birth, nationality, language, race or religion.

All inhabitants of Austria shall be entitled to the free exercise, whether public or private, of any creed, religion or belief, whose practices are not inconsistent with public order or public morals.

. . . . . .

ARTICLE 69.

Austria agrees that the stipulations in the foregoing Articles of this Section, so far as they affect persons belonging to racial, religious or linguistic minorities, constitute obligations of international concern and shall be placed under the guarantee of the League of Nations. They shall not be modified without the assent of a majority of the Council of the League of Nations. The Allied and Associated Powers represented on the Council severally agree not to withhold their assent from any modification in these Articles which is in due form assented to by a majority of the Council of the League of Nations.

Austria agrees that any Member of the Council of the League of Nations shall have the right to bring to the attention of the Council any infraction, or any danger of infraction, of any of these obligations, and that the Council may thereupon take such action and give such direction as it may deem proper and effective in the circumstances. . . .

. . . . .

ARTICLE 88.

The independence of Austria is inalienable otherwise than with the consent of the Council of the League of Nations. Consequently Austria undertakes in the absence of the consent of the said Council to abstain from any act which might directly or indirectly or by any means whatever compromise her independence, particularly, and until her admission to membership of the League of Nations, by participation in the affairs of another Power.

. . . . .

PART V.

MILITARY, NAVAL AND AIR CLAUSES.

In order to render possible the initiation of a general limitation of the armaments of all nations, Austria undertakes strictly to observe the military, naval and air clauses which follow.

ARTICLE 119.

Universal compulsory military service shall be abolished in Austria. The Austrian Army shall in future only be constituted and recruited by means of voluntary enlistment.

ARTICLE 120.

The total number of military forces in the Austrian Army shall not exceed 30,000 men, including officers and depot troops. . . .

ARTICLE 132.

The manufacture of arms, munitions and war material shall only be carried on in one single factory, which shall be controlled by and belong to the State, and whose output shall be strictly limited to the manufacture of such arms, munitions and war material as is necessary for the military forces and armaments referred to in Articles 120, 123, 129, 130 and 131.

The manufacture of sporting weapons is not forbidden, provided that sporting weapons manufactured in Austria taking ball cartridge are not of the same calibre as that of military weapons used in any European army. . . .

ARTICLE 134.

The importation into Austria of arms, munitions and war material of all kinds is strictly forbidden.

The manufacture for foreign countries and the exportation of arms, munitions and war material shall also be forbidden.

ARTICLE 135.

The use of flame throwers, asphyxiating, poisonous or other gases, and all similar liquids, materials or devices being prohibited, their manufacture and importation are strictly forbidden in Austria.

Material specially intended for the manufacture, storage or use of the said products or devices is equally forbidden.

The manufacture and importation into Austria of armoured cars, tanks or any similar machines suitable for use in war are equally forbidden.

. . . . .

ARTICLE 136.

From the date of the coming into force of the present Treaty all Austro-Hungarian warships, submarines included, are declared to be finally surrendered to the Principal Allied and Associated Powers.

All the monitors, torpedo boats and armed vessels of the Danube Flotilla will be surrendered to the Principal Allied and Associated Powers.

Austria will, however, have the right to maintain on the Danube for the use of the river police three patrol boats to be selected by the Commission referred to in Article 154 of the present Treaty.

. . . . .

ARTICLE 140.

The construction or acquisition of any submarine, even for commercial purposes, shall be forbidden in Austria.

. . . . .

ARTICLE 144.

The armed forces of Austria must not include any military or naval air forces.

No dirigible shall be kept.

. . . . .

ARTICLE 159.

So long as the present Treaty remains in force, Austria undertakes to submit to any investigation which the Council of the League of Nations, acting if need be by a majority vote, may consider necessary.

. . . . .

ARTICLE 177.

The Allied and Associated Governments affirm and Austria accepts the responsibility of Austria and her allies for causing the loss and damage to which the Allied and Associated Governments and their nationals have been subjected as a consequence of the war imposed upon them by the aggression of Austria-Hungary and her allies.

ARTICLE 178.

The Allied and Associated Governments recognise that the resources of Austria are not adequate, after taking into account the permanent diminutions of such resources which will result from other provisions of the present Treaty, to make complete reparation for such loss and damage.

The Allied and Associated Governments however require, and Austria undertakes, that she will make compensation as hereinafter determined for damage done to the civilian population of the Allied and Associated Powers and to their property during the period of the belligerency of each as an Allied and Associated Power against Austria by the said aggression by land, by sea and from the air, and in general damage as defined in Annex I hereto.[9]

7-12. DIVERS OPINIONS OF THE PARIS PEACE SETTLEMENT

7. THE VIEW OF COLONEL EDWARD M. HOUSE, JUNE 29, 1919 [10]

~~~~~~

Colonel Edward M. House, one of the senior American delegates to the Paris Peace Conference, had acted as President Wilson's personal representa-

---

[9] The articles in the Treaty of Trianon of June 4, 1920, with Hungary, respectively identical with or similar to the articles quoted above, are numbered 55, 60, 73, 103, 104, 115, 118, 119, 120, 124, 128, 143, 161, and 162.—*Ed.*

[10] C. Seymour, ed., *The Intimate Papers of Colonel House,* 4 vols., Houghton Mifflin Company, Boston, 1926-1928, vol. IV, pp. 487-489. Reprinted by permission of the publishers.

tive in Europe during the war years. He was also directing head of "The Inquiry," an American commission organized in September 1917 "to study the facts likely to come up in the Peace Conference at the end of the War." He made an especially interesting entry in his diary for the day following the signing of the Treaty of Versailles.

June 29, 1919: I am leaving Paris, after eight fateful months, with conflicting emotions. Looking at the Conference in retrospect there is much to approve and much to regret. It is easy to say what should have been done, but more difficult to have found a way of doing it.

The bitterness engendered by the war, the hopes raised high in many quarters because of victory, the character of the men having the dominant voices in the making of the Treaty, all had their influence for good or for evil, and were to be reckoned with. There seemed to be no full realization of the conditions which had to be met. An effort was made to enact a peace upon the usual lines. This should never have been attempted. The greater part of civilization had been shattered and history could guide us but little in the making of this peace.

How splendid it would have been had we blazed a new and better trail! However, it is to be doubted whether this could have been done, even if those in authority had so decreed, for the peoples back of them had to be reckoned with. It may be that Wilson might have had the power and influence if he had remained in Washington and kept clear of the Conference. When he stepped from his lofty pedestal and wrangled with representatives of other states upon equal terms, he became as common clay.

I wonder what motives actuated Clemenceau when he receded from his first position and chose to welcome the President into the arena where the debates concerning peace were to proceed day by day. I doubt whether he saw that its effect would be to lessen Wilson's commanding influence, and bring it nearer a level with that of Lloyd George and his own. It is more likely that he was content to accept my assurance that the President would readily acquiesce in having him, Clemenceau, preside over the Congress, and it may well be that he considered that France would fare better if Wilson could sit in conference and obtain an intimate knowledge of France's claims against the Central Powers.

To those who are saying that the Treaty is bad and should never have been made and that it will involve Europe in infinite difficulties in its

enforcement, I feel like admitting it. But I would also say in reply
that empires cannot be shattered and new states raised upon their ruins
without disturbance. To create new boundaries is always to create new
troubles. The one follows the other. While I should have preferred a
different peace, I doubt whether it could have been made, for the ingre-
dients for such a peace as I would have had were lacking at Paris. And
even if those of us like Smuts, Botha, and Cecil could have had our
will, as much trouble might have followed a peace of our making as
seems certain to follow this.

The same forces that have been at work in the making of this peace
would be at work to hinder the enforcement of a different kind of
peace, and no one can say with certitude that anything better than has
been done could be done at this time. We have had to deal with a situation pregnant with difficulties and one which could be met only by an
unselfish and idealistic spirit, which was almost wholly absent and
which was too much to expect of men come together at such a time
and for such a purpose.

And yet I wish we had taken the other road, even if it were less
smooth, both now and afterward, than the one we took. We would at
least have gone in the right direction and if those who follow us had
made it impossible to go the full length of the journey planned, the
responsibility would have rested with them and not with us.

8. THE VIEW OF A BRITISH ECONOMIST, 1919 [11]

*John M. Keynes, in his own words, "was temporarily attached to the Brit-
ish Treasury during the war and was their official representative at the
Paris Peace Conference up to June 7, 1919; he also sat as deputy for the Chancellor of the Exchequer on the Supreme Economic Council." He resigned
from these positions because of his disagreement with the policy of the conference "towards the economic problems of Europe."*

. . . The Treaty includes no provisions for the economic rehabilitation of Europe,—nothing to make the defeated Central Empires into
good neighbors, nothing to stabilize the new States of Europe, nothing
to reclaim Russia; nor does it promote in any way a compact of eco-

[11] J. M. Keynes, *The Economic Consequences of the Peace*, Harcourt, Brace and Howe,
New York, 1920, pp. 226-227, 296-297. Reprinted by permission of Mr. Keynes.

nomic solidarity amongst the Allies themselves; no agreement was reached at Paris for restoring the disordered finances of France and Italy, or to adjust the systems of the Old World and the New.

The Council of Four paid no attention to these issues, being preoccupied with others,—Clemenceau to crush the economic life of his enemy, Lloyd George to do a deal and bring home something which would pass muster for a week, the President to do nothing that was not just and right. It is an extraordinary fact that the fundamental economic problems of a Europe starving and disintegrating before their eyes, was the one question in which it was impossible to arouse the interest of the Four. Reparation was their main excursion into the economic field, and they settled it as a problem of theology, of politics, of electoral chicane, from every point of view except that of the economic future of the States whose destiny they were handling.

. . . . .

. . . For the immediate future events are taking charge, and the near destiny of Europe is no longer in the hands of any man. The events of the coming year will not be shaped by the deliberate acts of statesmen, but by the hidden currents, flowing continually beneath the surface of political history, of which no one can predict the outcome. In one way only can we influence these hidden currents,—by setting in motion those forces of instruction and imagination which change *opinion*. The assertion of truth, the unveiling of illusion, the dissipation of hate, the enlargement and instruction of men's hearts and minds, must be the means.

In this autumn of 1919, in which I write, we are at the dead season of our fortunes. The reaction from the exertions, the fears, and the sufferings of the past five years is at its height. Our power of feeling or caring beyond the immediate questions of our own material well-being is temporarily eclipsed. The greatest events outside our own direct experience and the most dreadful anticipations cannot move us.

. . . . .

We have been moved already beyond endurance, and need rest. Never in the lifetime of men now living has the universal element in the soul of man burnt so dimly.

9. THE VIEW OF A GERMAN NATIONALIST WRITER, MAY 28, 1919 [12]

Dr. Alfred von Wegerer, having served Germany as an officer during the World War, became a leading figure in the movement to destroy the so-called "War Guilt Thesis" upon the return of peace. In 1923 he founded and until 1937 he edited a scholarly monthly review devoted chiefly to research in the causes of the war (Die Kriegsschuldfrage, *after 1928 called* Berliner Monatshefte).

People and government have, during the most recent days, unambiguously made clear that we cannot sign the document which our enemies call a peace. One thing is certain, that any government which, by its signature, would confer upon this work of the devil (*Satansstück*) the halo of right, would, sooner or later, be driven out.

Has this peace come as a surprise to us? Sorry to say, we must answer yes.—No one had believed in such cunning madness. We all dreamed more or less of a peace by agreement and justice, read diligently and in good faith what the false prophet across the big pond promised us and all the world, and now we see how Old England and the revenge-filled chauvinist Clemenceau, continuously goaded by Foch, have pieced together a preventive peace reminiscent of the days of yore. There is not the faintest trace of any understanding of the times, of any foresight (*Weitblick*) into the future of the history of the peoples. A grey, bureaucrat's treaty (*Bureaufriede*), put together by small, narrow-minded politicians of hate and force. A few years will suffice to wash away all this wicked bungling. . . .

The cardinal points underlying the political stand to be taken are simple and natural: internal unity, a model constitution attuned to the life of the individual as well as that of the whole people, greatest increase of economic power, maintenance of the natural defensive strength and creation of a general ethic, upholding and drawing closer of Germandom outside the present or prospective national boundaries, winning of strong, natural allies.

For the immediate future our concern perforce will be merely to foster the internal unity and hammer away at the conscience of the

[12] A. von Wegerer, *Im Kampf gegen die Kriegsschuldlüge. Ausgewählte Aufsätze*, Quaderverlag G. m. b. H., Berlin, 1936, pp. 1-2. Reprint of his article on "Politische Zeitgedanken" in *Der Tag* (Berlin), May 28, 1919, No. 243. Reprinted by permission of the Quaderverlag.

world through notes, protests, standing protests, and communications of all sorts, until the charlatans at the head of the misled enemy nations are flung away and the field of right once more becomes free for the establishment of a true peoples' peace. Here it is necessary to inaugurate a grand propaganda which will place in the shadow everything that has hitherto been attempted. Film, pen, printer's ink, and brush must restlessly labor toward the goal, day and night, guided by the ablest spirits in the nation.

But for the immediate future even all this is of little help. Should the Entente invade us, then nothing is left but to remain cold-blooded, offer passive resistance wherever possible, and show contempt and pride. Even now the government must prepare the people for this eventuality and publish rules of conduct so that there may then be but a single grasp of the situation among the entire nation, including the female sex.

10. THE VIEW OF THE BRITISH MEMBER OF THE "BIG FOUR," JUNE 25, 1923 [13]

David Lloyd George, head of the British Delegation, spoke and wrote much on the peace settlement which he helped effect in 1918-1919. In a speech in 1923 he attacked those French and British critics of the Treaty of Versailles who denounced various portions thereof without taking into consideration the principles of the document as a whole.

In France there exist at least two or three schools of thought concerning the Versailles Treaty. There is one powerful section which has always regarded it as a treasonable pact, in which M. Clemenceau gave away solid French rights and interests in a moment of weakness under pressure from President Wilson and myself. That is the Poincaré-Barthou-Pertinax school. . . . It is the one which has brought Europe to its present state of confusion and despair.

There is the second school which reads into the Treaty powers and provisions which it does not contain, and never contemplated. These critics maintain stoutly that M. Briand and all other French Prime Ministers, with the exception of M. Poincaré, betrayed their trust by failing to enforce these imaginary stipulations. . . .

[13] D. Lloyd George, *Is It Peace?*, Hodder and Stoughton, London, 1923, pp. 208-211. Speech in London, June 25, 1923, on "The Treaty of Versailles and Its Critics." Reprinted by permission of the publishers.

In the background there is a third school which knows exactly what the Treaty means, but dare not say so in the present state of French public opinion. Perhaps they think it is better to bide their time. That time will come, and when it does arrive, let us hope it will not be too late to save Europe from the welter. . . .

In England we find at least three schools. There are the critics who denounce it as a brutal outrage upon international justice. It is to them a device for extorting incalculable sums out of an impoverished Germany as reparation for damages artificially worked up. Then there is the other extreme—the "Die-Hard" section—more influential since it became less numerous, who think the Treaty let Germany off much too lightly. In fact they are in complete agreement with the French Chauvinists as to the reprehensible moderation of its terms. In Britain also there is a third party which regards its provisions as constituting the best settlement, when you take into account the conflicting aims, interests, and traditions of the parties who had to negotiate and come to an agreement.

But take all these variegated schools together, or separately, and you will find not one in a thousand of their pupils could give you an intelligent and comprehensive summary of the main principles of the Treaty. . . . Controversialists generally are satisfied to concentrate on the articles in the Treaty which are obnoxious or pleasing to them as the case may be, and ignore the rest completely, however essential they may be to a true judgment of the whole. . . .

11. A HUNGARIAN VIEW OF THE TREATY OF TRIANON, 1933 [14]

Extremely bitter against the terms of the peace settlement were the Hungarians who, generally speaking, felt that they had received the harshest treatment at Paris. Among the most prominent and important critics of the Treaty of Trianon was Stephen Count Bethlen, scion of a noble and wealthy Transylvanian family and Premier of Hungary from April 1921 until August 1931.

In spite of . . . difficulties and obstacles the interior evolution of the [Dual] Monarchy was progressing [in the pre-war period] in the di-

[14] S. Bethlen, *The Treaty of Trianon and European Peace. Four Lectures Delivered in London in November 1933*, Longmans, Green and Company, London, 1934, pp. 157-160, 171. Reprinted by permission of the author and publishers.

rection of a gradual national emancipation of the small races forming the population. This would in due time have certainly led to an organic reconstruction of the constitution of the Monarchy, in which each of the races would have enjoyed autonomy to an extent varying according to the degree of civilisation, the national significance and importance of the various peoples.

However, the World War made an end to this evolution, and the Peace Treaty, in establishing the conditions now prevailing in those parts, created what I cannot but consider a most amateurish work.

The first of its effects was to establish three classes in which the peoples living on the territory of the former Monarchy were ranged according to their attitude in the war, but without taking the slightest heed of their historical development, their economical interests, or cultural importance. One group of these peoples was admitted to the rank of Associates, and these favourites were granted anything they desired and even more than they aspired to. This group comprised the Czechs, Serbs and Rumanians. The second category was formed of those small people who, in the eyes of the makers of the Peace Treaties, were perhaps less responsible for the war than the Hungarians and the Austro-Germans, but who had sided with these two chief culprits to the last, or, at least, had furnished no visible evidence of their intention to betray them. They were never asked what their desire was, but were simply allotted either to the Czechs, on the supposition that they belonged to the northern Slav races, or to the Serbs if they were of supposed southern Slav origin; a procedure in which nobody even thought of safeguarding in any form the national individuality and character of these peoples. This was the fate of the Slovaks and Ruthenians in the north and the Croats, Slovenes and Wends in the south. In consequence their conditions in the new Czechoslovakian Republic and in the Kingdom of Yugoslavia have become absolutely intolerable because they are considered not even as minorities. They belong to a special category of nations which we might most properly call the "oppressed majority."

The third group was formed of the vanquished Hungarians and Austro-Germans. The leading principle in dealing with these was to take away from them all territories where even infinitesimal traces of alien races might be found. One of the very intricate consequences of this procedure was, among other things, that three and a half million Magyars—no less than one-third of the Hungarian people—were put under foreign domination.

. . . . .

It was furthermore a grave mistake to carve geographic, historic and economic units into pieces and then leave them to their fate. This was bound to end in confusion, unrest and new disputes in which the great nations of Europe also must needs be involved sooner or later in consequence of their contrasting interests. It was a mistake to fail to recognise the political and economic duty the Monarchy had been accomplishing—as well as she might—for the benefit of Europe. It was an even graver mistake to substitute nothing for the destroyed organisation of the Monarchy: but—if they considered the methods of the former Monarchy by which the peaceful relations between the small nations had been maintained as unfit and incompatible with the principles of justice—the greatest mistake was to neglect the inauguration of some other and more suitable instrument in its stead, since they might well have realised that the paramount purpose of the Peace Treaties undoubtedly should have been the creation of an organisation where the peaceful relations and the prosperity of the small peoples would be provided for, and certainly not the preparation of the "bellum omnium contra omnes" in which everybody is at constant war against all the others. I am afraid also that Europe will one day have to pay heavily for this neglect and these omissions!

. . . . . .

As you see, there is a cloud of interrogation-marks hovering above the peoples of the Danube Basin. Their position is far from what it was before the war and there are many forces in Europe working to secure the leadership over these peoples, and to shape their future destiny in a form suiting the interests of one or the other of the Great Powers.

12. THE VIEW OF AN AMERICAN LEGAL EXPERT, 1939 [15]

There has been much loose talk concerning "revision" of the peace settlement, in particular of the Treaty of Versailles. The studied opinion on this question of an American student of international law is valuable and enlightening.

[15] W. E. Stephens, *Revisions of the Treaty of Versailles.* (In press; quotation represents closing paragraphs of the book.) By permission of the author and the Columbia University Press.

Among all the Articles of the Treaty of Versailles, which contemplate a variety of changes to be effected in the peace settlement, there is not a single provision which purports to confer upon a contracting State a legal right to free itself from its treaty commitments or to require a revision of the terms of the agreement.

The Principal Allied Powers dictated the terms of the Treaty in 1919 and imposed a settlement upon Germany which was intended to give them greater security and safeguard their position of supremacy. While they contemplated the relinquishment of some of the prerogatives of their commanding position as victors, such as the transitory arrangements, they did not propose to afford Germany an opportunity to escape the legal burdens imposed upon her in the Treaty. The lack of legal or moral restraint on the part of the Allied Powers to abstain from exercising compulsion to produce Germany's acceptance of the settlement did not presage a willingness on their part to grant Germany a right to escape what had been gained at terrific costs.

There was a general recognition of the necessity for providing permanent processes whereby the settlement of 1919 itself could be modified, but the question of treaty revision was so tied up with the requirements for national security, as they saw it, that the Allied Powers could not bring themselves to accept a definite commitment to revise the Treaty at a later date. The complexity of the problems pertaining to the conservation of the advantages gained during the war, made the victors extremely cautious in adopting any measures which might compromise their position of advantage. . . .

Sufficient facilities for revising the Treaty terms were made available to the contracting parties in case the willingness to revise should be present. Arrangements for the voluntary employment of certain agencies and procedures marked the extent of the Allies' acceptance of proposals for Treaty reconsideration and possible readjustments. . . . The chief drawback to the use of the machinery for modifying the settlement of 1919 has been the unwillingness of the contracting parties to coordinate their efforts and to forego whatever advantages might arise for them to bargain for some reward for their consent to a change.

The agencies created by the Treaty lacked the authority to decide and the power to enforce their decisions in many cases where action was needed. One of the most discouraging factors in the account of post-war efforts to achieve a modification of certain Treaty provisions has been the delay which regularly occurred between the acceptance of some scheme to effect a change and the actual inception of the new agreement.

The entire world has suffered from the misfortunes arising from the attempt to dictate a settlement of the war problems. At present there is great confusion regarding the status of the Peace Treaty and the rights and duties of the contracting parties as a result of the limited revisions of the original terms of the agreement, repudiation of various treaty commitments, negotiation of arrangements unrelated to the Peace Treaty, the execution of various stipulations, and the foregoing of contractual rights to avoid military conflicts. The failure of the contracting parties to make a more flexible arrangement for modifications or adjustments of the Treaty provisions may be considered a primary cause of the critical conditions in the field of international law and relations which now confront all nations. One cannot but wonder what the results might have been had the Allied Powers accepted at Paris the proposal which would have enabled the belligerent Powers to effect in a more orderly manner the revisions of the Treaty of Versailles.

☖ ☖ ☖

CHAPTER 2

THE LEAGUE OF NATIONS

13. SPEECH ACCOMPANYING PRESIDENT WILSON'S PRESENTATION OF THE DRAFT COVENANT TO THE PEACE CONFERENCE, FEBRUARY 14, 1919 [1]

President Wilson, who insisted that a constitution for a society of nations be written into the peace settlement, was made chairman of a special commission to draft such a covenant. The commission, composed of two representatives each from the United States, the British Empire, France, Italy, and Japan and one each from Belgium, Brazil, China, Portugal, Serbia, Greece, Poland, Rumania, and Czechoslovakia, reported back to a plenary session of the Paris Peace Conference on February 14, 1919—twenty days after its appointment. Wilson's speech in presenting the draft included the following remarks.

UNION OF WILLS THAT CANNOT BE RESISTED.

Fourteen nations were represented [on the committee that prepared the draft], among them all of those Powers which for convenience we have called the Great Powers, and among the rest a representation of the greatest variety of circumstances and interests. So that I think we are justified in saying that the significance of the result, therefore, had the deepest of all meanings, the union of wills in a common purpose, a union of wills which cannot be resisted, and which, I dare say, no nation will run the risk of attempting to resist.

Now as to the character of the document. While it has consumed some time to read this document, I think you will see at once that it is very simple, and in nothing so simple as in the structure which it suggests for a League of Nations—a body of delegates, an executive council, and a permanent secretariat.

---

[1] H. W. V. Temperley, ed., *A History of the Peace Conference of Paris*, 6 vols., Henry Frowde and Hodder & Stoughton, London, 1920-1924, vol. III, pp. 62-65. Reprinted by permission of the publishers.

When it came to the question of determining the character of the representation in the body of delegates, we were all aware of a feeling which is current throughout the world. Inasmuch as I am stating it in the presence of the official representatives of the various governments here present, including myself, I may say that there is a universal feeling that the world cannot rest satisfied with merely official guidance. There has reached us through many channels the feeling that if the deliberating body of the League of Nations was merely to be a body of officials representing the various governments, the peoples of the world would not be sure that some of the mistakes which preoccupied officials had admittedly made might not be repeated.

It was impossible to conceive a method or an assembly so large and various as to be really representative of the great body of the peoples of the world, because, as I roughly reckon it, we represent, as we sit around this table, more than twelve hundred million people. You cannot have a representative assembly of twelve hundred million people, but if you leave it to each government to have, if it pleases, one or two or three representatives, though only with a single vote, it may vary its representation from time to time, not only, but it may govern the choice of its several representatives.

Therefore, we thought that this was a proper and a very prudent concession to the practically universal opinion of plain men everywhere that they wanted the door left open to a variety of representation, instead of being confined to a single official body with which they could or might not find themselves in sympathy.

PROVISION FOR DISCUSSION.

And you will notice that this body has unlimited rights of discussion —I mean of discussion of anything that falls within the field of international relations—and that it is especially agreed that war or international misunderstandings, or anything that may lead to friction or trouble, is everybody's business, because it may affect the peace of the world.

And in order to safeguard the popular power so far as we could of this representative body, it is provided, you will notice, that when a subject is submitted, it is not to arbitration, but to discussion by the Executive Council. It can, upon the initiative of either of the parties to the dispute, be drawn out of the Executive Council on the larger form of the general body of delegates, because through this instrument we are depending primarily and chiefly upon one great force, and this is the moral force of the public opinion of the world—the pleasing and clarifying and compelling influences of publicity, so that intrigues can no longer have their coverts, so that designs that are sinister can at any time be drawn into the open, so that those things that are destroyed by the light may be promptly destroyed by the overwhelming light of the universal expression of the condemnation of the world.

Armed force is in the background in this programme, but it is in the background, and if the moral force of the world will not suffice, the physical force of the world shall. But that is the last resort, because this is intended as a constitution of peace, not as a league of war.

The simplicity of the document seems to me to be one of its chief virtues, because, speaking for myself, I was unable to see the variety of circumstances with which this League would have to deal. I was unable, therefore, to plan all the machinery that might be necessary to meet the differing and unexpected contingencies. Therefore, I should say of this document that it is not a strait-jacket, but a vehicle of life.

A LIVING THING IS BORN.

A living thing is born, and we must see to it what clothes we put on it. It is not a vehicle of power, but a vehicle in which power may be varied at the discretion of those who exercise it and in accordance with the changing circumstances of the time. And yet, while it is elastic, while it is general in its terms, it is definite in the one thing that we are called upon to make definite. It is a definite guarantee of peace. It is a definite guarantee by word against aggression. It is a definite guarantee against the things which have just come near bringing the whole structure of civilization to ruin.

Its purposes do not for a moment lie vague. Its purposes are declared, and its powers are unmistakable. It is not in contemplation that this should be merely a League to secure the peace of the world. It is a League which can be used for co-operation in any international matter. That is the significance of the provision introduced concerning labour. There are many ameliorations of labour conditions which can be effected by conference and discussion. I anticipate that there will be a very great usefulness in the Bureau of Labour which it is contemplated shall be set up by the League. Men and women and children who work have been in the background through long ages, and sometimes seemed to be forgotten, while governments have had their watchful and suspicious eyes upon the manœuvres of one another, while the thought of statesmen has been about structural action and the larger transactions of commerce and finance.

Now, if I may believe the picture which I see, there comes into the foreground the great body of the labouring people of the world, the men and women and children upon whom the great burden of sustaining the world must from day to day fall, whether we wish it to do so or not, people who go to bed tired and wake up without the stimulation of lively hope. These people will be drawn into the field of international consultation and help, and will be among the wards of the combined governments of the world. This is, I take leave to say, a very great step in advance.

Then, as you will notice, there is an imperative article concerning the publicity of all international agreements. Henceforth no member of the League can claim any agreement valid which it has not registered with the Secretary-General, in whose office, of course, it will be subject to the examination of anybody representing a member of the League. And the duty is laid upon the Secretary-General to publish every document of that sort at the earliest possible time.

I suppose most persons who have not been conversant with the business of foreign affairs do not realize how many hundreds of these agreements are made in a single year, and how difficult it might be to publish the more unimportant of them immediately, how uninteresting it would be to most of the world to publish them immediately, but even they must be published just as soon as it is possible for the Secretary-General to publish them.

PROTECTION OF THE HELPLESS.

Then there is a feature about this covenant which, to my mind, is one of the greatest and most satisfactory advances that have been made. We are done with annexations of helpless peoples, meant in some instances by some Powers to be used merely for exploitation. We recognized in the most solemn manner that the helpless and undeveloped peoples of the world, being in that condition, put an obligation upon us to look after their interests primarily before we use them for our interests; and that in all cases of this sort hereafter it shall be the duty of the League to see that the nations who are assigned as the tutors and advisors and directors of these peoples shall look to their interests and their development before they look to the interests and desires of the mandatory nation itself.

There has been no greater advance than this, gentlemen. If you look back upon the history of the world you will see how helpless peoples have too often been a prey to Powers that had no conscience in the matter. It has been one of the many distressing revelations of recent years that the Great Power which has just been, happily, defeated put intolerable burdens and injustices upon the helpless people of some of the colonies which it annexed to itself, that its interest was rather their extermination than their development, that the desire was to possess the land for European purposes and not to enjoy their confidence in order that mankind might be lifted in these places to the next higher level.

Now, the world, expressing its conscience in law, says there is an end of that, that our consciences shall be settled to this thing. States will be picked out which have already shown that they can exercise a conscience in this matter, and under their tutelage the helpless peoples of the world will come into a new light and into a new hope.

A PRACTICAL DOCUMENT.

So I think I can say of this document that it is at one and the same time a practical document and a human document. There is a pulse of sympathy in it. There is a compulsion of conscience throughout it. It is practical, and yet it is intended to purify, to rectify, to elevate. And I want to say that, so far as my observation instructs me, this is in one sense a belated document. I believe that the conscience of the world has long been prepared to express itself in some such way. We are not just now discovering our sympathy for these people and our interest in them. We are simply expressing it, for it has long been felt, and in the administration of the affairs of more than one of the great States represented here—so far as I know, all of the great States that are represented here—that humane impulse has already expressed itself in their dealings with their colonies, whose peoples were yet at a low stage of civilization.

We have had many instances of colonies lifted into the sphere of complete self-government. This is not the discovery of a principle. It is the universal application of a principle. It is the agreement of the great nations which have tried to live by these standards in their separate administrations to unite in seeing that their common force and their common thought and intelligence are lent to this great and humane enterprise. I think it is an occasion, therefore, for the most profound satisfaction that this humane decision should have been reached in a matter for which the world has long been waiting, and until a very recent period thought that it was still too early to hope.

Many terrible things have come out of this war, gentlemen, but some very beautiful things have come out of it. Wrong has been defeated, but the rest of the world has been more conscious than it ever was before of the majority of right. People that were suspicious of one another can now live as friends and comrades in a single family, and desire to do so. The miasma of distrust, of intrigue, is cleared away. Men are looking eye to eye and saying: "We are brothers and have a common purpose. We did not realize it before, but now we do realize it, and this is our covenant of friendship."

14. THE (AMENDED) COVENANT OF THE LEAGUE OF NATIONS [2]

The twenty-six articles of the League of Nations Covenant comprised the first twenty-six articles of each of the peace treaties. This circumstance, insisted on by Wilson lest the nations shelve indefinitely the drafting of such an instrument, was an important item in the decision of the United States Senate to refuse its consent to American ratification. The first meeting of the League Council took place in Paris on January 16, 1920, under the presidency of Léon Bourgeois of France. The first meeting of the Assembly took place in Geneva on November 15, 1920, under the presidency of Paul Hymans of Belgium.

The High Contracting Parties,

In order to promote international co-operation and to achieve international peace and security
    by the acceptance of obligations not to resort to war,
    by the prescription of open, just and honourable relations between nations,
    by the firm establishment of the understandings of international law as the actual rule of conduct among Governments,
    and by the maintenance of justice and a scrupulous respect for all treaty obligations in the dealings of organised peoples with one another,

Agree to this Covenant of the League of Nations.

---

[2] League of Nations, *Ten Years of World Co-operation*, Secretariat of the League of Nations, Geneva, 1930, pp. 417-430.

ARTICLE 1.

1. The original Members of the League of Nations shall be those of the Signatories which are named in the Annex to this Covenant and also such of those other States named in the Annex as shall accede without reservation to this Covenant. Such accession shall be effected by a Declaration deposited with the Secretariat within two months of the coming into force of the Covenant. Notice thereof shall be sent to all other Members of the League.

2. Any fully self-governing State, Dominion or Colony not named in the Annex may become a Member of the League if its admission is agreed to by two-thirds of the Assembly, provided that it shall give effective guarantees of its sincere intention to observe its international obligations, and shall accept such regulations as may be prescribed by the League in regard to its military, naval and air forces and armaments.

3. Any Member of the League may, after two years' notice of its intention so to do, withdraw from the League, provided that all its international obligations and all its obligations under this Covenant shall have been fulfilled at the time of its withdrawal.

ARTICLE 2.

The action of the League under this Covenant shall be effected through the instrumentality of an Assembly and of a Council, with a permanent Secretariat.

ARTICLE 3.

1. The Assembly shall consist of Representatives of the Members of the League.

2. The Assembly shall meet at stated intervals and from time to time as occasion may require at the Seat of the League or at such other place as may be decided upon.

3. The Assembly may deal at its meetings with any matter within the sphere of action of the League or affecting the peace of the world.

4. At meetings of the Assembly, each Member of the League shall have one vote, and may have not more than three Representatives.

ARTICLE 4.

1. The Council shall consist of Representatives of the Principal Allied and Associated Powers, together with Representatives of four other Members of the League. These four Members of the League shall be

selected by the Assembly from time to time in its discretion. Until the appointment of the Representatives of the four Members of the League first selected by the Assembly, Representatives of Belgium, Brazil, Spain and Greece shall be Members of the Council.

2. With the approval of the majority of the Assembly, the Council may name additional Members of the League, whose Representatives shall always be members of the Council; the Council with like approval may increase the number of Members of the League to be selected by the Assembly for representation on the Council.[3]

2 bis.[4] *The Assembly shall fix by a two-thirds majority the rules dealing with the election of the non-permanent Members of the Council, and particularly such regulations as relate to their term of office and the conditions of re-eligibility.*

3. The Council shall meet from time to time as occasion may require, and at least once a year, at the Seat of the League, or at such other place as may be decided upon.

4. The Council may deal at its meetings with any matter within the sphere of action of the League or affecting the peace of the world.

5. Any Member of the League not represented on the Council shall be invited to send a Representative to sit as a member at any meeting of the Council during the consideration of matters specially affecting the interests of that Member of the League.

6. At meetings of the Council, each Member of the League represented on the Council shall have one vote, and may have not more than one Representative.

ARTICLE 5.

1. Except where otherwise expressly provided in this Covenant or by the terms of the present Treaty, decisions at any meeting of the Assembly or of the Council shall require the agreement of all the Members of the League represented at the meeting.

2. All matters of procedure at meetings of the Assembly or of the Council, including the appointment of Committees to investigate particular matters, shall be regulated by the Assembly or by the Council and may be decided by a majority of the Members of the League represented at the meeting.

3. The first meeting of the Assembly and the first meeting of the

---

[3] The number of non-permanent members of the Council was increased to six on September 25, 1922, to nine on September 8, 1926, to ten on October 5, 1933, and to eleven on October 10, 1936.—*Ed.*

[4] This amendment (italics) came into force on July 29, 1926.—*Ed.*

Council shall be summoned by the President of the United States of America.

ARTICLE 6.

1. The permanent Secretariat shall be established at the Seat of the League. The Secretariat shall comprise a Secretary-General and such secretaries and staff as may be required.

2. The first Secretary-General shall be the person named in the Annex; thereafter the Secretary-General shall be appointed by the Council with the approval of the majority of the Assembly.

3. The secretaries and staff of the Secretariat shall be appointed by the Secretary-General with the approval of the Council.

4. The Secretary-General shall act in that capacity at all meetings of the Assembly and of the Council.

5.[5] *The expenses of the League shall be borne by the Members of the League in the proportion decided by the Assembly.*

ARTICLE 7.

1. The Seat of the League is established at Geneva.

2. The Council may at any time decide that the Seat of the League shall be established elsewhere.

3. All positions under or in connection with the League, including the Secretariat, shall be open equally to men and women.

4. Representatives of the Members of the League and officials of the League when engaged on the business of the League shall enjoy diplomatic privileges and immunities.

5. The buildings and other property occupied by the League or its officials or by Representatives attending its meetings shall be inviolable.

ARTICLE 8.

1. The Members of the League recognise that the maintenance of peace requires the reduction of national armaments to the lowest point consistent with national safety and the enforcement by common action of international obligations.

2. The Council, taking account of the geographical situation and circumstances of each State, shall formulate plans for such reduction for the consideration and action of the several Governments.

3. Such plans shall be subject to reconsideration and revision at least every ten years.

---

[5] This amendment (italics) came into force on August 13, 1924.—*Ed.*

4. After these plans shall have been adopted by the several Governments, the limits of armaments therein fixed shall not be exceeded without the concurrence of the Council.

5. The Members of the League agree that the manufacture by private enterprise of munitions and implements of war is open to grave objections. The Council shall advise how the evil effects attendant upon such manufacture can be prevented, due regard being had to the necessities of those Members of the League which are not able to manufacture the munitions and implements of war necessary for their safety.

6. The Members of the League undertake to interchange full and frank information as to the scale of their armaments, their military, naval and air programmes and the condition of such of their industries as are adaptable to warlike purposes.

ARTICLE 9.

A permanent Commission shall be constituted to advise the Council on the execution of the provisions of Articles 1 and 8 and on military, naval and air questions generally.

ARTICLE 10.

The Members of the League undertake to respect and preserve as against external aggression the territorial integrity and existing political independence of all Members of the League. In case of any such aggression or in case of any threat or danger of such aggression the Council shall advise upon the means by which this obligation shall be fulfilled.

ARTICLE 11.

1. Any war or threat of war, whether immediately affecting any of the Members of the League or not, is hereby declared a matter of concern to the whole League, and the League shall take any action that may be deemed wise and effectual to safeguard the peace of nations. In case any such emergency should arise the Secretary-General shall on the request of any Member of the League forthwith summon a meeting of the Council.

2. It is also declared to be the friendly right of each Member of the League to bring to the attention of the Assembly or of the Council any circumstance whatever affecting international relations which threatens to disturb international peace or the good understanding between nations upon which peace depends.

ARTICLE 12.[6]

1. The Members of the League agree that if there should arise between them any dispute likely to lead to a rupture they will submit the matter either to arbitration *or judicial settlement* or to enquiry by the Council, and they agree in no case to resort to war until three months after the award by the arbitrators *or the judicial decision* or the report by the Council.

2. In any case under this Article the award of the arbitrators *or the judicial decision* shall be made within a reasonable time, and the report of the Council shall be made within six months after the submission of the dispute.

ARTICLE 13.[7]

1. The Members of the League agree that whenever any dispute shall arise between them which they recognise to be suitable for submission to arbitration *or judicial settlement,* and which cannot be satisfactorily settled by diplomacy, they will submit the whole subject-matter to arbitration *or judicial settlement.*

2. Disputes as to the interpretation of a treaty, as to any question of international law, as to the existence of any fact which, if established, would constitute a breach of any international obligation, or as to the extent and nature of the reparation to be made for any such breach, are declared to be among those which are generally suitable for submission to arbitration *or judicial settlement.*

3. *For the consideration of any such dispute, the court to which the case is referred shall be the Permanent Court of International Justice, established in accordance with Article 14, or any tribunal agreed on by the parties to the dispute or stipulated in any convention existing between them.*

4. The Members of the League agree that they will carry out in full good faith any award *or decision* that may be rendered, and that they will not resort to war against a Member of the League which complies therewith. In the event of any failure to carry out such an award *or decision,* the Council shall propose what steps should be taken to give effect thereto.

ARTICLE 14.

The Council shall formulate and submit to the Members of the League for adoption plans for the establishment of a Permanent Court

---

[6] The material in italics came into force on September 26, 1924.—*Ed.*
[7] As under note 6.—*Ed.*

of International Justice. The Court shall be competent to hear and determine any dispute of an international character which the parties thereto submit to it. The Court may also give an advisory opinion upon any dispute or question referred to it by the Council or by the Assembly.

ARTICLE 15.

1.[8] If there should arise between Members of the League any dispute likely to lead to a rupture, which is not submitted to arbitration *or judicial settlement* in accordance with Article 13, the Members of the League agree that they will submit the matter to the Council. Any party to the dispute may effect such submission by giving notice of the existence of the dispute to the Secretary-General, who will make all necessary arrangements for a full investigation and consideration thereof.

2. For this purpose the parties to the dispute will communicate to the Secretary-General, as promptly as possible, statements of their case with all the relevant facts and papers, and the Council may forthwith direct the publication thereof.

3. The Council shall endeavour to effect a settlement of the dispute, and if such efforts are successful, a statement shall be made public giving such facts and explanations regarding the dispute and the terms of settlement thereof as the Council may deem appropriate.

4. If the dispute is not thus settled, the Council either unanimously or by a majority vote shall make and publish a report containing a statement of the facts of the dispute and the recommendations which are deemed just and proper in regard thereto.

5. Any Member of the League represented on the Council may make public a statement of the facts of the dispute and of its conclusions regarding the same.

6. If a report by the Council is unanimously agreed to by the members thereof other than the Representatives of one or more of the parties to the dispute, the Members of the League agree that they will not go to war with any party to the dispute which complies with the recommendations of the report.

7. If the Council fails to reach a report which is unanimously agreed to by the members thereof, other than the Representatives of one or more of the parties to the dispute, the Members of the League reserve to themselves the right to take such action as they shall consider necessary for the maintenance of right and justice.

[8] The amendment (italics) to the first paragraph of this article came into force on September 26, 1924.—*Ed.*

8. If the dispute between the parties is claimed by one of them, and is found by the Council, to arise out of a matter which by international law is solely within the domestic jurisdiction of that party, the Council shall so report, and shall make no recommendation as to its settlement.

9. The Council may in any case under this Article refer the dispute to the Assembly. The dispute shall be so referred at the request of either party to the dispute provided that such request be made within fourteen days after the submission of the dispute to the Council.

10. In any case referred to the Assembly, all the provisions of this Article and of Article 12 relating to the action and powers of the Council shall apply to the action and powers of the Assembly, provided that a report made by the Assembly, if concurred in by the Representatives of those members of the League represented on the Council and of a majority of the other Members of the League, exclusive in each case of the Representatives of the parties to the dispute, shall have the same force as a report by the Council concurred in by all the members thereof other than the Representatives of one or more of the parties to the dispute.

ARTICLE 16.

1. Should any Member of the League resort to war in disregard of its covenants under Articles 12, 13 or 15, it shall *ipso facto* be deemed to have committed an act of war against all other Members of the League, which hereby undertake immediately to subject it to the severance of all trade or financial relations, the prohibition of all intercourse between their nationals and the nationals of the covenant-breaking State, and the prevention of all financial, commercial or personal intercourse between the nationals of the covenant-breaking State and the nationals of any other State, whether a Member of the League or not.

2. It shall be the duty of the Council in such case to recommend to the several Governments concerned what effective military, naval or air force the Members of the League shall severally contribute to the armed forces to be used to protect the covenants of the League.

3. The Members of the League agree, further, that they will mutually support one another in the financial and economic measures which are taken under this Article, in order to minimise the loss and inconvenience resulting from the above measures, and that they will mutually support one another in resisting any special measures aimed at one of their number by the covenant-breaking State, and that they will take the necessary steps to afford passage through their territory to the forces of

any of the Members of the League which are co-operating to protect the covenants of the League.

4. Any Member of the League which has violated any covenant of the League may be declared to be no longer a Member of the League by a vote of the Council concurred in by the Representatives of all the other Members of the League represented thereon.

ARTICLE 17.

1. In the event of a dispute between a Member of the League and a State which is not a Member of the League, or between States not Members of the League, the State or States not Members of the League shall be invited to accept the obligations of membership in the League for the purposes of such dispute, upon such conditions as the Council may deem just. If such invitation is accepted, the provisions of Articles 12 to 16 inclusive shall be applied with such modifications as may be deemed necessary by the Council.

2. Upon such invitation being given the Council shall immediately institute an enquiry into the circumstances of the dispute and recommend such action as may seem best and most effectual in the circumstances.

3. If a State so invited shall refuse to accept the obligations of membership in the League for the purposes of such dispute, and shall resort to war against a Member of the League, the provisions of Article 16 shall be applicable as against the State taking such action.

4. If both parties to the dispute when so invited refuse to accept the obligations of membership in the League for the purposes of such dispute, the Council may take such measures and make such recommendations as will prevent hostilities and will result in the settlement of the dispute.

ARTICLE 18.

Every treaty or international engagement entered into hereafter by any Member of the League shall be forthwith registered with the Secretariat and shall as soon as possible be published by it. No such treaty or international engagement shall be binding until so registered.

ARTICLE 19.

The Assembly may from time to time advise the reconsideration by Members of the League of treaties which have become inapplicable and the consideration of international conditions whose continuance might endanger the peace of the world.

ARTICLE 20.

1. The Members of the League severally agree that this Covenant is accepted as abrogating all obligations or understandings *inter se* which are inconsistent with the terms thereof, and solemnly undertake that they will not hereafter enter into any engagements inconsistent with the terms thereof.

2. In case any Member of the League shall, before becoming a Member of the League, have undertaken any obligations inconsistent with the terms of this Covenant, it shall be the duty of such Member to take immediate steps to procure its release from such obligations.

ARTICLE 21.

Nothing in this Covenant shall be deemed to affect the validity of international engagements, such as treaties of arbitration or regional understandings like the Monroe doctrine, for securing the maintenance of peace.

ARTICLE 22.

1. To those colonies and territories which as a consequence of the late war have ceased to be under the sovereignty of the States which formerly governed them and which are inhabited by peoples not yet able to stand by themselves under the strenuous conditions of the modern world, there should be applied the principle that the well-being and development of such peoples form a sacred trust of civilisation and that securities for the performance of this trust should be embodied in this Covenant.

2. The best method of giving practical effect to this principle is that the tutelage of such peoples should be entrusted to advanced nations who by reason of their resources, their experience or their geographical position can best undertake this responsibility, and who are willing to accept it, and that this tutelage should be exercised by them as Mandatories on behalf of the League.

3. The character of the mandate must differ according to the stage of the development of the people, the geographical situation of the territory, its economic conditions and other similar circumstances.

4. Certain communities formerly belonging to the Turkish Empire

have reached a stage of development where their existence as independent nations can be provisionally recognised subject to the rendering of administrative advice and assistance by a Mandatory until such time as they are able to stand alone. The wishes of these communities must be a principal consideration in the selection of the Mandatory.

5. Other peoples, especially those of Central Africa, are at such a stage that the Mandatory must be responsible for the administration of the territory under conditions which will guarantee freedom of conscience and religion, subject only to the maintenance of public order and morals, the prohibition of abuses such as the slave trade, the arms traffic and the liquor traffic, and the prevention of the establishment of fortifications or military and naval bases and of military training of the natives for other than police purposes and the defence of territory, and will also secure equal opportunities for the trade and commerce of other Members of the League.

6. There are territories, such as South-West Africa and certain of the South Pacific Islands, which, owing to the sparseness of their population, or their small size, or their remoteness from the centres of civilisation, or their geographical contiguity to the territory of the Mandatory, and other circumstances, can be best administered under the laws of the Mandatory as integral portions of its territory, subject to the safeguards above mentioned in the interests of the indigenous population.

7. In every case of mandate, the Mandatory shall render to the Council an annual report in reference to the territory committed to its charge.

8. The degree of authority, control or administration to be exercised by the Mandatory shall, if not previously agreed upon by the Members of the League, be explicitly defined in each case by the Council.

9. A permanent Commission shall be constituted to receive and examine the annual reports of the Mandatories and to advise the Council on all matters relating to the observance of the mandates.

ARTICLE 23.

Subject to and in accordance with the provisions of international conventions existing or hereafter to be agreed upon, the Members of the League:

(a) will endeavour to secure and maintain fair and humane conditions of labour for men, women and children, both in their own countries and in all countries to which their commercial and industrial relations extend, and for that purpose will establish and maintain the necessary international organisations;

(b) undertake to secure just treatment of the native inhabitants of territories under their control;

(c) will entrust the League with the general supervision over the execution of agreements with regard to the traffic in women and children, and the traffic in opium and other dangerous drugs;

(d) will entrust the League with the general supervision of the trade in arms and ammunition with the countries in which the control of this traffic is necessary in the common interest;

(e) will make provision to secure and maintain freedom of communications and of transit and equitable treatment for the commerce of all Members of the League. In this connection, the special necessities of the regions devastated during the war of 1914-1918 shall be borne in mind;

(f) will endeavour to take steps in matters of international concern for the prevention and control of disease.

ARTICLE 24.

1. There shall be placed under the direction of the League all international bureaux already established by general treaties if the parties to such treaties consent. All such international bureaux and all commissions for the regulation of matters of international interest hereafter constituted shall be placed under the direction of the League.

2. In all matters of international interest which are regulated by general conventions but which are not placed under the control of international bureaux or commissions, the Secretariat of the League shall, subject to the consent of the Council and if desired by the parties, collect and distribute all relevant information and shall render any other assistance which may be necessary or desirable.

3. The Council may include as part of the expenses of the Secretariat the expenses of any bureau or commission which is placed under the direction of the League.

ARTICLE 25.

The Members of the League agree to encourage and promote the establishment and co-operation of duly authorised voluntary national

Red Cross organisations having as purposes the improvement of health, the prevention of disease and the mitigation of suffering throughout the world.

ARTICLE 26.

1. Amendments to this Covenant will take effect when ratified by the Members of the League whose Representatives compose the Council and by a majority of the Members of the League whose Representatives compose the Assembly.

2. No such amendments shall bind any Member of the League which signifies its dissent therefrom, but in that case it shall cease to be a Member of the League.

15. THE CHIEF DIFFERENCES BETWEEN THE DRAFT OF FEBRUARY 14, 1919, AND THE COVENANT AS ADOPTED ON APRIL 28, 1919 [9]

The draft covenant presented by President Wilson met with considerable criticism from the plenary session of the Paris Conference. Twenty-six important alterations were made before the document was finally adopted.

a.–There was a general re-arrangement of the articles, to make the order more logical.

b.–Certain drafting alterations were made to enable the Germans to sign the Covenant without thereby becoming Members of the League.

c.–The word "States" before "Members of the League" was left out, as not properly applying to the British Dominions and India.

d.–"Body of Delegates" and "Executive Council" became "Assembly" and "Council" respectively.

e.–Provision was made for the admission of new members to the Council, both permanent and elected, in order to cover the cases of Germany and Russia.

f.–States specially invited to sit on the Council are invited to sit "as members."

g.–The need of *unanimity* to give force to a decision of the Council or Assembly is expressly stated (except in specified cases).

[9] H. W. V. Temperley, ed., *A History of the Peace Conference of Paris,* 6 vols., Henry Frowde and Hodder & Stoughton, London, 1920-1924, vol. III, pp. 57-58. Reprinted by permission of the publishers.

h.–The Secretary-General's appointment by the Council must have the *approval* of the Assembly.

i.–The Secretariat and other positions under the League are opened to *women*.

k. (*sic*)–Candidates for admission to the League (not being original members) must adhere *without reservation*.

l.–Members of the League may withdraw from it on giving two years' notice.

m.–The Council is only to formulate plans for the reduction of armaments, and not *determine*. Plans are to be *revised every 10 years* at least.

n.–A prima facie definition of *matter suitable for arbitration* is included in Art. XIII.

o.–Art. XIV. The Court is empowered to give an *advisory opinion* to the Council.

p.–Art. XV. Where a unanimous recommendation cannot be had, Members reserve the right to take such action as they think fit.

q.–The Council is to make no recommendation in cases affecting a Member's *domestic jurisdiction*.

r.–When a dispute is transferred from the Council to the Assembly, the agreement of all the Council and *a majority of the Assembly* is effective.

s.–Art. XVI. A Covenant-breaking State may be expelled.

t.–Art. XVII. "Deemed necessary by the *Council*," instead of "by the League."

u.–New Arts. XXIII, XXV. The League is given an interest in White Slave Traffic, Opium Traffic, treatment of natives, prevention of disease, Red Cross.

v.–The Secretariat is to help and supply information in matters not under any existing Bureau.

w.–No Power need accept a *Mandate* against its will.

x.–The Commission on Mandates is to advise the *Council*, not the League.

y.–*Monroe Doctrine Article* (new Art. XXI) inserted.

z.–Amendments may be carried by a *bare majority* of the Assembly if the Council is unanimous.

zz.–*States dissenting* from an amendment carried by the majority *may withdraw*. Otherwise they are bound by it.

16. THE STATUTE OF THE PERMANENT COURT OF INTER-
NATIONAL JUSTICE, AS AMENDED IN 1936 *(Extracts)* [10]

*The protocol of signature of the statute which set up the "World Court"
was executed at Geneva on December 16, 1920. The statute came into force
in September 1921 after its ratification by twenty-eight states. A protocol to
revise the statute was opened for signature at Geneva on September 14, 1929,
and came into force on February 1, 1936. In addition to slightly modifying
eighteen of the original articles, the protocol of amendment added four new
ones (65-68) which clarified the procedure for advisory opinions. The first
ordinary session of the court was held from June 15 to August 12, 1922.
About sixty states eventually became members of the court, and of these
approximately two-thirds accepted the "Optional Clause" based on the
second paragraph of Article 36.*

ARTICLE 1.

A Permanent Court of International Justice is hereby established,
in accordance with Article 14 of the Covenant of the League of Nations. . . .[11]

ARTICLE 2.

The Permanent Court of International Justice shall be composed of
a body of independent judges, elected regardless of their nationality
from amongst persons of high moral character, who possess the qualifications required in their respective countries for appointment to the
highest judicial offices, or are jurisconsults of recognized competence in
international law.

· · · · ·

ARTICLE 4.

The members of the Court shall be elected by the Assembly and
by the Council from a list of persons nominated by the national groups
in the Court of Arbitration [organized under the Hague Conventions
of 1899 and 1907]. . . .

· · · · ·

---

[10] Permanent Court of International Justice *Publications, Series D. Acts and Documents Concerning the Organization of the Court. No. 1: Statute and Rules of Court,* 3rd
ed. (March 1936), A. W. Sijthoff's Publishing Company, Leyden, 1936, pp. 12-27.

[11] The statute thus incorporated by reference a provision empowering the court to
give advisory opinions. For Article 14 of the Covenant see Document No. 14.—*Ed.*

ARTICLE 9.

At every election, the electors shall bear in mind that not only should all the persons appointed as members of the Court possess the qualifications required, but the whole body also should represent the main forms of civilization and the principal legal systems of the world.

ARTICLE 10.

Those candidates who obtain an absolute majority of votes in the Assembly and in the Council shall be considered as elected.

In the event of more than one national of the same Member of the League being elected by the votes of both the Assembly and the Council, the eldest of these only shall be considered as elected.

. . . . .

ARTICLE 13.

The members of the Court shall be elected for nine years.

They may be re-elected.

They shall continue to discharge their duties until their places have been filled. Though replaced, they shall finish any cases they may have begun. . . .

. . . .

ARTICLE 16.

The members of the Court may not exercise any political or administrative function, nor engage in any other occupation of a professional nature. . . .

. . . . .

ARTICLE 18.

A member of the Court cannot be dismissed unless, in the unanimous opinion of the other members, he has ceased to fulfil the required conditions. . . .

. . . . .

ARTICLE 30.

The Court shall frame rules for regulating its procedure. . . .

ARTICLE 31.

Judges of the nationality of each of the contesting parties shall retain their right to sit in the case before the Court.

If the Court includes upon the Bench a judge of the nationality of one of the parties, the other party may choose a person to sit as a judge. Such person shall be chosen preferably from among those persons who have been nominated as candidates as provided in Articles 4 and 5.

If the Court includes upon the Bench no judge of the nationality of the contesting parties, each of these may proceed to select a judge as provided in the preceding paragraph. . . .

Should there be several parties in the same interest, they shall, for the purpose of the preceding provisions, be reckoned as one party only. . . .

. . . . .

ARTICLE 33.

The expenses of the Court shall be borne by the League of Nations, in such a manner as shall be decided by the Assembly upon the proposal of the Council.

ARTICLE 34.

Only States or Members of the League of Nations can be parties in cases before the Court. . . . . .

ARTICLE 36.

The jurisdiction of the Court comprises all cases which the parties refer to it and all matters specially provided for in treaties and conventions in force.

The Members of the League of Nations and the States mentioned in the Annex to the Covenant may, either when signing or ratifying the protocol to which the present Statute is adjoined, or at a later moment, declare that they recognize as compulsory *ipso facto* and without special agreement, in relation to any other Member or State accepting the same obligation, the jurisdiction of the Court in all or any of the classes of legal disputes concerning:

(*a*) the interpretation of a treaty;

(*b*) any question of international law;

(*c*) the existence of any fact which, if established, would constitute a breach of an international obligation;

(*d*) the nature or extent of the reparation to be made for the breach of an international obligation.

The declaration referred to above may be made unconditionally or on condition of reciprocity on the part of several or certain Members or States, or for a certain time.

In the event of a dispute as to whether the Court has jurisdiction, the matter shall be settled by the decision of the Court.[12]

. . . . .

ARTICLE 39.

The official languages of the Court shall be French and English. . . .

. . . . .

ARTICLE 46.

The hearing in Court shall be public, unless the Court shall decide otherwise, or unless the parties demand that the public be not admitted.

. . . . .

ARTICLE 55.

All questions shall be decided by a majority of the judges present at the hearing.

In the event of an equality of votes, the President or his deputy shall have a casting vote.

. . . . .

ARTICLE 60.

The judgment is final and without appeal. In the event of dispute as to the meaning or scope of the judgment, the Court shall construe it upon the request of any party.

. . . . .

ARTICLE 65.

Questions upon which the advisory opinion of the Court is asked shall be laid before the Court by means of a written request, signed either by the President of the Assembly or the President of the Council of the League of Nations, or by the Secretary-General of the League under instructions from the Assembly or Council.

---

[12] The second paragraph of this article forms the basis of the so-called "Optional Clause" which reads: "The undersigned, being duly authorized thereto, further declare, on behalf of their Government, that, from this date, they accept as compulsory *ipso facto* and without special Convention, the jurisdiction of the Court in conformity with Article 36, paragraph 2, of the Statute of the Court, under the following conditions: . . ."—*Ed.*

The request shall contain an exact statement of the question upon which an opinion is required, and shall be accompanied by all documents likely to throw light upon the question.

· · · · ·

ARTICLE 67.

The Court shall deliver its advisory opinion in open Court, notice having been given to the Secretary-General of the League of Nations and to the representatives of Members of the League, of States and of international organizations immediately concerned.

ARTICLE 68.

In the exercise of its ordinary functions, the Court shall further be guided by the provisions of the Statute which apply in contentious issues to the extent to which it recognizes them to be applicable.

17-19. THE INTERNATIONAL LABOR ORGANIZATION

17. THE CONSTITUTION OF THE I. L. O. *(Extracts from Part XIII of the Treaty of Versailles, June 28, 1919)* [13]

An important section of the peace settlement which met relatively little outspoken criticism, and which was therefore perhaps less familiar to the general public, was that dealing with the establishment of an International Labor Organization (I. L. O.) to promote the ideal of social justice throughout the world. This body, though sustained by League funds, was made autonomous and generally responsible only to itself and to public opinion. The first meeting of the General Conference took place in Washington in October 1919. The United States became a member of the I. L. O. on August 20, 1934, without assuming "any obligations under the Covenant of the League of Nations."

· · · · ·

Whereas the League of Nations has for its object the establishment of universal peace, and such a peace can be established only if it is based upon social justice;

---

[13] United States, 66th Congress, 1st Session, Senate Document No. 49, *Treaty of Peace with Germany*, Government Printing Office, Washington, 1919.

And whereas conditions of labour exist involving such injustice, hardship and privation to large numbers of people as to produce unrest so great that the peace and harmony of the world are imperilled; and an improvement of those conditions is urgently required: as, for example, by the regulation of the hours of work, including the establishment of a maximum working day and week, the regulation of the labour supply, the prevention of unemployment, the provision of an adequate living wage, the protection of the worker against sickness, disease and injury arising out of his employment, the protection of children, young persons and women, provision for old age and injury, protection of the interests of workers when employed in countries other than their own, recognition of the principle of freedom of association, the organisation of vocational and technical education and other measures;

Whereas also the failure of any nation to adopt humane conditions of labour is an obstacle in the way of other nations which desire to improve the conditions in their own countries;

The HIGH CONTRACTING PARTIES, moved by sentiments of justice and humanity as well as by the desire to secure the permanent peace of the world, agree to the following:

. . . . .

ARTICLE 387 [OF THE TREATY OF VERSAILLES].

A permanent organisation is hereby established for the promotion of the objects set forth in the Preamble.

The original Members of the League of Nations shall be the original Members of this organisation, and hereafter membership of the League of Nations shall carry with it membership of the said organisation.

ARTICLE 388.

The permanent organisation shall consist of:

(1) a General Conference of Representatives of the Members and,

(2) an International Labour Office controlled by the Governing Body described in Article 393.

. . . . .

ARTICLE 393.[14]

The International Labour Office shall be under the control of a Governing Body consisting of thirty-two persons:

[14] The General Conference in its fourth session (1922) adopted, by 82 votes to 2, with 6 abstentions, a draft amendment to this article which became effective on June 4, 1934. The amended version is here given.—Ed.

sixteen representing Governments,
eight representing the Employers, and
eight representing the Workers.

Of the sixteen persons representing Governments, eight shall be appointed by the Members of chief industrial importance, and eight shall be appointed by the Members selected for that purpose by the Government Delegates to the Conference excluding the Delegates of the eight Members mentioned above. Of the sixteen Members represented, six shall be non-European States.

Any question as to which are the Members of chief industrial importance shall be decided by the Council of the League of Nations.

The persons representing the Employers and the persons representing the Workers shall be elected respectively by the Employers' Delegates and the Workers' Delegates to the Conference. Two Employers' representatives and two Workers' representatives shall belong to non-European States.

The period of office of the Governing Body shall be three years.

The method of filling vacancies and of appointing substitutes and other similar questions may be decided by the Governing Body subject to the approval of the Conference.

The Governing Body shall, from time to time, elect one of its number to act as its Chairman, shall regulate its own procedure, and shall fix its own times of meeting. A special meeting shall be held if a written request to that effect is made by at least twelve of the representatives on the Governing Body.

．　．　．　．　．

Article 396.

The functions of the International Labour Office shall include the collection and distribution of information on all subjects relating to the international adjustment of conditions of industrial life and labour, and particularly the examination of subjects which it is proposed to bring before the Conference with a view to the conclusion of international conventions, and the conduct of such special investigations as may be ordered by the Conference.

It will prepare the agenda for the meetings of the Conference.

It will carry out the duties required of it by the provisions of this Part of the present Treaty in connection with international disputes.

It will edit and publish in French and English, and in such other languages as the Governing Body may think desirable, a periodical paper dealing with problems of industry and employment of international interest.

Generally, in addition to the functions set out in this Article, it shall have such other powers and duties as may be assigned to it by the Conference.

. . . . .

ARTICLE 399.

Each of the Members will pay the travelling and subsistence expenses of its Delegates and their advisers and of its Representatives attending the meetings of the Conference or Governing Body, as the case may be.

All the other expenses of the International Labour Office and of the meetings of the Conference or Governing Body shall be paid to the Director by the Secretary-General of the League of Nations out of the general funds of the League.

The Director shall be responsible to the Secretary-General of the League for the proper expenditure of all moneys paid to him in pursuance of this Article.

. . . . .

ARTICLE 405.

When the Conference has decided on the adoption of proposals with regard to an item in the agenda, it will rest with the Conference to determine whether these proposals should take the form: (*a*) of a recommendation to be submitted to the Members for consideration with a view to effect being given to it by national legislation or otherwise, or (*b*) of a draft international convention for ratification by the Members.

In either case a majority of two-thirds of the votes cast by the Delegates present shall be necessary on the final vote for the adoption of the recommendation or draft convention, as the case may be, by the Conference.

In framing any recommendation or draft convention of general application the Conference shall have due regard to those countries in which climatic conditions, the imperfect development of industrial organisation, or other special circumstances make the industrial conditions substantially different, and shall suggest the modifications, if any, which it considers may be required to meet the case of such countries.

A copy of the recommendation or draft convention shall be authenticated by the signature of the President of the Conference and of the

Director and shall be deposited with the Secretary-General of the League of Nations. The Secretary-General will communicate a certified copy of the recommendation or draft convention to each of the Members.

Each of the Members undertakes that it will, within the period of one year at most from the closing of the session of the Conference, or if it is impossible owing to exceptional circumstances to do so within the period of one year, then at the earliest practicable moment and in no case later than eighteen months from the closing of the session of the Conference, bring the recommendation or draft convention before the authority or authorities within whose competence the matter lies, for the enactment of legislation or other action.

In the case of a recommendation, the Members will inform the Secretary-General of the action taken.

In the case of a draft convention, the Member will, if it obtains the consent of the authority or authorities within whose competence the matter lies, communicate the formal ratification of the convention to the Secretary-General and will take such action as may be necessary to make effective the provisions of such convention.

If on a recommendation no legislative or other action is taken to make a recommendation effective, or if the draft convention fails to obtain the consent of the authority or authorities within whose competence the matter lies, no further obligation shall rest upon the Member.

In the case of a federal State, the power of which to enter into conventions on labour matters is subject to limitations, it shall be in the discretion of that Government to treat a draft convention to which such limitations apply as a recommendation only, and the provisions of this Article with respect to recommendations shall apply in such case.

The above Article shall be interpreted in accordance with the following principle:

In no case shall any Member be asked or required, as a result of the adoption of any recommendation or draft convention by the Conference, to lessen the protection afforded by its existing legislation to the workers concerned.

. . . . .

ARTICLE 416.

In the event of any Member failing to take the action required by Article 405, with regard to a recommendation or draft convention, any other Member shall be entitled to refer the matter to the Permanent Court of International Justice.

. . . . .

ARTICLE 422.

Amendments to this part of the present Treaty which are adopted by the Conference by a majority of two-thirds of the votes cast by the Delegates present shall take effect when ratified by the States whose representatives compose the Council of the League of Nations and by three-fourths of the Members.

ARTICLE 423.

Any question or dispute relating to the interpretation of this Part of the present Treaty or of any subsequent convention concluded by the Members in pursuance of the provisions of this Part of the present Treaty shall be referred for decision to the Permanent Court of International Justice.

. . . . .

ARTICLE 427.

The High Contracting Parties, recognising that the well-being, physical, moral and intellectual, of industrial wage-earners is of supreme international importance, have framed, in order to further this great end, the permanent machinery provided for in Section I and associated with that of the League of Nations.

They recognise that differences of climate, habits and customs, of economic opportunity and industrial tradition, make strict uniformity in the conditions of labour difficult of immediate attainment. But, holding as they do that labour should not be regarded merely as an article of commerce, they think that there are methods and principles for regulating labour conditions which all industrial communities should endeavour to apply, so far as their special circumstances will permit.

Among these methods and principles, the following seem to the High Contracting Parties to be of special and urgent importance:

First.—The guiding principle above enunciated that labour should not be regarded merely as a commodity or article of commerce.

Second.—The right of association for all lawful purposes by the employed as well as by the employers.

Third.—The payment to the employed of a wage adequate to maintain a reasonable standard of life as this is understood in their time and country.

Fourth.—The adoption of an eight-hour day or a forty-eight-hour week as the standard to be aimed at where it has not already been attained.

Fifth.—The adoption of a weekly rest of at least twenty-four hours, which should include Sunday wherever practicable.

Sixth.—The abolition of child labour and the imposition of such limitations on the labour of young persons as shall permit the continuation of their education and assure their proper physical development.

Seventh.—The principle that men and women should receive equal remuneration for work of equal value.

Eighth.—The standard set by law in each country with respect to the conditions of labour should have due regard to the equitable economic treatment of all workers lawfully resident therein.

Ninth.—Each State should make provision for a system of inspection in which women should take part, in order to ensure the enforcement of the laws and regulations for the protection of the employed.

Without claiming that these methods and principles are either complete or final, the High Contracting Parties are of opinion that they are well fitted to guide the policy of the League of Nations; and that, if adopted by the industrial communities who are Members of the League, and safeguarded in practice by an adequate system of such inspection, they will confer lasting benefits upon the wage-earners of the world.[15]

18. A SAMPLE DRAFT CONVENTION: DRAFT CONVENTION CONCERNING SICKNESS INSURANCE FOR AGRICULTURAL WORKERS, 1927 [16]

The following draft convention, included as an example, was adopted on June 15, 1927, during the tenth session of the General Conference of the I. L. O.

The General Conference of the International Labour Organisation of the League of Nations,

---

[15] These labor provisions of the Versailles Treaty are reproduced in full in Part XIII (Articles 332-372) of the Treaty of Saint-Germain with Austria, Part XIII (Articles 315-355) of the Treaty of Trianon with Hungary, and Part XII (Articles 249-289) of the Treaty of Neuilly with Bulgaria.—*Ed.*

[16] International Labour Office, *Official Bulletin*, vol. XII, pp. 131-135.

Having been convened at Geneva by the Governing Body of the International Labour Office, and having met in its Tenth Session on 25 May 1927, and

Having decided upon the adoption of certain proposals with regard to sickness insurance for agricultural workers, which is included in the first item of the Agenda of the Session, and

Having determined that these proposals shall take the form of a draft international convention,

adopts, this fifteenth day of June of the year one thousand nine hundred and twenty-seven, the following Draft Convention for ratification by the Members of the International Labour Organisation, in accordance with the provisions of Part XIII of the Treaty of Versailles and of the corresponding Parts of the other Treaties of Peace:

ARTICLE 1.

Each Member of the International Labour Organisation which ratifies this Convention undertakes to set up a system of compulsory sickness insurance for agricultural workers, which shall be based on provisions at least equivalent to those contained in this Convention.

ARTICLE 2.

The compulsory sickness insurance system shall apply to manual and non-manual workers, including apprentices, employed by agricultural undertakings.

It shall, nevertheless, be open to any Member to make such exceptions in its national laws or regulations as it deems necessary in respect of:

(a) Temporary employment which lasts for less than a period to be determined by national laws or regulations, casual employment not for the purpose of the employer's trade or business, occasional employment and subsidiary employment;

(b) Workers whose wages or income exceed an amount to be determined by national laws or regulations;

(c) Workers who are not paid a money wage;

(d) Out-workers whose conditions of work are not of a like nature to those of ordinary wage-earners;

(e) Workers below or above age-limits to be determined by national laws or regulations;

(f) Members of the employer's family.

It shall further be open to exempt from the compulsory sickness insurance system persons who in case of sickness are entitled by virtue of any laws or regulations, or of a special scheme, to advantages at least equivalent on the whole to those provided for in this Convention.

ARTICLE 3.

An insured person who is rendered incapable of work by reason of the abnormal state of his bodily or mental health shall be entitled to a cash benefit for at least the first twenty-six weeks of incapacity from and including the first day for which benefit is payable.

The payment of this benefit may be made conditional on the insured person having first complied with a qualifying period and, on the expiry of the same, with a waiting period of not more than three days.

Cash benefit may be withheld in the following cases:

(a) Where in respect of the same illness the insured person receives compensation from another source to which he is entitled by law; benefit shall only be wholly or partially withheld in so far as such compensation is equal to or less than the amount of the benefit provided by the present Article;

(b) As long as the insured person does not by the fact of his incapacity suffer any loss of the normal product of his labour, or is maintained at the expense of the insurance funds or from public funds; nevertheless, cash benefit shall only partially be withheld when the insured person, although thus personally maintained, has family responsibilities;

(c) As long as the insured person while ill refuses, without valid reason, to comply with the doctor's orders, or the instructions relating to the conduct of insured persons while ill, or voluntarily and without authorisation removes himself from the supervision of the insurance institutions.

Cash benefit may be reduced or refused in the case of sickness caused by the insured person's wilful misconduct.

ARTICLE 4.

The insured person shall be entitled free of charge, as from the commencement of his illness and at least until the period prescribed for the grant of sickness benefit expires, to medical treatment by a fully qualified medical man and to the supply of proper and sufficient medicines and appliances.

Nevertheless, the insured person may be required to pay such part of the cost of medical benefit as may be prescribed by national laws or regulations.

Medical benefit may be withheld as long as the insured person refuses, without valid reason, to comply with the doctor's orders or the instructions relating to the conduct of insured persons while ill, or neglects to make use of the facilities placed at his disposal by the insurance institution.

ARTICLE 5.

National laws or regulations may authorise or prescribe the grant of medical benefit to members of an insured person's family living in his household and dependent upon him, and shall determine the conditions under which such benefit shall be administered.

ARTICLE 6.

Sickness insurance shall be administered by self-governing institutions, which shall be under the administrative and financial supervision of the competent public authority and shall not be carried on with a view of profit. Institutions founded by private initiative must be specially approved by the competent public authority.

The insured persons shall participate in the management of the self governing insurance institutions on such conditions as may be prescribed by national laws or regulations.

The administration of sickness insurance may, nevertheless, be undertaken directly by the State where and as long as its administration is rendered difficult or impossible or inappropriate by reason of national conditions, and particularly by the insufficient development of the employers' and workers' organisations.

ARTICLE 7.

The insured persons and their employers shall share in providing the financial resources of the sickness insurance system.

It is open to national laws or regulations to decide as to a financial contribution by the competent public authority.

ARTICLE 8.

A right of appeal shall be granted to the insured person in case of dispute concerning his right to benefit.

ARTICLE 9.

It shall be open to States which comprise large and very thinly populated areas not to apply the Convention in districts where, by reason of the small density and wide dispersion of the population and the inadequacy of the means of communication, the organisation of sickness insurance, in accordance with this Convention, is impossible.

The States which intend to avail themselves of the exception provided by this Article shall give notice of their intention when communicating their formal ratification to the Secretary-General of the League of Nations. They shall inform the International Labour Office as to what districts they apply the exception and indicate their reasons therefor.

In Europe it shall be open only to Finland to avail itself of the exception contained in this Article.

ARTICLE 10.

The formal ratifications of this Convention under the conditions set forth in Part XIII of the Treaty of Versailles and in the corresponding Parts of the other Treaties of Peace shall be communicated to the Secretary-General of the League of Nations for registration.

ARTICLE 11.

This Convention shall come into force ninety days after the date on which the ratifications of two Members of the International Labour Organisation have been registered by the Secretary-General.

It shall be binding only upon those Members whose ratifications have been registered with the Secretariat.

Thereafter, the Convention shall come into force for any Member ninety days after the date on which its ratification has been registered with the Secretariat.

ARTICLE 12.

As soon as the ratifications of two Members of the International Labour Organisation have been registered with the Secretariat, the Secretary-General of the League of Nations shall so notify all the Members of the International Labour Organisation. He shall likewise notify them of the registration of ratifications which may be communicated subsequently by other Members of the Organisation.

ARTICLE 13.

Subject to the provisions of Article 11, each Member which ratifies this Convention agrees to bring the provisions of Articles 1, 2, 3, 4, 5,

6, 7, 8, and 9 into operation not later than 1 January 1929, and to take such action as may be necessary to make these provisions effective.

ARTICLE 14.

Each Member of the International Labour Organisation which ratifies this Convention engages to apply it to its colonies, possessions and protectorates, in accordance with the provisions of Article 421 of the Treaty of Versailles and of the corresponding Articles of the other Treaties of Peace.

ARTICLE 15.

A Member which has ratified this Convention may denounce it after the expiration of ten years from the date on which the Convention first comes into force, by an act communicated to the Secretary-General of the League of Nations for registration. Such denunciation shall not take effect until one year after the date on which it is registered with the Secretariat.

ARTICLE 16.

At least once in ten years, the Governing Body of the International Labour Office shall present to the General Conference a report on the working of this Convention and shall consider the desirability of placing on the Agenda of the Conference the question of its revision or modification.

ARTICLE 17.

The French and English texts of this Convention shall both be authentic.

19. LIST OF INTERNATIONAL LABOR CONVENTIONS ADOPTED BY THE INTERNATIONAL LABOR CONFERENCE, 1919-1937 [17]

In the eighteen-year period from 1919 to 1937, the General Conference of the I.L.O. adopted an average of about seven conventions every two years. The list was varied and interesting.

1. Hours of Work (Industry), 1919.
2. Unemployment, 1919.
3. Childbirth, 1919.

---

[17] International Labour Conference, Twenty-Fourth Session, Geneva, 1938, *Report of the Director, Appendix (15 March 1938)*, International Labour Office, Geneva, 1938, p. 64.

4. Night Work (Women), 1919.
5. Minimum Age (Industry), 1919.
6. Night Work (Young Persons), 1919.
7. Minimum Age (Sea), 1920.
8. Unemployment Indemnity (Shipwreck), 1920.
9. Placing of Seamen, 1920.
10. Minimum Age (Agriculture), 1921.
11. Right of Association (Agriculture), 1921.
12. Workmen's Compensation (Agriculture), 1921.
13. White Lead (Painting), 1921.
14. Weekly Rest (Industry), 1921.
15. Minimum Age (Trimmers and Stokers), 1921.
16. Medical Examination of Young Persons (Sea), 1921.
17. Workmen's Compensation (Accidents), 1925.
18. Workmen's Compensation (Occupational Diseases), 1925.
19. Equality of Treatment (Accident Compensation), 1925.
20. Night Work (Bakeries), 1925.
21. Inspection of Emigrants, 1926.
22. Seamen's Articles of Agreement, 1926.
23. Repatriation of Seamen, 1926.
24. Sickness Insurance (Industry, etc.), 1927.
25. Sickness Insurance (Agriculture), 1927.
26. Minimum Wage-Fixing Machinery, 1928.
27. Marking of Weight (Packages Transported by Vessels), 1929.
28. Protection against Accidents (Dockers), 1929.
29. Forced Labour, 1930.
30. Hours of Work (Commerce and Offices), 1930.
31. Hours of Work (Coal Mines), 1931.
32. Protection against Accidents (Dockers) (Revised), 1932.
33. Minimum Age (Non-Industrial Employment), 1932.
34. Fee-Charging Employment Agencies, 1933.
35. Old-Age Insurance (Industry, etc.), 1933.
36. Old-Age Insurance (Agriculture), 1933.
37. Invalidity Insurance (Industry, etc.), 1933.
38. Invalidity Insurance (Agriculture), 1933.
39. Survivors' Insurance (Industry, etc.), 1933.
40. Survivors' Insurance (Agriculture), 1933.
41. Night Work (Women) (Revised), 1934.

42. Workmen's Compensation (Occupational Diseases) (Revised), 1934.
43. Sheet-Glass Works, 1934.
44. Unemployment Provisions, 1934.
45. Underground Work (Women), 1935.
46. Hours of Work (Coal Mines) (Revised), 1935.
47. Forty-Hour Week, 1935.
48. Maintenance of Migrants' Pension Rights, 1935.
49. Reduction of Hours of Work (Glass-Bottle Works), 1935.
50. Recruiting of Indigenous Workers, 1936.
51. Reduction of Hours of Work (Public Works), 1936.
52. Holidays with Pay, 1936.
53. Officers Competency Certificates, 1936.
54. Holidays with Pay (Sea), 1936.
55. Shipowners' Liability (Sick and Injured Seamen), 1936.
56. Sickness Insurance (Sea), 1936.
57. Hours of Work and Manning (Sea), 1936.
58. Minimum Age (Sea) (Revised), 1936.
59. Minimum Age (Industry) (Revised), 1937.
60. Minimum Age (Non-Industrial Employment) (Revised), 1937.
61. Reduction of Hours of Work (Textiles), 1937.
62. Safety Provisions (Building), 1937.[18]

20. THE REGISTRATION OF TREATIES [19]

In a speech of January 8, 1918, before the United States Congress, President Wilson enunciated fourteen points as comprising "the only possible program" for world peace. The first of these points demanded: "Open covenants of peace, openly arrived at, after which there shall be no private international understandings of any kind but diplomacy shall proceed always frankly and in the public view." Article 18 of the League Covenant accordingly made it incumbent upon League members to register their future

[18] At the time this report was rendered, March 1938, the total number of ratifications of these conventions ranged from 34 for Spain, 33 for Chile, and 30 for Great Britain to 19 each for Hungary and Poland, 17 each for Finland and Germany, and 12 for China and to 1 each for Afghanistan and Liberia.—*Ed.*

[19] *Memorandum Approved by the Council of the League of Nations, Meeting in Rome, on 19th May, 1920, in re: the Registration and Publication of Treaties as Prescribed under Article 18 of the Covenant of the League of Nations,* in League of Nations, *Official Journal, 1st Year* (1920), pp. 154-157.

treaties with the Secretariat. The procedure to be followed was outlined by the Secretary-General and approved by the Council in May 1920. By the end of 1937 the League had published the texts of 4,100 international agreements in 177 volumes of its "Treaty Series." English translations (provided by the Secretariat if necessary) were regularly included.

1. One of the most important innovations in International Law established by the Covenant of Members of the League of Nations consists in the registration and publication of every Treaty or International Engagement entered into by any Member of the League.

Article 18 of the Covenant of the League of Nations, by which this has been provided for, reads as follows:

"Every Treaty or International Engagement entered into hereafter by any Member of the League shall be forthwith registered with the Secretariat and shall as soon as possible be published by it. No such Treaty or International Engagement shall be binding until so registered."

It is hardly necessary to dwell on the importance of an arrangement whereby publicity of Treaties and other International Engagements—and, as a preliminary thereto, their registration—will be secured.

Publicity has for a long time been considered as a source of moral strength in the administration of National Law. It should equally strengthen the laws and engagements which exist *between nations*. It will promote public control. It will awaken public interest. It will remove causes for distrust and conflict. Publicity alone will enable the League of Nations to extend a moral sanction to the contractual obligations of its Members. It will, moreover, contribute to the formation of a clear and indisputable system of International Law.

Since the satisfactory execution of the principles of Article 18 of the Covenant depends in the first place on the co-operation of the Governments of the Members of the League of Nations, the Secretary-General begs to present to the Members of the League in the following memorandum some suggestions whereby, in his opinion, the application of Article 18 may best be secured. The arrangements suggested have, of course, only a provisional character. Experience may, in the future, suggest modification and revision.

2. If the application of Article 18 is to conform to the best advantage with the objects of the League of Nations, an extensive interpretation

of its provisions should be adopted. The details of its applications have accordingly been worked out with this principle in view.

The aim of the following suggestions is to establish as far as possible a complete and reliable survey of the whole system of Treaties and International Engagements entered into after the coming into force of the Covenant of the League.

3. The provision that "every Treaty or International Engagement shall be forthwith registered with the Secretariat" leads to the following conclusions as regards the material which requires registration.

This material comprises not only every formal Treaty of whatsoever character and every International Convention, but also any other International Engagement or act by which nations or their Governments intend to establish legal obligations between themselves and another State, Nation or Government.

Agreements regarding the revision or the prolongation of Treaties form separate international engagements; they also should be registered under Article 18.

It is proposed, moreover, that the denunciation of any Treaty or Agreement should, if only for the sake of completeness, be included in the scheme of registration.

4. Article 18 refers to Treaties, etc., entered into "hereafter." It is thereby understood that registration is necessary for *all* Treaties, etc., which become, or *have* become finally binding so far as the acts between the Parties *inter se* are concerned, after the date of the coming into force of the Covenant (January 10th, 1920).

Treaties or Engagements which have finally come into force at an earlier date are not included; but the International Secretariat is authorised, if this appear desirable to the Contracting Parties, to extend the system of Treaty Registration so as to include Treaties and Engagements of an earlier date.

5. As no Treaties or International Engagements will be binding until registration with the International Secretariat has taken place, the latest date at which they should be presented for registration will be the date when, so far as the acts of the Parties *inter se* are concerned, they receive final binding force, and are intended to come into operation. It may prove convenient, however, for various reasons, for the Parties to present a Treaty or International Engagement for Registration as soon as the text has been finally decided upon, even if exchange of ratifications between them still has to take place at a later date. The Secretary-General will, of course, have to see that, if a Treaty or En-

gagement be published at this stage, it is made clear that the Parties have not yet finally entered into the Treaty or Engagement.

In the event of a Treaty or Engagement being presented for registration before it is finally entered into, the Parties will no doubt inform the Secretariat of the later act by which they definitely bring the Treaty into force.

6. It is suggested as a general principle that the Parties presenting a Treaty or Engagement for registration should do so by depositing a textual and complete copy thereof with all appurtenant declarations, protocols, ratifications, etc., at the Treaty Registration Bureau of the International Secretariat, accompanying it with an authentic statement that this text represents the full contents of the Treaty or Engagement into which the Parties intend to enter.

In case of necessity, the contents of a Treaty or Engagement can of course be transmitted to the International Secretariat by other means— for instance, by telegram—so long as it is established that the text is indisputably the one agreed upon between the Parties.

7. A certificate of Registration will be delivered to the Parties concerned, under the signature of the Secretary-General of the League of Nations, or of his Deputy. . . .

8. Treaties or International Engagements may be presented for Registration by one Party only, either in the name of all the Parties at the same time, or of that Party alone, as long as it is established that the text is that which has been agreed upon between the Parties.

9. Publication of a Treaty or Engagement registered with the Secretariat will be secured automatically and as soon as possible, by its inclusion in the Treaty Part of the League of Nations Journal. Copies of this Journal will be regularly forwarded to the Governments of all States Members of the League.

It is intended to give that part of the Journal in which the publication of Treaties and Engagements is effected a special form, convenient for placing separately in Law Libraries and in private studies.

The separate index for this Treaty Part of the League of Nations Journal will be published at regular intervals.

10. The Secretary-General of the League proposes to organise his system of Registration in the following manner, hoping that it may prove convenient alike to the Parties and to all those interested in the contents of Treaties and the relevant details.

A Register will be kept in chronological order, stating, with regard to each Treaty or other Engagement or International Act, the Parties between which it has been concluded, the title (short title if any), the date of signature, ratification and presentation for registration, and finally, the number under which it has been registered.

The actual texts presented to the Secretariat will be kept as an annex to this Register, each text being marked *ne varietur* by the Secretary-General or his Deputy.

Apart from the chronological Register, a second Register will be kept which will form to some extent an *état civil* of all Treaties and Engagements concerned. For every Treaty or Engagement a special page will be set apart as in a ledger, where all the data concerning it will be noted—including not only the Parties' signatures and ratifications, but also later adhesions, denunciations, etc. Notes relative to preparatory matter, discussions, and internal legislation arising out of the Treaties, etc., may also be added.

The Secretariat may on occasion be requested to deliver to States, Courts of Justice or private persons interested, certified extracts from this Register, attesting the existence and the status of International Treaties and Engagements, the moment of their coming into force, their ratification, their denunciations, the reservations entered in respect of them, etc., etc. The Secretary-General intends to make the Treaty Registration Office available for this purpose, but no legal liability for the contents of such extracts can be assumed by the Secretariat.

A general Index will be made to the Collection of Treaties and Engagements. It will be arranged in a way convenient for consultation.

11. The Treaty Registers of the International Secretariat will, moreover, include a special series of those Treaties and Conventions which, by some special provision or with some special object in view, are placed under the care of the Secretary-General. An instance of such a provision will be found in Article 405 in the Treaty of Versailles, according to which Draft Labour Conventions will be deposited with the Secretariat. The same applies to Labour Recommendations.

To these may be added other Draft Conventions and Recommendations which may be made by analogous organisations under the League of Nations.

12. It should be noted that by the provisions of Article 18 not only Treaties between Members of the League of Nations have to be registered, but also Treaties or Engagements entered into by a Member of the League with a State which has not yet been admitted into the League.

13. In connection with this last point, it has been suggested that the

system of Registration of Treaties by the Secretariat of the League of Nations should from the beginning be so extended as to admit of the Registration of Treaties, etc., made by and between States or Communities that have not yet been admitted as Members of the League of Nations. This would serve to complete the Registration of Treaties and the public collection of Treaties which will be formed by the Treaty Part of the League of Nations Journal. The Secretary-General therefore proposes, although the Registration will be for this part absolutely voluntary, to accept applications for the Registration of Treaties, etc., even if none of the Parties is at the time a Member of the League of Nations.

The Secretary-General of the League of Nations trusts that experience may show that the system of Registration and Publication of Treaties on the lines suggested in this Memorandum will work satisfactorily. He will be glad to receive suggestions for possible modifications of the present scheme.

21-23. THE LEAGUE AND MANDATES

21. TEXT OF A CLASS B MANDATE: THE BRITISH MANDATE FOR GERMAN EAST AFRICA [20]

Article 22 of the League Covenant made the League responsible for the well-being and development of the people who lived in the former German oversea possessions (except Kiaochow) and the former Turkish possessions on the Arabian Peninsula. The League might delegate certain of the more advanced nations to act as its stewards over these relatively backward areas, called mandates. These last were divided into three categories (A, B, and C mandates) according to the degree of their political development, their geographical position, and the level of their economic and social conditions. The C and B mandates were assigned by the Big Four at the Paris Peace Conference in 1919 and the A mandates were allotted at a special conference at San Remo in April 1920. The League Council confirmed these apportionments in a manner illustrated by the following example.

The Council of the League of Nations:

Whereas by Article 119 of the Treaty of Peace with Germany signed at Versailles on June 28th, 1919, Germany renounced in favour of the

[20] League of Nations, *Official Journal, 3rd Year 1922,* pp. 865-868.

Principal Allied and Associated Powers all her rights over her oversea possessions, including therein German East Africa; and

Whereas, in accordance with the treaty of June 11th, 1891, between Her Britannic Majesty and His Majesty the King of Portugal, the River Rovuma is recognised as forming the northern boundary of the Portuguese possessions in East Africa from its mouth up to the confluence of the River M'Sinje; and

Whereas the Principal Allied and Associated Powers agreed that, in accordance with Article 22, Part I (Covenant of the League of Nations), of the said treaty, a mandate should be conferred upon His Britannic Majesty to administer part of the former colony of German East Africa, and have proposed that the mandate should be formulated in the following terms; and

Whereas His Britannic Majesty has agreed to accept the mandate in respect of the said territory, and his undertaken to exercise it on behalf of the League of Nations in accordance with the following provisions; and

Whereas by the afore-mentioned Article 22, paragraph 8, it is provided that the degree of authority, control or administration to be exercised by the Mandatory, not having been previously agreed upon by the Members of the League, shall be explicitly defined by the Council of the League of Nations;

Confirming the said mandate, defines its terms as follows:

ARTICLE 1.

The territory over which a mandate is conferred upon His Britannic Majesty (hereinafter called the Mandatory) comprises that part of the territory of the former colony of German East Africa situated to the east of the following line: . . .

ARTICLE 2.

Boundary Commissioners shall be appointed by His Britannic Majesty and His Majesty the King of the Belgians to trace on the spot the line described in Article 1 above.

In case any dispute should arise in connection with the work of these commissioners, the question shall be referred to the Council of the League of Nations, whose decision shall be final.

The final report by the Boundary Commission shall give the precise description of this boundary as actually demarcated on the ground, the necessary maps shall be annexed thereto and signed by the commissioners. The report, with its annexes, shall be made in triplicate; one copy shall be deposited in the archives of the League of Nations, one shall be kept by the Government of His Majesty the King of the Belgians and one by the Government of His Britannic Majesty.

ARTICLE 3.

The Mandatory shall be responsible for the peace, order and good government of the territory, and shall undertake to promote to the utmost the material and moral well-being and the social progress of its inhabitants. The Mandatory shall have full powers of legislation and administration.

ARTICLE 4.

The Mandatory shall not establish any military or naval bases, nor erect any fortifications, nor organise any native military force in the territory except for local police purposes and for the defence of the territory.

ARTICLE 5.

The Mandatory:

(1) shall provide for the eventual emancipation of all slaves and for as speedy an elimination of domestic and other slavery as social conditions will allow;

(2) shall suppress all forms of slave trade;

(3) shall prohibit all forms of forced or compulsory labour, except for essential public works and services, and then only in return for adequate remuneration;

(4) shall protect the natives from abuse and measures of fraud and force by the careful supervision of labour contracts and the recruiting of labour;

(5) shall exercise a strict control over the traffic in arms and ammunition and the sale of spirituous liquors.

ARTICLE 6.

In the framing of laws relating to the holding or transfer of land, the Mandatory shall take into consideration native laws and customs, and shall respect the rights and safeguard the interests of the native population.

No native land may be transferred, except between natives, without the previous consent of the public authorities, and no real rights over native land in favour of non-natives may be created except with the same consent.

The Mandatory will promulgate strict regulations against usury.

ARTICLE 7.

The Mandatory shall secure to all nationals of States Members of the League of Nations the same rights as are enjoyed in the territory by his own nationals in respect of entry into and residence in the territory, the protection afforded to their person and property, the acquisition of property, movable and immovable, and the exercise of their profession or trade, subject only to the requirements of public order, and on condition of compliance with the local law.

Further, the Mandatory shall ensure to all nationals of States Members of the League of Nations, on the same footing as to his own nationals, freedom of transit and navigation, and complete economic, commercial and industrial equality; provided that the Mandatory shall be free to organise essential public works and services on such terms and conditions as he thinks just.

Concessions for the development of the natural resources of the territory shall be granted by the Mandatory without distinction on grounds of nationality between the nationals of all States Members of the League of Nations, but on such conditions as will maintain intact the authority of the local Government.

Concessions having the character of a general monopoly shall not be granted. This provision does not affect the right of the Mandatory to create monopolies of a purely fiscal character in the interest of the territory under mandate, and in order to provide the territory with fiscal resources which seem best suited to the local requirements; or, in certain cases, to carry out the development of natural resources either directly by the State or by a controlled agency, provided that there shall result therefrom no monopoly of the natural resources for the benefit of the Mandatory or his nationals, directly or indirectly, nor any preferential advantage which shall be inconsistent with the economic, commercial and industrial equality hereinbefore guaranteed.

The rights conferred by this article extend equally to companies and associations organised in accordance with the law of any of the Members of the League of Nations, subject only to the requirements of public order, and on condition of compliance with the local law.

Article 8.

The Mandatory shall ensure in the territory complete freedom of conscience and the free exercise of all forms of worship which are consonant with public order and morality; missionaries who are nationals of States Members of the League of Nations shall be free to enter the territory and to travel and reside therein, to acquire and possess property, to erect religious buildings and to open schools throughout the territory; it being understood, however, that the Mandatory shall have the right to exercise such control as may be necessary for the maintenance of public order and good government, and to take all measures required for such control.

Article 9.

The Mandatory shall apply to the territory any general international conventions already existing, or which may be concluded hereafter, with the approval of the League of Nations, respecting the slave trade, the traffic in arms and ammunition, the liquor traffic, and the traffic in drugs, or relating to commercial equality, freedom of transit and navigation, aerial navigation, railways, postal, telegraphic, and wireless communication, and industrial, literary and artistic property.

The Mandatory shall co-operate in the execution of any common policy adopted by the League of Nations for preventing and combating disease, including diseases of plants and animals.

Article 10.

The Mandatory shall be authorised to constitute the territory into a customs fiscal and administrative union or federation with the adjacent territories under his own sovereignty or control; provided always that the measures adopted to that end do not infringe the provisions of this mandate.

Article 11.

The Mandatory shall make to the Council of the League of Nations an annual report to the satisfaction of the Council, containing full information concerning the measures taken to apply the provisions of this mandate.

A copy of all laws and regulations made in the course of the year and affecting property, commerce, navigation or the moral and material well-being of the natives shall be annexed to this report.

ARTICLE 12.

The consent of the Council of the League of Nations is required for any modification of the terms of this mandate.

ARTICLE 13.

The Mandatory agrees that if any dispute whatever should arise between the Mandatory and another Member of the League of Nations relating to the interpretation or the application of the provisions of the mandate, such dispute, if it cannot be settled by negotiation, shall be submitted to the Permanent Court of International Justice provided for by Article 14 of the Covenant of the League of Nations.

States Members of the League of Nations may likewise bring any claims on behalf of their nationals for infractions of their rights under this mandate before the said Court for decision.

The present instrument shall be deposited in orginal in the archives of the League of Nations. Certified copies shall be forwarded by the Secretary-General of the League of Nations to all Members of the League.

Done at London, the twentieth day of July one thousand nine hundred and twenty-two.

22. DIRECTIONS FOR COMPILING ANNUAL REPORTS ON B AND C MANDATES [21]

Mandatory powers were required to render annual reports of their administration to the League Council. Late in 1920 a Permanent Mandates Commission was created to examine these reports and present facts and recommendations to the Council. The commission was given advisory powers only. In 1926 it drew up a revised questionnaire as a guide for the preparation of the annual reports.

The attached document replaces the former questionnaires for B and C mandated territories (documents C. 396 and 397. 1921). It has been drawn up with a view to facilitating the preparation of the annual

---

[21] *List of Questions Which the Permanent Mandates Commission Desires Should Be Dealt with in the Annual Reports of the Mandatory Powers for B and C Mandates,* in League of Nations, *VI. A. Mandates, 1926, VI. A. 16,* pp. 1-7. (Geneva, June 25, 1926.)

reports which, under the terms of Article 22 of the Covenant, mandatory Powers are required to furnish to the Council with regard to the territories for which they are responsible.

The document indicates, in the form of questions, the principal points upon which the Permanent Mandates Commission desires that information should be given in the annual reports.

Without asking that its questions should be necessarily reproduced in the reports, the commission considers it desirable that the reports should be drawn up in accordance with the general plan of the questionnaire.

A. STATUS OF THE TERRITORY.

1. Is there any organic law in which the mandatory Power has laid down and defined the status of the mandated territory? Please forward such changes as have been made in this organic law.

2. To what extent is the territory financially and administratively autonomous?

B. STATUS OF THE NATIVE INHABITANTS OF THE TERRITORY.

3. Has a special national status been granted to the native inhabitants? If so, what is the legal or current term used to describe this special status?

4. Do natives of the territory enjoy the same guarantees as regards the protection of their persons and property in the territory of the mandatory Power and in its colonies, protectorates and dependencies as the native inhabitants of each or any of the latter? If not, what treatment do they receive in this respect?

C. INTERNATIONAL RELATIONS.

5. What international treaties or conventions (general or special) apply to the territory?

6. How fully has effect been given, as a consequence of the stipulations of the Mandate, to the principle of economic equality for all Members of the League of Nations?

D. GENERAL ADMINISTRATION.

7. To what extent have legislative and executive powers been delegated to the chief Administrative Officer of the territory?

8. Does the chief Administrative Officer exercise these powers with the assistance of legislative, executive or advisory councils? If so, what are the powers of these councils? How are they constituted and do they include unofficial members and native members?

9. What are the different Government departments? How are they organised?

10. Into what administrative districts is the country divided? How are they organised?

11. How many officials are there?

How are they divided between the central administration, technical services (agriculture, public health, public works, etc.) and district administrations?

What is their origin and their nationality?

What are the conditions required for appointment?

What is the status of the officials? Are they entitled to a pension? Are advantages reserved to officials with a knowledge of the native languages?

12. Do natives take part in the general administration, and, if so, to what extent? Are any posts in the public service open to natives? Have any councils of native notables been created?

13. Are there any native communities organised under native rulers and recognised by the Government? What degree of autonomy do they possess and what are their relations with the Administration? Do village councils exist?

E. PUBLIC FINANCE.

14. Please forward the detailed budget of revenue and expenditure for the current fiscal year, and a similar statement for the last completed year of account.

Please attach a comparative table of the total revenue and expenditure, section by section, for each of the past five years.

15. Has the territory a public debt? If so, attach figures for the last five years.

16. Has the ordinary and extraordinary expenditure been covered by budgetary revenue or in some other way—either by public loans, or by advances or free grants by the mandatory Government?

In the latter case, state the conditions of the financial transactions involved.

17. Please give the annual and total amounts of advances and grants-in-aid by the mandatory Power to the mandated territory.

F. DIRECT TAXES.

18. What direct taxes—such as capitation, or income, or land taxes—are imposed: (a) On natives? (b) On non-natives?

19. Are the native direct taxes paid individually or collectively?

Are they applicable to all natives without distinction or only to able-bodied male adults? Is the rate of taxation the same throughout the territory or does it vary in different districts? Can a native pay in kind or only in money?

20. Is compulsory labour exacted in default of the payment of these taxes in cash or kind? If so, on what basis is the equivalent calculated?

21. What methods are employed to assess and collect the native taxes?

22. Is any portion of this tax handed over to the native chiefs or communities? Are chiefs salaried by the administration?

23. Are the native chiefs allowed to exact tribute or other levies in cash or in kind or in labour? If so, is this tribute in addition to the Government taxes?

G. INDIRECT TAXES.

24. What is the tariff of import and export duties? Are transit and statistical duties charged?

25. Are there any indirect duties in force other than import, export and transit duties?

26. Does the territory form part of a Customs union with neighbouring colonies and dependencies of the mandatory Power? If so, how are the Customs receipts and expenses divided?

27. Are the products of the mandated territory given preferential treatment when imported into the territory of the mandated Power, its colonies or dependencies, or do they pay the same duties as similar products from foreign countries?

H. TRADE STATISTICS.

28. Please forward comparative statistics concerning the general and special trade of the territory, showing both imports and exports for the past five years. (Please indicate the amount of imports and exports of Government material and stores.)

I. JUDICIAL ORGANISATION.

29. Please give a description of the judicial organisation, both civil and criminal.

30. How are the courts and tribunals of the various instances constituted?

31. Do they recognise native customary law, and if so, in what cases and under what conditions?

32. Are natives entitled to officiate in the courts and tribunals: for example, as assessors or members of the jury?

33. Does the judicial organisation include tribunals exclusively composed of natives? Are these tribunals under direct or indirect control of the mandatory Power? What powers do they exercise? Can they inflict punishments for which the law makes no provision? How are their sentences carried out?

34. Does the law inflict the penalties of corporal punishment, forced residence and deportation? If so, under what conditions and limitations?

35. Does the penitentiary system obviate the necessity of sending prisoners long distances for confinement?

J. POLICE.

36. Is there any police force apart from the armed forces proper? If so, what is its strength?

37. Are the police concentrated in centres under direct $\begin{cases} \text{European} \\ \text{Japanese} \end{cases}$ authority or distributed in detachments in the villages under native subalterns only?

K. DEFENCE OF THE TERRITORY.

38. Are any military forces maintained for the defence of the territory?

If so, how are they recruited, organised and armed? What is the period of service? What proportion of Europeans or Japanese do they include? What is their strength? Is it provided that discharged soldiers are called up as reservists in case of an emergency?

39. If the Territory has no armed forces of its own, what are the arrangements for its defence?

40. If military expenditure and expenditure on the police are included under the same item of the budget, please indicate separately the expenditure on each.

L. ARMS AND AMMUNITION.

41. What measures have been adopted to control the importation of arms and ammunition?

42. What number of arms, and quantity of ammunition of the different categories have been imported during the year, and what approximately is the number of such arms and the quantity of ammunition in the country?

43. Is the importation (with or without restrictions) allowed of "trade guns" (flint locks) and "trade powder" for self-defence, or for the protection of crops against wild animals, or for any other harmless purpose?

M. SOCIAL, MORAL AND MATERIAL CONDITION OF THE NATIVES.

44. What, generally speaking, are the measures adopted to promote the moral, social and material welfare of the natives?

As an indication, please state approximately the total revenue derived from the natives by taxation and the total amount of the expenditure on their welfare (education, public health, etc.).

45. Is the native population divided into distinct social castes? If so, does the law recognise these distinctions and privileges which may be attached thereto by native tradition and custom?

46. Does the slave trade or slave-dealing exist in any form? If so, what measures are taken for their suppression and what has been the success of these measures?

47. Does slavery still exist and, if so, in what form:

(a) In Moslem districts?
(b) In other districts?

Can a slave be emancipated under native customary law?

48. What measures are being taken to suppress slavery? What have been the results of these measures?

49. Do any of the following practices exist in the territory:

Acquisition of women by purchase disguised as payment of dowry or of presents to parents?

Purchase of children under the guise of adoption?
Pledging of individuals as security for debt?
Slavery for debts?
Are these practices penalised by law?

50. What is the status of freed slaves, especially women and children, in the native social organisation?

51. What is the social status of women? In particular, are polygamy and concubinage universal or prevalent? Are they recognised by law?

52. Can a native move about freely throughout the entire territory? Are there any regulations in regard to such movement? Is vagrancy a penal offence? If so, how is it defined?

N. CONDITIONS AND REGULATIONS OF LABOUR.

53. Have measures been taken in accordance with Part XIII of the Treaty of Versailles to ensure the application of conventions or recommendations of the International Labour Conference?

Please indicate such local circumstances, if any, as render these provisions inapplicable or ineffective.

54. Does the local supply of labour, in quantity, physical powers of resistance and aptitude for industrial and agricultural work conducted on modern lines appear to indicate that it is adequate, as far as can be foreseen, for the economic development of the territory?

Or does the Government consider it possible that sooner or later a proper care for the preservation and development of the native races may make it necessary to restrict for a time the establishment of new enterprises or the extension of existing enterprises and to spread over a longer term of years the execution of such large public works as are not of immediate and urgent necessity?

55. Are there any laws and regulations regarding labour, particularly concerning:

Labour contracts and penalties to which employers and employed are liable in the case of their breach?

Rates of wages and methods of payment?

Hours of work?

Disciplinary powers possessed by employers?

Housing and sanitary conditions in the camps or villages of workers?

Inspection of factories, workshops and yards?

Medical inspection before and on completion of employment; medical assistance to workers?

Compensation in the event of accident, disease or incapacity arising out of, and in the course of, employment?

Insurance against sickness, old age or unemployment?

56. Do labourers present themselves freely in sufficient numbers to satisfy the local demand for labour? Or has recruiting to be carried out in native centres more or less distant to make good shortage of labour?

57. Does the Administration recruit labour for the service of the Administration of other territories or for private employers? If so, under what conditions and safeguards?

58. Are private recruiting organisations or agents of employers permitted to recruit labour within the territory for service in the territory itself at a distance from the place of recruiting or in another country? If so, under what conditions and safeguards?

59. Please give a table showing the number of workers of each sex recruited (*a*) for Government work, (*b*) for private enterprise.

60. Indicate the nature of the work for which recruiting has taken place during the year (e.g., mines, porterage, agriculture, construction of railways, roads, etc.). Give, where possible, mortality and morbidity statistics among the workers.

61. Does the existing law provide for compulsory labour for essential public works and services?

What authority is competent to decide what are public works and services the essential nature of which justifies recourse to compulsory labour?

What payment is made to the workers?

May such compulsory labour be commuted for a money payment?

Are all classes of the population liable to such labour?

For what period can this labour be exacted?

62. How is the recruiting and supervision of compulsory labour organised?

63. Are any workers recruited from outside the territory? If so, by whom and under what conditions?

64. Are the contracts of such workers signed before departure from their native country? Give a specimen contract.

65. Is there any special officer charged with the duty of looking after those workers on arrival, allocating them to employers, seeing that the employer fulfils his obligations through the period of contract, and arranging for their repatriation or re-engagement?

66. Are they segregated, in camps, compounds or otherwise? What are the regulations in this matter? Has their presence in the territory given rise to any trouble with the native inhabitants?

67. Are these workers encouraged to bring their wives with them, and do they do so? Are they allowed to settle in the territory if they so wish?

68. Give the nationality of imported workers, the numbers of new arrivals, repatriations, deaths and the total present at the end of the year (men and women).

69. Are there any trade unions in the territory? If so, have these unions put forward any protests or demands?

O. LIBERTY OF CONSCIENCE AND WORSHIP.

70. Is freedom of exercise of all forms of worship and religious instruction ensured?

71. Has it been considered necessary, in the interest of public order and morality, to impose restrictions on the free exercise of worship or to enact regulations on the subject?

72. Are there any restrictions on missionaries, who are nationals of States not members of the League of Nations?

P. EDUCATION. [22]

73. State the general policy and principles adopted in regard to the education of the natives. How do the methods in use illustrate the application of the different characteristics of these principles?

74. Please give a brief analysis of the education budget indicating the amounts allocated respectively to

Government schools,
Non-Government schools,
Inspection of educational institutions.

75. Is official authorisation necessary for opening Non-Government educational institutions? If so, under what conditions is such authorisation granted?

76. Are Non-Government educational institutions subject to a compulsory official inspection, and, if so, how is it carried out?

77. What conditions are attached to any grants-in-aid made to Non-Government schools? On what basis are the grants made?

78. Please give a table showing the number of boys' schools of the different grades in the following categories:

Government schools.
Non-Government schools subsidised by the government.
Non-Government schools not subsidised.

State the numbers enrolled and the average attendance in each category of schools.

79. Please give the same information regarding girls' schools.

80. Is any vocational training, or instruction in agriculture, or domestic science given in the territory?

---

[22] Questions 73 to 84 refer only to the education of natives.

81. Are there any normal classes or training institutions for the education of native teachers?

82. Give some general indication of the curricula in each class of school mentioned above.

Do they include the teaching of a European or Japanese language, and if so, how far does this teaching go?

Does the curriculum in Government schools include religious instruction (compulsory or optional)?

83. What language is used as a medium of instruction?

84. What are the numbers of the teaching staff (Government and Non-Government, certificated and uncertificated)? How are they distributed among the different categories of schools?

85. Are there any schools for non-natives?

Q. ALCOHOL, SPIRITS AND DRUGS.

86. Are the natives much addicted to the use of alcohol and spirits?

87. What is the accepted definition of the terms "liquor traffic" and "trade spirits"?

88. Have legal methods concerning the liquor traffic been enacted to give effect to the mandates and the Convention of St. Germain of September 10th, 1919?

89. Is there any licensing system for the sale of imported alcoholic liquors?

90. What are the import duties on (a) spirituous liquors, (b) wines, (c) beer and other fermented beverages? Has any limit of strength of (b) and (c) been adopted? Are the duties higher or lower than those in the neighbouring countries?

91. What are the quantities of each class imported each year for the last five years, and what are the principal countries of origin?

92. What steps are taken to prevent smuggling and the illicit traffic in imported alcohol and spirits?

93. Is the process of distillation known to the natives? Have any measures been taken to restrict (a) the manufacture, (b) the sale, (c) the consumption of intoxicants manufactured by the natives?

94. Is any encouragement given to communities or associations which, for religious or other reasons, are trying to suppress the use of these intoxicants?

95. Is the population of the territory addicted to the use of drugs (including hashish and hemp)? If so, what measures are in force to prohibit or regulate their use?

R. PUBLIC HEALTH.

96. What health organisation is in charge of research work and the prevention, control and treatment of disease? State the work done by this organisation and the results observed.

97. Does this organisation train natives as medical and sanitary assistants, or women as midwives and as nurses? What is the method adopted?

98. How many doctors, both official and private, are there in the territory? Has official and private action as regards sanitation and preventive and curative medicine been co-ordinated?

99. What progress has been made in inducing the natives, especially the chiefs, to adopt sanitary reforms in the towns and villages?

100. What endemic or epidemic diseases have been responsible for the greatest mortality? Are there statistics regarding the morbidity and death rate attributable to these diseases? If no general statistics exist, please supply any which have been compiled for certain centres or certain specified areas.

101. Give any other information of importance from the epidemiological point of view, particularly as regards the spread of dangerous diseases, such as sleeping-sickness, etc., which are not covered by the preceding question.

102. Does the health organisation deal with the supervision of prostitution? What is the position with regard to prostitution?

S. LAND TENURE.

103. Is the Government's policy directed towards the exploitation of the arable land by the establishment of large agricultural undertakings under foreign management or by the development of the system of native small-holdings?

104. What are the various classes of property which, in view of their nature, origin or use, constitute the domain of the territory?

Under what item of the local budget do the revenues of this domain appear, or, in the case of the sale of such property, the sum realised?

Under what items of the local budget do the costs of exploiting such domain appear?

Are the recruiting and employment of the labour required for the exploitation of this domain regulated by the common law?

105. Does the law provide a definition of the term "vacant lands"? What authority is competent to decide whether land is vacant?

Does the law recognise the rights of use and enjoyment that may be exercised by the natives in the "vacant lands" (the right of gathering produce, cutting of wood, grazing, hunting, fishing, etc.)?

106. Has the mandatory Power acquired on its own account (and not in its capacity as Mandatory) any property or rights whatsoever in the territory? If so, what property or rights?

On what basis does the State's proprietary title rest?

Is this property subject to the same dues and charges as the property of private individuals?

Is the State subject to the ordinary regulations regarding the recruiting and employment of the labour needed for the exploitation of these lands?

How is the revenue of these lands employed?

107. What is the system of land registration in force?

Is it applicable to land owned or occupied by natives?

Is there a land registry department?

108. What is the native system of land tenure? Is it uniform through the territory? Have the natives any notion of the right of individual property?

Does the law recognise the right of natives to hold property as individuals?

109. Do the authorities exercise control over land transactions with a view to safeguarding the customary rights of the natives on such land?

What is the maximum term of land-leases to non-natives?

Does the law reserve land for the natives or native communities, from which they cannot be dispossessed for the benefit of non-natives?

110. Have the native chiefs the power of dispossessing existing occupiers and of granting the land to third parties? If so, have the persons dispossessed the right of appeal to the authorities?

111. What is the (approximate) proportion in the whole territory of:
Native land,
State land,
Land leased or sold to non-natives (including any property of the mandatory Power referred to in Section 106)?

112. What are the regulations with regard to expropriation for reasons of public utility? How is the compensation determined?

T. FORESTS.

113. State the main provisions of the forest law (if any). Does it provide for the protection of forests and for afforestation of cleared or waste lands?

U. MINES.

114. Is any legislation in force with regard to mines? What are the main provisions? If there is no special legislation on this subject, does the State claim the ownership of the sub-soil?

115. What mineral resources (a) are known to exist, (b) have been leased, (c) are actually exploited by the State or privately?

V. POPULATION.

116. What is the population of the territory in natives, coloured persons other than natives, Asiatics, Europeans and Americans? Are the figures supplied the result of a census or are they merely an estimate?

117. Please supply, if possible, quinquennial or decennial comparative statistics of the population.

118. Is there any considerable emigration from, or immigration into, the territory? If so, what are the causes?

What are the countries of destination or origin of emigrants and immigrants, respectively?

23. EXAMINATION OF AN ANNUAL REPORT: BRITISH REPORT ON TOGOLAND FOR 1932 [23]

Examination of the annual reports by the Permanent Mandates Commission was to be done in the presence of an accredited representative of the mandatory. He was expected to answer questions and clarify any obscure or doubtful points. The following sample examination was chosen mainly because of its brevity.

SIXTH MEETING.

Held on Wednesday, October 25th, 1933, at 4 p.m.

Mr. A. W. Cardinall, late District Commissioner, accredited representative of the mandatory Power, came to the table of the Commission.

WELCOME TO THE ACCREDITED REPRESENTATIVE.

The CHAIRMAN extended a welcome to Mr. Cardinall, who had been appointed accredited representative of the mandatory Power—a

---

[23] League of Nations, Permanent Mandates Commission, *Minutes of the Twenty-Fourth Session, Held at Geneva from October 23rd to November 4th, 1933*, Geneva, 1933, pp. 47-52. *(VI. A. Mandates 1933. VI. A. 3.)*

position which he had held the previous year—for the examination of the annual report on Togoland under British mandate.

OPENING OBSERVATIONS BY THE ACCREDITED REPRESENTATIVE.

Mr. CARDINALL.—I thank you, Mr. Chairman, for your kind words of welcome, and I should like to convey to you my deep appreciation of appearing once more before you. I trust that in my capacity of accredited representative I shall be of assistance to you.

I do not think it will be necessary for me to make any preliminary remarks with regard to the year under review, because, during 1932, the regime outlined in earlier reports has been inaugurated, so that, so far, there is little to mention, whilst appendices on the regime regulations will be found at the end of the report. The putting into force of those regulations, in so far as the southern section is concerned, has been postponed until 1933.

. . . . .

STATUS OF THE TERRITORY.

M. PALACIOS said that he had already remarked at previous sessions[24] of the Commission that in official documents the territory had often been called "British Sphere of Togoland."

In the laws the texts of which were annexed to the annual report, such as the Native Administration Ordinance 1932 (page 91) and the Native Administration Amendment Ordinance (page 112), this incorrect title was again used. The official description of the territory was "Togoland under British Mandate." Had the mandatory Power taken the necessary measures to ensure that in official documents the territory would always be described as "Togoland under British Mandate"?

Mr. CARDINALL said that the Ordinance giving effect to the title "Togoland under British Mandate," being dated July 1932, was subsequent to the two Native Administration Ordinances in question, which were enacted in May and June respectively.

ADMINISTRATIVE RE-ORGANISATION OF THE TERRITORY.

M. VAN REES, referring to the information on page 6 and following of the report, according to which the northern section of Togoland under British mandate, the Kusasi, Southern Mamprussi, Eastern Dagomba and Krachi districts had been re-organised in such a way that their boundaries now coincided with those of the three native States of Mamprussi, Dagomba and Gonja, and to the further statement

---

[24] See Minutes of the Twenty-Second Session, p. 170.

that that re-organisation had enabled the administrative officers to lay the foundations on which it was hoped to rebuild the States in question, enquired what was the meaning of this re-organisation. If it were merely a question of entrusting the three native States with the administration of certain neighbouring portions of the mandated territory, there could be no objection; but if, as might be inferred, the re-organisation had rather the character of a re-instatement of certain parts of the territory under mandate in the native political entities of the Gold Coast in order to reconstitute these entities in the form in which they had existed before the delimitation of the frontier between the Gold Coast and German Togoland, there was risk that such a step might infringe the territorial integrity of the territory under mandate the maintenance of which was one of the fundamental principles of the mandates system.

Mr. CARDINALL replied that there was no question of political administration—if by political administration was meant European administration. Those areas which were included in the administration of the three native States would still, from a political standpoint, be quite separate. Even if any question of political administration had been involved, the territorial gain would be on the side of the territory under mandate, as reference to the map would show.

M. VAN REES did not contest the fact that the re-organisation might be of benefit to the inhabitants of the northern part of the territory under mandate. But, in the event of the emancipation of this territory, how could that be achieved without dismembering again the three native States, if in reality the regions which were or would be united thereto formed an integral part of those States? That was a point which struck at the very roots of the mandates institution and which had led M. Van Rees to ask for further explanations.

Mr. CARDINALL said that he would refer the question, which was hypothetical, to the Government, in order that the position might be clarified.

M. SAKENOBE noted that it had not yet been found possible to evolve for the Krachi Division a constitution which met with acceptance by all the subordinate chiefs, and that the head chief exercised little control over his people. He enquired whether it would not be possible to appoint as a native authority over that area the chief of the Kete Krachi, under whose leadership the people had formerly grouped themselves for purposes of protection.

Mr. CARDINALL said that he had lived in the locality for many years. The chief of the Krachi had been misinterpreted to the British—and to the Germans—as a true political chief. Although he had been treated as such for years, he had been in reality the Fetish head of a large confederation which had been formed to protect the settlers from the Ashanti and which stretched far into the mountains to what was now territory under French mandate. The difficulty at present was to find out what was the recognised political constitution.

M. RAPPARD asked how it could be that the real chief should not have made his claims known.

Mr. CARDINALL explained that many of the villages in the Krachi Division were originally simply migratory and hunting outposts, of which the political chiefs might be living at some considerable distance.

M. SAKENOBE, referring to the amalgamation of the three northern States with non-mandated areas, enquired how inhabitants of the mandated territory were distinguished from other members of the population.

Mr. CARDINALL replied that no distinction was made.

APPLICATION IN THE TERRITORY UNDER MANDATE OF LEGISLATION PROMULGATED IN THE GOLD COAST AND ASHANTI, AND NORTHERN TERRITORIES.

Lord LUGARD enquired which of the Gold Coast and Ashanti laws were operative in Togoland, and asked that the next report might contain an entire list of the Ordinances which did—or alternatively did not—apply to north or south Togoland.

Mr. CARDINALL stated that, as the southern section was treated as an integral part of the eastern portion of the Gold Coast, all Gold Coast Ordinances applied to it automatically, except such as were specifically excluded by the Governor; the northern section similarly had the Ordinances of the northern territories applied to it.

JUDICIAL ORGANISATION.

Lord LUGARD, referring to a statement in the report that native tribunals had been appointed "in each of the divisions which is a member of a State" (paragraph 31), enquired whether, in the event of a division not being a member of a State, it had no native tribunal at all.

Mr. CARDINALL said that the Ordinance under which that provision was established had only come into force in February 1933. An explanation of the position would be given in the next report.

Lord LUGARD commented on the statement that there was nothing to prevent any case, "Whatever may be the amount or issue involved," reaching the Privy Council (paragraph 31); that seemed to allow of any amount of appeals—the bugbear of the Gold Coast.

Mr. CARDINALL said that it would be difficult to take away the right of appeal, even in land cases.

Lord LUGARD pointed out that, in Nigeria, disputes regarding tribal boundaries were, he understood, now settled by the executive officer with an appeal to the Governor, as head of the Executive, and not to the courts.

He asked what powers the native councils possessed to impose rates and make by-laws.

Mr. CARDINALL referred the Commission to Part II, Section 8, of the Native Administration Ordinance of 1932, which specified the powers of the native authority. Section 12 defined the means by which judgments could be enforced.

CONCESSIONS.

Lord LUGARD enquired if the Concessions Ordinance and Minerals Ordinance applied to the southern part of the mandated territory. He pointed out that, in the Gold Coast, which was singular among British possessions, the minerals were possessed by the natives. Was the mineral ownership vested in the natives in Togoland?

Mr. CARDINALL replied that ownership was vested in the people.

Lord LUGARD asked whether the position was the same for lands, and whether the chiefs in Togoland could grant concessions of land or minerals to concessionaires.

Mr. CARDINALL answered the first question in the affirmative, and stated in reply to the second that concessions could only be granted through the operation of the Concessions Ordinance, under which, in the interests of the natives, applications were referred to the Supreme Court. He would ask for a fuller statement to be included in the 1933 report.

Lord LUGARD enquired whether, under the Concessions Ordinance, the Government had the right to exact royalties or whether royalties were payable to the chiefs. The Government, he understood, levied 5 per cent on profits, and charged license fees for prospecting and mining.

Mr. CARDINALL said that, in the Gold Coast, there was an export duty on gold and diamonds.

He stated, in reply to a further question by Lord Lugard, that there were as yet no minerals of any value known in the southern part of the territory and that there was now no mining of any sort, though gold had been found in small quantities some years ago. The Mining Concessions Ordinance applied to the northern part, but no mining activities were being carried on there at present.

Lord LUGARD asked that information might be given in the next report stating whether, in the event of minerals being found, the royalties would go to the native chiefs or to the finances of the territory.

PUBLIC FINANCE.

M. RAPPARD noted that the finances of the territory under mandate were bound up with those of the neighbouring territory and was glad to learn once again (paragraph 60 of the report) that the continued deficit in the accounts was covered by the Gold Coast and that the subsidies granted by the latter were treated as grants-in-aid which it was not the intention of the Gold Coast Government to recover. That would preclude any notion that the deficit was a repayable debt on the mandated territory.

He enquired whether the form of administration adopted had had the effect of transferring outside the mandated territory posts and administrative services, and whether that would mean a loss of revenue for the territory (posts and telegraphs, legal fees, etc.).

Mr. CARDINALL said that the situation would remain unchanged. The new division of the territory had not involved any change in the District Commissioners' courts or in the post offices and did not imply any diminution of revenue.

M. RAPPARD observed that direct taxation had not yet been introduced, but pointed out that a levy on the salaries of civil servants might be regarded as coming within that category.

Mr. CARDINALL agreed that this was so.

TRADE: DEVELOPMENT OF TRANSPORT BY ROAD.

M. MERLIN directed attention to the fact that goods which were formerly purchased in the French zone were being obtained in increasing quantities in the Gold Coast (paragraph 65 of the report). He asked how that had come about, and enquired whether roads were being used instead of railways.

Mr. CARDINALL said that the position was due to the uneconomical manner—uneconomical from the standpoint of the mandated territory—in which lorries were run by the African owners, whose petrol costs were often only $4\frac{1}{2}d.$ per ton-mile, and who could compete with any railway running down to Lomé. The situation was that goods that used to come by rail now—temporarily—came by road.

M. SAKENOBE asked for further information concerning the marketing of the products of the Jasikan-Ahamansu cacao belt; he noted that the main part of that cacao area was as yet unopened by any official road system (paragraph 193).

Mr. CARDINALL referred to the map and pointed out that it was impossible in the present state of the country's finances to extend in that region the main road running north and south. When the country's finances improved, each part of the territory would be dealt with in turn, and the cacao-producing region would naturally be given due consideration.

CATTLE.

M. SAKENOBE congratulated the mandatory Power on having immunised in-contact cattle against rinderpest (page 73). He asked that statistics of cattle might be given in the next report.

ARMS AND AMMUNITION.

M. SAKENOBE said that he could not reconcile the statistics for the number of shot-guns (182) licensed during 1931 in the southern section with the statement that "the Commissioner in charge of the southern section may, in his discretion, grant a total of twenty-four permits each year" (paragraphs 91 and 92).

Mr. CARDINALL explained that shot-guns were licensed annually. The figure of 182 would include renewals granted in 1931, together with new licences, which might not exceed twenty-four in any one year. There would thus be an ascending figure for each successive year. Flint-locks, on the contrary, had a life licence.

Lord LUGARD commented on the increased sale of gunpowder, which, according to the report, was regarded as an indication that the people had had more money to spend; that was hardly borne out by the reference to the severe effects of the trade depression (paragraph 97).

MORAL CONDITIONS OF THE NATIVES.

Mlle. DANNEVIG felt that something should be done to remedy the deplorable moral situation evidenced by the statement in the report that "at present it is not uncommon for a man to countenance repeated acts of adultery in order to enrich himself with the fines which are imposed on the offender." She enquired by whom the fines, varying according to the husband's rank from 7s. 6d. to £2, were imposed (paragraph

99). She noted that there was no definite rule as to the number of times a husband might claim the adultery fee before the wife was classed as a prostitute, but that popular opinion placed it at six. That appeared to be quite contrary to normal standards of morality.

Mr. CARDINALL said that the fines were imposed by the native courts. Section 47 (2) of the Native Administration Ordinance of 1932 was aimed partly at ameliorating the existing state of affairs, and Section 56 enabled the District Commissioner to exercise control. In those matters, it was hoped eventually to build up a common law practice of precedents and stated cases such as obtained in the United Kingdom. Thus customary law, which was naturally elastic, would be formed along lines accepted generally by civilised nations. The whole matter was one of education, and in actual practice a fine could not now be enforced if a woman were guilty of a sixth adultery offence.

CINEMATOGRAPH.

Lord LUGARD enquired whether cinematograph films were being exhibited in the territory, whether special measures had been taken to regulate the use of the cinematograph among the population, and whether films of educative value were being shown to the natives.

Mr. CARDINALL replied that he knew of no cinemas operating in the north and said that he would make enquiries in regard to the south. A Cinematograph Ordinance controlled the industry and the censorship imposed thereby was considered satisfactory.

LABOUR.

Mr. WEAVER expressed his thanks for the description of the manner in which road work was divided up among the villages (paragraph 48 of the report). He asked whether there was any Government control in the case of a road being constructed against the advice of the District Commissioner.

Mr. CARDINALL said that in such cases the work was so purely voluntary that it would be impossible to regulate it; more likely than not, the road was not even economically wanted.

Mr. WEAVER noted that minor communal services were apportioned among the people according to their fitness to perform them and that the men undertook the heavier work. As regards the maintenance of roads linking their villages with the main-road system, he observed that in the Cameroons such work was no longer classed amongst minor communal services but was paid compulsory labour.

Mr. CARDINALL said that the Administration was trying to go

on those same lines in Togoland, and referred the Commission to the statement (paragraph 114 of the report) that a draft Ordinance would shortly be enacted giving full effect to the requirements of the Forced Labour Convention.

Mr. WEAVER asked whether any natives were employed in the Ashanti goldfields. It would be interesting to know whether there was any movement of labour out of the territory.

Mr. CARDINALL was unable to give any information on the subject. There was, he said, a tribal occupational tendency, one tribe, for instance, being chiefly interested in plate-laying on the railways; the choice was quite voluntary.

Mr. WEAVER congratulated the mandatory Power on the success of the co-operative system in connection with cacao, and hoped that the system would in course of time prove equally successful for cotton. He suggested that co-operation on the lines of the "Better Living Societies" in India might help towards the solution of the problem of excessive expenditure and the consumption of liquor at funeral ceremonies, etc.

EDUCATION.

Mlle. DANNEVIG observed that progress seemed to have been made in education in the southern section of the territory; parents, she noted, were ready to pay school fees, notwithstanding the economic depression. Very little was said, however, about education in the northern section (paragraph 142 of the report), which comprised a population of 170,000; no Government schools existed and, in 1932, there was only one mission school—at Kete Krachi, the most southerly district. The Roman Catholic Mission, it was stated, proposed to open another school near the boundary between the northern and southern sections.

She enquired whether the mandatory Power was considering the possibility of creating schools in the northern part of the territory. It was stated that there was little demand there for education, though a number of children whose homes were in the mandated territory attended schools in the Gold Coast. The Commission would be interested to know the attitude of the chiefs in the matter.

Mr. CARDINALL replied that both financial and political issues were involved. Most of the northern territory had, until recently, been inhabited by people who used their bows and arrows on every occasion. There was a mission school at Yendi and children could also attend a school close to the frontier.

Great interest was taken in education in the southern section of the territory, where the school attendance was proportionately larger than in any other part of the Gold Coast administration.

ALCOHOL AND SPIRITS.

Count de PENHA GARCIA felt that, so far as consumption was concerned, the brief but comprehensive account given in the report for 1932 showed little change in the liquor situation in the territory since the advent of the mandatory Power. Alcohol played an important part in the life of the people, from their birth to their death, and no ceremony, whether social or contractual, was complete without it. The mandatory Power had not been idle in the matter; it had taken steps to increase the licence fees for retail stores, to reduce the hours of sale, and to impose higher Customs tariffs on imported liquors. All those measures had, however, proved unavailing, and had had an unlooked-for effect in the form of an alarming increase in illicit distillation. Natives had become expert in the making of alembics—a full description was given in the report—and samples of liquor had been produced containing over 70 per cent of alcohol (paragraph 152). The Commission would be glad to know what measures had been taken, or were contemplated, by the Administration to combat that practice. It seemed preferable that the natives should have access to less deleterious beverages than those of their own distilling. He asked that information might be given in the next report as to whether, in the Mandatory's view, the increase in illicit distillation was the result of higher import duties and the increased charge for licences.

Mr. CARDINALL agreed that the problem was a most difficult one, and stated that public opinion was against the Government in police prosecutions and investigations.

PUBLIC HEALTH.

The CHAIRMAN said that, according to the report for 1931, there had been reason to think that sleeping-sickness was very widespread in the Dagomba District, in the north of the territory. The report for 1932 (paragraph 162) stated that it was also prevalent in the southern Mamprussi area. The main focus of the disease had, it appeared, been discovered. The Commission would be glad to know what measures the Administration had taken to cope with it.

The annual report for Togoland under French mandate (page 79) also spoke of a focus in that territory, close to the frontier of the territory under British mandate. Were the French and British authorities taking concerted action against the disease?

Mr. CARDINALL said that he would ask that full particulars should be given in the next report.

PETITIONS.

M. PALACIOS, in his capacity as Rapporteur, recalled that a petition had been received from the chief and inhabitants of Woamé in Togoland under French mandate, in which they claimed the right to land situated in the territory under British mandate and which the inhabitants of Honuta, in the latter territory, also claimed. The Government of the United Kingdom had not sent any observations on that petition.

The CHAIRMAN referred to a letter dated September 25th, 1932, from a certain Anku Satchie, President of the Natural Rulers' Society, of Togoland under British mandate, stating that, on the same date, he had sent a petition to the League through the intermediary of the mandatory Power. That petition had not yet reached the League.

CLOSE OF THE HEARING.

The CHAIRMAN expressed the Commission's thanks to Mr. Cardinall for his valuable co-operation in the examination of the annual report.

24. A SAMPLE MINORITIES TREATY (CZECHOSLOVAKIA,
SEPTEMBER 10, 1919) (Extracts) [25]

The boundary adjustments of the peace settlement created a serious problem of national minorities. President Wilson realized at the time that nothing was "more likely to disturb the peace of the world than the treatment which might in certain circumstances be meted out to minorities." Hence, through special minorities guarantees, about thirty million people scattered throughout central and eastern Europe were placed under League guardianship. Minorities guarantees were written into the peace treaties with Austria, Hungary, Bulgaria, and Turkey. Special minorities treaties were signed, sometimes under protest, by Poland, Rumania, Greece, Yugoslavia, and Czechoslovakia. The Czechoslovak treaty is herewith reproduced. It was signed at Saint-Germain-en-Laye on September 10, 1919, and became effective on July 16, 1920.

. . . . .

[25] *Extract from the Treaty between the United States of America, the British Empire, France, Italy and Japan and Czechoslovakia, Signed at Saint-Germain-en-Laye on September 10th, 1919,* in League of Nations, *Protection of Linguistic, Racial and Religious Minorities by the League of Nations. Provisions Contained in the Various Instruments at Present in Force,* Geneva, 1927, pp. 90-94.

Whereas the peoples of Bohemia, of Moravia and of part of Silesia, as well as the peoples of Slovakia, have decided of their own free will to unite, and have in fact united, in a permanent union for the purpose of forming a single sovereign independent State under the title of the Czecho-Slovak Republic; and

Whereas the Ruthene peoples to the south of the Carpathians have adhered to this union, and

Whereas the Czecho-Slovak Republic in fact exercises sovereignty over the aforesaid territories and has already been recognised as a sovereign independent State by the other High Contracting Parties;

The United States of America, the British Empire, France, Italy and Japan on the one hand, confirming their recognition of the Czecho-Slovak State as a sovereign and independent member of the Family of Nations within the boundaries which have been or may be determined in accordance with the terms of the Treaty of Peace with Austria of even date;

Czecho-Slovakia on the other hand, desiring to conform her institutions to the principles of liberty and justice, and to give a sure guarantee to all the inhabitants of the territories over which she has assumed sovereignty;

The High Contracting Parties, anxious to assure the execution of Article 57 of the said Treaty of Peace with Austria;[26]

Have . . . agreed as follows:

CHAPTER I.

ARTICLE 1.

Czecho-Slovakia undertakes that the stipulations contained in Articles 2 to 8 of this Chapter shall be recognised as fundamental laws and that no law, regulation or official action shall conflict or interfere with these stipulations, nor shall any law, regulation or official action prevail over them.

ARTICLE 2.

Czecho-Slovakia undertakes to assure full and complete protection of life and liberty to all inhabitants of Czecho-Slovakia without distinction of birth, nationality, language, race or religion.

---

[26] This article reads: "The Czecho-Slovak State accepts and agrees to embody in a Treaty with the Principal Allied and Associated Powers such provisions as may be deemed necessary by these Powers to protect the interests of inhabitants of that State who differ from the majority of the population in race, language or religion."—*Ed.*

All inhabitants of Czecho-Slovakia shall be entitled to the free exercise, whether public or private, of any creed, religion or belief, whose practices are not inconsistent with public order or public morals.

ARTICLE 3.

Subject to the special provisions of the Treaties mentioned below, Czecho-Slovakia admits and declares to be Czecho-Slovak nationals *ipso facto* and without the requirement of any formality German, Austrian or Hungarian nationals habitually resident or possessing rights of citizenship (*pertinenza, Heimatsrecht*), as the case may be, at the date of the coming into force of the present Treaty in territory which is or may be recognised as forming part of Czecho-Slovakia under the Treaties with Germany, Austria or Hungary respectively, or under any Treaties which may be concluded for the purpose of completing the present settlement.

Nevertheless, the persons referred to above who are over eighteen years of age will be entitled under the conditions contained in the said Treaties to opt for any other nationality which may be open to them. Option by a husband will cover his wife and option by parents will cover their children under eighteen years of age. . . .

. . . . .

ARTICLE 6.

All persons born in Czecho-Slovak territory who are not born nationals of another State shall *ipso facto* become Czecho-Slovak nationals.

ARTICLE 7.

All Czecho-Slovak nationals shall be equal before the law and shall enjoy the same civil and political rights without distinction as to race, language or religion.

Differences of religion, creed or confession shall not prejudice any Czecho-Slovak national in matters relating to the enjoyment of civil or political rights, as for instance admission to public employments, functions and honours, or the exercise of professions and industries.

No restriction shall be imposed on the free use by any Czecho-Slovak national of any language in private intercourse, in commerce, in religion, in the press or publication of any kind, or at public meetings.

Notwithstanding any establishment by the Czecho-Slovak Government of an official language, adequate facilities shall be given to Czecho-Slovak nationals of non-Czech speech for the use of their language, either orally or in writing, before the courts.

ARTICLE 8.

Czecho-Slovak nationals who belong to racial, religious or linguistic minorities shall enjoy the same treatment and security in law and in fact as the other Czecho-Slovak nationals. In particular, they shall have an equal right to establish, manage and control at their own expense, charitable, religious and social institutions, schools and other educational establishments, with the right to use their own language and to exercise their religion freely therein.

ARTICLE 9.

Czecho-Slovakia will provide in the public educational system in towns and districts in which a considerable proportion of Czecho-Slovak nationals of other than Czech speech are residents adequate facilities for ensuring that the instruction shall be given to the children of such Czecho-Slovak nationals through the medium of their own language. This provision shall not prevent the Czecho-Slovak Government from making the teaching of the Czech language obligatory.

In towns and districts where there is a considerable proportion of Czecho-Slovak nationals belonging to racial, religious or linguistic minorities, these minorities shall be assured an equitable share in the enjoyment and application of the sums which may be provided out of public funds under the State, municipal or other budget, for educational, religious or charitable purposes.

CHAPTER II.

ARTICLE 10.

Czecho-Slovakia undertakes to constitute the Ruthene territory south of the Carpathians within frontiers delimited by the Principal Allied and Associated Powers as an autonomous unit within the Czecho-Slovak State, and to accord to it the fullest degree of self-government compatible with the unity of the Czecho-Slovak State.

ARTICLE 11.

The Ruthene territory south of the Carpathians shall possess a special Diet. This Diet shall have powers of legislation in all linguistic, scholastic and religious questions, in matters of local administration, and in other questions which the laws of the Czecho-Slovak State may assign to it. The Governor of the Ruthene territory shall be appointed by the President of the Czecho-Slovak Republic and shall be responsible to the Ruthene Diet.

ARTICLE 12.

Czecho-Slovakia agrees that officials in the Ruthene territory will be chosen as far as possible from the inhabitants of this territory.

ARTICLE 13.

Czecho-Slovakia guarantees to the Ruthene territory equitable representation in the legislative assembly of the Czecho-Slovak Republic, to which Assembly it will send deputies elected according to the constitution of the Czecho-Slovak Republic. These deputies will not, however, have the right of voting in the Czecho-Slovak Diet upon legislative questions of the same kind as those assigned to the Ruthene Diet.

ARTICLE 14.

Czecho-Slovakia agrees that the stipulations of Chapters I and II so far as they affect persons belonging to racial, religious or linguistic minorities constitute obligations of international concern and shall be placed under the guarantee of the League of Nations. They shall not be modified without the consent of a majority of the Council of the League of Nations. The United States, the British Empire, France, Italy and Japan hereby agree not to withhold their assent from any modification in these Articles which is in due form assented to by a majority of the Council of the League of Nations.

Czecho-Slovakia agrees that any member of the Council of the League of Nations shall have the right to bring to the attention of the Council any infraction, or any danger of infraction, of any of these obligations, and that the Council may thereupon take such action and give such direction as it may deem proper and effective in the circumstances. . . .

. . . . .

25. THE LEAGUE COMMISSIONER'S REPORT ON THE FINANCIAL
RECONSTRUCTION OF HUNGARY, 1926 *(Extracts)* [27]

*Valuable financial assistance was rendered by the League to some of the
smaller states of the world. The financial reconstruction of Hungary, with
League aid, was conspicuously successful. The League commissioner whose
final report is given below was Jeremiah Smith, Jr., of Boston.*

To the Council of the League of Nations:

I have the honour to submit to the Council of the League of Nations
my Twenty-fifth and final Report. Owing to my attendance at the
meeting of the Council in Geneva during the period when the monthly
report for May ordinarily would have been prepared, this report covers
the months of both May and June 1926.

I. TERMINATION OF BUDGET CONTROL AND GENERAL SUPERVISION.

The fiscal year of the Hungarian Government ended on June 30th,
and provisional accounts show a budget surplus for the year of approximately 62 million gold crowns. Closed accounts may be expected to
show a somewhat larger surplus.

Since the reconstruction plan came into operation on May 1st, 1924,
the Hungarian Government has completed two full financial years,
each with a substantial budget surplus. As this result had long been
foreseen, the Council of the League of Nations, at its meeting held in
Geneva on June 10th, after hearing the report of the Financial Committee of the Council, declared: "that, the financial stability of Hungary
being assured, the functions of the Commissioner-General shall be
brought to an end on June 30th, 1926, in pursuance of para. 10 of
Article VI of Protocol II."

As Article VI of Protocol II established the control of the budget
and the general supervision of the execution of the reconstruction programme by a Commissioner-General, the termination of his duties puts
an end to any such control and supervision, and Hungary now assumes
full responsibility for the management of its own finances. While the
level of the budget is somewhat higher than that contemplated in the
original programme of reconstruction, there seems no substantial reason

---

[27] From the *Twenty-Fifth (Final) Report by the Commissioner-General of the League
of Nations for Hungary, May 1st–June 30th, 1926,* in League of Nations, *Official Journal
1926,* pp. 1176-1178.

to doubt that it can be maintained permanently at the present level. Whether it is so maintained or not is merely a question of capable administration, and depends, under ordinary circumstances, upon two factors. One of these is the continuance of a sound and conservative policy by the National Bank in the maintenance of the currency; the other is reasonably prudent management of the budget.

The management of the Hungarian National Bank has been sound and prudent; it has ample reserves of foreign exchange, and there is every reason to believe that the present policy will be continued.

Undoubtedly great pressure will be brought to bear upon the Government to increase the level of expenditure for all sorts of purposes, but strong reasons of a practical nature exist which should prevent the budget from again becoming unbalanced. In case a deficit should be created through excessive expenditure, recourse cannot well be had to foreign borrowing to cover this deficit, for the practical reason that the Peace Treaty prevents Hungary from giving security for any foreign loan without the consent of the Reparation Commission, which is not likely to be obtained for such purpose, and, without security, foreign loans would be difficult, if not impossible, to obtain; recourse can no longer be had to inflation, because the National Bank has the sole monopoly of note issue, is divorced from Government control and is forbidden by its Statutes to lend money to the Government except against adequate security. Under existing conditions, it would be difficult, if not impossible to issue a domestic loan (which must rank after reparations as a charge on the assets of the Hungarian State) for the purpose of raising funds to cover a budget deficit. Possibly Treasury bills might be issued to local financial institutions, but this resource is extremely limited in extent. Therefore, if the budget should again become unbalanced, the only recourse open to the Government is to raise taxes, and the unpopularity of such a measure should prove a strong practical deterrent from engaging in unwise and excessive expenditure.

While the control of the budget and the general supervision of the execution of the reconstruction plan are terminated by the discharge of the Commissioner-General, two questions still remained to be dealt with, the details of which were settled by the decision of the Council. One of these questions is the management of the revenues assigned as security for the Reconstruction Loan, which is governed by the terms of the original Protocol; the other question is not governed by the Protocol and concerns the disposition of the unexpended balance of the Reconstruction Loan. In these two cases the Council adopted the following procedure, which is the same as that previously established in the case of Austria:

(a) Under the terms of Protocol II (Art. XI, 1), the Trustees of the Reconstruction Loan succeed to the duties of the Commissioner-General in the control of the special account of the revenues pledged for the security of the Reconstruction Loan, and, after retaining the amounts necessary to meet the service of the Loan, are to transfer the balance to the Hungarian Government.

(b) The Reconstruction Loan issued in 1924 produced a net amount of approximately 253 million gold crowns, which was to be used for the purpose of meeting budget deficits during a period of two and a-half years, which it was contemplated might be necessary to balance the budget. About 70 million gold crowns was used for this purpose for the budget year ending June 30th, 1924, and none of the Reconstruction Loan has been used for a similar purpose since that date. From time to time, the expenditure of 100 million gold crowns additional from the Reconstruction Loan has been authorised by the Council of the League of Nations, on the recommendation of the Financial Committee, for capital investments by the Hungarian Government, of which 50 million gold crowns was to be spent during the budget year ended June 30th, 1926, and 50 million gold crowns was authorised in December 1925 for the budget year July 1st, 1926–June 30th, 1927. The balance remaining—approximately 81 million gold crowns—is to be retained in liquid form in a separate account managed by a person to be appointed by the Financial Committee, except in so far as it is released for expenditure within the budget for such purposes as the Council, on the recommendation of the Financial Committee, may from time to time approve, and for this purpose the Financial Committee has appointed M. ter Meulen, who will have the assistance of an agent residing at Budapest. Inasmuch as the capital investment programme of the Hungarian Government has been fully provided for up to July 1st, 1927, it was deemed unnecessary at this stage to authorise any releases beyond that date.

On making his final report, the Commissioner-General takes this occasion to express his thanks to the Council of the League and its competent organisations, and especially the Financial Committee, for the support, advice and assistance which he has constantly received from them, and, further, to express his gratitude to the Hungarian

Government and the Hungarian people for the uniform kindness and courtesy with which he has been treated by all with whom he has come in contact. Without the co-operation of both the Government and the people, it would have been impossible to make any satisfactory progress with the reconstruction plan, and this has been completely given at every stage of the work.

II. OBJECTS AND RESULTS OF THE RECONSTRUCTION PLAN.

The causes which made it necessary for Hungary to ask the League of Nations for assistance in 1923 have been admirably stated in the preface to the documents relating to the reconstruction plan, which were issued by the League of Nations in April 1924. Briefly summarised, they are as follows:

Disorganisation caused by the war and consequent loss of territory, political difficulties, internal and external, which followed the Armistice, the undetermined liability for reparations and the difficulty of reorganising a political and commercial establishment designed for a much larger country presented obstacles which could not be overcome. The budget became unbalanced, current expense was met from note inflation, which produced a continually increasing depreciation of the currency, and the only means of arresting it became a foreign loan to meet the budget deficit during the period necessary for financial reorganisation. The League entrusted the preparation of a suitable plan to its Financial Committee. The entire success of this experiment depended upon the preparation of the plan and too much praise cannot be given to the Financial Committee of the League for the ability shown in this task. The Committee had the wisdom and courage to prepare a plan based upon sound financial principles which had been tested under normal conditions. Many people doubted the efficacy of such a plan under the abnormal conditions which prevailed at that time in Hungary, but the Committee rejected many of the theories which were then being put forward as necessary to correct abnormal conditions and preferred to rely upon principles which had stood the test of time. The result has vindicated the judgment of the Committee.

The principal features of the plan were:

(1) Definite settlement of the reparation liability for 20 years, which was obtained through a decision of the Reparation Commission, fixing annual payments on account of reparations until 1944, at an average rate of 10 million gold crowns a year.

(2) The stoppage of inflation through the creation of a central bank of issue, with the exclusive privilege of issuing banknotes, divorced from political control and forbidden to loan money to the State or any of its subdivisions without adequate security. The ultimate adoption of the free exchange of notes for gold is contemplated by this plan.

(3) The issue of an international loan, secured on some of the most productive revenues of the State, for the purpose of covering budget deficits until June 30th, 1926, when it was expected that the budget would be in a state of permanent equilibrium.

(4) The preparation of a budget covering the period up to June 30th, 1926, and the appointment of a Commissioner-General to supervise the execution of the whole programme and to control the expenditure of the proceeds of the Loan as well as the revenues pledged to secure the service of the Loan, with power to regulate expenditure and revenue in case the Government should fall behind the reconstruction programme.

(5) The adoption of a centralised system of Treasury receipts and disbursements, which would give exact knowledge of the cash position of the Treasury at all times.

The execution of the plan has proved even more successful than anticipated. As was expected, there was a large deficit for the financial year ending June 30th, 1924, which was met from the proceeds of the Reconstruction Loan. Since July 1st, 1924, the budget has been in a state of equilibrium, and it has been unnecessary to expend any of the proceeds of the Reconstruction Loan for budgetary deficits. This surprising result is not due to reductions in expenditure—for none was contemplated by the plan—but to unexpected increases in the estimated revenue of the State over the conservative estimates of the plan due to the stabilisation of the currency and the increased confidence which followed it. The currency has been stable since the National Bank was opened on June 24th, 1924, and the Bank has ample reserves for the maintenance of the currency.

It should not be forgotten that the Financial Committee of the League, in its original report pointed out that the problem which confronted Hungary was a double one: financial and budgetary on the one hand and economic on the other. It further pointed out that the responsibility of the League should be expressly limited to remedying the budgetary and financial position. "The necessary economic adaptation must be effected by Hungary itself; the essential contribution (of the League) is to give a stable basis on which this adaptation can take place." The League has now done all that it undertook to do—*i.e.*, to create a sound budgetary and financial position, which is necessary to establish a firm foundation for the future upon which the complete economic recovery of Hungary can take place. Economic conditions have slowly and steadily improved since the plan became effective, and if the present position is maintained by Hungary itself, the economic conditions should continue to improve until they reach at least the normal pre-war conditions.

• • • • •

Ʊ Ʊ Ʊ

CHAPTER 3

REPARATION, DEBTS, DEPRESSION

26. THE GERMAN REPARATION BILL, MAY 5, 1921 [1]

The tasks of compiling Germany's reparation debt and formulating a method of payment were entrusted by the Paris Peace Conference to a special Reparation Commission. This body, which came to be composed of one representative each from Great Britain, France, Italy, and Belgium, announced its plan on April 28, 1921. The indemnity figure stipulated (132 billion gold marks) was three times as high as that proposed by economic experts at the conference, but it was endorsed by the Allied Governments and presented to Germany on May 5. Six days later the government of Chancellor Joseph Wirth accepted the bill, to prevent an Allied occupation of the Ruhr area.

COVERING LETTER.

No. 13/279.

Paris, May 5, 1921.

The Reparation Commission.
To the Kriegslastenkommission.

The Reparation Commission has the honour to notify to the German Government, in the enclosed document, the Schedule of Payments prescribing the time and manner for securing and discharging the entire obligation of Germany for reparation under Articles 231, 232 and 233 of the Treaty of Versailles.

(*Signed*) DUBOIS.
JOHN BRADBURY.
SALVAGO RAGGI.
DELACROIX.

---

[1] Reparation Commission, *Publications, III: Official Documents Relative to the Amount of Payments to be Effected by Germany under Reparations Account,* vol. I (May 1, 1921-July 1, 1922), His Majesty's Stationery Office, London, 1922, pp. 4-9.

SCHEDULE OF PAYMENTS.

Prescribing the time and manner for securing and discharging the entire obligation of Germany for reparation under Articles 231, 232 and 233 of the Treaty of Versailles.

The Reparation Commission has, in accordance with Article 233 of the Treaty of Versailles, fixed the time and manner for securing and discharging the entire obligation of Germany for Reparation under Articles 231, 232 and 233 of the Treaty — as follows:

This determination is without prejudice to the duty of Germany to make restitution under Article 238 or to other obligations under the Treaty.

ARTICLE 1.

Germany will perform in the manner laid down in this Schedule her obligation to pay the total fixed in accordance with Articles 231, 232 and 233 of the Treaty of Versailles by the Commission, viz., 132 milliards of gold marks less:

(*a*) The amount already paid on account of Reparation, (*b*) sums which may from time to time be credited to Germany in respect of State properties in ceded territories, etc., and (*c*) any sums received from other enemy or ex-enemy Powers in respect of which the Commission may decide that credit should be given to Germany, plus the amount of the Belgian debt to the Allies, the amounts of these deductions and addition to be determined later by the Commission.

ARTICLE 2.

Germany shall create and deliver to the Commission in substitution for bonds already delivered or delivered under paragraph 12 (*c*) of Annex II of Part VIII (Reparation) of the Treaty of Versailles the bonds hereafter described.

A.—Bonds for the amount of 12 milliards gold marks.

These bonds shall be created and delivered at latest on July 1, 1921. There shall be an annual payment from fund (*sic*) to be provided by Germany as prescribed in this Schedule in each year from May 1, 1921, equal in amount to 6 per cent. of the nominal value of the issued bonds, out of which there shall be paid interest at 5 per cent. per annum payable half-yearly on the bonds outstanding at any time, and the balance to sinking fund for the redemption of the bonds by annual drawings at par.

These bonds are hereinafter referred to as bonds of Series (A).

B.—*Bonds for a further amount of 38 milliards gold marks.*

These bonds shall be created and delivered at the latest on November 1, 1921.

There shall be an annual payment from funds to be provided by Germany as prescribed in this Schedule in each year from November 1, 1921, equal in amount to 6 per cent. of the nominal value of the issued bonds out of which there shall be paid interest at 5 per cent. per annum payable half-yearly on the bonds outstanding at any time and the balance to sinking fund for the redemption of the bonds by annual drawings at par.

These bonds are hereinafter referred to as bonds of Series (B).

C.—*Bonds for 82 milliards of gold marks, subject to such subsequent adjustment by creation or cancellation of bonds as may be required under Article 1.*

These bonds shall be created and delivered to the Reparation Commission, without coupons attached, at the latest on 1st November, 1921. They shall be issued by the Commission as and when it is satisfied that the payments which Germany is required to make in pursuance of this schedule are sufficient to provide for the payment of interest and sinking fund on such bonds. There shall be an annual payment from funds to be provided by Germany as prescribed in this schedule in each year from the date of issue by the Reparation Commission equal in amount to 6 per cent. of the nominal value of the issued bonds out of which shall be paid interest at 5 per cent. per annum payable half-yearly on the bonds outstanding at any time and the balance to sinking fund for the redemption of the bonds by annual drawings at par.

The German Government shall supply to the Commission couponsheets for such bonds as and when issued by the Commission.

These bonds are hereinafter referred to as bonds of Series (C).

ARTICLE 3.

The bonds provided for in Article 2 shall be signed by the German Government as bearer bonds, in such form and in such denominations as the Commission shall prescribe for the purpose of making them marketable, and shall be free of all German taxes and charges of every description present or future.

Subject to the provisions of Articles 248 and 251 of the Treaty of Versailles, these bonds shall be secured on the whole of the assets and revenues of the German Empire and the German States, and in particular on the assets and revenues specified in Article 7 of this schedule. The Service of bonds of Series (A), (B) and (C) shall be a first, second and third charge respectively on said assets and revenues and shall be met by payments to be made by Germany under this schedule.

ARTICLE 4.

Germany shall pay in each year until the redemption of the bonds provided for in Article 2 by means of the sinking funds attached thereto:—

(1) The sum of 2 milliard gold marks;

(2) (a) A sum equivalent to 25 per cent. of the value of her exports in each period of twelve months starting from May 1, 1921, as determined by the Commission,

or

(b) Alternately an equivalent amount as fixed in accordance with any other index proposed by Germany and accepted by the Commission;

(3) A further sum equivalent to 1 per cent. of the value of her exports as above defined or[,] alternately, an equivalent amount fixed as provided in (b) above.

Provided always that when Germany shall have discharged her obligations under this schedule, other than her liability in respect of outstanding Bonds, the amount to be paid in each year under this paragraph shall be reduced to the amount required in that year to meet the interest and sinking fund on the bonds then outstanding.

Subject to the provisions of Article 5 the payments to be made in respect of paragraph (1) above shall be made quarterly on or before January 15, April 15, July 15, and October 15 each year and the payments in respect of paragraphs (2) and (3) above shall be made quarterly on or before February 15, May 15, August 15 and November 15, and calculated on the basis of the exports in the last quarter but one preceding that quarter, the first payment to be made on or before November 15, 1921, to be calculated on the basis of the exports in the three months ending July 31, 1921.

Article 5.

Germany shall pay within 25 days from this notification one milliard gold marks in gold or approved foreign currencies or approved foreign bills or in drafts at three months on the German Treasury endorsed by approved German banks and payable in pounds sterling in London, in francs in Paris, in dollars in New York or any currency in any other place designated by the Commission. These payments will be treated as the first two quarterly instalments of payments provided in Article 4 (1°).

Article 6.

The Commission will[,] within 25 days from this notification, in accordance with paragraph 12 A (d), Annex II of the Treaty as amended, establish the special Sub-Commission to be called the Committee of Guarantees.

The Committee of Guarantees will consist of representatives of the Allied Powers now represented on the Reparation Commission, including a representative of the United States of America in the event of that Government desiring to make the appointment.

The Committee shall co-opt not more than three representatives of nationals of other Powers whenever it shall appear to the Commission that a sufficient portion of the bonds to be issued under this schedule is held by nationals of such Powers to justify their representation on the Committee of Guarantees.

Article 7.

The Committee of Guarantees will be charged with the duty of securing the application of Articles 241 and 248 of the Treaty of Versailles.

It shall supervise the application to the service of the Bonds provided for in Article 2 of the funds assigned as security for the payments to be made by Germany under Article 4. The funds to be so assigned shall be:

(a) The proceeds of all German maritime and land Customs duties, and in particular the proceeds of all Import and Export duties;

(b) Proceeds of a levy of 25 per cent. on the value of all exports from Germany except those exports upon which a levy of not less than 25 per cent. is applied under the legislation referred to in Article 9;

(c) The proceeds of such direct or indirect taxes or any other funds as may be proposed by the German Government and accepted

by the Committee of Guarantees in addition to or in substitution
for the funds specified in (*a*) and (*b*) above.

The assigned funds shall be paid to accounts to be opened in the
name of the Committee and supervised by it, in gold or in foreign
currencies approved by the Committee.

The equivalent of the 25 per cent. levy referred to in paragraph (*b*)
shall be paid in German currency by the German Government to the
exporter.

The German Government shall notify to the Committee of Guarantees any proposed action which may tend to diminish the proceeds of
any of the assigned funds and shall, if the Committee demand it, substitute some other approved funds.

The Committee of Guarantees shall be charged further with the duty
of conducting on behalf of the Commission the examination provided
for in paragraph 12 (*b*) of Annex II to Part VIII of the Treaty of
Versailles and of verifying on behalf of the Commission, and if necessary of correcting, the amount declared by the German Government
as the value of German exports for the purpose of the calculation of
the sum payable in each year or quarter under Article 4 (2) and the
amounts of the funds assigned under this Article to the service of the
bonds.

The Committee shall be entitled to take such measures as it may
deem necessary for the proper discharge of its duties.

The Committee of Guarantees is not authorised to interfere in German administration.

ARTICLE 8.

In accordance with paragraph 9 (2) of Annex II as amended[,] Germany shall on demand, subject to the prior approval of the Commission, provide such material and labour as any of the Allied Powers
may require towards the restoration of the devastated areas of that
Power, or to enable any Allied Power to proceed with the restoration
or the development of its industrial or economic life. The value of
such material and labour shall be determined in each case by a valuer
appointed by Germany and a valuer appointed by the Power concerned, and, in default of agreement, by a referee nominated by the
Commission.

This provision as to valuation does not apply to deliveries under Annexes III, IV, V, and VI to Part VIII of the Treaty.[2]

ARTICLE 9.

Germany shall take every necessary measure of legislative and administrative action to facilitate the operation of the German Reparation (Recovery) Act, 1921, in force in the United Kingdom, and of any similar legislation enacted by any Allied Power, so long as such legislation remains in force. Payments effected by the operation of such legislation shall be credited to Germany on account of the payments to be made by her under Article 4 (2).

The equivalent in German currency shall be paid by the German Government to the exporter.

ARTICLE 10.

Payment for all services rendered, all deliveries in kind and all receipts under Article 9 shall be made to the Reparation Commission by the Allied Power receiving the same in cash or current coupons within one month of the receipt thereof, and shall be credited to Germany on account of the payments to be made by her under Article 4.

ARTICLE 11.

The sum payable under Article 4 (3) and any surplus receipts by the Commission under Article 4 (1) and (2) in each year, not required for the payment of interest and sinking fund on bonds outstanding in that year, shall be accumulated and applied so far as they will extend, at such times as the Commission may think fit, by the Commission in paying simple interest not exceeding 2½ per cent. per annum, from May 1, 1921, to May 1, 1926, and thereafter at a rate not exceeding 5 per cent. on the balance of the debt not covered by the bonds then issued.

The interest on such balance of the debt shall not be cumulative. No interest thereon shall be payable otherwise than as provided in this paragraph.

ARTICLE 12.

The present schedule does not modify the provisions securing the execution of the Treaty of Versailles, which are applicable to the stipulations of the present schedule.

---

[2] These annexes relate mainly to specific replacements in kind, such as replacements of merchant vessels, cattle, and coal.—*Ed.*

27. THE BALFOUR NOTE OF AUGUST 1, 1922 [3]

As a step toward easing the European financial situation, the British in 1922 announced their willingness, in effect, to cancel all war debts and reparation due them provided the United States likewise remitted her war debts.

Foreign Office, August 1, 1922.

Your Excellency,

As your Excellency is aware, the general question of the French debt to this country has not as yet been the subject of any formal communication between the two Governments, nor are His Majesty's Government anxious to raise it at the present moment. Recent events, however, leave them little choice in the matter, and they feel compelled to lay before the French Government their views on certain aspects of the situation created by the present condition of international indebtedness.

Speaking in general terms, the war debts, exclusive of interest, due to Great Britain at the present moment amount in the aggregate to about £3,400,000,000, of which Germany owes £1,450,000,000, Russia £650,000,000, and our allies £1,300,000,000. On the other hand, Great Britain owes the United States about a quarter of this sum—say £850,000,000, at par of exchange, together with interest accrued since 1919.

No international discussion has yet taken place on the unexampled situation partially disclosed by these figures; and, pending a settlement which would go to the root of the problem, His Majesty's Government have silently abstained from making any demands upon their allies, either for the payment of interest or the repayment of capital. But, if action in the matter has hitherto been deemed inopportune, this is not because His Majesty's Government either underrate the evils of the present state of affairs, or because they are reluctant to make large sacrifices to bring it to an end. On the contrary, they are prepared, if such a policy formed part of a satisfactory international settlement, to remit all the debts due to Great Britain by our allies in respect of loans, or by Germany in respect of reparations.

---

[3] From letter of the Earl of Balfour to the French and other ambassadors, August 1, 1922, in *Despatch to the Representatives of France, Italy, Serb-Croat-Slovene State, Roumania, Portugal and Greece at London Respecting War Debts. Presented to Parliament by Command of His Majesty*, Misc. No. 5 (1922), Cmd. 1737, His Majesty's Stationery Office, London, 1922, pp. 2-4.

Recent events, however, make such a policy difficult of accomplishment. With the most perfect courtesy, and in the exercise of their undoubted rights, the American Government have required this country to pay the interest accrued since 1919 on the Anglo-American debt, to convert it from an unfunded to a funded debt, and to repay it by a sinking fund in twenty-five years. Such a procedure is clearly in accordance with the original contract. His Majesty's Government make no complaint of it; they recognise their obligations and are prepared to fulfil them. But evidently they cannot do so without profoundly modifying the course which, in different circumstances, they would have wished to pursue. They cannot treat the repayment of the Anglo-American loan as if it were an isolated incident in which only the United States of America and Great Britain had any concern. It is but one of a connected series of transactions, in which this country appears sometimes as debtor, sometimes as creditor, and, if our undoubted obligations as a debtor are to be enforced, our not less undoubted rights as a creditor cannot be left wholly in abeyance.

His Majesty's Government do not conceal the fact that they adopt this change of policy with the greatest reluctance. It is true that Great Britain is owed more than it owes, and that, if all inter-Allied war debts were paid, the British Treasury would, on balance, be a large gainer by the transaction. But can the present world situation be looked at only from this narrow financial standpoint? It is true that many of the Allied and Associated Powers are, as between each other, creditors or debtors, or both. But they were, and are, much more. They were partners in the greatest international effort ever made in the cause of freedom; and they are still partners in dealing with some, at least, of its results. Their debts were incurred, their loans were made, not for the separate advantage of particular States, but for a great purpose common to them all, and that purpose has been, in the main, accomplished.

To generous minds it can never be agreeable, although, for reasons of State, it may perhaps be necessary, to regard the monetary aspect of this great event as a thing apart, to be torn from its historical setting and treated as no more than an ordinary commercial dealing between traders who borrow and capitalists who lend. There are, moreover, reasons of a different order, to which I have already referred, which increase the distaste with which His Majesty's Government

adopt so fundamental an alteration in method of dealing with loans
to allies. The economic ills from which the world is suffering are due
to many causes, moral and material, which are quite outside the scope
of this despatch. But among them must certainly be reckoned the
weight of international indebtedness, with all its unhappy effects upon
credit and exhange, upon national production and international trade.
The peoples of all countries long for a speedy return to the normal.
But how can the normal be reached while conditions so abnormal are
permitted to prevail? And how can these conditions be cured by any
remedies that seem at present likely to be applied?

For evidently the policy hitherto pursued by this country of refusing
to make demands upon its debtors is only tolerable so long as it is
generally accepted. It cannot be right that one partner in the common
enterprise should recover all that she has lent, and that another, while
recovering nothing, should be required to pay all that she has borrowed.
Such a procedure is contrary to every principle of natural justice and
cannot be expected to commend itself to the people of this country.
They are suffering from an unparalleled burden of taxation, from
an immense diminution in national wealth, from serious want of employment, and from the severe curtailment of useful expenditure. These
evils are courageously borne. But were they to be increased by an
arrangement which, however legitimate, is obviously one-sided, the
British taxpayer would inevitably ask why he should be singled out to
bear a burden which others are bound to share.

To such a question there can be but one answer, and I am convinced
that Allied opinion will admit its justice. But while His Majesty's
Government are thus regretfully constrained to request the French
Government to make arrangements for dealing to the best of their
ability with Anglo-French loans, they desire to explain that the amount
of interest and repayment for which they ask depends not so much
on what France and other Allies owe to Great Britain as on what Great
Britain has to pay America. The policy favoured by His Majesty is,
as I have already observed, that of surrending their share of German
reparation, and writing off, through one great transaction, the whole
body of inter-Allied indebtedness. But, if this be found impossible of
accomplishment, we wish it to be understood that we do not in any
event desire to make a profit out of any less satisfactory arrangement.
In no circumstances do we propose to ask more from our debtors

than is necessary to pay to our creditors. And, while we do not ask for more, all will admit that we can hardly be content with less. For it should not be forgotten, though it sometimes is, that our liabilities were incurred for others, not for ourselves. The food, the raw material, the munitions required by the immense military and naval efforts of Great Britain and half the £2,000,000,000 advanced to allies were provided, not by means of foreign loans, but by internal borrowing and war taxation. Unfortunately, a similar policy was beyond the power of other European nations. Appeal was therefore made to the Government of the United States; and under the arrangement then arrived at the United States insisted, in substance if not in form, that, though our allies were to spend the money, it was only on our security that they were prepared to lend it. This co-operative effort was of infinite value to the common cause, but it cannot be said that the rôle assigned in it to this country was one of special privilege or advantage.

Before concluding I may be permitted to offer one further observation in order to make still clearer the spirit in which His Majesty's Government desire to deal with the thorny problem of international indebtedness.

In an earlier passage of this despatch I pointed out that this, after all, is not a question merely between allies. Ex-enemy countries also are involved; for the greatest of all international debtors is Germany. Now His Majesty's Government do not suggest that, either as a matter of justice or expediency, Germany should be relieved of her obligation to the other allied States. They speak only for Great Britain; and they content themselves with saying once again that, so deeply are they convinced of the economic injury inflicted on the world by the existing state of things that this country would be prepared (subject to the just claims of other parts of the Empire) to abandon all further right to German reparation and all claims to repayment by allies, provided that this renunciation formed part of a general plan by which this great problem could be dealt with as a whole and find a satisfactory solution. A general settlement would, in their view, be of more value to mankind than any gains that could accrue even from the most successful enforcement of legal obligations.

I have, &c.
BALFOUR.

28. THE DECLARATION OF GERMAN DEFAULT BY THE REPARA-
TION COMMISSION, DECEMBER 26, 1922 [4]

Dissatisfied with the rate of German reparation payments and indignant over a Berlin request for a total moratorium from the middle of 1922 until the end of 1924, France appealed to the Reparation Commission to declare Germany in default on the delivery of telegraph poles. Over the protest of its British member, the commission found Germany in such default and soon thereafter in general default. This declaration was used as the legal basis for the French-Italian-Belgian occupation of the Ruhr district—the heart of German industry—in January 1923.

On the 20th October, 1922, the French Delegation requested the Commission to declare Germany in default as regards its obligation to furnish timber to France during 1922. Under the above order all the sawn timber (55,000 M³) should have been delivered to France before the 30th September, 1922, and the 200,000 telegraph poles ordered by France should have been tendered in uncreosoted condition before the 30th November, 1922. The position on the 30th September, 1922, was as follows:

Category of timber	Amount ordered	Contracts made by German Government	Per cent.	Amount due on 30th Sept.	Amount received in Germany by French Agents at 30th Sept.	Per cent. of the order	Des-patched	Per cent. of the order
Sawn Wood	53,000	54,935	100	55,000	17,417	31.5	15,950	29
Telegraph Poles	200,000	75,694	38	145,000*	46,133	23.0	40,047	20

*On the assumption that the rate of delivery was constant.

On the 30th November, the deliveries were still considerably in arrears and, on the 1st December, the Commission formally heard the representatives of the German Government on the subject.

On the 26th December, 1922, after careful examination of the German defence, the Commission took the following decision:

"(1) It was unanimously decided that Germany had not executed in

[4] Reparation Commission, *Publications, V: Report on the Work of the Reparation Commission from 1920 to 1922,* His Majesty's Stationery Office, London, 1923, pp. 141-143.

their entirety the orders passed under Annex IV, Part VIII of the Treaty of Versailles, for deliveries of timber to France during 1922.

(2) It was decided by a majority, the British Delegate voting against this decision, that this non-execution constituted a default by Germany in her obligations within the meaning of paragraph 17 of Annex II.[5]

(3) It was decided by a majority, the British Delegate abstaining from voting, to recall to the Governments concerned that in its letter of March 21st, 1922, fixing the payments to be made by Germany during the current year, the Commission had made the following statement:

'If the Reparation Commission finds, in the course of the year 1922, that deliveries in kind called for by France or her nationals, or by any other Power entitled to reparation or its nationals, in accordance with the procedure laid down by the Treaty or in virtue of a procedure approved by the Reparation Commission and within the limits of the figures above indicated have not been effected by reason of obstruction on the part of the German Government or on the part of its organisations, or by reason of a breach of the procedure of the Treaty or of a procedure approved by the Reparation Commission, additional equivalent cash payments shall be exacted from Germany at the end of 1922 in replacement of the deliveries not effected.'

(4) It was decided on the present occasion to understand by the phrase 'interested Powers' in paragraph 17 of Annex II, Great Britain, France, Italy and Belgium. A copy of the letter addressed to these four Governments would be despatched to the Government of the United States of America."[6]

The importance of this decision notifying the formal default by Ger-

---

[5] This paragraph read: "In case of default by Germany in the performance of any obligation under this part of the present Treaty, the Commission will forthwith give notice of such default to each of the interested Powers and may make such recommendations as to the action to be taken in consequence of such default as it may think necessary."—*Ed.*

[6] On the same day the Commission adopted the following formal interpretation of paragraph 17 of Annex II:

"The Reparation Commission in the exercise of its powers of interpretation under paragraph 12 of Annex II, Part VIII of the Treaty of Versailles, decided that the word 'default' in paragraph 17 of the said Annex had the same meaning as the expression 'voluntary default' in paragraph 18 of the same Annex."

many by a majority vote, has been such that it has appeared advisable to reproduce in full in Appendix XXXV[7] the minutes of the meeting at which the German hearing took place, and the relevant part of the minutes of the meeting at which the default was declared.

29. OFFICIAL BRITISH VIEW ON THE ILLEGALITY OF THE RUHR OCCUPATION (Extracts) [8]

The British Government was strongly opposed to the occupation of the Ruhr as a means of stimulating German payment and so informed France. The opposing views of Great Britain and France on the reparation question were a factor in the virtual termination in 1923 of the Entente Cordiale of 1904.

31. France and Belgium hold that the occupation has been effected in virtue of the authority conferred by paragraph 18 of annex II to Part VIII of the Treaty [of Versailles]. The German Government have consistently contended that such an operation does not, on a proper interpretation of that paragraph, fall within the category of "economic and financial prohibitions and reprisals and in general such other measures as the respective Governments may determine to be necessary in the circumstances."

32. The highest legal authorities in Great Britain have advised His Majesty's Government that the contention of the German Government is well founded, and His Majesty's Government have never concealed their view that the Franco-Belgian action in occupying the Ruhr, quite apart from the question of expediency, was not a sanction authorised by the Treaty itself. . . .

33. The French Government have endeavoured to convict His Majesty's Government of inconsistency in now refusing to acknowledge the legality of the occupation of the Ruhr under paragraph 18 of annex II, when on two former occasions they joined in the presentation of ultimata threatening such occupation, and when in 1920 they

---

[7] *See* page 240 [of the Report].

[8] Note of the Marquess Curzon of Kedleston to the French and Belgian Ambassadors, August 11, 1923, in *Correspondence with the Allied Governments Respecting Reparation Payments by Germany. Presented to Parliament by Command of His Majesty,* Misc. No. 5 (1923), Cmd. 1943, His Majesty's Stationery Office, London, 1923, pp. 55-60.

actually participated in the occupation of Düsseldorf, Duisburg and Ruhrort. There is no inconsistency. The action then taken or threatened was never claimed to be in pursuance of the Reparation Clauses of the Treaty. The Allies jointly decided to threaten Germany with the occupation of further territory just as they might have threatened her with a renewal of war, for her failure to perform her Treaty obligations, some of which had no connection whatever with Reparations.

34. In the view of His Majesty's Government, it cannot legitimately be claimed that the measures which the Allies are, under paragraph 18 of annex II, authorised to take in certain emergencies, include the military occupation of territory. Such occupation forms the subject of the special provisions of Part XIV of the Treaty, dealing with Guarantees. It is the right to occupy the left bank of the Rhine and the bridgeheads, which has been given to the Allies "as a guarantee for the execution of the Treaty." Moreover, article 430 particularly stipulates that if the Reparation Commission finds that Germany refuses to observe the whole or part of her obligations under the Treaty with regard to reparations, the whole or part of the occupied territories, which may already have been evacuated, "will be immediately reoccupied." It would have been idle to stipulate expressly for such reoccupation in case of default on reparations, if the Allies had already an unlimited right to occupy any German territory under another clause of the Treaty.

. . . . . .

38. The parallel which the French Government seek to draw with German action in 1871 can hardly be sustained. It is true that Germany refused to quit the French departments which she occupied with her forces until the indemnity of 5 milliards [francs] had been paid. But this occupation was expressly provided for by the Preliminaries of Peace of 1871. No similar authority can be cited in the case of the Ruhr, and the real analogy in the present case is the occupation of the left bank of the Rhine, as provided for by the treaty, and from this no one has proposed to depart.

. . . . .

52. It is admitted that Germany can only make substantial payments if, by the restoration of her public finance and a stabilisation of her currency, a surplus is made available for reparation on her budget. Moreover, this surplus must be in a form in which it can be made available for external payments over the foreign exchanges. External

debts cannot be paid by the collection of depreciating paper marks. In the view of His Majesty's Government forcible interference with the economic life of Germany, even if it be consistent with the terms of the Treaty of Versailles, cannot assist in the necessary restoration. Not only will it prevent the realisation of any surplus for reparation, but, by intensifying the disorder of German finance and currency, it will have the gravest reactions on trade.

53. His Majesty's Government, therefore, regard as doomed to failure the method pursued by the French and Belgian Governments to secure reparations. In spite of wholesale seizures, the occupation of the Ruhr by France and Belgium has produced, at great cost, less receipts for the Allies, notably of coal and coke, than were forthcoming in the previous year. Moreover, His Majesty's Government feel that the resulting situation involves great and growing danger to the peaceful trade of the world and, not least, of this country. His Majesty's Government regard a continuance of the present position as fraught with the gravest risks, both economic and political. They consider the impartial fixation of Germany's liability at a figure not inconsistent with her practical power of making payment a matter of great urgency; and they have suggested what appears to them to be an appropriate means to this end.

• • • • • •

30. CONTRAST OF SECOND (YOUNG) AND FIRST (DAWES) EXPERTS' PLANS [9]

Although the Experts' (Dawes) Plan of 1924 served a useful purpose in temporarily easing the reparation situation and hence also the general tension in post-war Europe, it suffered from certain obvious defects. In the Experts' (Young) Plan of 1929 an attempt was made to remove these weaknesses as indicated below.

The Dawes Plan, although drawn up at a time of intense crisis, has by a test lasting nearly five years justified by facts the postulates on which it was based as regards both the restoration of the public finances of Germany and her economic recovery.

---

[9] *Report of the Committee of Experts on Reparations. Presented to Parliament by the Financial Secretary to the Treasury by Command of His Majesty, June, 1929*, Cmd. 3343, His Majesty's Stationery Office, London, June, 1929, pp. 29-31.

It may be well to summarise briefly the points of advantage—whether to Germany or her Creditors—claimed for the new proposal, which justify a departure from a scheme that has in the past rendered signal service.

The Plan drawn up by the Committee to afford a definite solution of the Reparation question accompanies a reduction in the existing obligations of Germany by an essential modification in their financial and political status. In so far as the creditors are relinquishing substantial advantages in the face value of payments due under the Dawes Plan, they are doing so only by reason of those improvements in intrinsic and available values which arise from the practicability and certainty of commercialisation and mobilisation within a reasonable period and in its attendant financial and economic psychology.

Among the modifications, which are considered specially important, are the following:

(1) *Fixation of the period and the debt.*

The Dawes Plan imposes in virtue of the Index of Prosperity increasing annuities, of which the number are not fixed. The new programme indicates a definite number of fixed annuities.

(2) *Disappearance of the Index of Prosperity.*

Only estimates, which vary very widely, of the ultimate effect of the Index of Prosperity can at this date be made. But in no circumstances could Germany benefit therefrom, and the disappearance of this element of uncertainty is wholly to her benefit.

(3) *Attainment of financial autonomy.*

Under the Dawes Plan Germany can only obtain the discharge of her obligations in marks by the existence of a system of transfer protection which involves a measure of external control. This brings attendant limiting effects on German credit and financial independence which render difficult, if not impossible, any mobilisation of the German debt. The new plan would be abandoning the fundamental purposes for which it was intended if it did not cancel this clause and leave to Germany the obligation of facing her engagements on her own untrammelled responsibility.

(4) *Postponement safeguards.*

Nevertheless, if an exceptional emergency interrupts the normal course of economic life to which the scheme is adapted, Germany can, on her own initiative, resort to certain measures of temporary relief.

The annuity is divided into two parts, of which one is subject to postponement of transfer and payment. Germany will thus be enabled under certain circumstances temporarily to relieve her balance of payments, and will in fact enjoy the advantages of a form of transfer protection without its attendant limitations.

(5) *Deliveries.*

While the Dawes Plan reluctantly accepted the expedient of deliveries in kind, the new Plan, in spite of the desire of the creditor Powers to dispose freely of their shares of the annuities, recognises the undesirability of a sudden cessation of the system at present in force. The creditors are therefore to take deliveries in kind for ten years, but in decreasing amounts beginning with 750 millions.

(6) *Mobilisation.*

From the point of view of the creditor Powers an essential feature of the new Plan which induces them to agree to reduction on their claims that leave them burdened with a considerable part of their expenditure for the damages caused by the war, is the fact that the annuity is paid in a form lending itself to mobilisation.

(7) *Financial organisation.*

The organisation and machinery of the Dawes Plan were based on the conviction that it must find its proper guarantee in the interest of all parties to carry it out in good faith. In aiming as it did at the transference of the Reparation payments from the political to the economic and business sphere, it presumed constant co-operation of debtor and creditors alike. The new system goes further along the same road, replacing the collaboration of separate administrative and governmental organisations by common work in a purely financial institution, in the management of which Germany is to have an appropriate part. The present administrative organisations cannot have all the elasticity necessary for banking transactions of the magnitude of the payment and transfer of the annuities; but the new Bank [for International Settlements] in close association with the banks of issue and with the banking facilities at its command will have all the necessary means of effecting these operations without disturbance to the German economy or to the economy of other countries. In addition it will be in a position to open up to trade new possibilities of development. The operations which it is to undertake cannot be disturbed or hampered without irreparable damage to the credit of the countries concerned. This assurance should make it possible to limit the guarantees established under the present system for the protection of the rights of the creditors, to the minimum required for the prompt and facile commercialisation of the mobilisable part of the annuity.

(8) *Summary*.

The proposed plan continues and completes the work begun by the Dawes Plan, which the position alike of Germany and of the other countries made it impossible to do more than indicate in outline in 1924. By the final reduction and fixation of the German debt, by the establishment of a progressive scale of annuities, and by the facilities which the new Bank offers for lessening disturbance in the payment of the annuities, it sets the seal on the inclusion of the German debt in the list of international settlements. If it involves appreciable reduction of payments to the creditor countries on what might have been anticipated under the continued operation of the Dawes Plan, it at the same time eliminates the uncertainties which were inherent in that Plan and were equally inimical to the interest of the debtor and to the creditors, by substituting a definite settlement under which the debtor knows the exact extent of his obligations.

31-32. THE PROPOSED AUSTRO-GERMAN CUSTOMS ACCORD OF 1931

31. THE VIENNA PROTOCOL, MARCH 19, 1931 [10]

An increasingly bad economic situation in Europe led to the formulation or attempted formulation in 1930-1931 of numerous relief plans, such as the French proposal for the establishment of a European federation and the holding of a series of economic and grain conferences in various European capitals. The only important understanding actually reached, however, was a proposed customs accord between Germany and Austria.

In pursuance of the conversation which took place in Vienna at the beginning of March, 1931, the German Government and the Austrian Government have agreed to enter forthwith into negotiations for a treaty to assimilate the tariff and economic policies of their respective countries on the basis and within the limits of the following principles.

---

[10] Permanent Court of International Justice, *Publications, Series A/B., Judgments, Orders and Advisory Opinions*, A. W. Sijthoffs' Publishing Company, Leyden, 1931, No. 41, pp. 99-102.

I.

(1) While completely maintaining the independence of the two States and fully respecting the obligations undertaken by them towards other States, the treaty is intended to initiate a reorganization of European economic conditions by regional agreements.

(2) More especially both Parties will, in the treaty, unconditionally declare their willingness to enter into negotiations for a similar arrangement with any other country expressing such a desire.

II.

(1) Germany and Austria will agree on a tariff law and a customs tariff which shall be put into force in both customs areas concurrently with the treaty and for the period of its validity.

(2) During the validity of the treaty, amendments to the tariff law and the customs tariff may only be effected by agreement between the two Parties.

III.

(1) As long as the treaty remains in force, the exchange of goods between the two countries shall not be subject to any import or export duties.

(2) In the treaty the two Governments will come to an agreement as to whether internal customs duties will be necessary, and, if so, for what specified categories of goods and for what period.

IV.

In the treaty the two Governments will reach an agreement for a provisional arrangement regarding the turnover tax and the exchange of those goods for which, at the present time, monopolies or excise duties prevail in either of the two countries.

V.

(1) The Customs Administration of each of the two countries shall be independent of that of the other and shall remain under the exclusive control of its own Government. Furthermore, each country shall bear the expenses of its own Customs Administration.

(2) Both Governments, whilst fully respecting the above principle, will enact special measures of a technical character to provide for the uniform execution of the tariff law, the customs tariff and the other tariff regulations.

VI.

(1) In the German customs area the customs duties shall be levied

by the German Customs authorities and in the Austrian customs area by the Austrian Customs authorities.

(2) After deducting the special expenses arising out of the application of the treaty, the amount of the duties received shall be apportioned between the two countries according to a quota.

(3) In the agreements to be reached regarding this point, care will be taken not to prejudice the liens on customs revenues existing in either country.

VII.

(1) No import, export or transit prohibitions shall exist as between Germany and Austria. Such exceptions as may prove to be requisite for reasons of public security, public health or matters of a similar nature shall be specified in the treaty as precisely as possible.

(2) In place of the Agreement on the Diseases of Animals concluded between Germany and Austria on July 12th, 1924, the two Governments will conclude and put into force as soon as possible, and in any case not later than one year after the entry into operation of the treaty, a fresh agreement regulating the traffic in animals and animal products between Germany and Austria in accordance with the regulations which govern internal traffic in Germany and Austria, the same conditions being given.

VIII.

The rights appertaining to individual and juridical persons of the one Party in the territory of the other in respect of domicile, industry, taxation, etc., shall be regulated in the treaty on the basis of the relevant provisions of the Austro-German Commercial Treaty now in force. On the same basis regulations will also be agreed upon concerning railway and shipping traffic between the two Parties.

IX.

(1) Each of the two Governments, even after the entry into operation of the treaty, shall retain in principle the right to conclude commercial treaties with third States on their own behalf.

(2) In the relevant negotiations with third States, the German and the Austrian Governments will see that the interests of the other contracting Party are not violated in contravention of the tenor and purpose of the treaty to be concluded.

(3) So far as it seems opportune and possible with a view to effecting a simple, speedy and uniform settlement of the commercial relations with third States, the German Government and the Austrian Govern-

ment will conduct joint negotiations for the conclusion of commercial treaties with third States. Even in this case, however, Germany and Austria will each on its own behalf, sign and ratify a separate commercial treaty and will only arrange for a simultaneous exchange of the ratifications with the third State in question.

X.

The two Governments will, at a suitable time, take the steps necessary to bring into accord with one another and with the tenor and purpose of the treaty, to be concluded, the existing commercial treaties concluded by Germany and Austria with third States so far as they contain tariff rates fixed by commercial treaties with other countries or so far as they would interfere with the execution of the existing import and export prohibitions and other regulations for the exchange of goods.

XI.

(1) To ensure a smooth working of the treaty, an Arbitral Committee composed of members of the two Parties on the lines of complete parity shall be provided for. This Committee will have to deal with the following matters:

> (a) settlement by arbitration of differences of opinion arising between the two Parties as to the interpretation and application of the treaty;

> (b) to bring about a compromise in cases where the treaty provides for a special agreement between the two Parties or in which, according to the tenor of the treaty, the realization of the intentions of one Party depends upon the consent of the other, provided that in such cases agreement cannot be reached between the two Parties.

(2) A decision of the Arbitral Committee in cases (a) and (b) referred to above shall have binding effect on both Parties, a majority of votes being sufficient. The President of the Committee shall have a casting vote. Complete parity in choosing the President shall be provided for in the treaty.

(3) Should either of the Governments be of the opinion that a decision of the Arbitral Committee in any of the cases mentioned under 1 (b) infringes its vital economic interests, it shall be entitled to terminate the treaty on giving six months' notice. Such notice of termination may also be given during the first period of three years mentioned under XII (2).

XII.

(1) The treaty to be concluded shall be ratified and shall enter into operation at the end of a period to be fixed in the treaty which extends from the date of the exchange of ratifications.

(2) The treaty may be denounced at any time upon one year's notice, but not so as to terminate it before the end of the third year after its entry into operation except in the case mentioned under XI (3).

(3) Notice may only be given in virtue of a law of the country denouncing the treaty.

32. ADVISORY OPINION OF THE PERMANENT COURT ON THE PROPOSED CUSTOMS ACCORD, SEPTEMBER 5, 1931 [11]

Several powers, particularly France and the Little Entente, professed to see in the proposed customs accord a veiled political union between the two German states and hence exerted diplomatic and financial pressure to prevent its consummation. The legality of the proposal was questioned and eventually (September 5, 1931) the Permanent Court of International Justice gave an eight-to-seven advisory opinion that the accord would violate Austria's promise in the First Geneva Protocol (1922) not to jeopardize her independence. Two days before the advisory opinion was made public, Germany and Austria had renounced the proposed pact. The following selection contains the court's opinion as well as the text of the First Geneva Protocol.

Austria, owing to her geographical position in central Europe and by reason of the profound political changes resulting from the late war, is a sensitive point in the European system. Her existence, as determined by the treaties of peace concluded after the war, is an essential feature of the existing political settlement which has laid down in Europe the consequences of the break-up of the Austro-Hungarian Monarchy.

It was in view of these circumstances that the Treaty of Peace concluded at Saint-Germain on September 10th, 1919, provided as follows:

---

[11] Permanent Court of International Justice, *Publications, Series A/B., Judgments, Orders and Advisory Opinions,* A. W. Sijthoffs' Publishing Company, Leyden, 1931, No. 41, pp. 42-54.

"Article 88

The independence of Austria is inalienable otherwise than with the consent of the Council of the League of Nations. Consequently, Austria undertakes in the absence of the consent of the said Council to abstain from any act which might directly or indirectly or by any means whatever compromise her independence, particularly, and until her admission to membership of the League of Nations, by participation in the affairs of another Power."

It was, more particularly, in view of the same circumstances that, when Austria was given the financial and economic assistance necessary to her independence, the Protocols of October 4th, 1922, were drawn up and signed at Geneva, of which Protocol No. I runs as follows:

"PROTOCOL No. I.

[*Translation*]

DECLARATION.

THE GOVERNMENT OF HIS BRITANNIC MAJESTY, THE GOVERNMENT OF THE FRENCH REPUBLIC, THE GOVERNMENT OF HIS MAJESTY THE KING OF ITALY, AND THE GOVERNMENT OF THE CZECHOSLOVAK REPUBLIC,

Of the one part,

At the moment of undertaking to assist Austria in her work of economic and financial reconstruction,

Acting solely in the interests of Austria and of the general peace, and in accordance with the obligations which they assumed when they agreed to become Members of the League of Nations,

Solemnly declare:

That they will respect the political independence, the territorial integrity and the sovereignty of Austria;

That they will not seek to obtain any special or exclusive economic or financial advantage calculated directly or indirectly to compromise that independence;

That they will abstain from any act which might be contrary to the spirit of the conventions which will be drawn up in common with a view to effecting the economic and financial reconstruction of Austria, or which might prejudicially affect the guarantees demanded by the Powers for the protection of the interests of the creditors and of the guarantor States;

And that, with a view to ensuring the respect of these principles by all nations, they will, should occasion arise, appeal, in accordance with the regulations contained in the Covenant of the League of Nations, either individually or collectively, to the Council of the League, in order that the latter may consider what measures should be taken, and that they will conform to the decisions of the said Council.

THE GOVERNMENT OF THE FEDERAL REPUBLIC OF AUSTRIA,

Of the other part,

Undertakes, in accordance with the terms of Article 88 of the Treaty of Saint-Germain, not to alienate its independence; it will abstain from any negotiations or from any economic or financial engagement calculated directly or indirectly to compromise this independence.

This undertaking shall not prevent Austria from maintaining, subject to the provisions of the Treaty of Saint-Germain, her freedom in the matter of customs tariffs or commercial or financial agreements, and, in general, in all matters relating to her economic régime or her commercial relations, provided always that she shall not violate her economic independence by granting to any State a special régime or exclusive advantages calculated to threaten this independence.

The present Protocol shall remain open for signature by all the States which desire to adhere to it.

In witness whereof the undersigned, duly authorized for this purpose, have signed the present Declaration (Protocol I).

Done at Geneva in a single copy, which shall be deposited with the Secretariat of the League of Nations and shall be registered by it without delay, on the fourth day of October, one thousand nine hundred and twenty-two.

(Signed)	BALFOUR.	*(Signed)*	SEIPEL."
(")	G. HANOTAUX.		
(")	IMPERIALI.		
(")	KRČMÁŘ.		
(")	POSPIŠIL.		

Spain and Belgium acceded to this Protocol.

It will be seen that these provisions, without imposing any absolute veto upon Austria, simply require her to abstain or, in certain circumstances, to obtain the consent of the Council of the League of Nations.

By a Protocol drawn up at Vienna on March 19th, 1931, Germany and Austria agreed to conclude a treaty with a view to assimilating the tariff and economic policies of the two countries on the basis and principles laid down in that Protocol, thereby resulting in the establishment of a customs union régime.

There is nothing in this Protocol which provides for any consent by the Council of the League of Nations. In point of fact, however, the Protocol was communicated by the German and Austrian Governments themselves to the British, French and Italian Governments, among others, and the British Government brought the matter before the Council.

It was in these circumstances that the Council requested the Court to give an advisory opinion on the following question:

"Would a régime established between Germany and Austria on the basis and within the limits of the principles laid down by the Protocol of March 19th, 1931, the text of which is annexed to the present request, be compatible with Article 88 of the Treaty of Saint-Germain and with Protocol No. I signed at Geneva on October 4th, 1922?"

Accordingly, the Court has not to consider the conditions under which the Austro-German customs union might receive the Council's consent. The only question the Court has to settle is whether, from the point of view of law, Austria could, without the consent of the Council, conclude with Germany the customs union contemplated in the Vienna Protocol of March 19th, 1931, without committing an act which would be incompatible with the obligations she has assumed under the provisions quoted above.

I.—Firstly, as regards the undertakings assumed by Austria in Article 88 of the Treaty of Saint-Germain:

When—as had previously been provided in Article 80 of the Treaty of Peace concluded with Germany on June 28th, 1919—the Treaty of Saint-Germain laid down that the independence of Austria was inalienable, except with the consent of the Council of the League of Nations, that Treaty imposed upon Austria, who in principle has sovereign control over her own independence, an obligation not to alienate that independence, except with the consent of the Council of the League of Nations.

If we consider the general observations at the beginning of the present Opinion concerning Austria's present status, and irrespective of the definition of the independence of States which may be given by legal doctrine or may be adopted in particular instances in the practice of States, the independence of Austria, according to Article 88 of the Treaty of Saint-Germain, must be understood to mean the continued existence of Austria within her present frontiers as a separate State with sole right of decision in all matters economic, political, financial or other with the result that that independence is violated, as soon as there is any violation thereof, either in the economic, political, or any other field, these different aspects of independence being in practice one and indivisible.

If by the régime contemplated by the Austro-German Protocol of 1931 Austria does not alienate her independence, the Council's consent on this matter is obviously not necessary. In the other event, however, it is essential.

By "alienation," as mentioned in Article 88, must be understood any voluntary act by the Austrian State which would cause it to lose its independence or which would modify its independence in that its sovereign will would be subordinated to the will of another Power or particular group of Powers, or would even be replaced by such will.

Further, since the signatory Powers to the Treaty of Saint-Germain other than Austria have in Article 88 approved this inalienability by Austria of her independence, they are themselves clearly bound not to participate in acts involving alienation.

Having thus stipulated the inalienability of Austria's independence otherwise than with the consent of the Council of the League of Nations, Article 88 provides: "Consequently, Austria undertakes in the absence of the consent of the said Council to abstain from any act which might directly or indirectly or by any means whatever compromise her independence, particularly, and until her admission to membership of the League of Nations, by participation in the affairs of another Power."

There is no doubt that the word "consequently" connects the first and second sentences in the article. But, although the undertaking given by Austria in this second sentence to abstain from certain acts, which might directly or indirectly compromise her independence, refers to the observance of the inalienability of her independence laid down in the first sentence, it does not follow that the acts from which Austria has undertaken to abstain are, as a consequence, necessarily acts of alienation proper, that is, acts which would directly cause her to lose her independence or would modify it, as stated above.

Moreover, the undertaking given by Austria to abstain from "any act which might directly or indirectly or by any means whatever compromise her independence" can only be interpreted to refer to "any act calculated to endanger" that independence, in so far, of course, as can reasonably be foreseen.

An act calculated to endanger cannot be assimilated to the danger itself, still less to the consummation of that danger, any more than a threatened loss or risk can be assimilated to a loss or risk which actually materializes.

In any case, if more is wanted, the "participation in the affairs of another Power" mentioned at the end of Article 88 as an example— which ceased to be of practical application upon Austria's entry into the League of Nations—of an act which might, pending such entry, compromise her independence, cannot possibly be assimilated to an act of alienation.

II.—As regards the Protocol signed at Geneva on October 4th, 1922, by Austria, France, Great Britain, Italy and Czechoslovakia, and subsequently acceded to by Belgium and Spain, it cannot be denied that, although it took the form of a declaration, Austria did assume thereby certain undertakings in the economic sphere.

From the standpoint of the obligatory character of international engagements, it is well known that such engagements may be taken in the form of treaties, conventions, declarations, agreements, protocols, or exchanges of notes.

That Austria's undertakings in the 1922 Protocol fall within the scope of the obligations undertaken by her in Article 88 of the Treaty of Saint-Germain appears from the express or implied reference made to that provision in the Protocol.

Accordingly, the "economic independence" expressly mentioned in the last paragraph of Austria's undertakings in the 1922 Protocol refers in the economic sphere to "the independence of Austria" within the meaning of Article 88 of the Peace Treaty, so that, as has been shown, a violation of this "economic independence" would be a violation of "the independence of Austria."

Thus also the grant of a special régime or exclusive advantages calculated to threaten Austria's independence within the meaning of the last paragraph of the 1922 Protocol would be one of these acts which might compromise Austria's independence within the meaning of Article 88.

But this in no way prevents the undertakings assumed by Austria in a special and distinct instrument open to the accession of all Powers, whether signatory to the Peace Treaty or not, and to which in fact a

Power non-signatory to the Peace Treaty (i.e. Spain) did accede, from possessing their own value and on that account a binding force complete in itself and capable of independent application.

Thus Spain, who was not a Party to the Peace Treaty and who consequently cannot invoke Article 88, would, on the contrary, be entitled to rely on the 1922 Protocol as the only instrument to which she is a Party, in order to enforce Austria's express undertakings in that Protocol.

It has been argued that the first part of the 1922 Protocol containing the declaration by France, Great Britain, Italy and Czechoslovakia and, by accession, Belgium and Spain, is a simple restatement of the undertaking given by States Members of the League of Nations in Article 10 of the Covenant to respect the territorial integrity and political independence of each Member. Similarly, this part has been regarded as a simple reaffirmation of the obligation assumed by the signatory Powers of the Treaty of Saint-Germain not to participate in any acts not compatible with the inalienability of Austria's independence.

It was therefore submitted that Austria's undertakings ought to be regarded merely as the exact counterpart of the undertakings of the other Powers and, accordingly, as a mere repetition of Article 88 of the Peace Treaty.

As regards the Covenant of the League of Nations, however, while it certainly contains an undertaking to respect the territorial integrity and political independence of each Member and even to preserve as against external aggression this territorial integrity and political independence, it must be observed that it contains neither any undertaking on the part of States not to alienate their own independence, of which they alone are in principle entitled to dispose, nor any undertaking not to seek economic advantages calculated to compromise the independence of another State which is free to dispose of it as it pleases.

Furthermore, as regards Article 88, it has been shown that even admitting that Austria's undertakings in the 1922 Protocol are covered by this article, nevertheless they constitute undertakings possessing their own value and consequently are capable of independent application as would be the case if, for instance, Spain sought to enforce them.

Similarly, no useful comparison can be drawn between other customs unions, numerous examples of which have been and still continue to be furnished by political history, and the customs union contemplated in the Austro-German Protocol.

In fact, it has not been shown that any of the countries bound by customs unions had undertaken in any way to abstain from any act, negotiations or economic engagement calculated to compromise its economic independence, or to abstain from granting to another Power a special régime or exclusive advantages calculated to threaten that independence.

In sum, the provisions of the 1922 Protocol create for Austria undertakings obligatory in themselves, special undertakings from the economic standpoint, i.e. undertakings not only not to alienate her independence, but, from the special economic standpoint, undertakings to abstain from any negotiations or from any economic or financial engagement calculated directly or indirectly to compromise that independence and still more precisely and definitely, undertakings not to violate her economic independence by granting to any State a special régime or exclusive advantages calculated to threaten this independence.

III.—That being so, a consideration of the Austro-German Protocol of March 19th, 1931, the full text of which is annexed hereto, leads to the following results.

By the Protocol of Vienna of 1931, the German and Austrian Governments agreed to enter into negotiations for a treaty "to assimilate the tariff and economic policies of their respective countries" (*Angleichung der zoll- und handelspolitischen Verhältnisse*) on the basis and within the limits of the principles laid down in that Protocol (Preamble).

While declaring that the independence of the two States and full respect for their international engagements are to be completely maintained (Art. I), both Governments undertook (Art. II) to agree on a tariff law and customs tariff which are to be put into force simultaneously and concordantly in Germany and Austria and the technical execution of which shall be uniform, although each country will enforce its application by means of its own administration (Art. V), the customs receipts being apportioned according to a quota to be fixed (Art. VI, No. 2).

As between Germany and Austria, export and import duties are in principle to be removed (Art. III). There will be, subject to inevitable exceptions necessary for public health and security, no import, export or transit prohibitions (Art. VII, No. 1). As regards exchange of goods between the two countries, the turnover tax and commodities forming the subject of monopolies or excise duties will provisionally be regulated by agreement (Art. IV).

As regards the economic treaty régime, Article IX, while declaring that both Governments retain in principle (*grundsätzlich*) the right to conclude commercial treaties "on their own behalf," provides on the other hand that the German and Austrian Governments will see that the interests of the other Party are not violated in contravention of the tenor and purpose of the customs union treaty, i.e. the assimilation of the tariff and economic policies of both countries; the negotiations, Article IX continues, will, as far as possible, be conducted jointly and, notwithstanding that treaties are to be signed and ratified separately, exchanges of ratifications are to be simultaneous (Art. IX, Nos. 2 and 3).

From the point of view of form, therefore, Austria will certainly possess commercial treaties concluded, signed and ratified by herself. But in reality, and without its being necessary to consider in this connection whether Article IX does or does not imply that there may be limitations other than those set out in Nos. 2 and 3, to the right of concluding "treaties" on her own account, it will suffice to note the provisions for joint negotiations, for regard for the interests of the other Party, and the undertaking to the effect that one Party will not ratify without the other.

Lastly, the necessary consequence of this new economic treaty régime will be the modification of Austria's existing treaty régime, which must of course be brought into accord with the projected customs union treaty (Art. X).

Furthermore, disputes which may arise in connection with the interpretation and application of the customs union treaty are to be submitted for arbitration to a paritative arbitral committee (Art. XI, No. 1 *a*), whose duty it will also be to bring about a compromise in cases where the treaty provides for a special arrangement or in cases where the treaty makes the realization of the intentions of one Party dependent upon the consent of the other (Art. XI, No. 1 *b*).

Lastly, the treaty, which is to be concluded for an unspecified duration, may be denounced after three years; it may be denounced before the conclusion of this period, should either of the two countries consider that a decision of the arbitral committee infringes its vital economic interests (Art. XII, and Art. XI, No. 3).

IV.—It is not and cannot be denied that the régime thus established certainly fulfils "the requirements of a customs union: uniformity of customs law and customs tariff; unity of the customs frontiers and of the customs territory vis-à-vis third States; freedom from import and export duties in the exchange of goods between the partner States; apportionment of the duties collected according to fixed quota" (Austrian Memorial, p. 4).

Properly speaking, what has to be considered here is not any particular provision of the Protocol of 1931, but rather the Protocol as a whole or, better still—to use the actual terms of the question put by the Council—"the régime" to be established on the basis of this Protocol.

It can scarcely be denied that the establishment of this régime does not in itself constitute an act alienating Austria's independence, for Austria does not thereby cease, within her own frontiers, to be a separate State, with its own government and administration; and, in view, if not of the reciprocity in law, though perhaps not in fact, implied by the projected treaty, at all events of the possibility of denouncing the treaty, it may be said that legally Austria retains the possibility of exercising her independence.

It may even be maintained, if regard be had to the terms of Article 88 of the Treaty of Peace, that since Austria's independence is not strictly speaking endangered, within the meaning of that article, there would not be, from the point of view of law, any inconsistency with that article.

On the other hand, it is difficult to deny that the projected régime of customs union constitutes a "special régime" and that it affords Germany, in relation to Austria, "advantages" which are withheld from third Powers.

It is useless to urge that the Austro-German Protocol of 1931 (Art. I, No. 2) provides that negotiations are to be entered into for a similar arrangement with any other country expressing a desire to that effect.

It is clear that this contingency does not affect the immediate result of the customs union as at present projected between Germany and Austria.

Finally, if the régime projected by the Austro-German Protocol of Vienna in 1931 be considered as a whole from the economic standpoint adopted by the Geneva Protocol of 1922, it is difficult to maintain that this régime is not calculated to threaten the economic independence of Austria and that it is, consequently, in accord with the undertakings specifically given by Austria in that Protocol with regard to her economic independence.

FOR THESE REASONS,

The Court,

by eight votes to seven,

is of opinion that:

A régime established between Germany and Austria, on the basis and within the limits of the principles laid down by the Protocol of March 19th, 1931, would not be compatible with Protocol No. I signed at Geneva on October 4th, 1922.

Done in English and French, the French text being authoritative, at the Peace Palace, The Hague, this fifth day of September, one thousand nine hundred and thirty-one, in two copies, one of which is to be placed in the archives of the Court, and the other to be forwarded to the Council of the League of Nations.

(Signed) M. ADATCI,
President.

(Signed) Å. HAMMARSKJÖLD,
Registrar.

M. Guerrero, Count Rostworowski, MM. Fromageot, Altamira, Urrutia and Negulesco, whilst concurring in the above Opinion, declare that, in their opinion, the régime of customs union projected by the Austro-German Protocol of March 19th, 1931, since it would be calculated to threaten the independence of Austria in the economic sphere, would constitute an act capable of endangering the independence of that country and would, accordingly, be not only incompatible with Protocol No. I of Geneva of October 4th, 1922, but also and in itself incompatible with Article 88 of the Treaty of Saint-Germain of September 10th, 1919.

M. Anzilotti, whilst concurring in the operative portion of the present Opinion, declares that he is unable to agree in regard to the grounds on which it is based, and accordingly has delivered the separate opinion which follows hereafter.[12]

MM. Adatci and Kellogg, Baron Rolin-Jaequemyns, Sir Cecil Hurst, MM. Schücking, van Eysinga and Wang, declaring that they are unable to concur in the Opinion given by the Court and availing themselves of the right conferred on them by Article 71 of the Rules of Court, have delivered the joint dissenting opinion which follows hereafter.

(Initialled) M. A.
(Initialled) Å. H.

---

[12] The eighth majority vote came from Judge Bustamente, who endorsed the opinion exactly as it stood.—*Ed.*

33. THE INTERGOVERNMENTAL-DEBT MORATORIUM, 1931-1932 [13]

On June 20, 1931, President Herbert Hoover, in the interest of economic recovery, proposed a one-year world moratorium on intergovernmental debts. The scheme was well received except in France, where the government insisted that it be integrated with the Young Plan. The resulting delay probably deprived the plan of some of its potential value. In the end, the entire proceeding served chiefly to advertise Germany's financial exhaustion and the bitterness of Franco-German relations. The terminal dates of the moratorium were July 1, 1931, and June 30, 1932.

Resolved by the Senate and House of Representatives of the United States of America in Congress assembled, That in the case of each of the following countries: Austria, Belgium, Czechoslovakia, Estonia, Finland, France, Germany, Great Britain, Greece, Hungary, Italy, Latvia, Lithuania, Poland, Rumania, and Yugoslavia, the Secretary of the Treasury, with the approval of the President, is authorized to make, on behalf of the United States, an agreement with the government of such country to postpone the payment of any amount payable during the fiscal year beginning July 1, 1931, by such country to the United States in respect of its bonded indebtedness to the United States, except that in the case of Germany the agreement shall relate only to amounts payable by Germany to the United States during such fiscal year in respect of the costs of the Army of Occupation.

SEC. 2. Each such agreement on behalf of the United States shall provide for the payment of the postponed amounts, with interest at the rate of 4 per centum per annum beginning July 1, 1933, in ten equal annuities, the first to be paid during the fiscal year beginning July 1, 1933, and one during each of the nine fiscal years following, each annuity to be payable in one or more installments.

SEC. 3. No such agreement shall be made with the government of any country unless it appears to the satisfaction of the President that such government has made, or has given satisfactory assurance of willingness and readiness to make, with the government of each of the other countries indebted to such country in respect of war, relief, or reparation debts, an agreement in respect of such debts substantially

---

[13] *The Statutes at Large of the United States of America from December 1931 to March 1933,* Government Printing Office, Washington, 1933, vol. 47, pt. 1, pp. 3-4 (House Joint Res. 147).

similar to the agreement authorized by this joint resolution to be made
with the government of such creditor country on behalf of the United
States.

SEC. 4. Each agreement authorized by this joint resolution shall be
made so that payments of annuities under such agreement shall, unless
otherwise provided in the agreement (1) be in accordance with the
provisions contained in the agreement made with the government of
such country under which the payment to be postponed is payable,
and (2) be subject to the same terms and conditions as payment under
such original agreement.

SEC. 5. It is hereby expressly declared to be against the policy of
Congress that any of the indebtedness of foreign countries to the United
States should be in any manner canceled or reduced; and nothing in
this joint resolution shall be construed as indicating a contrary policy,
or as implying that favorable consideration will be given at any time
to a change in the policy hereby declared.

Approved, December 23, 1931.

34. "THE END OF REPARATIONS" AT THE LAUSANNE CONFERENCE, 1932 [14]

*Early in 1932, Chancellor Heinrich Brüning of Germany made it clear
that Germany would not be able to renew the Young Plan payments after
the expiration of the moratorium. Meanwhile Great Britain had found it
necessary once more to "go off the gold standard" and even France had
begun to feel the adverse effects of prolonged and widespread depression.
Another reparation conference was therefore called for June 1932 at Lausanne. This, it was hoped, would not merely reach a "lasting settlement"
of the reparation issue but would agree on "the measures necessary to solve
the other economic and financial difficulties which are responsible for and
may prolong the present world crisis."*

AGREEMENT WITH GERMANY.

The Government of His Majesty the King of the Belgians, the
Government of the United Kingdom of Great Britain and Northern

[14] *Final Act of the Lausanne Conference. Lausanne, July 9, 1932. Presented by the
Secretary of State for Foreign Affairs to Parliament by Command of His Majesty,* Misc.
No. 7 (1932), Cmd. 4126, His Majesty's Stationery Office, London, 1932, pp. 5-15.

Ireland, the Government of Canada, the Government of the Commonwealth of Australia, the Government of New Zealand, the Govern-
ment of the Union of South Africa, the Government of India, the Gov-
ernment of the French Republic, the Government of the Greek
Republic, the Government of His Majesty the King of Italy, the
Government of His Majesty the Emperor of Japan, the Government
of the Republic of Poland, the Government of the Republic of Portugal,
the Government of His Majesty the King of Roumania, the Government of the Czechoslovak Republic and the Government of His
Majesty the King of Yugoslavia (hereinafter described as the creditor
Governments), and the Government of the German Reich,

Recognising that the legal validity of the Agreements signed at The
Hague on the 20th January, 1930, is not in question,

But concerned by the economic difficulties resulting from the present
crisis,

And being desirous to make, so far as they are concerned, the necessary efforts to ensure the confidence which is indispensable to the development of normal economic and financial relations between the
nations,

The undersigned, duly authorised to that effect by their respective
Governments,

Have agreed as follows:—

Declaration.

The Powers signatory of the present Agreement have assembled at
Lausanne to deal with one of the problems resulting from the war,
with the firm intention of helping to create a new order, permitting
the establishment and development of confidence between the nations
in a mutual spirit of reconciliation, collaboration and justice.

They do not claim that the task accomplished at Lausanne, which
will completely put an end to Reparations, can alone assure that peace
which all the nations desire. But they hope that an achievement of such
significance and so arduously attained will be understood and appre-
ciated by all the pacific elements in Europe and the world, and that
it will be followed by fresh achievements.

These further successes will be more readily won if the nations will
rally to this new effort in the cause of real peace, which can only be
complete if it is applied both in the economic and in the political sphere
and rejects all possibility of resort to arms or to violence.

The signatory Powers will make every effort to resolve the problems which exist at the present moment or may arise subsequently in the spirit which has inspired the present Agreement.

ARTICLE 1.

The German Government shall deliver to the Bank for International Settlements German Government 5 per cent. redeemable bonds, to the amount of three milliard reichsmarks gold of the present standard of weight and fineness, to be negotiated under the following arrangements:—

(1) The Bank for International Settlements shall hold the bonds as trustee.

(2) The Bonds shall not be negotiated by the Bank for International Settlements before the expiry of three years from the signature of the present Agreement. Fifteen years after the date of the said signature the Bonds which the Bank for International Settlements has not been able to negotiate shall be cancelled.

(3) After the above period of three years the Bank for International Settlements shall negotiate the Bonds by means of public issues on the markets as and when possible, in such amounts as it thinks fit, provided that no issue shall be made at a rate below 90 per cent.

The German Government shall have the right at any time to redeem at par, in whole or in part, the Bonds not yet issued by the Bank for International Settlements. In determining the terms of issue of the Bonds, the Bank for International Settlements shall take into account the desirability of giving to the German Government the right to redeem the Bonds after a reasonable period.

(4) The Bonds shall carry interest at 5 per cent. and sinking fund at 1 per cent. as from the date on which they are negotiated. They shall be free of all German taxes, present and future.

(5) The proceeds of the Bonds, as and when issued, shall be placed to a special account, the allocation of which shall be settled by a further agreement in due course between the Governments, other than Germany, signatory to the present Agreement.

(6) If any foreign loan is issued by the German Government, or with its guarantee, at any time after the coming into force of the present Agreement, the German Government shall offer to apply up to the equivalent of one-third of the net cash proceeds of the loan raised to the purchase of Bonds held by the Bank for International Settlements.

The purchase price shall be such that the net yield on the Bonds so purchased would be the same as the net yield of the loan so raised. This paragraph does not refer to loans for a period of not more than twelve months.

(7) If, after five years from the signature of the present Agreement, the Bank for International Settlements considers that the credit of the German Government is restored, but the quotations of its loans remain none the less below the minimum price of issue fixed under paragraph (3) above, the minimum price may be varied by a decision of the Board of the Bank for International Settlements, which decision shall require a two-thirds majority.

Further, at the request of the German Government, the rate of interest may be reduced below 5 per cent. if issues can be made at par.

(8) The Bank for International Settlements shall have power to settle all questions as to the currency and denomination of bonds issued, and also all questions as to charges and costs of issue, which it shall have the right to deduct from the proceeds of the issue. In considering any questions relating to the issue of Bonds, the Board of the Bank for International Settlements shall take the advice of the President of the Reichsbank, but decisions may be made by a majority vote.

Article 2.

On its coming into force the present Agreement will put to an end and be substituted for the reparation régime provided for in the agreement with Germany, signed at The Hague on the 20th January, 1930, and the agreements signed at London on the 11th August, 1931, and at Berlin on the 6th June, 1932; the obligations resulting from the present Agreement will completely replace the former obligations of Germany comprised in the annuities of the "New Plan."

Article 3.

Consequently, Articles 1, 2, 4, 5, 7, 8, 9, and 12 and Annexes I, III, IV, V, Va, VI, VIa, VII, IX, X and Xa of the said agreement with Germany are definitely abrogated.

Article 4.

The Protocol signed at London on the 11th August, 1931, and the Protocol supplementary thereto signed at Berlin on the 6th June, 1932, are abrogated. Consequently, the provisional receipts handed to the

Bank for International Settlements by the German Railway Company under the said Protocol of the 11th August, 1931, will be returned to it.

ARTICLE 5.

The debt certificate of the German Government and the certificate of the German Railway Company referred to in Article 7 and in Annexes III and IV of The Hague Agreement shall, with the coupons attached, be returned to the German Government and to the German Railway Company respectively.

ARTICLE 6.

Nothing in the present Agreement alters or affects Article 3 (Liquidation of the past), Article 6 (so far as concerns the corporate existence of the Bank for International Settlements), or Article 10 (Immunities of the Bank for International Settlements) of The Hague Agreement.

ARTICLE 7.

The Signatory Governments declare that nothing in the present Agreement diminishes or varies or shall be deemed to diminish or vary the rights of the bondholders of the German External Loan, 1924, or of the German Government International 5½ per cent. Loan, 1930.

Any necessary adaptation of the machinery relating to the manner in which the obligations of the German Government with respect to the German External Loan, 1924, and with respect to the German Government International 5½ per cent. Loan, 1930, will be discharged will be subject to mutual arrangement between the German Government, on the one hand, and the Bank for International Settlements, Fiscal Agent of the Trustees of the German External Loan, 1924, and Trustee of the German Government International 5½ per cent. Loan, 1930, on the other hand.

ARTICLE 8.

The present Agreement will, on its coming into force, be notified by the Government of the French Republic to the Bank for International Settlements with a view to the application by the Bank of the provisions which affect it; the said Government will also inform the Bank, for the purposes of its Statutes, that the "New Plan" is no longer in effect.

ARTICLE 9.

Any disputes, whether between the Governments signatory of the present Agreement, or between one or more of those Governments and the Bank for International Settlements, as to the interpretation or application of this Agreement shall be referred to the Arbitration Tribunal set up under Article 15 of The Hague Agreement with Germany. The relevant provisions of that Article and of Annex XII of the said Agreement will for this purpose be applicable.

Article 10.

The present Agreement, of which the English and French texts are both authentic, shall be ratified, and the ratifications shall be deposited at Paris.

The Governments whose seat is outside Europe will be entitled merely to notify the French Government, through their diplomatic representatives in Paris, that their ratification has been given; in that case they must transmit the instrument of ratification as soon as possible.

As soon as the present Agreement has been ratified by the Governments of Germany, Belgium, France, Great Britain and Northern Ireland, Italy and Japan, it shall come into force between those Governments whose ratifications have been deposited or notified at that date. It shall come into force in respect of every other signatory Government on the date of notification or deposit of ratification.

The French Government will transmit to all the signatory Governments and to the Bank for International Settlements a certified copy of the *Procès-verbal* of the deposit of each ratification, and a certified copy of each notification.

Article 11.

The present Agreement may be signed at any time up to the date on which it first comes into force in accordance with Article 10, by any Government signatory to the Agreement signed at The Hague on the 20th January, 1930.

After that date any of the said Governments may accede to the present Agreement by means of a notification addressed to the Government of the French Republic, which will transmit to the other Contracting Governments and to the Bank for International Settlements a certified copy of such notification. In that case the Agreement will come into force for the Government concerned on the date of such accession.

Done at Lausanne, the 9th day of July, 1932, in a single copy which will remain deposited in the archives of the Government of the French Republic, which will transmit certified copies to each of the signatory Governments.

. . . .

RESOLUTION RELATING TO A WORLD ECONOMIC AND FINANCIAL CONFERENCE.

The Conference, apart from the questions already dealt with, has further undertaken to decide upon "the measures necessary to solve the other economic and financial difficulties which are responsible for, and may prolong, the present world crisis."

The main questions of this order which demand examination are as follows:

(a) *Financial Questions.*

    Monetary and credit policy.

    Exchange difficulties.

    The level of prices.

    The movement of capital.

(b) *Economic Questions.*

    Improved conditions of production and trade interchanges, with particular attention to—

    Tariff policy.

    Prohibitions and restrictions of importation and exportation, quotas and other barriers to trade.

    Producers' agreements.

The Conference emphasises in particular the necessity of restoring currencies to a healthy basis and of thereby making it possible to abolish measures of exchange control and to remove transfer difficulties; further, the Conference is impressed with the vital need of facilitating the revival of international trade.

To achieve the above purposes—

The Conference decides to invite the League of Nations to convoke at a convenient date and at a place to be fixed (not necessarily Geneva) a Conference on Monetary and Economic Questions.

The Conference decides to entrust the preliminary examination of these complex questions, which are closely interdependent, to an authoritative committee of experts.

. . . .

35. THE LAUSANNE "GENTLEMEN'S AGREEMENT," JULY 2, 1932 [15]

The Lausanne Agreement was widely hailed until it was revealed that Great Britain, France, Italy, and Belgium had come to the following supplementary agreement. Since the United States had consistently maintained its unwillingness to accept any official relation between reparation and war debts, Americans now resented what appeared to them an attempt by certain powers to pass responsibility for the world financial crisis on to their country. The Lausanne reparation provisions therefore were not put into force and the Young Plan technically remained in effect; but few intergovernmental debt payments were made after the expiry of the world moratorium on June 30, 1932.

PROCÈS-VERBAL.

The Lausanne Agreement will not come into final effect until after ratification as provided for in the Agreement. So far as the Creditor Governments on whose behalf this *Procès-verbal* is initialled [Belgium, Great Britain, France, Italy] are concerned, ratification will not be effected until a satisfactory settlement has been reached between them and their own creditors. It will be open to them to explain the position to their respective Parliaments, but no specific reference to it will appear in the text of the agreement with Germany. Subsequently, if a satisfactory settlement about their own debt is reached, the aforesaid Creditor Governments will ratify and the agreement with Germany will come into full effect. But if no such settlement can be obtained, the agreement with Germany will not be ratified; a new situation will have arisen and the Governments interested will have to consult together as to what should be done. In that event, the legal position, as between all the Governments, will revert to that which existed before the Hoover Moratorium.

The German Government will be notified of this arrangement.

July 2, 1932.

[15] *Further Documents Relating to the Settlement Reached at the Lausanne Conference. Presented by the Secretary of State for Foreign Affairs to Parliament by Command of His Majesty,* Misc. No. 8 (1932), Cmd. 4129, His Majesty's Stationery Office, London, 1932, p. 3.

36-38. The World (London) Monetary and Economic Conference, 1933

36. THE AGENDA OF THE CONFERENCE, 1933 *(Extracts)*[16]

In accordance with Part V of the final act of the Lausanne Conference, the League Council made preparations for the holding of a world monetary and economic conference in London in 1933. On January 19, 1933, a preparatory commission of experts submitted the agenda for the gathering.

PART I.

A. INTRODUCTION.

The Preparatory Commission of Experts has been given the task of preparing a draft annotated agenda for the forthcoming Monetary and Economic Conference. In undertaking this task, we have been guided by the terms of reference transmitted to us by the Council of the League of Nations, and by certain preliminary discussions recorded in the Final Act of the Lausanne Conference. This Conference, having arrived at far-reaching decisions with regard to the pressing problem of reparations payments, invited the League of Nations to convoke a World Conference "to decide upon the measures to solve the other economic and financial difficulties which are responsible for, and may prolong, the present world crisis." In this message from Lausanne, we have found the clearest indication of our general mandate.

Before setting forth the problems which require solution, we wish to call attention to the gravity of the situation with which the world is confronted.

Unemployment has recently been estimated by the International Labour Office as involving at least thirty million workers. Even this huge total, which does not include the workers' families or other dependants, is probably an underestimate. The burden of suffering and demoralisation resulting from unemployment of such proportions is appalling.

Wholesale commodity prices—expressed in gold—have declined since

---

[16] League of Nations, Monetary and Economic Conference, *Draft Annotated Agenda Submitted by the Preparatory Commission of Experts* (Series II. Economic and Financial 1933. II. Spec. 1.), Geneva, 1933, pp. 5-9.

October 1929 by roughly a third; raw material prices on the average by 50 to 60 per cent. In the middle of December [1932], at Winnipeg, the price of wheat fell to the lowest level recorded in any primary market for wheat during the past four centuries. Such price declines have produced profound disturbances in the economic system. They have thrown completely out of adjustment prevailing costs of the various factors of production, have made business enterprise generally unremunerative, and have seriously disorganised practically all the world markets.

World stocks of agricultural products and of other raw materials continue to accumulate. The index of world stocks for 1932 was double that for 1925. Huge accumulations thus overhang some of the principal markets and burden the processes of orderly price readjustment.

Industrial production has been drastically curtailed, particularly in those trades producing capital equipment. The depths which have been reached in some instances are illustrated by the position of the United States steel industry, which, at the close of 1932, was operating at only 10 per cent of capacity.

The international flow of goods, hindered by currency disorders and restricted by a multiplicity of new governmental interventions, has been reduced to incredibly low levels. The total value of world trade in the third quarter of 1932 was only about one-third of that in the corresponding period of 1929. The fall during the three-year period was continuous.

Moreover, the quantum of goods in foreign trade appears to have fallen by at least 25 per cent; by far the largest fall on record.

As a result of price-declines and the fall in the volume of production and trade, national incomes in many countries have fallen, it is estimated, by more than 40 per cent. The revenues of Governments, as a consequence, have suffered sharp reductions, while expenditures have shown no corresponding decline. The inevitable result has been a series of budget deficits which, in some cases, have reached unprecedented proportions.

Only a handful of countries now retain free and uncontrolled goldstandard currency systems. Almost half the countries of the world are off the gold standard, and, in some forty countries, exchange restrictions have been imposed.

Currency disorganisation, price-declines, curtailment of trade have thrown into sharp relief the vast and difficult problems of indebtedness with which many, if not most, countries are confronted. As matters now stand, there are countries the total value of whose export trade has fallen below the sums required for external debt service alone.

Facts such as these indicate the extremities to which the forces of disintegration have already carried the economic and financial world. Further losses of ground cannot be contemplated without the gravest forebodings. . . .

Nevertheless, recovery will be halting and restricted if unaccompanied by broad measures of reconstruction. Three years of world-wide dislocation have generated a vast network of restraints upon the normal conduct of business. In the field of international trade, prohibitions, quotas, clearing agreements, exchange restrictions—to mention only some of the most widely employed forms of regulation—throttle business enterprise and individual initiative. Defensively intended, and in many instances forced by unavoidable monetary and financial emergencies, these measures have developed into a state of virtual economic warfare. It is not only in the field of trade that this tension exists. In the difficult sphere of international monetary and currency relations and in the world capital markets, free international co-operation has given place to complex and harassing regulations designed to safeguard national interests. If a full and durable recovery is to be effected, this prevailing conflict of national economies must be resolved.

The measures to be adopted to this end constitute the problem which the Governments must shortly face in London. In essence, the necessary programme is one of economic disarmament. In the movement towards economic reconciliation, the armistice was signed at Lausanne; the London Conference must draft the Treaty of Peace. Failure in this critical undertaking threatens a world-wide adoption of ideals of national self-sufficiency which cut unmistakably athwart the lines of economic development. . . .

B. GENERAL PROGRAMME OF THE CONFERENCE.

The programme of reconstruction which we deem it necessary for Governments to undertake is set out below. In this programme, the problem of inter-Governmental indebtedness has not been included, because it lies outside our terms of reference. In our opinion, however, it is essential that this question shall be settled and that the settlement shall relieve the world of further anxiety concerning the disturbing effects of such payments upon financial, economic and currency stability. Until there is such a settlement, or the definite prospect of such a settlement, these debts will remain an insuperable barrier to economic and financial reconstruction. We therefore attach the greatest importance to the early resumption and successful conclusion of negotiations upon this problem.

. . . . . .

The principal questions which the Governments have to consider can be summarised as follows:

1. In the field of monetary and credit policy, the objective must be the restoration of an effective international monetary standard to which the countries which have abandoned the gold standard can wisely adhere. Each Government must, of course, remain free to decide when and under what conditions it could adopt such a standard, and we do not suggest that this can or should be done without the most careful preparation. The notes appended clearly show that there are a great number of economic as well as financial conditions which must be fulfilled before the restoration of an international gold standard can be a practical possibility. Moreover, it will be necessary to provide effective safeguards against such a restoration of the gold standard leading to a fresh breakdown. The question has to be considered whether measures can be taken, with the co-operation of Central Banks on the lines of the recommendations suggested in the report of the Gold Delegation of the League of Nations, to ensure a greater stability of price-levels in the future.

2. The unprecedented fall of commodity prices in recent years has caused a growing disequilibrium between costs and prices, has immensely increased the real burden of all debts and fixed charges, has made business more and more unprofitable, and has resulted in a continuous and disastrous increase of unemployment throughout the world. Some increase in the level of world prices is highly desirable and would be the first sign of world recovery. The Conference will no doubt wish to explore all possibilities of counteracting this fall in prices. One of the methods that should be considered is the continuation and development, where monetary conditions permit, of a general policy of easy money designed to promote a healthy expansion of business.

At the same time, the question requires to be considered whether, particularly in the case of certain primary commodities where large stocks are overhanging the markets, a better level of prices could not be obtained by the regulation of exports or production. Such an arrangement could be of special importance in the case of wheat, the cultivation of which represents the livelihood of a large proportion of mankind.

Of course, any rise in prices which might be obtained by such means can, in the long run, be maintained only by a general improvement of trade such as would follow from the abolition of present-day restrictions and the restoration of financial confidence.

3. The abolition of exchange restrictions is an essential condition of world recovery. For this purpose, the Governments concerned must take internal measures necessary to secure the stability of their budgets and of their economic systems. In some cases, however, these efforts will not be sufficient so long as there is a mass of short-term foreign debts, which may at any moment be withdrawn; in other cases, even the service of the long-term debts entails great difficulties. These difficulties will require careful treatment. The objective must be to restore the confidence of the foreign lending markets, and much depends on the future level of prices.

. . . . .

4. Finally, there must be greater freedom of international trade. It has already been pointed out that one of the most significant features of the present crisis is the fall which has taken place, not only in the value, but in the quantum of world trade. This fall has been partly caused, and has certainly been intensified, by the growing network of restrictions which have been imposed on trade in recent years. Every country seeks to defend its economy by imposing restrictions on imports, which in the end involve a contraction in its exports. All seek to sell but not to buy. Such a policy must inevitably lead to an increasing paralysis of international trade. Governments should set themselves to re-establish the normal interchange of commodities.

In the first instance, every effort should be made to secure a general agreement for the progressive relaxation, and the complete abrogation at the earliest possible date, of the emergency measures—prohibitions, quotas, etc.—imposed as a result of the crisis. At the same time, it will be necessary for the Governments to reconsider recent economic tendencies in so far as these are reflected in excessive tariffs, and to arrive at understandings for the moderation and stabilising of tariff policies in the future. Action in this direction has an intimate bearing upon the stabilisation of currencies, as it is impossible to maintain an international monetary system except on the basis of an international economic system. The great creditor nations have a special responsibility in this respect.

Such is the general outline of the problems before the Conference as we see them.

· · · · ·

37. DECLARATION OF PRESIDENT ROOSEVELT AGAINST THE TEMPORARY STABILIZATION OF CURRENCIES, JULY 3, 1933 [17]

Sixty-seven nations were represented at the opening session of the World (London) Monetary and Economic Conference on June 12, 1933. Questions of world monetary policy and trade barriers soon led to serious disagreement. France, Italy, and other gold-standard nations held that all discussion of the lowering or removal of trade barriers must follow a general stabilization of world currencies. Great Britain seemed to have no fixed policy, but the United States, having recently devaluated her currency, refused to join any move for general stabilization at least until a sufficient rise in prices had been effected at home. Herewith follows the emphatic declaration of President Franklin D. Roosevelt on this subject.

I would regard it as a catastrophe amounting to a world tragedy if the great Conference of Nations, called to bring about a more real and permanent financial stability and a greater prosperity to the masses of all nations, should, in advance of any serious effort to consider these broader problems, allow itself to be diverted by the proposal of a purely artificial and temporary experiment affecting the monetary exchange of a few nations only. Such action, such diversion, shows a singular lack of proportion and a failure to remember the larger purposes for which the Economic Conference originally was called together.

I do not relish the thought that insistence on such action should be made an excuse for the continuance of the basic economic errors that underlie so much of the present world-wide depression.

The world will not long be lulled by the specious fallacy of achieving a temporary and probably an artificial stability in foreign exchange on the part of a few large countries only.

The sound internal economic system of a nation is a greater factor

---

[17] United States, Department of State, *Press Releases,* July 8, 1933, Government Printing Office, Washington, 1933, pp. 15-16.

in its well-being than the price of its currency in changing terms of the currencies of other nations.

It is for this reason that reduced cost of government, adequate government income, and ability to service government debts are all so important to ultimate stability. So, too, old fetishes of so-called international bankers are being replaced by efforts to plan national currencies with the objective of giving to those currencies a continuing purchasing power which does not greatly vary in terms of the commodities and need of modern civilization. Let me be frank in saying that the United States seeks the kind of dollar which a generation hence will have the same purchasing and debt-paying power as the dollar value we hope to attain in the near future. That objective means more to the good of other nations than a fixed ratio for a month or two in terms of the pound or franc.

Our broad purpose is the permanent stabilization of every nation's currency. Gold or gold and silver can well continue to be a metallic reserve behind currencies, but this is not the time to dissipate gold reserves. When the world works out concerted policies in the majority of nations to produce balanced budgets and living within their means, then we can properly discuss a better distribution of the world's gold and silver supply to act as a reserve base of national currencies.

Restoration of world trade is an important partner both in the means and in the result. Here also temporary exchange fixing is not the true answer. We must rather mitigate existing embargoes to make easier the exchange of products which one nation has and the other nation has not.

The Conference was called to better and perhaps cure fundamental economic ills. It must not be diverted from that effort.

38. FINAL RESOLUTION OF THE WORLD (LONDON) MONETARY AND ECONOMIC CONFERENCE, JULY 27, 1933 [18]

On July 27, 1933, the World (London) Monetary and Economic Conference adjourned, having achieved little in the way of lasting remedy. The listlessness that marked the closing meetings of the assemblage was well illustrated by the wording of its final resolution.

---

[18] League of Nations, Monetary and Economic Conference, *Reports Approved by the Conference on July 27th, 1933, and Resolutions Adopted by the Bureau and the Executive Committee* (Series II. Economic and Financial 1933. II. Spec. 4.), London, 1933, p. 5.

The Conference,

Empowers the President, Vice-President, and Bureau;

(1) To take whatever action they may consider likely to promote its success, whether by the convocation of any committee set up by the Conference or of representatives of States especially concerned in any particular problem or by reference to experts for study of any special question;

(2) To determine the date of the re-assembling of the Conference.

39. THE JOHNSON DEBT-DEFAULT ACT, APRIL 13, 1934 [19]

The wholesale defaults on European government-debt payments to the United States after 1932 aroused much resentment among the American people. While Finland alone continued to meet her obligations in full, the other European states, it seemed to many Americans, were spending on war preparations sums that rightfully should have been repaid to the United States. The popular feeling was reflected in congressional action on future foreign lending.

Be it enacted by the Senate and House of Representatives of the United States of America in Congress assembled, That hereafter it shall be unlawful within the United States or any place subject to the jurisdiction of the United States for any person to purchase or sell the bonds, securities, or other obligations of, any foreign government or political subdivision thereof or any organization or association acting for or on behalf of a foreign government or political subdivision thereof, issued after the passage of this Act, or to make any loan to such foreign government, political subdivision, organization, or association, except a renewal or adjustment of existing indebtedness while such government, political subdivision, organization, or association, is in default in the payment of its obligations, or any part thereof, to the Government of the United States. Any person violating the provisions of this Act shall upon conviction thereof be fined not more than $10,000 or imprisoned for not more than five years, or both.

SEC. 2. As used in this Act the term "person" includes individual,

---

[19] *The Statutes at Large of the United States of America from March 1933 to June 1934,* Government Printing Office, Washington, 1934, vol. 48, pt. 1, p. 574 (Public. No. 151).

partnership, corporation, or association other than a public corporation
created by or pursuant to special authorization of Congress, or a
corporation in which the Government of the United States has or exercises a controlling interest through stock ownership or otherwise.

Approved, April 13, 1934.

40. THE ROME PROTOCOL (No. II), 1934 [20]

*Though the rise to power of Hitler in 1933 foreshadowed an Italo-German
entente, Mussolini at first manifested little sympathy with Germany's desire
to absorb Austria. For strategic and economic reasons Italy favored Austrian
independence, or, preferably, Austrian membership in a bloc including Hungary and dominated from Rome. The personal friendship which developed
among the three premiers—Mussolini, Dollfuss, and Gömbös—furthered this
policy, and in March 1934 three protocols were signed at Rome. The
signatories agreed to consult frequently on important affairs, to co-operate in
broader European policies, and to conclude bilateral trade agreements calculated to widen Austria's market for manufactures and Hungary's market
for grain. The bilateral trade treaties were duly negotiated but they brought
no appreciable upswing in the economic life of any of the signatories.*

The Austrian, Italian and Hungarian Governments, being anxious
to develop economic relations between Italy and Austria, Italy and
Hungary, and Austria and Hungary by giving a fresh impetus to the
exchange of goods with a view to overcoming unsound tendencies
towards autarchy (*sic*) and so to promote by concrete measures the work
of economic reconstruction of the Danubian States, in accordance
with the spirit of the decision taken of the Stresa Conference and with
the principles laid down in the Danubian Memorandum presented by
Italy and dated September 29th, 1933,
    Have agreed as follows:

ARTICLE 1.

The Austrian, Italian and Hungarian Governments undertake to
extend the agreements at present in force, to facilitate reciprocal exports
and thus by degrees to make their national economic systems mutually

---

[20] "Protocol No. II between Austria, Hungary and Italy Regarding the Development
of Economic Relations. Signed at Rome, March 17th, 1934," in League of Nations, *Treaty
Series 1934-1935*, vol. CLIV, p. 295.

supplement one another. For this purpose, new bilateral agreements shall be concluded by May 15th, 1934.

ARTICLE 2.

The Austrian, Italian and Hungarian Governments decide to take the necessary steps to remedy the difficulties encountered by Hungary as a result of the fall in the price of wheat.

The agreements on this point shall be concluded as soon as possible and in any case by May 15th, 1934.

ARTICLE 3.

The three Governments undertake to facilitate and develop as much as possible the transit trade through the Adriatic ports. Bilateral agreements for this purpose shall be concluded as rapidly as possible.

ARTICLE 4.

The three Governments shall set up a permanent commission of three experts, who shall follow the development of mutual economic relations and shall make concrete proposals in the spirit of the present Protocol for the development of their mutual trade.

The present Protocol is drawn up in three copies, . . .

41. MONETARY AGREEMENT OF SEPTEMBER 25, 1936, AMONG FRANCE, GREAT BRITAIN, AND THE UNITED STATES [21]

The failure of the World (London) Monetary and Economic Conference to relieve either the trade or currency phases of international economic rivalry led to further commercial undercutting through the voluntary depreciation of currencies. In September 1936 the financial authorities of the United States, Great Britain, and France decided to check this evil, at least temporarily, through a tripartite stabilization agreement.

1. His Majesty's Government, after consultation with the United States Government and the French Government, join with them in affirming a common desire to foster those conditions which will safeguard peace and will best contribute to the restoration of order in

---

[21] Press Release in *The Times* (London), September 26, 1936. Parallel official statements were issued by the French and United States Governments.

international economic relations, and to pursue a policy which will tend to promote prosperity in the world and to improve the standard of living.

2. His Majesty's Government must, of course, in its policy towards international monetary relations, take into full account the requirements of internal prosperity of the countries of the Empire, as corresponding considerations will be taken into account by the Governments of France and of the United States of America. They welcome this opportunity to reaffirm their purpose to continue the policy which they have pursued in the course of recent years, one constant object of which is to maintain the greatest possible equilibrium in the system of international exchanges and to avoid to the utmost extent the creation of any disturbance of that system by British monetary action. His Majesty's Government share with the Governments of France and the United States the conviction that the continuation of this twofold policy will serve the general purpose which all governments should pursue.

3. The French Government inform His Majesty's Government that, judging that the desired stability of the principal currencies cannot be ensured on a solid basis except after the re-establishment of a lasting equilibrium between the various economic systems, they have decided with this object to propose to their Parliament the readjustment of their currency. His Majesty's Government have, as also the United States Government, welcomed this decision in the hope that it will establish more solid foundations for the stability of international economic relations. His Majesty's Government, as also the Governments of France and of the United States of America, declare their intention to continue to use the appropriate available resources so as to avoid as far as possible any disturbance of the basis of international exchanges resulting from the proposed readjustment. They will arrange for such consultation for this purpose as may prove necessary with the other two Governments and the authorized agencies.

4. His Majesty's Government are moreover convinced, as are also the Governments of France and the United States of America, that the success of the policy set forth above is linked with the development of international trade. In particular, they attach the greatest importance to action being taken without delay to relax progressively the present system of quotas and exchange controls with a view to their abolition.

5. His Majesty's Government, in common with the Governments of France and the United States of America, desire and invite the co-operation of the other nations to realize the policy laid down in the

present Declaration. They trust that no country will attempt to obtain an unreasonable competitive exchange advantage and thereby hamper the effort to restore more stable economic relations which it is the aim of the three Governments to promote.

42. FACTORS IN THE GREAT DEPRESSION [22]

The definitive analysis of the causes of the Great Depression has not yet been written. The following selection, however, offers a useful summary of certain factors in the depression as it affected Europe.

Between 1920 and 1930 Europe and the world at large passed through a complete business cycle with post-war complications. The liquidation of war and the readjustment to peace was a huge task, even for countries that had been spared revolution or loss of territory. Trade channels had been blocked; some markets had become impoverished; some industries had swollen equipment and labor force; currencies were in chaos; rates of wages, interest, and taxes had found new levels; and many countries had expanded production greatly to supply their own needs or to feed markets formerly served by the belligerents.

By 1925 Europe had made a remarkable recovery in many directions. Its output of wheat, corn, rye, beet, wool, potatoes, coal, iron, and steel was near or above pre-War levels, and its production of the new goods— oil, electricity, electrical appliances, automobiles, and rayon—was mounting. Coal, shipbuilding, shipping, steel, cottons and woolens were sick from lack of buyers or from excess capacity, fierce competition, and fallen prices. Not one of Britain's staple export industries had regained its pre-War position in 1929, and two-fifths of the unemployed army of a million workers belonged to these industries. Germany's experience was similar: export markets were more easily lost than regained. Meanwhile, farmers everywhere complained that the price of their produce had fallen too near the cost of production, but that the price of the industrial goods they had to buy remained too high. But while some industries lost customers, others found new ones. In the first place, the devastated areas must be rebuilt; the supply of houses, offices, shops and public buildings must catch up with the demand; suburban "dormitories" were required for those who commuted between a city job

---

[22] H. Heaton, *Economic History of Europe,* Harper & Brothers, New York, 1936, pp. 652-655. Reprinted by permission of the publishers.

and a semi-rural home, while roads must be made or improved to bear the growing load of motor traction. The construction industry was busy, and according to one estimate employed about 14 per cent of the industrial workers of western Europe in 1925. This construction, supplemented by the equipping of new industries and the remodeling of old ones, gave much work to the capital goods industries. In the second place, the demand for new comforts and luxuries, though less strong in Europe than in North America, was broad enough to bring new industries and service occupations into being. Hence the decline in the number of weavers, miners, and shipbuilders was more than counterbalanced by the growth of employment in virtually new occupations, ranging from the making of cars and cycles to the preservation of feminine beauty and the sale of prepared foods.

The expansion of production was encouraged by these capital and consumption needs, by the protection governments were willing to give, by the behavior of prices, and by the comparative ease with which capital could be obtained at home, in London or in New York. The stream of American capital, like the English one a century earlier, ran high to other continents till 1928, and British investors resumed their export of loans and investments, though on a smaller scale than before 1914. After falling rapidly in 1920, prices recovered somewhat and remained fairly steady (in countries with stable currencies) at 40 to 60 per cent above pre-War levels. The trend was slowly downward, but the movement was not marked enough to check production, and schemes for price maintenance helped to keep some prices at a level that encouraged producers to expand output.

The rest of the story is world history rather than European. Till 1928 production and purchase advanced at about the same pace; but hints of saturation then began to be evident, prices of foodstuffs and raw materials began to fall a little more quickly, and surplus stocks grew large enough to overshadow the market. By mid-1929 the prices of minerals were breaking, wool brought much lower prices in the auction rooms, while bumper wheat crops in 1928 and the reentry of Russia wrecked grain prices. This fall came just at a time when the flow of capital to primary producing countries was checked. London, Paris, and New York ceased to export loans, for the money could earn more in the boiling stock markets of New York and London. Hence the debtor primary producers had to pay for their imports and pay their interest bills by sending out produce that was shrinking rapidly in value and by supplementing it with gold from their bank reserves.

The silver countries were also hit by a rapid fall in the price of silver.

The depression of 1929 thus began largely as a result of increasing stringency in the agricultural borrowing countries; but other factors played their part. The most urgent replacement and reequipment demands of Europe were eventually met. The flow of American capital, which had financed much reconstruction and had allowed some Europeans to pay their debts and buy goods with borrowed money, came to an end. Instead, there must now be a greater flow of payments to America, and this stream was swollen by funds going to be lent or used for speculation in stocks. Since America was not a great market for European goods, the transfer was made partly in gold. The concentration of gold in New York and Paris weakened the credit basis of many European banking systems, and forced central banks to raise their rates in order to protect reserves from depletion.

Meanwhile Europeans had been sucked into a stock and promotion boom of their own, in which borrowers as well as banks—especially the "industrial banks"—were deeply involved. In January, 1929, an Italian bank came to grief after "bulling the Bourse." A Belgian bank nearly foundered after financing an unhappy cork trust. A big Viennese bank nearly sank under the load of embarrassed firms it was carrying, and a Rothschild had to withdraw funds from New York to save it. Just at that moment (September) the arrest of a flashy British promoter for forging stock certificates upset London, sent stock prices diving down, forced the Bank to raise its rate, compelled investors to sell American stocks to get funds, drove British lenders to pull their loans out of the New York call market, and thus added one more cloud to the Manhattan horizon. Within a month the sky showed nothing but clouds; the major boom in America and the minor boom in Europe had ended. To the fall in prices of primary products was added that in the price of all salable things, but especially of those pieces of paper that had poured out of the financial mills of the electrical, oil, public utilities, and non-ferrous metal magnates.

For three years, till the summer of 1932, gloom grew relentlessly deeper in every part of the world. . . . The volume of world trade declined about a quarter, and its value about two-thirds. In every country the all-absorbing political problem was to find ways that would bring relief and lead to recovery. Ancient landmarks were swept away, the reestablished gold standards were abandoned, imports were almost throttled. The reparations problem was solved by abandoning payment, and the interallied debts were settled in the same way. . . .

The boom of the nineteen-twenties was the thirteenth—and the greatest—since Waterloo. The depression that followed was the fourteenth—and the deepest. In the second half of 1932 signs appeared to prompt the hope that the worst was over. Prices, production, volume of trade and employment began to rise, were checked by the American crisis early in 1933, and then resumed their ascent. The long depression, like a severe long war, left deep scars on the body politic and economic; but only an incorrigible optimist would assert that the sight of these scars will keep the business world from eagerly embracing its fourteenth boom or precipitating its fifteenth depression. . . .

43-46. THE QESTION OF TERRITORIAL EXPANSION

43. THE "HAVES" VS. THE "HAVE-NOTS" VIEW [23]

The strong spirit of economic nationalism manifested in Germany, Italy, and Japan in the decade of the 'thirties and the reluctance of the imperial powers to accede to the territorial demands of these states led some observers to speak in terms of a conflict of interests between the "Haves" and the "Have-nots." Messrs. Simonds and Emeny did much to popularize this interpretation of recent international relations.

By reason of their physical circumstances, the Great Powers may be divided into two classes, the "Haves" and the "Have-nots." Of these, the first class, to which the British Empire, France, Russia, and the United States belong, is composed of the nations whose territories are large and rich and whose ethnic unity has been achieved. The second class of Great Powers, which are characterized by lands that are relatively exiguous and poor in material resources, include Japan, Italy, and Germany. In the case of Germany, moreover, the situation is further aggravated by lack of ethnic unity, because of the inclusion of important German minorities within the boundaries of some of Germany's immediate neighbors.

For the first group of states, the Haves which are sated and therefore satisfied, security through the maintenance of the status quo is the sole objective of national policy. Having, their chief purpose is to hold. For

---

[23] F. H. Simonds and B. Emeny, *The Great Powers in World Politics. International Relations and Economic Nationalism,* rev. ed., New York, 1937, pp. 33-37. Used by permission of American Book Company, publishers.

the group of Have-nots, on the other hand, their present situation being precarious, through deprivation of many of the essentials of security and power, the acquisition of what they lack assumes primary consideration.

In theory the existing disparity between the "Have" and the "Have-not" Powers might be abolished in one of two ways: the sated states might consent to sacrificing a portion of their territory or that of some smaller nations as a means of restoring the balance of material wealth; or they might share with the "Have-nots" equal rights and security in investment and trade in their own resources. In practice, however, no relief by such means is discoverable for the less fortunate states; for both solutions run counter to the basic principles of sovereignty, which holds the national territory and the control of its resources to be inalienable. Faithful to that principle, states are rarely willing to cede their land voluntarily to others, and never to surrender any part of their right to the privileged exploitation of their national wealth.

The fact that forty-two millions of French not merely possess a homeland area large and rich enough to satisfy their needs and their aspirations, but also control a vast colonial empire, while a large number of Italians are crowded into a narrow peninsula and were, up to the conquest of Ethiopia, extremely poor in colonial territories, has appeared to Italian thought clearly the consequence of accidents of history and not of the operation of divine law.

In the same way, the fact that the sixty-five millions who constitute the white population of the British Commonwealth own and exploit the well-nigh inexhaustible resources of an empire on which the sun never sets, while the same number of Germans are cooped up in a relatively insignificant and economically insufficient region of Central Europe, is explicable to the German mind only in terms of luck, of the good fortune which enabled Great Britain to achieve national unity centuries before Germany.

It is customary to think of the territory of a state in the same fashion as of the private property of an individual; but it is evident that there is here a double contrast. Within states, courts and police uphold titles and maintain lawful owners in possession of their land, which was acquired by the lawful processes of inheritance, purchase, or barter. By contrast, in the matter of national territory not only is there lacking any international authority to maintain the present owner in possession, but also that nation's title almost invariably derives from war.

In Europe, at least, all present frontiers are derived from former conquests. As a consequence, states which were anciently possessors of provinces, until their eviction through defeat in war, still regard the present tenure as based upon neither legal nor moral warrant. Furthermore, such states are entitled to believe that the present tenure may also prove transitory like the past.

The student of international affairs, then, is confronted with two mutually exclusive conceptions of national policy, the first static, and the second dynamic. Here, too, he also touches the very heart of the problem of peace in the contemporary world, which is posed by the demand of one group of peoples for security based upon the status quo, and of another for a prosperity, prestige, or ethnic unity obtainable only by a modification of that status quo. And the collision between these conceptions is as old as history and has obviously been hitherto, an inescapable concomitant of the nation states system.

Today, as always in the past, the static theory is naturally embraced by those states which already have prosperity and now seek security. . . . Thus it is found to be the familiar thesis of the peoples of such states that mankind has, at last, reached the point where the territorial division of the earth's surface has become immutable because the title of the present possessors is both legally and morally imprescriptible; morally, because it can be assailed only by war—and war has now been adjudged a crime. . . .

Against that thesis, however, there must be set the contention of those countries which, being dissatisfied with the status quo, advance the dynamic theory. . . . Why, Italian Fascism, German National Socialism, and Japanese Militarism demand, should the traditional ebb and flow in the fortunes of states be interrupted merely to suit the views of those peoples which happen at the moment to be sated and therefore satisfied? . . .

44. RAW MATERIALS AND WAR ECONOMY [24]

The following paragraphs call attention to an interesting and frequently overlooked aspect of the raw-material problem.

It is primarily the importance of raw materials in preparations for war, combined with the present menace of war, which makes them centers of friction and international dispute. Before much progress can

---

[24] E. Staley, *Raw Materials in Peace and War,* Council on Foreign Relations, New York, 1937, pp. 36, 238-239. Reprinted by permission of the Council on Foreign Relations.

be made in attacking peacetime raw material problems . . . the dominance of the idea of war economy must be broken, and this can be done only if measures can be taken which remove the ever-present "assumption of violence." This cannot be accomplished by redistributing sovereignty over raw material sources. Indeed, we may say that it is measures not primarily directed at raw material problems as such which offer the only hope of making raw material problems soluble. Under circumstances of more secure peace, much of the friction over raw materials that seems so alarming today would simply disappear.

. . . . .

The strategic importance of raw materials in wartime makes them centers of conflict in the continuous struggle for power forced upon the nations by the ever-present risk of war. There is no solution for such conflicts, and there can be no real hope of successfully applying methods of peaceful change to raw material problems except by removing the necessity for framing national policies in terms of power. Were raw material problems not complicated by the constant fear of war, they would not be particularly difficult or dangerous. It is only with reference to war potential or under conditions of intense economic nationalism, resulting in large part from fear of war, that current slogans relating to the "have" and "have-not" nations possess any relevance to raw materials discussions.

45. A GERMAN NATIONAL-ECONOMIC VIEW ON THE NEED FOR COLONIES, 1937 [25]

After the advent of Adolf Hitler to power, the Berlin Government placed increasing emphasis on the economic and financial need of Germany to regain her lost colonies. Dr. Hjalmar Schacht, while Minister of Economics, advanced the argument with precision and clarity.

A particularly ridiculous charge to which Germany has often to listen in connection with her colonial demands is that colonies in general and her former colonies in particular are valueless, and that it would not do Germany any good if her colonies were returned to her. This immediately prompts the retort: If the colonies are so bad, why do you keep them? It is also misleading to refer to the minor part played

[25] H. Schacht, "Germany's Colonial Demands," in *Foreign Affairs*, January 1937, pp. 230-234. Reprinted by permission of the Council on Foreign Relations.

by the colonies in Germany's pre-war foreign trade. I have already pointed out that before the war free trade prevailed on a large scale and that Germany had valuable resources in the form of foreign investments. Consequently, it was not necessary before the war for Germany to develop her colonies with particular energy. It nevertheless is astonishing what Germany did with her colonies before the war without any great effort. They had been in her possession, on the average, for only some twenty-five years, from the end of the eighties and the beginning of the nineties. But during those twenty-five years Germany did more with her colonies than other countries had done in two hundred and fifty years.

At the outbreak of the World War, that is, after two decades of German administration, the German colonies had ceased to be a burden on the mother country. In fact, the financial balance was so well established that even the colonial railway loans had been paid for by the earnings of the colonies. Only the seven thousand police troops were supported by the mother country. During the fifteen years before the war, the external trade of the German colonies had increased seven-fold. That happened in a time when Germany did not experience a scarcity of raw materials and foreign currency, in a time when world trade had not been interrupted by political and economic mistrust, in a time when the struggles of different currency systems were not being fought out, in a time, therefore, when Germany had no particular need to intensify her trade with her colonies. Today, when there no longer is free trade in the world, when Germany is crushed by foreign debt and harassed by the lack of raw materials and valuta, if her colonies were returned to her she would proceed to develop them with far greater intensity. A large part of the food supplies and raw materials which we now lack could be furnished by them.

Of course there are short-sighted people who declare that if Germany got back her colonies they would compete with the other countries which supply raw materials, to the disadvantage of these latter. This is simply the eternally recurring, short-sighted, unbusinesslike attitude of all those people who are constantly afraid of any new development. It was this attitude which found expression in England in the nineties, when it was said that every Englishman would be the richer if only Germany were crushed.

. . . . .

I therefore wish to name two conditions essential to the solution of Germany's raw material problem. First, Germany must produce her raw materials on territory under her own management. Second, this colonial territory must form part of her own monetary system. Colonial raw materials cannot be developed without considerable investments. Colonial markets are not of the kind that can live by the personal needs of the population. Shirts and hats for the negroes and ornaments for their wives do not constitute an adequate market. Colonial territories are developed by the building of railways and roads, by automobile traffic, radio and electric power, by huge plantations, etc. From the moment that the German colonies came under the Mandate Powers, Germany was cut off from the delivery of goods required for such investments. In 1913, for example, Germany's exports to Tanganyika formed 52.6 per cent of that area's imports. In 1935 they formed 10.7 per cent. The British Mandate Power as a matter of course places its orders in England and not in Germany or elswhere. That is the reason why Germany needs colonial territories which she herself administers. Since, however, the development of colonies depends upon long term investments, and these investments cannot be made by the native negro population, the German currency system must prevail in the colonial territories, so that the required investments may be made with German credits. These, then, are Germany's two basic demands in the colonial field: that she have territories under German management and included in the German monetary system.

All the other questions involved—sovereignty, army, police, law, the churches, international collaboration—are open to discussion. They can all be solved by means of international co-operation so long as nothing unworthy is imputed against the honor of Germany. The German colonial problem is not a problem of imperialism. It is not a mere problem of prestige. It is simply and solely a problem of economic existence. Precisely for that reason the future of European peace depends upon it.

46. "DO COLONIES PAY?" [26]

Partisans in the dispute regarding the economic value of colonies seemed often to overlook certain important factors which must be considered in answering the question, "Do colonies pay?" The following extract seeks to make clear the chief elements that require recognition in any such effort.

[26] Royal Institute of International Affairs, *The Colonial Problem. A Report by a Study Group of Members of the Royal Institute of International Affairs,* Oxford University Press, New York, 1937, pp. 41-44. Reprinted by permission of the Royal Institute of International Affairs and the Oxford University Press.

If . . . an attempt were made to assess the economic value of a colony to a metropolitan Power, the value to be measured would not be the whole of the economic benefits derived from the relations between the colony and the metropolitan country; but only that part of them derived from the particular relationship between the colony and the possessing Power. For some, at least, of these benefits might still be obtainable if the colony were independent, or were administered by another Power. What has to be computed is the value in economic terms which the metropolitan country derives from the special advantages conferred upon it by sovereignty over the colony. In practice, this means the benefits derived from preferential export and import duties or from partial or total exclusion of foreign goods, making the trade of the metropolitan Power with the colony more profitable than that of other countries; the value of special opportunities to the investors of the metropolitan country, either in being first in the field and reaping the initial profits, if any, in reselling their claims at enhanced prices or in excluding foreigners completely from participation; and the value to metropolitan nationals of special opportunities of settlement. Against the additional value so obtained from the actual possession of the colony must be set the expenses incurred in administration and, where colonial defence can be separated from national defence in general, the cost of naval and military establishments.

If it were merely a question of finding out how much total benefit the metropolitan Power derived from the colony, the question would be easier to answer; and in most cases the answer would be that the benefits were less than those which could be derived from trade with and investment in independent countries, as in these latter there would be no cost of administration and defence to set off against profits. If equality of opportunity in every respect could be secured, there would be scant support from business men for the possession of colonies, though perhaps an increased support from humanitarians. It is the special advantages derived from possession that make a colony an asset; without these, the objections raised by the Manchester school in the last century against the cost of maintaining colonies once more become valid.

But the value of these advantages to the metropolitan Power is for many reasons hard to estimate. In the first place, many colonies have been annexed not so much to obtain special advantages for the metropolitan country as to prevent another country from obtaining even greater advantages for itself. Colonies, that is to say, are sometimes acquired and maintained more in order to insure against exclusion than to exclude others. An Open Door colony under one's own sovereignty may be preferable to a highly protected colony under another's. In such a case, the value of possesson is to be considered as the prevention of the loss which would have been caused by an exclusive economic régime imposed by another Power. Again, the advantage derived from possession has often been merely the greater trade and investment under a European than under an indigenous administration.

Even though a country has no trade with any colony, it may, nevertheless, share in the profits of colonial enterprises. Its trade with foreign countries may be increased as a result of their trade with colonies, and its investors may find more profitable employment for their capital both at home and abroad through the increased opportunities which result from the development of colonies, even though none of their capital is invested directly in colonial territory. . . .

· · · · ·

According to the various underlying assumptions, the query "Do colonies pay?" may therefore be answered in general terms; but one that will satisfy everyone is probably impossible, not only because of lack of factual data, but also because of the difficulty of analysing the behaviour of a great number of independent variables. We may, however, . . . set forth the various items of debit and credit which would have to be drawn up for the whole period of a colony's existence as a preliminary to answering this question. . . .

Subject to the reservations noted above, the metropolitan country will credit the colony with:

1. The interest received by investors in the metropolitan country on capital invested in the colony. This will include interest on loans raised by the central and local governments of the colony and the interest and dividends paid by private enterprises.

2. The benefits accruing to consumers in the metropolitan country as the result of the cheaper imports which the relatively low cost of production in the colony may enable them to obtain. . . .

3. The benefits accruing to producers in the metropolitan country as the result of the direct and indirect profits on their exports (including invisible exports) to the colony. Indirect profits will include the advantages to be gained through an increase in the size of the producers' total output by the enlargement of their market. Such benefits may be shared with other than metropolitan producers.

4. Both the Government and individuals in the colony may make money payments to the Government or individuals in the metropolitan country, for defence, administration, family remittances, and for charitable or other purposes.

On the other side of the account the metropolitan country will debit the colony with:

1. The losses of metropolitan investors on their investments in the colony.

2. Losses of traders and others doing business with the colony, whether as importers or exporters.

3. Subsidies, grants, and subventions, directly or indirectly made by the Government or the citizens of the metropolitan Power to the Government or inhabitants of the colony. These would include the cost of the defence and administration of the colony, grants made by individuals to medical, educational, or other services, and the costs of tariffs and other preferences in favour of the colony.

4. Finally, the cost of acquisition, by purchase or other means, of the colony should be included.

Enough has been said to show that the question of the economic value of colonies involves a complex of calculations which are by no means simple in themselves, and which have varying reactions one on another. . . .

☒ ☒ ☒

CHAPTER 4

SECURITY AND ARMAMENTS

47-49. The Foreign Policies of Certain Powers

47. THE FOREIGN POLICY OF FRANCE (JULES CAMBON) [1]

The following selections represent authoritative résumés of some recent European foreign policies. This first summary was written by Jules Cambon, French Ambassador to Germany during the eight years before the World War.

To sum up. If in the past France has sometimes given herself over to the spirit of conquest, either she was led to do so in the enthusiasm of victory after attacks had been launched against her, or because she felt that she was carrying the torch of liberty to the peoples of other nations. Even then, in the hours of their greatest triumphs, our statesmen (knowing how quickly the French spirit can change) thought like Talleyrand that the surest foundation of peace lay in the reëstablishment of the balance of power. This view we still hold.

Of course the situation is not precisely the same today as formerly. At Geneva discussions are carried on in public, and for that reason a preoccupation with the principle of the balance of power seems out of date. But it would be a mistake to take this view. There are groups, cabals and oppositions inside the League of Nations, and though political action may take new forms, at heart it is the same. National aspirations are the expression of national interests, and these, as I have said, persist through the ages because human nature does not change. They condition the relations of peoples, and according to circumstances bring them together or set them one against the other. So it was with France and England; they had long been enemies, but they united at last in the face of a common danger. It is true that by the Briand-

---

[1] *The Foreign Policy of the Powers: France, Germany, Great Britain, Italy, Japan, Soviet Russia, the United States,* Council on Foreign Relations, New York, 1935, pp. 22-24. Reprinted by permission of the Council on Foreign Relations.

193

Kellogg Pact most of the nations have solemnly renounced war, but in 1914 how little the most solemn engagements were worth when the German Chancellor, Bethmann-Hollweg, declared that necessity knows no law! We therefore are under compulsion to neglect nothing which can guarantee us against the danger of war.

When I have said that security has always been the cardinal aim of France, that term must be understood in its fullest sense. There is a France outside our own frontiers. Just as England cannot permit her communications with India to be menaced in Egypt, and just as the United States considers that one of her elementary interests is to safeguard the Panama Canal, just so France must guard her communications with her possessions in North Africa and preserve her freedom of action in the Mediterranean. Here we touch the problem of the relations of states at its most delicate point. For it is when states come into direct contact that practical accommodations become imperative.

Security! The term signifies more indeed than the maintenance of the homeland of a people, or even of their territories beyond the seas. It also means the maintenance of the world's respect for them, the maintenance of their economic interests, everything, in a word, which goes to make up the grandeur, the life itself, of the nation. But all peoples have not the same ideal; each follows what it considers to be its national interests in accordance with its own traditions. If the nations are to live in peace, those who direct the foreign affairs of each state must try diligently and long to understand and respect the aspirations of others. For by a statesman's comprehension of the forces which direct the destiny of nations one measures the breadth and depth of his genius.

48. THE FOREIGN POLICY OF ITALY (DINO GRANDI) [2]

The following summary of Italian foreign policy was written by Dino Grandi, at one time Italian Foreign Minister and then Italian Ambassador to Great Britain.

The affinity of Italian foreign policy with the foreign policy of England grew steadily throughout the nineteenth century and during the early years of the twentieth. . . .

[2] *The Foreign Policy of the Powers: France, Germany, Great Britain, Italy, Japan, Soviet Russia, the United States,* Council on Foreign Relations, New York, 1935, pp. 98-101. Reprinted by permission of the Council on Foreign Relations.

This understanding has been renewed of late years by the similarity of our views as to the best way of facing Europe's political exigencies, a common dislike for the rigidity of abstract formulæ, and an innate sense of justice in the two peoples—justice based on an understanding of mankind, which alone makes it possible to settle problems in reality and not merely in form. Justice and legality are not identical. There are treaties, pacts and agreements which must be respected and honestly carried out; but over and above treaties, pacts and agreements there are the claims of good sense and equity which must be satisfied. International problems are not merely matters for legal and coercive settlement; they are essentially problems of social order, and social order is maintained only by an earnest effort to satisfy the needs of the peoples.

We are satisfied that during these last years Italy has made this effort. No problem has left us indifferent or lacking in zeal, still less, hostile. Never has Italy refused to recognize the just rights of others. Ever since the signing of the Treaty of Versailles, France has insisted on her need for security. We did not hesitate to guarantee this security, and took a solemn pledge to this effect by signing the Locarno Treaty. The German nation has claimed and still claims freedom. From the close of the war to the present time it is true to say that Italy has never neglected any occasion, however slight, to help Germany arrange for a term to be put to international control over her domestic concerns, to remove over-burdensome obligations in the political, military and financial domains, and to assist the German people to resume its place on an equal footing in the consortium of free nations.

But Italy also has her own problems to solve, and ones no less formidable than those of safety, liberty, and the resumption of economic relations with neighboring countries. Ours is a vital problem that involves our very existence and future, a future of peace, tranquillity and work for a population of 42 million souls, which will number 50 million in another fifteen years. Can this population live and prosper in a territory half the size of Spain and Germany and lacking raw materials and natural resources to meet its vital needs, pent up, moreover, in a closed sea beyond which its commerce lies, a sea the outlets of which are owned by other nations? Meanwhile all the nations of the world are raising barriers against the development of trade, the movement of capital, and emigration, denationalizing whoever crosses their frontiers to enter, I do not say their own homes, but even their protectorates and colonies.

During the years that Mussolini has been Head of the Italian Government this problem has grown steadily more acute. At the beginning it hardly existed in the consciousness of Europe, which regarded our foreign policy as permanently bound up with and circumscribed by the Adriatic conflict. Today it forms part of the general situation of European reconstruction, which nobody is any longer able to envisage without taking into account the satisfaction of Italy's vital needs.

Thus the first constructive phase of our foreign policy is closed. Fascism has placed Italy's problem before Europe, not as an isolated one to be considered apart from others, but as one factor of the comprehensive European problem, which demands a single organic settlement. In this, I think, consists the deepest and more real significance of the Duce's foreign policy.

49. THE FOREIGN POLICY OF THE SOVIET UNION (KARL RADEK) [3]

The foreign policy of the Soviet Union was described as follows by Karl Radek, former editor of Izvestia *and former secretary of the Communist International. In January 1937 he was sentenced to prison for his alleged part in a Trotskyite conspiracy against the Soviet Union.*

The Soviet Union does not close the door to the possibility of striking a deal with imperialistic Powers which are waging a struggle against other imperialistic Powers, if the latter attack the Soviet Union; but in entering into such an agreement the Soviet Union would not accept any responsibility for the specific purposes pursued by the imperialistic Powers parties to the agreement. Never and under no conditions would it participate in the plundering of other nations, because participation in such a plunder would be contrary to the international solidarity of the workers. But against an attacking imperialism, agreement is permissible with any opponent in order to defeat an enemy invading Soviet territory.

I think I have named the fundamental principles of Soviet policy and have explained their interdependence. They are all derived from the basic fact that imperialism is unable to solve the great problems which

[3] *The Foreign Policy of the Powers: France, Germany, Great Britain, Italy, Japan, Soviet Russia, the United States,* Council on Foreign Relations, New York, 1935, pp. 140-142. Reprinted by permission of the Council on Foreign Relations.

mankind has to face today. A new imperialistic war will not solve them. It will lead to an immense destruction of productive forces, to unexampled sufferings among the masses of the people, and will achieve nothing except a new re-shuffling of the possessions of the capitalist world.

The Soviet Union is an enemy of imperialistic wars which arise from the fact that capitalism is no longer in a position to develop the productive forces of the human race, but that it is still capable of attempting to seize a piece of land which is being reserved for the exploitation of a given national bourgeoisie. That is how the world is pushed toward immense new upheavals. We are therefore certain that the masses, thrust into the turmoil of new wars, will seek a way out along the same road that was followed by the Soviet proletariat in 1917.

The object of the Soviet Government is to save the soil of the first proletariat state from the criminal folly of a new war. To this end the Soviet Union has struggled with the greatest determination and consistency. The defense of peace and of the neutrality of the Soviet Union against all attempts to drag it into the whirlwind of a world war is the central problem of Soviet foreign policy.

The Soviet Union follows the policy of peace because peace is the best condition for building up a socialist society. Fighting for the maintenance of peace, accepting obligations of neutrality toward the struggling camps of the imperialists, the Soviet Union has at the same time raised the military preparedness of the country to a level which answers the demands of national defense and the requirements of modern warfare. Its neutrality is a positive factor which the imperialistic Powers which have not yet lost the sense of realities will not fail to appreciate. Those of them which are unable to realize the importance of Soviet neutrality or are forced by the insoluble difficulties of their own position to risk an adventurous war against that huge country, with its dozens of millions of men united by a common desire for peace, a desire for peaceful creative work—to those Powers will be given the proofs that the generation which laid down the foundations of socialism is also capable of defending them with iron energy. And we are convinced that, irrespective of what might be the course of the war and who might be responsible for its origins, the only victor that would emerge from it would be the Soviet Union leading the workers of the whole world; for it alone has a banner which, in case of a war, can become the banner of the masses of the entire world.

50-51. The Washington Conference Treaties, 1921-1922

50. THE WASHINGTON NAVAL TREATY, 1922 *(Extracts)* [4]

Probably because the Paris Peace Conference ignored the question of the freedom of the seas, it appeared in 1920-1921 that the pre-war Anglo-German naval rivalry might be replaced by an equally dangerous Anglo-American naval rivalry. Moreover, should war break out, Great Britain might well be supported by Japan under the terms of the Anglo-Japanese alliance which had been renewed in 1911 for ten years. To avoid these dangers, President Warren G. Harding invited eight powers to attend a conference at Washington in the winter of 1921-1922 to discuss naval limitation and Pacific relations. The conference drafted seven treaties, of which two five-power agreements concerned naval limitation. One of these, relating to the outlawry of poison gas and restrictions on submarine warfare, was not ratified and hence never came into force. The other, the ratifications of which were exchanged on August 17, 1923, and which is reproduced in part below, limited certain classes of naval tonnage.

Article 1.

The Contracting Powers agree to limit their respective naval armament as provided in the present Treaty.

. . . . .

Article 4.

The total capital ship replacement tonnage of each of the Contracting Powers shall not exceed in standard displacement, for the United States, 525,000 tons (533,400 metric tons); for the British Empire, 525,000 tons (533,400 metric tons); for France, 175,000 tons (177,800 metric tons); for Italy, 175,000 tons (177,800 metric tons); for Japan, 315,000 tons (320,040 metric tons).

Article 5.

No capital ship exceeding 35,000 tons (35,560 metric tons) standard

---

[4] *Treaty between the British Empire, France, Italy, Japan and the United States of America for the Limitation of Naval Armament. Signed at Washington, February 6, 1922. Presented by the Secretary of State for Foreign Affairs to Parliament by Command of His Majesty*, Treaty Series No. 5 (1924), Cmd. 2036, His Majesty's Stationery Office, London, 1924, pp. 3-17.

displacement shall be acquired by, or constructed by, for, or within the jurisdiction of, any of the Contracting Powers.

ARTICLE 6.

No capital ship of any of the Contracting Powers shall carry a gun with a calibre in excess of 16 inches (406 millimetres).

ARTICLE 7.

The total tonnage for aircraft carriers of each of the Contracting Powers shall not exceed in standard displacement, for the United States, 135,000 tons (137,160 metric tons); for the British Empire, 135,000 tons (137,160 metric tons); for France, 60,000 tons (60,960 metric tons); for Italy, 60,000 tons (60,960 metric tons); for Japan, 81,000 tons (82,296 metric tons).

. . . . .

ARTICLE 14.

No preparations shall be made in merchant ships in time of peace for the installation of warlike armaments for the purpose of converting such ships into vessels of war, other than the necessary stiffening of decks for the mounting of guns not exceeding 6-inch (152 millimetres) calibre.

. . . . .

ARTICLE 19.

The United States, the British Empire and Japan agree that the *status quo* at the time of the signing of the present Treaty, with regard to fortifications and naval bases, shall be maintained in their respective territories and possessions specified hereunder:—

1. The insular possessions which the United States now holds or may hereafter acquire in the Pacific Ocean, except (*a*) those adjacent to the coast of the United States, Alaska and the Panama Canal Zone, not including the Aleutian Islands, and (*b*) the Hawaiian Islands;

2. Hong Kong and the insular possessions which the British Empire now holds or may hereafter acquire in the Pacific Ocean, east of the meridian of 110° east longitude, except (*a*) those adjacent to the coast of Canada, (*b*) the Commonwealth of Australia and its territories, and (*c*) New Zealand;

3. The following insular territories and possessions of Japan in the

Pacific Ocean, to wit: the Kurile Islands, the Bonin Islands, Amami-Oshima, the Loochoo Islands, Formosa and the Pescadores, and any insular territories or possessions in the Pacific Ocean which Japan may hereafter acquire.

The maintenance of the *status quo* under the foregoing provisions implies that no new fortifications or naval bases shall be established in the territories and possessions specified; that no measures shall be taken to increase the existing naval facilities for the repair and maintenance of naval forces, and that no increase shall be made in the coast defences of the territories and possessions above specified. This restriction, however, does not preclude such repair and replacement of worn-out weapons and equipment as is customary in naval and military establishments in time of peace.

. . . . .

ARTICLE 21.

If during the term of the present Treaty the requirements of the national security of any Contracting Power in respect of naval defence are, in the opinion of that Power, materially affected by any change of circumstances, the Contracting Powers will, at the request of such Power, meet in conference with a view to the reconsideration of the provisions of the Treaty and its amendment by mutual agreement. . . .

ARTICLE 22.

Whenever any Contracting Power shall become engaged in a war which in its opinion affects the naval defence of its national security, such Power may after notice to the other Contracting Powers suspend for the period of hostilities its obligations under the present Treaty other than those under Articles XIII and XVII [forbidding the reconversion of a scrapped vessel and the use of a vessel being built or already constructed for another Power], provided that such Power shall notify the other Contracting Powers that the emergency is of such a character as to require such suspension.

The remaining Contracting Powers shall in such case consult together with a view to agreement as to what temporary modifications, if any, should be made in the Treaty as between themselves. Should such consultation not produce agreement, duly made in accordance with the constitutional methods of the respective Powers, any one of said Contracting Powers may, by giving notice to the other Contracting

Powers, suspend for the period of hostilities its obligations under the present Treaty, other than those under Articles XIII and XVII.

On the cessation of hostilities the Contracting Powers will meet in conference to consider what modifications, if any, should be made in the provisions of the present Treaty.

Article 23.

The present Treaty shall remain in force until the 31st December, 1936, and in case none of the Contracting Powers shall have given notice two years before that date of its intention to terminate the Treaty, it shall continue in force until the expiration of two years from the date on which notice of termination shall be given by one of the Contracting Powers, whereupon the Treaty shall terminate as regards all Contracting Powers. . . .

51. THE QUADRUPLE AGREEMENTS RELATING TO PACIFIC INSULAR POSSESSIONS, 1921-1922 [5]

At the Washington Conference there were also signed two four-power treaties relating to the status of the Pacific insular possessions of the United States, Great Britain, France, and Japan. Ratified on August 17, 1923, these agreements definitely terminated the Anglo-Japanese Alliance of 1911.

TREATY . . . RELATING TO . . . INSULAR POSSESSIONS . . . .
DECEMBER 13, 1921.

I.

The High Contracting Parties agree as between themselves to respect their rights in relation to their insular possessions and insular dominions in the region of the Pacific Ocean.

If there should develop between any of the High Contracting Parties a controversy arising out of any Pacific question and involving their said rights which is not satisfactorily settled by diplomacy and is likely

[5] *Treaty between the British Empire, France, Japan and the United States of America Relating to Their Insular Possessions and Insular Dominions in the Pacific Ocean, and Accompanying Declaration, together with Treaty Supplementary to the above Treaty. . . . Signed at Washington, December 13, 1921, and February 6, 1922. Presented by the Secretary of State for Foreign Affairs to Parliament by Command of His Majesty,* Treaty Series No. 6 (1924), Cmd. 2037, His Majesty's Stationery Office, London, 1924, pp. 3-5, 6.

to affect the harmonious accord now happily subsisting between them, they shall invite the other High Contracting Parties to a joint conference to which the whole subject will be referred for consideration and adjustment.

II.

If the said rights are threatened by the aggressive action of any other Power, the High Contracting Parties shall communicate with one another fully and frankly in order to arrive at an understanding as to the most efficient measures to be taken, jointly or separately, to meet the exigencies of the particular situation.

III.

This Treaty shall remain in force for ten years from the time it shall take effect, and after the expiration of said period it shall continue to be in force subject to the right of any of the High Contracting Parties to terminate it upon twelve months' notice.

IV.

This Treaty shall be ratified as soon as possible in accordance with the constitutional methods of the High Contracting Parties and shall take effect on the deposit of ratifications, which shall take place at Washington, and thereupon the agreement between Great Britain and Japan, which was concluded at London on the 13th July, 1911, shall terminate. . . .

DECLARATION ACCOMPANYING THE TREATY OF DECEMBER 13, 1921.

In signing the Treaty this day between the United States of America, the British Empire, France and Japan, it is declared to be the understanding and intent of the Signatory Powers:

1. That the Treaty shall apply to the Mandated Islands in the Pacific Ocean; provided, however, that the making of the Treaty shall not be deemed to be an assent on the part of the United States of America to the mandates and shall not preclude agreements between the United States of America and the Mandatory Powers respectively in relation to the mandated islands. . . .

TREATY . . . SUPPLEMENTARY TO THE QUADRUPLE PACIFIC TREATY . . . .
FEBRUARY 6, 1922.

The United States of America, the British Empire, France and Japan have, through their respective Plenipotentiaries, agreed upon the following stipulations supplementary to the Quadruple Treaty signed at Washington on the 13th December, 1921:

The term "insular possessions and insular dominions" used in the aforesaid Treaty shall, in its application to Japan, include only Karafuto (or the southern portion of the island of Sakhalin), Formosa and the Pescadores, and the islands under the mandate of Japan.

. . . . .

52. A POST-WAR TREATY OF ARBITRATION (AUSTRIA AND HUNGARY, 1923) [6]

The early post-war period witnessed the negotiation of a whole series of treaties of friendship, arbitration, and conciliation. The following treaty between Austria and Hungary (signed on April 10, 1923, at Budapest and effective from July 14, 1923) may be taken as an example of this type of agreement.

The Kingdom of Hungary and the Republic of Austria, the Governments of which have mutually declared that their policy is directed towards the promotion of peace, and that, in order to avoid anything which might impede the attainment of this object, they have recognised the necessity of keeping in close touch in regard to any questions which may arise affecting both countries, being animated by a desire to contribute towards the maintenance and safeguarding of peace in Central Europe and to establish the principle of compulsory arbitration in their mutual relations,

Have resolved to conclude an agreement for this purpose and have appointed as their Plenipotentiaries:

For His Highness the Regent of the Kingdom of Hungary:

Councillor Geza Daruváry von Daruvár, Royal Hungarian Minister of Justice, Acting Head of the Royal Hungarian Ministry of Foreign Affairs, and

For the Federal President of the Republic of Austria:

M. Franz Calice, Envoy Extraordinary, and Minister Plenipotentiary,

---

[6] League of Nations, *Treaty Series 1923*, vol. XVIII, pp. 99-101. English translation by the Secretariat of the League of Nations.

Who, having communicated their full powers found in good and due form, have agreed upon the following provisions:

ARTICLE 1.

The High Contracting Parties undertake that, in the event of any dispute arising between them in future, they will first of all endeavour to reach an agreement by means of a friendly understanding.

If, however, it should prove impossible in this way to settle the dispute, no matter what its nature may be, it shall be submitted, after an agreement has been reached by the two Parties, to an arbitrator or arbitrators specially appointed for the purpose.

As a rule, any arbitration courts which may be set up from time to time shall sit alternately in Vienna and Budapest.

The two Governments may, if they consider it expedient, refer the dispute to the Permanent Court of International Justice.

The High Contracting Parties shall not apply to a court of arbitration until they have drawn up a special agreement in which the facts of the dispute and the points to be decided are accurately stated.

ARTICLE 2.

The foregoing provisions shall also apply to disputes arising out of circumstances which occurred before the conclusion of this Agreement.

ARTICLE 3.

The present Agreement shall be ratified and the instruments of ratification shall be exchanged as soon as possible at Budapest. The Agreement shall enter into force on the fifteenth day after the exchange of the ratifications.

The text of the agreement shall be communicated to the Secretariat of the League of Nations.

ARTICLE 4.

Should one of the High Contracting Parties denounce this Agreement, the denunciation shall not come into force until one year after it has been communicated in writing to the other Contracting Party.

In faith whereof the Plenipotentiaries of both Parties have signed this Agreement and have thereto affixed their seals.

Done in duplicate at Budapest on April 10, 1923, in Hungarian and German texts authentic.

(*L. S.*) DARUVÁRY.
(*L. S.*) F. CALICE.

53. THE PROTOCOL FOR THE PACIFIC SETTLEMENT OF INTERNATIONAL DISPUTES, 1924 [7]

The failure of the powers to accept a draft Treaty of Mutual Assistance unanimously adopted by the Fourth Assembly of the League of Nations in September 1923 eventually led Premiers MacDonald and Herriot of Great Britain and France, respectively, to seek some formula whereby "arbitration, security, and disarmament" might become recognized as the basis of all future international relations. In September 1924, accordingly, they jointly introduced a resolution before the Fifth Assembly of the League reopening the entire question of war and peace. The result was the unanimous adoption by the Assembly on October 2, 1924, of the so-called Geneva Protocol, the only document thus far drawn up which gave real promise of preventing future wars by clearly defining the aggressor in future conflicts and providing seemingly effective guarantees to defeat the aims of potential aggressors. But the protocol was never ratified, for Great Britain, now under the leadership of Premier Stanley Baldwin and Foreign Secretary Austen Chamberlain, disapproved of world-wide commitments and sanctions and evidently distrusted compulsory arbitration as a means of preserving peace.

Animated by the firm desire to ensure the maintenance of general peace and the security of nations whose existence, independence or territories may be threatened;

Recognising the solidarity of the members of the international community;

Asserting that a war of aggression constitutes a violation of this solidarity and an international crime;

Desirous of facilitating the complete application of the system provided in the Covenant of the League of Nations for the pacific settlement of disputes between States and of ensuring the repression of international crimes; and

For the purpose of realising, as contemplated by Article 8 of the Covenant, the reduction of national armaments to the lowest point consistent with national safety and the enforcement by common action of international obligations;

The undersigned, duly authorised to that effect, agree as follows:

[7] League of Nations, *Official Journal,* Special Supplement No. 23, Records of the Fifth Assembly, Annex II to A. 135, 1924, pp. 498-502.

Article 1.

The signatory States undertake to make every effort in their power to secure the introduction into the Covenant of amendments on the lines of the provisions contained in the following articles.

They agree that, as between themselves, these provisions shall be binding as from the coming into force of the present Protocol and that, so far as they are concerned, the Assembly and the Council of the League of Nations shall thenceforth have power to exercise all the rights and perform all the duties conferred upon them by the Protocol.

Article 2.

The signatory States agree in no case to resort to war either with one another or against a State which, if the occasion arises, accepts all the obligations hereinafter set out, except in case of resistance to acts of aggression or when acting in agreement with the Council or the Assembly of the League of Nations in accordance with the provisions of the Covenant and of the present Protocol.

Article 3.

The signatory States undertake to recognise as compulsory, *ipso facto* and without special agreement, the jurisdiction of the Permanent Court of International Justice in the cases covered by paragraph 2 of Article 36 of the Statute of the Court, but without prejudice to the right of any State, when acceding to the special protocol provided for in the said Article and opened for signature on December 16th, 1920, to make reservations compatible with the said clause.

Accession to this special protocol, opened for signature on December 16th, 1920, must be given within the month following the coming into force of the present Protocol.

States which accede to the present Protocol after its coming into force must carry out the above obligation within the month following their accession.

Article 4.

With a view to render more complete the provisions of paragraphs 4, 5, 6, and 7 of Article 15 of the Covenant, the signatory States agree to comply with the following procedure:

1. If the dispute submitted to the Council is not settled by it as provided in paragraph 3 of the said Article 15, the Council shall

endeavour to persuade the parties to submit the dispute to judicial settlement or arbitration.

2. (a) If the parties cannot agree to do so, there shall, at the request of at least one of the parties, be constituted a Committee of Arbitrators. The Committee shall so far as possible be constituted by agreement between the parties.

(b) If within the period fixed by the Council the parties have failed to agree, in whole or in part, upon the number, the names and the powers of the arbitrators and upon the procedure, the Council shall settle the points remaining in suspense. It shall with the utmost possible despatch select in consultation with the parties the arbitrators and their President from among persons who by their nationality, their personal character and their experience, appear to it to furnish the highest guarantees of competence and impartiality.

(c) After the claims of the parties have been formulated, the Committee of Arbitrators, on the request of any party, shall through the medium of the Council request an advisory opinion upon any points of law in dispute from the Permanent Court of International Justice, which in such case shall meet with the utmost possible despatch.

3. If none of the parties asks for arbitration, the Council shall again take the dispute under consideration. If the Council reaches a report which is unanimously agreed to by the members thereof other than the representatives of any of the parties to the dispute, the signatory States agree to comply with the recommendations therein.

4. If the Council fails to reach a report which is concurred in by all its members, other than the representatives of any of the parties to the dispute, it shall submit the dispute to arbitration. It shall itself determine the composition, the powers and the procedure of the Committee of Arbitrators and, in the choice of the arbitrators, shall bear in mind the guarantees of competence and impartiality referred to in paragraph 2 (b) above.

5. In no case may a solution, upon which there has already been a unanimous recommendation of the Council accepted by one of the parties concerned, be again called in question.

6. The signatory States undertake that they will carry out in full good faith any judicial sentence or arbitral award that may be rendered and that they will comply, as provided in paragraph 3 above, with the solutions recommended by the Council. In the event of a State failing to carry out the above undertakings, the Council

shall exert all its influence to secure compliance therewith. If it
fails therein, it shall propose what steps should be taken to give
effect thereto, in accordance with the provision contained at the end
of Article 13 of the Covenant. Should a State in disregard of the
above undertakings resort to war, the sanctions provided for by
Article 16 of the Covenant, interpreted in the manner indicated in
the present Protocol, shall immediately become applicable to it.

7. The provisions of the present article do not apply to the settlement of disputes which arise as the result of measures of war taken
by one or more signatory States in agreement with the Council or
the Assembly.

ARTICLE 5.

The provisions of paragraph 8 of Article 15 of the Covenant shall
continue to apply in proceedings before the council.

If in the course of an arbitration, such as is contemplated in Article
4 above, one of the parties claims that the dispute, or part thereof,
arises out of a matter which by international law is solely within the
domestic jurisdiction of that party, the arbitrators shall on this point
take the advice of the Permanent Court of International Justice through
the medium of the Council. The opinion of the Court shall be binding
upon the arbitrators, who, if the opinion is affirmative, shall confine
themselves to so declaring in their award.

If the question is held by the Court or by the Council to be a matter
solely within the domestic jurisdiction of the State, this decision shall
not prevent consideration of the situation by the Council or by the
Assembly under Article 11 of the Covenant.

ARTICLE 6.

If in accordance with paragraph 9 of Article 15 of the Covenant a
dispute is referred to the Assembly, that body shall have for the settlement of the dispute all the powers conferred upon the Council as to
endeavouring to reconcile the parties in the manner laid down in
paragraphs 1, 2, and 3 of Article 15 of the Covenant and in paragraph
1 of Article 4 above.

Should the Assembly fail to achieve an amicable settlement:

If one of the parties asks for arbitration, the Council shall proceed
to constitute the Committee of Arbitrators in the manner provided
in sub-paragraphs (a), (b), and (c) of paragraph 2 of Article 4
above.

If no party asks for arbitration, the Assembly shall again take the dispute under consideration and shall have in this connection the same powers as the Council. Recommendations embodied in a report of the Assembly, provided that it secures the measure of support stipulated at the end of paragraph 10 of Article 15 of the Covenant, shall have the same value and effect, as regards all matters dealt with in the present Protocol, as recommendations embodied in a report of the Council adopted as provided in paragraph 3 of Article 4 above.

If the necessary majority cannot be obtained, the dispute shall be submitted to arbitration and the Council shall determine the composition, the powers and the procedure of the Committee of Arbitrators as laid down in paragraph 4 of Article 4 above.

ARTICLE 7.

In the event of a dispute arising between two or more signatory States, these States agree that they will not, either before the dispute is submitted to proceedings for pacific settlement or during such proceedings, make any increase of their armaments or effectives which might modify the position established by the Conference for the Reduction of Armaments provided for by Article 17 of the present Protocol, nor will they take any measure of military, naval, air, industrial or economic mobilisation, nor, in general, any action of a nature likely to extend the dispute or render it more acute.

It shall be the duty of the Council, in accordance with the provisions of Article 11 of the Covenant, to take under consideration any complaint as to infraction of the above undertakings which is made to it by one or more of the States parties to the dispute. Should the Council be of opinion that the complaint requires investigation, it shall, if it deems it expedient, arrange for enquiries and investigations in one or more of the countries concerned. Such enquiries and investigations shall be carried out with the utmost possible despatch and the signatory States undertake to afford every facility for carrying them out.

The sole object of measures taken by the Council as above provided is to facilitate the pacific settlement of disputes and they shall in no way prejudice the actual settlement.

If the result of such enquiries and investigations is to establish an infraction of the provisions of the first paragraph of the present Article, it shall be the duty of the Council to summon the State or States guilty of the infraction to put an end thereto. Should the State or States in question fail to comply with such summons, the Council shall declare them to be guilty of a violation of the Covenant or of the present Protocol, and shall decide upon the measures to be taken with a view to end as soon as possible a situation of a nature to threaten the peace of the world.

For the purposes of the present Article decisions of the Council may be taken by a two-thirds majority.

ARTICLE 8.

The signatory States undertake to abstain from any act which might constitute a threat of aggression against another State.

If one of the signatory States is of opinion that another State is making preparations for war, it shall have the right to bring the matter to the notice of the Council.

The Council, if it ascertains that the facts are as alleged, shall proceed as provided in paragraphs 2, 4, and 5 of Article 7.

ARTICLE 9.

The existence of demilitarised zones being calculated to prevent aggression and to facilitate a definite finding of the nature provided for in Article 10 below, the establishment of such zones between States mutually consenting thereto is recommended as a means of avoiding violations of the present Protocol.

The demilitarised zones already existing under the terms of certain treaties or conventions, or which may be established in future between States mutually consenting thereto, may at the request and at the expense of one or more of the conterminous States, be placed under a temporary or permanent system of supervision to be organised by the Council.

ARTICLE 10.

Every State which resorts to war in violation of the undertakings contained in the Covenant or in the present Protocol is an aggressor. Violation of the rules laid down for a demilitarised zone shall be held equivalent to resort to war.

In the event of hostilities having broken out, any State shall be presumed to be an aggressor, unless a decision of the Council, which must be taken unanimously, shall otherwise declare:

1. If it has refused to submit the dispute to the procedure of pacific settlement provided by Articles 13 and 15 of the Covenant

as amplified by the present Protocol, or to comply with a judicial sentence or arbitral award or with a unanimous recommendation of the Council, or has disregarded a unanimous report of the Council, a judicial sentence or an arbitral award recognising that the dispute between it and the other belligerent State arises out of a matter which by international law is solely within the domestic jurisdiction of the latter State; nevertheless, in the last case the State shall only be presumed to be an aggressor if it has not previously submitted the question to the Council or the Assembly, in accordance with Article 11 of the Covenant.

2. If it has violated provisional measures enjoined by the Council for the period while the proceedings are in progress as contemplated by Article 7 of the present Protocol.

Apart from the cases dealt with in paragraphs 1 and 2 of the present Article, if the Council does not at once succeed in determining the aggressor, it shall be bound to enjoin upon the belligerents an armistice, and shall fix the terms, acting, if need be, by a two-thirds majority and shall supervise its execution.

Any belligerent which has refused to accept the armistice or has violated its terms shall be deemed an aggressor.

The Council shall call upon the signatory States to apply forthwith against the aggressor the sanctions provided by Article 11 of the present Protocol, and any signatory State thus called upon shall thereupon be entitled to exercise the rights of a belligerent.

ARTICLE 11.

As soon as the Council has called upon the signatory States to apply sanctions, as provided in the last paragraph of Article 10 of the present Protocol, the obligations of the said States, in regard to the sanctions of all kinds mentioned in paragraphs 1 and 2 of Article 16 of the Covenant, will immediately become operative in order that such sanctions may forthwith be employed against the aggressor.

Those obligations shall be interpreted as obliging each of the signatory States to co-operate loyally and effectively in support of the Covenant of the League of Nations, and in resistance to any act of aggression, in the degree which its geographical position and its particular situation as regards armaments allow.

In accordance with paragraph 3 of Article 16 of the Covenant the signatory States give a joint and several undertaking to come to the assistance of the State attacked or threatened, and to give each other mutual support by means of facilities and reciprocal exchanges as regards the provision of raw materials and supplies of every kind, openings of credits, transport and transit, and for this purpose to take all measures in their power to preserve the safety of communications by land and by sea of the attacked or threatened State.

If both parties to the dispute are aggressors within the meaning of Article 10, the economic and financial sanctions shall be applied to both of them.

ARTICLE 12.

In view of the complexity of the conditions in which the Council may be called upon to exercise the functions mentioned in Article 11 of the present Protocol concerning economic and financial sanctions, and in order to determine more exactly the guarantees afforded by the present Protocol to the signatory States, the Council shall forthwith invite the economic and financial organisations of the League of Nations to consider and report as to the nature of the steps to be taken to give effect to the financial and economic sanctions and measures of co-operation contemplated in Article 16 of the Covenant and in Article 11 of this Protocol.

When in possession of this information, the Council shall draw up through its competent organs:

1. Plans of action for the application of the economic and financial sanctions against an aggressor State;

2. Plans of economic and financial co-operation between a State attacked and the different States assisting it;

and shall communicate these plans to the Members of the League and to the other signatory States.

ARTICLE 13.

In view of the contingent military, naval and air sanctions provided for by Article 16 of the Covenant and by Article 11 of the present Protocol, the Council shall be entitled to receive undertakings from States determining in advance the military, naval and air forces which they would be able to bring into action immediately to ensure the fulfilment of the obligations in regard to sanctions which result from the Covenant and the present Protocol.

Furthermore, as soon as the Council has called upon the signatory States to apply sanctions, as provided in the last paragraph of Article

10 above, the said States may, in accordance with any agreements which they may previously have concluded, bring to the assistance of a particular State, which is the victim of aggression, their military, naval and air forces.

The agreements mentioned in the preceding paragraph shall be registered and published by the Secretariat of the League of Nations. They shall remain open to all States Members of the League which may desire to accede thereto.

ARTICLE 14.

The Council shall alone be competent to declare that the application of sanctions shall cease and normal conditions be re-established.

ARTICLE 15.

In conformity with the spirit of the present Protocol, the signatory States agree that the whole cost of any military, naval or air operations undertaken for the repression of an aggression under the terms of the Protocol, and reparation for all losses suffered by individuals, whether civilians or combatants, and for all material damage caused by the operations of both sides, shall be borne by the aggressor State up to the extreme limit of its capacity.

Nevertheless, in view of Article 10 of the Covenant, neither the territorial integrity nor the political independence of the aggressor State shall in any case be affected as the result of the application of the sanctions mentioned in the present Protocol.

ARTICLE 16.

The signatory States agree that in the event of a dispute between one or more of them and one or more States which have not signed the present Protocol and are not Members of the League of Nations, such non-Member States shall be invited, on the conditions contemplated in Article 17 of the Covenant, to submit, for the purpose of a pacific settlement, to the obligations accepted by the States signatories of the present Protocol.

If the State so invited, having refused to accept the said conditions and obligations, resorts to war against a signatory State, the provisions of Article 16 of the Covenant, as defined by the present Protocol, shall be applicable against it.

ARTICLE 17.

The signatory States undertake to participate in an International

Conference for the Reduction of Armaments which shall be convened by the Council and shall meet at Geneva on Monday, June 15th, 1925. All other States, whether Members of the League or not, shall be invited to this Conference.

In preparation for the convening of the Conference, the Council shall draw up with due regard to the undertakings contained in Articles 11 and 13 of the present Protocol, a general programme for the reduction and limitation of armaments, which shall be laid before the Conference and which shall be communicated to the Governments at the earliest possible date, and at the latest three months before the Conference meets.

If by May 1st, 1925, ratifications have not been deposited by at least a majority of the permanent Members of the Council and ten other Members of the League, the Secretary-General of the League shall immediately consult the Council as to whether he shall cancel the invitations or merely adjourn the Conference to a subsequent date to be fixed by the Council so as to permit the necessary number of ratifications to be obtained.

ARTICLE 18.

Wherever mention is made in Article 10, or in any other provision of the present Protocol, of a decision of the Council, this shall be understood in the sense of Article 15 of the Covenant, namely, that the votes of the representatives of the parties to the dispute shall not be counted when reckoning unanimity or the necessary majority.

ARTICLE 19.

Except as expressly provided by its terms, the present Protocol shall not affect in any way the rights and obligations of Members of the League as determined by the Covenant.

ARTICLE 20.

Any dispute as to the interpretation of the present Protocol shall be submitted to the Permanent Court of International Justice.

ARTICLE 21.

The present Protocol, of which the French and English texts are both authentic, shall be ratified.

The deposit of ratifications shall be made at the Secretariat of the League of Nations as soon as possible.

States of which the seat of government is outside Europe will be entitled merely to inform the Secretariat of the League of Nations that their ratification has been given; in that case, they must transmit the instrument of ratification as soon as possible.

So soon as the majority of the permanent Members of the Council and ten other Members of the League have deposited or have effected their ratifications, a *procès-verbal* to that effect shall be drawn up by the Secretariat.

After the said *procès-verbal* has been drawn up, the Protocol shall come into force as soon as the plan for the reduction of armaments has been adopted by the Conference provided for in Article 17.

If within such period after the adoption of the plan for the reduction of armaments as shall be fixed by the said Conference, the plan has not been carried out, the Council shall make a declaration to that effect; this declaration shall render the present Protocol null and void.

The grounds on which the Council may declare that the plan drawn up by the International Conference for the Reduction of Armaments has not been carried out, and that in consequence the present Protocol has been rendered null and void, shall be laid down by the Conference itself.

A signatory State which, after the expiration of the period fixed by the Conference, fails to comply with the plan adopted by the Conference, shall not be admitted to benefit by the provisions of the present Protocol.

In faith whereof the undersigned, duly authorised for this purpose, have signed the present Protocol.

Done at Geneva, on the second day of October, nineteen hundred and twenty-four, in a single copy, which will be kept in the archives of the Secretariat of the League and registered by it on the date of its coming into force.

54. THE LOCARNO PACT, 1925 [8]

Following the rejection of the Geneva Protocol, the powers of western Europe accepted a scheme calculated at least to identify future aggressors in one of Europe's many sore-spots—the Rhineland. Owing largely to the initiative of the German Foreign Minister, Gustav Stresemann, an interna-

---

[8] *Treaty of Mutual Guarantee between Germany, Belgium, France, Great Britain and Italy, October 16, 1925,* in League of Nations, *Treaty Series 1926-1927,* vol. LIV, pp. 291-297.

tional conference was held at Locarno in Switzerland in October 1925 at which the so-called Locarno Pact was negotiated. It came into force on September 14, 1926, after Germany entered the League, and remained effective until renounced by Germany on March 7, 1936. (See Document No. 70.)

The President of the German Reich, His Majesty the King of the Belgians, the President of the French Republic, His Majesty the King of the United Kingdom of Great Britain and Ireland and of the British Dominions beyond the Seas, Emperor of India, and His Majesty the King of Italy;

Anxious to satisfy the desire for security and protection which animates the peoples upon whom fell the scourge of the war of 1914-1918;

Taking note of the abrogation of the treaties for the neutralisation of Belgium, and conscious of the necessity of ensuring peace in the area which has so frequently been the scene of European conflicts;

Animated also with the sincere desire of giving to all the signatory Powers concerned supplementary guarantees within the framework of the Covenant of the League of Nations and the treaties in force between them;

Have determined to conclude a treaty with these objects, and have appointed as their plenipotentiaries:

[Names of Plenipotentiaries omitted]

Who, having communicated their full powers, found in good and due form, have agreed as follows:—

ARTICLE 1.

The High Contracting Parties collectively and severally guarantee, in the manner provided in the following Articles, the maintenance of the territorial *status quo* resulting from the frontiers between Germany and Belgium and between Germany and France, and the inviolability of the said frontiers as fixed by or in pursuance of the Treaty of Peace signed at Versailles on June 28, 1919, and also the observance of the stipulations of Articles 42 and 43 of the said treaty concerning the demilitarised zone.

ARTICLE 2.

Germany and Belgium, and also Germany and France, mutually undertake that they will in no case attack or invade each other or resort to war against each other.

This stipulation shall not, however, apply in the case of:

(1) The exercise of the right of legitimate defence, that is to say, resistance to a violation of the undertaking contained in the previous paragraph or to a flagrant breach of Articles 42 or 43 of the said Treaty of Versailles, if such breach constitutes an unprovoked act of aggression and by reason of the assembly of armed forces in the demilitarised zone immediate action is necessary;

(2) Action in pursuance of Article 16 of the Covenant of the League of Nations;

(3) Action as the result of a decision taken by the Assembly or by the Council of the League of Nations or in pursuance of Article 15, paragraph 7, of the Covenant of the League of Nations, provided that in this last event the action is directed against a State which was the first to attack.

ARTICLE 3.

In view of the undertakings entered into in Article 2 of the present Treaty, Germany and Belgium, and Germany and France, undertake to settle by peaceful means and in the manner laid down herein all questions of every kind which may arise between them and which it may not be possible to settle by the normal methods of diplomacy:

Any question with regard to which the Parties are in conflict as to their respective rights shall be submitted to judicial decision, and the Parties undertake to comply with such decision.

All other questions shall be submitted to a conciliation commission. If the proposals of this commission are not accepted by the two Parties, the question shall be brought before the Council of the League of Nations, which will deal with it in accordance with Article 15 of the Covenant of the League.

The detailed arrangements for effecting such peaceful settlement are the subject of special Agreements signed this day.

ARTICLE 4.

(1) If one of the High Contracting Parties alleges that a violation of Article 2 of the present Treaty or a breach of Articles 42 or 43 of the Treaty of Versailles has been or is being committed, it shall bring the question at once before the Council of the League of Nations.

(2) As soon as the Council of the League of Nations is satisfied that such violation or breach has been committed, it will notify its finding

without delay to the Powers signatory of the present Treaty, who severally agree that in such case they will each of them come immediately to the assistance of the Power against whom the act complained of is directed.

(3) In case of a flagrant violation of Article 2 of the present Treaty or of a flagrant breach of Articles 42 or 43 of the Treaty of Versailles by one of the High Contracting Parties, each of the other Contracting Parties hereby undertakes immediately to come to the help of the Party against whom such a violation or breach has been directed as soon as the said Power has been able to satisfy itself that this violation constitutes an unprovoked act of aggression and that by reason either of the crossing of the frontier or of the outbreak of hostilities or of the assembly of armed forces in the demilitarised zone immediate action is necessary. Nevertheless, the Council of the League of Nations, which will be seized of the question in accordance with the first paragraph of this Article, will issue its findings, and the High Contracting Parties undertake to act in accordance with the recommendations of the Council, provided that they are concurred in by all the Members other than the representatives of the Parties which have engaged in hostilities.

ARTICLE 5.

The provisions of Article 3 of the present Treaty are placed under the guarantee of the High Contracting Parties as provided by the following stipulations:

If one of the Powers referred to in Article 3 refuses to submit a dispute to peaceful settlement or to comply with an arbitral or judicial decision and commits a violation of Article 2 of the present Treaty or a breach of Articles 42 or 43 of the Treaty of Versailles, the provisions of Article 4 of the present Treaty shall apply.

Where one of the Powers referred to in Article 3, without committing a violation of Article 2 of the present Treaty or a breach of Articles 42 or 43 of the Treaty of Versailles, refuses to submit a dispute to peaceful settlement or to comply with an arbitral or judicial decision, the other Party shall bring the matter before the Council of the League of Nations, and the Council shall propose what steps shall be taken; the High Contracting Parties shall comply with these proposals.

ARTICLE 6.

The provisions of the present Treaty do not affect the rights and obligations of the High Contracting Parties under the Treaty of Versailles or under arrangements supplementary thereto, including the Agreements signed in London on August 30, 1924.

ARTICLE 7.

The present Treaty, which is designed to ensure the maintenance of peace, and is in conformity with the Covenant of the League of Nations, shall not be interpreted as restricting the duty of the League to take whatever action may be deemed wise and effectual to safeguard the peace of the world.

ARTICLE 8.

The present Treaty shall be registered at the League of Nations in accordance with the Covenant of the League. It shall remain in force until the Council, acting on a request of one or other of the High Contracting Parties notified to the other signatory Powers three months in advance, and voting at least by a two-thirds' majority, decides that the League of Nations ensures sufficient protection to the High Contracting Parties; the Treaty shall cease to have effect on the expiration of a period of one year from such decision.

ARTICLE 9.

The present Treaty shall impose no obligation upon any of the British dominions, or upon India, unless the Government of such dominion, or of India, signifies its acceptance thereof.

ARTICLE 10.

The present Treaty shall be ratified and the ratifications shall be deposited at Geneva in the archives of the League of Nations as soon as possible.

It shall enter into force as soon as all the ratifications have been deposited and Germany has become a Member of the League of Nations.

The present Treaty, done in a single copy, will be deposited in the archives of the League of Nations, and the Secretary-General will be requested to transmit certified copies to each of the High Contracting Parties.

In faith whereof the above-mentioned Plenipotentiaries have signed the present Treaty.

Done at Locarno, October 16, 1925.

55. THE PARIS (BRIAND-KELLOGG) PACT, 1928 [9]

On April 6, 1927, the French Foreign Minister, Aristide Briand, proposed the negotiation of a Franco-American treaty "mutually outlawing war." After several months of correspondence the American Secretary of State, Frank B. Kellogg, suggested the drafting of a general anti-war pact open to all nations. Most League powers responded readily to this plan for, upon signing the League Covenant, they had already promised to regard war only as a means of last recourse. On August 27, 1928, then, the representatives of fifteen invited states signed the Treaty for the Renunciation of War, in Paris. It became effective on March 2, 1929, and soon received numerous additional adherences. Eventually it appeared, ironically, that the Paris Pact gave rise to a new phenomenon in international relations, the "undeclared war."

The President of the German Reich, the President of the United States of America, His Majesty the King of the Belgians, the President of the French Republic, His Majesty the King of Great Britain, Ireland and the British Dominions beyond the Seas, Emperor of India, His Majesty the King of Italy, His Majesty the Emperor of Japan, the President of the Republic of Poland, the President of the Czechoslovak Republic,

Deeply sensible of their solemn duty to promote the welfare of mankind;

Persuaded that the time has come when a frank renunciation of war as an instrument of national policy should be made to the end that the peaceful and friendly relations now existing between their peoples may be perpetuated;

Convinced that all changes in their relations with one another should be sought only by pacific means and be the result of a peaceful and orderly process, and that any signatory Power which shall hereafter seek to promote its national interests by resort to war should be denied the benefits furnished by this Treaty;

Hopeful that, encouraged by their example, all the other nations of the world will join in this humane endeavor and by adhering to the present Treaty as soon as it comes into force bring their peoples within

---

[9] United States, Department of State, *The General Pact for the Renunciation of War, Text of the Pact as Signed, Notes and Other Papers,* Government Printing Office, Washington, 1928, pp. 1-3.

the scope of its beneficent provisions, thus uniting the civilized nations of the world in a common renunciation of war as an instrument of their national policy;

Have decided to conclude a Treaty and for that purpose have appointed as their respective Plenipotentiaries:

[*Names of Plenipotentiaries omitted.*]

who, having communicated to one another their full powers found in good and due form have agreed upon the following articles:

ARTICLE 1.

The High Contracting Parties solemnly declare in the names of their respective peoples that they condemn recourse to war for the solution of international controversies, and renounce it as an instrument of national policy in their relations with one another.

ARTICLE 2.

The High Contracting Parties agree that the settlement or solution of all disputes or conflicts of whatever nature or of whatever origin they may be, which may arise among them, shall never be sought except by pacific means.

ARTICLE 3.

The present Treaty shall be ratified by the High Contracting Parties named in the Preamble in accordance with their respective constitutional requirements, and shall take effect as between them as soon as all their several instruments of ratification shall have been deposited at Washington.

This Treaty shall, when it has come into effect as prescribed in the preceding paragraph, remain open as long as may be necessary for adherence by all the other Powers of the world. Every instrument evidencing the adherence of a Power shall be deposited at Washington and the Treaty shall immediately upon such deposit become effective as between the Power thus adhering and the other Powers parties hereto.

It shall be the duty of the Government of the United States to furnish each Government named in the Preamble and every Government subsequently adhering to this Treaty with a certified copy of the Treaty and of every instrument of ratification or adherence. It shall also be the duty of the Government of the United States telegraphically to

notify such Governments immediately upon the deposit with it of
each instrument of ratification or adherence.

In faith whereof the respective Plenipotentiaries have signed this
Treaty in the French and English languages both texts having equal
force, and hereunto affix their seals.

*Done at Paris, the twenty-seventh day of August in the year one
thousand nine hundred and twenty-eight.*

56-57. THE PROJECT OF A EUROPEAN UNION

56. FRENCH MEMORANDUM ON THE ORGANIZATION OF A EUROPEAN FEDERAL UNION, MAY 1, 1930 *(Extracts)* [10]

*The increasingly noticeable effects of the Great Depression led, among
other things, to a French proposal for the organization of a European federal
union. The plan had political as well as economic aspects and came to
naught.*

At a preliminary meeting held in Geneva on September 9th, 1929,
at the request of the French representative, the authorised representatives of the twenty-seven European States which are Members of the
League of Nations were invited to consider the advantages of an agreement between the interested Governments having as its object the
creation, among the nations of Europe, of some kind of federal bond
establishing between them a system of constant solidarity, and allowing
them, whenever necessary, to get into touch immediately to study,
discuss and settle problems likely to be of common interest.

Having unanimously recognised the need for some effort in this
direction, the representatives who were consulted all undertook to
recommend to their respective Governments the consideration of the
question which had been directly submitted to them by the French
representative, who had also taken the opportunity, on September 5th,
of raising the matter before the Tenth Assembly of the League of
Nations. . . .

The proposal examined by twenty-seven European Governments
found its justification in the very definite feeling of collective responsi-

---

[10] League of Nations, *Documents Relating to the Organisation of a System of European Federal Union,* Geneva, 1930, pp. 9-14.

bility in face of the danger which threatens the peace of Europe, from the political as well as from the economic and social points of view, as a result of the essential lack of unity in the organisation of Europe. . . .

No one to-day doubts that the lack of cohesion in the grouping of the material and moral forces of Europe does in fact constitute the most serious obstacle to the development and efficiency of all political or judicial institutions on which the foundations of any universal organisation of peace tend to be based. This dispersion of energy does not limit less seriously, in Europe, the possibilities of enlarging the economic market, the attempts at intensifying and ameliorating industrial production, and thereby every guarantee against labour crises, which are sources of both political and social instability. Moreover, the danger of such division is still further increased by the extent of the new frontiers (more than 20,000 kilometres of Customs barriers) which the peace treaties have had to create, in order to satisfy national aspirations in Europe.

The very activities of the League of Nations, whose responsibilities are rendered all the more heavy by the fact that it is a universal organisation, might meet with serious obstruction in Europe if these territorial divisions were not counteracted at the earliest moment by a bond of solidarity enabling the nations of Europe to realise at last the geographical unity of Europe, and to bring about, within the framework of the League, one of the regional understandings which the pact has formally recommended. . . .

It is in no way proposed to form a European group outside the League of Nations, but, on the contrary, to bring European interests into harmony under the control of, and in conformity with, the spirit of the League of Nations, by creating within its universal organisation an organisation which, for being limited, would be all the more effective. . . .

Far from constituting a fresh tribunal for the settlement of disputes, the European association, which could not be called upon in such matters to use its good offices except in a purely consultative capacity, would not be competent to deal fully with particular problems for the settlement of which a special procedure of the League of Nations or some other expressly defined procedure has been laid down by the Covenant or by treaties. . . .

Accordingly, the French representative was careful, from the be-

ginning, to avoid all ambiguity when, taking the initiative at the first
European reunion, he expressed the opinion that it should include
only representatives of the States which are Members of the League of
Nations,[11] and should meet at Geneva on the occasion of the Tenth
Assembly—that is to say, in the atmosphere and within the framework
of the League of Nations. . . .

The policy of European union, towards which must tend the present
search for the link of solidarity between the Governments of Europe,
implies, in effect, a conception absolutely contrary to that which formerly led to the creation in Europe of Customs unions, tending to
abolish internal Customs barriers in order to erect on the boundary
of the whole community a stiffer barrier—that is to say, in order to
create, in practice, a weapon against the States situated outside these
unions. . . .

It is in the light of these observations and inspired by the general
anxiety mentioned at the beginning of this Memorandum that the
Government of the Republic, in conformity with the procedure laid
down at the first European reunion of September 9th, 1929, have the
honour to submit to-day for consideration by the Governments concerned a statement of the different points on which they are invited to
give their opinion.

I.

Need for a General Agreement, however Summary It May Be, to
Affirm the Principle of the Moral Union of Europe and to
Place Formally on Record the Existence of the Solidarity
Established between the States of Europe.

. . . . .

II.

Need for Machinery Which Will Secure for the European Union
the Organs Essential for the Accomplishment of Its Task.

. . . . .

III.

Need for Laying down in Advance the Essential Principles Which
Shall Determine the General Conceptions of the European

---

[11] This position automatically excluded the Soviet Union, which was not a League
member at the time.—*Ed.*

COMMITTEE AND GUIDE IT IN THE ENQUIRIES WHICH IT MAKES FOR
THE PURPOSE OF PREPARING THE PROGRAMME OF THE EUROPEAN
ORGANISATION.

. . . . .

IV.

ADVISABILITY OF RESERVING, EITHER FOR THE NEXT EUROPEAN CONFER-
ENCE OR FOR THE FUTURE EUROPEAN COMMITTEE, THE STUDY OF ALL
QUESTIONS OF PRACTICAL APPLICATION.

. . . . .

The Government of the Republic are very anxious to receive before
July 15th the replies of the Governments consulted, with any observations or spontaneous suggestions which they might care to add to their
communications. . . .

57. GENERAL CONCLUSIONS DRAWN FROM THE REPLIES TO THE FRENCH MEMORANDUM OF MAY 1, 1930, ON A EUROPEAN FEDERAL UNION [12]

*The French memorandum of May 1, 1930, on a European federal union
was answered by twenty-six states. The full texts of the replies may be
found on pages 17-66 of the League reference cited for the present document. The following general conclusions drawn from the replies were made
public by France on September 8, 1930.*

According to its own conception of its duties, it is not for the reporting Government [France]—after merely giving an analytical summary
of the opinions independently expressed by all the Governments consulted—to attempt to draw substantive conclusions. . . .

From among these indications, however, it is the duty of the Rapporteur to extract the most urgent—that is to say, those which seem
to call for immediate discussion.

All the Governments consulted share the French Government's
desire to place the proposed Union definitely under the moral authority

---

[12] League of Nations, *Documents Relating to the Organisation of a System of European Federal Union*, Geneva, 1930, p. 77.

of the League of Nations. The European Conference should begin to discuss this point fairly promptly so as to have sufficient time to consider the conditions and the form in which the Assembly's views ought to be ascertained.

Several Governments, moreover, have proposed that representatives of States which are not Members of the League should be invited to attend the meetings of the European Conference from the beginning. Here, again, before the point is discussed at all, consideration must be given to the propriety of ascertaining the feeling of the League.

The British Government's proposal that the consultation itself, in its present form, should be brought to the Assembly's notice, would mean in practice an equally prompt discussion.

The same would apply to any declaration, resolution or draft motion which it might, as the outcome of the first European meeting, seem proper to communicate to the Assembly. . . .

Such are the immediate and preliminary obligations that seem incumbent upon this first European Conference; . . . If, as has been asserted unanimously and with conviction, this Union answers to a vital European need, it will be the task of the forces of evolution, aided by the will of the peoples, to insure its regular and unimpeded development.

September 8th, 1930.

58. THE LONDON NAVAL TREATY, 1930 *(Extracts)* [13]

~~~~~~

In October 1929 Premier MacDonald came to visit President Hoover in the United States. One of the results of their conversations was the calling of a five-power naval conference in London on January 21, 1930. There, on April 22, 1930, the United States, Great Britain, Japan, France, and Italy signed the London Naval Treaty, but the two last, because of their rivalry for control of the western Mediterranean, withheld their signatures from the most vital parts of the agreement. The final document, therefore, which was proclaimed on January 1, 1931, partook of the nature of a tripartite agreement among the United States, Great Britain, and Japan. Especially interesting was Article 21, the "escalator clause."

~~~~~~

---

[13] League of Nations, *Treaty Series 1931*, vol. CXII, pp. 66-91.

PART I.

ARTICLE 1.

The High Contracting Parties agree not to exercise their rights to lay down the keels of capital ship replacement tonnage during the years 1931-1936, inclusive, as provided in . . . the Treaty for the Limitation of Naval Armament signed between them at Washington on the 6th February, 1922, . . .

. . . . .

PART III.

The President of the United States of America, His Majesty the King of Great Britain, Ireland and the British Dominions beyond the Seas, Emperor of India, and His Majesty the Emperor of Japan, have agreed as between themselves to the provisions of this Part III:

. . . . .

ARTICLE 16.

1. The completed tonnage in the cruiser, destroyer and submarine categories which is not to be exceeded on the 31st December, 1936, is given in the following table:

Categories	United States	British Commonwealth of Nations	Japan
Cruisers:			
(a) with guns of more than 6.1-inch (155 mm.) calibre.	180,000 tons (182,880 metric tons)	146,800 tons (149,149 metric tons)	108,400 tons (110,134 metric tons)
(b) with guns of 6.1-inch calibre or less.	143,500 tons (145,796 metric tons)	192,200 tons (195,275 metric tons)	100,450 tons (102,057 metric tons)
Destroyers	150,000 tons (152,400 metric tons)	150,000 tons (152,400 metric tons)	150,000 tons (152,400 metric tons)
Submarines	52,700 tons (53,543 metric tons)	52,700 tons (53,543 metric tons)	52,700 tons (53,543 metric tons)

2. Vessels which cause the total tonnage in any category to exceed the figures given in the foregoing table shall be disposed of gradually during the period ending on the 31st December, 1936.

3. The maximum number of cruisers of sub-category (a) shall be as follows: for the United States, eighteen; for the British Commonwealth of Nations, fifteen; for Japan, twelve.

. . . . .

Article 21.

If, during the term of the present Treaty, the requirements of the national security of any High Contracting Party in respect of vessels of war limited by Part III of the present Treaty are, in the opinion of that Party, materially affected by new construction of any other Power other than those who have joined in Part III of this Treaty, that High Contracting Party will notify the other Parties to Part III as to the increase required to be made in its own tonnages within one or more of the categories of such vessels of war, specifying particularly the proposed increases and the reasons therefor, and shall be entitled to make such increase. Thereupon the other Parties to Part III of this Treaty shall be entitled to make a proportionate increase in the category or categories specified; and the said other Parties shall promptly advise with each other through diplomatic channels as to the situation thus presented.

PART IV.

Article 22.

The following are accepted as established rules of International Law:

(1) In their action with regard to merchant ships, submarines must conform to the rules of International Law to which surface vessels are subject.

(2) In particular, except in case of persistent refusal to stop on being duly summoned, or of active resistance to visit or search, a warship, whether surface vessel or submarine, may not sink or render incapable of navigation a merchant vessel without having first placed passengers, crew and ship's papers in a place of safety. For this purpose the ship's boats are not regarded as a place of safety unless the safety of the passengers and crew is assured, in the existing sea and weather conditions, by the proximity of land, or the presence of another vessel which is in a position to take them on board.

The High Contracting Parties invite all other Powers to express their assent to the above rules.

PART V.

Article 23.

The present Treaty shall remain in force until the 31st December, 1936, subject to the following exceptions:

(1) Part IV shall remain in force without limit of time;

(2) The provisions of Articles 3, 4 and 5, and of Article 11 and Annex II to Part II so far as they relate to aircraft carriers, shall remain in force for the same period as the Washington Treaty.

Unless the High Contracting Parties should agree otherwise by reason of a more general agreement limiting naval armaments, to which they all become parties, they shall meet in conference in 1935 to frame a new treaty to replace and to carry out the purposes of the present Treaty, it being understood that none of the provisions of the present Treaty shall prejudice the attitude of any of the High Contracting Parties at the conference agreed to.

. . . . .

Done at London, the twenty-second day of April, nineteen hundred and thirty.

59. THE GREAT POWERS AND DISARMAMENT, 1932-1934 [14]

Early in 1931 the League Council, in accordance with its obligations under Article 8 of the Covenant, summoned the world's first disarmament conference to meet at Geneva on February 2, 1932. When the delegates, representing about sixty states, assembled, they were presented with a draft disarmament convention compiled by a preparatory commission. This document, to which were appended numerous reservations, indicated the methods of limitation that might be adopted but left all concrete decisions as to ratios and figures to be decided by the conference itself. Unable to agree on any vital point, the conference dragged on to a weary adjournment in July 1932. Then, on February 2, 1933, after the powers had recognized in principle Germany's right to equality in armaments, the conference reassembled; but in June, having accomplished virtually nothing, it adjourned until October 16. Two days before the delegates regathered, news came of Germany's withdrawal (because of her impatience with these dilatory tactics) from the conference and intended withdrawal from the League. The conference thereupon acted only to adjourn. Finally, after several further adjournments, it reassembled in May 1934. The situation at that point was well described in the appended quotation.

[14] J. W. Wheeler-Bennett, *The Pipe Dream of Peace. The Story of the Collapse of Disarmament,* William Morrow & Company, New York, 1935, pp. 227-230. Reprinted by permission of the publishers.

The respective positions of the Great Powers, therefore, on the eve of the reassembly of the General Commission of the Conference on 29th May [1934] was (*sic*) as follows:—

Germany, in the Note to Great Britain of 16th April, had assumed a not unreasonable attitude. She had agreed to the postponement of the reduction of armaments of other Powers for five years after the signature of a Convention; had accepted the proposals for supervision and control of armaments contained in the British Memorandum of 29th January, and was agreeable, on the basis of reciprocity, to the regulations suggested by the British Government for ensuring the non-military character of the S.A. and S.S.[15] On the other hand, she had insisted upon her 300,000 men for the *Reichswehr* and upon "a defensive air force of short-range machines, not including bombing planes, from the beginning of the Convention, the numerical strength of which would not exceed 30 per cent of the combined air forces of Germany's neighbours or 50 per cent of the military aircraft possessed by France (in France itself and in the French North African territories) whichever figure was the less." This would suffice Germany for the first five years of a ten years' Convention, "but after those five years she claims that the necessary reduction and increases should be made so that she should attain full equality of numbers with the principal Air Powers at the end of the ten years of the Convention." She refused to discuss the question of her return to the League until after the question of disarmament and of equality of rights had been settled, and by the publication of her military estimates on 29th March had given notice to the world that in her claims and intention to rearm she remained adamant, . . .

Great Britain, though her action had been belated, had made an honest effort to bridge the gulf between Germany and France. She had gone a long way in her concessions to the German point of view regarding rearmament and, in the matter of French security, had made a considerable departure from her traditional policy, first in offering to participate in a Pact of Consultation and, later, in asking France what form of "guarantees" she really did consider necessary to her security.

France alone had remained consistent and had steadfastly refused to consider any agreement which recognized the immediate rearmament

---

[15] The Storm Troops (*Sturmabteilungen*) and so-called Elite Guards (*Schutzstaffeln*). —*Ed.*

of Germany. She had considered the British offer to consult in the event of a breach of the Disarmament Convention as insufficient and . . . her interest in "guarantees" had waned as British interest in that subject had increased. Finally, she had seized upon the publication of the German military estimates to terminate the diplomatic exchanges and to call for a return to Geneva and the Policy of October, 1933.

The attitude of *Italy* had perhaps been the most helpful of all, for she had not only put forward a very practical plan of her own, but had also declared her willingness to agree to any formula acceptable to the other nations.

In effect, therefore, the position had undergone little change since the withdrawal of Germany from the Conference, save that she had made further progress towards her own rearmament. No success had attended the efforts to bridge the gap between Paris and Berlin, and in endeavouring to do so a definite rift had occurred between Great Britain and France. Failing to secure the required degree of support from her former ally, France had turned more and more towards the Soviet Union, and was not unhopeful of securing not only the entry of the U.S.S.R. into the League of Nations, but also a pact of mutual guarantee with that country. . . .[16]

The proposals of the *Soviet Union,* which were discussed by MM. Litvinoff and Barthou[17] in a conversation of great importance on the evening of 18th May, were for a definite European Pact of Non-Aggression and Mutual Assistance. . . .

The General Commission of the Disarmament Conference reassembled on 29th May [1934], after an interval of seven months, in an atmosphere of gloom and fatalistic pessimism. On all sides it was felt that the meeting partook of the character of a "wake," and interest was concentrated mainly upon the nature of the funeral orations. Disarmament had been dead for some considerable time; the chances of limitation of armaments were by this time of the slimmest, and rearmament seemed to be the word of the moment.[18]

---

[16] The Soviet Union became a member of the League in September 1934; a Franco-Soviet pact of mutual assistance was signed on May 2, 1935.—*Ed.*

[17] Foreign ministers of the Soviet Union and France, respectively.—*Ed.*

[18] The conference dispersed once more, after a few days of wrangling. Thereafter all the Great Powers voted increasing armament appropriations and Germany made it clear that equality she would achieve—if not in disarmament, then in rearmament.—*Ed.*

60. THE WITHDRAWAL OF GERMANY FROM THE DISARMAMENT CONFERENCE, 1933 [19]

The note announcing Germany's withdrawal from the World Disarmament Conference was both clear and brief.

TELEGRAM FROM THE GERMAN MINISTER FOR FOREIGN AFFAIRS TO MR. HENDERSON. [20]

Berlin, October 14, 1933.

On behalf of the German Government, I have the honour to make to you the following communication:—

In the light of the course which recent discussions of the Powers concerned have taken in the matter of disarmament, it is now clear that the Disarmament Conference will not fulfil what was its sole object, namely, general disarmament. It is also clear that this failure of the conference is due solely to the unwillingness on the part of the highly-armed States to carry out their contractual obligation to disarm. This renders impossible the satisfaction of Germany's recognised claim to equality of rights, and the condition on which the German Government agreed at the beginning of this year again to take part in the work of the conference thus no longer exists.

The German Government is accordingly compelled to leave the Disarmament Conference.

BARON VON NEURATH.

61. PAN-AMERICAN (ARGENTINE) ANTI-WAR TREATY OF NON-AGGRESSION AND CONCILIATION, 1933 *(Extracts)* [21]

Four days before Germany left the World Disarmament Conference, six states in the western hemisphere (Argentina, Brazil, Chile, Mexico, Paraguay, and Uruguay) signed a treaty of non-aggression at Rio de Janeiro. This agreement, signed October 10, 1933, contained an interesting provision

---

[19] *Proceedings of the Bureau of the Disarmament Conference, Geneva, October 14, 1933. Presented by the Secretary of State for Foreign Affairs to Parliament by Command of His Majesty,* Misc. No. 5 (1933), Cmd. 4437, His Majesty's Stationery Office, London, 1933, p. 11.

[20] Arthur Henderson was president of the conference.—*Ed.*

[21] *The Statutes at Large of the United States of America from January 1935 to June 1936,* Government Printing Office, Washington, 1936, vol. 49, pt. 2, pp. 3375-3378.

that the signatories would refuse to recognize territorial changes brought about through violence. Numerous adherences, including that of the United States, followed, and President Franklin D. Roosevelt proclaimed the treaty on March 11, 1936.

ARTICLE 1.

The high contracting parties solemnly declare that they condemn wars of aggression in their mutual relations or in those with other states, and that the settlement of disputes or controversies of any kind that may arise among them shall be effected only by the pacific means which have the sanction of international law.

ARTICLE 2.

They declare that as between the high contracting parties territorial questions must not be settled by violence, and that they will not recognize any territorial arrangement which is not obtained by pacific means, nor the validity of the occupation or acquisition of territories that may be brought about by force of arms.

ARTICLE 3.

In case of noncompliance, by any state engaged in a dispute, with the obligations contained in the foregoing articles, the contracting states undertake to make every effort for the maintenance of peace. To that end they will adopt in their character as neutrals a common and solidary attitude; they will exercise the political, juridical, or economic means authorized by international law; they will bring the influence of public opinion to bear, but will in no case resort to intervention, either diplomatic or armed; subject to the attitude that may be incumbent upon them by virtue of other collective treaties to which such states are signatories.

ARTICLE 4.

The high contracting parties obligate themselves to submit to the conciliation procedure established by this treaty the disputes specially mentioned and any others that may arise in their reciprocal relations, . . . in all controversies which it has not been possible to settle by diplomatic means within a reasonable period of time.

. . . . .

ARTICLE 15.

The present treaty shall be ratified by the high contracting parties as soon as possible, in accordance with their respective constitutional procedures.

The original treaty and the instruments of ratification shall be deposited in the Ministry of Foreign Relations and Worship of the Argentine Republic, which shall communicate the ratifications to the other signatory states. The treaty shall go into effect between the high contracting parties 30 days after the deposit of the respective ratifications, and in the order in which they are effected.

ARTICLE 16.

This treaty shall remain open to the adherence of all states. . . .

ARTICLE 17.

The present treaty is concluded for an indefinite time, but may be denounced on 1 year's notice, on the expiration of which the effects thereof shall cease for the denouncing state, and remain in force for the other states which are parties thereto, by signature or adherence. . . .

62. THE PACT OF ROME, 1933 [22]

The intensity of the international rivalry demonstrated at the failing disarmament conference led Premier Benito Mussolini to suggest a four-power pact among the great western states guaranteeing peace for at least a stated period. The result of this proposal was the initialling (June 7, 1933) and eventual signing (July 15, 1933) of the Pact of Rome of ten years' (stated) duration. As first suggested by Mussolini, the pact was to be fairly specific, particularly with respect to possible treaty revisions, but when Poland and the Little Entente objected to this as possibly endangering the rights of the smaller nations, France insisted that the original terms be made more general.

. . . . .

ANNEX.

AGREEMENT OF UNDERSTANDING AND CO-OPERATION.

. . . . .

---

[22] *Despatch to His Majesty's Ambassador at Rome in Regard to the Agreement of Understanding and Co-operation between France, Germany, Italy, and the United Kingdom, London, June 7, 1933. Presented by the Secretary of State for Foreign Affairs to Parliament by Command of His Majesty, Cmd. 4342, His Majesty's Stationery Office, London, 1933, pp. 6-9.*

ARTICLE 1.

The High Contracting Parties will consult together as regards all questions which appertain to them. They undertake to make every effort to pursue, within the framework of the League of Nations, a policy of effective co-operation between all Powers with a view to the maintenance of peace.

ARTICLE 2.

In respect of the Covenant of the League of Nations, and particularly articles 10, 16 and 19, the High Contracting Parties agree to examine between themselves and without prejudice to decisions which can only be taken by the regular organs of the League of Nations, all proposals relating to methods and procedure calculated to give due effect to these articles.

ARTICLE 3.

The High Contracting Parties undertake to make every effort to ensure the success of the Disarmament Conference and, should questions which particularly concern them remain in suspense on the conclusion of that Conference, they reserve the right to re-examine these questions between themselves in pursuance of the present agreement with a view to ensuring their solution through the appropriate channels.

ARTICLE 4.

The High Contracting Parties affirm their desire to consult together as regards all economic questions which have a common interest for Europe and particularly for its economic restoration, with a view to seeking a settlement within the framework of the League of Nations.

ARTICLE 5.

The present agreement is concluded for a period of ten years from the date of its entry into force.

If, before the end of the eighth year, none of the High Contracting Parties shall have notified to the others his intention to terminate the agreement, it shall be regarded as renewed and will remain in force indefinitely, each of the High Contracting Parties possessing in that event the right to terminate it by a declaration to that effect on giving two years' notice.

. . . . .

63. THE STRESA RESOLUTION, 1935 *(Extracts)* [23]

Germany's denunciation, on March 16, 1935, of the military restrictions of the Versailles Treaty precipitated a meeting (already previously contemplated) of representatives of Great Britain, France, and Italy at Stresa from April 11 to 14. The principles there affirmed or reaffirmed might have had far-reaching consequences for the future of European international relations—had they really been put into practice.

The Representatives of the Governments of Italy, France and the United Kingdom have examined at Stresa the general European situation in the light of the results of the exchanges of views which have taken place in recent weeks, of the decision taken on the 16th March by the German Government, and of the information obtained by British Ministers during the visits recently paid by them to several European capitals. Having considered the bearing of this situation on the policy defined in the arrangements reached respectively in Rome and in London, they found themselves in complete agreement on the various matters discussed.   . . . . .

They confirmed the Anglo-French-Italian declarations of the 17th February and the 27th September, 1934, in which the three Governments recognised that the necessity of maintaining the independence and integrity of Austria would continue to inspire their common policy.   . . . . .

It was regretfully recognised that the method of unilateral repudiation adopted by the German Government, at a moment when steps were being taken to promote a freely negotiated settlement of the question of armaments, had undermined public confidence in the security of a peaceful order. . . .

. . . . .

The following joint Declaration was made by the Representatives of Italy and the United Kingdom in reference to the Treaty of Locarno:—

The Representatives of Italy and of the United Kingdom, the

---

[23] *Joint Resolution of the Stresa Conference, Including the Anglo-Italian Declaration and the Final Declaration, Stresa, April 14, 1935. Presented by the Secretary of State for Foreign Affairs to Parliament by Command of His Majesty,* Misc. No. 2 (1935), Cmd. 4880, His Majesty's Stationery Office, London, 1935, pp. 2-4.

Powers which participate in the Treaty of Locarno only in the capacity of guarantors, formally reaffirm all their obligations under that Treaty, and declare their intention, should the need arise, faithfully to fulfil them.

. . . . .

The three Powers, the object of whose policy is the collective maintenance of peace within the framework of the League of Nations, find themselves in complete agreement in opposing, by all practicable means, any unilateral repudiation of treaties which may endanger the peace of Europe, and will act in close and cordial collaboration for this purpose.

64. THE FRANCO-SOVIET TREATY OF MUTUAL ASSISTANCE, 1935 *(Extracts)* [24]

French and Soviet fears of Germany's military renaissance, France's desire to gain access to the great oil resources and a larger share of the foreign trade of the Soviet Union, and Moscow's growing uneasiness over the Nazi denunciations of communism and references to eastward fields of expansion, led to the signing, on May 2, 1935, of a Franco-Soviet five-year pact of mutual assistance. Ratifications were exchanged on March 27, 1936. In the autumn of 1938, following the four-power settlement of Germany's claims in Czechoslovakia, it appeared for a time that France might be weaned away from this post-war parallel of the Franco-Russian Alliance of 1894.

ARTICLE 1.

In the event of France or the U.S.S.R. being threatened with, or in danger of, attack on the part of a European State, the U.S.S.R., and, reciprocally, France, undertake to proceed mutually to immediate consultation as regards the measures to be taken for the observance of the provisions of Article 10 of the Covenant of the League of Nations.

ARTICLE 2.

In the event of France or the U.S.S.R., in the circumstances specified in Article 15, paragraph 7, of the League of Nations Covenant, being

[24] *Correspondence Showing the Course of Certain Diplomatic Discussions Directed Towards Securing an European Settlement, June 1934 to March 1936. Presented by the Secretary of State for Foreign Affairs to Parliament by Command of His Majesty,* Misc. No. 3 (1936), Cmd. 5143, His Majesty's Stationery Office, London, 1936, pp. 26-29.

the object, in spite of the genuinely peaceful intentions of both countries, of an unprovoked attack on the part of a European State, the U.S.S.R., and, reciprocally, France, shall immediately give each other aid and assistance.

ARTICLE 3.

In consideration of the fact that under Article 16 of the Covenant of the League of Nations any member of the League who has recourse to war contrary to the obligations undertaken in Articles 12, 13 and 15 of the Covenant is *ipso facto* considered as having committed an act of war against all the other members of the League, France, and, reciprocally, the U.S.S.R. undertake in the event of one of them being the object, in these circumstances and in spite of the genuinely peaceful intentions of both countries, of an unprovoked attack on the part of a European State, to give each other immediately aid and assistance in execution of Article 16 of the Covenant.

The same obligation is assumed in the event of France or the U.S.S.R. being the object of an attack on the part of a European State in the circumstances specified in Article 17, paragraphs 1 and 3 of the Covenant of the League of Nations.[25]

. . . . .

PROTOCOL OF SIGNATURE.

. . . . .

II. The joint purpose of both Governments being in no way to invalidate by the present Treaty the obligations previously undertaken by France and the U.S.S.R. towards third countries, in published treaties, it is agreed that effect shall not be given to the provisions of the aforesaid Treaty in a way which, being inconsistent with the treaty obligations assumed by one of the contracting parties, would expose the latter to sanctions of an international character.

. . . . .

IV. The two Governments declare that the negotiations which have just resulted in the signature of the present Treaty were originally started with a view to drawing up a security agreement covering all the countries of North-Eastern Europe, namely, the U.S.S.R., Germany, Czechoslovakia, Poland and the Baltic States neighbours of the

---

[25] For texts of all League Covenant articles, see Doc. No. 14.—*Ed.*

U.S.S.R.; besides this agreement a treaty of assistance between the U.S.S.R., France and Germany was to have been concluded, under which each of these three States would be pledged to come to the assistance of that one among them which had been the object of an attack by one of these three States. . . .

Done at Paris, this 2nd day of May, 1935.

Pierre Laval.

Vladimir Potemkin.

65. THE ANGLO-GERMAN NAVAL AGREEMENT OF 1935 [26]

On May 21, 1935, Reichsführer Adolf Hitler outlined the German position on thirteen "present issues." The eighth issue concerned armaments, and here Hitler repeated a previous declaration that "the limitation of the German navy is placed at 35 per cent" of the British Commonwealth navy. This statement led to Anglo-German naval conversations in London which culminated on June 18, 1935, in an exchange of notes. The agreement aroused protests not merely in Great Britain but in France and Italy where it was felt that the British were condoning a new violation of the Versailles Treaty. To this charge the British First Lord of the Admiralty replied in parliament (June 21, 1935) saying: "Germany is already constructing a fleet which is outside the limits laid down in the Versailles Treaty; what we have done is, by agreement with Germany, to circumscribe the effects which might flow from this unilateral decision of Germany." On April 28, 1939, Germany declared the agreement of 1935 to have been "nullified" by Britain's new "encirclement policy."

SIR SAMUEL HOARE TO HERR VON RIBBENTROP.

Foreign Office, June 18, 1935.

Your Excellency,

During the last few days the representatives of the German Government and His Majesty's Government in the United Kingdom have been engaged in conversations, the primary purpose of which has been to prepare the way for the holding of a general conference on the

---

[26] *Exchange of Notes between His Majesty's Government in the United Kingdom and the German Government Regarding the Limitation of Naval Armaments, London, June 18, 1935. Presented by the Secretary of State for Foreign Affairs to Parliament by Command of His Majesty,* Treaty Series No. 22 (1935), Cmd. 4953, His Majesty's Stationery Office, London, 1935, pp. 2-4.

subject of the limitation of naval armaments. I have now much pleasure in notifying your Excellency of the formal acceptance by His Majesty's Government in the United Kingdom of the proposal of the German Government discussed at those conversations that the future strength of the German navy in relation to the aggregate naval strength of the Members of the British Commonwealth of Nations should be in the proportion of 35:100. His Majesty's Government in the United Kingdom regard this proposal as a contribution of the greatest importance to the cause of future naval limitation. They further believe that the agreement which they have now reached with the German Government, and which they regard as a permanent and definite agreement as from to-day between the two Governments, will facilitate the conclusion of a general agreement on the subject of naval limitation between all the naval Powers of the world.

2. His Majesty's Government in the United Kingdom also agree with the explanations which were furnished by the German representatives in the course of the recent discussions in London as to the method of application of this principle. These explanations may be summarised as follows:—

(*a*) The ratio of 35:100 is to be a permanent relationship, *i.e.,* the total tonnage of the German fleet shall never exceed a percentage of 35 of the aggregate tonnage of the naval forces, as defined by treaty, of the Members of the British Commonwealth of Nations, or, if there should in future be no treaty limitations of this tonnage, a percentage of 35 of the aggregate of the actual tonnages of the Members of the British Commonwealth of Nations.

(*b*) If any future general treaty of naval limitation should not adopt the method of limitation by agreed ratios between the fleets of different Powers, the German Government will not insist on the incorporation of the ratio mentioned in the preceding sub-paragraph in such future general treaty, provided that the method therein adopted for the future limitation of naval armaments is such as to give Germany full guarantees that this ratio can be maintained.

(*c*) Germany will adhere to the ratio 35:100 in all circumstances, *e.g.,* the ratio will not be affected by the construction of other Powers. If the general equilibrium of naval armaments, as normally maintained in the past, should be violently upset by any abnormal and exceptional construction by other Powers, the German Government reserve the right to invite His Majesty's Government in the United Kingdom to examine the new situation thus created.

(*d*) The German Government favour, in the matter of limitation of naval armaments, that system which divides naval vessels into categories, fixing the maximum tonnage and/or armament for vessels in each category, and allocates the tonnage to be allowed to each Power by categories of vessels. Consequently, in principle, and subject to (*f*) below, the German Government are prepared to apply the 35 per cent. ratio to the tonnage of each category of vessel to be maintained, and to make any variation of this ratio in a particular category or categories dependent on the arrangements to this end that may be arrived at in a future general treaty on naval limitation, such arrangements being based on the principle that any increase in one category would be compensated for by a corresponding reduction in others. If no general treaty on naval limitation should be concluded, or if the future general treaty should not contain provision creating limitation by categories, the manner and degree in which the German Government will have the right to vary the 35 per cent. ratio in one or more categories will be a matter for settlement by agreement between the German Government and His Majesty's Government in the United Kingdom, in the light of the naval situation then existing.

(*e*) If, and for so long as, other important naval Powers retain a single category for cruisers and destroyers, Germany shall enjoy the right to have a single category for these two classes of vessels, although she would prefer to see these classes in two categories.

(*f*) In the matter of submarines, however, Germany, while not exceeding the ratio of 35:100 in respect of total tonnage, shall have the right to possess a submarine tonnage equal to the total submarine tonnage possessed by the Members of the British Commonwealth of Nations. The German Government, however, undertake that, except in the circumstances indicated in the immediately following sentence, Germany's submarine tonnage shall not exceed 45 per cent. of the total of that possessed by the Members of the British Commonwealth of Nations. The German Government reserve the right, in the event of a situation arising which in their opinion makes it necessary for Germany to avail herself of her right to a percentage of submarine tonnage exceeding the 45 per cent. above mentioned, to give notice to this effect to His Majesty's Government in the United Kingdom, and agree that the matter shall be the subject of friendly discussion before the German Government exercise that right.

(*g*) Since it is highly improbable that the calculation of the 35 per cent. ratio should give for each category of vessels tonnage figures exactly divisible by the maximum individual tonnage permitted for ships in that category, it may be necessary that adjustments should be made in order that Germany shall not be debarred from utilising her tonnage to the full. It has consequently been agreed that the German Government and His Majesty's Government in the United Kingdom will settle by common accord what adjustments are necessary for this purpose, and it is understood that this procedure shall not result in any substantial or permanent departure from the ratio 35:100 in respect of total strengths.

3. With reference to sub-paragraph (c) of the explanations set out above, I have the honour to inform you that His Majesty's Government in the United Kingdom have taken note of the reservation and recognise the right therein set out, on the understanding that the 35:100 ratio will be maintained in default of agreement to the contrary between the two Governments.

4. I have the honour to request your Excellency to inform me that the German Government agree that the proposal of the German Government has been correctly set out in the preceding paragraphs of this note.

I have the honour to be, &c.

SAMUEL HOARE.

66. THE LONDON NAVAL TREATY, 1936 *(Extracts)* [27]

Under Article 23 of the London Naval Treaty of 1930 the signatory powers were obliged to meet in conference in 1935 to replace and carry out the purposes of that agreement. On December 29, 1934, moreover, Japan gave notice of her intention to terminate the Washington Naval Treaty of 1922 on December 31, 1936, for the continuance of an unequal "upper limit" in favor of the United States and Great Britain suggested a "moral superiority" which was humiliating to Tokyo. A new London naval conference therefore assembled on December 7, 1935, representing the United States, the British Commonwealth, Japan, France, and Italy. The Japanese delegation soon withdrew, and the Italian delegation, for reasons "concerned with political events unrelated to the conference," failed to sign the final (tripartite) agreement of March 25, 1936. It was proclaimed on August 6,

[27] United States, Department of State, *Limitation of Naval Armament. Treaty between the United States of America and Other Powers,* Treaty Series, No. 919, Government Printing Office, Washington, 1937, pp. 8-35.

1937, both Germany and the Soviet Union having meanwhile (July 17, 1937) adhered. In view of the delicate Asiatic situation the Soviet Union was not required to give the stipulated information with respect to her Far Eastern fleet provided no ship of this group were transferred to the Baltic or Black seas. On December 2, 1938, Italy finally also adhered to the document. See the next document (No. 67) for further modifications of the treaty.

. . . . .

ARTICLE 2.

After the date of the coming into force of the present Treaty, no vessel exceeding the limitations as to displacement or armament prescribed by this Part of the present Treaty shall be acquired by any High Contracting Party or constructed by, for or within the jurisdiction of any High Contracting Party.

. . . . .

ARTICLE 4.

(1) No capital ship shall exceed 35,000 tons (35,560 metric tons) standard displacement.

(2) No capital ship shall carry a gun with a calibre exceeding 14 in. (356 mm.); provided however that if any of the Parties to the Treaty for the Limitation of Naval Armament signed at Washington on the 6th February, 1922, should fail to enter into an agreement to conform to this provision prior to the date of the coming into force of the present Treaty, but in any case not later than the 1st April, 1937, the maximum calibre of gun carried by capital ships shall be 16 in. (406 mm.).

(3) No capital ship of sub-category (a), the standard displacement of which is less than 17,500 tons (17,780 metric tons), shall be laid down or acquired prior to the 1st January, 1943.

(4) No capital ship, the main armament of which consists of guns of less than 10 in. (254 mm.) calibre, shall be laid down or acquired prior to the 1st January, 1943.

ARTICLE 5.

(1) No aircraft carrier shall exceed 23,000 tons (23,368 metric tons) standard displacement or carry a gun with a calibre exceeding 6.1 in. (155 mm.).

(2) If the armament of any aircraft carrier includes guns exceeding 5.25 in. (134 mm.) in calibre, the total number of guns carried which exceed that calibre shall not be more than ten.

ARTICLE 6.

(1) No light surface vessel of sub-category (*b*) exceeding 8,000 tons (8,128 metric tons) standard displacement, and no light surface vessel of sub-category (*a*) shall be laid down or acquired prior to the 1st January, 1943.

(2) Notwithstanding the provisions of paragraph (1) above, if the requirements of the national security of any High Contracting Party are, in His opinion, materially affected by the actual or authorised amount of construction by any Power of light surface vessels of sub-category (*b*), or of light surface vessels not conforming to the restrictions of paragraph (1) above, such High Contracting Party shall, upon notifying the other High Contracting Parties of His intentions and the reasons therefor, have the right to lay down or acquire light surface vessels of sub-categories (*a*) and (*b*) of any standard displacement up to 10,000 tons (10,160 metric tons) subject to the observance of the provisions of Part III of the present Treaty. Each of the other High Contracting Parties shall thereupon be entitled to exercise the same right.

(3) It is understood that the provisions of paragraph (1) above constitute no undertaking expressed or implied to continue the restrictions therein prescribed after the year 1942.

ARTICLE 7.

No submarine shall exceed 2,000 tons (2,032 metric tons) standard displacement or carry a gun exceeding 5.1 in. (130 mm.) in calibre.

· · · · ·

ARTICLE 9.

No preparations shall be made in merchant ships in time of peace for the installation of warlike armaments for the purpose of converting such ships into vessels of war, other than the necessary stiffening of decks for the mounting of guns not exceeding 6.1 in. (155 mm.) calibre.

· · · · ·

Article 11.

(1) Each of the High Contracting Parties shall communicate every year to each of the other High Contracting Parties information, as hereinafter provided, regarding His annual programme for the construction and acquisition of all vessels of the categories and sub-categories mentioned in Article 12 (*a*), whether or not the vessels concerned are constructed within His own jurisdiction, and periodical information giving details of such vessels and of any alterations to vessels of the said categories or sub-categories already completed.

(2) For the purposes of this and the succeeding Parts of the present Treaty, information shall be deemed to have reached a High Contracting Party on the date upon which such information is communicated to His Diplomatic Representatives accredited to the High Contracting Party by whom the information is given.

(3) This information shall be treated as confidential until published by the High Contracting Party supplying it.

. . . . .

Article 22.

No High Contracting Party shall, by gift, sale or any mode of transfer, dispose of any of His surface vessels of war or submarines in such manner that such vessel may become a surface vessel of war or a submarine in any foreign navy. This provision shall not apply to auxiliary vessels.

. . . . .

Article 24.

(1) If any High Contracting Party should become engaged in war, such High Contracting Party may, if He considers the naval requirements of His defence are materially affected, suspend, in so far as He is concerned, any or all of the obligations of the present Treaty, provided that He shall promptly notify the other High Contracting Parties that the circumstances require such suspension, and shall specify the obligations it is considered necessary to suspend.

(2) The other High Contracting Parties shall in such case promptly consult together, and shall examine the situation thus presented with a view to agreeing as to the obligations of the present Treaty, if any, which each of the said High Contracting Parties may suspend. Should such consultation not produce agreement, any of the said High Con-

tracting Parties may suspend, in so far as He is concerned, any or all of
the obligations of the present Treaty, provided that He shall promptly
give notice to the other High Contracting Parties of the obligations
which it is considered necessary to suspend.

(3) On the cessation of hostilities, the High Contracting Parties
shall consult together with a view to fixing a date upon which the
obligations of the Treaty which have been suspended shall again become
operative, and to agreeing upon any amendments in the present Treaty
which may be considered necessary.

. . . . .

ARTICLE 27.

The present Treaty shall remain in force until the 31st December,
1942.

. . . . .

ARTICLE 29.

None of the provisions of the present Treaty shall constitute a precedent for any future Treaty.

. . . . .

*Done in London the 25th day of March, nineteen hundred and
thirty-six.*

67. LONDON (NAVAL ARMAMENTS) PROTOCOL, JUNE 30, 1938 [28]

*The persistent refusal of Japan to furnish information respecting its naval-
construction plans led the three signatories of the London Naval Treaty of
1936 to modify this agreement through a protocol signed in London on
June 30, 1938, and effective from the same date.*

[Released for publication June 30, 12 noon]

Following the refusal of Japan to furnish information with regard

[28] United States, Department of State, *Press Releases*, Saturday, July 2, 1938, vol. XIX,
No. 457, pp. 10-11, and United States, Department of State, *Limitation of Naval Arma-
ment, Protocol between the United States of America, the French Republic, and the
United Kingdom of Great Britain and Northern Ireland, Modifying the Treaty of March
25, 1936 (Treaty Series No. 919)*, Executive Agreement Series, No. 127, Government
Printing Office, Washington, 1938, pp. 1-3.

to its naval construction, or its plans for future construction, the powers parties to the London Naval Treaty of 1936—that is, the United States, Great Britain, and France—mutually reached the decision to depart from the limits of the treaty in the battleship category and, on April 1, exchanged notes announcing their intention to escalate.

Under the terms of the treaty, the next step following the formal announcement of intention to escalate is consultation over a period of 3 months to determine whether new limits can be fixed and if so what these new limits will be. Accordingly, the representatives of the three powers met at London on April 12 and at intervals thereafter in order to explore the possibilities of limitation.

All three powers, in this consultation, took the ground that, in view of all the circumstances, there must be a departure from the limits of the treaty. The United States, wishing to maintain in effect naval limitation insofar as possible, informed the other signatory powers of its willingness to accept a new limitation of 45,000 tons on the size and 16 inches in the armament of capital ships. When it is decided to build larger capital ships, these limitations are, from a technical point of view, believed most nearly to correspond with the naval defense needs of the United States.

The protocol signed today at London by the signatories to the London treaty of 1936 gives formal approval to the fixing of the new limitation to the tonnage of capital ships. . . . The text [of the protocol] is as follows:

"Whereas by Article Four (1) of the Treaty for the Limitation of Naval Armaments signed in London on the 25th March, 1936, it is provided that no capital ship shall exceed 35,000 tons (35,560 metric tons) standard displacement;

"And whereas by reason of Article Four (2) of the said Treaty the maximum calibre of gun carried by capital ships is 16 inches (406 mm.);

"And whereas on the 31st March, 1938, His Majesty's Government in the United Kingdom of Great Britain and Northern Ireland and the Government of the United States of America gave notice under paragraph (2) of Article 25 of the said Treaty of their decision to exercise the right provided for in paragraph (1) of the said Article to depart from the limitations and restrictions of the Treaty in regard to the upper limits of capital ships of subcategory (a);

"And whereas consultations have taken place as provided in paragraph (3) of Article 25, with a view to reaching an agreement in order to reduce to a minimum the extent of the departures from the limitations and restrictions of the Treaty;

"The undersigned, duly authorized by their respective Governments, have agreed as follows:

"One. As from this day's date the figure of 35,000 tons (35,560 metric tons) in Article Four (1) of the said Treaty shall be replaced by the figure of 45,000 tons (45,720 metric tons).

"Two. The figure of 16 inches (406 mm.) in Article Four (2) remains unaltered.

"Three. The present protocol, of which the French and English texts shall both be equally authentic, shall come into force on this day's date.

"In faith whereof the undersigned have signed the present protocol.

"Done in London the 30th day of June 1938."

68. THE GERMAN-JAPANESE ANTI-COMMUNIST PACT, 1936 [29]

As a concrete manifestation of the harmony of their ideologies, Germany and Japan, on November 25, 1936, signed an Anti-Communist Pact. Italy adhered to the document on November 6, 1937, and Hungary on February 24, 1939.

The Government of the German Reich and the Imperial Japanese Government,

Avowing that it is the aim of the Communist International, called Komintern, to destroy and overpower the existing States by all available means,

Convinced that the toleration of the interference of the Communist International in the domestic affairs of the nations endangers not only their own domestic tranquillity and social welfare but threatens world peace as a whole,

Have, in the desire to coöperate against the communist work of destruction, agreed as follows:

ARTICLE 1.

The High Contracting Parties agree to keep each other informed concerning the activities of the Third International, to consult upon

---

[29] Germany, *Reichsgesetzblatt*, vol. II, 1937, No. 4, pp. 28-30.

the necessary defense measures and to execute these measures in close coöperation with each other.

ARTICLE 2.

The High Contracting Parties will mutually invite third Powers, whose domestic peace is threatened by the disruptive work of the Communist International, to take defense measures in the spirit of this agreement or to participate in the agreement.

ARTICLE 3.

The German and Japanese texts of this agreement are equally authentic. It becomes effective from the date of signature and is valid for a period of five years. The High Contracting Parties will mutually agree, in good time prior to the expiration of this period, concerning the continued form of their coöperation.

In witness whereof the undersigned, duly authorized by their respective Governments, have signed and set seal to this agreement.

Done in duplicate at Berlin, the 25th November 1936, that is, the 25th November in the 11th year of the Showa-Period.

JOACHIM VON RIBBENTROP   VICOMTE KINTOMO MUSHAKOJI

Minister Extraordinary and Pleni-   *Imperial Japanese Minister Ex-*
potentiary of the German   *traordinary and Plenipoten-*
Reich.   *tiary.*

SUPPLEMENTARY PROTOCOL TO THE AGREEMENT AGAINST THE COMMUNIST INTERNATIONAL

Pursuant to this day's signature of the Agreement against the Communist International, the undersigned Plenipotentiaries have agreed as follows:

a) The competent authorities of the two High Contracting Parties will coöperate closely in the exchange of information regarding the activity of the Communist International and on the educational and defense measures that shall be taken.

b) The competent authorities of the two High Contracting Parties will invoke severe measures, within the framework of existing laws, against those who, at home or abroad, directly or indirectly, serve the Communist International or further its subversive work.

c) To facilitate the coöperation of the competent authorities of the two High Contracting Parties as defined in (a) above, a permanent commission shall be established. This commission shall weigh and advise upon the necessary further defense measures that shall be taken to combat the subversive activities of the Communist International.

Berlin, the 25th November 1936, . . .

69. THE MONTREUX STRAITS CONVENTION, JULY 20, 1936 *(Extracts)* [30]

The failure of most disarmament moves and the growing tension in Europe led to a demand in Turkey that the country be allowed to fortify the area of the Straits at Constantinople, demilitarized under the provisions of the Treaty of Lausanne of 1923. Eventually, on April 10, 1936, the Ankara Government requested the Lausanne signatories and the League to consider revision of the relevant treaty terms. Turkey's legal approach, at a time when unilateral renunciations of treaty restrictions were resorted to by other states, and a general feeling that Italy's Ethiopian venture was perhaps tied up with other Italian aims in the eastern Mediterranean, predisposed most of the powers concerned to look favorably upon the republic's request. Hence, on July 20, 1936, Bulgaria, France, Great Britain, Greece, Japan, Rumania, the Soviet Union, Turkey, and Yugoslavia signed a convention allowing the refortification of the Straits. Turkey lost no time in proceeding to remilitarize the zone.

ARTICLE 1.

The High Contracting Parties recognise and affirm the principle of freedom of transit and navigation by sea in the Straits.

The exercise of this freedom shall henceforth be regulated by the provisions of the present Convention.

ARTICLE 2.

In time of peace, merchant vessels shall enjoy complete freedom of transit and navigation in the Straits, by day and by night, under any

---

[30] *Convention Regarding the Régime of the Straits, Montreux, July 20, 1936. Presented by the Secretary of State for Foreign Affairs to Parliament by Command of His Majesty,* Treaty Series No. 30 (1937), Cmd. 5551, His Majesty's Stationery Office, London, 1937, pp. 7-23, 33.

flag and with any kind of cargo, without any formalities, except as provided in article 3 below. . . .

ARTICLE 3.

All ships entering the Straits by the Ægean Sea or by the Black Sea shall stop at a sanitary station near the entrance to the Straits for the purpose of the sanitary control prescribed by Turkish law within the framework of international sanitary regulations. . . .

ARTICLE 4.

In time of war, Turkey not being belligerent, merchant vessels, under any flag or with any kind of cargo, shall enjoy freedom of transit and navigation in the Straits subject to the provisions of articles 2 and 3. . . .

ARTICLE 5.

In time of war, Turkey being belligerent, merchant vessels not belonging to a country at war with Turkey shall enjoy freedom of transit and navigation in the Straits on condition that they do not in any way assist the enemy.

Such vessels shall enter the Straits by day and their transit shall be effected by the route which shall in each case be indicated by the Turkish authorities.

. . . . .

ARTICLE 10.

In time of peace, light surface vessels, minor war vessels and auxiliary vessels, whether belonging to Black Sea or non-Black Sea Powers, and whatever their flag, shall enjoy freedom of transit through the Straits without any taxes or charges whatever, provided that such transit is begun during daylight and subject to the conditions laid down in article 13 and the articles following thereafter.

Vessels of war other than those which fall within the categories specified in the preceding paragraph shall only enjoy a right of transit under the special conditions provided by articles 11 and 12.

ARTICLE 11.

Black Sea Powers may send through the Straits capital ships of a tonnage greater than that laid down in the first paragraph of article 14, on condition that these vessels pass through the Straits singly, escorted by not more than two destroyers.

ARTICLE 12.

Black Sea Powers shall have the right to send through the Straits, for the purpose of rejoining their base, submarines constructed or purchased outside the Black Sea, provided that adequate notice of the laying down or purchase of such submarines shall have been given to Turkey.

Submarines belonging to the said Powers shall also be entitled to pass through the Straits to be repaired in dockyards outside the Black Sea on condition that detailed information on the matter is given to Turkey.

In either case, the said submarines must travel by day and on the surface, and must pass through the Straits singly.

ARTICLE 13.

The transit of vessels of war through the Straits shall be preceded by a notification given to the Turkish Government through the diplomatic channel. The normal period of notice shall be eight days; but it is desirable that in the case of non-Black Sea Powers this period should be increased to fifteen days. . . .

ARTICLE 14.

The maximum aggregate tonnage of all foreign naval forces which may be in course of transit through the Straits shall not exceed 15,000 tons, except in the cases provided for in article 11 and in Annex III [relating to certain Japanese over-age training ships] to the present Convention.

The forces specified in the preceding paragraph shall not, however, comprise more than nine vessels. . . .

ARTICLE 15.

Vessels of war in transit through the Straits shall in no circumstances make use of any aircraft which they may be carrying.

. . . . .

ARTICLE 17.

Nothing in the provisions of the preceding articles shall prevent a naval force of any tonnage or composition from paying a courtesy visit of limited duration to a port in the Straits at the invitation of the Turkish Government. Any such force must leave the Straits by the same route as that by which it entered. . . .

ARTICLE 18.

(1) The aggregate tonnage which non-Black Sea Powers may have in that sea in time of peace shall be limited as follows:—

(*a*) Except as provided in paragraph (*b*) below, the aggregate tonnage of the said Powers shall not exceed 30,000 tons;

(*b*) If at any time the tonnage of the strongest fleet in the Black Sea shall exceed by at least 10,000 tons the tonnage of the strongest fleet in that sea at the date of the signature of the present Convention, the aggregate tonnage of 30,000 tons mentioned in paragraph (*a*) shall be increased by the same amount, up to a maximum of 45,000 tons. . . .

(*c*) The tonnage which any one non-Black Sea Power may have in the Black Sea shall be limited to two-thirds of the aggregate tonnage provided for in paragraphs (*a*) and (*b*) above. . . .

(2) Vessels of war belonging to non-Black Sea Powers shall not remain in the Black Sea more than twenty-one days, whatever be the object of their presence there.

ARTICLE 19.

In time of war, Turkey not being belligerent, warships shall enjoy complete freedom of transit and navigation through the Straits under the same conditions as those laid down in articles 10 to 18.

Vessels of war belonging to belligerent Powers shall not, however, pass through the Straits except in cases arising out of the application of article 25 of the present Convention, and in cases of assistance rendered to a State victim of aggression in virtue of a treaty of mutual assistance binding Turkey, concluded within the framework of the Covenant of the League of Nations, and registered and published in accordance with the provisions of article 18 of the Covenant. . . .

ARTICLE 20.

In time of war, Turkey being belligerent, the provisions of articles 10 to 18 shall not be applicable; the passage of warships shall be left entirely to the discretion of the Turkish Government.

ARTICLE 21.

Should Turkey consider herself to be threatened with imminent danger of war she shall have the right to apply the provisions of article 20 of the present Convention. . . .

Should the Turkish Government make use of the powers conferred by the first paragraph of the present article, a notification to that effect shall be addressed to the High Contracting Parties and to the Secretary-General of the League of Nations.

If the Council of the League of Nations decide by a majority of two-thirds that the measures thus taken by Turkey are not justified, and if such should also be the opinion of the majority of the High Contracting Parties signatories to the present Convention, the Turkish Government undertakes to discontinue the measures in question. . . .

. . . . .

ARTICLE 25.

Nothing in the present Convention shall prejudice the rights and obligations of Turkey, or of any of the other High Contracting Parties members of the League of Nations, arising out of the Covenant of the League of Nations.

ARTICLE 26.

The present Convention shall be ratified as soon as possible.

The ratifications shall be deposited in the archives of the Government of the French Republic in Paris.

. . . . .

ARTICLE 28.

The present Convention shall remain in force for twenty years from the date of entry into force.

The principle of freedom of transit and navigation affirmed in article 1 of the present Convention shall however continue without limit of time.

If, two years prior to the expiry of the said period of twenty years, no High Contracting Party shall have given notice of denunciation to the French Government the present Convention shall continue in force until two years after such notice shall have been given. Any such notice shall be communicated by the French Government to the High Contracting Parties.

In the event of the present Convention being denounced in accordance with the provisions of the present article, the High Contracting Parties agree to be represented at a conference for the purpose of concluding a new Convention.

. . . . .

70. THE GERMAN DENUNCIATION OF THE LOCARNO AGREEMENT AND THE DECISION TO REMILITARIZE THE RHINELAND, MARCH 7, 1936 [31]

On the ground that the Franco-Soviet pact of 1935 had deprived the Locarno agreement of its "inner meaning" Germany, on March 7, 1936, informed the Belgian, British, and French governments that she no longer regarded herself as being bound by the terms of that treaty. Consequently Germany also felt free to remilitarize the Rhineland and German soldiers reëntered the hitherto forbidden zone on the very day of Hitler's announcement. These actions caused some consternation abroad, but no real effort was made to apply sanctions or take reprisals.

[*Translation.*]

MEMORANDUM.

Immediately after being informed of the Pact between France and the Union of Socialist Soviet Republics (*sic*), concluded on the 2nd May, 1935,[32] the German Government drew the attention of the other signatory Powers of the Locarno Rhine Pact to the fact that the obligations, which France has undertaken in the new Pact, are not compatible with her obligations arising out of the Rhine Pact.[33] The German Government then explained their point of view in full detail and in both its legal and political aspects—in its legal aspect in the German Memorandum of the 25th May, 1935, in its political aspect in the many diplomatic conversations which followed on that Memorandum. It is also known to the Governments concerned that neither their written replies to the German Memorandum, nor the arguments brought forward by them through the diplomatic channel or in public declarations, were able to invalidate the German Government's point of view.

In fact, all the diplomatic and public discussions which have taken place since May 1935 regarding these questions, have only been able to confirm on all points the view expressed by the German Government at the outset.

---

[31] *Memorandum by the German Government Respecting the Franco-Soviet Treaty, the Treaty of Locarno and the Demilitarised Zone in the Rhineland. Communicated to the Secretary of State for Foreign Affairs by the German Ambassador on March 7, 1936. Presented by the Secretary of State for Foreign Affairs to Parliament by Command of His Majesty,* Germany No. 1 (1936), Cmd. 5118, His Majesty's Stationery Office, London, 1936, pp. 3-6.

[32] See Document No. 64.—*Ed.*

[33] See Document No. 54.—*Ed.*

1. It is an undisputed fact that the Franco-Soviet Pact is exclusively directed against Germany.

2. It is an undisputed fact that in the Pact France undertakes, in the event of a conflict between Germany and the Soviet Union, obligations which go far beyond her duty as laid down in the Covenant of the League of Nations, and which compel her to take military action against Germany even when she cannot appeal either to a recommendation or to an actual decision of the Council of the League.

3. It is an undisputed fact that France, in such a case, claims for herself the right to decide on her own judgment who is the aggressor.

4. It is thereby established that France has undertaken towards the Soviet Union obligations which practically amount to undertaking in a given case to act as if neither the Covenant of the League of Nations, nor the Rhine Pact, which refers to the Covenant, were valid.

This result of the Franco-Soviet Pact is not removed by the fact that France, in the Pact, makes the reservation that she does not wish to be bound to take military action against Germany if by such action she would expose herself to a sanction on the part of the guarantor Powers, Italy and Great Britain. As regards this reservation, the decisive fact remains that the Rhine Pact is not based only on the obligations of Great Britain and Italy as guarantor Powers, but primarily on the obligations established in the relations between France and Germany. Therefore it matters only whether France, in undertaking these treaty obligations, has kept herself within the limits imposed on her so far as Germany is concerned by the Rhine Pact.

This, however, the German Government must deny.

The Rhine Pact was intended to achieve the object of securing peace in Western Europe by providing that Germany on the one hand and France and Belgium on the other hand, in their relation to one another, should renounce for all future time the use of military force. If at the time of the conclusion of the Pact certain exceptions to this renunciation of war going beyond the right of self-defence were admitted, the political reason for this, as is generally known, lay solely in the fact that France had already undertaken certain obligations towards Poland and Czechoslovakia, which she did not wish to sacrifice to the conception of absolute security in the West. Germany, with her own clear conscience in regard to the matter, at the time accepted these limitations on the renunciation of war. She did not raise exceptions to the treaties with Poland and Czechoslovakia, laid by France on the table at Locarno, solely on the obvious condition that these treaties were in conformity with the construction of the Rhine Pact, and contained no sort of provisions regarding the application of article 16 of the Covenant of the League of Nations, such as those contained in the new Franco-Soviet agreements. The contents of these special agreements, as then notified to the German Government, fulfilled this condition. The exceptions admitted in the Rhine Pact were not, it is true, specifically confined to Poland and Czechoslovakia, but were formulated as an abstract principle. Nevertheless, the intention of all the negotiations relating to these questions was merely to find a compromise between the renunciation of war by Germany and France, and the wish of France to maintain the obligations which she had already undertaken towards her allies. If, therefore, France now utilises the abstract provisions of the Rhine Pact, which permit the possibility of war, in order to conclude a fresh alliance against Germany with a Power highly armed in a military sense; if she thus further, and in so decisive a manner, restricts the scope of the renunciation of war agreed upon with Germany; and if in this connection, as shown above, she does not even observe the fixed formal limits, she has created an entirely new situation, and has destroyed the political system of the Rhine Pact, not only in theory but also in fact.

The latest debates and decisions of the French Parliament have shown that France, in spite of the German representations, is determined to put the pact with the Soviet Union definitely into force. A diplomatic conversation has even revealed that France already regards herself as bound by her signature of this pact on the 2nd May, 1935. In the face of such a development of European politics, the German Government, if they do not wish to neglect or to abandon the interests of the German people which they have the duty of safeguarding, cannot remain inactive.

The German Government have continually emphasised during the negotiations of the last years their readiness to observe and fulfil all the obligations arising from the Rhine Pact as long as the other contracting parties were ready on their side to maintain the pact. This obvious and essential condition can no longer be regarded as being fulfilled by France. France has replied to the repeated friendly offers and peaceful assurances made by Germany by infringing the Rhine Pact through a military alliance with the Soviet Union exclusively directed against Germany. In this manner, however, the Locarno Rhine Pact has lost its inner meaning and ceased in practice to exist. Consequently, Germany regards herself for her part as no longer bound by this dissolved treaty. The German Government are now constrained to face the new situation created by this alliance, a situation which is rendered more acute by the fact that the Franco-Soviet Treaty has been supplemented by a Treaty of Alliance between Czechoslovakia and the Soviet Union exactly parallel in form. In accordance with the fundamental right of a nation to secure its frontiers and ensure its possibilities of defence, the German Government have to-day restored the full and unrestricted sovereignty of Germany in the demilitarised zone of the Rhineland.

In order, however, to avoid any misinterpretation of their intentions and to establish beyond doubt the purely defensive character of these measures, as well as to express their unchangeable longing for a real pacification of Europe between States which are equals in rights and equally respected, the German Government declare themselves ready to conclude new agreements for the creation of a system of peaceful security for Europe on the basis of the following proposals:—

(1) The German Government declare themselves ready to enter at once into negotiations with France and Belgium with regard to the creation of a zone demilitarised on both sides, and to give their agreement in advance to any suggestion regarding the depth and nature thereof on the basis of full parity.

(2) The German Government propose, for the purpose of ensuring the sanctity and inviolability of the boundaries in the West, the conclusion of a non-aggression pact between Germany, France and Belgium, the duration of which they are ready to fix at twenty-five years.

(3) The German Government desire to invite Great Britain and Italy to sign this treaty as guarantor Powers.

(4) The German Government agree, in case the Netherlands Government should so desire and the other Contracting Parties consider it appropriate, to bring the Netherlands into this treaty system.

(5) The German Government are prepared, in order to strengthen further these security agreements between the Western Powers, to conclude an air pact calculated to prevent in an automatic and effective manner the danger of sudden air attacks.

(6) The German Government repeat their offer to conclude with the States bordering Germany in the East non-aggression pacts similar to that with Poland. As the Lithuanian Government have

in the last few months corrected their attitude towards the Memel Territory to a certain extent, the German Government withdraw the exception which they once made regarding Lithuania and declare their readiness, on condition that the guaranteed autonomy of the Memel territory is effectively developed, to sign a non-aggression pact of this nature with Lithuania also.

(7) Now that Germany's equality of rights and the restoration of her full sovereignty over the entire territory of the German Reich have finally been attained, the German Government consider the chief reason for their withdrawal from the League of Nations to be removed. They are therefore willing to re-enter the League of Nations. In this connexion they express the expectation that in the course of a reasonable period the question of colonial equality of rights and that of the separation of the League Covenant from its Versailles setting may be clarified through friendly negotiations.

71-72. BELGIAN NEUTRALITY REAFFIRMED, 1936-1937

71. DECLARATION BY KING LEOPOLD III ON THE POSITION OF BELGIUM, OCTOBER 14, 1936 (Extracts) [34]

The apparent inability or unwillingness of Great Britain and France to co-operate in holding Germany in check as of yore, led the Belgian King to declare before his parliament, on October 14, 1936, that henceforth the little kingdom should follow a purely Belgian policy, unhampered by alliances and neutral in any disputes among her neighbors.

Our military policy, like our foreign policy, which of necessity determines the former, ought to be based, not on preparing for a more or less victorious war as member of a coalition, but on fending off war from our territory.

The reoccupation of the Rhineland, in violation of the spirit and letter of the Locarno Pact, has virtually restored us to our pre-war international position.

---

[34] Translation of text reproduced in French in Royal Institute of International Affairs, *Documents on International Affairs 1936* (Ed. by Stephen Heald), Oxford University Press, London, 1937, pp. 225-227. "Text furnished by the Belgian Embassy in London."

Our geographic location requires us to maintain a military establishment such as would dissuade any one of our neighbors from using
our territory to attack another state. In fulfilling this mission, Belgium contributes in a conspicuous manner to the peace of western
Europe and *ipso facto* earns the right to the respect and, if necessary,
the assistance of all the States that are interested in this peace.

On these points I believe Belgian opinion to be unanimous.

But our obligations must not go beyond this. Any policy of alliance
with a single country would weaken our external position and create—
rightly or wrongly—internal dissension. An alliance, even a purely
defensive one, would not achieve the desired end, for, however prompt
the aid of an ally, it would not come until after the invader's blow,
which would be a lightning-like one. . . .

. . . . .

That is why we must, as the minister of foreign affairs recently said,
pursue a policy "exclusively and entirely Belgian." That policy should
aim resolutely at placing us outside any conflicts of our neighbors; it
corresponds to our national ideal.

. . . . .

In resolving the military problem in a spirit of high patriotic comprehension, you will restore to the country simultaneously with the
serenity of spirit necessary to meet foreign emergencies, the cir-
cumambient serenity indispensable to national prosperity.

You will thus have established once more before the country that the
essential preoccupation of the government of national union is to place
above all else the higher interest of Belgium.

72. THE ANGLO-FRENCH GUARANTEE OF ASSISTANCE TO BELGIUM, 1937 [35]

*Six months after the Belgian declaration, on April 24, 1937, the British
and French governments endorsed the stand taken by the Brussels authorities.*

[35] *Documents Exchanged between His Majesty's Government in the United Kingdom
and the French Government and the Belgian Government Concerning the International
Position of Belgium, Brussels, April 24, 1937. Presented by the Secretary of State for
Foreign Affairs to Parliament by Command of His Majesty,* Belgium No. 1 (1937), Cmd.
5437, His Majesty's Stationery Office, London, 1937, pp. 2-3.

NO. 1.

JOINT COMMUNICATION TO THE BELGIAN MINISTER FOR FOREIGN
AFFAIRS BY HIS MAJESTY'S AMBASSADOR AND THE FRENCH
AMBASSADOR AT BRUSSELS ON APRIL 24, 1937.

In accordance with instructions received from their respective Governments, His Majesty's Ambassador and the French Ambassador have the honour to make the following communication to the Belgian Government:—

1. The Governments of the United Kingdom of Great Britain and Northern Ireland and of the French Republic have not failed during the last few months to give their full attention to the desire of the Belgian Government to have the international rights and obligations of Belgium clarified in certain respects where this is rendered necessary by her geographical position and by the delays which may still occur before the negotiation and conclusion of the general Act intended to replace the Treaty of Locarno.

2. The Government of the United Kingdom and the Government of the Republic, being anxious to give full expression to their sympathy with this desire of the Belgian Government, have agreed to make the following declaration:—

3. The said Governments have taken note of the views which the Belgian Government has itself expressed concerning the interests of Belgium, and more particularly—

(1) the determination expressed publicly and on more than one occasion by the Belgian Government: (*a*) to defend the frontiers of Belgium with all its forces against any aggression or invasion, and to prevent Belgian territory from being used, for purposes of aggression against another State, as a passage or as a base of operations by land, by sea or in the air; (*b*) to organise the defence of Belgium in an efficient manner for this purpose;

(2) the renewed assurances of the fidelity of Belgium to the Covenant of the League of Nations and to the obligations which it involves for Members of the League.

4. In consequence, taking into account the determination and assurances mentioned above, the Government of the United Kingdom and the Government of the Republic declare that they consider Belgium to be now released from all obligations towards them resulting from either the Treaty of Locarno or the arrangements drawn up in London on the 19th March, 1936, and that they maintain in respect of Belgium the

undertakings of assistance which they entered into towards her under the above-mentioned instruments.

5. The Government of the United Kingdom and the Government of the Republic agree that the release of Belgium from her obligations, as provided for in paragraph 4 above, in no way affects the existing undertakings between the United Kingdom and France.

Esmond Ovey.   J. Laroche

Brussels, April 24, 1937.

NO. 2.

COMMUNICATION FROM THE BELGIAN MINISTER FOR FOREIGN AFFAIRS TO HIS MAJESTY'S AMBASSADOR. [36]

[Translation.]

M. l'Ambassadeur,   *Brussels, April 24, 1937.*

The Royal Government has taken note with great satisfaction of the declaration communicated to it this day by the Government of the United Kingdom of Great Britain and Northern Ireland. It thanks the Government of the United Kingdom warmly for this communication. I avail, &c.

P. H. Spaak.

73. THE ANGLO-ITALIAN MEDITERRANEAN AGREEMENT OF JANUARY 2, 1937 [37]

The increasing ill-feeling between Great Britain and Italy over the Ethiopian and other incidents received at least a temporary check on January 2, 1937, when the two countries issued a mutually reassuring statement of their respective aims in the Mediterranean. In the same month the two governments reached agreement on the grazing and watering rights of some of the tribes in their neighboring East-African colonies and on Italian colonial transit rights in British Somaliland.

His Majesty's Government in the United Kingdom and the Italian Government;

---

[36] A similar communication was addressed to the French Ambassador at Brussels.

[37] *Declaration by His Majesty's Government in the United Kingdom and the Italian Government Regarding the Mediterranean, Rome, January 2,1937. Presented by the Secretary of State for Foreign Affairs to Parliament by Command of His Majesty,* Treaty Series No. 14 (1937), Cmd. 5429, His Majesty's Stationery Office, London, 1937, p. 2.

Animated by the desire to contribute increasingly, in the interests of the general cause of peace and security, to the betterment of relations between them and between all the Mediterranean Powers, and resolved to respect the rights and interests of those Powers;

Recognise that the freedom of entry into, exit from, and transit through, the Mediterranean is a vital interest both to the different parts of the British Empire and to Italy, and that these interests are in no way inconsistent with each other;

Disclaim any desire to modify or, so far as they are concerned, to see modified the *status quo* as regards national sovereignty of territories in the Mediterranean area;

Undertake to respect each other's rights and interests in the said area;

Agree to use their best endeavours to discourage any activities liable to impair the good relations which it is the object of the present declaration to consolidate.

This declaration is designed to further the end of peace and is not directed against any other Power.

ERIC DRUMMOND.   G. CIANO.

Rome, January 2, 1937.

74. THE ANGLO-ITALIAN AGREEMENTS OF 1938 *(Extracts)* [38]

On April 16, 1938, the representatives of Great Britain and Italy arrived at a whole series of agreements regulating future relations between the two states. This procedure was in accord with the views of Premier Neville Chamberlain that the peace of Europe required co-operation rather than competition between the so-called democratic and totalitarian states. But the April agreement was not to come into force until some definite steps had been taken in the direction of withdrawal of foreign fighters from the scene of the Spanish civil war. Finally, on November 16, 1938, seven months after the signature of the agreements, they came into force.

---

[38] *Agreement between the United Kingdom and Italy Consisting of a Protocol with Annexes and Exchanges of Notes, . . . Rome, April 16, 1938. Presented by the Secretary of State for Foreign Affairs to Parliament by Command of His Majesty,* Treaty Series No. 31 (1938), Cmd. 5726, His Majesty's Stationery Office, London, 1938, pp. 4-30.

PROTOCOL.

The Government of the United Kingdom of Great Britain and
Northern Ireland and the Italian Government, animated by the desire
to place the relations between the two countries on a solid and lasting
basis and to contribute to the general cause of peace and security, have
decided to undertake conversations in order to reach agreement on
questions of mutual concern;

and the said conversations have taken place;

His Excellency the Right Honourable the EARL OF PERTH,
G.C.M.G., C.B., His Majesty's Ambassador Extraordinary and
Plenipotentiary at Rome, and

His Excellency Count GALEAZZO CIANO di CORTELLAZZO,
Minister for Foreign Affairs,

duly authorised for that purpose by their respective Governments, have
drawn up the present Protocol and have signed the Agreements and
Declarations annexed hereto, each of which shall be regarded as a
separate and self contained instrument:—

(1) Reaffirmation of the Declaration of the 2nd January, 1937, regarding the Mediterranean, and of the Notes exchanged on the
   31st December, 1936;

(2) Agreement regarding the Exchange of Military Information;

(3) Agreement regarding certain Areas in the Middle East;

(4) Declaration regarding Propaganda;

(5) Declaration regarding Lake Tsana;

(6) Declaration regarding the Military Duties of Natives of Italian
   East Africa;

(7) Declaration regarding the free Exercise of Religion and the
   Treatment of British Religious Bodies in Italian East Africa;

(8) Declaration regarding the Suez Canal.

The said instruments shall take effect on such date as the two Governments shall together determine. Except in so far as any of them contain
provisions with regard to their revision or duration, each of the said
instruments shall remain in force indefinitely, but should either Government at any time consider that a change of circumstances renders the
revision of any of these instruments necessary, the two Governments
will consult together with a view to such revision.

. . . . .

Done at Rome, in duplicate, the 16th April, 1938, in the English and Italian languages, both of which shall have equal force.

PERTH. CIANO.

NO. 2.

ANNEX 1.

. . . . . .

The Government of the United Kingdom and the Italian Government hereby reaffirm the Declaration signed in Rome on the 2nd January, 1937 [Cmd. 5429], regarding the Mediterranean, and the Notes exchanged between the two Governments on the 31st December, 1936 [Cmd. 5348], regarding the *status quo* in the Western Mediterranean.

. . . . . .

NO. 3.

ANNEX 2.

. . . . .

The Government of the United Kingdom and the Italian Government agree that in the month of January each year a reciprocal exchange of information shall take place through the Naval, Military and Air Attachés in London and Rome regarding any major prospective administrative movements or redistribution of their respective naval, military and air forces. This exchange of information will take place in respect of such forces stationed in or based on—

(1) overseas possessions of either Party (which phrase shall for this purpose be deemed to include protectorates and mandated territories) in or with a seaboard on the Mediterranean, the Red Sea or the Gulf of Aden, and

(2) territories in Africa other than those referred to in paragraph (1) above and lying in an area bounded on the west by longitude 20° east and on the south by latitude 7° south.

Such an exchange of information will not necessarily preclude the occasional communication of supplementary military information should either Party consider that the political circumstances of the moment make it desirable.

The two Governments further agree to notify each other in advance of any decision to provide new naval or air bases in the Mediterranean east of longitude 19° east and in the Red Sea or approaches thereto.

. . . . .

NO. 4.

ANNEX 3.

. . . . .

The Government of the United Kingdom of Great Britain and Northern Ireland and the Italian Government,

being desirous of ensuring that there shall be no conflict between their respective policies in regard to the areas in the Middle East referred to in the present agreement, . . .

have agreed as follows:—

ARTICLE 1.

Neither Party will conclude any agreement or take any action which might in any way impair the independence or integrity of Saudi Arabia or of the Yemen.

ARTICLE 2.

Neither Party will obtain or seek to obtain a privileged position of a political character in any territory which at present belongs to Saudi Arabia or to the Yemen or in any territory which either of those States may hereafter acquire.

ARTICLE 3.

The two Parties recognise that, in addition to the obligations incumbent on each of them in virtue of Articles 1 and 2 hereof, it is in the common interest of both of them that no other Power should acquire or seek to acquire sovereignty or any privileged position of a political character in any territory which at present belongs to Saudi Arabia or to the Yemen or which either of those States may hereafter acquire, . . .

. . . . .

ARTICLE 5.

(1) The two Parties agree that it is in the common interest of both of them that there shall be peace between Saudi Arabia and the Yemen and within the territories of those States. But, while they will at all times exert their good offices in the cause of peace, they will not intervene in any conflict which, despite their good offices, may break out between or within those States.

(2) The two Parties also recognise that it is in the common interest of both of them that no other Power should intervene in any such conflict.

. . . . .

ARTICLE 8.

(1) Should either Party at any time give notice to the other that they consider that a change has taken place in the circumstances obtaining at the time of the entry into force of the present Agreement, such as to necessitate a modification of the provisions of the Agreement, the two Parties will enter into negotiations with a view to the revision or amendment of any of the provisions of the Agreement.

(2) At any time after the expiration of a period of ten years from the entry into force of this Agreement either Party may notify the other of its intention to determine the Agreement. Any such notification shall take effect three months after the date on which it is made.

NO. 5.

ANNEX 4.

. . . . .

The two Governments welcome the opportunity afforded by the present occasion to place on record their agreement that any attempt by either of them to employ the methods of publicity or propaganda at its disposal in order to injure the interests of the other would be inconsistent with the good relations which it is the object of the present Agreement to establish and maintain between the two Governments and the peoples of their respective countries.

. . . . . .

NO. 6.

ANNEX 5.

. . . .

The Italian Government confirm to the government of the United Kingdom the assurance given by them to the Government of the United Kingdom on the 3rd April, 1936, and reiterated by the Italian Minister for Foreign Affairs to His Majesty's Ambassador at Rome on the 31st December, 1936, to the effect that the Italian Government were fully conscious of their obligations towards the Government of the United Kingdom in the matter of Lake Tsana and had no intention whatever of overlooking or repudiating them.

. . . . .

NO. 9.

ANNEX 8.

. . . . .

The Government of the United Kingdom and the Italian Government hereby reaffirm their intention always to respect and abide by the provisions of the Convention signed at Constantinople on the 29th October, 1888, which guarantees at all times and for all Powers the free use of the Suez Canal.

. . . . .

NO. 11.

EXCHANGE OF NOTES BETWEEN UNITED KINGDOM AND ITALY.

ITALIAN ASSURANCES IN REGARD TO POLICY IN SPAIN, SPANISH POSSESSIONS OVERSEAS AND THE SPANISH ZONE OF MOROCCO; AND UNITED KINGDOM INTENTIONS CONCERNING THE CLARIFICATION OF THE POSITION OF MEMBERS OF THE LEAGUE IN REGARD TO THE SITUATION IN ETHIOPIA.

(*a*)

. . . . .

[*Translation*]

The Minister for Foreign Affairs.

Your Excellency,   *Rome, April 16, 1938.*

Your Excellency will remember that, in the course of our recent conversations, I gave Your Excellency certain assurances regarding the policy of the Italian Government in connexion with Spain. I now wish to reaffirm those assurances and to place them on record.

First, the Italian Government have the honour to confirm their full adherence to the United Kingdom formula for the proportional evacuation of the foreign volunteers from Spain, and pledge themselves to give practical and real application to such an evacuation at the moment and on the conditions which shall be determined by the Non-Intervention Committee on the basis of the above-mentioned formula.

I desire secondly to reaffirm that if this evacuation has not been completed at the moment of the termination of the Spanish civil war, all remaining Italian volunteers will forthwith leave Spanish territory and all Italian war material will simultaneously be withdrawn.

I wish thirdly to repeat my previous assurance that the Italian Government have no territorial or political aims, and seek no privileged economic position, in or with regard to either Metropolitan Spain, the Balearic Islands, any of the Spanish possessions overseas, of the Spanish Zone of Morocco, and that they have no intention whatever of keeping any armed forces in any of the said territories.

I avail, &c.

CIANO.

(b)

Lord Perth to Count Ciano.

Your Excellency,
British Embassy,
Rome, April 16, 1938.

In reply to Your Excellency's Note of to-day's date, I have the honour to take note of the reaffirmation contained therein of the assurances which Your Excellency has already given me, during the course of our recent conversations, regarding the policy of the Italian Government in connexion with Spain. His Majesty's Government in the .United Kingdom, to whom I shall not fail to transmit this communication, will, I feel sure, be gratified at its contents. In this connexion I hardly need to remind Your Excellency that His Majesty's Government regard a settlement of the Spanish question as a prerequisite of the entry into force of the Agreement between our two Governments.

I have further the honour to inform Your Excellency that His Majesty's Government, being desirous that such obstacles as may at present be held to impede the freedom of member States as regards recognition of Italian sovereignty over Ethiopia should be removed, intend to take steps at the forthcoming meeting of the Council of the League of Nations for the purpose of clarifying the situation of member States in this regard.

I avail, &c.

PERTH.

NO. 12.

EXCHANGE OF NOTES BETWEEN UNITED KINGDOM AND ITALY.

· · · · ·

[*Translation.*]

The Minister for Foreign Affairs.

Your Excellency,
Rome, April 16, 1938.

I have the honour to inform Your Excellency that the Italian Government have decided to accede to the Naval Treaty signed in London on the 25th March, 1936 [Cmd. 5561], in accordance with the procedure laid down in Article 31 of that Treaty. This accession will take place so soon as the instruments annexed to the Protocol signed this day come into force.

In advising Your Excellency of the foregoing I desire to add that the Italian Government intend in the meantime to act in conformity with the provisions of the aforesaid Treaty.

I avail, &c.

CIANO.

75. THE CHAMBERLAIN-HITLER PEACE AVOWAL, SEPTEMBER 30, 1938 [39]

In addition to producing an agreement regarding the settlement of Germany's claims to the Sudetenland and other areas in Czechoslovakia (See Document No. 215), the conference of Premiers Chamberlain, Daladier, Hitler, and Mussolini in Munich on September 30, 1938, produced an interesting "joint resolution" of the British and German leaders on the matter of future relations between their respective peoples.

Mr. Chamberlain, receiving representatives of the British Press yesterday [September 30] before his departure from Munich, said:—

"I have always been of the opinion that if we could get a peaceful solution to the Czechoslovak question it would open the way generally to appeasement in Europe.

"This morning I had a talk with the Führer, and we both signed the following declaration:—

" 'We, the German Führer and Chancellor and the British Prime Minister, have had a further meeting to-day and are agreed in recognising that the question of Anglo-German relations is of the first importance for the two countries and for Europe.

" 'We regard the agreement signed last night and the Anglo-German Naval Agreement as symbolic of the desire of our two peoples never to go to war with one another again.

" 'We are resolved that the method of consultation shall be the method adopted to deal with any other questions that may concern our two countries, and we are determined to continue our efforts to remove possible sources of difference and thus to contribute to assure the peace of Europe.' "

[39] *The Times* (London), October 1, 1938, p. 12.

CHAPTER 5

GREAT BRITAIN AND ITS EMPIRE

76. SOME OF THE EFFECTS OF THE WAR IN GREAT BRITAIN [1]

The following comments on various aspects of the social and moral consequences of the World War to Great Britain are taken from a work by an ex-editor of The Economist. *The opinions expressed were not his own, but those of "a number of correspondents in quite different walks of life and with varied knowledge of different classes of society to whom [he] appealed for aid." Extract "a" was written by Mr. John Bright Clark, "a grandson of the great John Bright" and a leading member of the Boot and Shoe Manufacturers' Federation. Extract "b" was sent to Mr. Hirst "by a civil servant, who held a high position in one of the Local Government and Public Health Departments during the War and for some years afterwards." The comment under "c" was from a letter by "a woman who took high honours at Cambridge, and has had much experience as a teacher and lecturer in one of the provincial universities." Another woman, "an Oxford graduate, an acute observer of society," submitted the material in extract "d." A "prominent member of the Labour Party" contributed the views in extract "e," and "f" was penned by "a Yorkshirewoman, whose politics are Liberal, of a type now regarded as old-fashioned." The last item, "g," represented the views of "C. R. Hone, now Bishop of Pontefract, who has taken a keen interest in social questions."*

a. As to business, I think generally there is more initiative—not so much of a tendency to keep in old ruts.

There is also less secrecy; that is to say, there is more general research, and more readiness among people in business to be friendly with, and exchange information with, others who may be their competitors, rather than being afraid of them and keeping at a distance. . . .

Coming to more general things, it seems to me that the younger

[1] F. W. Hirst, *The Consequences of the War to Great Britain,* Oxford University Press, London, 1934, pp. 64, 66, 69-70, 71, 74-76, 76-77, 78-79, 80-81, 85. Reprinted by permission of the publishers.

generation are much more independent, and take much more their own line, without reference to the preceding generation than was the case when I was growing up. At the same time, as far as I know them, although there is perhaps rather more inclination to pleasure, yet I find them very keen, straight, and public spirited, and with their sympathies and ideals in the right place.

. . . . .

b. As to morals and religion, I should say the post-War generation is more natural, laxer in morals and freer in thought: the War made many people wonder what was the use of religion and dealt some shrewd blows to Sunday observance. Possibly increased contact with the Continent has extended Sunday games and amusements and divested us of some of our British "hypocrisy," which I always thought was not so much a claim that Englishmen did not sin as a readiness to repress by law or convention the doing of things which in other countries are openly practised or tolerated.

. . . . .

c. The general attitude of modern students is that the elder generation—their teachers, religious leaders, and politicians, though no doubt well-intentioned, are "back numbers" and cannot appreciate modern literature, art, morality, or social movements.

. . . . .

d. The post-war generation suffers from a sort of inward instability, a lack of character, due, probably, to the somewhat hysterical atmosphere of their childhood. There seems nowadays to be no desire to provide for the future or look beyond to-morrow. The war shattered that sense of security which brooded over Victorian homes, and made men buy estates and lay down cellars against their own old age and for the benefit of their sons. Many of those who so "laid up treasure on earth" either perished themselves or saw their hoards destroyed, and the present generation is convinced of the futility of providing for an uncertain to-morrow. Neither life nor property was sacred in war; why then make a home and learn to love it only to have it snatched from you? . . .

The second main tendency seems to be towards uniformity in every sphere. Mass destruction has led to mass production and the loss of individuality. Four years in a khaki uniform accustoms the eye to a drab sameness and four years of learning to obey orders saps initiative. It is only fair to say that the latter condemnation applies more to the private soldier and its consequences are only too evident among the working classes to-day. In an officer, on the other hand, self-reliance and a deep sense of responsibility could not but be developed, and there must be among them still many whose characters were inestimably enriched by their wartime training.

This tendency towards uniformity shows itself also in the breaking down of barriers which formerly existed between class and class and group and group. War-time economy and ration tickets did much towards bridging the gulf which was fixed between the way of living of rich and poor, and both the new rich and the new poor have learnt that the old social orders were not immutable, that the roles of Lazarus and his patron *are* interchangeable.

Levelling was inevitable in a period when a duke's son served under his gardener's boy; or a duke's daughter hoed turnips while her "social inferiors" were buying themselves fur coats out of their earnings in the munition factories. It is significant that you seldom hear nowadays the phrase which was once so common: "I know my station."

In the same way the line which formerly demarcated so clearly the province of women from that of men has now become so blurred as to be often scarcely visible. During the war, women perforce undertook men's jobs and showed unexpected capability. Since then they have managed, not without a good deal of ill-feeling, to retain their footing in business and most of the professions, not to mention the now all-important world of sport.

Just as the sphere of women is now less sharply differentiated from that of men, so have the nursery and the drawing-room drawn closer together. Those who were children during the war undoubtedly missed the influence—and the bullying—of elder brothers and fathers who were fighting; and to this lack of discipline (which has persisted long after the cause of it has been removed) can be added the indulgence shown to their remaining children by women who had lost husbands and sons. Before the War (in better class families at least) children were kept apart from their elders, had their own good plain food in the nursery and found their own simple amusements. Now they mix more freely with their elders, sit down to table with them, play the same games, and expect and get much more attention and amusement. . . .

. . . . .

e. Post-War people, as compared with pre-War people, have lost confidence in things human and divine. The awful massacre, waste, cruelty, and injustice of the War shook belief in a benevolent Deity and a providential dispensation. Commercial morality was undermined by War profiteering and contrast of the fortunes and high incomes made by those who stayed at home with the low wages of those who risked life and limb in the foul miseries of trench warfare. Subordinates were infected by the dishonesty of the bosses. The idea of "eat, drink, and be merry" spread, and habits of thrift and saving diminished, . . .

The long depression and unemployment have also had a demoralizing effect. There is a good deal of despairing bitterness and a lack of enterprise, perhaps, among those who find it difficult to get jobs. . . . There is also a general distrust of politicians and statesmen.

. . . . .

f. In seeking for the biggest disturbance caused by the War, I should say that we have lost most heavily in our ideals. Speaking very generally, every one nowadays is more out for himself or herself, and the idea of personal service for others has been thrust into the background. The idea that the State will step in to relieve unemployment, *expecting no return,* has broken the morale of the workers, and the fierce competition in the professions and industries, allied with heavy taxation, has caused the middle classes to become more self-centered, with the result that leisure time is spent in pleasures all ready provided by professionals, and intelligent recreation has almost disappeared. . . .

. . . . .

g. It is surprising to hear from many chaplains, and from men who served in the ranks, that the War had curiously little effect on the religious outlook of the majority of the men. Those who had deep religious convictions on the whole tended to maintain them, despite the horrors and shocks to faith through which they passed; those who were irreligious or indifferent for the most part remained so. Superficial ideas of religion and of prayer, which regard prayer as a prophylactic against danger, were certainly shattered, but deeper and worthier convictions persisted through all the storm and stress. The fact that so few were affected was no doubt partly due to the life of a soldier being mainly a matter of routine from day to day, and cheerfulness and fatalism were the governing ideas encouraged in the Army. "It is good policy for a soldier to suppress thought and emotion." The historic sergeant was right when he said to an officer: "It would never do, sir, to let the men take this 'ere War seriously." . . .

In conclusion it seems true to say that the effect of the War on religion in England was for a time definitely detrimental in alienating many from religious faith, and in breaking down habits of religious observance; but it seems doubtful whether its influence in these directions has been long enduring, or permanent in character. On the other hand, the influence of war service in overcoming denominational differences and prejudices promises to have a more enduring effect; and experiences learnt through the War have awakened the Church to a more active recognition of its responsibilities in the promotion of international peace, and have stimulated efforts to give a more intelligent and coherent presentation of the Christian Faith to meet the needs of the rising generation.

77. BRITISH WOMEN IN INDUSTRY [2]

The question of women in industry was a serious one in post-war Great Britain where the females considerably outnumbered the males in the total population. Miss Brittain, a staunch champion of the rights of women, and author of the popular Testament of Youth *and some interesting novels, published a careful study of the problem in 1928.*

During the War women passed rapidly into trades hitherto considered unsuitable for them, such as transport, munitions, motor manufacture and shipbuilding, and were found to be specially well-adapted to organisation, supervision and process work of all kinds. Work hitherto thought too heavy or too highly skilled was made quite feasible by means of lifting tackle (now generally considered desirable for men also) and special training, as well as by the more adequate nourishment of the worker. Numbers of women were brought back into manual labour, often of the most strenuous kind; in agriculture, for instance, they were employed in forestry and timber cutting, as well as in dairies and on farms.

In industry the temporary relaxation of Trade Union regulations led to women being universally employed to replace or supplement

---

[2] V. Brittain, *Women's Work in Modern England,* Noel Douglas, London, 1928, pp. 8-15, 200-201. Reprinted by permission of the publishers, now Williams and Norgate, Ltd.

men. Various organisations for direct war service, such as those of the hospital workers and the Army, Navy and Air Force Auxiliary Corps, were recruited from luxury trades, private domestic service, retired women, women normally unoccupied, and girls leaving school.

Statistics given by the War Cabinet Committee on Women in Industry in Great Britain and Ireland show that the 5,966,000 women who were employed in July, 1914, had increased by July, 1918, to 7,311,000. Of these the greatest increase was in Industry (exclusive of agriculture, transport and domestic service), in which the number of women rose from 2,178,600 to 2,970,600. Commerce came second with an increase of 429,000, National and Local Government third with 198,000 new members, and the Professions fourth with an increase of 110,000. The only form of occupation where the numbers declined was domestic service, which showed a decrease of 400,000. In individual trades the greatest increase was in the metal (*i.e.,* munitions) trade, where the numbers of women employed rose from 170,000 in July, 1914, to 594,000 in July, 1918.

Because of this increase in numbers, as well as owing to the efficiency shown by women in every type of occupation, the Women's Employment Committee foresaw an extension of openings for women not only in industry, but in the higher branches of commerce, and believed that employers would gladly continue to use them after the War in the work formerly done by men in shops, such as managing, buying and travelling. Especially they predicted great opportunities in the Local Government Service, and particularly, as the result of the investigation conducted by Dame Adelaide Anderson, in the Health and Sanitary Services.

These sanguine hopes were doomed to disappointment. The War had certainly given the world an object lesson in woman's achievement, but men in general showed a disturbing tendency to be appalled rather than encouraged by this demonstration of unexpected ability. Mrs. Barbara Drake, in her book *Women in Trade Unions,* points out that the years from 1914 to 1918 had not so much solved old problems of female labour or raised new ones, as they had brought to a head the long dispute between employers upholding their right to exploit "cheap and docile" labour, and the Trade Unions endeavouring to restrict or to forbid women's employment.

With the end of the necessity which had provoked war-time agreements, both sides were anxious to return to the old advantageous positions. While employers were quite ready to offer "equal pay by results" in trades to which women were not well adapted, they were most opposed to it in such industries as engineering and aircraft wood-working, in the light processes of which women notoriously excelled men.

The immediate result of demobilisation was to add a sentimental argument to the already familiar economic and social arguments against the work of women. The Restoration of the Pre-War Practices Act, which became law in July, 1918, effectually dispelled any lingering optimism as to the improvement of women's position in industry owing to the War. Women were discharged wholesale; they were not only turned out of old industries, but out of many new ones sufficiently resembling the old to come under the Act. By the autumn of 1919 three-quarters of a million of the women employed at the time of the Armistice had been dismissed, and the position of women in general could "certainly not be described as enviable."

. . . . .

The disintegrating effect of demobilisation, followed by three years of trade depression and the closing of many factories which employed women, soon reflected itself in the woman's Trade Union movement. By 1923 the number of organised women was reduced to 480,000, a figure little more than half that of 1913. Whether the amalgamation in 1920 of the National Federation of Women Workers with the National Union of General Workers has really been of advantage to women is still a disputed point. In 1919 Mr. R. H. Glanfield and Mr. Ben H. Morgan, two members of the Women's Employment Committee, emphatically dissented from their colleagues as to the advantages of mixed Trade Unions.

"Until," they stated, "the prejudices that exist in the ranks of male workers against women workers in many trades have diminished, the interests of women cannot, in our opinion, be so well served through the medium of a mixed Union where women are in a minority."

Certainly, and in spite of the established fact that differences of capacity between individuals of the same sex vary at least as much as the differences between the sexes, the membership of mixed unions both in industry and in the professions seems in many cases to perpetuate that traditional "inferiority complex" which is the worst enemy of women workers in all ranks of life, and causes women to accept the idea of a "woman's" wage or salary being necessarily less than that of a man.

. . . . .

In spite of the set-back to women's work which immediately followed the War, the past nine years have seen the breaking of many ancient barriers. The otherwise unsatisfactory Sex Disqualification (Removal) Act [1919] opened many new professions to women, though progress in the professions as well as in industry has been retarded by the trade depression following the post-war boom, and again by the black year of 1926 which eclipsed the temporary revival of 1924-1925. Though the census of 1921 showed that in professional occupations women out-numbered men by 359,982 to 306,830, this excess is explained by the fact that teaching and nursing are still preponderantly women's occupations, and account for 86 per cent. of the total number of women in professions.

In spite, however, of a situation in which the occupations of women are so much less varied than those of men while their tastes and gifts are equally diversified, one of the most encouraging features of the 1921 Census was that which showed an increase in the numbers of women returned under the more learned professions. In medicine, for instance, the 477 women doctors of 1911 had become 1,253 by 1921. In the veterinary branch of surgery the women, though still a mere handful, had increased from 2 to 24. Women architects had multiplied from 7 to 49, while there were 147 women Nonconformist ministers as compared with only 3 in 1911. In four occupations, those of engineer, barrister, solicitor and police, in which no women were returned in 1911, the numbers in 1921 had respectively become 46, 20, 17 and 278 (130 of these being employed in Greater London).

In industry in general, post-war conditions, as has already been noted, compare favourably with those of the pre-1914 period, owing to the establishment of Trade Boards which were designed to eliminate sweating and which now regulate the wages of about two million women, and to the increase of welfare work in factories, from which, except in the questionable and much disputed case of special sex protection, men and women benefit alike.

. . . . .

Apart from the obvious requirements of more training and better organisation, the progress of women in the future appears to depend mainly upon the development of their power, as exhibited during the War, to grasp the need for a professional attitude, greater efficiency, a deeper sense of responsibility, and an increased willingness to adventure. Until time and education bring, as they are bound to bring, these changes, the limiting division of "men's work" and "women's work" will continue to exist in fields where its necessity is long past.

A woman Factory Inspector is as capable of judging the circumstances and work of men as she is of investigating the conditions and achievements of women; a woman lawyer is as competent to conduct a case of manslaughter or a libel suit as to draft Bills on behalf of women's societies. It is undoubtedly true that at the present time work for women offers to women the best prospects in most occupations, but to regard this stage as anything but a transition to more complete opportunities would be to put definite limits to woman's future field of employment, and to deprive the community of that general standard of efficiency which can only be attained when every form of work is done by the person most competent to do it, irrespective of height, weight, religion, race or sex.

"It is not only," states the Minority Report of the War Cabinet Committee, "that the exclusion of women, as women, from any occupation into which they seek an entry is a restriction on the liberty of more than half the population. Any such narrowing of the field of selection, and any limitation of the choice of occupation, necessarily detracts, to an unknown degree, from that utilisation of every available talent upon which maximum productivity depends."

The widening by women of their fields of work will be an advantage not only to themselves but to society as a whole, for any given community thrives, not by setting limits here, nor by putting restrictions there, but by offering more opportunities and an ever-widening freedom to those vital qualities of energy and initiative which, wherever they may be found, are alone capable of carrying forward the boundaries of civilisation.

78. THE ENFRANCHISEMENT OF WOMEN IN GREAT BRITAIN

In recognition of the services rendered by women during the World War and in line with the general European trend towards democracy immediately following the war, the British Parliament enfranchised women by two acts of 1918 and 1928, respectively.

a. THE ACT OF FEBRUARY 6, 1918 [3]

. . . . .

[3] *Representation of the People Act, 1918,* in *The Public General Statutes* [of Great Britain] *1917-18,* Council of Law Reporting, London, 1918, p. 255.

4.—(1) A woman shall be entitled to be registered as a parliamentary elector for a constituency . . . if she—

(*a*) has attained the age of thirty years; and

(*b*) is not subject to any legal incapacity; and

(*c*) is entitled to be registered as a local government elector in respect of the occupation in that constituency of land or premises (not being a dwelling-house) of a yearly value of not less than five pounds or of a dwelling-house, or is the wife of a husband entitled to be so registered.

· · · · ·

b. THE ACT OF JULY 2, 1928 [4]

· · · · ·

1. For the purpose of providing that the parliamentary franchise shall be the same for men and women, subsections (1) and (2) of section four of the Representation of the People Act, 1918 . . . shall be repealed and the following section shall be substituted for sections (1) and (2) of that Act:—

(*Section to be substituted for the said section one.*)

".—(1) A person shall be entitled to be registered as a parliamentary elector for a constituency . . . if he or she is of full age and not subject to any legal incapacity; and

(*a*) Has the requisite residence qualification; or

(*b*) has the requisite business premises qualification; or

(*c*) is the husband or wife of a person entitled to be so registered in respect of a business premises qualification.

· · · · ·

79. THE TARIFF ACT OF AUGUST 19, 1921 *(Extracts)* [5]

As one means of reviving industry in Great Britain in 1921, parliament approved a high-tariff measure defended by Premier Lloyd George as necessary to "shield unstable key industries." In the course of debate the prime minister defined key industries as those "essential for war." The chemical and optical industries were the ones chiefly affected by the act.

---

[4] *Representation of the People (Equal Franchise) Act, 1928,* in *The Public General Acts* [of Great Britain] *1928,* Council of Law Reporting, London, 1928, p. 28.

[5] *The Safeguarding of Industries Act, 1921,* in *The Public General Statutes* [of Great Britain], *1921,* Council of Law Reporting, London, 1922, pp. 260-261, 270-271.

Most Gracious Sovereign,

We, Your Majesty's most dutiful and loyal subjects, the Commons of the United Kingdom of Great Britain and Ireland in Parliament assembled, with a view to the safeguarding of certain special industries and the safeguarding of employment in the United Kingdom against the effects of the depreciation of foreign currencies and the disposal of imported goods at prices below the cost of production, have freely and voluntarily resolved to give and grant unto Your Majesty the several duties hereinafter mentioned; and do therefore most humbly beseech Your Majesty that it may be enacted, and be it enacted by the King's most Excellent Majesty, by and with the advice and consent of the Lords Spiritual and Temporal, and Commons, in this present Parliament assembled, and by the authority of the same, as follows:—

. . . . .

1.—(1) Subject to the provisions of this Act, there shall be charged, levied, and paid on goods specified in the Schedule to this Act, on the importation thereof into the United Kingdom, duties of customs equal to one-third of the value of the goods. . . .

. . . . .

SCHEDULE.

Goods chargeable with Duty.

Optical glass and optical elements, whether finished or not, microscopes, field and opera glasses, theodolites, sextants, spectroscopes and other optical instruments.

Beakers, flasks, burettes, measuring cylinders, thermometers, tubing, and other scientific glassware and lamp-blown ware, evaporating dishes, crucibles, combustion boats, and other laboratory porcelain.

Galvanometers, pyrometers, electroscopes, barometers, analytical and other precision balances, and other scientific instruments, gauges and measuring instruments of precision of the types used in engineering machine shops and viewing rooms, whether for use in such shops or rooms or not.

Wireless valves and similar rectifiers, and vacuum tubes.

Ignition magnetos and permanent magnets.

Arc-lamp carbons.

Hosiery latch needles.

Metallic tungsten, ferro-tungsten and manufactured products of metallic tungsten, and compounds (not including ores or minerals) of thorium, cerium and the other rare earth metals.

All synthetic organic chemicals (other than synthetic organic dye-stuffs, colours and colouring matters imported for use as such, and organic intermediate products imported for their manufacture), ana-lytical re-agents, all other fine chemicals (except sulphate of quinine of vegetable origin) and chemicals manufactured by fermentation processes.

80. THE ANGLO-RUSSIAN TRADE AGREEMENT, 1921 *(Extracts)* [6]

The economic situation in Great Britain in 1921 was so serious that the government, for fear of having Russia place its large industrial orders else-where, concluded a trade treaty with the Russian Socialist Federated Soviet Republic. Communism, indeed, had made so little headway in western Europe that the London authorities evidently lost their earlier fear of con-tacts with the Bolshevik state. In Russia, on the other hand, the attempt at pure communism had failed, and coincident with the adoption of the New Economic Policy at home the Moscow Government was ready to enter into a business truce with the West. The trade treaty, which conferred de facto, *but not* de jure, *recognition on Russia, was abrogated on May 26, 1927, when Anglo-Soviet diplomatic relations were severed by the British Government following the alleged discovery of Soviet anti-British activities in London.*

Whereas it is desirable in the interests both of Russia and of the United Kingdom that peaceful trade and commerce should be resumed forthwith between these countries, and whereas for this purpose it is necessary pending the conclusion of a formal general peace treaty between the Governments of these countries by which their economic and political relations shall be regulated in the future, that a prelim-inary agreement should be arrived at between the Government of the United Kingdom and the Government of the Russian Socialist Federal Soviet Republic, hereinafter referred to as the Russian Soviet Gov-ernment.

The aforesaid parties have accordingly entered into the present agreement for the resumption of trade and commerce between the countries.

[6] *Trade Agreement between His Britannic Majesty's Government and the Government of the Russian Socialist Federal Soviet Republic, Signed at London, March 16, 1921,* in League of Nations, *Treaty Series 1921,* vol. IV, pp. 128-136.

The present agreement is subject to the fulfilment of the following conditions, namely:

(a) That each party refrain from hostile action or undertakings against the other, and from conducting outside of its own borders any official propaganda, direct or indirect, against the institutions of the British Empire or the Russian Soviet Republic respectively, and more particularly that the Russian Soviet Government refrains from any attempt by military or diplomatic or any other form of action or propaganda to encourage any of the peoples of Asia in any form of hostile action against British interests or the British Empire especially in India and in the independent State of Afghanistan.

   The British Government gives a similar particular undertaking to the Russian Soviet Government in respect of the countries which formed part of the former Russian Empire and which have now become independent.

. . . . . .

It is understood that the term "conducting any official propaganda" includes the giving by either party of assistance or encouragement to any propaganda conducted outside its own borders.

. . . . .

Both parties agree not to impose or maintain any form of blockade against each other, and to remove forthwith all obstacles hitherto placed in the way of the resumption of trade between the United Kingdom and Russia in any commodities which may be legally exported from or imported into their respective territories to or from any other foreign country, and not to exercise any discrimination against such trade, as compared with that carried on with any other foreign country, or to place any impediments in the way of banking, credit and financial operations for the purpose of such trade, but subject always to legislation generally applicable in the respective countries. It is understood that nothing in this article shall prevent either party from regulating the trade in arms and ammunition under general provisions of law which are applicable to the imports of arms and ammunition from, or their export to foreign countries.

Nothing in this Article shall be construed as over-riding the provisions of any general international convention which is binding on either party by which the trade in any particular article is or may be regulated (as for example, the Opium Convention).

. . . . .

(3) The British and other Governments having already undertaken the clearances of the seas adjacent to their own coasts and also certain parts of the Baltic from mines for the benefit of all nations, the Russian Soviet Government on their part undertake to clear the sea passages to their own ports.

The British Government will give the Russian Soviet Government any information in their power as to the position of mines which will assist them in clearing passages to the ports and shores of Russia.

The Russian Government, like other nations, will give all information to the International Mine Clearance Committee about the areas they have swept, and also what areas still remain dangerous. They will also give all information in their possession about the minefields laid down by the late Russian Governments since the outbreak of war in 1914 outside Russian territorial waters, in order to assist in their clearance.

Provided that nothing in this section shall be understood to prevent the Russian Government from taking, or require them to disclose any measures they may consider necessary for the protection of their ports.

(4) Each party may nominate such number of its nationals as may be agreed from time to time as being reasonably necessary to enable proper effect to be given to this agreement, having regard to the conditions under which trade is carried on in its territories, and the other party shall permit such persons to enter its territories, and to sojourn and carry on trade there, provided that either party may restrict the admittance of any such persons into any specified areas, and may refuse admittance to or sojourn in its territories to any individual who is *persona non grata* to itself, or who does not comply with this agreement or with the conditions precedent thereto.

. . . . .

(5) Either party may appoint one or more official agents, to a number to be mutually agreed upon, to reside and exercise their functions in the territories of the other, who shall personally enjoy the rights and immunities set forth in the preceding article, and also immunity from arrest and search provided that either party may refuse to admit any individual as an official agent who is *persona non grata* to itself, or may require the other party to withdraw him should it find it necessary to

do so on ground of public interest or security. Such agents shall have access to the authorities of the country in which they reside for the purpose of facilitating the carrying out of this agreement, and of protecting the interests of their nationals.

Official agents shall be at liberty to communicate freely with their own Government and with other official representatives of their Government in other countries by post, by telegraph and wireless telegraphy in cypher, and to receive and despatch couriers with sealed bags subject to a limitation of 3 kilog. per week which shall be exempt from examination.

Telegrams and radiotelegrams of official agents shall enjoy any right of priority over private messages that may be generally accorded to messages of the official representatives of foreign Governments in the United Kingdom and Russia respectively.

Russian official agents in the United Kingdom shall enjoy the same privileges in respect of exemption from taxation, central or local, as are accorded to the official representatives of other foreign Governments. British official agents in Russia shall enjoy equivalent privileges, which, moreover, shall in no case be less than those accorded to the official agents of any other country.

The official agents shall be the competent authorities to visa the passports of persons seeking admission, in pursuance of the preceding article, into the territories of the parties.

. . . . .

(11) Merchandise, the produce or manufacture of one country, imported into the other in pursuance of this agreement, shall not be subjected therein to compulsory requisition on the part of the Government or of any local authority.

. . . . .

(13) The present agreement shall come into force immediately and both parties shall at once take all necessary measures to give effect to it. It shall continue in force unless and until replaced by the treaty contemplated in the preamble so long as the conditions laid down both in the articles of the agreement and in the preamble are observed by both sides. Provided that at any time after the expiration of twelve months from the date on which the agreement comes into force, either party may give notice to terminate the provisions of the preceding articles, and on the expiration of six months from the date of such notice those articles shall terminate accordingly.

Provided also that in the event of the infringement by either party at any time of any of the provisions of this agreement or of the conditions referred to in the preamble, the other party shall immediately be free from the obligations of the agreement. Nevertheless, it is agreed that before taking any action inconsistent with the agreement the aggrieved party shall give the other party a reasonable opportunity of furnishing an explanation or remedying the default.

· · · · ·

(14) This agreement is drawn and signed in the English language. But it is agreed that as soon as may be a translation shall be made into the Russian language and agreed between the parties. Both texts shall then be considered authentic for all purposes.

Signed at London, this 16th day of March 1921.

R. S. HORNE.
L. KRASSIN.

81. THE "ZINOVIEFF LETTER," 1924 *(Extracts)* [7]

During the British electoral campaign of 1924, following the dissolution of parliament by Premier J. Ramsay MacDonald, the cause of the Labor Party was seriously hurt by the publication in The Times *(London) of a letter said to have been written by the president of the Third International, Gregory Zinovieff, to British communists, urging them to prepare for revolution. The Soviets branded the document a forgery and its authenticity has not been established, but at the time it effectively hurt the Laborites who, in the opinion of many voters, seemed guilty of condoning unbridled communist propaganda. The treaty mentioned in the first paragraph of the letter refers to two conventions signed in London on August 8, 1924, involving* de jure *recognition of the Soviet state and the rehabilitation of financial and commercial relations between the two countries. The Conservative Government which came to power after the election of 1924 notified Moscow on November 21, 1924, that it would not submit the documents to parliament for ratification.*

[7] *The Times* (London), October 25, 1924, p. 12.

Very Secret.

To the Central Committee, British Communist Party.

Executive Committee,
    Third
Communist International
    Presidium.

Sept. 15, 1924, Moscow.

Dear Comrades,

The time is approaching for the Parliament of England to consider the Treaty concluded between the Governments of Great Britain and the S.S.S.R. for the purpose of ratification. The fierce campaign raised by the British *bourgeoisie* around the question shows the majority of the same, together with reactionary circles, are against the Treaty for the purpose of breaking off an agreement consolidating the ties between the proletariats of the two countries leading to the restoration of normal relations between England and the S.S.S.R.

* * * * * * *

Keep close observation over the leaders of the Labour Party, because these may easily be found in the leading strings of the *bourgeoisie*. The foreign policy of the Labour Party as it is already represents an inferior copy of the policy of the Curzon Government. Organize a campaign of disclosure of the foreign policy of MacDonald.

The Ikki [Executive Committee, Third (Communist) International] will willingly place at your disposal the wide material in its possession regarding the activities of British Imperialism in the Middle and Far East. In the meanwhile, however, strain every nerve in the struggle for the ratification of the Treaty, in favour of a continuation of negotiations regarding the regulation of relations between the S.S.S.R. and England. A settlement of relations between the two countries will assist in the revolutionizing of the international and British proletariat not less than a successful rising in any of the working districts of England, as the establishment of close contact between the British and Russian proletariat, the exchange of delegations and workers, &c., will make it possible for us to extend and develop the propaganda of ideas of Leninism in England and the Colonies. Armed warfare must be preceded by a struggle against the inclinations to compromise which are embedded among the majority of British workmen, against the ideas of evolution and peaceful extermination of capitalism. Only then will it be possible to count upon complete success of an armed insurrection. . . .

　　　• • • • •

From your last report it is evident that agitation-propaganda work in the Army is weak, in the Navy a very little better. Your explanation that the quality of the members attracted justifies the quantity is right in principle; nevertheless, it would be desirable to have cells in all the units of the troops, particularly among those quartered in the large centres of the country, and also among factories working on munitions and at military store depôts. We request that the most particular attention be paid to these latter.

In the event of danger of war, with the aid of the latter and in contact with the transport workers, it is possible to paralyze all the military preparations of the *bourgeoisie* and make a start in turning an imperialist war into a class war. . . .

　　　• • • • •

The military section of the British Communist Party, so far as we are aware, further suffers from a lack of specialists, the future directors of the British Red Army.

It is time you thought of forming such a group, which, together with the leaders, might be, in the event of an outbreak of active strife, the brain of the military organization of the party.

　　　• • • • •

Desiring you all success, both in organization and in your struggle.

With Communist Greetings,
President of the Presidium of the IKKI,
ZINOVIEFF.

Member of the Presidium,
McMANUS.
Secretary KUUSINEN.

卍 卍 卍

82. THE GREAT STRIKE, 1926 [8]

The following comments on the "general strike" called by the General Council of the Trades Union Congress in May 1926 were written by the editor of the London Daily Herald, *which had Labor Party affiliations. According to the foreword, "This rough diary of events was written and dictated at odd moments during the Unforgettable Nine Days to keep a friend at a distance informed as to what went on. . . . Its only merit is that it recorded things as they happened and as they came to the knowledge of one who was in the thick of it all."*

FIRST DAY [MAY 4]

. . . . .

The first sign that this morning is not as other mornings came about nine o'clock. Telephone bell rang. Voice of a friend, an American business man, offering to call with his car and take me to the office.

"You're very kind, but why?"

"If I don't you'll have to walk."

"But I always walk."

"Gee!—Well, this strike isn't going to worry you Britishers much if that's the way you take it."

Walking to-day, I must admit, was less agreeable than it usually is. The quiet road towards Regent's Park and the Park itself I had pretty much to myself, as I generally do. But as soon as I got out of the Park near Portland Road Station, I found the streets filled—and frequently blocked—by more continuous streams of traffic than I had ever seen in any city before.

I think there was a vague idea that when the omnibuses were taken off, the roads would be strangely clear. The taking off of the omnibuses was the signal for every sort and condition of motor car to come out. Traffic was far more tangled, far more often held up, and far slower than usual. Many who drove could have got to their places of business more quickly if they had walked.

Thousands of bicycles added to the confusion. All who could bring out and ride machines—no matter how old, how rusty—were threading their way through the cars. Carts and lorries filled with lucky

---

[8] H. Fyfe, *Behind the Scenes of the Great Strike,* The Labour Publishing Company, Ltd., London, 1926, pp. 9-10, 40-42, 55-56, 60, 79. Reprinted by permission of Mr. Fyfe.

clerks and typists who had asked for lifts, rumbled along among big, expensive, shining sports cars and limousines. Taxi-cabs are still plying, and there is little difficulty in finding one free.

. . . . .

THIRD DAY [MAY 6]

. . . . .

. . . not less marvellous than the completeness of the stoppage, the instant obedience to orders shown by those who were told to leave their work, is the absence of disturbances, the determination of the strikers to give no pretext whatever for the employment of the armed force which the Cabinet has so plentifully prepared.

Even the sentries outside Buckingham Palace have been put into field service kit. They no longer glow in scarlet; khaki is their only wear.

This causes comment, not very complimentary to the King, who has no more to do with it than you or I. He is roughly criticised, too, because of the Royal Arms appearing on the *British Gazette;* it is regarded as HIS paper by millions who don't know the ways of the Stationery Office. Many complained as well of HIS proclamation about the State of Emergency, which was signed by him as a matter of form. The impression that he is taking sides against the mass of working people is curiously widespread.

"Tomfool," by the way, has written some very delightful verses on the office-workers walking to the City. In the broadcasting of news this was spoken of as "The Great Trek." Here is what her quick brains made of it. (I suppose you know it is Eleanor Farjeon.)

> "It's the great, great Trek
>   Through the thronged city streets,
> It's the trek to the shops
>   And the tall office-seats;
> The roads are thick with people
>   Cheek by jowl, neck and neck,
> As the Walkers through the city
>   Make the great, great Trek.
>
> "It's the great, great Trek
>   On the road that is unseen
> To the goal of the future—
>   And the obstacles between

> Will seek to daunt the hearts
> And hold the march in check
> Of the Workers who are following
> The great, great Trek.

> "Oh, the way is hard to go,
> And the end is far to see,
> And the progress may be slow,
> And the body weary be,
> Yet something in men's spirits
> (What it is who shall reck?)
> Keeps them dogged as they plod
> On the great, great Trek.

> "There's a hope men must reach for,
> And a wrong men must break,
> In the teeth of all hardships
> For their child's child's sake.
> When the new hope is planted
> On the old wrong's wreck,
> Their child's child shall thank them
> For the Great, Great Trek."

I suppose there must be some to whom trekking is hard, but I can't say I have seen any evidence of it myself.

A girl in a shop told Mrs. S. that she gets home far more comfortably and quickly than she did in normal times. "I used to hang about a long time for an omnibus and then stand or sit all squeezed up. Now I can get a seat in a car whenever I want it, and it takes me right to my door."

A certain number of people, I am sure, take rides for fun. It's a chance that has never come their way before. One boy I know strolled out one morning at Battersea, where he lives, was offered a lift to Kew, took it, then got another to Richmond, was next taken into the City— to Liverpool Street Station— and finally, by two or three stages, reached Battersea again in time for tea! He said he'd had a most enjoyable day.

It's an ill wind that blows nobody good!

* * * * *

The streets have become dangerous. Motors are allowed to break the speed regulations, and numbers of drivers are driving without licenses—

in Cabinet service! There are lots of smashes—not bad ones, bonnets stoved in and mud guards bent and steering gear twisted.

One can't feel very safe in going to one's office even. We journalists are not on strike because our union, unfortunately, is not affiliated to the T.U.C. But the office is surrounded by pickets of other unions who eye one suspiciously. One has to enter the building by a back door which is closely guarded. The atmosphere generally suggests that anything may happen.

. . . . .

FIFTH DAY [MAY 8]

. . . . .

Here is another illustration of good feeling between strikers and police.

An official employed in anti-strike work had to go down to the East End of London in search of two policemen who were wanted for some purpose. He asked in a public-house where he could find them. The place was full of strikers; one of them said he knew, but before he would tell, the official must buy a *British Worker,* and he must read the leading article!

To the delight of the strikers, he good-humouredly produced his penny and read the article through. Then he was taken into a room behind the bar where the two policemen were taking a rest, the strikers having promised to keep order while they did so.

. . . . .

There has been a lot of excitement among the electricians. Some of them were anxious to cut off all current, not only power but light, so as to "hasten the victory." They don't like being at work while so many have stopped. They feel it isn't "the right thing."

The General Council has told them to carry on. It would be madness to plunge large parts of the country into darkness. Panic would be created, ruffianism would be let loose. No one will be allowed to come out with official sanction until the General Council gives instructions. Union authority is over-ridden. Some unions don't quite take this in. The engineering trades will probably be called out on Wednesday; this will mean putting the second line into the fight.

. . . . .

SIXTH DAY [MAY 9]

. . . . .

Interesting to study the type of woman who comes out again now in the uniform she used to wear in wartime. She is frumpy, hard-featured, hard-eyed. She cannot attract attention in ordinary times, so she jumps at the opportunity to push herself into prominence now.

The stiff line of the black helmet across the brow lends the face a look of resolution, but the mouth and chin are usually, so far as I have noticed, weakly shaped, denoting conceit rather than self-reliance.

I should be sorry to have to depend on any of these uniformed spinsters for help in an emergency.

. . . .

NINTH DAY [MAY 12]

. . . . .

An American staying in London came into the office just now and told me one of the comical incidents which are occurring on the railways (as well as some tragic ones), while amateurs are trying to take the places of skilled men.

He travelled from Warwick Avenue tube station to Baker Street. The first hitch was a stop in the tunnel, which put all the lights out. When the alarm caused by this had subsided, the train crawled along until Baker Street was reached.

There the American, who was standing on the platform of the car next the locomotive, heard an agonised voice calling to the conductor: "I say, Bill, I can't start the darned thing. Give me the instructions."

The conductor handed him a clip of leaflets; in a few minutes a z-z-z-z-z sound from the locomotive began suddenly and as suddenly ended.

Then the voice again: "Bill, I've touched the wrong handle and the brake's gone fut. Send for the chief engineer."

"We shan't be long," the conductor told the passengers; but most of them got out and walked!

83. THE TRADE DISPUTES AND TRADE UNIONS ACT, JULY 29, 1927 [9]

After the end of the British general strike in May 1926, the Conservative Government determined to prevent future similar contingencies by law. It therefore proposed and secured the passage of the following act.

[9] *The Public General Acts of Great Britain 1927,* Council for Law Reporting, London, 1928, pp. 328-338.

Be it enacted by the King's most Excellent Majesty, by and with the advice and consent of the Lords Spiritual and Temporal, and Commons, in this present Parliament assembled, and by the authority of the same, as follows:

1.—(1) It is hereby declared—

(a) that any strike is illegal if it—

(i) has any object other than or in addition to the furtherance of a trade dispute within the trade or industry in which the strikers are engaged; and

(ii) is a strike designed or calculated to coerce the Government either directly or by inflicting hardship upon the community; and

(b) that any lock-out is illegal if it—

(i) has any object other than or in addition to the furtherance of a trade dispute within the trade or industry in which the employers locking-out are engaged; and

(ii) is a lock-out designed or calculated to coerce the Government either directly or by inflicting hardship upon the community:

and it is further declared that it is illegal to commence, or continue, or to apply any sums in furtherance or support of, any such illegal strike or lock-out.

For the purposes of the foregoing provisions—

(a) A trade dispute shall not be deemed to be within a trade or industry unless it is a dispute between employers and workmen, or between workmen and workmen, in that trade or industry, which is connected with the employment or non-employment or the terms of the employment, or with the conditions of labour, of persons in that trade or industry; and

(b) without prejudice to the generality of the expression "trade or industry" workmen shall be deemed to be within the same trade or industry if their wages or conditions of employment are determined in accordance with the conclusions of the same joint industrial council, conciliation board or other similar body, or in accordance with agreements made with the same employer or group of employers.

(2) If any person declares, instigates, incites others to take part in or otherwise acts in furtherance of a strike or lock-out, declared by this Act to be illegal, he shall be liable on summary conviction to a fine not exceeding ten pounds or to imprisonment for a term not exceeding three

months, or on conviction on indictment to imprisonment for a term not exceeding two years:

Provided that no person shall be deemed to have committed an offence under this section or at common law by reason only of his having ceased work or refused to continue to work or to accept employment.

(3) Where any person is charged before any court with an offence under this section, no further proceedings in respect thereof shall be taken against him without the consent of the Attorney-General except such as the court may think necessary by remand (whether in custody or on bail) or otherwsie to secure the safe custody of the person charged, but this subsection shall not apply to Scotland, or to any prosecution instituted by or on behalf of the Director of Public Prosecutions.

(4) The provisions of the Trade Disputes Act, 1906, shall not, nor shall the second proviso to subsection (1) of section two of the Emergency Powers Act, 1920, apply to any act done in contemplation or furtherance of a strike or lock-out which is by this Act declared to be illegal, and any such act shall not be deemed for the purposes of any enactment to be done in contemplation or furtherance of a trade dispute:

Provided that no person shall be deemed to have committed an offence under any regulations made under the Emergency Powers Act, 1920, by reason only of his having ceased work or having refused to continue to work or to accept employment.

2.—(1) No person refusing to take part or to continue to take part in any strike or lock-out which is by this Act declared to be illegal, shall be, by reason of such refusal or by reason of any action taken by him under this section, subject to expulsion from any trade union or society, or to any fine or penalty, or to deprivation of any right or benefit to which he or his legal personal representatives would otherwise be entitled, or liable to be placed in any respect either directly or indirectly under any disability or at any disadvantage as compared with other members of the union or society, anything to the contrary in the rules of a trade union or society notwithstanding.

(2) No provisions of the Trade Union Acts, 1871 to 1917, limiting the proceedings which may be entertained by any court, and nothing in the rules of a trade union or society requiring the settlement of disputes in any manner shall apply to any proceeding for enforcing any right or exemption secured by this section, and in any such proceeding the court may, in lieu of ordering a person who has been expelled from membership of a trade union or society to be restored to membership,

order that he be paid out of the funds of the trade union or society such sum by way of compensation or damages as the court thinks just.

(3) As respects any strike or lock-out before the passing of this Act but since the first day of May, nineteen hundred and twenty-six, which, according to the law as declared by this Act, was illegal, this section shall have effect as if it had been in operation when the strike or lock-out took place.

3.—(1) It is hereby declared that it is unlawful for one or more persons (whether acting on their own behalf or on behalf of a trade union or of an individual employer or firm, and notwithstanding that they may be acting in contemplation or furtherance of a trade dispute) to attend at or near a house or place where a person resides or works or carries on business or happens to be, for the purpose of obtaining or communicating information or of persuading or inducing any person to work or to abstain from working, if they so attend in such numbers or otherwise in such manner as to be calculated to intimidate any person in that house or place, or to obstruct the approach thereto or egress therefrom, or to lead to a breach of the peace; and attending at or near any house or place in such numbers or in such manner as is by this subsection declared to be unlawful shall be deemed to be a watching or besetting of that house or place within the meaning of section seven of the Conspiracy, and Protection of Property Act, 1875.

(2) In this section the expression "to intimidate" means to cause in the mind of a person a reasonable apprehension of injury to him or to any member of his family or to any of his dependants or of violence or damage to any person or property, and the expression "injury" includes injury to a person in respect of his business, occupation, employment or other source of income, and includes any actionable wrong.

(3) In section seven of the Conspiracy, and Protection of Property Act, 1875, the expression "intimidate" shall be construed as having the same meaning as in this section.

(4) Notwithstanding anything in any Act, it shall not be lawful for one or more persons, for the purpose of inducing any person to work or to abstain from working, to watch or beset a house or place where a person resides or the approach to such a house or place, and any person who acts in contravention of this subsection shall be liable on summary conviction to a fine not exceeding twenty pounds or to imprisonment for a term not exceeding three months.

4.—(1) It shall not be lawful to require any member of a trade union to make any contribution to the political fund of a trade union unless he has (at some time after the commencement of this Act and before he is first after the thirty-first day of December, nineteen hundred and twenty-seven, required to make such a contribution)* delivered at the head office or some branch office of the trade union, notice in writing in the form set out in the First Schedule to this Act of his willingness to contribute to that fund and has not withdrawn the notice in manner hereinafter provided; and every member of a trade union who has not delivered such a notice as aforesaid, or who, having delivered such a notice, has withdrawn it in manner hereinafter provided, shall be deemed for the purposes of the Trade Union Act, 1913, to be a member who is exempt from the obligation to contribute to the political fund of the union, and references in that Act to a member who is so exempt shall be construed accordingly:

Provided that, if at any time a member of a trade union who has delivered such a notice as aforesaid gives notice of withdrawal thereof, delivered at the head office or at any branch office of the trade union, he shall be deemed for the purposes of this subsection to have withdrawn the notice as from the first day of January next after the delivery of the notice of withdrawal.

For the purposes of this subsection, a notice may be delivered personally or by any authorised agent and any notice shall be deemed to have been delivered at the head or a branch office of a trade union if it has been sent by post properly addressed to that office.[10]

. . . . .

* The parentheses, which do not appear in the act itself, have been inserted for clarity's sake.—*Ed.*

[10] *First Schedule.*

Form of Political Fund Contribution Notice.

Name of Trade Union...
Name of member's branch (if any)...

Political Fund (Contribution Notice).

I hereby give notice that I am willing, and agree, to contribute to the Political Fund of the   Union and I understand that I shall, in consequence, be liable to contribute to that Fund and shall continue to be so liable unless I deliver at the head office, or some branch office, of the Union a written notice of withdrawal: I also understand that after delivering such a notice of withdrawal I shall still continue to be liable to contribute to the political fund until the next following first day of January.

A................ B................

Address ....
Membership number (if any)..............
..............day of ...., 19...

5.—(1) Amongst the regulations as to the conditions of service in His Majesty's civil establishments there shall be included regulations prohibiting established civil servants from being members, delegates, or representatives of any organisation of which the primary object is to influence or affect the remuneration and conditions of employment of its members, unless the organisation is an organisation of which the membership is confined to persons employed by or under the Crown and is an organisation which complies with such provisions as may be contained in the regulations for securing that it is in all respects independent of, and not affiliated to, any such organisation as aforesaid the membership of which is not confined to persons employed by or under the Crown or any federation comprising such organisations, that its objects do not include political objects, and that it is not associated directly or indirectly with any political party or organisation:

Provided that the regulations made in compliance with the provisions of this section shall not prevent—

(*a*) any person who is at the commencement of this Act an established civil servant from remaining a member of any trade union or organisation not composed wholly or mainly of persons employed by or under the Crown of which he had, at the commencement of this Act, been a member for more than six months, if under the rules thereof there had on the fourth day of April, nineteen hundred and twenty-seven, accrued or begun to accrue to him a right to any future payment during incapacity, or by way of superannuation, or on the death of himself or his wife, or as provision for his children; or

(*b*) any person employed at the commencement of this Act by or under the Crown who thereafter becomes an established civil servant from remaining, so long as he is not appointed to a position of supervision or management, a member of any trade union or organisation, not composed wholly or mainly of persons employed by or under the Crown, of which he is a member at the date when he so becomes an established civil servant, if under the rules thereof there has at that date accrued, or begun to accrue, to him a right to any future payment during incapacity, or by way of superannuation, or on the death of himself or his wife, or as provision for his children; or

(*c*) a person who in addition to being an established civil servant is, apart from his service as such, also engaged in some other employment or occupation from being a member, delegate, or representative of any trade union or organisation, of which the primary object is to influence or affect the remuneration or conditions of employment of persons engaged in that employment or occupation.

(2) Subject as hereinafter provided, any established civil servant who contravenes the regulations made under this section shall be disqualified for being a member of the Civil Service:

Provided that, in the case of a first offence, a civil servant shall forthwith be warned by the head of his department, and the said disqualification shall not take effect if within one month after such warning the civil servant ceases to contravene the said regulations.

. . . . .

6.—(1) It shall not be lawful for any local or other public authority to make it a condition of the employment or continuance in employment of any person that he shall or shall not be a member of a trade union, or to impose any condition upon persons employed by the authority whereby employees who are or who are not members of a trade union are liable to be placed in any respect either directly or indirectly under any disability or disadvantage as compared with other employees.

(2) It shall not be lawful for any local or other public authority to make it a condition of any contract made or proposed to be made with the authority, or of the consideration or acceptance of any tender in connection with such a contract, that any person to be employed by any party to the contract shall or shall not be a member of a trade union.

. . . . .

7.—Without prejudice to the right of any person having a sufficient interest in the relief sought to sue or apply for an injunction to restrain any application of the funds of a trade union in contravention of the provisions of this Act, an injunction restraining any application of the funds of a trade union in contravention of the provisions of section one of this Act may be granted at the suit or upon the application of the Attorney-General.

. . . . .

8.—(1) This Act may be cited as the Trade Disputes and Trade Unions Act, 1927, . . .

. . . . .

84. SPEECH OF THE PRINCE OF WALES (LATER EDWARD VIII) TO THE MANCHESTER CHAMBER OF COMMERCE UPON HIS RETURN FROM A SOUTH AMERICAN TOUR, MAY 12, 1931 (Extracts) [11]

The "Prince of Wales," the later Edward VIII, undertook a number of good-will tours, notably to South America, in an apparent effort to stimulate British sales to that continent. Upon his return from these trips he delivered some frank addresses to British business men urging them to alter their traditional and old-fashioned business methods. One such talk is herewith quoted.

. . . . .

The first thing (I) learned was that in South America the prestige of Great Britain as a manufacturing country is by no means what it was, and I regret to have to tell you that that feeling exists not only among South Americans but also among the British communities resident there.

. . . . .

I have formed the impression from my experiences in the last three months that we in this country have a tendency to adhere too closely to pre-War types of manufactures and to forget what a change in taste has come over the world in the last 10 years. It is a world-wide change, as evident here as abroad. We used to sell our goods mainly on their quality and durability. Today the majority of people desire goods that won't last so long. They want something cheaper, and also they have got into the habit of looking forward to replacements as immediate improvements and new inventions come along. Also they have, I believe, got into the habit of liking a change for the sake of a change. Haven't we got that habit ourselves? Are we not jealous when somebody we know has got a newer article than we have? The taste of the world is in fact becoming as fickle as women's fashions.

If we are to succeed in meeting competition we must be prepared to manufacture the class of goods which South America is looking for, and which our competitors are providing. There is no reason why we should not turn out such goods, maintaining at the same time a degree of higher quality over that supplied by our competitors. To compete with foreign prices we should sacrifice some of the high finish and

[11] *The Times* (London), May 13, 1931, p. 9.

solidity we have been accustomed to give, without affecting their mechanical efficiency and usefulness. South American mentality and the whole atmosphere of the sub-continent calls for goods of a brighter rather than of a sombre character. It is very important indeed to appeal to the eye in this way.

I came across many instances in which the principal of a manufacturing firm in this country had been amply rewarded by undertaking a personal visit to South America in order to understand the change of outlook which is evidenced in South America today, and to grasp to the full the potentialities of that valuable market. It is essential that such visits should be made by the heads, or responsible officers, of British firms fairly frequently, so that they can make a careful study of the requirements, customs, and regulations of those countries.

. . . . .

You will find such visits more profitable in all ways than those of subordinate representatives, and it would be found very advantageous to spend a little time in studying the language of the country that you are going to visit. Not only will the South American be flattered that you have taken the trouble to acquire something of his language, but it will help you to get into the life and the atmosphere of South America very much better. . . .

. . . . .

The question of language applies even more strongly to correspondence and to the issue of catalogues and handbooks. It will save the South American's time and please him at the same time.

. . . . .

I am sorry to say we are sadly behind the times in the field of advertising, and are not sufficiently prone to blow our own trumpet, and when we have done something or invented something we do not broadcast it sufficiently and are too apt to leave the world in ignorance of it. I know many Englishmen sneer at the North American idea of publicity and describe their methods of boasting as vulgar. It is entirely a matter of opinion, and the fact remains that our friends in the United States do get away with it and, to use a phrase of their own, they put their goods across. If we are going to put our goods across we must take a leaf out of their book.

One of the first things we need to do is to improve the present very inadequate British News Service in South America. Events of national and commercial and sporting importance are not reported adequately, and, if reported at all, are reported too late or are not given enough prominence. To grasp the extent to which the influence of the United States has penetrated the commercial and industrial world of South America, you must realize the daily experiences of the average business man resident in one of the great States there. His telephone was of North American manufacture; 99 times out of 100 his car came from United States; his newspaper was well stocked with news from that quarter of the world; his office furniture and equipment was something up to date and efficient from the same source, and when he finished his day's work and went home, and his mind turned to relaxation, he would find his American radio and his American gramophone, or American films in the "movie" theatres waiting to entertain him—films portraying the life and culture of the United States, but with captions printed in his own language. And any time after dark he would find the manufactured goods of the United States attractively and prominently advertised on illuminated signs in every available position in the city. Well, we may hope that he will be pleased, when he takes off his shirt at night to see if it is clean enough to wear the next day, when he finds that that article at least comes from Manchester.

. . . . .

I advocate most strongly the system of group representation, not only for non-competitive trades, but for competing firms as well. In short, the abolition of the old-fashioned system of multiple agencies and its substitution by united trade selling organizations. There are still too many agents and too much internal throat-cutting by individual competing firms. Let us try to get every order for Great Britain at the best possible price, and decide afterwards which firm is to execute it when once it has been entered upon our national order books.

. . . . .

I am sure we could do more to open the doors of our universities and of our technical colleges, and even of our manufacturing plants to South American students, anxious to obtain technical training. Let us do that and ensure their preference in after life for British machinery and British products.

. . . . .

85. CONDITIONS IN THE "DISTRESSED" OR "SPECIAL" AREAS [12]

Economic conditions in Great Britain apparently were worst in several so-called "depressed" or, more euphemistically, "special" areas. The situations were studied and analyzed by special investigating commissions and some remedial measures were effected. The reports from which the following material was taken were written by P. Malcolm Stewart. Additional materials may be found in Reports of Investigations into the Industrial Conditions in Certain Depressed Areas of I.—West Cumberland and Haltwhistle; II.—Durham and Tyneside; III.—South Wales and Monmouthshire; IV.—Scotland. Presented by the Minister of Labour to Parliament by Command of His Majesty, *Cmd. 4728, London, His Majesty's Stationery Office, 1934, and in* Commissioner for the Special Areas in Scotland. Final Report by Sir H. Arthur Rose, Baronet. Presented by the Secretary of State for Scotland to Parliament by Command of His Majesty, July, 1936, *Cmd. 5245, London, His Majesty's Stationery Office, 1936.*

a.

. . . . .

25. The Special Areas are in their present unfortunate position owing to the decline of the main industries, coal mining, ship building and iron and steel, which attracted such large numbers of workers to them during the nineteenth century under more prosperous conditions. It seems unlikely that these industries will again employ the numbers engaged in them even up to ten years ago. During the period of prosperity large communities with full equipment of railways, roads, houses, schools and other municipal and social services were created. Many millions of pounds were spent in building up these services. A large proportion of the inhabitants have been associated with the Areas for several generations; they are bound to the Areas by ties of home and family and religion, by local patriotism and, especially in Wales, by a fervent national spirit and, sometimes, a distinctive language. It is natural, therefore, that wherever one goes in these Areas one should be

---

[12] *First Report of the Commissioner for the Special Areas (England and Wales). Presented by the Minister of Labour to Parliament by Command of His Majesty, July 1935,* Cmd. 4957, His Majesty's Stationery Office, London, 1935, pp. 14-16; *Second Report of the Commissioner for the Special Areas (England and Wales). Presented by the Minister of Labour to Parliament by Command of His Majesty, February 1936,* Cmd. 5090, His Majesty's Stationery Office, London, 1936, pp. 4-6, 68-69.

met by the demand that something should be done to attract fresh industries to the Area. This is the general request, and I regard it as at once the most important and the most difficult of my duties to try to satisfy it. I have given more time and personal attention to this side of my work than to any other, but it must be frankly admitted that up to the present the results have been negligible. Many of the negotiations I have initiated with this end in view were necessarily confidential, and it would only prejudice the present slender chances of success if I were to give a full account of them. The following paragraphs will, however, indicate the main lines on which I have been working.

26. In the first place I approached a number of the larger and more prosperous firms in the country in the hope that I might persuade them to open new branches of their industry in one or other of the Special Areas. Without exception they were sympathetic to my representations, but except in one case they had good reasons which made it impossible for them to accede to my request. . . .

．　．　．　．　．

29. Some hundreds of new factories have been established in recent years in the Midlands and South, but very few in the Special Areas. Why is this so? The main reasons appear to fall in the following categories:—

(1) Inaccessibility to markets. This applies particularly to Cumberland. . . .

(2) High rates. These probably have a deterrent effect on employers out of proportion to their real significance. . . .

(3) Fear of industrial unrest. This fear is very general and is bred from past disputes mainly in the coal-mining industry. It prevails particularly with regard to South Wales, but the facts scarcely warrant the attitude adopted. Statistics apart from those of coal-mining do not justify the fear which undoubtedly exists in the minds of many employers. . . .

(4) The fact that the areas are, and for some years have been, suffering from industrial depression. This factor, coupled with the common application to them of the term "depressed" or "distressed" areas, has itself a deterrent effect. While it is true that "trade brings trade," the converse unfortunately is equally true. Unemployment undermines business confidence and reduces purchasing power. A vicious circle is thus set up. . . .

(5) Difficulty in obtaining finance to start new industries. . . .

b.

. . . . .

10. The circular letter referred to in paragraph 28 of my First Report, which was issued, with the assistance of the Federation of British Industries, to firms outside the Special Areas, invited them to complete and return a questionnaire on the possibility of their establishing a new industry or a branch of their business in one of the Special Areas. The questions to which replies were sought were as follows:—

(1) Have you established any works or branches of your business in any of the Special Areas during the past few years?

(2) Have you considered within the past five years the choice of a site in one of the Special Areas? If the answer to the above is "yes," would you say whether you have been deterred by:—

   (*a*) High rates;
   (*b*) Fear of labour trouble;
   (*c*) Inaccessibility;
   (*d*) Technical trade reasons;
   (*e*) Other reasons (if possible please indicate nature).

(3) Are you now prepared to consider choice of a site in one of the Special Areas for a new works or any extension of your business? . . .

A map accompanied each questionnaire, showing the districts covered by the Special Areas, and at the suggestion of the Federation a short article was inserted in their Journal, explaining the objects I had in view in circulating the questionnaire. The completion and return of the questionnaire entailed no expense and involved the minimum of labour.

. . . . .

13. A total of 5,829 copies of the questionnaire were circulated with the following result:—

(1) 4,066 firms did not reply;
(2) 1,313 gave unqualified negative replies to all questions;
(3)   386 gave qualified negatives to all questions;
(4)   64 answered at least one question in the affirmative.

While I acknowledge gratefully the courtesy of those firms who returned the questionnaire and in some instances accompanied their reply with a sympathetic and helpful letter, I regret the lack of interest in the Special Areas shown by the large majority who made no response.

· · · · ·

17. The major points which the questionnaire has brought out are:—
(1) The lack of interest in the Special Areas shown by industry in general. . . .
(2) The smallness of the number who had during the last few years set up works of any kind in the Special Areas;
(3) The even smaller number now ready to consider opening up a factory or branch;
(4) The diverse nature of the reasons given for neglecting the Special Areas.

· · · · ·

255. . . . Probably the most serious human problem of the Special Areas is that presented by unemployment among young men between 18 and 21. . . .

256. Many of these young persons have done practically no work; they have been brought up in a home where the father has been continuously out of work, and they have little or no conception that a man's ordinary occupation should be such as will provide the means of subsistence for himself and for his family. They have seen their own families and their friends kept for years by the State, and they have come to accept this as a normal condition of life. It is hardly surprising in the circumstances that young persons with this background and upbringing should be ready victims of all manner of demoralizing influences. In short, these young persons present in my view the most tragic aspect of the problem of the Special Areas and one fraught with great danger to the State.

· · · · ·

86. THE PLATFORM OF THE LABOR PARTY, 1928 [13]

The following summary of the legislative and administrative proposals of the British Labor Party in 1928 is unusually complete and frank for a document of its type.

[13] *Labour and the Nation,* rev. ed., The Labour Party, London, 1928, pp. 52-55. Reprinted by permission.

SUMMARY

The Labour Party asks for power. If granted power, it will use it both to lay the foundations of a new social order, and to relieve immediate distress, by carrying out, as rapidly as Parliamentary opportunity permits, the policy embodied in "Labour and the Nation," of which the following legislative and administrative measures are a summary:—

I. INDUSTRIAL LEGISLATION

1. The Repeal of the Trade Unions Act and the Restoration of Trade Union Rights.
2. The establishment of a 48-hour week.
3. The improvement and extension of Factory Acts, Mines Regulation Acts, Workmen's Compensation Acts, Merchant Shipping Acts, Minimum Wage Acts, and other industrial legislation.
4. The establishment and enforcement of international labour standards.

II. UNEMPLOYMENT

1. The establishment of adequate provision for unemployed workers, under the control of a National Authority.
2. The amendment of the Unemployment Insurance Acts, the establishment of the scale of benefits recommended by the Labour Party in its evidence before the Blanesburgh Committee, and the extension of the principle of Unemployment Insurance to classes of workers at present outside its scope.
3. The withdrawal from the Labour market of children under 15, with the necessary provision of maintenance allowances.
4. The improvement of the provision made for widows and orphans and for the veterans of industry.
5. The repeal of the Eight Hours Act in the coal industry.
6. The transference and migration of unemployed miners.
7. The establishment of a superannuation scheme for aged miners.

III. THE DEVELOPMENT OF INDUSTRY AND TRADE

1. The establishment of a National Economic Committee to advise the Government as to economic policy, and of a National Development and Employment Board to prepare schemes for the development of national resources.
2. The control of the Bank of England by a public Corporation, including representatives of the Treasury, the Board of Trade, Industry, Labour and the Co-operative Movement; the encouragement

of Co-operative and Municipal banking; the promotion of an International Conference, as proposed at Genoa in 1922, with a view to the regulation of the value of gold by international agreement; and the introduction of such further changes in the banking and financial system as will secure that the available supply of credit and savings is used to the greatest national advantage.

3. The transference to public ownership of the coal, transport, power, and life insurance industries.

4. The appointment of a Commission to prepare a scheme for the reconstruction of the cotton industry.

5. The relief of industry by the readjustment of the relations between national and local finance and by the taxation of land values.

6. The protection of the consumer against exploitation and the extension of the powers of the Food Council.

7. The establishment of the fullest possible publicity with regard to costs and profits.

8. The promotion of scientific research, with a view to the improvement of industrial technique.

9. The extension of the powers of the Economic Section of the League of Nations.

IV. AGRICULTURE AND RURAL LIFE

1. The transference of land to public ownership.

2. The establishment of security of tenure for efficient farmers.

3. The provision of credit on easy terms.

4. The stabilisation of prices by the collective purchase of imported grain and meat.

5. The elimination of waste by the development of collective marketing.

6. The establishment of efficient services of electrical power and transport in rural areas.

7. The protection of the agricultural worker by the establishment of an adequate minimum wage, effectively enforced, and of reasonable hours of labour.

8. The improvement of the services of health, housing and education in rural districts.

9. The provision of facilities for the acquisition of land, both for small holdings and for allotments.

10. The introduction of legislation to abolish the evils of the tied cottage, and the rapid development of housing schemes in rural areas.

11. The development of the fishing industry, and the improvement of the conditions of fishermen and their dependents.

V. THE DEVELOPMENT OF THE SOCIAL SERVICES

1. The passage of legislation to enable the larger local authorities to undertake such services as their citizens may desire, subject to due safeguards in respect of efficiency and capital expenditure.
2. The provision of an adequate supply of houses at rents within the means of the workers, the establishment of cottage homes for the aged, the continuance and strengthening of the Rent Restriction Acts, and prevention of profiteering in land and building materials.
3. Slum clearance and the extension of town and regional planning.
4. The provision of medical care before and after child-birth, and the extension and improvement of the school medical service.
5. The amendment of the Health Insurance Acts, and the extension of insurance, including additional medical benefits, to the dependents of insured workers and to sections of the population at present outside its scope.
6. The improvement of pensions for the aged and of the allowances provided for widows and orphans.
7. The break-up of the Poor Law.

VI. EDUCATION AND THE CARE OF CHILDHOOD

1. The creation of a democratic system of education, adequately financed, free from the taint of class distinctions, and organised as a continuous whole from the Nursery School to the University.
2. The fullest possible provision for the physical well-being of children, by the establishment of the necessary number of open-air Nursery Schools, other open-air schools, and special schools for defective children, by the extension of school meals and by the further development of the school medical service.
3. The adequate staffing of Primary Schools and the drastic reduction in the size of classes.
4. The improvement of school buildings, and the provision of books, equipment and amenities on a generous scale.
5. The regrading and development of education in such a way as to secure primary education for all children up to 11, and free secondary education, of varying types, for all children above that age.
6. The extension of the school-leaving age to 15, with a view to its being raised to 16 as soon as that further reform shall be practicable, and the necessary provision of maintenance allowances.

7. The establishment of easy access to Universities and to other places of higher education, and the provision of adequate financial assistance for them.

VII. FINANCIAL POLICY.

1. The progressive reduction of expenditure on armaments.
2. The abolition of taxes upon the necessaries of life and of protective duties.
3. The increase of the death duties upon large estates.
4. The further graduation of the income tax so as to relieve the smaller, and increase the contribution from the larger incomes.
5. The establishment of an additional graduated surtax on incomes from property of over £500 per annum.
6. The taxation of land values.

VIII. INTERNATIONAL PEACE AND CO-OPERATION

1. The renunciation by international treaty, without reservation or qualification, of the use of war as an instrument of national policy, and the negotiation through the League of Nations of international agreements.
2. The reduction of armaments, by international agreement, to the minimum required for police purposes, with due provision for the employment elsewhere of workers who are displaced, and opposition to compulsory military service.
3. The immediate signature of the Optional Clause, the consequent acceptance of the Jurisdiction of the Permanent Court of International Justice in all justiciable disputes, and the signature of the General Act of Arbitration, Conciliation and Judicial Settlement, drafted and approved by the Assembly of the League of Nations in 1928.
4. The repudiation of the agreement with regard to military and naval forces which the Conservative Government has attempted to negotiate with France.
5. The immediate and unconditional withdrawal of all foreign troops from the Rhineland.
6. The promotion of international economic co-operation, as recommended by the International Economic Conference of 1927, and cordial co-operation with the International Labour Office.
7. The establishment of the fullest possible publicity with regard to international relations and policy, the publication of any international agreement not yet disclosed, or disclosed only imperfectly,

and the submission of all international engagements to the House of Commons.

8. The systematic use of the League of Nations to promote the utmost possible measure of co-operation between the nations of the world.

9. The establishment of diplomatic and commercial relations with the Russian Government.

IX. THE BRITISH COMMONWEALTH OF NATIONS

1. The establishment of the closest possible co-operation, on terms of complete equality, between Great Britain and the Dominions.

2. The recognition of the right of the Indian people to self-government and self-determination, and the admission of India to the British Commonwealth of Nations on an equal footing with the self-governing Dominions.

3. The establishment of safeguards against the exploitation of indigenous peoples by European capital, the prevention of forced labour and of injurious or inequitable conditions of employment, the protection of such people in the occupation of their land and in the exercise of civic rights, the development among them of the services of health and education, and their preparation, by all possible means, for full self-government at the earliest practicable date.

4. The strengthening and extension of the authority of the Mandates Commission of the League of Nations.

5. The development, in co-operation with the other States composing it, of the economic resources of the British Commonwealth of Nations, and the establishment of machinery for the advice and supervision of intending emigrants.

X. POLITICAL DEMOCRACY

1. The maintenance of the unquestioned supremacy of the House of Commons.

2. Uncompromising resistance to the establishment of a second chamber with authority over finance and power to hamper the House of Commons and defeat democratic decisions.

3. The abolition of plural voting.

4. The establishment of full civil and political rights for Civil Servants.

5. Drastic legislation against corrupt practices at elections, and the abolition of practices which confer special political advantages upon wealth.

6. The establishment of complete publicity with regard to Party

funds, and the termination of the practice of selling so-called honours.

7. The creation of separate legislative assemblies in Scotland, Wales and England, with autonomous powers in matters of local concern.

87. SOME OF THE POLICIES ADVOCATED BY THE BRITISH FASCISTS [14]

During the second Labor Government under Premier MacDonald (June 5, 1929, to August 24, 1931), the Labor Party suffered important defections when Sir Oswald Mosley, a man of wealth, and some of his friends became convinced that the government was not striving sufficiently hard to remedy the bad economic conditions. Then, in September 1932, Mosley founded the British Union of Fascists, a black-shirted group which patterned its ideology and ritual upon the Italian and Nazi models. Eventually, following a number of street fights, the British Fascists were forbidden to wear their uniforms or practice their semi-military tactics. For the text of this law see Document No. 94.

The first act of a Fascist Parliament will be to confer upon Government complete power of action by order. M.P.s will no longer be employed in hanging about the lobbies of the House of Commons, gossiping and intriguing in the smoke-room and obstructing the nation's business by endless and irrelevant discussion in the Chamber. Fascist M.P.s will be the spearheads of the Government's drive to action in carrying through executive measures in their own localities and constituencies. . . . The Parliamentary system, in fact, will immediately be transformed from a system which produces windbags to a system which produces men of action.

. . . . .

Fascism . . . does not shrink from empty taunts of dictatorship and is prepared openly to defend before the people the power which it demands as necessary to meet the problems which confront the nation. But something more is necessary than the taking of power on paper to deal with present problems.

It is necessary to have behind Government an instrument of steel, tested and tried in the ordeal of struggle and sacrifice, which will neither

---

[14] O. Mosley, *Blackshirt Policy*, B. U. F. Publications, Ltd., London, 1934, pp. 10, 12, 15-16, 25-26, 41, 61-62, 71. Reprinted by permission of Abbey Supplies Limited, London.

bend nor break in national emergency. Such an instrument means Fascism, for it can never come from those organisations of old women, tea-fights, conferences and compromises of which the old Parties consist.

. . . . .

. . . it is the wearing of the Blackshirt and the spirit of those who wear it which have been by far the biggest factors in the early success of Fascism. The Blackshirt is to us the symbol of service to and love of country; it is the emblem of men and women who are not afraid to stand up before all the world and to proclaim their faith. . . .

Beyond the supreme value of this symbol of faith, there are many practical reasons for wearing the Blackshirt. It brings down one of the great barriers of class by removing differences of dress, and one of the objects of Fascism is to break the barriers of class. Already the Blackshirt has achieved within our ranks that classless unity which we will ultimately secure within the nation as a whole.

Again, the Blackshirt is necessary for the very practical reason that it enables us to distinguish friend from foe in the fight which Red violence forces upon us. . . .

. . . . .

The solution [for the economic crisis] presented by Fascism is the Corporate State. As the name implies, this means a nation organised as the human body, with each organ performing its individual function, but working in harmony with the whole, and co-related with the general purpose by a directive and controlling intelligence, which, in the case of the nation, is Fascist Government. The Corporate State is, in fact, a completely new conception of an organised nation, differing as widely from the present Capitalistic State as it does from the Socialist conception of the State. No idea is more erroneous than the belief sedulously fostered by our Socialist enemies, that Fascism is merely a revival of Capitalism. . . .

In simple definition, Capitalism is the system by which capital uses the nation for its own purposes; Fascism is the system by which the nation uses capital for its own purposes.

. . . . .

(Our assailants) say that "economic nationalism" is fatal to world peace, because "other nations will follow our example and economic rivalry between highly organised nations will lead to world war."

Let us first inquire what this economic rivalry will be about. If other nations followed our example and were self-contained, where would such an international struggle arise? At present such rivalry exists in the struggle for markets under the present international system. Unorganised nations with diminishing home markets strive to sell abroad their surplus in international competition.

But under national organisation that necessity would cease to exist because each nation would be able to dispose of its present surplus at home by reason of the increased purchasing power of its home market. So far, therefore, from other nations following our example in national organisation, and thus increasing economic rivalry between nations, that process will bring this international rivalry to an end.

. . . . .

We have had enough of the slop of Democracy in Foreign as in Domestic affairs. We are no more prepared to enter into undefined commitments which may lead to the slaughter of our people in alien quarrels than we are prepared to leave Britain defenceless in an armed Europe. A Fascist Government in Britain will immediately increase British Air strength to the level of the strongest Power in Europe and will put the Fleet in proper condition. . . .

. . . . .

Party warfare will be brought to an end [after a Fascist victory at the polls] and every energy of the country will be devoted to the task of national reconstruction. Parliament will be brought together at regular intervals to review the work of the Government in short sessions. M.P.s will be armed with practical points of suggestion and criticism gained in actual administrative experience, for the whole network of local administration will be swept away and replaced by a system in which a local Fascist M.P. from the area will be the responsible executive officer of local government.

88. ELECTION OF A SPEAKER TO THE HOUSE OF COMMONS, NOVEMBER 3, 1931 [15]

Because it affords a good example of an interesting political performance, the following description of the election of a Speaker of the House of Commons is included in this collection.

[15] *Parliamentary Debates, House of Commons,* Fifth Series, vol. 259, His Majesty's Stationery Office, London, 1931, pp. 2-10.

. . . . .

Colonel Sir GEORGE COURTHOPE (*addressing himself to the Clerk of the House, who, standing up, pointed to him and then sat down*): Sir Horace Dawkins,—It is our duty, in response to the Gracious Message from the Throne, to choose our Speaker, and I rise to move the election, for the third time, of Captain FitzRoy. I do so with a grateful appreciation of the honour conferred upon me by my selection for this task, but with grave doubts as to my fitness to perform it adequately, and yet with keen delight in the opportunity which it gives to me to pay some tribute to an old friend and colleague. The office which we have to fill is no light one, for the Speaker is the custodian of the honour of this House. For some five and a-half centuries the Speaker of the House of Commons has been the centre and the symbol of Parliamentary development. Around him have grown up, now by strife, now by peaceful evolution, our Constitution, our institutions, our democracy. He is the very focus of a system, deep-rooted in the past, but ever growing with the changing years, which has won the admiration and the envy of the world.

The Speaker must fulfil many functions. He is our mouth-piece, the guardian of our privileges, the interpreter of our traditions, the judge of our behaviour, and the guide of all our efforts. Each new Parliament presents new problems. . . . This new Parliament, without precedent in the nature and size of its majority, charged with a stupendous task at a time of grave danger, filled with new faces, impelled by new forces—this Parliament may well make unusual calls upon him who occupies the Chair.

And what of the man whom I propose that we should set there? Captain FitzRoy is well known to most of us, for he entered this House more than 30 years ago, and, with one short interval, has served here ever since. We, who have been his colleagues, know how well he served. It would take too long to catalogue his achievements, but let me mention one. Captain FitzRoy did more than anyone to bring the industry of agriculture to the forefront of Parliamentary consideration. Incidentally, he is himself an enlightened practical farmer, and as good a judge of shorthorn cattle as he is of Members of this House. During two Parliaments he filled with distinction the office of Deputy-Chairman of Ways and Means. When three and a half years ago he was unanimously elected Speaker, he brought to his high office not only the experience of long and honourable service in this House and in his country, but all the best qualities of a soldier, a sportsman, an English gentleman. He has already added lustre to the illustrious line of Speakers under whose hands "freedom has slowly broadened down from precedent to precedent." Captain FitzRoy has won our respect by his impartiality, our admiration by his wisdom and his patience, and our affection by his good-humoured tolerance of our shortcomings. He possesses those most important members, an ear that sometimes fails to hear, and an eye that cannot see what is better left unseen. He has well and truly upheld the privileges of the Commons, the dignity of Parliament, the authority of the Chair, the rights of private Members, and the protection of minorities. In short, he has been a good Speaker; let us keep him. In the full assurance that he will fill his high office in the future with the same ability and distinction that he has displayed in such ample measure in the past, I beg to move, "That Captain the Right Hon. Edward Algernon FitzRoy do take the Chair of this House as Speaker."

Mr. W. THORNE: Sir Horace Dawkins,—I beg to second the Motion.

As an old Member of this House, with 27 years' consecutive service, and in accordance with the unanimous wish of the party with which I am associated, it gives me very great pleasure to second this Motion which has been so ably moved by my hon. and gallant Friend the Member for Rye (Sir G. Courthope). I should like, in the first place, to express the hope that Mr. Speaker-Elect will have the best of good health and strength to preside over this Parliament, which I guess will last for the next four or five years—[*Interruption*]—at least, I think so. . . .

·   ·   ·   ·   ·

The only other thing that I want to say is that I understand that one of the chief things that I have to do is to take Mr. Speaker-Elect by the hand and walk him up to the Chair. That is not a very big job for me, because, as a man who has had the pleasure of taking four women to the altar, with all the attendant domestic, family and financial obligations in front of me, I am quite sure it will be a very easy job for me to take Captain FitzRoy by the hand. I want to assure Captain FitzRoy and the House, with all the sincerity at my command, that it gives me very great pleasure to second this Motion.

The House then unanimously called CAPTAIN EDWARD AL-GERNON FITZROY to the Chair.

Captain FITZROY (*who, standing up in his place, was received with general cheers*): Sir Horace Dawkins,—In accordance with ancient usage, I rise to submit myself to the will of the House. In doing so, I must say how keenly I appreciate the honour that has been conferred upon me by the way in which the hon. and gallant Member for Rye (Sir G. Courthope) and the hon. Member for Plaistow (Mr. Thorne) have moved and seconded the Motion that I should be again placed in the Chair. I cannot conceive of a better combination of Mover and Seconder of a Motion such as this than that of the two hon. Members who have done it to-day. They have both been Members of this House for a very long time, and, during all the time that I have known them, I should think I am right in saying that on 99 questions out of 100 they have been diametrically opposed to one another; and on the hundredth occasion upon which they have agreed, their agreement has been about myself. . . .

This is really the only occasion on which I have an opportunity of addressing the House, and hon. Members, perhaps, will excuse me if I make one or two remarks. Since I first came into this House, now a good many years ago, it appears to me that every year more Members wish to take part in our Debates. It is quite true that you cannot put a quart into a pint pot, nor can you get more than a certain number of speakers into any one Debate, but I believe that, with a little trouble and consideration for others, we could get more speakers into a Debate if hon. Members would always try to make their speeches as short as possible. Might I say, without offence, that Ministers are not always the soul of brevity. It is astonishing, if you try, what a lot can be said in the course of 15 or 20 minutes, and I can safely say that some of the best and most effective speeches I have heard in the House have not taken more than 20 minutes. It is painful to me on many occasions to find how many Members who wish to speak I am unable to call, and I can assure the House that it would be the greatest gratification to me if, in our big Debates at any rate, many more Members could catch my eye. . . .

. . . . .

The House then having again unanimously called CAPTAIN ED-WARD ALGERNON FITZROY to the Chair, he was taken out of his place and conducted to the Chair by SIR GEORGE COURTHOPE and MR. THORNE.

Mr. SPEAKER-ELECT (*standing on the upper step*): Before I take my seat in the Chair of this House, I should like to offer the House

my grateful thanks for the great honour they have conferred upon me
and to assure them that, so long as I retain their confidence, I will give
all my strength to the service of this House.

Mr. SPEAKER-ELECT *sat down in the Chair.*

*Then the Mace (which before lay under the Table) was placed upon
the Table.*

The PRIME MINISTER (Mr. Ramsay MacDonald): Mr. Speaker-
Elect, I am very happy indeed to be the first to congratulate you upon
your election to the Chair, and at the same time to congratulate this
House upon your decision. You will, as has already been pointed out,
I dare say, have a very difficult task during the opening weeks of your
Speakership. There is a great multitude of unknown faces and an unusual proportion of Members who are but apprentices in the mysterious
arts and crafts of the House of Commons. They are very happy, however, in having you as their guide through those difficult ways. . . .

We ask you to preside over us, knowing that the rights both of
majorities and minorities will be safe in your keeping, that you will
preserve the liberties and the dignities of this House, and that with
impartial care you will conduct our business and maintain our reputation among the representative institutions of the whole world. We on
our part pledge ourselves to you to maintain your authority and to
assist in every possible way to make your task as easy as it can possibly
be made. I shall follow your injunction, at any rate to begin with, and
I offer you, on behalf of the whole House, our very hearty congratula-
tions and our most sincere thanks for having put yourself in our hands.

89. EXPULSION OF THE SUPPORTERS OF THE NATIONAL GOVERN-
MENT FROM THE BRITISH LABOR PARTY, SEPTEMBER 1931 [16]

*On August 24, 1931, Premier MacDonald tendered King George V the
resignation of the second Labor Government. One day later he reassumed
control—with a new "National Ministry" composed of members drawn
from all three major parties. Thereupon MacDonald and several other Labor
leaders who endorsed his course were expelled from membership in the
Labor Party.*

[16] P. Snowden, *An Autobiography,* 2 vols., Ivor Nicholson and Watson, Ltd., London, 1934, vol. II, pp. 986-987. Reprinted by permission of Lady Snowden and of the
publishers.

Previous to the General Election [1931] I and other Labour members who had supported the National Government were expelled from the Labour Party. The letter conveying this intimation to me I reproduce in full without comment. It speaks for itself!

THE LABOUR PARTY

"Transport House,
"Smith Square,
"London, S.W.1,
"1st October 1931.

"Dear Mr. Snowden,

"The National Executive Committee, at its meeting on Monday, 28th September, gave anxious consideration to the political situation and the developments which point to a grouping of the opponents of the Labour Party and an attack upon it at an impending Election.

"It was strongly felt that no distinction could be made in the attitude of the National Executive Committee to the actions and negotiations leading to the threatened anti-Labour combination from that shown in the establishment of the New Party by Sir Oswald Mosley earlier in the present year.

"Consequently it decided that Members of Parliament and others who are associated or in future associate themselves with the present Government thereby cease to be members of the Labour Party.

"It is my duty to convey this information to you and to express the regret of the Executive Committee that the decisions of representative Committees of the movement which have already been approved by the Trade Union Congress at Bristol and which will undoubtedly be approved at the Annual Conference of the Party at Scarborough have not been accepted by certain of its representatives, amongst whom are numbered some who have been largely responsible for the creation of its policy and practice.

"Yours sincerely,
"G. R. SHEPHERD."
(National Agent.)

꒭ ꒭ ꒭

90-92. THE BRITISH CABINET'S AGREEMENT TO DIFFER, 1932

90. THE DECISION OF THE CABINET, JANUARY 22, 1932 [17]

As a consequence of the parliamentary election of October 27, 1931, the National Government (supported by Conservatives, National Liberals, and National Laborites) won a huge majority. The premiership was retained by MacDonald, reëlected as a National Laborite, but his control was by leave of the Conservatives, who alone had a majority of more than three hundred. To maintain the appearance of unity, the National Ministry included eleven Conservatives, five National Liberals, and four National Laborites. Since these men found it difficult to agree on all important issues, the unusual step was taken of permitting individual members of the cabinet to dissent from the majority view "by speech and vote." This cabinet "agreement to differ" was announced in the following text. A discussion of "collective responsibility" in the British Cabinet may be found in W. I. Jennings, Cabinet Government, The Macmillan Company, New York, 1936, pp. 217-227.

The Cabinet has had before it the report of its Committee on the Balance of Trade, and, after prolonged discussion, it has been found impossible to reach a unanimous conclusion on the Committee's recommendations.

The Cabinet, however, is deeply impressed with the paramount importance of maintaining national unity in the presence of the grave problems that now confront this country and the whole world.

It has accordingly determined that some modification of usual Ministerial practice is required, and has decided that Ministers who find themselves unable to support the conclusions arrived at by the majority of their colleagues on the subject of import duties and cognate matters are to be at liberty to express their views by speech and vote.

The Cabinet, being essentially united on all other matters of politics, believes that by this special provision it is best interpreting the will of the nation and the needs of the times.

---

[17] *The Manchester Guardian Weekly,* January 29, 1932, p. 84. The text of the press announcement and a discussion of the factors that led to the decision may also be found in the memoirs of one of the prominent members of the cabinet involved: P. Snowden, *An Autobiography,* 2 vols., Ivor Nicholson and Watson, Ltd., London, 1934, vol. II, pp. 1003-1017.

91. DEFENSE OF THE CABINET'S DECISION BY HOME SECRETARY SIR HERBERT SAMUEL (LIBERAL), JANUARY 23, 1932 [18]

The publication in January 1932 of the British Cabinet's "agreement to differ" aroused much criticism. Sir Herbert Samuel, Home Secretary, defended it as follows.

When the formation of a National Government on a non-party basis was first mooted during the financial crisis of last summer, it was obvious that differences of opinion on the tariff issue might make co-operation impossible. Those differences were kept in abeyance at that time and during the general election; but it is essential now that definite decisions should be taken.

The Cabinet recently appointed a committee that included nearly half its members to consider the question of the balance of trade, and that committee by a large majority resolved in favour of certain proposals.

I dissented from some of the most important, and in a memorandum put forward an alternative policy. Lord Snowden also expressed his disagreement, and when the matter came before the Cabinet Sir Donald Maclean and Sir Archibald Sinclair shared the opinion that a case had not been established in favour of the measures in question, and that they were open to grave objections in the national interests.

In those circumstances the courses that were open were these. The four Ministers who held that view might have agreed to subordinate their opinions on the ground that larger issues predominated and might have concurred in the action proposed by the majority.

This we could not do. We had undertaken to exercise our own judgments on the questions involved, and having done that and reached the conclusion that the course proposed was not sound, we were obliged to say so and to vote in Parliament accordingly. Any other action would have been inconsistent with political sincerity.

There remained only two courses. One was to accept as inevitable the break-up of the National Government. In view of the international character of the chief problems with which we are confronted and the importance of maintaining, so far as possible, a united front in attacking them, this would have been most regrettable.

---

[18] *The Manchester Guardian Weekly,* January 29, 1932, p. 92.

It would, I am sure, have been deplored by the nation at large. The four dissentient Ministers are in full agreement with our colleagues on the great issues of disarmament, reparations, war debts, and currency, as well as on India and on national economy. We should be reluctant to withhold any contribution of ours which might be thought useful in dealing with those problems. Nor could we leave out of account the position of the Prime Minister, to whom the country is under such great obligations. His resignation was desired by no one. But to expect him to remain as the head of a Government which, by the withdrawal of one of the political parties constituting it, would have been deprived in large measure of its claim to the title National, would obviously be to subject him to serious embarrassment.

The only other course was frankly to suspend in this instance and for the time being the rule which has long prevailed of the collective responsibility of Ministers; to give latitude to the members of the Government who dissented on these matters, and consequently to those who shared their view in the two Houses of Parliament and in the constituencies, to express their opinions by speech and by vote without withholding their general support from the National Government as such. . . .

It is said that the plan is unprecedented, anomalous, illogical. That is undoubtedly true. But those considerations do not perturb us at all.

The basis of the last general election was open to the same criticisms. Our Constitution, happily, is elastic and adaptable. If this temporary measure is better on the whole than the alternatives that are open, that is what matters most. . . .

92. CRITICISM OF THE "NEW FREEDOM FOR MINISTERS" BY AN AUTHORITY ON GOVERNMENT (HAROLD J. LASKI) [19]

The following letter by Professor Harold J. Laski of the University of London may be taken as an example of the type of criticism that followed the announcement of the British Cabinet's "agreement to differ."

. . . The abandonment of the principle of collective Cabinet responsibility is defended . . . as though it affected only one single item in the Government's policy. But, in fact, a change so momentous in our fiscal

---

[19] Letter in *The Manchester Guardian Weekly*, January 29, 1932, p. 92.

policy affects the whole range of our domestic, Imperial, and international affairs. Where do the responsibilities of the dissident Ministers cease? Is their "freedom" ended when they have voted against the new tariff? Or are they to be allowed to carry their opposition over the whole area of contentious issues to which the new tariff will give rise? Will they take part in Cabinet discussions of these matters? Are we to have two kinds of Cabinets—a united Cabinet which discusses matters not arising out of the tariff, and one, consisting of the majority, which will discuss the tariff and its implications?

And where does the new principle end? If a Cabinet Minister should suddenly . . . develop a sense of loyalty to the Covenant of the League, could he attack Sir John Simon's desertion of it in the House of Commons? . . .

Mr. MacDonald, moreover, might well go farther. Since dissent on matters of major import no longer implies a need for resignation, it is surely possible to end official opposition by taking Mr. Lansbury and Sir Stafford Cripps into the Cabinet. It is true that they would dissent from the majority policy on tariffs, India, Manchuria, and disarmament. But they would accept the Children Bill, the new Town Planning Bill, the London Traffic Bill. . . . Indeed I do not see why Mr. Lansbury and Sir Stafford Cripps should not be admitted to the Conservative Party. Though they dissent from its major doctrines, they could be permitted to vote against them; and there are non-controversial matters on which common ground could be found. Mr. MacDonald has opened up new vistas of party rationalisation. The saving in expenditure on agents, meetings, literature ought to be immense. . . .

93. REJECTION BY THE BRITISH LABOR PARTY OF A UNITED FRONT WITH THE COMMUNIST PARTY, 1937 [20]

The efforts of the British Communists to tempt the Labor Party into a "United Front" were as unsuccessful as they were frequent. The official Labor summaries of these proposals and of the fate of the suggestion in 1937 are given in the following material.

[20] *Report of the Thirty-Seventh Annual Conference of the Labour Party, Bournemouth, 1937,* The Labour Party, London, 1937, pp. 268-270, 156, 164. Reprinted by permission.

*a. STATEMENT OF THE NATIONAL EXECUTIVE COMMITTEE OF THE
BRITISH LABOR PARTY ISSUED TO THE PARTY AND
TO THE PRESS IN JANUARY 1937*

To all Members of Affiliated Organisations

For more than three months a persistent campaign has been proceeding on behalf of what its promoters describe as "Working Class Unity." Its promoters are the Communist Party, the I.L.P.,[21] and the Socialist League. The campaign is being conducted by means of a large number of public meetings and through the press owned by these three bodies. Large sums of money, the sources of which are not disclosed, are obviously being spent on this Campaign. Its object is to bring the Communist Party and the I.L.P. within the Labour Party. Members of the Labour Party who are taking part in this Campaign are acting in clear defiance of repeated and emphatic decisions of the Annual Conferences of the Party.

This statement of the essential facts is, therefore, issued in order to enable members of the Party to deal with misrepresentation and misinformed criticism.

PAST PARTY DECISIONS

Only last autumn the most strenuous efforts were made to induce the Trades Union Congress and the Labour Party to admit the Communist Party to our counsels or, alternatively, to join with the Communist Party in "United Front" activities. These efforts were unsuccessful.

At Party Conferences in London in 1924, at Liverpool in 1925, at Margate in 1926, at Birmingham in 1928, and at Southport in 1934, proposals of a similar character were discussed and emphatic decisions against association with Communist activity were registered.

In the recent "Appeal for Loyalty," issued by the National Executive Committee [of the Labour Party] on January 12 last, reference was made to the Southport Conference decision.

The National Executive Committee recommended to that Conference:

> "That united action with the Communist Party, or organisations ancillary or subsidiary thereto, without the sanction of the National Executive Committee, is incompatible with membership of the Labour Party."

The Conference adopted the recommendation by 1,820,000 votes to 89,000 votes.

---

[21] The Independent Labor Party, founded in 1893 chiefly through the efforts of a Scottish ex-miner and trade-union leader, J. Keir Hardie.—*Ed.*

In making this recommendation, the National Executive Committee sought and secured full powers to deal with persons who indulged in such action.

At the same Conference, the National Executive Committee reported applications from the Communist Party and the Independent Labour Party for "United Front" action. The National Executive Committee's refusal to entertain this proposal was endorsed by the Conference by so overwhelming a majority that no count was taken.

Despite these repeated rebuffs, the Communist Party again applied for affiliation to the Labour Party in November, 1935, but in fulfilment of previous Conference decisions the application was refused by the National Executive Committee.

As the Communist Campaign for affiliation was carried on through the Constituency and Local Labour Parties as well as the National Trade Unions and their Branches, the National Council of Labour, on behalf of the industrial, political and Parliamentary sections of the Movement, published in July, 1936, a statement entitled "British Labour and Communism," which set out in detailed and authenticated terms the vital distinctions between the policy of the British Labour Movement and that of the Communist International. By quotations from speeches of Communist leaders, it was clearly shown that, in spite of their proposal for a "United Front," the Communist International remained bitterly hostile to the policy and to the democratic basis of Socialist Parties such as the British Labour Party.

THE EDINBURGH CONFERENCE DISCUSSIONS

At Edinburgh last October [1936], the Annual Conference was asked to approve the following Resolution, submitted by the Edinburgh Trades and Labour Council:

"This Conference, recognising the need for the unity of the Working-Class Movement, instructs the National Executive Committee to accept the affiliation of the Communist Party on the conditions laid down by the Party Constitution."

This was defeated by 1,728,000 to 592,000.

The National Executive Committee's refusal to accept the Communist Party's application for affiliation put forward in November, 1935, was endorsed without a further vote and the Statement, "British Labour and Communism," was approved. It had also been approved by the Trades Union Congress at Plymouth a month earlier.

The following Resolution was also submitted to the Edinburgh Conference, on behalf of the Amalgamated Engineering Union:

"That this Conference calls for the adoption of a policy which will unify all political bodies engaged in working-class propaganda, and remove all obstacles which at present stand in the way of complete unity.

"It views with dismay the widespread preparations for war and the increasing tendencies towards Fascism.

"Believing that the present division and conflict between the various sections of the working-class movement is a negation of the principles of Socialism and a hindrance to its progress, the Conference instructs the National Executive Committee immediately to meet representatives of all working-class bodies to bring about a 'United Front.' "

To this the following Amendment was moved on behalf of the South-East Essex Divisional Labour Party:

"That this Conference instructs the National Executive Committee to take all practicable steps to mobilise the support of all peace-loving and democratic citizens in the struggle for peace and the fight against Fascism."

After discussion, the Amendment was defeated by 1,933,000 votes to 190,000, and the Resolution was defeated by 1,805,000 to 435,000.

No single proposal has ever received such frequent consideration, nor been more repeatedly and emphatically repudiated by Annual Conferences of the Party.

It is the duty of the National Executive Committee to give effect between Annual Conferences to Conference decisions. It cannot, therefore, remain inactive in view of recent events.

THE SOCIALIST LEAGUE AND THE "UNITED FRONT"

Within a few weeks of the Edinburgh Conference, negotiations were begun by the Socialist League, an affiliated organisation, with the Communist Party and the Independent Labour Party for the purpose of initiating a so-called "Unity Campaign" on the lines specifically condemned by that Conference. Later, the terms of an agreement were drawn up and arrangements made for their simultaneous submission to the three organisations concerned. It was this circumstance which led the National Executive Committee to issue an "Appeal to the Movement for Party Loyalty" on January 12 last [1937].

A Special Conference of the Socialist League opened in London on January 16. The leaders of the League contended that the proposed

"Unity Campaign" would not invalidate the League's continued affiliation to the Labour Party. When this was challenged and proved to be inaccurate, the leaders of the League claimed and secured support for their proposals as a vote of confidence in their leadership.

The National Executive Committee, therefore, on January 27, issued the following Statement, a copy of which was sent to the Socialist League:

"The National Executive Committee of the Labour Party regrets that the Socialist League has taken action which its National Council must have known would be contrary to the cause of unity in the ranks of Labour, and would render the League ineligible for continued affiliation to the Labour Party, especially having regard to the statement on Party loyalty issued by the Executive dated January 12, 1937.

"The National Executive Committee resolves that the Socialist League, having acted at a Special Conference on January 16–17, 1937, on the recommendation of its National Council in direct defiance of Labour Party Conference decisions, be disaffiliated from the Labour Party, nationally and locally.

"The National Executive Committee appeals to all members of the Socialist League who are loyal to the Labour Party to recognise the new situation created by the Socialist League decision, and to continue their work for Socialism through the Labour Party."

Against this decision the Socialist League protested, but proceeded with the "Unity Campaign" in association with the Communist Party and the I.L.P., without any reference to the views of the Constituency Parties in the areas where meetings were held, or to the opinions of Labour Members representing some of these Constituencies in Parliament, or of Labour Candidates, who had been selected to fight others.

Owing to the imminence of the County Council Elections throughout the country, the National Executive Committee deferred further decision on the matter until its March meeting.

THE CHOICE OF LOYALTIES

At that meeting the National Executive Committee, in view of the continuance of the campaign, felt itself compelled to declare that membership of the Socialist League was incompatible with membership of the Labour Party. It, therefore, decided that, as from June 1 next, continued membership of the League will render its members ineligible for membership of the Party. It also decided that Annual Conference decisions regarding united action with the Communist Party shall be applied.

These decisions have been taken with the greatest reluctance, but unless a small minority is to be permitted to defy the will of the majority, there is no alternative.

The Communist Party claims to be "a voluntary organisation based on iron discipline," demanding "unbounded loyalty to the Party" as the chief characteristic of its membership. It takes not only its money, but also its orders from Moscow and must obey them slavishly. Mr. Harry Pollitt, at the "Unity Campaign" meeting in London on April 3, stated: "It is said I take my orders from Stalin. I plead guilty."

The Labour Party has never exercised an iron discipline nor does it demand unthinking loyalty. It encourages free discussion and it has been tolerant in its fellowship. It seeks a loyalty to its general principles, based on understanding and democratic consent. In this particular case, the National Executive Committee has not acted hastily, but only after its appeal for loyalty has been completely disregarded.

OUR WORK FOR TO-DAY AND TO-MORROW

Acting on an undertaking given at the Edinburgh Conference, the National Executive Committee has just published an immediate Programme of practical measures which a Labour Government with an effective majority would endeavour to carry into law within the lifetime of a single Parliament.

This "Short Programme" has already received wide publicity and support, and it is intended to concentrate our propaganda upon it during the coming months, both by the issue of further literature and by a nation-wide Campaign of Demonstrations and Conferences.

To this work the National Executive Committee calls on all Party members to contribute their individual and collective efforts. It calls for a real, and not a sham, unity. The real United Front is that of the Socialist, Trade Union, and Co-operative Movements.

It is the duty and privilege of Party members through their Trade Unions, their Constituency and Local Parties, their Women's Sections, their Leagues of Youth, and their Co-operative Societies, to help to win the British people for Socialism, for Democracy, and for Peace, to conquer political power and to drive the present Government from office.

It is a matter for deep regret that some members of the Party, instead of concentrating all their efforts on this great work, have preferred to embark on a disruptive campaign, which distracts the attention of the Movement and diverts valuable time and energy from more important tasks.

The National Executive Committee hopes that, even now, these members will abandon this campaign and will loyally join in the constructive activities of the Party. If not, the Party must go forward without them.

(For the National Executive Committee.)

J. S. MIDDLETON,

January, 1937   *Secretary.*

b. THE BOURNEMOUTH CONFERENCE VOTES UPHOLDING THE VIEWS OF THE NATIONAL EXECUTIVE COMMITTEE, 1937

THE CHAIRMAN [of the Bournemouth Conference][22]: The question of the United Front arises on the Annual Report of the Executive, pages 25 to 28 [of the Conference Report], with which has to be read Appendix VII.[23] By way of a reminder, may I say in regard to the Report, beginning on page 25 and ending on page 28, that in this section there are two sections—one of which relates to the action of the Executive in regard to the Socialist League—and the second to the re-affirmation of policy regarding the United Front. If anyone desires to move the reference back of these sections he should open the debate in that way. We should have a debate common to those two sections and at the end, if a motion to refer back is proposed, we should take two votes, one on the section relating to the Socialist League and the other regarding the United Front policy.

. . . . .

(At the end of the debate) a Card Vote was taken on the motion for the reference back of the paragraphs relating to the Socialist League, which resulted as follows:—

For the Reference Back................. 373,000

Against the Reference Back...........1,730,000

The motion was thereupon declared lost.

A Card Vote was then taken on the reference back of the remaining paragraphs, including the following sentence:

---

[22] The chairman was Mr. Hugh Dalton.—*Ed.*

[23] Appendix VII is the selection quoted as "*a*" of this Document.—*Ed.*

"This section of the Report, if adopted by the Annual Conference, will be accepted as a reaffirmation of the Party's rejection of the United Front policy as previously recorded at the Southport and Edinburgh Conferences."

The voting resulted as follows:—

   For the Reference Back............... 331,000
   Against the Reference Back...........2,116,000

The Motion was thereupon declared lost.

94. PROHIBITION OF POLITICAL UNIFORMS AND SEMI-MILITARY
  ORGANIZATIONS, DECEMBER 18, 1936 *(Extracts)* [24]

A growing number of political street fights in London and other cities led to the passage of an act, effective from January 1, 1937, prohibiting the wearing of political uniforms, such as the blackshirt, and the formation of semi-military organizations.

    . . . . .

1.—(1) Subject as hereinafter provided, any person who in any public place or at any public meeting wears uniform signifying his association with any political organisation or with the promotion of any political object shall be guilty of an offence:

Provided that, if the chief officer of police is satisfied that the wearing of any such uniform as aforesaid on any ceremonial, anniversary, or other special occasion will not be likely to involve risk of public disorder, he may, with the consent of a Secretary of State, by order permit the wearing of such uniform on that occasion either absolutely or subject to such conditions as may be specified in the order.

    . . . . .

2.—(1) If the members or adherents of any association of persons, whether incorporated or not, are—

 (*a*) organised or trained or equipped for the purpose of enabling

[24] *The Public Order Act, 1936*, in *The Public General Acts* [of Great Britain] *1936-37*, vol. III, Council of Law Reporting, London, 1938, pp. 60-67.

them to be employed in usurping the functions of the police or of the armed forces of the Crown; or

(*b*) organised and trained or organised and equipped either for the purpose of enabling them to be employed for the use or display of physical force in promoting any political object, or in such manner as to arouse reasonable apprehension that they are organised and either trained or equipped for that purpose;

then any person who takes part in the control or management of the association, or in so organising or training as aforesaid any members or adherents thereof, shall be guilty of an offence under this section: . . .

(2) No prosecution shall be instituted under this section without the consent of the Attorney-General.

. . . . .

(6) Nothing in this section shall be construed as prohibiting the employment of a reasonable number of persons as stewards to assist in the preservation of order at any public meeting held upon private premises, or the making of arrangements for that purpose or the instruction of the persons to be so employed in their lawful duties as stewards, or their being furnished with badges or other distinguishing signs.

3.—(1) If the chief officer of police, having regard to the time or place at which and the circumstances in which any public procession is taking place and to the route taken or proposed to be taken by the procession, has reasonable ground for apprehending that the procession may occasion serious public disorder, he may give directions imposing upon the persons organising or taking part in the procession such conditions as appear to him necessary for the preservation of public order, including conditions prescribing the route to be taken by the procession and conditions prohibiting the procession from entering any public place specified in the directions:

Provided that no conditions restricting the display of flags, banners, or emblems shall be imposed under this subsection except such as are reasonably necessary to prevent risk of a breach of the peace.

. . . . .

4.—(1) Any person who, while present at any public meeting or on the occasion of any public procession, has with him any offensive weapon, otherwise than in pursuance of lawful authority, shall be guilty of an offence. . . .

              . . . . .

5.—Any person who in any public place or at any public meeting uses threatening, abusive or insulting words or behaviour with intent to provoke a breach of the peace or whereby a breach of the peace is likely to be occasioned, shall be guilty of an offence.

              . . . . .

7. . . . (3) A constable may without warrant arrest any person reasonably suspected by him to be committing an offence under section one, four or five of this Act.

              . . . . .

10. . . . (3) This Act shall come into operation on the first day of January nineteen hundred and thirty-seven.

95-96. THE ABDICATION OF EDWARD VIII

95. RENUNCIATION OF THE THRONE BY EDWARD VIII, DECEMBER 10, 1936 [25]

On December 10, 1936, King Edward VIII renounced the throne to which he had succeeded upon the death (January 20, 1936) of his father, George V. The abdication was brought about by serious differences of view between the king and his ministers, particularly Premier Stanley Baldwin. The dispute, which in the opinion of many was based upon the king's alleged desire to participate actively in governmental affairs, was brought to a crisis by Edward's wish to marry morganatically a twice-divorced woman of American birth. The royal letter of abdication was read to the House of Commons by the Speaker.

The PRIME MINISTER (Mr. Baldwin) at the Bar, acquainted the House that he had a Message from His Majesty the King to this House, signed by His Majesty's own hand. And he presented the same to the House, and it was read out by Mr. Speaker as followeth, all the Members of the House being uncovered.

[25] Great Britain, *Parliamentary Debates, House of Commons,* vol. 318, pp. 2175-2176.

Fort Belvedere,
Sunningdale,
Berkshire.

Members of the House of Commons,

After long and anxious consideration, I have determined to renounce the Throne to which I succeeded on the death of My father, and I am now communicating this, My final and irrevocable decision. Realising as I do the gravity of this step, I can only hope that I shall have the understanding of My peoples in the decision I have taken and the reasons which have led Me to take it. I will not enter now into My private feelings, but I would beg that it should be remembered that the burden which constantly rests upon the shoulders of a Sovereign is so heavy that it can only be borne in circumstances different from those in which I now find Myself. I conceive that I am not overlooking the duty that rests on Me to place in the forefront the public interest, when I declare that I am conscious that I can no longer discharge this heavy task with efficiency or with satisfaction to Myself.

I have accordingly this morning executed an Instrument of Abdication in the terms following:—

"I, Edward VIII, of Great Britain, Ireland, and the British Dominions beyond the Seas, King, Emperor of India, do hereby declare My irrevocable determination to renounce the Throne for Myself and for my descendants, and My desire that effect should be given to this Instrument of Abdication immediately.

In token whereof I have hereunto set My hand this tenth day of December, nineteen hundred and thirty-six, in the presence of the witnesses whose signatures are subscribed.

(Signed) EDWARD R. I.

My execution of this Instrument has been witnessed by My three brothers, Their Royal Highnesses the Duke of York, the Duke of Gloucester and the Duke of Kent.

I deeply appreciate the spirit which has actuated the appeals which have been made to Me to take a different decision, and I have, before reaching My final determination, most fully pondered over them. But My mind is made up. Moreover, further delay cannot but be most injurious to the peoples whom I have tried to serve as Prince of Wales and as King and whose future happiness and prosperity are the constant wish of My heart.

I take My leave of them in the confident hope that the course which
I have thought it right to follow is that which is best for the stability
of the Throne and Empire and the happiness of My peoples. I am
deeply sensible of the consideration which they have always extended
to Me both before and after My accession to the Throne and which I
know they will extend in full measure to My successor.

I am most anxious that there should be no delay of any kind in giving
effect to the Instrument which I have executed and that all necessary
steps should be taken immediately to secure that My lawful successor,
My brother, His Royal Highness, the Duke of York, should ascend the
Throne.

EDWARD R. I.

96. THE DECLARATION OF ABDICATION ACT, 1936 [26]

*A law giving effect to the letter of abdication of King Edward VIII was
passed on December 11, 1936. The throne thereupon went to Edward's
brother, the Duke of York, who was crowned George VI on May 12, 1937.*

AN ACT TO GIVE EFFECT TO HIS MAJESTY'S DECLARATION OF
ABDICATION; AND FOR PURPOSES CONNECTED THEREWITH.
[11th DECEMBER 1936.]

WHEREAS His Majesty by His Royal Message of the tenth day of
December in this present year has been pleased to declare that He is
irrevocably determined to renounce the Throne for Himself and His
descendants, and has for that purpose executed the Instrument of Abdication set out in the Schedule to this Act, and has signified His desire
that effect thereto should be given immediately;

And whereas, following upon the communication to His Dominions
of His Majesty's said declaration and desire, the Dominion of Canada
pursuant to the provisions of section four of the Statute of Westminster,
1931, has requested and consented to the enactment of this Act, and the
Commonwealth of Australia, the Dominion of New Zealand, and the
Union of South Africa have assented thereto:

Be it therefore enacted by the King's most Excellent Majesty, by and
with the advice and consent of the Lords Spiritual and Temporal, and
Commons, in this present Parliament assembled, and by the authority
of the same, as follows:—

1.—(1) Immediately upon the Royal Assent being signified to this

<hr>

[26] *The Public General Acts* [of Great Britain], *1936-1937,* London, 1937, pp. 9-10.

Act the Instrument of Abdication executed by His present Majesty on the tenth day of December, nineteen hundred and thirty-six, set out in the Schedule to this Act, shall have effect, and thereupon His Majesty shall cease to be King and there shall be a demise of the Crown, and accordingly the member of the Royal Family then next in succession to the Throne shall succeed thereto and to all the rights, privileges, and dignities thereunto belonging.

(2) His Majesty, His issue, if any, and the descendants of that issue, shall not after His Majesty's abdication have any right, title or interest in or to the succession to the Throne, and section one of the Act of Settlement shall be construed accordingly.

(3) The Royal Marriages Act, 1772, shall not apply to His Majesty after His abdication nor to the issue, if any, of His Majesty or the descendants of that issue.

2. This Act may be cited as His Majesty's Declaration of Abdication Act, 1936.

SCHEDULE.

I, Edward the Eighth, of Great Britain, Ireland, and the British Dominions beyond the Seas, King, Emperor of India, do hereby declare My irrevocable determination to renounce the Throne for Myself and for My descendants, and My desire that effect should be given to this Instrument of Abdication immediately.

In token whereof I have hereunto set My hand this tenth day of December, nineteen hundred and thirty-six, in the presence of the witnesses whose signatures are subscribed.

EDWARD R. I.

Signed at Fort Belvedere
   in the presence of
     ALBERT.
     HENRY.
     GEORGE.

97. SPEECH ON FOREIGN POLICY BY NEVILLE CHAMBERLAIN
(Extracts) [27]

The Conservative Neville Chamberlain, who took office as premier in May 1937, hoped to bring lasting peace to Europe through the friendly co-operation of Great Britain, France, Germany, and Italy. Upon the resigna-

[27] Great Britain, *Parliamentary Debates, House of Commons,* February 21, 1938, vol. 332, pp. 53-54, 64.

tion of his foreign secretary, Anthony Eden, in February 1938—because of
the latter's opposition to a policy which involved making increasing con-
cessions to the demands of the dictatorially-controlled states—Chamberlain
felt it incumbent upon him to explain his views to parliament.

~~~~~~

In order that the House may have before it as complete a picture as
possible of the events which have led up to the present situation [the
resignation of Foreign Secretary Anthony Eden], I must ask for their
indulgence while I endeavour to state once again my own views upon
certain aspects of foreign policy—views which have never altered, and
which have been shared by all my colleagues. On a former occasion I
described that policy as being based upon three principles—first, on the
protection of British interests and the lives of British nationals; secondly, on the maintenance of peace, and, as far as we can influence it,
the settlement of differences by peaceful means and not by force; and,
thirdly, the promotion of friendly relations with other nations who are
willing to reciprocate our friendly feelings and who will keep those
rules of international conduct without which there can be neither
security nor stability.

It is not enough to lay down general principles. If we truly desire
peace, it is, in my opinion, necessary to make a sustained effort to
ascertain, and if possible remove, the causes which threaten peace and
which now, for many months, have kept Europe in a state of tension
and anxiety. There is another fact which points in the same direction.
We are in this country now engaged upon a gigantic scheme of
rearmament which most of us believe to be essential to the maintenance
of peace. Other countries are doing the same. Indeed, we were the
last of the nations to rearm, but this process of general rearmament has
been forced upon us all, because every country is afraid to disarm lest
it should fall a victim to some armed neighbour. I recognise the force
of that hard fact, but I have never ceased publicly to deplore what seems
to me a senseless waste of money, for which everyone will have to pay
dearly, if they are not paying for it already. I cannot believe that,
with a little good will and determination, it is not possible to remove
genuine grievances and to clear away suspicions which may be entirely unfounded.

For these reasons, then, my colleagues and I have been anxious to
find some opportunity of entering upon conversations with the two
European countries with which we have been at variance, namely,

Germany and Italy, in order that we might find out whether there was any common ground on which we might build up a general scheme of appeasement in Europe. . . .

. . . . .

The peace of Europe must depend upon the attitude of the four major Powers—Germany, Italy, France and ourselves. For ourselves, we are linked to France by common ideals of democracy, of liberty and Parliamentary government. France need not fear that the resignation of my right hon. Friend upon this issue signifies any departure from the policy of the closest friendship with France of which he has been such a distinguished exponent. I count myself as firm a friend of France as my right hon. Friend. The difference between him and me will never mean that there is any difference between us about our relations with France. On the other side we find Italy and Germany linked by affinities of outlook and in the forms of their government. The question that we have to think of is this: Are we to allow these two pairs of nations to go on glowering at one another across the frontier, allowing the feeling between the two sides to become more and more embittered, until at last the barriers are broken down and the conflict begins which many think would mean the end of civilisation? Or can we bring them to an understanding of one another's aims and objects, and to such discussion as may lead to a final settlement? If we can do that, if we can bring these four nations into friendly discussion, into a settling of their differences, we shall have saved the peace of Europe for a generation. . . .

98. THE IMPERIAL CONFERENCE OF 1926 ON INTER-IMPERIAL RELATIONS [28]

The relations between Great Britain and her dominions were greatly altered as a result of the exigencies of the World War, the dependence of the mother country on the help of her colonies, the independent signature of the peace treaties by the dominions, and their full-fledged membership in the League of Nations. Then, in the post-war years, the dominions from time to time performed acts, such as the signature of bilateral treaties with other

---

[28] *Imperial Conference, 1926. Summary of Proceedings. Presented to Parliament by Command of His Majesty, November, 1926,* Cmd. 2768, His Majesty's Stationery Office, London, 1926, pp. 13-15.

states, which obviously came within the category of sovereign powers. The Imperial Conference of 1926, in a document known as the Balfour Report, affirmed this new dominion status in principle, but it remained for later actual legislation (See Document No. 99) to give legal force to the views there expressed.

REPORT OF INTER-IMPERIAL RELATIONS COMMITTEE.
I. INTRODUCTION.

We were appointed at the meeting of the Imperial Conference on the 25th October, 1926, to investigate all the questions on the Agenda affecting Inter-Imperial Relations. Our discussions on these questions have been long and intricate. We found, on examination, that they involved consideration of fundamental principles affecting the relations of the various parts of the British Empire *inter se,* as well as the relations of each part to foreign countries. For such examination the time at our disposal has been all too short. Yet we hope that we may have laid a foundation on which subsequent Conferences may build.

II. STATUS OF GREAT BRITAIN AND THE DOMINIONS.

The Committee are of opinion that nothing would be gained by attempting to lay down a Constitution for the British Empire. Its widely scattered parts have very different characteristics, very different histories, and are at very different stages of evolution; while, considered as a whole, it defies classification and bears no real resemblance to any other political organization which now exists or has ever yet been tried.

There is however, one most important element in it which, from a strictly constitutional point of view, has now, as regards all vital matters, reached its full development—we refer to the group of self-governing communities composed of Great Britain and the Dominions. Their position and mutual relation may be readily defined. *They are autonomous Communities within the British Empire, equal in status, in no way subordinate one to another in any aspect of their domestic or external affairs, though united by a common allegiance to the Crown and freely associated as members of the British Commonwealth of Nations.*

A foreigner endeavouring to understand the true character of the British Empire by the aid of this formula alone would be tempted to think that it was devised rather to make mutual interference impossible than to make mutual co-operation easy.

Such a criticism, however, completely ignores the historic situation. The rapid evolution of the Oversea Dominions during the last fifty years has involved many complicated adjustments of old political machinery to changing conditions. The tendency towards equality of status was both right and inevitable. Geographical and other conditions made this impossible of attainment by the way of federation. The only alternative was by the way of autonomy; and along this road it has been steadily sought. Every self-governing member of the Empire is now the master of its destiny. In fact, if not always in form, it is subject to no compulsion whatever.

But no account, however accurate, of the negative relations in which Great Britain and the Dominions stand to each other can do more than express a portion of the truth. The British Empire is not founded upon negations. It depends essentially, if not formally, on positive ideals. Free institutions are its life-blood. Free co-operation is its instrument. Peace, security, and progress are among its objects. Aspects of all these great themes have been discussed at the present Conference; excellent results have been thereby obtained. And, though every Dominion is now, and must always remain, the sole judge of the nature and extent of its co-operation, no common cause will, in our opinion, be thereby imperilled.

Equality of status, so far as Britain and the Dominions are concerned, is thus the root principle governing our Inter-Imperial Relations. But the principles of equality and similarity, appropriate to *status,* do not universally extend to function. Here we require something more than immutable dogmas. For example, to deal with questions of diplomacy and questions of defence, we require also flexible machinery—machinery which can, from time to time, be adapted to the changing circumstances of the world. This subject also has occupied our attention. The rest of this Report will show how we have endeavoured not only to state political theory, but to apply it to our common needs.

99. THE STATUTE OF WESTMINSTER, DECEMBER 11, 1931 [29]

A committee representing Great Britain and the dominions was appointed in 1929 to report on a method for making legal the new status toward which the dominions had been moving in recent years. The Imperial Conference

[29] *The Public General Acts of Great Britain, 1932,* Council of Law Reporting, London, 1933, pp. 13-17.

of 1930 accepted the report which this committee eventually rendered and soon thereafter the necessary steps were taken in each dominion to give it the force of law. The passage of the Statute of Westminster by the British Parliament in December 1931 completed the legalization of the new commonwealth relationship.

Whereas the delegates of His Majesty's Governments in the United Kingdom, the Dominion of Canada, the Commonwealth of Australia, the Dominion of New Zealand, the Union of South Africa, the Irish Free State and Newfoundland, at Imperial Conferences holden at Westminster in the years of our Lord nineteen hundred and twenty-six and nineteen hundred and thirty did concur in making the declarations and resolutions set forth in the Reports of the said Conferences:

And whereas it is meet and proper to set out by way of preamble to this Act that, inasmuch as the Crown is the symbol of the free association of the members of the British Commonwealth of Nations, and as they are united by a common allegiance to the Crown, it would be in accord with the established constitutional position of all the members of the Commonwealth in relation to one another that any alteration in the law touching the Succession to the Throne or the Royal Style and Titles shall hereafter require the assent as well of the Parliaments of all the Dominions as of the Parliament of the United Kingdom:

And whereas it is in accord with the established constitutional position that no law hereafter made by the Parliament of the United Kingdom shall extend to any of the said Dominions as part of the law of that Dominion otherwise than at the request and with the consent of that Dominion:

And whereas it is necessary for the ratifying, confirming and establishing of certain of the said declarations and resolutions of the said Conferences that a law be made and enacted in due form by authority of the United Kingdom:

And whereas the Dominion of Canada, the Commonwealth of Australia, the Dominion of New Zealand, the Union of South Africa, the Irish Free State and Newfoundland have severally requested and consented to the submission of a measure to the Parliament of the United Kingdom for making such provision with regard to the matters aforesaid as is hereafter in this Act contained:

Now, therefore, be it enacted by the King's most Excellent Majesty by and with the advice and consent of the Lords Spiritual and Temporal, and Commons, in this present Parliament assembled, and by the authority of the same, as follows:—

1. In this Act the expression "Dominion" means any of the following Dominions, that is to say, the Dominion of Canada, the Commonwealth of Australia, the Dominion of New Zealand, the Union of South Africa, the Irish Free State and Newfoundland.

2.—(1) The Colonial Laws Validity Act, 1865, shall not apply to any law made after the commencement of this Act by the Parliament of a Dominion.

(2) No law and no provision of any law made after the commencement of this Act by the Parliament of a Dominion shall be void or inoperative on the ground that it is repugnant to the law of England, or to the provisions of any existing or future Act of Parliament of the United Kingdom, or to any order, rule or regulation made under any such Act, and the powers of the Parliament of a Dominion shall include the power to repeal or amend any such Act, order, rule or regulation in so far as the same is part of the law of the Dominion.

3. It is hereby declared and enacted that the Parliament of a Dominion has full power to make laws having extra-territorial operation.

4. No Act of Parliament of the United Kingdom passed after the commencement of this Act shall extend or be deemed to extend, to a Dominion as part of the law of that Dominion, unless it is expressly declared in that Act that that Dominion has requested, and consented to, the enactment thereof.

5. Without prejudice to the generality of the foregoing provisions of this Act, sections seven hundred and thirty-five and seven hundred and thirty-six of the Merchant Shipping Act, 1894, shall be construed as though reference therein to the Legislature of a British possession did not include reference to the Parliament of a Dominion.

6. Without prejudice to the generality of the foregoing provisions of this Act, section four of the Colonial Courts of Admiralty Act, 1890 (which requires certain laws to be reserved for the signification of His Majesty's pleasure or to contain a suspending clause), and so much of section seven of that Act as requires the approval of His Majesty in Council to any rules of Court for regulating the practice and procedure of a Colonial Court of Admiralty, shall cease to have effect in any Dominion as from the commencement of this Act.

7.—(1) Nothing in this Act shall be deemed to apply to the repeal, amendment or alteration of the British North American Acts, 1867 to 1930, or any order, rule or regulation made thereunder.

(2) The provisions of section two of this Act shall extend to laws made by any of the Provinces of Canada and to the powers of the legislatures of such Provinces.

(3) The powers conferred by this Act upon the Parliament of Canada or upon the legislatures of the Provinces shall be restricted to the enactment of laws in relation to matters within the competence of the Parliament of Canada or of any of the legislatures of the Provinces respectively.

8. Nothing in this Act shall be deemed to confer any power to repeal or alter the Constitution or the Constitution Act of the Commonwealth of Australia or the Constitution Act of the Dominion of New Zealand otherwise than in accordance with the law existing before the commencement of this Act.

9.—(1) Nothing in this Act shall be deemed to authorise the Parliament of the Commonwealth of Australia to make laws on any matter within the authority of the States of Australia, not being a matter within the authority of the Parliament or Government of the Commonwealth of Australia.

(2) Nothing in this Act shall be deemed to require the concurrence of the Parliament or Government of the Commonwealth of Australia in any law made by the Parliament of the United Kingdom with respect to any matter within the authority of the States of Australia, not being a matter within the authority of the Parliament or Government of the Commonwealth of Australia, in any case where it would have been in accordance with the constitutional practice existing before the commencement of this Act that the Parliament of the United Kingdom should make that law without such concurrence.

(3) In the application of this Act to the Commonwealth of Australia the request and consent referred to in section four shall mean the request and consent of the Parliament and Government of the Commonwealth.

10.—(1) None of the following sections of this Act, that is to say, sections two, three, four, five and six, shall extend to a Dominion to which this section applies as part of the law of that Dominion, unless that section is adopted by the Parliament of the Dominion, and any Act of that Parliament adopting any section of this Act may provide that the adoption shall have effect either from the commencement of this Act or from such later date as is specified in the adopting Act.

(2) The Parliament of any such Dominion as aforesaid may at

any time revoke the adoption of any section referred to in subsection (1) of this section.

(3) The Dominions to which this section applies are the Commonwealth of Australia, the Dominion of New Zealand and Newfoundland.

11. Notwithstanding anything in the Interpretation Act, 1889, the expression "Colony" shall not, in any Act of the Parliament of the United Kingdom passed after the commencement of this Act, include a Dominion or any Province or State forming part of a Dominion.

12. This Act may be cited as the Statute of Westminster, 1931.

100. POSSIBILITIES OF MIGRATION FROM THE UNITED KINGDOM TO THE DOMINIONS [30]

The continued seriousness of the economic situation in Great Britain and the desire to bind the commonwealth more closely together for defense purposes led to the appointment in February 1936 of an Oversea Settlement Board (headed by the Marquess of Hartington who, in May 1938, succeeded to the title of Duke of Devonshire) to consider specific proposals for schemes of migration within the empire. The report of the board contains (p. 7) a table showing the number of Migrants of British Nationality from the United Kingdom to other parts of the British Empire from 1913 through 1937. For each year from 1931 through 1937 there was a balance inward to the United Kingdom.

SUMMARY.

99. The problem before us is how to strengthen the Empire by means of migration from the United Kingdom to the oversea Dominions.[31] It is both a difficult and an urgent problem, and it can only be solved if the Governments and peoples concerned realize its importance and are prepared to co-operate wholeheartedly in the measures necessary for its solution. . . .

100. The problem is also one of importance in view of the interest

---

[30] *Report of the Oversea Settlement Board, May 1938. Presented by the Secretary of State for Dominion Affairs to Parliament by Command of His Majesty, June 1938,* Cmd. 5766, His Majesty's Stationery Office, London, 1938, pp. 34-38.

[31] The term "Dominions" is used in this report to include Canada, Australia, New Zealand, and the Union of South Africa.—*Ed.*

shown throughout the world in the development of the less closely settled countries. . . .

101. Although the population possibilities of the oversea Dominions are often exaggerated we have assumed as a legitimate hypothesis that each is capable of supporting a substantially larger population than at present.

102. We believe that the full development of the oversea Dominions . . . will add weight not only to the influence of each of the Dominions in which it takes place but also to that of the British Commonwealth as a whole in the councils of the world. This development should be brought about so far as possible by people of British stock.

103. Both in the United Kingdom and the Dominions the birth rate of the British stock shows a downward trend and the population is growing older in its composition. The seriousness of this situation is obvious from the point of view of the social and economic life of the community and of defence.

104. Migration from the United Kingdom to the oversea Dominions since 1919, despite a large measure of State assistance, has never approached in volume that of the years prior to 1914, and from 1931 onwards the inward has exceeded the outward movement.

. . . . .

106. The unfavourable economic conditions which have discouraged migration in recent years appear to be passing away but the progress made towards a renewal of migration has not thus far been commensurate with the improvement in economic conditions. . . .

107. The position of the oversea Dominions as relatively thinly populated areas facing a highly competitive world demands that the natural increase of population should be supplemented by immigration, and action should be taken without loss of time while the United Kingdom is still able to supply migrants. It can no longer be assumed as axiomatic that the migration of large numbers of persons from the United Kingdom to the Dominions is in the interests of the United Kingdom, if those interests could be considered in isolation from those of the Dominions. Even now, it is only from the point of view of the strengthening of the Empire as a whole that the encouragement of migration from the United Kingdom can be justified. . . .

108. It follows that if the Dominions are to obtain the United Kingdom migrants whom they need it lies with them to create the conditions which will attract such migrants, and to co-operate in meas-

ures for enabling new migrants to take advantage of the opportunities which await them overseas.

109. We recognize that, having regard to the nature of population trends, both in the United Kingdom and in the Dominions, it may be desirable that the growth of British stock in the Dominions from natural increase and migration should be supplemented by a carefully regulated flow of other immigrants of assimilable types.

110. A regular flow of migration will require full co-operation and partnership between participating countries. A planned policy will be essential. The burden of any financial assistance to encourage migration should be equitably shared.

. . . . .

113. A greater measure of planned co-operation than has existed in the past is in our opinion desirable if full advantage is to be taken of the opportunities afforded by industrial expansion in the Dominions for the absorption of migrants from this country. It seems to us desirable that there should exist in the Dominions, in so far as it does not exist already, machinery through which the current needs of the Dominions for specific types of workers may be ascertained as precisely as possible and through which these needs may be correlated with the supply available in this country.

. . . . .

115. As regards specific methods of migration, our view is that financial assistance should not be given, save in very exceptional circumstances, to schemes of land settlement and development, but that reliance should be placed primarily upon "infiltration." A process of infiltration can most effectively be facilitated by the nomination system whereby persons resident in the United Kingdom may be nominated by individuals or approved organizations overseas for the grant of assisted passages. . . . Facilities for the migration of single women are especially important.

. . . . .

117. . . . . we favour the establishment under appropriate conditions of reduced passage rates which while bringing the cost of the passage within the reach of the average person desiring to proceed overseas yet leave the settler on arrival overseas within the category of an unassisted immigrant.

118. Everything possible should be done to familiarize the population

of this country with the Dominions and the conditions of life overseas, for example, by giving greater prominence to Empire subjects in the curricula of schools and by making an increased use of such media as films. Any means of bringing about closer intercourse between the various parts of the Empire should be encouraged, e. g., by the cheapening of methods of communication, the encouragement of visits by representative United Kingdom workers to the Dominions and of representative Dominion workers to the United Kingdom, organized visits or temporary exchanges of school children, teachers and others, and reduction in the cost of return tickets between this country and the Dominions.

101. PROCLAMATION OF THE PROVISIONAL GOVERNMENT OF AN IRISH REPUBLIC, 1916 [32]

Irish discontent with British rule crystallized in 1916 in a so-called Easter Rebellion. The uprising was mainly the work of a society known as Sinn Fein ("We Ourselves") which, originally founded to improve the welfare of the Irish masses and foster Irish national sentiment, had recently become thoroughly identified with the republican movement. On Easter Monday, April 24, 1916, Sinn Feiners seized some public buildings in Dublin and issued the following proclamation from Liberty Hall. The rebellion was put down with severity.

POBLACHT NA H EIREANN.
THE PROVISIONAL GOVERNMENT
OF THE
IRISH REPUBLIC
TO THE PEOPLE OF IRELAND.

IRISHMEN AND IRISHWOMEN: In the name of God and of the dead generations from which she receives her old tradition of nationhood, Ireland, through us, summons her children to her flag and strikes for her freedom.

Having organised and trained her manhood through her secret revolutionary organisation, the Irish Republican Brotherhood, and through

---

[32] F. P. Jones, *History of the Sinn Fein Movement and the Irish Rebellion of 1916*, P. J. Kenedy & Sons, New York, 1917, reduced facsimile following page 284. Reprinted by permission of the publisher.

her open military organisations, the Irish Volunteers and the Irish Citizen Army, having patiently perfected her discipline, having resolutely waited for the right moment to reveal itself, she now seizes that moment, and, supported by her exiled children in America and by gallant allies in Europe, but relying in the first on her own strength, she strikes in full confidence of victory.

We declare the right of the people of Ireland to the ownership of Ireland, and to the unfettered control of Irish destinies, to be sovereign and indefeasible. The long usurpation of that right by a foreign people and government has not extinguished the right, nor can it ever be extinguished except by the destruction of the Irish people. In every generation the Irish people have asserted their right to national freedom and sovereignty; six times during the past three hundred years they have asserted it in arms. Standing on that fundamental right and again asserting it in arms in the face of the world, we hereby proclaim the Irish Republic as a Sovereign Independent State, and we pledge our lives and the lives of our comrades-in-arms to the cause of its freedom, of its welfare, and of its exaltation among the nations.

The Irish Republic is entitled to, and hereby claims, the allegiance of every Irishman and Irishwoman. The Republic guarantees religious and civil liberty, equal rights and equal opportunities to all its citizens, and declares its resolve to pursue the happiness and prosperity of the whole nation and of all its parts, cherishing all the children of the nation equally, and oblivious of the differences carefully fostered by an alien government, which have divided a minority from the majority in the past.

Until our arms have brought the opportune moment for the establishment of a permanent National Government, representative of the whole people of Ireland and elected by the suffrages of all her men and women, the Provisional Government, hereby constituted, will administer the civil and military affairs of the Republic in trust for the people.

We place the cause of the Irish Republic under the protection of the Most High God, Whose blessing we invoke upon our arms, and we pray that no one who serves that cause will dishonour it by cowardice, inhumanity, or rapine. In this supreme hour the Irish nation must, by its valour and discipline and by the readiness of its children to sacrifice themselves for the common good, prove itself worthy of the august destiny to which it is called.

Signed on Behalf of the Provisional Government,

THOMAS J. CLARKE,

SEAN MACDIARMADA,   THOMAS MACDONAGH,

P. H. PEARSE,   EAMONN CEANNT,

JAMES CONNOLLY,   JOSEPH PLUNKETT.[33]

102. THE ANGLO-IRISH TREATY OF DECEMBER 6, 1921 *(Extracts)* [34]

The failure of the Home Rule Act of 1920 to satisfy those Irishmen who lived in the twenty-six counties south and west of the six "Ulster" counties eventually led to two London conferences between British and Irish leaders. The second conference, convened in October 1921, sought a formula whereby "the association of Ireland with the community of nations known as the British Empire could best be reconciled with Irish national aspirations." Early in the morning of December 6, 1921, the British and Irish negotiators, headed by Premier Lloyd George and Arthur Griffith (founder of Sinn Fein), respectively, signed a treaty which, in effect, was the birth certificate of a new dominion, the Irish Free State. Northern Ireland, as the six counties comprising most of the province of Ulster now officially were called, maintained a separate existence under British parliamentary control in accordance with the provisions of the Home Rule Act of 1920.

1. Ireland shall have the same constitutional status in the Community of Nations known as the British Empire as the Dominion of Canada, the Commonwealth of Australia, the Dominion of New Zealand, and the Union of South Africa, with a Parliament having powers to make laws for the peace, order and good government of Ireland and an Executive responsible to that Parliament, and shall be styled and known as the Irish Free State.

4. The oath to be taken by Members of the Parliament of the Irish Free State shall be in the following form:—

[33] All seven signatories to this document were later executed.—*Ed.*

[34] *The Public General Statutes of Great Britain 1922,* Council of Law Reporting, London, 1923, pp. 658-660.

I . . . do solemnly swear true faith and allegiance to the Constitution of the Irish Free State as by law established and that I will be faithful to H. M. King George V., his heirs and successors by law, in virtue of the common citizenship of Ireland with Great Britain and her adherence to and membership of the group of nations forming the British Commonwealth of Nations.

. . . . .

11. Until the expiration of one month from the passing of the Act of Parliament for the ratification of this instrument, the powers of the Parliament and the Government of the Irish Free State shall not be exercisable as respects Northern Ireland and the provisions of the Government of Ireland Act, 1920, shall so far as they relate to Northern Ireland remain of full force and effect, and no election shall be held for the return of members to serve in the Parliament of the Irish Free State for constituencies in Northern Ireland, unless a resolution is passed by both Houses of the Parliament of Northern Ireland in favour of the holding of such elections before the end of the said month.

12. If before the expiration of the said month, an address is presented to His Majesty by both Houses of the Parliament of Northern Ireland to that effect, the powers of the Parliament and Government of the Irish Free State shall no longer extend to Northern Ireland, and the provisions of the Government of Ireland Act, 1920, (including those relating to the Council of Ireland) shall so far as they relate to Northern Ireland, continue to be of full force and effect, and this instrument shall have effect subject to the necessary modifications.

Provided that if such an address is so presented a Commission consisting of three persons, one to be appointed by the Government of the Irish Free State, one to be appointed by the Government of Northern Ireland and one who shall be Chairman to be appointed by the British Government shall determine in accordance with the wishes of the inhabitants, so far as may be compatible with economic and geographic conditions, the boundaries between Northern Ireland and the rest of Ireland, and for the purposes of the Government of Ireland Act, 1920, and of this instrument, the boundary of Northern Ireland shall be such as may be determined by such Commission.

. . . . .

103. THE CONSTITUTION OF IRELAND, 1937 *(Extracts)* [35]

The Irish Free State, on October 25, 1922, adopted a constitution which, having been accepted by the British Parliament without change, was proclaimed on December 6, 1922. Thereafter, particularly during the presidency of Eamon de Valera (1932-1937), the Irish Free State strove to dissociate itself more and more from Great Britain. By the end of 1936 all constitutional references to the king and the governor-general had been dropped. Then, in June 1937, the unicameral Irish Parliament approved the draft of another constitution, which was enacted by popular vote on July 1, 1937, and became effective on December 29, 1937. The first president chosen under the new instrument of government was the Protestant Professor Douglas Hyde.

In the Name of the Most Holy Trinity, from Whom is all authority and to Whom, as our final end, all actions both of men and States must be referred,

We, the people of Éire,

Humbly acknowledging all our obligations to our Divine Lord, Jesus Christ, Who sustained our fathers through centuries of trial,

Gratefully remembering their heroic and unremitting struggle to regain the rightful independence of our Nation,

And seeking to promote the common good, with due observance of Prudence, Justice and Charity, so that the dignity and freedom of the individual may be assured, true social order attained, the unity of our country restored, and concord established with other nations,

Do hereby adopt, enact, and give to ourselves this Constitution.

THE NATION

ARTICLE 1.

The Irish nation hereby affirms its inalienable, indefeasible, and sovereign right to choose its own form of Government, to determine its relations with other nations, and to develop its life, political, economic and cultural, in accordance with its own genius and traditions.

---

[35] Ireland, Stationery Office, *Constitution of Ireland* (Text in English and Gaelic), Stationery Office, Dublin, 1937, pp. 4-116.

ARTICLE 2.

The national territory consists of the whole island of Ireland, its islands and the territorial seas.

ARTICLE 3.

Pending the re-integration of the national territory, and without prejudice to the rights of the Parliament and Government established by this Constitution to exercise jurisdiction over the whole of that territory, the laws enacted by that Parliament shall have the like area and extent of application as the laws of Saorstát Eireann[36] and the like extraterritorial effect.

THE STATE

ARTICLE 4.

The name of the State is *Éire,* or, in the English language, *Ireland*.

· · · · ·

ARTICLE 8.

1. The Irish language as the national language is the first official language.

2. The English language is recognised as a second official language.

3. Provision may, however, be made by law for the exclusive use of either of the said languages for any one or more official purposes, either throughout the State or in any part thereof.

· · · · ·

ARTICLE 10.

1. All natural resources, including the air and all forms of potential energy, within the jurisdiction of the Parliament and Government established by this Constitution and all royalties and franchises within that jurisdiction belong to the State subject to all estates and interests therein for the time being lawfully vested in any person or body. . . . .

· · · · ·

THE PRESIDENT

ARTICLE 12.

1. There shall be a President of Ireland (*Uachtarán na hÉireann*),

---

[36] The Irish Free State.—*Ed.*

hereinafter called the President, who shall take precedence over all other persons in the State. . . .

2. 1° The President shall be elected by direct vote of the people.

2° Every citizen who has the right to vote at an election for members of Dáil Eireann shall have the right to vote at an election for President.

3° The voting shall be by secret ballot and on the system of proportional representation by means of the single transferable vote.

3. 1° The President shall hold office for seven years. . . .

2° A person who holds, or who has held, office as President, shall be eligible for re-election to that office once, but only once. . . .

4. 1° Every citizen who has reached his thirty-fifth year of age is eligible for election to the office of President.

2° Every candidate for election, not a former or retiring President, must be nominated either by

    i. not less than twenty persons, each of whom is at the time a member of one of the Houses of the Oireachtas, or

    ii. by the Councils of not less than four administrative Counties (including County Boroughs) as defined by law. . . .

4° Former or retiring Presidents may become candidates on their own nomination.

5° Where only one candidate is nominated for the office of President it shall not be necessary to proceed to a ballot for his election. . . .

9. The President shall not leave the State during his term of office save with the consent of the Government. . . .

ARTICLE 13.

1. 1° The President shall, on the nomination of Dáil Eireann, appoint the Taoiseach, that is, the head of the Government or Prime Minister. . . .

2. 1° Dáil Eireann shall be summoned and dissolved by the President on the advice of the Taoiseach.

2° The President may in his absolute discretion refuse to dissolve Dáil Eireann on the advice of a Taoiseach who has ceased to retain the support of a majority in Dáil Eireann. . . .

3. 1° Every Bill passed or deemed to have been passed by both Houses of the Oireachtas shall require the signature of the President for its enactment into law. . . .

9. The powers and functions conferred on the President by this

Constitution shall be exercisable and performable by him only on the advice of the Government, save where it is provided by this Constitution that he shall act in his absolute discretion or after consultation with or in relation to the Council of State, . . .

. . . . .

THE NATIONAL PARLIAMENT

Constitution and Powers

ARTICLE 15.

1. 1° The National Parliament shall be called and known, and is in this Constitution generally referred to, as the Oireachtas.

2° The Oireachtas shall consist of the President and two Houses, viz.: a House of Representatives to be called Dáil Eireann and a Senate to be called Seanad Eireann. . . .

6. 1° The right to raise and maintain military or armed forces is vested exclusively in the Oireachtas.

2° No military or armed force, other than a military or armed force raised and maintained by the Oireachtas, shall be raised or maintained for any purpose whatsoever. . . .

Dáil Eireann

ARTICLE 16.

1. 1° Every citizen without distinction of sex who has reached the age of twenty-one years, and who is not placed under disability or incapacity by this Constitution or by law, shall be eligible for membership of Dáil Eireann.

2° Every citizen without distinction of sex who has reached the age of twenty-one years who is not disqualified by law and complies with the provisions of the law relating to the election of members of Dáil Eireann, shall have the right to vote at an election for members of Dáil Eireann. . . .

2. . . . 2° The number of members shall from time to time be fixed by law, but the total number of members of Dáil Eireann shall not be fixed at less than one member for each thirty thousand of the population, or at more than one member for each twenty thousand of the population. . . .

5. The same Dáil Eireann shall not continue for a longer period than

seven years from the date of its first meeting: a shorter period may be
fixed by law. . . .

. . . . .

Seanad Eireann

ARTICLE 18.

1. Seanad Eireann shall be composed of sixty members, of whom
eleven shall be nominated members and forty-nine shall be elected
members.

2. A person to be eligible for membership of Seanad Eireann must
be eligible to become a member of Dáil Eireann.

3. The nominated members of Seanad Eireann shall be nominated
by the Taoiseach with their prior consent.

4. The elected members of Seanad Eireann shall be elected as follows:

    i. Three shall be elected by the National University of Ireland.

    ii. Three shall be elected by the University of Dublin.

    iii. Forty-three shall be elected from panels of candidates consti-
        tuted as hereinafter provided.

5. Every election of the elected members of Seanad Eireann shall be
held on the system of proportional representation by means of the single
transferable vote, and by secret postal ballot.

6. The members of Seanad Eireann to be elected by the Universities
shall be elected on a franchise and in the manner to be provided by law.

7. 1° Before each general election of the members of Seanad Eireann
to be elected from panels of candidates, five panels of candidates shall be
formed in the manner provided by law containing respectively the
names of persons having knowledge and practical experience of the
following interests and services, namely:—

    i. National Language and Culture, Literature, Art, Education
       and such professional interests as may be defined by law for
       the purpose of this panel;

    ii. Agriculture and allied interests, and Fisheries;

    iii. Labour, whether organised or unorganised;

    iv. Industry and Commerce, including banking, finance, ac-
        countancy, engineering and architecture;

    v. Public administration and social services, including voluntary
       social activities.

2° Not more than eleven and, subject to the provisions of Article 19 hereof, not less than five members of Seanad Eireann shall be elected from any one panel.

8. A general election for Seanad Eireann shall take place not later than ninety days after a dissolution of Dáil Eireann, . . .

ARTICLE 19.

Provision may be made by law for the direct election by any functional or vocational group or association or council of so many members of Seanad Eireann as may be fixed by such law from the corresponding panels of candidates constituted under Article 18 of this Constitution.

Legislation

ARTICLE 20.

1. Every bill initiated in and passed by Dáil Eireann shall be sent to Seanad Eireann and may, unless it be a Money Bill, be amended in Seanad Eireann and Dáil Eireann shall consider any such amendment. . . .

3. A Bill passed by either House and accepted by the other House shall be deemed to have been passed by both Houses.

Money Bills

ARTICLE 21.

1. 1° Money Bills shall be initiated in Dáil Eireann only.

2° Every Money Bill passed by Dáil Eireann shall be sent to Seanad Eireann for its recommendations.

2. 1° Every Money Bill sent to Seanad Eireann for its recommendations shall, at the expiration of a period not longer than twenty-one days after it shall have been sent to Seanad Eireann, be returned to Dáil Eireann, which may accept or reject all or any of the recommendations of Seanad Eireann.

2° If such Money Bill is not returned by Seanad Eireann to Dáil Eireann within such twenty-one days or is returned within twenty-one days with recommendations which Dáil Eireann does not accept, it shall be deemed to have been passeed by both Houses at the expiration of the said twenty-one days.

ARTICLE 25.

. . . 4. . . . 5° An official translation of every law enacted by the Oireachtas in the Irish language shall be issued in the English language and an official translation of every law enacted by the Oireachtas in the English language shall be issued in the Irish language.

. . . . . .

THE GOVERNMENT

ARTICLE 28.

1. The Government shall consist of not less than seven and not more than fifteen members who shall be appointed by the President in accordance with the provisions of this Constitution. . . .

4. 1° The Government shall be responsible to Dáil Eireann. . . .

6. 1° The Taoiseach shall nominate a member of the Government to be the Tánaiste.

2° The Tánaiste shall act for all purposes in the place of the Taoiseach if the Taoiseach should die, or become permanently incapacitated, until a new Taoiseach shall have been appointed. . . .

7. 1° The Taoiseach, the Tánaiste and the member of the Government who is in charge of the Department of Finance must be members of Dáil Eireann.

2° The other members of the Government must be members of Dáil Eireann or Seanad Eireann, but not more than two may be members of Seanad Eireann. . . .

INTERNATIONAL RELATIONS

ARTICLE 29.

1. Ireland affirms its devotion to the ideal of peace and friendly co-operation amongst nations founded on international justice and morality.

2. Ireland affirms its adherence to the principle of the pacific settlement of international disputes by international arbitration or judicial determination. . . .

THE COUNCIL OF STATE

ARTICLE 31.

1. There shall be a Council of State to aid and counsel the President. . . .

2. The Council of State shall consist of the following members:

    i. As *ex-officio* members: the Taoiseach, the Tánaiste, the Chief Justice, the President of the High Court, the Chairman of Dáil Eireann, the Chairman of Seanad Eireann, and the Attorney General.

    ii. Every person able and willing to act as a member of the Council of State who shall have held the office of President, or the office of Taoiseach, or the office of Chief Justice, or the office of President of the Executive Council of Saorstát Eireann.

    iii. Such other persons, if any, as may be appointed by the President under this Article to be members of the Council of State.

3. The President may at any time and from time to time by warrant under his hand and Seal appoint such other persons as, in his absolute discretion, he may think fit, to be members of the Council of State, but not more than seven persons so appointed shall be members of the Council of State at the same time. . . .

. . . . .

THE FAMILY

ARTICLE 41.

1. 1° The State recognises the Family as the natural primary and fundamental unit group of Society, and as a moral institution possessing inalienable and imprescriptible rights, antecedent and superior to all positive law.

2° The State, therefore, guarantees to protect the Family in its constitution and authority, as the necessary basis of social order and as indispensable to the welfare of the Nation and the State. . . .

3. . . . 2° No law shall be enacted providing for the grant of a dissolution of marriage.

3° No person whose marriage has been dissolved under the civil law of any other State but is a subsisting valid marriage under the law for the time being in force within the jurisdiction of the Government and Parliament established by this Constitution shall be capable of contracting a valid marriage within that jurisdiction during the lifetime of the other party to the marriage so dissolved.

. . . . .

PRIVATE PROPERTY

ARTICLE 43.

1. 1° The State acknowledges that man, in virtue of his rational being, has the natural right, antecedent to positive law, to the private ownership of external goods.

2° The State accordingly guarantees to pass no law attempting to abolish the right of private ownership or the general right to transfer, bequeath, and inherit property.

2. 1° The State recognises, however, that the exercise of the rights mentioned in the foregoing provisions of this Article ought, in civil society, to be regulated by the principles of social justice.

2° The State, accordingly, may as occasion requires, delimit by law the exercise of the said rights with a view to reconciling their exercise with the exigencies of the common good.

RELIGION

ARTICLE 44.

1. . . . 2° The State recognises the special position of the Holy Catholic Apostolic and Roman Church as the guardian of the Faith professed by the great majority of the citizens. . . .

2. 1° Freedom of conscience and the free profession and practice of religion are, subject to public order and morality, guaranteed to every citizen.

2° The State guarantees not to endow any religion. . . .

. . . . .

ARTICLE 63.

. . . In case of conflict between the Irish and the English texts [of the Constitution], the Irish text shall prevail.

104. THE ANGLO-IRISH AGREEMENTS OF 1938 (Extracts) [37]

In the Irish election campaign of 1932, the keynote sounded by Fianna Fáil, the party of de Valera, was political and economic self-sufficiency.

[37] *Agreements between the Government of the United Kingdom and the Government of Eire, Signed at London on 25th April, 1938. Presented by the Secretary of State for Dominion Affairs to Parliament by Command of His Majesty, April 1938,* Cmd. 5728, His Majesty's Stationery Office, London, 1938, pp. 2-12.

Specifically, de Valera advocated abolition of the oath to the king required by the treaty of 1921 (Document No. 102), the raising of a high tariff wall, and retention by the Irish Treasury of £5,000,000 annually, collected from Irish peasants as land-purchase instalments and due British bondholders under financial agreements of 1921, 1923, and 1926. In the new parliament de Valera, supported by his own and the Laborite deputies, was elected (March 1932) president of the Executive Council in place of William Cosgrave, who had held that post since 1923. When de Valera then tried to carry out his election promises, the British Government refused to accept either the unilateral abrogation of the treaty oath clause or the repudiation of the annuity payments. A conflict ensued which, manifested chiefly in the form of a tariff war, lasted from July 1932 until April 1938. In this fight the Irish were the greater sufferers for, whereas Great Britain purchased nine-tenths of the exports of the Free State, the latter took only one-twelfth of the British exports. The agreements of 1938 became effective on May 19.

The Government of the United Kingdom and the Government of Eire, being desirous of promoting relations of friendship and good understanding between the two countries, of reaching a final settlement of all outstanding financial claims of either of the two Governments against the other, and of facilitating trade and commerce between the two countries, have, subject to Parliamentary confirmation, entered into the Agreements hereinafter set forth:—

AN AGREEMENT REGARDING ARTICLES 6 AND 7 OF THE ARTICLES OF AGREEMENT OF DECEMBER 6, 1921

The Government of the United Kingdom and the Government of Eire have agreed as follows:—

1. The Provisions of Articles 6 and 7 of the Articles of Agreement for a Treaty between Great Britain and Ireland signed on the 6th day of December, 1921, and of the Annex thereto shall cease to have effect.[38]

2. Thereafter the Government of the United Kingdom will transfer to the Government of Eire the Admiralty property and rights at Berehaven, and the harbour defences at Berehaven, Cobh (Queenstown) and Lough Swilly now occupied by care and maintenance parties fur-

[38] This treaty, partly reproduced in Document No. 102, recognized dominion status for the Irish Free State. Articles 6 and 7 thereof reserved to Great Britain authority over the three Irish naval bases mentioned in Article 2 of the agreement here quoted.—*Ed.*

nished by the United Kingdom, together with buildings, magazines, emplacements, instruments and fixed armaments with ammunition therefor at present at the said ports.

3. The transfer will take place not later than the 31st December, 1938. In the meantime the detailed arrangements for the transfer will be the subject of discussion between the two Governments.

Done in duplicate at London, this 25th day of April, 1938.

·　·　·　·　·

A FINANCIAL AGREEMENT

The Government of the United Kingdom and the Government of Eire have agreed as follows:—

1. The Government of Eire agree to pay to the Government of the United Kingdom on or before the 30th November, 1938, the sum of £10,000,000 sterling.

2. Subject to the provisions of Article 3 of this Agreement, payment of the sum specified in Article 1 shall constitute a final settlement of all financial claims of either of the two Governments against the other arising out of matters occurring before the date of this Agreement.[39]

3. The provisions of Article 2 of this Agreement shall not affect—

    (i) payments made or liabilities incurred by one Government to the other in respect of agency services or ordinary inter-governmental transactions, whether for goods supplied, services rendered, disbursements made, or otherwise;

    (ii) the payment of £250,000 a year [until 1987] by the Government of Eire to the Government of the United Kingdom in respect of damage to property [during "the trouble"] under the Agreement of the 3rd December, 1925;

    (iii) any payments made or to be made in pursuance of arrangements which have been or may hereafter be reached between the two Governments in respect of the following matters:—

        (*a*) Unredeemed Bank notes;

        (*b*) Withdrawal of United Kingdom silver coin from Eire;

        (*c*) Trustee Savings Banks;

        (*d*) Double Taxation.

4. The Government of the United Kingdom undertake to abolish,

---

[39] The sum of £10,000,000 therefore was to represent full settlement for the land-purchase instalments (£5,000,000 annually) that were due British bondholders under the Anglo-Irish agreements of 1921, 1923, and 1926 and that had been suspended by President Eamon de Valera in 1932.—*Ed.*

as from the date on which the accompanying Trade Agreement between the United Kingdom and Eire comes into force pursuant to Article 19 thereof, the duties of customs chargeable under the Irish Free State (Special Duties) Act, 1932, on articles imported from Eire into the United Kingdom, or exported from Eire to any other country and thence brought into the United Kingdom.

5. The Government of Eire undertake to abolish, as from the date on which the accompanying Trade Agreement between the United Kingdom and Eire comes into force pursuant to Article 19 thereof, the duties of Customs known as Customs (Emergency) Duties (Tariff list Reference Nos. 280, 281 and 288) chargeable on goods produced or manufactured in the United Kingdom and imported into Eire.

Done in duplicate at London, this 25th day of April, 1938.

. . . . .

A TRADE AGREEMENT

The Government of the United Kingdom and the Government of Eire have agreed as follows:—

ARTICLE 1.

(1) The Government of the United Kingdom undertake that goods grown, produced or manufactured in, and consigned from, Eire, which, on the day on which this Agreement comes into force, are liable to duty under the Import Duties Act, 1932, or under Section 1 of the Ottawa Agreements Act, 1932, and also such goods which are on that day free of duty, shall enjoy entry free of customs duty into the United Kingdom. This paragraph does not apply to goods which, on the day on which this Agreement comes into force, are liable to duty both under the Import Duties Act, 1932, or the Ottawa Agreements Act, 1932, and under some other enactment.

(2) Provided that as regards eggs, poultry, butter, cheese and other milk products, the undertaking contained in the first paragraph of this Article shall operate only until the 20th August, 1940.

. . . . .

ARTICLE 3.

(1) The Government of Eire, recognising that it is the policy of the Government of the United Kingdom to promote the orderly marketing of agricultural products, declare their readiness to co-operate in any

arrangements made or approved by that Government for this purpose, and the Government of the United Kingdom, for their part, will not seek to regulate the quantity of any such goods produced in Eire and imported into the United Kingdom unless it appears to them that the orderly marketing of such goods cannot otherwise be procured. . . .

ARTICLE 4.

(1) The Government of Eire undertake to consult from time to time with the Government of the United Kingdom as to the quantities of eggs and poultry to be exported from Eire to the United Kingdom, and to exercise such control of exports as may be necessary to make effective any agreement so reached. . . .

ARTICLE 11.

(1) The Government of Eire undertake that goods produced or manufactured in the United Kingdom shall be entitled to admission into Eire at the preferential rate of duty wherever such a rate exists and that existing margins between the full and the preferential rates shall not be reduced.

. . . . .

ARTICLE 15.

Except to the extent that may be necessary to maintain production in Eire on an economic basis or to secure the effective operation of schemes for orderly marketing of agricultural products, the Government of Eire undertake to withdraw the export bounties or subsidies that have been paid in respect of goods exported from Eire to the United Kingdom. In particular they undertake to withdraw export bounties and subsidies in so far as the intention of such payments has been to counteract the effect of duties of customs on such goods on importation into the United Kingdom, in all cases where such duties have been abolished.

ARTICLE 16.

It being the intention of the Government of Eire that coal, coke and manufactured fuel of United Kingdom origin shall continue to be imported into Eire in not less than the proportion which such coal, coke and manufactured fuel formed of total imports of those products into Eire in the year 1937, they undertake to abolish the present control by licence of the importation of coal and to admit into Eire, coal, coke and manufactured fuel of United Kingdom origin free of duty and to charge a duty of not less than 3s. per ton on coal, coke and manufactured fuel of other origin.

. . . . .

ARTICLE 19.

This Agreement shall come into force on a date to be mutually agreed between the two Governments. It shall remain in force for a period of three years from the date of its coming into force and, unless notice of termination shall have been given by either Government to the other six months before the expiry of that period, it shall remain in force until the expiry of six months from the date on which notice of termination is given.

Done in duplicate at London, this 25th day of April, 1938.

Signed on behalf of the Government of the United Kingdom:	*Signed on behalf of the Government of Eire:*
NEVILLE CHAMBERLAIN.	ÉAMON DE VALÉRA.
JOHN SIMON.	SEÁN F. LEMASS.
SAMUEL HOARE.	SEÁN MACENTEE.
MALCOLM MACDONALD.	SÉAMAS O RIAIN.
W. S. MORRISON.	

105. THE ANGLO-EGYPTIAN TREATY OF AUGUST 26, 1936 *(Extracts)* [40]

~~~~~~

When the World War broke out, Egypt, though officially occupied by the British since January 1883, was still technically part of the Ottoman Empire. Then, in December 1914, Great Britain announced that "the suzerainty of Turkey over Egypt is terminated" and herself extended a protectorate over the land of the Nile. There was so much dissatisfaction in Egypt over the continued exercise of British control before, during, and after the World War that, eventually, spurred perhaps by Fascist Italian activities in the Mediterranean, the London authorities granted virtual independence to the Egyptians. "Virtual" because, as was pointed out, the "facts

---

[40] *Treaty of Alliance between His Majesty, in Respect of the United Kingdom, and His Majesty the King of Egypt . . . London, August 26, 1936. Presented by the Secretary of State for Foreign Affairs to Parliament by Command of His Majesty,* Treaty Series No. 6 (1937), Cmd. 5360, His Majesty's Stationery Office, London, 1937, pp. 4-14.

of modern warfare" made essential some close relationship among technical equals. Ratifications of the Anglo-Egyptian Treaty of Alliance of 1936 were exchanged on December 22, 1936. In accordance with her promise, Great Britain then helped arrange for a meeting of the powers that had capitulatory rights in Egypt. As a consequence, the Montreux Convention[41] was signed May 8, 1937, providing for the gradual abolition of extraterritoriality by 1949. On May 26, 1937, Egypt became a member of the League of Nations.

ARTICLE 1.

The military occupation of Egypt by the forces of His Majesty the King and Emperor is terminated.

ARTICLE 2.

His Majesty the King and Emperor will henceforth be represented at the Court of His Majesty the King of Egypt and His Majesty the King of Egypt will be represented at the Court of St. James's by Ambassadors duly accredited.

ARTICLE 3.

Egypt intends to apply for membership to the League of Nations. His Majesty's Government in the United Kingdom, recognising Egypt as a sovereign independent State, will support any request for admission which the Egyptian Government may present in the conditions prescribed by Article 1 of the Covenant.

ARTICLE 4.

An alliance is established between the High Contracting Parties with a view to consolidating their friendship, their cordial understanding and their good relations.

ARTICLE 5.

Each of the High Contracting Parties undertakes not to adopt in relation to foreign countries an attitude which is inconsistent with the alliance, nor to conclude political treaties inconsistent with the provisions of the present treaty.

[41] The text of the Montreux Convention may be found in *Final Act, Convention and other Documents Regarding the Abolition of the Capitulations in Egypt, Montreux, May 8, 1937. Presented by the Secretary of State for Foreign Affairs to Parliament by Command of His Majesty*, Treaty Series No. 55 (1937), Cmd. 5630, His Majesty's Stationery Office, London, 1937.

ARTICLE 6.

Should any dispute with a third State produce a situation which involves a risk of rupture with that State, the High Contracting Parties will consult each other with a view to the settlement of the said dispute by peaceful means, in accordance with the provisions of the Covenant of the League of Nations and of any other international obligations which may be applicable to the case.

ARTICLE 7.

Should, notwithstanding the provisions of Article 6 above, either of the High Contracting Parties become engaged in war, the other High Contracting Party will, subject always to the provisions of Article 10 below, immediately come to his aid in the capacity of an ally.

The aid of His Majesty the King of Egypt in the event of war, imminent menace of war or apprehended international emergency will consist in furnishing to His Majesty the King and Emperor on Egyptian territory, in accordance with the Egyptian system of administration and legislation, all the facilities and assistance in his power, including the use of his ports, aerodromes and means of communication. It will accordingly be for the Egyptian Government to take all the administrative and legislative measures, including the establishment of martial law and an effective censorship, necessary to render these facilities and assistance effective.

ARTICLE 8.

In view of the fact that the Suez Canal, whilst being an integral part of Egypt, is a universal means of communication as also an essential means of communication between the different parts of the British Empire, His Majesty the King of Egypt, until such time as the High Contracting Parties agree that the Egyptian Army is in a position to ensure by its own resources the liberty and entire security of navigation of the Canal, authorises His Majesty the King and Emperor to station forces in Egyptian territory in the vicinity of the Canal, in the zone specified in the Annex to this Article, with a view to ensuring in co-operation with the Egyptian forces the defence of the Canal. The detailed arrangements for the carrying into effect of this Article are contained in the Annex hereto. The presence of these forces shall not constitute in any manner an occupation and will in no way prejudice the sovereign rights of Egypt.

It is understood that at the end of the period of twenty years specified in Article 16 the question whether the presence of British forces is no longer necessary owing to the fact that the Egyptian Army is in a position to ensure by its own resources the liberty and entire security of navigation of the Canal may, if the High Contracting Parties do not agree thereon, be submitted to the Council of the League of Nations for decision in accordance with the provisions of the Covenant in force at the time of signature of the present treaty or to such other person or body of persons for decision in accordance with such other procedure as the High Contracting Parties may agree.

Annex to Article 8.

1. Without prejudice to the provisions of Article 7, the numbers of the forces of His Majesty the King and Emperor to be maintained in the vicinity of the Canal shall not exceed, of the land forces, 10,000, and of the air forces, 400 pilots, together with the necessary ancillary personnel for administrative and technical duties. These numbers do not include civilian personnel, *e.g.*, clerks, artisans and labourers.

．　．　．　．　．

11. Unless the two Governments agree to the contrary, the Egyptian Government will prohibit the passage of aircraft over the territories situated on either side of the Suez Canal and within 20 kilometres of it, except for the purpose of passage from east to west or *vice versa* by means of a corridor 10 kilometres wide at Kantara. This prohibition will not, however, apply to the forces of the High Contracting Parties or to genuinely Egyptian air organisations or to air organisations genuinely belonging to any part of the British Commonwealth of Nations operating under the authority of the Egyptian Government.　．　．　．　．

ARTICLE 10.

Nothing in the present treaty is intended to or shall in any way prejudice the rights and obligations which devolve, or may devolve, upon either of the High Contracting Parties under the Covenant of the League of Nations or the Treaty for the Renunciation of War signed at Paris on August 27, 1928.

ARTICLE 11.

While reserving liberty to conclude new conventions in future, modifying the agreements of the 19th January and the 10th July, 1899, the

High Contracting Parties agree that the administration of the Sudan shall continue to be that resulting from the said agreements. The Governor-General shall continue to exercise on behalf of the High Contracting Parties the powers conferred upon him by the said agreements.

The High Contracting Parties agree that the primary aim of their administration in the Sudan must be the welfare of the Sudanese.

Nothing in this article prejudices the question of sovereignty over the Sudan.

2. Appointments and promotions of officials in the Sudan will in consequence remain vested in the Governor-General, who, in making new appointments to posts for which qualified Sudanese are not available, will select suitable candidates of British and Egyptian nationality.

3. In addition to Sudanese troops, both British and Egyptian troops shall be placed at the disposal of the Governor-General for the defence of the Sudan.

4. Egyptian immigration into the Sudan shall be unrestricted except for reasons of public order and health.

5. There shall be no discrimination in the Sudan between British subjects and Egyptian nationals in matters of commerce, immigration or the possession of property. . . .

ARTICLE 12.

His Majesty the King and Emperor recognises that the responsibility for the lives and property of foreigners in Egypt devolves exclusively upon the Egyptian Government, who will ensure the fulfilment of their obligations in this respect.

ARTICLE 13.

His Majesty the King and Emperor recognises that the capitulatory régime now existing in Egypt is no longer in accordance with the spirit of the times and with the present state of Egypt.

His Majesty the King of Egypt desires the abolition of this régime without delay.

Both High Contracting Parties are agreed upon the arrangements with regard to this matter as set forth in the Annex to this Article.

Annex to Article 13.

1. It is the object of the arrangements set out in this Annex:—

   (i) To bring about speedily the abolition of the Capitulations in Egypt with the disappearance of the existing restrictions on Egyptian sovereignty in the matter of the application of Egyptian legislation (including financial legislation) to foreigners as its necessary consequences;

(ii) To institute a transitional régime for a reasonable and not unduly prolonged period to be fixed, during which the Mixed Tribunals will remain and will, in addition to their present judicial jurisdiction, exercise the jurisdiction at present vested in the Consular Courts.

At the end of this transitional period the Egyptian Government will be free to dispense with the Mixed Tribunals.

2. As a first step, the Egyptian Government will approach the Capitulatory Powers as soon as possible with a view to (*a*) the removal of all restrictions on the application of Egyptian legislation to foreigners, and (*b*) the institution of a transitional régime for the Mixed Tribunals as provided in paragraph 1 (ii) above.

3. His Majesty's Government in the United Kingdom, as the Government of a Capitulatory Power and as an ally of Egypt, are in no way opposed to the arrangements referred to in the preceding paragraph and will collaborate actively with the Egyptian Government in giving effect to them by using all their influence with the Powers exercising capitulatory rights in Egypt.

. . . . .

ARTICLE 15.

The High Contracting Parties agree that any difference on the subject of the application or interpretation of the provisions of the present treaty which they are unable to settle by direct negotiations shall be dealt with in accordance with the provisions of the Covenant of the League of Nations.

ARTICLE 16.

At any time after the expiration of a period of twenty years from the coming into force of the treaty, the High Contracting Parties will, at the request of either of them, enter into negotiations with a view to such revision of its terms by agreement between them as may be appropriate in the circumstances as they then exist. In case of the High Contracting Parties being unable to agree upon the terms of the revised treaty, the difference will be submitted to the Council of the League of Nations for decision in accordance with the provisions of the Covenant in force at the time of signature of the present treaty or to such other person or body of persons for decision in accordance with such procedure as the High Contracting Parties may agree. It is agreed that any revision of this treaty will provide for the continuation of the Alliance between the High Contracting Parties in accordance with the principles contained in Articles 4, 5, 6 and 7. Nevertheless, with the consent of both High Contracting Parties, negotiations may be entered into at any time after the expiration of a period of ten years after the coming into force of the treaty, with a view to such revision as afore-said.

ARTICLE 17.

The present treaty is subject to ratification. Ratifications shall be exchanged in Cairo as soon as possible. The Treaty shall come into force on the date of the exchange of ratifications, and shall thereupon be registered with the Secretary-General of the League of Nations.

In witness whereof the above-named plenipotentiaries have signed the present treaty and affixed thereto their seals.

Done at London in duplicate this 26th day of August, 1936.

106. GANDHI'S PLEA FOR NON-VIOLENT RESISTANCE [42]

Mohandas Karamchand Gandhi, who professed to abhor violence, was the leading advocate in post-war India of passive resistance or material and spiritual non-coöperation (satyagraha) as a means of forcing political con-cessions from the British. The following quotations are from a compilation made by a close friend of Gandhi.

For me the law of Satyagraha, the law of love is an eternal principle. For the past thirty years I have been preaching and practising Saty-agraha. The principles of Satyagraha, as I know it today, constitute a gradual evolution. . . . . .

The term Satyagraha was coined by me in South Africa to express the force that the Indians there used for full eight years. . . .

Its root meaning is holding on to truth. Hence truth-force. I have also called it Love-force, or Soul-force. In the application of Satyagraha I discovered in the earliest stages that pursuit of truth did not admit of violence being inflicted on one's opponent; but that he must be

---

[42] M. K. Gandhi, *Satyagraha in Gandhiji's Own Words (1910 to 1935),* Congress Golden Jubilee Brochure No. 1, All India Congress Committee, Allahabad, 1935, pp. 8-10.

weaned from error by patience and sympathy. . . . And patience
means self-suffering. So the doctrine came to mean vindication of truth
not by infliction of suffering on the opponent, but on one's self.

Carried out to its utmost limit, this force is independent . . . of
physical force or violence. Indeed, violence is the negation of this great
spiritual force, which can only be cultivated or wielded by those who
will entirely eschew violence. It is a force that may be used by individuals as well as by communities. It may be used as well in political
as in domestic affairs. Its universal applicability is a demonstration of
its permanence and invincibility. It can be used alike by men, women,
and children. It is totally untrue to say that it is a force to be used only
by the weak so long as they are not capable of meeting violence by
violence. It is impossible for those who consider themselves to be weak
to apply this force. Only those who realise that there is something in
man which is superior to the brute nature in him, and that the latter
always yields to it, can effectively be Satyagrahis. This force is to violence, and therefore to all tyranny, all injustice, what light is to darkness.
In politics, its use is based upon the immutable maxim that Government
of the people is possible only so long as they consent either consciously
or unconsciously to be governed.

And therefore the struggle on behalf of the people mostly consists
in opposing error in the shape of unjust laws. When you have failed
to bring the error home to the law-giver by way of petitions and the
like, the only remedies open to you, if you do not wish to submit to
error, are to compel him to yield to you either by physical force or by
suffering in your own person, by inviting the penalty for the breach of
his laws. Hence Satyagraha largely appears to the public as Civil
Disobedience or Civil Resistance. It is civil in the sense that it is not
criminal.

107. THE ECONOMIC OUTLOOK FOR INDIA [43]

*The following appraisal of the economic outlook for India is from the
work of a leading British woman authority on the subject.*

We must now consider [the questions] referring to the present and
the future, of which the first is whether or not the way has been pre-

---

[43] V. Anstey, *The Economic Development of India,* 3rd ed., Longmans, Green and
Company, London, 1936, pp. 473-478, 487. Reprinted by permission of the publishers.

pared for a great forward movement that will bring India into economic line with the industrialized countries of the West.

My own conclusion is that from the purely material, technical point of view there is no reason why rapid advance should not be made. India has at least her fair share of natural advantages, and there is no evidence to show that under favourable conditions Indian workers—supervisory, technical, and manual—are not capable of becoming as efficient as the inhabitants of other countries who work under similar conditions. The climate itself has advantages as well as disadvantages, and scientific research has already done much, and should do more, to reduce the latter and increase the former. But I am convinced that no such rapid advance can take place in the absence of fundamental social reorganization. No amount of protection, no efforts of Government to promote scientific research and propaganda, to assist new industries, or improve communications and public works, will effect any radical improvement in the economic condition of the people, unless certain obstacles are removed that affect economic progress fundamentally. Three classes of obstacles may be distinguished.

First and foremost, it must be definitely recognized that general prosperity in India can never be rapidly or substantially increased so long as any increase in the income of individuals is absorbed not by a rise in the standard of life, but by an increase in the population. The population problem lies at the root of the whole question of India's economic future, and it is useless to try to bilk the fact. It is difficult to avoid the conclusion that no matter how productivity is increased, economic organization is improved, public health is promoted or industrialization progresses, the standard of life of the masses will not and cannot be raised to a satisfactory level until changes have been introduced which will enable the size of the population to be better adjusted to economic resources. At present, on account of the strength and universality of certain customs and institutions, no satisfactory adjustment is secured. The requisite reforms fall within the social rather than the economic sphere, and belong to a domain from which the present Government is excluded both by popular desire and deliberate policy. It is a curious paradox that nothing would end British rule in India more quickly than any attempt to introduce just those reforms which would do most to improve the well-being of the masses. A well-proportioned decrease in the birth-rate would unquestionably result in an increase in income per head, which would enable each individual to procure and utilize more knowledge and capital, and would enable the State to raise a larger revenue which it could expend in spreading economic, as well as general education, and in initiating and assisting new economic projects.   . . . . .

The second fundamental obstacle to economic progress in India is the present uneconomic outlook of the people. The results of particular economic tendencies and measures depend upon the milieu within which they work. In discussing the working of economic laws in India the same assumptions cannot at present be made as in America or Western Europe. Failure to recognize this fact can only cause disappointment by leading to the adoption of measures which have proved efficacious in the West, but which are not appropriate to Indian conditions. Even the laws of supply and demand depend upon certain assumptions with regard to social conditions and the economic nature of man, which, as a matter of fact, are not always justified. For instance, it cannot be assumed in India (nor everywhere else for that matter) that an increase in the price of labour will necessarily lead to an increase in the supply of labour. New industries can only be a success if they attract a supply of labour suitable in quantity and quality to the requirements. To the extent that labour is not mobile and is not attracted by higher wages, it will be impossible, or at least extremely difficult, to extend large-scale modern industries on a commercial basis in India. "One cannot help feeling that, until you can push ahead with primary education and get the workers to find useful ways of spending their money, they are not going to have any incentive to earn more."

Again, in India it cannot be assumed that if the Government stands on one side private individuals will seize the most promising openings and initiate enterprises that are likely to prove remunerative. Neither capital nor labour is mobile, and competition does not tend to produce an equality of returns from the marginal doses of labour and capital. The truth is that an economic outlook does not prevail, and that, as long as the economic motive cannot be relied upon, it is extraordinarily difficult to predict the results of economic measures or in any way to influence or to guide economic development. If there is to be economic achievement, there must be economic effort, and economic effort can only result from the adoption of an economic outlook and from a readiness to modify social customs and institutions in the interests of material development. A static social ideal cannot coexist with a progressive economic ideal. The ascetic hermit cannot expect his cell to be lit with electricity and warmed by central heating. Modern methods of production depend upon division of labour, large-scale production, and the application of science to production, and these presuppose a certain level of education, regular disciplined work and, above all, economic ambition. An increase in prosperity can only be expected from the co-operative efforts of the members of a community in which the economic motive prevails. It need not, however, be assumed that the economic motive must prevail to the exclusion of all others.

The conclusion is that a change in the outlook of the people, whereby they may become willing to change their social customs and institutions in the interests of economic progress, is a fundamental condition of such progress in India. The chief social reforms that are relevant to the problem of economic development have already been considered at some length in previous chapters, and include the removal of religious and caste hindrances to efficient production, to the mobility and efficiency of labour, and to economic expenditure and consumption; reforms with regard to the social ideals of the people, which will engender a more widespread and intense desire to render social service; and reforms with regard to the social and economic position of women.

The third fundamental obstacle to economic progress in India is the lack of co-operation between the Government and the governed. Apart from fundamental constitutional changes the Government can facilitate such co-operation only by adhering most strictly to a policy which definitely aims not only at good government, but also at the elimination of any possible causes of suspicion of its motives. Insufficient attention has often been paid in the past to the necessity of conciliating public opinion in economic matters, but a change in policy in this respect has recently appeared; for instance, in the adoption of "discriminating protection," the repeal of the cotton excise, the purchase of stores in India, the institution of rupee tenders, the limitation of direct financial aid to companies registered in India, and in the establishment of a Reserve Bank. The new Constitution [1935], particularly by the grant of Provincial Autonomy, should do much to stimulate public interest and co-operation in economic and social development. . . . A great forward step would be taken if it was realized how limited is the power of the Government over economic development, and what great need there is for voluntary economic effort on the part of individuals. To imagine, for instance, that all that is necessary in order to induce industrialization in India is to adopt protective tariffs, or grant bounties on production, is entirely to misunderstand the factors at work, and grossly to overrate the powers of Government and the potentialities of Governmental economic policy.

Although the power of the Government has been overrated, it is none the less true that the part played by the Government in the economic life of the country must necessarily be greater in India than in most other countries, owing partly to the scarcity of natural leaders in economic matters, and partly to the attitude and position deliberately assumed by the Government in India. After all, it has been the political connection with England that has brought about intimate economic contact between India and the West, been responsible for the "opening-up" of India, the establishment of large-scale factory and plantation industries, and for the existence of economic anachronisms within the country. Many of India's most pressing present-day economic problems are due to this connection, and the Government ought, therefore, to assume at least part responsibility for finding a solution. The difficulty is that no solution can be found without the whole-hearted co-operation of the people, and that it is particularly difficult for a "foreign" Government to obtain that co-operation, and to raise the revenue necessary for the performance of extensive economic and social functions. It can be concluded that until fully responsible government is conceded it is to be expected, on the one hand, that Government policy will be subject to drastic criticism, and, on the other, that too much reliance will tend to be placed upon it.   . . . . .

In conclusion it can be said that India's economic future depends, in the main, not upon the inauguration of particular schemes of development, or the adoption of particular lines of policy, but upon more fundamental social reforms and reorganization, directed towards controlling the size of the population, breaking up the existing over-rigid social stratification, stimulating social enterprise and energy, promoting education, and replacing the forms by the spirit of religion. . . .

108. POLITICAL THOUGHT IN BRITISH INDIA [44]

This penetrating summary of political thought in India appeared in the report of the Simon Commission which was appointed in 1927, representing all three major British parties, and which published its findings in two volumes in 1930. The report was not popular in India.

Political thought in British India to-day is derived from Europe. The

[44] *Report of the Indian Statutory* (Simon) *Commission. Presented by the Secretary of State for the Home Department to Parliament by Command of His Majesty,* vol. 1, Cmd. 3568, His Majesty's Stationery Office, London, 1930, p. 406.

keen intelligence of the educated Indian has been stimulated by study of Western institutions. It is remarkable how the theories and phrases of political science as expounded in England and America have been adopted and absorbed. But the sudden impact of ideas drawn from the experience and conditions of other peoples in other climates is bound to have a disturbing effect. Down to thirty or forty years ago India stood entirely outside the influence of the course of political ideas which at length produced democratic self-government in some other parts of the world. But in the last generation she has been swayed, at one and the same time, by the force of several conceptions which in Europe had followed a certain sequence. Thus, the struggle for power between rival religious communities, the rise of an intense national spirit, the spread of toleration, the growth of democracy, and the controversies of socialism, mark fairly well-defined epochs in European history. But, in India, these various influences are contending side by side for the allegiance of the politically-minded. The growth of national self-consciousness is retarded by communal separatism. The movement towards Western industrialism is countered by the return to the spinning wheel. The equality of Asiatic and European is proclaimed, while the clash of Brahmin and non-Brahmin, or caste and outcast, is intensified. Ultra-democratic constitutions are propounded, although the long process which was a necessary antecedent to democracy in Europe, viz. the breaking down of class and communal and occupational barriers, has only just begun. Indian political thought finds it tempting to fore-shorten history, and is unwilling to wait for the final stage of a prolonged evolution. It is impatient of the doctrine of gradualness.

109. EXTRACTS FROM THE CONSTITUTION OF THE INDIAN NATIONAL CONGRESS, 1934 [45]

The Indian National Congress was founded at Bombay in 1885 by a group of patriotic Hindus interested in discussing social and political questions affecting Indian life. By 1926 the Congress, which had been holding annual meetings, asked for dominion status for India, and within another decade most of its members demanded outright independence. The following resolutions were adopted by the Congress meeting at Bombay in October 1934.

[45] All India Congress Committee, General Secretary, *Constitution of the Indian National Congress, as Amended at the Bombay Session, October 1934,* Congress House, Bombay, 1934, pp. 1, 2, 9, 15.

ARTICLE 1.

The object of the Indian National Congress is the attainment of *Poorna Swaraj* (Complete Independence) by all legitimate and peaceful means.

. . . . .

ARTICLE 3.

(a) Any person over the age of 18 years who believes in Article 1 shall, on making a written declaration to that effect and presenting an application . . . be entitled to be placed on the register of Congress members. . . .

. . . . .

ARTICLE 9.

(a) The Annual Session shall be ordinarily held during the month of February or March. The said Session shall be held at the place decided upon at the preceding Session or such other place as may be determined by the Working Committee. . . .

. . . . .

ARTICLE 17.

(a) The proceedings of the Congress, the All India Congress Committee and the Working Committee shall ordinarily be conducted in Hindustani; the English language or any provincial language may be used if the speaker is unable to speak Hindustani or whenever permitted by the President. . . .

110. THE BALFOUR DECLARATION, NOVEMBER 2, 1917 [46]

As an element in war-time strategy, British Foreign Secretary Arthur James Balfour wrote the following letter to Baron Edmond de Rothschild, leader of the Jewish community in Great Britain. The policy of the declaration was accepted by the principal Allied Powers at the San Remo Conference in April 1920, and its text was embodied in the mandate approved by the League Council in July 1922.

[46] Facsimile in L. Stein, *Zionism*, Ernest Benn, London, 1925, Frontispiece. Reprinted by permission of the publishers.

Foreign Office
November 2nd, 1917

Dear Lord Rothschild,

I have much pleasure in conveying to you, on behalf of His Majesty's Government, the following declaration of sympathy with Jewish Zionist aspirations which has been submitted to, and approved by, the Cabinet.

"His Majesty's Government view with favour the establishment in Palestine of a National Home for the Jewish people, and will use their best endeavours to facilitate the achievement of this object, it being clearly understood that nothing shall be done which may prejudice the civil and religious rights of existing non-Jewish communities in Palestine, or the rights and political status enjoyed by Jews in any other country."

I should be grateful if you would bring this declaration to the knowledge of the Zionist Federation.

Yours sincerely,

(Signed) ARTHUR JAMES BALFOUR.

111. OFFICIAL STATEMENT OF BRITISH POLICY IN PALESTINE, 1930 [47]

The efforts of the British to fulfil their obligations to the Jewish people as assumed in the Balfour Declaration aroused the bitter opposition of the Arabs in Palestine and in neighboring Arabic states. The Arabs held that the declaration conflicted with Britain's war-time promises of Arabian independence and with the principle of self-determination, for, in 1922, the Holy Land contained about eight times as many Arabs as Jews. When the discontent of the Arabs crystallized in a violent anti-Jewish outbreak in 1929, the British authorities appointed several commissions to investigate the cause of the difficulties. Then, in October 1930, the British Government published what it described as "a clear and full statement of policy, designed to remove . . . misunderstanding." This statement is the source of the following selection.

---

[47] *Palestine. Statement of Policy by His Majesty's Government in the United Kingdom. Presented by the Secretary of State for the Colonies to Parliament by Command of His Majesty, October 1930,* Cmd. 3692, His Majesty's Stationery Office, London, 1930, pp. 3-23.

1. The Report of the Special Commission, under the Chairmanship of Sir Walter Shaw, which was published in April, gave rise to acute controversy, in the course of which it became evident that there is considerable misunderstanding about the past actions and future intentions of His Majesty's Government in the United Kingdom in regard to the administration of Palestine. It was realised that the publication of a clear and full statement of policy, designed to remove such misunderstanding and the resultant uncertainty and apprehension, was a matter of urgent importance.

. . . . .

3. Many of the misunderstandings which have unhappily arisen on both sides appear to be the result of a failure to appreciate the nature of the duty imposed upon His Majesty's Government by the terms of the Mandate. The next point, therefore, which His Majesty's Government feel it necessary to emphasise, in the strongest manner possible, is that in the words of the Prime Minister's statement in the House of Commons on the 3rd April last, "a double undertaking is involved, to the Jewish people on the one hand and to the non-Jewish population of Palestine on the other."

Much of the agitation which has taken place during the past year seems to have arisen from a failure to realise the full import of this fundamental fact. Both Arabs and Jews have assailed the Government with demands and reproaches based upon the false assumption that it was the duty of His Majesty's Government to execute policies from which they are, in fact, debarred by the explicit terms of the Mandate.

The Prime Minister, in the statement above referred to, announced, in words which could not have been made more plain, that it is the intention of His Majesty's Government to continue to administer Palestine in accordance with the terms of the Mandate, as approved by the Council of the League of Nations. "That," said Mr. Ramsay MacDonald, "is an international obligation from which there can be no question of receding." In spite of so unequivocal a statement, the hope seems to have been entertained that, by some means or other, an escape could be found from the limitations plainly imposed by the terms of the Mandate. It must be realised, once and for all, that it is useless for Jewish leaders on the one hand to press His Majesty's Government to conform their policy in regard, for example, to immigration and land, to the aspirations of the more uncompromising sections of Zionist opinion. That would be to ignore the equally important duty of the

Mandatory Power towards the non-Jewish inhabitants of Palestine. On the other hand, it is equally useless for Arab leaders to maintain their demands for a form of Constitution, which would render it impossible for His Majesty's Government to carry out, in the fullest sense, the double undertaking already referred to. His Majesty's Government have reason to think that one of the reasons for the sustained tension and agitation on both sides has been the creation by misguided advisers of the false hope that efforts to intimidate and to bring pressure to bear upon His Majesty's Government would eventually result in forcing them into a policy which weighted the balances in favour of the one or the other party.

It becomes, therefore, essential that at the outset His Majesty's Government should make it clear that they will not be moved, by any pressure or threats, from the path laid down in the Mandate, and from the pursuit of a policy which aims at promoting the interests of the inhabitants of Palestine, both Arabs and Jews, in a manner which shall be consistent with the obligations which the Mandate imposes.

. . . . .

9. The preceding paragraphs contain an exposition of the general principles which have to be taken into account as governing policy in Palestine and in the limiting conditions under which it must be carried out. The practical problems with which His Majesty's Government are faced in Palestine must now be considered in detail.

These may be regarded as falling roughly under three heads:—

    (1) Security,
    (2) Constitutional development,
    (3) Economic and Social development.

They will be dealt with in that order.

. . . . .

(2) Constitutional Development.

11. Reference has already been made to the demands of Arab leaders for a form of constitution which would be incompatible with the mandatory obligations of His Majesty's Government. It is, however, the considered opinion of His Majesty's Government that the time has now come when the important question of the establishment of a measure of self-government in Palestine must, in the interests of the community as a whole, be taken in hand without further delay.

It may be convenient, in the first instance, to give a brief résumé of the history of this question since the establishment of the civil administration.

In October 1920 there was set up in Palestine an Advisory Council composed in equal parts of official and nominated unofficial members. Of the ten unofficial members, four were Moslems, three were Christians and three were Jews.

On the 1st September, 1922, the Palestine Order in Council was issued, setting up a Government in Palestine under the Foreign Jurisdiction Act. Part 3 of the Order in Council directed the establishment of a Legislative Council to be composed of the High Commissioner as President, with ten other official members, and 12 elected non-official members. The procedure for the selection of the non-official members was laid down in the Legislative Council, Order in Council, 1922, and in February and March 1923 an attempt was made to hold elections in accordance with that procedure.

The attempt failed owing to the refusal of the Arab population as a whole to co-operate (a detailed report of these elections is contained in the papers relating to the elections for the Palestine Legislative Council, 1923, published as Command Paper 1889).

The High Commissioner thereupon suspended the establishment of the proposed Legislative Council, and continued to act in consultation with an Advisory Council as before.

Two further opportunities were given to representative Arab leaders in Palestine to co-operate with the Administration in the government of the country, first, by the reconstitution of a nominated Advisory Council, but with membership conforming to that proposed for the Legislative Council, and, secondly, by a proposal for the formation of an Arab Agency. It was intended that this Agency should have functions analogous to those entrusted to the Jewish Agency by Article 4 of the Palestine Mandate.

Neither of these opportunities was accepted and accordingly, in December 1923, an Advisory Council was set up consisting only of official members. This position still continues; the only change being that the Advisory Council has been enlarged by the addition of more official members as the Administration developed.

. . . . .

(3) *Economic and Social Development.*

14. Under this head the practical problems to be considered are mainly concerned with questions relating to land, immigration and unemployment. These three questions are intimately interrelated, with political as well as economic aspects, and upon their solution must depend any advance that can be hoped for towards settled conditions of peace and prosperity in Palestine.

. . . . .

15. As a result of these extensive and elaborate investigations, certain conclusions have emerged and certain facts have been established which will now be set out briefly:—

(1) *Land.*

It can now be definitely stated that at the present time and with the present methods of Arab cultivation there remains no margin of land available for agricultural settlement by new immigrants, with the exception of such undeveloped land as the various Jewish agencies hold in reserve.

There has been much criticism in the past in regard to the relatively small extent of State land which has been made available for Jewish settlement. It is, however, an error to imagine that the Palestine Government is in possession of large areas of vacant land which could be made available for Jewish settlement. The extent of unoccupied areas of Government land is negligible. The Government claims considerable areas which are, in fact, occupied and cultivated by Arabs. Even were the title of the Government to these areas admitted, and it is in many cases disputed, it would not be possible to make these areas available for Jewish settlement, in view of their actual occupation by Arab cultivators and of the importance of making available additional land on which to place the Arab cultivators who are now landless.

The provision of a margin available for settlement depends upon the progress made in increasing the productivity of the land already occupied.

. . . . .

17. The condition of the Arab fellah leaves much to be desired, and a policy of land development is called for if an improvement in his conditions of life is to be effected.

The sole agencies which have pursued a consistent policy of land development have been the Jewish Colonisation organisations, public and private.

The Jewish settlers have had every advantage that capital, science and organisation could give them. To these and to the energy of the settlers themselves their remarkable progress is due. On the other hand, the Arab population, while lacking the advantages enjoyed by the Jewish settlers, has, by the excess of births over deaths, increased with great rapidity, while the land available for its sustenance has decreased by about a million dunams. This area has passed into Jewish hands.

18. Reference has been made to the energy evinced and the remarkable progress made in Jewish land settlement. It would be unjust to accept the contention, which has been advanced in the course of the controversy regarding relations between Jews and Arabs in Palestine, that the effect of Jewish settlement upon the Arab population has in all cases been detrimental to the interests of the Arabs. This is by no means wholly true, but it is necessary in considering this aspect of the problem to differentiate between colonisation by such bodies as the Palestine Jewish Colonisation Association (commonly known as the P.I.C.A.) and colonisation under Zionist auspices.

In so far as the past policy of the P.I.C.A. is concerned, there can be no doubt that the Arab has profited largely by the installation of the Colonies, and relations between the colonists and their Arab neighbors have in the past been excellent. The cases which are now quoted by the Jewish authorities in support of the contention that the effect of Jewish colonisation on the Arabs in the neighborhood has been advantageous, are cases relating to colonies established by the P.I.C.A. before colonisation financed from the Palestine Foundation Fund, which is the main financial instrument of the Jewish Agency, came into existence.

Some of the attempts which have been made to prove that Zionist colonisation has not had the effect of causing the previous tenants of land acquired to join the landless class have on examination proved to be unconvincing, if not fallacious.

19. Moreover, the effect of Jewish colonisation on the existing population is very intimately affected by the conditions on which the various Jewish bodies hold, utilise and lease their land. It is provided by the Constitution of the Enlarged Jewish Agency, signed at Zürich on the 14th August, 1929 (Article 3 (d) and (e)), that the land acquired shall be held as the "inalienable property of the Jewish people," and that in "all the works or undertakings carried out or furthered by the Agency,

it shall be deemed to be a matter of principle that Jewish labour shall be employed." Moreover, by Article 23 of the draft lease, which it is proposed to execute in respect of all holdings granted by the Jewish National Fund, the lessee undertakes to execute all works connected with the cultivation of the holdings only with Jewish labour. Stringent conditions are imposed to ensure the observance of this undertaking.

An undertaking binding settlers in the Colonies of the Maritime Plain to hire Jewish workmen only, whenever they may be obliged to hire help, is inserted in the Agreement for the repayment of advances made by the Palestine Foundation Fund. Similar provision is contained in the Agreement for the Emek Colonies.

These stringent provisions are difficult to reconcile with the declaration at the Zionist Congress of 1921 of "the desire of the Jewish people to live with the Arab people in relations of friendship and mutual respect, and, together, with the Arab people, to develop the homeland common to both into a prosperous community which would ensure the growth of the peoples."

20. The Jewish leaders have been perfectly frank in their justification of this policy. The Executive of the General Federation of Jewish Labour, which exercises a very important influence on the direction of Zionist policy, has contended that such restrictions are necessary to secure the largest possible amount of Jewish immigration and to safeguard the standard of life of the Jewish labourer from the danger of falling to the lower standard of the Arab.

However logical such arguments may be from the point of view of a purely national movement, it must, nevertheless, be pointed out that they take no account of the provisions of Article 6 of the Mandate, which expressly requires that, in facilitating Jewish immigration and close settlement by Jews on the land, the Administration of Palestine must ensure that "the rights and position of other sections of the population are not prejudiced." . . . . .

29. The situation revealed by exhaustive examination of the various economic, political and social factors involved, makes it clear that Palestine has reached a critical moment in its development. In the past it may be said that the Government has left economic and social forces to operate with the minimum of interference or control, but it has become increasingly clear that such a policy can no longer continue. It is only the closest co-operation between the Government and the leaders of the Arab and Jewish communities that can prevent Palestine

from drifting into a situation which would imperil, on the one hand, the devoted work of those who have sought to build up the Jewish National Home, and, on the other, the interests of the majority of the population who at present possess few resources of their own with which to sustain the struggle for existence. What is required is that both races should consent to live together and to respect each other's needs and claims. To the Arabs His Majesty's Government would appeal for a recognition of the facts of the situation, and for a sustained effort at co-operation in obtaining that prosperity for the country as a whole by which all will benefit. From the Jewish leaders, His Majesty's Government ask a recognition of the necessity for making some concession on their side in regard to the independent and separatist ideals which have been developed in some quarters in connection with the Jewish National Home, and for accepting it as an active factor in the orientation of their policy that the general development of the country shall be carried out in such a way that the interests of the Arabs and Jews may each receive adequate consideration, with the object of developing prosperity throughout the country under conditions which will give no grounds for charges of partiality upon the one side or upon the other, but will permit of the Arab and Jewish communities developing in harmony and contentment.

112. THE PEEL REPORT ADVOCATING PARTITION, 1937 [48]

The continuance of violent manifestations in Palestine led to the appointment of the Peel Commission in May 1936 to study the underlying causes of the disturbances and make recommendations. The result of the commission's labors was embodied in a report of July 1937. It advocated the abolition of the mandate and the division of Palestine into a Jewish state, an Arab state, and a neutral (British-controlled) area. The plan aroused protests from all sides and was shelved, with League endorsement, while another commission was despatched to ascertain more facts.

CONCLUSIONS AND RECOMMENDATIONS.

1. We will now briefly recapitulate in pursuance of our terms of reference the conclusions and recommendations which we have set

[48] Great Britain, Palestine Royal Commission, *Report. Presented by the Secretary of State for the Colonies to Parliament by Command of His Majesty, July, 1937*, Cmd. 5479, His Majesty's Stationery Office, London, 1937, pp. 363-364, 380-392, 394-395.

out in this part of our Report. The underlying causes of the disturb-ances, or (as we regard it) the rebellion, of 1936 are, first, the desire of the Arabs for national independence; secondly, their antagonism to the establishment of the Jewish National Home in Palestine, quickened by their fear of Jewish domination. Among contributory causes were the effect on Arab opinion of the attainment of national independence by Iraq, Trans-Jordan, Egypt, Syria and the Lebanon; the rush of Jewish immigrants escaping from Central and Eastern Europe; the inequality of opportunity enjoyed by Arabs and Jews respectively in placing their case before Your Majesty's Government and the public; the growth of Arab mistrust; Arab alarm at the continued purchase of Arab land by Jews; the intensive character and the "modernism" of Jewish nationalism; and lastly the general uncertainty, accentuated by the ambiguity of certain phrases in the Mandate, as to the ultimate intentions of the Mandatory Power. This uncertainty has aggravated all the difficulties of the situation and in particular has (a) stimulated the Jewish desire to expand and consolidate their position in Palestine as quickly as possible, and (b) made it possible for the Arabs to interpret the conciliatory policy of the Palestine Government and the sympathetic attitude of some of its officials as showing that the British determination to implement the Balfour Declaration is not sincere.

2. We have found that, though the Arabs have benefited by the development of the country owing to Jewish immigration, this has had no conciliatory effect. On the contrary, improvement in the economic situation in Palestine has meant the deterioration of the political situa-tion.

3. The Palestine Government have attempted to discharge the con-tradictory obligations of the Mandatory under conditions of great diffi-culty by "holding the balance" between Jews and Arabs. Repeated attempts to conciliate either race have only increased the trouble. The situation in Palestine has reached a deadlock. The Administration has from the start been driven to work at high pressure under peculiar difficulties. The steps taken by the Palestine Government to enforce respect for law and order have proved ineffectual. The elementary duty of providing public security has not been discharged. Endeavours to control the alienation of land by Arabs to Jews have not been successful. In the hills there is no more room for further close settlement by Jews; in the plains it should only be allowed under certain restrictions. There has been great delay in the preparation of a record of rights: the ascer-tainment and registration of Government ownership in land has been

slow and unsatisfactory. The concession to the Palestine Electric Corporation has obstructed any development of irrigation from the River Jordan; and more might have been done to test the possibilities of irrigation in the south of the Gaza Sub-district and in Beersheba. Great efforts are being made to effect a radical change in the methods of cultivation by the Arab *fellah,* but this can only be accomplished after many years and after an extension of primary education.

4. As regards immigration the Mandate has been fully implemented, but the attempts to regulate it have been unsatisfactory, unacceptable to Arabs and Jews alike. . . .

5. In the matter of finance, the revenues of Palestine have increased rapidly, but far too large a proportion has had to be devoted towards meeting the charges of public security. . . .

6. The standard of social services in Palestine is higher than in the average British Colony or Indian Province, but the difficulty of providing services in one State for two distinct communities with two very different standards of living is apparent. . . .

7. As regards the development of local autonomy or self-governing institutions, this also has been hampered by the difficulty of combining what are virtually two civilizations in one system. The restrictions which the Mandatory Power found it necessary to impose in the interests of rural boards or backward municipalities have been resented by the larger towns. The attempts to create a local legislature have been unsuccessful and should not be revived.

. . . . .

A PLAN OF PARTITION.

1. We return, then, to Partition as the only method we are able to propose for dealing with the root of the trouble.

. . . . .

4. The Mandate for Palestine should terminate and be replaced by a Treaty System in accordance with the precedent set in Iraq and Syria.

5. A new Mandate for the Holy Places should be instituted to fulfil the purposes defined in Section 2 below.

6. Treaties of Alliance should be negotiated by the Mandatory with the Government of Trans-Jordan and representatives of the Arabs of Palestine on the one hand and with the Zionist Organisation on the other. These Treaties would declare that, within as short a period as

may be convenient, two sovereign independent States would be established—the one an Arab State, consisting of Trans-Jordan united with that part of Palestine which lies to the east and south of a frontier such as we suggest in Section 3 below; the other a Jewish State consisting of that part of Palestine which lies to the north and west of that frontier.

7. The Mandatory would undertake to support any requests for admission to the League of Nations which the Governments of the Arab and the Jewish States might make in accordance with Article I of the Covenant.

8. The Treaties would include strict guarantees for the protection of minorities in each State. . . .

. . . . .

2. The Holy Places.

10. The partition of Palestine is subject to the overriding necessity of keeping the sanctity of Jerusalem and Bethlehem inviolate and of ensuring free and safe access to them for all the world. . . .

11. A new Mandate, therefore, should be framed with the execution of this trust as its primary purpose. An enclave should be demarcated extending from a point north of Jerusalem to a point south of Bethlehem, and access to the sea should be provided by a corridor extending to the north of the main road and to the south of the railway, including the towns of Lydda and Ramle, and terminating at Jaffa.

12. We regard the protection of the Holy Places as a permanent trust. . . . It is not intended that in course of time they should stand by themselves as a wholly self-governing community.

. . . . . .

14. We think it would accord with Christian sentiment in the world at large if Nazareth and the Sea of Galilee (Lake Tiberias) were also covered by this Mandate. . . .

. . . . .

3. The Frontier.

17. The natural principle for the Partition of Palestine is to separate the areas in which the Jews have acquired land and settled from those which are wholly or mainly occupied by Arabs. . . . the Jewish lands and colonies are mostly to be found in the Maritime Plain between Al Majdal and Mount Carmel, in the neighbourhood of Haifa, in the Plain of Esdraelon and the Valley of Jezreel, and in the east of

Galilee, i.e., south of Tiberias, on the shores of the Lake, near Safad, and in the Huleh Basin. The rest of Galilee and the northern part of the plain of Acre are almost wholly in Arab occupation. So also is the central hill-country of old Samaria and Judaea—except for Jerusalem and its vicinity. The towns of Nablus, Jenin and Tulkarm, the last an outpost on the edge of the Maritime Plain, are centres of Arab nationalism. Except in and near Jerusalem and at Hebron, there are practically no Jews between Jenin and Beersheba. This Arab block extends eastwards to the River Jordan between the Dead Sea and Beisan. In the area stretching south and southeast of Beersheba to the Egyptian frontier, the Jews have bought some isolated blocks of land but the population is entirely Arab.

18. This existing separation of the area of Jewish land and settlement from that of wholly or mainly Arab occupation seems to us to offer a fair and practicable basis for Partition, provided that, in accordance with the spirit of our obligations, (1) a reasonable allowance is made within the boundaries of the Jewish State for the growth of population and col- onization, and (2) reasonable compensation is given to the Arab State for the loss of land and revenue. This last is one of the reasons we give in paragraph 23 below for suggesting the payment of a subvention by the Jewish State to the Arab State in the event of Partition coming into force.   .   .   .   .   .

20. Starting from Ras an Naqura, [the suggested frontier line] follows the existing northern and eastern frontier of Palestine to Lake Tiberias and crosses the Lake to the outflow of the River Jordan whence it continues down the river to a point a little north of Beisan. It then cuts across the Beisan Plain and runs along the southern edge of the Valley of Jezreel and across the Plain of Esdraelon to a point near Megiddo, whence it crosses the Carmel ridge in the neighbourhood of the Megiddo Road. Having thus reached the Maritime Plain, the line runs southwards down its eastern edge, curving west to avoid Tulkarm, until it reaches the Jerusalem-Jaffa corridor near Lydda. South of the Corridor it continues down the edge of the Plain to a point about 10 miles south of Rehovot, whence it turns west to the sea.

.   .   .   .   .

4. Inter-State Subvention.

23. As we have explained in an earlier chapter, the Jews contribute more *per capita* to the revenues of Palestine than the Arabs, and the

Government has thereby been enabled to maintain public services for the Arabs at a higher level than would otherwise have been possible. Partition would mean, on the one hand, that the Arab Area would no longer profit from the taxable capacity of the Jewish Area. On the other hand, (1) the Jews would acquire a new right of sovereignty in the Jewish Area: (2) that Area, as we have defined it, would be larger than the existing area of Jewish land and settlement: (3) the Jews would be freed from their present liability for helping to promote the welfare of Arabs outside that Area. It seems to us, therefore, not unreasonable to suggest that the Jewish State should pay a subvention to the Arab State when Partition comes into effect. . . .

. . . . .

5. British Subvention.

25. The Inter-State Subvention would adjust the financial balance in Palestine; but it must be remembered that the plan we are submitting involves the inclusion of Trans-Jordan in the Arab State. The taxable capacity of Trans-Jordan is very low and its revenues have never sufficed to meet the cost of its administration. From 1921 to the present day it has received grants-in-aid from the United Kingdom, which have amounted to a total sum of £1,253,000 or an average of about £78,000 a year. Grants have also been made towards the cost of the Trans-Jordan Frontier Force, and loans to the amount of £60,575, of which about £30,000 has been repaid, have been provided for earthquake-relief and the distribution of seed.

26. The Mandate for Trans-Jordan ought not in our opinion to be relinquished without securing, as far as possible, that the standard of administration should not fall too low through lack of funds to maintain it; and it is in this matter, we submit, that the British people might fairly be asked to do their part in facilitating a settlement. . . .

27. We recommend, therefore, that in the event of the Treaty System coming into force, Parliament should be asked to make a grant of £2,000,000 to the Arab State.

6. Tariffs and Ports.

28. The Arab and Jewish States, being sovereign independent States, would determine their own tariffs. Subject to the terms of the Mandate, the same would apply to the Mandatory Government.

29. . . . . It would greatly ease the position and it would promote the

interests of both the Arab and Jewish States if they could agree to impose identical customs-duties on as many articles as possible, and if the Mandatory Government, likewise, could assimilate its customs-duties as far as might be with those of one or both of the two States.

. . . . .

10. Exchange of Land and Population.

. . . . .

36. If Partition is to be effective in promoting a final settlement it must mean more than drawing a frontier and establishing two States. Sooner or later there should be a transfer of land and, as far as possible, an exchange of population.

. . . . .

47. Such is the plan of Partition which we submit to the consideration of Your Majesty's Government. We believe that it fulfils the essential conditions of Partition and demonstrates that, if Palestine ought to be divided, it can be divided.

. . . . .

CONCLUSION.

. . . . .

2. The advantages to the Arabs of Partition on the lines we have proposed may be summarized as follows:—

(i) They obtain their national independence and can operate on an equal footing with the Arabs of the neighbouring countries in the cause of Arab unity and progress.

(ii) They are finally delivered from the fear of being "swamped" by the Jews and from the possibility of ultimate subjection to Jewish rule.

(iii) In particular, the final limitation of the Jewish National Home within a fixed frontier and the enactment of a new Mandate for the Holy Places, solemnly guaranteed by the League of Nations, removes all anxiety lest the Holy Places should ever come under Jewish control.

(iv) As a set-off to the loss of territory the Arabs regard as theirs, the Arab State will receive a subvention from the Jewish State. It will also, in view of the backwardness of Trans-Jordan, obtain a grant of £2,000,000 from the British Treasury; and, if an arrangement can be made for the exchange of land and population, a further grant will be made for the conversion, as far as may prove possible, of uncultivable land in the Arab State into productive land from which the cultivators and the State alike will profit.

3. The advantages of Partition to the Jews may be summarized as follows:—

(i) Partition secures the establishment of the Jewish National Home and relieves it from the possibility of its being subjected in the future to Arab rule.

(ii) Partition enables the Jews in the fullest sense to call their National Home their own: for it converts it into a Jewish State. Its citizens will be able to admit as many Jews into it as they themselves believe can be absorbed. They will obtain the primary objective of Zionism—a Jewish nation, planted in Palestine, giving its nationals the same status in the world as other nations give theirs. They will cease at last to live a "minority life."

· · · · ·

6. There is no need to stress the advantage to the British people of a settlement in Palestine. We are bound to honour to the utmost of our power the obligations we undertook in the exigencies of war towards the Arabs and the Jews. . . . Partition offers a possibility of finding a way through them, a possibility of obtaining a final solution of the problem which does justice to the rights and aspirations of both the Arabs and the Jews and discharges the obligations we undertook towards them twenty years ago to the fullest extent that is practicable in the circumstances of the present time.

· · · · ·

113. SUMMARY OF THE ARAB DEMANDS IN PALESTINE, 1937 [49]

"It was not till we had announced the date on which we intended to leave the country," declared the Peel Commission on page 130 of its Report

[49] Great Britain, Palestine Royal Commission, *Minutes of Evidence Heard at Public Sessions (with Index)*, Colonial No. 134, His Majesty's Stationery Office, London, 1937, pp. 297-298. Reprinted by permission of the Controller of His Britannic Majesty's Stationery Office.

(Document No. 112), "that the [Arab] Higher Committee decided to abandon its 'Boycott' and co-operate with us in trying to find the way to peace in Palestine; and when at last they came before us, headed by the Mufti [Moslem religious head] of Jerusalem, the first words of the prepared statement he made to us, were these: 'The Arab cause in Palestine is one which aims at national independence. In its essence it does not differ from similar movements amongst the Arabs in all other Arab territories.' And at the close of his statement . . . he summed up the Arab demands"—as quoted in the appended selection.

Testimony of His Eminence Haj Amin Effendi El-Husseini, President of the Arab Higher Committee, January 12, 1937:

In conclusion I wish to add that the Arabs cannot see any benefit or hope of reform from the introduction of changes of a subsidiary nature and unless the grievances, fundamental as they are, are remedied and their causes removed, the evil will continue and the grievances will intensify. It is the firm belief of the Arabs that the proper and fundamental treatment of the situation will be found in the three *(sic)* following measures:—

1. The abandonment of the experiment of the Jewish National Home, which originated in the Balfour Declaration and which has proved to be a failure, and the reconsideration of all the consequences which resulted from this experiment and which prejudiced the rights of the Arabs and imperilled their national existence.

2. The immediate and complete stoppage of Jewish immigration.

3. The immediate and complete prohibition of the sale of Arab land to the Jews.

4. The solution of the Palestine problem on the same basis as that on which were solved the problems of Iraq, Syria and the Lebanon, namely, by the termination of the Mandate and by the conclusion of a treaty between Great Britain and Palestine, by virtue of which a national and independent government in constitutional form will be established, on which national elements will be represented, and which will guarantee justice, progress, and prosperity to all.

The policy of establishing a National Home for the Jews in this country must inevitably lead to continued anxiety and disturbances and will make of the Holy Land which of all countries in the world should enjoy peace and tranquillity the permanent scene of disorders. I am confident that it will be in the interests of everyone to abandon this impracticable attempt which aims at establishing a National Home for one people in the country of some other people, which is already fully populated and which is surrounded by oceans of countries belonging to the Arab people, who hold this country in the highest degree of veneration. Those people will never abandon this country at any time or under any circumstances. I refer now to the Moslem world, to the Arab and Moslem worlds, who attach great religious importance to this country.

114. BRITISH OFFICIAL STATEMENT ON PALESTINE, NOVEMBER 1938 [50]

Early in 1938 another Palestine commission, headed by Sir John Woodhead, was appointed, this time to draw up a "more precise and detailed scheme" than the Peel Plan for settling the Palestinian troubles. The Woodhead Commission reported in October 1938 [Cmd. 5854] and on the basis of its proposals the British Government invited to a London conference representatives of the Palestinian Arabs and those of neighboring states, and delegates of the Jewish Agency for Palestine. The conference assembled February 7, 1939, and dispersed in March without having come to an agreement.

1. The Royal Commission, presided over by the late Earl Peel, published its report in July, 1937, and proposed a solution of the Palestine problem by means of a scheme of partition under which independent Arab and Jewish States would be established while other areas would be retained under mandatory administration.[51] In their statement of policy following upon the publication of the report, His Majesty's Government in the United Kingdom announced their general agreement with the arguments and conclusions of the Royal Commission, and expressed the view that a scheme of partition on the general lines recommended by the Commission represented the best and most hopeful solution of the deadlock.

---

[50] *Palestine. Statement by His Majesty's Government in the United Kingdom. Presented by the Secretary of State for the Colonies to Parliament by Command of His Majesty, November, 1938,* Cmd. 5893, His Majesty's Stationery Office, London, 1938, pp. 2-4.

[51] See Document No. 112.—*Ed.*

2. The proposal of the Commission was framed in the light of the information available at the time, and it was generally recognized that further detailed examination would be necessary before it could be decided whether such a solution would prove practicable. This proposal was subsequently discussed in Parliament and at meetings of the Permanent Mandates Commission and the Council and Assembly of the League of Nations, when His Majesty's Government received authority to explore the practical application of the principle of partition. A despatch of 23rd December, 1937, from the Secretary of State for the Colonies to the High Commissioner for Palestine [Cmd. 5634], announced the intention of His Majesty's Government to undertake the further investigations required for the drawing up of a more precise and detailed scheme. It was pointed out that the final decision could not be taken in merely general terms and that the further enquiry would provide the necessary material on which to judge, when the best possible partition scheme had been formulated, its equity and practicability. The despatch also defined the functions and terms of reference of the technical Commission who were appointed to visit Palestine for the purpose of submitting in due course to His Majesty's Government proposals for such a detailed scheme.

3. His Majesty's Government have now received the report of the Palestine Partition Commission who have carried out their investigations with great thoroughness and efficiency, and have collected material which will be very valuable in the further consideration of policy. Their report is now published [Cmd. 5854], together with a summary of their conclusions. It will be noted that the four members of the Commission advise unanimously against the adoption of the scheme of partition outlined by the Royal Commission. In addition to the Royal Commission's scheme, two other schemes described as plans B and C are examined in the report. One member prefers plan B. Two other members, including the Chairman, consider that plan C is the best scheme of partition which, under the terms of reference, can be devised. A fourth member, while agreeing that plan C is the best that can be devised under the terms of reference, regards both plans as impracticable. The report points out that under either plan, while the budget of the Jewish State is likely to show a substantial surplus, the budgets of the Arab State (including Trans-Jordan) and of the Mandated Territories are likely to show substantial deficits. The Commission reject as impracticable the Royal Commission's recommendation for a direct subvention from the Jewish State to the Arab State. They think that, on economic

grounds, a customs union between the States and the Mandated Territories is essential and they examine the possibility of finding a solution for the financial and economic problems of partition by means of a scheme based upon such a union. They consider that any such scheme would be inconsistent with the grant of fiscal independence to the Arab and Jewish States. Their conclusion is that, on a strict interpretation of their terms of reference, they have no alternative but to report that they are unable to recommend boundaries for the proposed areas which will afford a reasonable prospect of the eventual establishment of self-supporting Arab and Jewish States.

4. His Majesty's Government, after careful study of the Partition Commission's report, have reached the conclusion that this further examination has shown that the political, administrative and financial difficulties involved in the proposal to create independent Arab and Jewish States inside Palestine are so great that this solution of the problem is impracticable.

5. His Majesty's Government will therefore continue their responsibility for the government of the whole of Palestine. They are now faced with the problem of finding alternative means of meeting the needs of the difficult situation described by the Royal Commission which will be consistent with their obligations to the Arabs and the Jews. His Majesty's Government believe that it is possible to find these alternative means. They have already given much thought to the problem in the light of the reports of the Royal Commission and of the Partition Commission. It is clear that the surest foundation for peace and progress in Palestine would be an understanding between the Arabs and the Jews, and His Majesty's Government are prepared in the first instance to make a determined effort to promote such an understanding. With this end in view, they propose immediately to invite representatives of the Palestinian Arabs and of neighbouring States on the one hand and of the Jewish Agency on the other, to confer with them as soon as possible in London regarding future policy, including the question of immigration into Palestine. As regards the representation of the Palestinian Arabs, His Majesty's Government must reserve the right to refuse to receive those leaders whom they regard as responsible for the campaign of assassination and violence.

6. His Majesty's Government hope that these discussions in London may help to promote agreement as to future policy regarding Palestine. They attach great importance, however, to a decision being reached at an early date. Therefore, if the London discussions should not produce

agreement within a reasonable period of time, they will take their own decision in the light of their examination of the problem and of the discussions in London, and announce the policy which they propose to pursue.

7. In considering and settling their policy His Majesty's Government will keep constantly in mind the international character of the Mandate with which they have been entrusted and their obligations in that respect.

🙢 🙢 🙢

CHAPTER 6

FRANCE

115. THE DESTRUCTION CAUSED BY THE WAR IN FRANCE [1]

When the World War came to a close, internal conditions in France were chaotic. The northern tenth of the country had the appearance of wasteland. Borrowing heavily and spending liberally on reconstruction, the French were aggrieved that German reparation payments failed to match French restoration expenditures. The following summary was written by one of Clémenceau's ablest assistants at the Paris Peace Conference. More detailed statistics may be found in the official Bulletin des Régions Liberées, *published from July 21, 1919, onwards.*

If France insists upon the execution of the [Versailles] treaty it is not solely because it is a contract; it is because its non-execution would very shortly place her in an impasse.

The war bled us terribly. Out of our population of less than 38,000,000 there were mobilized 8,500,000; 5,300,000 of them were killed or wounded (1,500,000 killed, 800,000 *mutilés,* 3,000,000 wounded), not counting 500,000 men who have come back to us from German prisons in very bad physical condition.

Almost 4,000,000 hectares[2] of land were devastated, together with 4,000 towns and villages; 600,000 buildings were destroyed, among them 20,000 factories and work-shops, besides 5,000 kilometers of railroads and 53,000 kilometers of roads. About 1,400,000 head of cattle were carried off. Altogether, a quarter of our productive capital was annihilated.

The financial consequences of the annihilation of all these resources bear down on us heavily today. The war cost us 150 billions of francs. The damage to property and persons comes to 200 billions. Our ordi-

---

[1] A Tardieu, "The Policy of France," in *Foreign Affairs,* vol. I (1922-1923), pp. 12-13. Reprinted by permission of the Council on Foreign Relations.

[2] A hectare is the equivalent of 2.471 acres.—*Ed.*

nary budget has increased from 4½ billions to 25 billions; our debt from 36 billions to 330 billions. Since the armistice we have spent on reconstruction and pensions a total of 90 billions, and we have received from Germany in one form or another less than two billions of gold marks (about six billions of francs), or about six per cent of what we have had to spend on restoring our provinces—a task as yet but half completed.

     .   .   .   .   .

If you will go back for a moment to the expense figures which I have just cited, you will find that in the last two years France has spent on reconstruction and pensions 7½ billions of dollars, or $5,700 a minute, while in the same period Germany has only spent 500 millions of dollars, or $381 a minute. In other words, we have accumulated a deficit of $5,319 every minute; and it is we who have paid it, in place of Germany who was responsible for creating the damage.

We think that this cannot go on. You would think the same in our place. The interest and amortization on the sums borrowed by us since the armistice to make up for Germany's default have cost us 4½ billions of francs a year. The interest on our debt absorbs 55 per cent of our taxes. We ask that all this be ended. Who can say it is not a legitimate demand?

116. THE DARIAC REPORT, MAY 28, 1922 *(Extracts)* [3]

During the early years of the Franco-German reparation struggle it appeared that Frenchmen such as Raymond Poincaré were less interested in financial contributions than in "a wedding of Ruhr coke with Lorraine iron," for the coal in the northern French fields was poorly suited to the Lorraine iron ore. On May 28, 1922, Adrien Dariac, president of the finance commission of the Chamber of Deputies, rendered a report on such a project to Poincaré. The report was not adopted by the French Government.

The following is the full text of the report presented recently to the French Government (and not yet published in France) by M. Dariac, who was sent by M. Poincaré as a commissioner to report on the economics and the industry of the Rhine province. . . .

---

[3] *The Manchester Guardian Weekly,* November 3, 1922, pp. II-III of Cover. Reprinted by permission.

TEXT OF THE REPORT

It will be remembered that the occupation of the Düsseldorf bridge-head was provoked by the ill will which Germany showed in meeting her engagements in 1921. It was after the London agreement of May 5, 1921, and the ultimatum which resulted from it, that it was decided to adopt the military sanctions consisting of the occupation of Düsseldorf, Duisburg, Ruhrort, and the neighbouring region, and the economic sanctions consisting of the control of the Rhenish Customs and the establishment of a Customs barrier at the limit of our zone of occupation. The economic sanctions were dropped in September, 1921, following the German acceptance of the ultimatum; but the military sanctions have remained in force as a means of pressure on our former enemies.

The feature of this region of occupation is its very accentuated industrial character, which makes of it a pledge in our hands of quite the first importance for the recovery of the sums which Germany has undertaken to pay us.

In existing circumstances, indeed, the Ruhr, and in particular the region of Düsseldorf, Duisburg, Ruhrort, which we are occupying, and which forms its head, constituted the principal element of German wealth, which is based entirely on iron and coal, their transformations and their derivatives. The majority of the great German consortiums have been formed there, have their headquarters and establishments there, and the ten or twelve industrialists who direct them rule, directly or indirectly, but absolutely, the economic destinies of Germany. (Metallurgy, coal, coal derivatives, dyestuffs, manures, shipping companies, import and export of raw materials or manufactured goods.)

. . . . .

The figures for the whole of the French production before the war are obviously unable to compare with the production of the Ruhr, the extent of which, however, does not equal that of a small French Department. . . .

. . . . .

It is this industrial power alone which has made the greatness and prosperity of Germany; from the agricultural point of view, before the war, and despite an intensive culture unrivalled in Europe, Germany bought abroad nearly three milliard gold marks' worth of foodstuffs of every sort (wheat, barley, rice, maize, coffee, fruits, wine, oils, cattle, etc.). This means in effect that Germany's food was only assured through the production of her industries, (coal, dyestuffs, metals, chemicals and textile industries, etc.)

"In Germany," as Vogler, Stinnes's chief lieutenant, has said, "the potato is a coal by-product."

The large-scale industry, the "heavy industry" of the Ruhr, concentrated entirely in the hands of a few individuals, is thus called to play a decisive part in the events which will unfold themselves in Germany's future.

In this field the Stinnes, the Thyssens, the Krupps, the Haniels, the Kloeckners, the Funkes, the Mannesmanns, and some three or four others play in Germany an economic rôle analogous to that of the Carnegies, the Rockefellers, the Harrimans, the Vanderbilts, and the Goulds in America; they also carry on a political activity unknown among the American billionaires.

．．．．．

And, in fact, if the paper mark plunges down day after day, the means of production of the Stinnes and Thyssens and Krupps and Haniels and their colleagues remain intact and are worth gold. This is what gives value to our occupation of the country.

No doubt we do not hold the whole of the Ruhr, but by our simple occupation at present we hold in reality the whole of its industrial production under our domination.

We occupy, indeed, the greater part of the basin, in which there have been established the blast furnaces which produce the cast-iron, as well as the ports of the Ruhr and the Rhine through which these blast furnaces are supplied with ores. Thus we cut in two the metallurgical establishments; we can, when we wish, separate from their coal, their ore, their cast-iron and steel production, the connected and complementary establishments which only complete their products in unoccupied Germany; we can utterly disorganise the industry of the potentates of Düsseldorf, Duisburg, and Ruhrort.

．．．．．

So long as we maintain our present position on the Rhine we shall thus constitute a constant menace for the ten or twelve masters of German industry who are in reality financially the masters of Germany.

From this point of view it is very regrettable that we have been led to abandon the economic sanctions which accompanied our occupation of Düsseldorf in 1921; the Customs barrier established between the occupied zone and free Germany, if it did not give great results in immediate return, nevertheless was in its simple presence a reminder that the circulation of the products between the factories producing crude metal and the factories working upon it was at our mercy, and that we could, by a simple raising of tariffs, either levy a virtually unlimited tithe upon the German metal industry or completely disorganise it.

And this perspective alone would have been of a sort which would suggest to the German Government, or its councils, suitable means for facilitating the rapid payment of its war debt.

But recriminations avail nothing.

In the existing circumstances, how can we profit by the pledge which we thus hold?

To begin with, there is one question which should be outside all debate: we cannot dream of abandoning this pledge.

. . . . .

To begin with, it is possible that the mere menace will inspire the German Government, counselled and assisted by the industrialists of the Ruhr, themselves desirous of evading a constraint of which they feel that we alone are the masters, with proposals which would be of a nature to give us satisfaction for the moment. But let us not be deceived: if the great industrialists concede to the German Government credits and facilities for the payment of the first arrears of its debt— a thing they will not do without good guarantees secured on the railways or other State property,—it will be in order to endeavour to rid themselves of the Nessus' shirt which the occupation of the Düsseldorf bridgehead constitutes for them.

Three years' experience has shown us how little confidence we can place in German good-will; let us beware, then, of abandoning a pledge which we can have available for exploiting if this good-will, always uncertain, should begin to flag.

. . . . .

It is clear how the possession of the pledge which we now hold in the Ruhr invests our action of persuasion or constraint with suppleness.

And finally, without employing constraint, is it not possible to imagine a utilisation of the Ruhr by a collaboration, a friendly *entente* between France and the Allies on the one part and Germany on the other, with permanent control of its means of production?

The Rhine separates two great metallurgical regions; on one side the Ruhr, with its nine million tons of cast-iron (1913 yield), absorbing annually 18 to 25 million tons of ore; on the other side, the Lorraine region (including the Saar), the productive capacity of which is also nine million tons of cast-iron.

The ironmasters of the Ruhr have available (in times of normal production) indefinite quantities of coal, but quite insufficient quantities of ore, since the new Germany produces no more than seven to eight million tons, for a consumption which before the war amounted to 48 million tons and would still easily reach 30 millions.

On the other hand, the ironmasters in the Lorraine group have available twice as much ore as they can work. . . . On the other hand, they absolutely require for their blast furnaces the coke of the Ruhr.

Hackneyed conclusion, a hundred times repeated: the French metal industry cannot live without the German coke, the German metal industry can only reach half its full development if it is deprived of French ore.

. . . . .

Cannot France envisage the exchange of German metallurgical coke and French ore as a friendly exploitation offering the bases of a true industrial association?

We cannot demand that Germany shall pay enormous sums for 35 years, and on the other hand we are afraid of seeing her industries develop in the proportion which would permit her to assure the payment of the debts which she has acknowledged. But so long as we are on the right bank of the Rhine and are masters of 45 million tons a year of ore we shall be in a position to play a decisive part in the German metal industry, demanding a control of production in return.

And no doubt this will be the solution of the future. . . .

. . . . .

The Rhinelander certainly does not love the Prussian, a greedy and disagreeable functionary, installed in this kindly country, with his concern for strict discipline and his spirit of authority.

There is a Rhenish psychology, complex enough and yet easily unravelled. These marches have been the prize of every victory, the ransom of every defeat; men at arms have heavily tramped down their soil. The troops of Louis XIV., of Louis XV., of Napoleon succeeded one another there, and were replaced by those of Frederick the Great or of Blücher. Geographically, intellectually their pole is on the west. Acts of force, the great disasters of the end of the Empire, cast them politically into the Prussian system.

Reluctantly the populations accepted it; but this Prussian system has presented itself to them under the aspect of ordered progress, of economic prosperity, of various reforms, and if its unpleasing rigidity was at first revolting to these people of semi-Latin culture, who had lived in the secular anarchy of a historical subdivision but had been immersed in belles-lettres and had experienced the sweetness of a beneficent liberty and of perhaps uncertain but still real democratic aspirations, they forgave these martinets with their barrack-room methods and their dry discipline in consideration of an unprecedented prosperity which seemed to secure the hegemony of Europe to Prussian Germany.

There came the great catastrophe of 1918. In the first months of 1919 the Rhineland expected modifications in its national status. It anticipated French annexation, or autonomy, and if the first of these eventualities awakened, if not resistance—the Rhenish populations are sufficiently malleable to accept the decisions of force—at least disquietude, the second appeared, on the whole, to be desired. The Versailles peace arrived at a third solution: inter-Allied occupation for five, ten, or fifteen years, but with the maintenance of the Rhineland within the German unit. The most that has been done has been to impose certain inter-Allied organisations on the solid texture of the administrative organisation of the Reich; the Prussian functionary has remained, and with him the prospective of a future in no way differing from the past.

Instead of . . . autonomy . . . it was in the main a case of the *status quo.* . . .

There followed the events of 1920-21. . . .

The Rhenish populations attentively followed the development of the crisis; anxious as to their destinies, they awaited French statements which might define them. If the military occupation was to be pro-

longed, they foresaw certain collaborations, which would be very difficult if this occupation was to be precarious.

Forcible words were followed by feeble actions; . . . the London
Conference reduced our rights, curtailed our claim, gave the populations
of Rhenish Prussia or of the Bavarian palatinate the clear impression
that our country had embarked on the path of concessions, that France,
though unpaid, would not realise the pledge which she held in her
hand, this Rhineland prepared to adapt herself to fresh formulæ, but
prudent and insufficiently heroic to break with her lord of yesterday,
who, once our soldiers were gone, would remain her lord of to-morrow.
May, 1921, was for us, from Mainz to Cologne, the painful period in
which our policy of abandonment made its appearance.

Prussian propaganda was encouraged by this bankruptcy.

It redoubled in intensity; it affirmed that, with the bad times over,
the Reich was soon to recover the mastery of its western provinces.

In face of this campaign the Rhinelanders drew back more, and since
then the situation has become more delicate. The French Government
therefore owes it to itself, . . . to practise a Rhenish policy based on
collaboration in the economic field, a policy of conciliation and of
rapprochement towards the populations.

. . . . .

The first act of this policy is the financial organisation of the Rhineland; a Customs barrier placed on the east facing Germany and razed
on the west facing France, to avoid the economic strangulation which
would result from a double fiscal wall diminishing the exchange of
goods and comprising the industrial life of the Rhinelands; a budget
separate from that of the Reich; the substitution of a healthy currency
for the damaged mark.

The second act is the replacement of Prussian by Rhenish functionaries.

The third is the extension of the powers of the High Commission
and the convocation of an elected assembly.

These are doubtless ambitious projects, but if executed wisely and
discerningly in proportion as Germany slips out of her engagements
they would be amply justified. It is a long-drawn-out policy, in which
a well-considered diplomacy must apply one after another the successive links of a well-thought-out course of action which, little by little,
will detach from Germany a free Rhineland under the military guard
of France and Belgium.

117. DEPRECIATION AND STABILIZATION (1928) OF THE FRANC [4]

The difficult post-war internal and foreign developments caused the French franc to decline in value until, in July 1926, it was worth only two cents—about one-tenth of its pre-war quotation. So critical was the situation that group lines were temporarily effaced in the Chamber of Deputies and Raymond Poincaré formed a National Union Ministry which, with little reconstitution, guided the destinies of France from July 1926 to July 1929. In this period the franc was stabilized and revalued at four cents—a procedure involving a virtual repudiation of four-fifths of the internal debt. But in the elections of 1928 Poincaré's policies were upheld and he soon came to be regarded as the "Savior of the Franc." The processes of depreciation and stabilization are here described in authoritative fashion.

The French franc lost eighty per cent of its value as a result of the World War. It fell from an exchange value of 19.29 cents in 1914 to 3.90 cents in 1928, and its internal purchasing power fell to the same extent. Such depreciation . . . has caused notable changes in France. In the first place, the temporary loss in financial prestige and power has been considerable. In the second place, production has come to be dominated more and more by large manufacturing units and corporate forms of enterprise. The results of this change are likely to persist. In the third place, the shift of power from the middle classes to the industrial leaders and to those with more flexible incomes appears to have changed the character of French life and ideals to a notable extent. Other results of depreciation might be mentioned, but these are perhaps the most striking.

. . . . .

At the close of the war, the most immediate influence working against the franc was the unfavorable balance of trade. The second in direct relation was the internal debt, which bore with it the threat of inflation or repudiation, and, therefore, of depreciation on both the commodity and the exchange markets. . . . Of course, the increase in the internal debt of France was a serious matter; it had risen from 32½ billion francs to 140 billion francs at the end of 1918. . . . Thus it was the

[4] From E. L. Dulles, *The French Franc 1914-1928. The Facts and Their Interpretation,* New York, 1929, pp. 1, 9-10, 11-12, 412-414, 418, 437-438. By permission of The Macmillan Company, publishers.

twofold strain of interest and capital expenditures which made necessary the inflation of later years. The internal debt practically doubled
during the eight years following the armistice.

. . . . .

Shortly after the armistice the complexities of the problem began to
be seen. The United States did not come forward with offers of reconstruction help, and England and France had serious differences in
regard to the peace treaty and reparations. Furthermore, the troubles
in Germany made it apparent that she could not pay the reparation bill
at once. These political events so absorbed the ablest statesmen that
the first decline of the franc, unpegged in 1919, passed almost unno-
ticed. The sudden drop, due in the first instance to the technical situation of the foreign exchange markets, was accentuated as the general
position of France appeared in a more unfavorable light. The increased
insistence on reparations, which became more and more important in
French internal politics, led to ever-growing friction without. France
went on spending money on reconstruction with a growing debt and
a diminishing prospect of financial recovery, and the turn of speculation
against France was the direct result.

It was natural that, as the size of budget expenditures and loans for
reconstruction purposes increased, there were heated political struggles
over questions which should have been settled mainly by impartial
technical experts. . . . As the difficulties became more evident, efforts
to overcome them became all the more desperate. Meanwhile, relations
between England and France were strained to the danger point on
several occasions, and various unsound financial measures were used to
postpone the bitter disillusionment of the French electors. The complications thus introduced into the external and internal political situations cannot be measured and appraised in the same manner in which
one can measure the volume of trade or the level of prices. They were,
none the less, the most important result of the reconstruction tangle,
and a prime cause of the depreciation of the franc.

. . . . .

The French problem of stabilization was . . . different from that
of any other nation. This was true, first, because of her economic
situation, and second, because of her political conditions. The instability
of political life . . . was aggravated in matters of finance by the strong
influence of the *rentier* class. It was natural that the large number of

government bond holders formed a serious obstacle to early stabilization. Since they had pocketed a very considerable loss in the value of their securities, they felt that their interests should be given some weight in the choice of the new value of the franc. It was, therefore, not possible to come quickly to the final decision because of strong public sentiment favoring a higher gold value. . . .

A second reason for the delay in stabilization was the condition of the internal debt, which was peculiar to the French situation. The large mass of short-time credits . . . made the situation difficult to handle from a technical point of view. . . .

Then, in the third place, the external debts of France were troublesome. They interfered, not so much because there was urgent need of payment, as because they prevented securing the foreign credits which were considered necessary for stabilization. . . .

These three factors are the inevitable outgrowth of the war and reconstruction expenditures. It was the budget deficits which led to depreciation, and therefore to the heavy losses sustained by the *rentier*. It was the cost of reconstruction which increased the internal debt, and made it impossible to discharge external debts. If the severe crises attributable to government embarrassment in handling the debt and the budget in 1924 and 1926 could have been avoided, if the budget could have been passed with reasonable speed in 1925, there is no reason to suppose that France would have found stabilization impossible in 1925 or 1926. It is important, then, to realize that the French difficulties were a combination of the exceptionally heavy postwar burdens and a political system unadapted to handling such difficult problems.

. . . . .

The last plunge of the franc in 1926 led almost inevitably to the recovery which followed so quickly. . . .

. . . . .

. . . It was sufficient to divert attention from the underlying difficulties until more constructive measures could be passed.

. . . . .

The final act of stabilization of June 25, 1928, . . . increased confidence and economic activity. . . .

Stabilization at the existing rate of exchange was . . . welcomed in all quarters as the proper and desirable solution of the monetary problem. . . .

To the student of monetary theory . . . there are four main points of interest in the provisions for stabilization. In the first place, it is significant that by the act of stabilization France passed almost imperceptibly to a full gold standard in place of the limping standard which had existed before the war. Then, in the second place, the new law did away with the former system of fixing the upper limit of the note circulation at a definite figure, and substituted the minimum ratio of gold to sight liabilities as the determinant. In the third place, in contrast to the procedure in other countries, France secured no large foreign loans to facilitate stabilization. And, finally, as has been said above, the legal act of stabilization brought no adverse economic reaction, but rather hastened the recovery of industry which was, already, fairly general.

118. A RESUMÉ OF THE FRENCH SOCIAL INSURANCE LAW, 1930 [5]

Frequent attempts were made in France after the war to secure the passage of a general social insurance law. On April 5, 1928, such an act, adopted in the previous month, was actually promulgated. But the objections of various groups and certain technical difficulties held up its enforcement for two years. Then, during the premiership of the Rightist André Tardieu, a revised act was passed (April 1930) which became effective on July 1, 1930. The supporters of the law described it "as perhaps the most important event" in the history of the Third Republic; its detractors claimed that it would "further sap the sturdy individualism" which had made France great. The extracts given below were taken from a summary translation made by the United States Department of Labor.

SYSTEM FOR COMMERCIAL, INDUSTRIAL, AND DOMESTIC WORKERS

All wage earners are compulsorily insured if their wages do not exceed 15,000 francs [then $600], or 18,000 francs in cities of more than 200,000 inhabitants and in certain industrial districts to be determined later. The maximum is increased for children over 6 weeks and under 16

[5] United States, Department of Labor, *Monthly Labor Review*, vol. XXXI, No. 3, September 1930, pp. 629-639; original text in France, *Journal Officiel*, May 1, 1930, pp. 4819-4833.

years of age by 2,000 francs for the first child, 4,000 francs for two children, and 10,000 francs for three or more children for the first class of insured persons, while for workers living in the cities of more than 200,000 the increase is 2,000 francs, 4,000 francs, and 7,000 francs, respectively, making a maximum in either case of 25,000 francs [then $1000].

. . . . .

The insurance system is financed by equal contributions by the employer and the worker, supplemented by certain contributions by the State. For the purpose of fixing the amount of the contributions the employees are divided annually into five classes. The classes and amount of contributions are as follows:

CONTRIBUTIONS TO SOCIAL INSURANCE OF SPECIFIED WAGE CLASSES

WAGE CLASS	CONTRIBUTION	
	Per day	Per month
	Francs	Francs
Under 2,400 francs per year (8 francs per day)	0.50	12.00
2,400 to 4,500 francs per year (8 to 15 francs per day)	1.00	24.00
4,500 to 6,000 francs per year (15 to 20 francs per day)	1.50	36.00
6,000 to 9,600 francs per year (20 to 32 francs per day)	2.00	48.00
9,600 to 15,000 or 18,000 francs per year* (32 to 50 or 60 francs per day)	3.50	80.00

*According to population of place of residence.

In each case the amount of the contribution is divided equally between the employer and the workman. It will be seen, therefore, that the daily dues of the French workman vary from 25 centimes to 1.75 francs, representing on the average 8 per cent of the annual wages. The payment is made in the form of stamps affixed to cards held by each insured person. The employee's share of the contribution is withheld from his pay, the employer being responsible for the payment of both shares. The insurance contributions are divided into two equal parts, one of which is reserved to cover the old-age risks and the other to cover the risks of sickness, maternity, invalidity, and death.

. . . . .

Liability to compulsory insurance ceases at 60 years, at which age the insured person becomes eligible for a pension. The wage earner may defer retirement, however, from year to year. In this case he continues to be insured against sickness and death but is exempt from all deductions on this account.

SICK BENEFITS

Insured persons receive both general and special medical care, medicines and appliances, treatment in hospitals or sanatoriums, necessary surgical operations and preventive treatment. The medical care is provided in case of illness or accident except in case of occupational diseases or industrial accidents which are subject to workmen's compensation. An insured person has free choice of a physician. . . .

Medical benefits are due from the date of the illness and are given until recovery or for a maximum period of six months to the wage earner, his wife, and his dependent children under 16 years of age. Any relapse occurring within two months is considered as a continuation of the original illness.

The cost of the benefits is borne by the fund or repaid by it to the insured person according to the conditions specified in the contracts. At the same time the insured person is required to bear part of the medical expenses amounting to 15 per cent if his wages are less than 15 francs per day and 20 per cent if his wages are over that amount; for pharmaceutical and other costs his share is fixed uniformly at 15 per cent. The total medical and pharmaceutical costs may not exceed in any case, per day of sickness and beginning with the first medical consultation, 50 per cent of the average basic daily wage for the preceding year. In case of sickness requiring special treatment, however, this maximum may be exceeded. The costs of hospitalization are borne by the fund but these costs, excluding doctors' fees, may not exceed the lowest rate charged in public hospitals for paying patients.

In order to be entitled to sick benefits the insured person must have paid the statutory contributions for 60 days during the 3 months or for 240 days during the 12 months preceding the illness.

. . . . .

The daily cash benefit amounts to half the average daily wage of the class to which the insured person belongs. The payment of the cash benefit dates regularly from the sixth day of sickness (from the fourth day if the insured person has three dependent children) and lasts until recovery or for a maximum period of six months. If hospital treatment is required, the daily benefit is reduced by a third if the insured person has dependent children or relatives, by one-half if the insured person is married but without other dependents, and by three-quarters in all other cases. When the illness lasts more than 15 days, the insurance fund pays, for each workday beginning with the sixteenth, that part of the insured person's contribution which is allotted to the old-age pension fund.

. . . . . .

MATERNITY BENEFITS

A woman worker, compulsorily insured, and the wife of an insured person are entitled to medical care and medicines during pregnancy and for the six months following childbirth.

An insured woman worker is also entitled to a daily cash benefit, amounting to half the basic wage on which she was paying contributions previous to pregnancy; this benefit is paid for the six weeks before and the six weeks following childbirth if she ceases work entirely during that period and if she has paid contributions for 60 days during the three months or for 240 days during the 12 months preceding the pregnancy. A monthly nursing benefit is paid during the period of nursing but for a period not to exceed nine months. . . .

. . . . .

INVALIDITY INSURANCE

Insured persons who are incapacitated as a result either of sickness or of accident not covered by the workmen's compensation act, so that their working capacity is reduced at least two-thirds, are after six months entitled to an invalidity pension. If the insured person contests the decision as to the degree of incapacity, a new examination of his records is necessary and the technical commission passes upon his case. Final appeal may be made to the standing committee of the Superior Council.

. . . . .

In order to receive an invalidity benefit a person must have been a member of the fund at least two years and have made payments representing at least 480 days of work during the two years preceding the sickness or accident.

. . . . .

OLD-AGE INSURANCE

Insured persons are entitled to retirement at the age of 60 years but if they choose may defer retirement indefinitely. For the transition period during which the system is being put into effect a minimum delay of five years is required before retirement pension is allowed.

The retirement pensions amount to 40 per cent of the average annual wages for persons between the ages of 60 and 65 who have paid into the scheme for at least 30 years a minimum contribution covering 240 days' labor each year. This pension is increased one-tenth for all insured persons who have brought up three or more children to the age of 16 years. . . .

.　.　.　.　.

The insured person can claim his pension at the age of 55 if he has contributed to the fund for at least 25 years, since the age of 16. This last condition is not enforced in the case of ex-service men. There is a corresponding reduction in the amount of the pension for persons who retire at this earlier age.

.　.　.　.　.

DEATH BENEFITS

Death benefits payable to the heirs of insured persons are fixed at 20 per cent of the average annual wages. The minimum amount is 1,000 francs for persons who have made their payments regularly, but may not exceed two-thirds of the annual wages of the deceased. The benefit is paid to the surviving husband or wife or other heirs. At least one year's contribution toward the death benefit must have been made.

.　.　.　.　.

GUARANTY DURING UNEMPLOYMENT

Persons of French nationality who are compulsorily insured and who are involuntarily unemployed through lack of work, are exempted from payment of the social-insurance contribution for a maximum period of 4 months in any 12-month period, the payment being guaranteed by the fund. Such persons must have been affiliated to the social insurance system for an entire year before the period of unemployment and have made the payments required for sickness insurance.

The unemployment guaranty is secured by a tax of 1 per cent on the total contributions. This amount is deposited in the general insurance fund, but financially and juridically the account is separate from the other insurance resources. When the amount of the fund is greater than the total deposits in the last year recorded, various grants may be made from this surplus to authorized unemployment funds on permission from the permanent section of the Superior Council on Social Insurance. The amount of these grants may not exceed 33 per cent of the benefits paid by these funds during the preceding year.

· · · · ·

VOLUNTARY INSURANCE

Farmers and agriculturists not covered by compulsory insurance, artisans, small proprietors, nonsalaried intellectual workers, and in general all persons who, without being on a salary, live principally on the products of their labor may take out voluntary insurance if they are of French nationality and their earnings do not exceed the limits set for those compulsorily insured. . . .

The voluntarily insured person may fix the amount of his contribution but it may not exceed 10 per cent of his annual earnings or be less than 240 francs per year unless he is insured only against the old-age risk, when the minimum is 120 francs per year. Voluntarily insured persons may be covered for all or part of the risks included in the law but they may not be insured for sick benefits to exceed 25 francs per workday, for a death benefit in excess of 3,600 francs, and for disability and old-age benefit in excess of 8,000 francs. Sickness insurance ceases at the age of 65.

· · · · ·

If the income of a person voluntarily insured exceeds at any time the maximum allowed, the insured person is notified that within six months from the date of the notification he will cease to be entitled to sickness insurance and that the contributions he continues to pay will be appropriated to insurance against death, invalidity, and old age, unless he prefers to reduce his contribution by an amount corresponding to the share set apart for the sickness insurance. Voluntarily insured persons who become wage earners may maintain their rights acquired under voluntary insurance.

· · · · ·

A compulsorily insured person whose annual wages pass beyond the prescribed maximum ceases to be subject to compulsory insurance as from January 1, following such an increase, but he may be admitted to voluntary insurance within the limits established for that type of insurance.

SPECIAL SYSTEM FOR AGRICULTURAL WORKERS

Insurance is compulsory for all wage earners employed in argicultural and forestry occupations whose earnings do not exceed those for the different classes of workers in industry and commerce. Included among those subject to insurance in addition to regular farm or forestry workers are wage earners employed by rural artisans and contractors for threshing and other agricultural operations; the staffs of farmers' associations, cooperative societies, and other agricultural associations; and tenant farmers *(métayers)* who usually work alone or with the help of members of their family, and who do not own any part of the livestock at the time they enter into the agreement. The owners of property thus rented are considered employers. The members of the family of a farmer who work with him and for him regularly without receiving remuneration in cash are not liable to compulsory insurance.

. . . . .

The contribution, half of which is paid by the insured and half by the employer, proprietor, or tenant, consists of two parts, the contribution covering the risks of sickness, maternity, and death amounting to 10 francs per month equally divided between the employer and the insured, while the contribution covering the old-age risk amounts to 2 per cent of the basic wage. For the purpose of fixing the latter contribution agricultural workers are divided into the same wage classes as workers in commerce and industry. . . .

. . . . .

TRANSITIONAL PROVISIONS

. . . . .

Employees of the State, the departments, and communes, the railroads, street railways and other public utilities, miners and quarry workers, registered seamen and other maritime workers, and the personnel of national theatres, who are already insured in special funds, will be transferred to the new system within one year from the time the present law goes into effect. . . .

GENERAL REGULATIONS

Pensions up to a maximum of 2,400 francs are not transferable and can not be seized for debt except for the payment of the costs of hospitalization.

In computing the income tax, the amounts paid to the insurance fund are deducted from the total income by both employers and employees.

Insurance benefits are suspended during military service or in case of war.

. . . . .

ADMINISTRATION OF INSURANCE FUNDS

. . . . .

Insurance funds must open special accounts for the different types of risks covered.

. . . . .

The law creates a Superior Social Insurance Council which, under the chairmanship of the Minister of Labor, has general supervision of the administration of the act. The council will be composed of 61 members, including 18 representatives of insured persons, 5 representatives of employers, 2 hospital representatives, 2 representatives of medical associations, 1 representative each of dental, pharmacists', and midwives' associations, together with representatives of Parliament, the funds, and the administrative department concerned. The general supervision of the enforcement of the act will be under the present old-age pension inspection service of the Ministry of Labor.

The funds for the operation of the law are derived from the contributions of employers and workers, from the State subsidy, and from miscellaneous sources such as the appropriations of the savings effected in expenditure or public assistance by reason of the operation of the social insurance law, the duty paid to the State by the Bank of France, the gambling tax, and the proceeds of fines, gifts, legacies, etc. The funds which receive and disburse these sums include the General Guaranty Fund which is administered by a council of 20 members under the supervision of the Minister of Labor and has general supervision of the Augmentation and Solidarity Fund and the Guaranty and Equalization Fund. The Augmentation and Solidarity Fund guarantees the minimum legal pension for invalidity and old age, reimbursement for family expenses, and the expenses connected with the liquidation of the former retirement law, as well as administrative and management expenses.

The Guaranty Fund is intended eventually to cover the annual deficits of the insurance funds and to guard against insolvency.

119. THE FRENCH IMPORT-QUOTA SYSTEM [6]

One of the most interesting and effective weapons of modern economic nationalism is the so-called import-quota system, first applied in the post-war period by France. Its purpose and history are well described below.

Excepting the Hawley-Smoot Tariff itself, the French policy of customs quotas, conceived during the first half of the year 1931 and applied with constantly increasing vigor during the year following July 1931, has occasioned more caustic attacks from the nations of the world, and particularly from the United States, and more patriotic defense from the French than any other single policy followed by any country during the depression period. . . .

There are no just grounds for particular condemnation of France for the method employed for the "protection" of her market during the present hysteria. If it is objected that quotas constitute a particularly vicious method of restricting imports and torpedoing treaties, it must be replied that its viciousness consists largely in its being more effective, and, of course, quotas are immediately and absolutely effective in checking imports. . . .

WHY FRANCE ADOPTED THE QUOTA SYSTEM

France was the last of the great trading nations of the world to experience the devastating effects of the world depression. As a consequence of her inflation a few years earlier her wage rates and other costs in 1930 were low in comparison with those of other countries, and thus during that year she was able to escape serious depression. With the continued fall in world prices, however, France began to experience serious difficulties in 1931. As prices in other countries fell, French imports tended to increase, while the high prices of French products, the decrease in world demand, and rising tariff barriers abroad restricted her export trade. The trade balance, normally deficitary, grew more

---

[6] J. M. Jones, Jr., *Tariff Retaliation. Repercussions of the Hawley-Smoot Bill,* University of Pennsylvania Press, Philadelphia, 1934, pp. 139-142, 144-146. Reprinted by permission of the publishers.

so to an alarming extent. Action for the protection of her home market was considered necessary. Restricted foreign markets had been responded to by France during 1930 and the first half of 1931 by straight tariff increases, but for a very particular reason it became impossible in 1931 further to protect her market in that fashion. The reason consisted in the fact that 70 per cent of her tariff duties were consolidated for definite periods in a few commercial treaties, these duties being generalized to a wide range of foreign countries in most-favored-nation treaties. The result? She resorted to establishing import contingents on selected products and allotting import quotas to foreign nations. This system left foreign nations with empty treaties but left France with freedom to restrict imports to whatever degree desired while leaving tariff rates unchanged.

THE TWO PHASES OF THE FRENCH QUOTA SYSTEM

Beginning with the decree of July 16, 1931, placing the imports of coal upon a quota basis, there followed in rapid succession a series of decrees appearing throughout the remainder of the year 1931 contingenting the importation of raw materials and foodstuffs, namely: flax, wines, woods, animals and meats, chemical fertilizers, fish, poultry and eggs, furniture and brooms, natural flowers, hams and milk, chicory and chicory roots, sugar, bananas, and canned fish. Beginning with the decree of January 7, 1932, contingents upon manufactured products appeared in rapid succession until on July 16, as a result of forty-six additional decrees published in the *Journal Officiel,* 1,131 items, or one-seventh of the total list of all products covered by the French tariff were subjected to contingenting upon their importation into France.

The application of the French customs quota policy, then, is divided into two distinct phases, the first consisting in the contingenting of foodstuffs and raw products during the half year following July 1931, and the second consisting in the contingenting of manufactured products during the first half of the year 1932. The chief reason for this rather clear division is that the farmers and producers of raw products were the first in France to suffer acute distress, to demand protection, and to receive it. However, the manufacturers watched with jealous eyes the liberal distribution of the contents of the "pork barrel" to the agriculturists, and as their own industries began to suffer increasing difficulties they began insistently to demand the contingenting of imports of manufactured products. Meanwhile, events in the international field were developing propitiously for their demands.

· · · · ·

OBJECTS OF THE FRENCH CUSTOMS QUOTA POLICY

In its very inception, then, as well as in its application the French customs quota system primarily was based upon the fact that France had 70 percent of her tariff duties "consolidated" in commercial treaties, the basis of the system being the treaty concluded with Germany in 1927 and supplementary treaties with Belgium, Switzerland, and Italy. These fixed or consolidated duties were extended to approximately fifty foreign countries by most-favored-nation treaties. Thus, in seeking to restrict imports, the French Government found itself obstructed in an effective use of the tariff, inasmuch as Germany refused to agree to a cancelation of her commercial treaty with France in which the majority of French tariff duties were fixed. Consequently the French Government resorted to customs quotas which, although they circumscribed its treaties, were even more effective than tariffs and enabled it even better to enforce a greater measure of reciprocity in foreign trade.

The legal basis of the French quota system is, appropriately enough, a law which originally empowered the Government to retaliate against foreign countries which placed unreasonable restrictions upon French commerce. This law of March 29, 1910, incorporated as Article 17 of the Customs Code, authorized the Government "to undertake immediately in case measures devised by foreign countries are of a nature to impede French Commerce, all dispositions appropriate to the circumstances."

· · · · ·

According to statements emanating from official sources there were two chief objects of the customs quota policy: First, to protect the national market from ruinous importation, to reserve the national market to national production, and to redress the deficitary trade balance; and second, to create a barrier against importation behind which the Government could proceed with the denunciation of France's most-favored-nation treaties, to secure tariff liberty, and to proceed with the negotiation of new treaties strictly on the basis of mutual concessions, abandoning the unconditional most-favored-nation clause. A third object, unproclaimed by French officials, to be sure, but discovered clearly enough in the operation of the system, was the promotion of European solidarity with complementary discrimination against the United States.

120. THE STAVISKY SCANDAL [7]

In December 1933 there came to light a financial scandal involving the municipal pawnshop of Bayonne and its director, the notorious Alexandre Stavisky. It appeared that highly-placed officials must have been implicated in the misdeeds, and excited mobs gathered in the larger cities demanding an investigation and punishment of the guilty parties. Royalist and other opposition papers published incendiary notices which seemed further to arouse the public—already exercised over the government's budgetary difficulties, the reduction of civil-service salaries and pensions, the delicate foreign situation, the tendency of the lower house to debate but do nothing, and the uncovering of other scandals overshadowed only by the Stavisky case. When the rumor spread that official efforts were being made to cover up the crime, France appeared close to revolution. The effort of Premier Edouard Daladier on February 6, 1934, to protect the deputies against intimidation by placing armed guards around the Palais Bourbon and its approaches, precipitated a minor insurrection. President Albert Lebrun thereupon asked ex-President Gaston Doumergue to leave his retirement and form a government that would have the confidence of the people and save the country from civil war. The following description of these events was written by an able foreign journalist.

. . . Until a few years before his death (Stavisky) was known only to the underworld of Paris,—not to the cap-and-muffler underworld, but to the top-hat underworld,—the *milieu*—who derive their income from gambling dens, bookmaking, cocaine, brothels, white-slave traffic, and more or less questionable financial transactions. Many of his intimate "collaborators" bore to the end the mark of the *milieu*. But during the last years of his career he succeeded in embellishing his list of acquaintances with some people of greater personal distinction. . . .

. . . . .

He was born in Kiev, in Russia, in 1886, the son of an honest and hard-working Jewish dentist. While Stavisky was still a small boy, his family emigrated to France, where his father began by setting up a practice in the old Jewish quarter north of the Hotel de Ville,—a

[7] A. Werth, *France in Ferment*, Harper & Brothers, New York, 1934, pp. 79-98, 161. Reprinted by permission of the publishers.

quarter from which—to quote a French writer—so many crooks and so many remarkable men have come. . . .

He not only became naturalised, but at some moment of his career (probably while he was still with his parents) he was converted to Catholicism; and French was practically his native language. Without this respectable middle-class background during his boyhood, Stavisky might not have been so successful.

    . . . . .

Up till 1926, Stavisky had been little more than an ordinary crook. . . . But by 1926, when financial speculation was at its height in France, Stavisky had grown more ambitious. That year he defrauded a stock-broker of no less than 7,500,000 francs,—about £70,000; and when, after two months' search, the police discovered him at a villa at Marly-le-Roy, where they arrested him in the midst of a sumptuous dinner party, the papers, in describing the episode, referred to him for the first time as "the king of crooks." . . .

    . . . . .

And then, in 1927 the "king of crooks" was released—"provisionally released"—before his case had come up for trial. Early in January, 1934, the papers disclosed that Stavisky had employed the services of four lawyer-deputies, one of whom was a Vice-President of the Chamber, and another an ex-Minister. Was it they who had wangled it? No sooner was Stavisky out of jail than he gave full vent to his financial genius. The Municipal Pawnshop at Orléans was one of his first victims. He arranged things in such a way that false or valueless jewelry was valued at the price of real jewelry; but before the scandal had time to develop, Stavisky was already engaged in the Bayonne racket, and the losses of the Orléans pawnshop were paid out of the future losses of the Municipal Pawnshop of Bayonne. Stavisky's economic system consisted, indeed, in a succession of increasingly large swindles; in this way all the swindles but the last one,—if ever there was to be a last one— were no longer swindles. The system, according to Stavisky, had the advantage of bringing capital into circulation; and, speaking to a Minister one day, he claimed in all earnestness (though without describing his system in detail) to have discovered a cure for unemployment in Europe. It was Stavisky's tragedy that his Hungarian Bonds scheme broke down; if it had succeeded, the Bayonne Bonds would have all

been repaid and the Bayonne Pawnshop would never have acquired its
unenviable notoriety. . . .

. . . . . .

The crowning achievement of Stavisky's career was the Bayonne
Affair. Although pawnshops—called *Crédits Municipaux*—have a semi-
official standing in France, it was Stavisky who gained control of the
Bayonne Pawnshop as soon as it was founded. The task of putting
a municipal pawnshop to the very special uses to which the Credit
Municipal of Bayonne was put could not have been carried out
single-handedly. The people who are alleged to have been particularly
active in promoting Stavisky's scheme were Tissier, the manager of the
pawnshop, Cohen, the valuer, whom Stavisky had brought from Orléans,
and, above all, Garat, the most influential person in Bayonne;—the man
who was both the mayor of the town and its deputy in Parliament.
Singularly enough—but this was discovered much later,—the Bayonne
Pawnshop never belonged to the Association of French Pawnbroking
Establishments; apparently such membership in the Association would
have presented certain drawbacks.

Beside securing the co-operation of the Mayor of Bayonne, Stavisky
found other means of consolidating the official standing of his pawnshop. In June, 1932, he obtained through the invaluable Dubarry, who
was "a friend of every Cabinet Minister," two letters signed by M.
Dalimier, at that time Minister of Labour in the Herriot Government
of 1932, recommending for investment Municipal Credit Bonds in general and the bonds of the Bayonne Pawnbroking Establishment in
particular. How and why M. Dalimier signed or was made to sign
those letters, was later to become the subject of a lengthy inquiry; but
early in January [1934], when the *Action Française*[8] produced the letters
for the first time, the public was merely confronted with the bare fact
that the Bayonne swindle had been carried out "with the help of a
Cabinet Minister,"—and not even of an ex-Minister but of one who
was the Minister of Colonies in the Government of the day. The
Bayonne Bonds were issued to the extent of something like 200 million
francs; the counterfoils of the bonds and the control slips showed a very
much smaller amount, which was more in harmony with the modest

---

[8] The *Action Française*, a royalist daily, had an estimated circulation of 80,000. With
Léon Daudet and Charles Maurras as its political editors it was in the forefront of anti-
parliamentary and anti-republican organs. Its language was vigorous, to say the least.—*Ed.*

dimensions of Bayonne; and these counterfoils alone had been shown to the officials who, from time to time, used to examine the books of the *Crédit Municipal*. Only one official of the Ministry of Commerce was formally charged with complicity. The worthless bonds were sold mainly to insurance companies, though a few millions worth were also passed on to the Social Insurance Fund; the number of small private investors—most of them belonging to the Bayonne district,—who subscribed to the bonds was comparatively small. . . . . . . many well-informed financiers knew long before the explosion of the Stavisky bomb that the amount of the pawnbroking bonds issued by large towns like Lille, Le Havre and Nantes was incomparably smaller than the amount issued by the little town of Bayonne. There were, indeed, strong suspicions in financial quarters that there was something queer about the Bayonne Bonds; and some of the small "financial" papers used to allude to this fact from time to time; though in most cases they were silenced immediately afterwards by the most obvious method. There was one "financial" journalist who was actually presented with a parcel of Bayonne Bonds. . . . . . . his campaign ceased at once. Another indiscreet journalist was beaten up by an ex-boxer, a member of Stavisky's bodyguard, in a café in the Champs-Élysées.

The Bayonne swindle seems to have come to the surface at the end of November [1933], following a complaint from one of the bond-holding companies; but for some obscure reason the authorities hesitated to take prompt action. Tissier, the manager of the *Crédit Municipal*, was the first man to be arrested; but even he was not arrested until December 23rd. As for Stavisky, his name was first mentioned in the Paris Press on December 30th in the following discreet little paragraph:

"Bayonne, December 29th. A warrant has been issued by the Parquet of Bayonne against a person named Serge-Alexandre Stavisky, aged 47, of Russian origin, who has already been involved in various financial adventures, in particular at Orléans, when he was charged with the same offence as the director of the local Pawnbroking Establishment" (*Echo de Paris,* December 30th).

That was a week after Tissier had been arrested. What had been happening to Stavisky, Tissier's chief, in the meantime? When the police called at the Claridge Hotel on Christmas Day, the financier had departed in an unknown direction. He must have been warned of the coming visit several days before; for on December 23rd, the day of Tissier's arrest, he obtained a passport in the name of Niemen at the Préfecture de Police. Niemen was an ex-boxer, and a member of the financier's bodyguard; but while the passport was made out to him, the photograph and description in the passport were Stavisky's. . . .

Most of the facts contained in this brief outline of Stavisky's life and career came to the knowledge of the general public during the first week in January [1934]. The excitement was enormous, for it was more than obvious that: (1) had not somebody "protected" Stavisky, his "provisional freedom" would never have been extended nineteen times, and over a period of six years; (2) that had he not been "protected"—and this protection implied the co-operation of politicians, lawyers, doctors, the judiciary and the police—he would not have been able to pose as a "king of Paris and Deauville," still less to carry on during those six years his financial operations; (3) that had he not received the conscious or unconscious assistance of Garat, Dubarry and others, the Bayonne swindle would never have succeeded; and (4) but for some important connections in the police, he would not have escaped. Lastly, it seemed obvious that none of these people would have protected Stavisky had it not been in their interest to do so.

There was a loud cry throughout France: *"Les noms, les noms!"* Who was to blame? Parliament, whose authority was just then at a low ebb, was, naturally, suspected of being the chief culprit. What was still worse, a member of the Government was found to have been mixed up in the dirty business. *"Les noms, les noms!"*—the public continued to clamour. Never in all the history of the Third Republic had the anti-Parliamentary and anti-Government Press been given such an undreamed-of opportunity. All right, they would give the public enough names to make them sick of the Republic and of the Chamber of Deputies.

The attack was led by the *Action Française*.

. . . . .

The official Havas agency published the following story on the Monday night [January 8, 1934]:

"Chamonix, January 8th. The detective service of the Sûreté Générale has discovered the crook Stavisky in a villa rented at Chamonix by one of his friends.

"In this villa only one room was heated. The policemen knocked at the door, and, receiving no reply, they forced the door. At that moment Stavisky fired a bullet through his head.

"A doctor who was called in at once was unable to say how serious

the wound was. Soon afterwards it was learned that the crook was in
a state of coma, and that there was no hope for his recovery."

⋆ ⋆ ⋆ ⋆ ⋆

A later message said that Stavisky had died without regaining consciousness.

Nine out of ten people in Paris did not believe a word of the "official"
version.

The word "suicide" made people smile, or made them angry. "The
police have murdered him. He knew too much." The official version
was torn to shreds. Dozens of details were produced on all sides to
disprove it. The conviction that Stavisky had not killed himself was
shared by Communists and Socialists, Royalists and Reactionaries, and
by the man in the street. . . .

⋆ ⋆ ⋆ ⋆ ⋆

It was not until much later that a number of statements were made
which, while showing almost conclusively that Stavisky shot himself,
suggested equally clearly that he had committed suicide "by persuasion."
The "persuasion" . . . [came] . . . from the police themselves . . . .

— — — — —

The rioters in the Place de la Concorde [on the night of February 6,
1934] were not only Royalists and Fascists but included also thousands
of people who . . . simply came out to protest against *les voleurs*. The
word *voleurs* comprised a whole range of notions—Stavisky, parliamentary corruption, bad business, Hitler, Daladier's mental shiftiness
and a thousand other things. *À bas les voleurs!* was a sharp but inarticu-
late outburst of anger against Parliament, the culprit or the scapegoat of
all ills. But what they wanted instead of Parliament, few of them could
say; the most that they knew was that they wanted somebody instead
of Daladier, instead of Chautemps, instead of the Radicals [Radical
Socialists], instead of the *Cartel des Gauches*. Perhaps the Royalists
alone knew exactly what they wanted; they wanted a king. But even
they knew that that was not a practical proposition, and were content
to shout against Parliament. The others, too, were only more or less
anti-parliamentary; and if the Royalists, the Jeunesses Patriotes, the
Croix de Feu and the rest of them had broken into the Chamber, they
would have quarrelled the moment they crossed the threshold.

121. THE CONSTITUTION OF THE RADICAL SOCIALIST PARTY, ADOPTED AT THE LYON CONGRESS, MARCH 30, 1935 *(Extracts)* [9]

Among the most important political groups in the Third Republic has been the Radical and Radical Socialist Party, led, in the post-war period, by such men as Edouard Herriot, Edouard Daladier, Camille Chautemps, and Albert Sarraut. Representing mainly small farmers, retail merchants, and in general the middle bourgeoisie, it has frequently exercised control over the governments. It stands for conciliation in foreign affairs, anti-clericalism, and broad social reform to be introduced at a moderately rapid rate. Its constitution is reproduced as an interesting example of such instruments.

Article 1.

An association to be known as the *Parti républicain, radical et radical-socialiste* is hereby formed from the members of those groups, delegates and newspapers willing to accept the present constitution. The national offices of the party will be located in Paris.

The party program [platform] constitutes its charter. All members are obliged to observe the program, as well as the constitution and by-laws of the party.

Article 2.

Admission to membership is open to:

(1) all individuals belonging to the groups indicated in articles 4 and 7 [dealing with local committees and regional organizations] provided they meet their annual assessments and receive party cards for the current year;

(2) all members of Parliament who belong to a local party committee and who pay annual dues of 1000 francs, provided they refrain from participating in any ministry which does not depend upon a majority drawn from the left;

(3) newspapers which support party policies, are enrolled in a "county" party organization *(fédération départementale)* and pay annual dues of 25 francs; and

(4) all party workers and representatives on local committees who carry party cards. . . . . .

---

[9] Translation by W. R. Sharp in W. E. Rappard et al., *Source Book on European Governments,* D. Van Nostrand Company, Inc., New York, 1937, pp. II-19-26. Courtesy of D. Van Nostrand Company, Inc.

Article 5.

Enrollment at Party headquarters is compulsory. Each organization must report annually in January, in addition to the total amount of its dues, a list of its officers, with the number of their membership cards. . . .

. . . . .

Article 9.

Members of the [National Party] Congress include
  (1) all members of the national executive committee, *ex officio*,
  (2) the editors of each newspaper belonging to the Party,
  (3) delegates elected by county federations and other local groups or committees, and
  (4) elective members of the national committee.
The Congress meets annually in the city which is designated by the preceding Congress. . . .

. . . . .

Article 11.

During the interval between meetings of the congress, Party affairs are administered by an executive committee, which has authority to establish smaller committees and a secretariat from among its membership.

Article 12.

The function of the executive committee is to discuss all questions affecting the Party and take such steps as may be desirable in its interest.

Specifically, the committee rules on matters relative to party organization, propaganda, and discipline.

Article 13.

The members of the executive committee are annually elected by the congress. Only those who have belonged for at least two years to a subordinate party committee are eligible for election.

The following are members of the executive committee *ex officio*, provided they are registered as members of a local or county committee:
  (1) senators, deputies, general councillors, district councillors, and municipal councillors in cities of at least 50,000 population;
  (2) honorary presidents and vice-presidents, ex-presidents, and general secretaries of the Party;

(3) the president and general secretary of each county federation; and

(4) the president and general secretary of each county youth organization of the Party. . . .

Further, upon nomination by each county federation a month in advance, the congress will annually appoint, for a one year term, dues-paying members of the executive committee in the ratio of one delegate per 100,000 population or additional fraction thereof. . . .

Finally, the congress will designate, after nomination as indicated above, additional delegates to the executive committee in the ratio of one for every 200 dues-paying party members or additional fraction thereof.

All these delegates are eligible for re-election. . . .

Women who belong to the Party shall be represented on the executive committee. To this end, the secretariat . . . shall present to each congress a list of ten women in addition to those already included in the list of names nominated by the county federations.

ARTICLE 14.

The executive committee, by secret ballot, selects from among its members a secretariat which, under its permanent control, is charged with the handling of current business.

This secretariat is composed of thirty-three members elected for two years. . . .   .

ARTICLE 20.

In the exercise of its powers, the executive committee is restricted as follows:

(1) Appeals from all its decisions may be taken to the next Congress . . . where they will be examined *en bloc* by the Congress.

(2) More particularly, the secretariat may always refer any resolution voted in a meeting where fewer than 150 members were present, to a subsequent meeting to which provincial delegates are especially called.

. . . . .

ARTICLE 22.

Party funds are derived:

(1) from selling party cards;

(2) from annual dues assessed upon groups, committees, federations and newspapers;

(3) from annual dues paid by members of the executive committee . . . ;

(4) from gifts and subscriptions; and

(5) from selling brochures.

. . . . .

ARTICLE 26.

The management of the funds of the executive committee shall be confided to a general treasurer appointed by the committee, and to a finance commission under the control of the committee.

. . . . .

ARTICLE 29.

The present constitution may be amended by the party congress after insertion on its agenda, discussion in a plenary session of the executive committee, and upon recommendation by the committee on rules and organization and of the conference of federation presidents and general secretaries.

122. THE PROGRAM OF THE POPULAR FRONT, JANUARY 1936 [10]

Early in 1936 the French parties of the Left (Radical Socialist, Socialist, and Communist) combined and agreed to contest the elections of April-May 1936 as the Popular Front. The union was the result, among other reasons, of a noticeable increase in the activities of various groups of so-called fascists. Its program was clear and direct.

I. DEFENSE OF LIBERTY

1. General amnesty for political prisoners.
2. Against the fascist leagues:
   (a) Disarmament and effective dissolution of all quasi-military organizations, in conformance with the law.
   (b) Enforcement of laws against the provocation of rioting or against attacks upon the security of the State. . . .
3. The press:

---

[10] Translation by W. R. Sharp in W. E. Rappard et al., *Source Book on European Governments,* D. Van Nostrand Company, Inc., New York, 1937, pp. II-31-34. Courtesy of D. Van Nostrand Company, Inc.

(a) Abrogation of decree-laws restricting freedom of opinion.

(b) Reform of the press by the adoption of legislation:

    (i) effectively suppressing journalistic blackmailing; and

    (ii) assuring to journalists decent means of existence, obliging them to make public the sources of their income, putting an end to private monopolies of commercial advertising and the scandals of financial publicity, and, finally, preventing the formation of newspaper "trusts."

(c) Organization of government radio broadcasting with a view to insuring accuracy of information and equality to all political and social groups using the radio.

4. Trade-union liberties:

(a) Application of and respect for the labor rights of all.

(b) Respect for the right of women to work.

5. Education and liberty of conscience:

(a) Strengthening of the public schools not only by adequate appropriations, but by such reforms as the raising of the compulsory school age to 14 years and, in secondary schools, the imposition of more rigorous standards of admission.

(b) Guarantees, to pupils and teachers alike, of full liberty of conscience, particularly by respecting academic "neutrality," "secularization" and the civil rights of teachers.

II. DEFENSE OF PEACE

1. To appeal for popular support, especially from labor, for the maintenance and organization of peace.

2. To coöperate internationally, within the *cadre* of the League of Nations, for collective security, by defining aggression and by applying sanctions automatically and concertedly in case of aggression.

3. To strive incessantly to change from an "armed" to a "disarmed" peace, by agreements first to limit and then to reduce and control armaments generally and simultaneously.

4. To nationalize war industries and suppress the private traffic in arms.

5. To repudiate secret diplomacy, and undertake public negotiations for the purpose of bringing back to Geneva those States that have withdrawn, without, however, weakening in any way the constitutional principles of the League of Nations: collective security and indivisible peace.

6. To render more flexible the procedure envisaged by the Covenant of the League for the peaceful revision of treaties dangerous to the peace of the world.

7. To extend, notably in eastern and central Europe, the system of security pacts open to all, following the principles of the Franco-Soviet pact.

III. ECONOMIC DEMANDS

1. Restoration of consumer purchasing power destroyed or reduced by the economic depression:

    (*a*) by measures against unemployment and the industrial crisis—
    - (i) institution of a national unemployment fund,
    - (ii) reduction of the working week without lowering the weekly wage,
    - (iii) provision of more work for youth by establishing adequate retirement pensions for industrial workers, and
    - (iv) rapid execution of a program of useful public works by the joint efforts of central and local governments and private capital.

    (*b*) by measures dealing with the agricultural and commercial crisis—
    - (i) revalorization of agricultural products, combined with an attack upon speculation and the high cost of living, in such a way as to reduce the spread between wholesale and retail prices;
    - (ii) in order to eliminate the "tithe" now levied by speculators upon producers and consumers, the creation of a national cereal administration;
    - (iii) support to agricultural coöperatives, the sale of fertilizer at low cost by national agencies; the development of agricultural credit, and the reduction of agricultural rents; and
    - (iv) suspension of foreclosures and the alleviation of mortgages on property. . . .

2. Stoppage of the plunder of savings and a better organization of credit by:

    (*a*) regulation of the banking profession,
    (*b*) regulation of the balance-sheets of banks and private corporations,

(c) stricter regulation of the powers of officers of private corporations,

(d) denial to retired civil servants of the right to sit on corporate boards of directors, and

(e) in order to free credit and savings from being dominated by an economic oligarchy, transformation of the Bank of France from a private into a public institution. . . .

3. A financial housecleaning by:

(a) regulation of war contracts along with the nationalization of munitions industries;

(b) elimination of waste in civil as well as military administration;

(c) institution of a war pensions fund;

(d) a democratic reform of the tax system with a view to stimulating economic recovery, the creation of additional revenue by taxing large fortunes, the rate to increase rapidly upon increments in excess of 75,000 francs [then about $5000], reorganization of inheritance duties, and taxes on monopolistic profits without affecting adversely retail prices;

(e) suppression of fraud in handling securities by rigorously putting into use the fiscal identification certificate recently voted by Parliament; and

(f) checks on the flight of capital by confiscating funds held in concealment abroad or their equivalent in France.

123. A SUMMARY OF LEGISLATION UNDER THE POPULAR FRONT, 1936-1937 [11]

The first French Popular Front Government was organized on June 4, 1936, under Premier Léon Blum, leader of the Socialist Party. With a rapidity which delighted some and frightened others, the Blum Government proceeded to carry out the promises of the electoral campaign of April-May 1936. A comparison of the following summary of these activities with the Popular Front Program reproduced in Document No. 122 will clearly illustrate this fact.

[11] J. C. de Wilde, "The New Deal in France," in *Foreign Policy Reports,* vol. XIII, No. 12, September 1, 1937, pp. 141-146. Reprinted by permission of the Foreign Policy Association.

During the first few months of its administration the Blum cabinet kept Parliament busy enacting laws ameliorating conditions of labor. An act of June 20 [1936] gave workers and employees in industry, commerce and the liberal professions a minimum annual paid vacation of fifteen days after one year's continuous employment in any enterprise. For the first time, thousands of workers enjoyed an extended holiday in the summer of 1936.

More leisure for employees was provided by the 40-hour week statute which became law on June 21. The government was directed to introduce the 40-hour week in all industrial and commercial establishments, either on its own initiative or at the request of workers' or employers' organizations. It was stipulated that there should be no decline in weekly pay or in the standard of living. At the beginning, care was taken not to introduce a blanket 40-hour week too rapidly; the first decree, applicable to coal mining, was not signed until September 25, 1936. Thereafter the pace greatly accelerated, so that by June 1937 about sixty decrees had been promulgated. According to statistics of the factory and mine inspection service covering employment in concerns with a hundred workers or more, the 40-hour week had been applied to 94 per cent of the workers at the beginning of May 1937. Application of the law did not prove such a stimulus to employment as the government had hoped. Owing to the difficulty of controlling enforcement and to the pressure of labor unions, the decrees generally provided for a five-day week in most industries, and in retail trade, banking and insurance. In Paris the application of this stipulation to shops aroused such protest that an exception was made for the duration of the 1937 Exposition. Many plants and offices, however, were compelled to close two days a week, thus curtailing the volume of possible re-employment, and in some instances even reducing production. During the year ending in May 1937 enterprises employing a hundred persons or over, to which the 40-hour week had been applied, showed an increase of only 125,645 or 6.4 per cent in the number of workers. Probably not even all of this increase was due to the shorter working week.

Paid vacations and the 40-hour week created a serious problem of leisure, especially since increased consumption of alcohol followed immediately in the wake of these innovations. The government tackled this problem with considerable success. A special under-secretariat for sports and leisure was created in the Ministry of Public Health and capably directed by Léo Lagrange. "Lagrange railway tickets" were made available at 40 per cent reduction to workers on holiday travel. Special excursions were made even cheaper, and a certain number of Mediterranean cruises were also organized. Youth hostels were encouraged, sport facilities created, and the democratization of winter sports was initiated.

To implement the Matignon accord,[12] a law of June 24, 1936 outlined the procedure for the conclusion of collective labor agreements. At the request of any labor union or employers' association the Minister of Labor was directed to bring about a meeting of a mixed commission to negotiate an agreement for any branch of industry or commerce in any region or for the whole country. In the event of disagreement the Minister of Labor was empowered to mediate. The law required that all collective labor contracts provide for (1) freedom of organization and speech for workers, (2) election of shop councils in concerns employing more than ten persons, (3) minimum wages by categories of workers and by regions, (4) dismissal notice, (5) regulation of apprenticeship, (6) procedure for settling disputes concerning application of the agreement, and (7) means of revising the contract. The Minister of Labor was authorized to make collective accords of this type obligatory for all employers and employees in the branch of industry or commerce and in the region or regions included within the contract's field of application. This law and the 1936 strike-wave gave an extraordinary impulse to the conclusion of collective agreements. Between mid-June and mid-December 1936, the texts of 2336 such contracts were communicated to the Ministry of Labor.

Higher wages, paid holidays, the 40-hour week and collective labor agreements imposed a considerable burden on many enterprises. The smaller industrialists and merchants were particularly hard hit, for they were financially unable to rationalize their establishments in order to meet part of the cost. The government provided partial relief through more liberal extension of credit. A limited debt moratorium was also accorded to merchants, industrialists and artisans who did not have to pay a general income tax in 1935 or were not subject to profit taxes during that year. For the most part, however, business men were left to bear or shift the cost to the best of their ability. Many medium-sized enterprises organized themselves into cartels; and a large number

---

[12] On June 7, 1936, in the Hotel Matignon, Premier Blum succeeded in getting representatives of capital and labor to accept an agreement for ending the wave of sit-down strikes which had begun in Paris at the end of May and rapidly spread to the provinces. It proved virtually impossible fully to enforce the accord.—*Ed.*

of small entrepreneurs simply discharged the few workers they employed and returned to the old artisan system of hiring apprentices.

In order to reduce unemployment Parliament not only passed the
40-hour week law, but extended the school-leaving age from 13 to 14
and gave its sanction to an extensive program of public works. The
latter program, approved by law of August 18, 1936, contemplated an
expenditure of 20 billion francs over a three-year period, in addition
to previously adopted projects. . . . The money was to be raised by
loans.
. . . . .

Since France is still agricultural to a large extent the Popular Front
government did not neglect the peasants. One of its major legislative
enactments was that establishing a National Wheat Office designed to
curb speculation and undue profits of middlemen, as well as to insure
farmers a remunerative price. Complete control over the marketing of,
and foreign trade in, wheat was vested in a central council of 51 members, 29 representing the wheat growers, 9 the consumers, 9 the millers,
bakers and grain trade, and 4 the Ministries of Agriculture, Finance,
National Economy and the Interior. Similarly constituted committees
in each *département* were set up to advise the council, allot wheat sales
among the millers and facilitate the formation of cooperatives. Farmers
were obliged to declare the area sown in the spring and the amount
harvested in the fall. The central council was directed to estimate the
national production in June of each year. In August the council, by
a three-fourths vote, was to fix the price of wheat for the crop year
at a level giving the commodity approximately the same purchasing
power as in the period 1911-1913. The determination of flour and bread
prices, however, was left in the hands of the local prefects and mayors.
The wheat price was applicable only for quantities sold within market
quotas which were to be determined for each farmer selling over 50
quintals on the basis of "normal production." Any amount produced
in excess of the quota could be sold only to cooperatives or, through
their agency, to the Wheat Office, and at a differential price fixed by the
council. In case of a harvest in excess of domestic consumption the
council was empowered to determine the quantities to be stored or
exported. Similarly in the event of a deficit, the council was to fix
the amount of bread grain and flour to be imported. While the law
directed the council to scale the domestic sale of wheat, provision was
made whereby those farmers belonging to cooperatives could obtain
immediate payment for their crop.

For the first year the operation of the Wheat Office was greatly facilitated by the relatively poor harvest of 1936 which left no surplus. . . .

. . . . . .

In addition to the laws ameliorating the condition of labor and
agriculture, Parliament enacted certain reforms at the instance of the
Popular Front cabinet. One of the most important of these was the law
of July 24, 1936 which took the Bank of France from the hands of the
"financial and industrial oligarchy" and subordinated it more effectively
to the will of the central government. The Bank had long been
anathema to the Left. Ever since Napoleon founded this Central Bank
in 1800, it had been under the control of private interests. Only the 200
largest stockholders had the right to elect the Board of Regents. In
fact, direction of the Bank had become a semi-hereditary prerogative
of some fifty leading families. As against the fifteen seats under private
control, the government held only three—those of the Governor and the
two Vice-Governors, who were named directly by the President of the
Republic. According to the Left, the Governor often fell under the
influence of the Board of Regents. The latter could put him under
obligation by providing the 100 shares of the Bank (normally worth
over a million francs) required to qualify him for office, or by enabling
a retiring Governor to procure lucrative posts in industry or banking.

The Bank exercised great influence over the economic and financial
life of France. Through its own banking facilities and the ability to
rediscount paper offered by other banks, it largely controlled the credit
machinery of the country. More important, whenever the government
was financially embarrassed, the Bank could at times influence the
state's economic policies by its power to grant or withhold direct or
indirect advances to the Treasury. Leftist governments had felt the
Bank's power after the elections of 1924 and 1932. Even governments
of the Centre had not been immune. . . .[13]

. . . . .

Nationalization of arms manufacture dealt the "oligarchy" another
blow. This step was taken, however, not only to curb the alleged
malevolent influence of "war profiteers," but also to secure improved
coordination of arms production and pave the way for possible international action to control and reduce armaments. A law of August 11,

[13] For the text of the new bank law, see Document No. 124.—*Ed.*

1936 permitted the government, until March 31, 1937, to nationalize in whole or in part only those concerns manufacturing or trading in weapons actually used in fighting, such as war planes, tanks, warships, gas masks, guns, rifles and ammunition. Those not nationalized were made subject to sweeping state control.

In applying this law the government faced the problem at what stage the manufacture of war implements would have to be nationalized. A thoroughgoing nationalization program completely eliminating the private "vested interest" in war and armament would really have entailed expropriation of the basic industries—iron and steel, and chemical. The government was not prepared to go so far. War Minister Daladier indicated in the Chamber on July 16, 1936 that he would nationalize only "enterprises which demand specialized equipment and installations." In other words, expropriation would be confined to those plants or parts of factories actually manufacturing specialized war material in its last stages. In accordance with this program, about a dozen factories were expropriated by the Ministers of War and Navy and converted into state enterprises managed directly by state engineers. Government bonds were given in compensation.[14]

Aviation companies working for the Ministry of Air have not been nationalized outright because it was thought better to leave some scope for individual initiative in an industry still in full evolution. For aviation a "mixed régime" was created. The state took over two-thirds of the capital of airplane factories—a measure which proved a boon to most stockholders since many companies were in a precarious financial condition. To coordinate production and administer these capital interests, six aeronautical construction companies were organized, each including all plants within a given geographic region. The government also controlled these companies.

.   .   .   .   .

One of the primary aims of the Popular Front was to combat the various Fascist and semi-Fascist organizations in France. In October 1935 the Laval government had been compelled to accept a law authorizing the dissolution of "all associations having the character of groups of combat or private militias" and prohibiting the carrying of arms. No action had been taken under this law, however, except for the dissolution of all Royalist organizations in February 1936 after one of their members had assaulted Léon Blum on the street. Soon after taking power—on June 18—the Blum government promulgated decrees dis-

---

[14] For the text of one of the nationalization decrees, see Document No. 125.—*Ed.*

solving the leading semi-Fascist group, Colonel de La Rocque's *Croix de Feu,* and minor organizations, including the *Francistes,* the *Jeunesses Patriotes* and the *Solidarité Française.* The *Croix de Feu,* however, almost immediately reconstituted itself as a political party called the *Parti Social Français.* . . .

More dangerous for the government has been the Fascist *Parti Populaire Français* founded in June 1936 by Jacques Doriot, a former Communist leader and the mayor of the Paris working-class suburb of Saint-Denis. This party was chiefly characterized by rabid opposition to the Communists, whom Doriot attacked as the servants of Moscow and the party of civil war. It bitterly opposed the Franco-Soviet pact which, Doriot claimed, would be utilized by the Soviet Union to embroil France in an ideological crusade against Germany and Italy. To make France really secure the French Popular party advocated an agreement with Germany and a *rapprochement* with Italy. Its domestic program was much less specific. It recommended intensive development of French overseas territories and the erection of the French Empire into a more or less self-sufficient unit. Closer regulation of production and control of profits were also listed among its demands. The party, however, did not appear to envisage a completely totalitarian state.

. . . . .

The financial problem was undoubtedly the most serious one which the Popular Front had to face throughout its tenure in power. The Blum government was ultimately shipwrecked on the rock of financial difficulties. . . .

124. REFORM OF THE BANK OF FRANCE, JULY 24, 1936 [15]

Among the most important items in the Popular Front program was reform of the Bank of France, an institution dating from 1800. Through the years, direction of the bank had traditionally become the prerogative of about fifty prominent families, and whereas fifteen directors' seats were privately controlled, the government commanded only three. The following law curtailed the influence of the chief stockholders, increased the influence of the state, and aimed at making the bank's governors entirely independent of private financial interests.

[15] France, Assemblée Nationale, *Journal Officiel de la République Française,* vol. 68, No. 173, July 25, 1936, pp. 7810-7811.

LAW TO AMEND AND PERFECT THE LAWS AND STATUTES GOVERNING THE BANK OF FRANCE

. . . . .

ARTICLE 1.

The General Assembly is composed of all stockholders of French nationality. Each member has the right to one vote, whatever the number of shares he may possess.

ARTICLE 2.

The General Assembly names three auditors. It receives an annual account of all the transactions of the Bank.

ARTICLE 3.

The Governor and two Vice-Governors need not be possessors of any Bank stock.

ARTICLE 4.

The Governor must take an oath before the President of the Republic that he will well and faithfully direct the affairs of the Bank in conformity with the laws and statutes.

ARTICLE 5.

The Governor receives an annual salary from the Bank equivalent to that of the Vice-President of the Council of State [Vice-Premier]. . . .

. . . . .

ARTICLE 7.

During the exercise of their functions, the Governor and Vice-Governors are forbidden to participate in any way, through work or counsel, in any private industrial, commercial, or financial enterprise.

ARTICLE 8.

The Governor and Vice-Governors, upon retirement, continue to receive their salaries for three years with the proviso that they do not, during this period, occupy any public office. During the same interval they are, furthermore, forbidden to lend their aid to any private enterprises and to receive therefrom any remuneration for work or counsel.

Article 9.

The Bank is administered by twenty councillors and supervised by three auditors. The Governor, Vice-Governors, councillors, and auditors form the General Council. The auditors have a consultative voice.

Two councillors are chosen by the stockholders, nine represent the economic and social groups [of the nation], and nine represent the collective interests of the nation.

The councillors are selected as follows:

I.—Two are elected by the General Assembly from among the manufacturers or merchants, excluding persons connected by work or counsel or administratively with any banking establishment.

II.—One is designated by the National Economic Council from among its vice-presidents;

One is chosen by the Superior Commission of Savings Banks from among its members;

One is chosen by secret ballot of the personnel of the Bank of France;

Six are chosen by the Minister of Finance from lists of three names each presented by each of the following organizations: the National Confederation of Consumers' Coöperatives, the General Confederation of French Artisans, the Assembly of the Presidents of the Chambers of Commerce of France, the General Confederation of Labor, the Permanent Assembly of Presidents of Chambers of Agriculture, and the commercial sections of the National Economic Council.

These last will provisionally be selected by the Minister of Commerce from the best qualified representatives of small business.

III.—Three will represent the Ministers of Finance, National Economy, and the Colonies.

Six are members ex-officio:

The President of the financial section of the Council of State;

The director of the general movement of funds [at the Treasury];

The general director of the *Caisse des Dépôts et Consignations;*

The governor of the *Crédit Foncier;*

The general director of the *Crédit National;*

The general director of the *Caisse Nationale du Crédit Agricole.*

No member of Parliament may be a member of the General Council.

ARTICLE 10.

The councillors who are elected or are chosen by the Ministers from lists presented by special groups may not hold office for more than three consecutive years. One-third of these councillors must be replaced each year. Retiring councillors may not be reëlected or reappointed until after a lapse of three years.

ARTICLE 11.

The General Council of the Bank may delegate all or some of its powers to a Permanent Committee comprising the Governor, the Vice-Governors, and four councillors one of whom is to be chosen by the Minister of Finance and three of whom are to be designated by the General Council.

· · · · ·

ARTICLE 17.

A decree will set the date of application of the present law. The General Council is regularly constituted from the time of the election or appointment of fifteen members.

The present Law, deliberated upon and adopted by the Senate and the Chamber of Deputies, is to be executed as a Law of the State.

Done at Paris, July 24, 1936.

125. NATIONALIZATION OF A FRENCH WAR-MATERIALS PLANT, 1937 [16]

In the name of more efficient production, the Popular Front Government secured the passage of a law (August 11, 1936) empowering the state to nationalize war-materials plants. The following decree of nationalization applied to the extensive works at Le Creusot of the Schneider Company.

The President of the French Republic,
On the advice of the Minister of War and National Defense;
By virtue of the law of August 11, 1936, on the nationalization of the manufacture of war materials;
By virtue of the decree of August 14, 1936, defining the list of ma-

---

[16] France, Assemblée Nationale, *Journal Officiel de la République Française,* vol. 69, No. 61, March 13, 1937, p. 3060.

terials subject to the provisions of the law of August 11, 1936, on the nationalization of the manufacture of war materials;

By virtue of the decree of November 6, 1936, supplementing the aforesaid decree;

The Council of Ministers consenting,

Decrees:

ARTICLE 1.

The workshops, plant, and special machinery used at Le Creusot by the firm of Schneider and Co. for the manufacture of war materials are expropriated for the use of the French State.

The expropriation applies to:

1. The parcels of land, whether built on or not, occupied by the aforesaid workshops and plant, shown in pink on the detailed plans and designated in the supporting detailed survey; these accompanying documents were prepared on March 10, 1937, by the Chief Engineer at Dijon;

2. The materiel, implements, and stocks of all kinds, including the products in process of being manufactured or assembled and the furnishings at present in the expropriated parts or in unexpropriated workshops and warehouses at Le Creusot of the firm of Schneider and Co. which are intended for the manufacture of war materials and which shall be established by an inventory carried out by both parties.

ARTICLE 2.

Possession of the establishments shall be taken by the services of the Ministry of War on a date to be fixed by decree of the Minister of War and National Defense.

ARTICLE 3.

The Minister of War and National Defense is charged with the execution of this decree, which shall be inserted in the *Journal Officiel*.

Done at Paris, March 11, 1937.

126. THE REORGANIZATION OF THE FRENCH RAILWAYS, 1937 [17]

The French railway system (private and state-owned) was completely reorganized in 1937 in an effort to provide more efficient service while

---

[17] Societé Nationale des Chemins de Fer Français, Mimeographed Report, September 1937; transl. taken from *The French Say* (now *French Opinion*), New York, January 1938, pp. 1-3.

simultaneously reducing (and eventually removing) the customary deficit
which annually had to be made up by the national government. The regula-
tions governing the new system are summarized below. A useful discussion
of the subject may be found in United States, Department of Commerce,
Foreign Railway News, *vol. XIII, Special Issue, November 10, 1937: "Na-*
tionalization of French Railways and Its Effect on the Transport Coordina-
tion Problem."

~~~~~~

The reorganization of the French Railways in 1937 has its charter in
two fundamental documents:

1. An Agreement reached on August 31, 1937, between the Minister
of Public Works, representing the French Government, and representatives of the five privately owned railways, the two State owned railways
and the two Paris belt line companies.

2. A Decree-law of the same date, validating the agreement and
containing certain supplementary provisions.

Let us examine rapidly the essential characteristics of the reorganization of the French railways which became effective on January 1, 1938.

Liquidation of Existing Railway Companies

The first step of this reorganization was to do away with the old division of the railways into distinct and separate lines and companies,
and to create a NATIONAL COMPANY OF FRENCH RAIL-
WAYS, which received the right to operate and administer all the
railways in France from January 1, 1938, to December 31, 1982.

The Agreement of 1921 had left operation and administration of the
lines to each individual railway company, and had merely introduced
an element of financial stability through the creation of a general reserve
fund, together with some administrative co-ordination through a Directing Committee and a Higher Railway Council. But the Agreement of
August 31, 1937, on the contrary, establishes complete unification in
the operation and administration of all railways in France.

In the new National Company of French Railways, the capitalization
(1,419,000,000 francs) is divided between the State and the former Railway Companies in the following proportions:

1. 49 per cent of the capital stock, in the form of A shares, is allotted
to the former Railway Companies in compensation for their contributions in rolling stock and stores.

2. 51 per cent of the capital stock, in the form of B shares, is allotted

to the State in compensation for its contributions in rolling stock and stores that belonged to the railways already owned by the State (State Railways and the Railways of Alsace-Lorraine) and also in compensation for sums advanced by the State to the common reserve fund for railways.

The A and B shares are to receive interest at the rate of 6 per cent per annum. The A shares are to be retired progressively from the present date until December 31, 1982, and are to be replaced progressively on retirement by J shares (Actions de Jouissance) similar to the dividend shares which already exist in the capitalization of the railway companies.

It is to be noted that both A and J shares distributed to the companies will be non-transferable until December 31, 1955, after which date they may be distributed among the shareholders of the private companies in prorata to their holdings.

The amounts paid to the private companies as interest and amortization on A shares may not be distributed to the shareholders before December 31, 1955, but whenever the National Company is able to show a balance of revenue and expenditures, the private companies may distribute up to 20 per cent of their annual receipts on A shares.

Administration and Operation of the National Company of French Railways

The National Company of French Railways is administered by a Board of Directors consisting of 33 members until December 31, 1955. On this Board, the majority of the Directors represent the State, the former Railway Companies being represented by 12 Directors. In addition, the railway employees are represented by 4 delegates sitting with the Board of Directors.

After December 31, 1955, the 12 Directors representing the liquidated Railway Companies are to be replaced by only 6 members, who are to represent the holders of A and B shares.

The President of the Board of Directors must be chosen from among the Directors representing the State; he is to be named by a Cabinet decree. The President is to be assisted by two Vice-Presidents, one of whom is chosen from the representatives of the State, and one from the Directors representing the former Railway Companies.

Besides the Board of Directors, an Executive Committee is organized which includes, until December 31, 1955, the President of the Board of Directors, the two Vice-Presidents of the Board and 8 members, 4 of whom are selected from the Directors representing the State and 4 from the Directors representing the former Railway Companies.

As for the operation of the National Company of French Railways, it is to be in the hands of a General Manager, seconded by an Assistant General Manager. There will also be a General Secretary. These officers are to be appointed by the Board of Directors with the approval of the Minister of Public Works.

These measures show that the State is assured of complete control over the administration and operation of the National Company of French Railways.

Financial Organization

The Agreement of August 31, 1937, contemplates that the National Railway Company will eventually be able to strike a balance between all revenues and expenditures.

With this in view, the agreement stipulates that at the end of each fiscal year, the Board of Directors shall approve the budget for the coming year, and shall provide for receipts at least equal to the total expenses and charges of all kinds accrued and incumbent on the National Company of French Railways for that year. To obtain this result, in case sufficient reserve funds representing previous surpluses are not available, the Board of Directors should arrive at a balanced budget by increasing or by adjusting freight and passenger rates. Likewise, the Board of Directors is bound to take such measures at any time and on every occasion when conditions change sufficiently to threaten the balance which it has established for the budget.

The changes in rates proposed by the Board of Directors under these circumstances, in order to establish or to maintain a balanced budget, must be submitted in the form of notification to the Supreme Council of Transportation, and these new rates will become effective if, within 30 days, the Minister of Public Works makes no objection.

In case the new rates are rejected by the Minister of Public Works, the agreement stipulates that the Cabinet must immediately ask Parliament to vote the National Company of French Railways a credit equal to the amount that was to be gained through the proposed increase in rates. This credit is to be put at the immediate disposal of the National Company of French Railways. In case the necessary credit is not voted within two months, the increased rates proposed by the National Company of French Railways will become effective.

It is clear that the Agreement of 1937 has sought in every way to assure the financial solvency of the National Company of French Railways, since it has provided that the rate increases proposed by the Company become effective in cases when they have not obtained the approval of the Cabinet or of Parliament.

The agreement has also provided that the Minister of Public Works has the right to ask for rate reductions, but in such an event, also, the Cabinet must ask Parliament to vote a credit covering the loss that such reduction would be expected to cause to the National Company of French Railways, and the rate reduction does not become effective until Parliament has voted the credit.

Here, again, we see that the concern for the financial solvency of the National Company of French Railways supercedes all other considerations.

In order to further assure this financial solvency, the Agreement of 1937 provides that the National Company will be reimbursed each year for the cost of the transportation service given to the Postal Service. With this in view, a contract is to be entered into between the National Company of French Railways and the Postal Service in order to fix the price of these services, and if such contract is not concluded by January 1, 1939, these services shall be paid for from that date henceforth at regular commercial rates.

This stipulation is made in an effort to abolish one of the principal causes of the railway deficits. . . .

However, the agreement does not expect the budget of the National Company to be fully balanced until 1943. Until this is achieved, the deficit will be covered by advances from the French Treasury, to be repaid later, when the National Company shows a profit.

If, after this period of five years, any given year shows a deficit, this deficit is to be met, first of all by the reserve funds of the National Company, and then by direct loans made by the State. These advances are interest-bearing and must be reimbursed to the State Treasury at the latest on December 31 of the year following the one in which they were granted. These loans will be carried as expenses, i.e., as sums to be reimbursed on the budget of the following year; they will in this manner receive their place in the financial budget for the year in which they are to be repaid, and will be considered as a part of the expenses and charges to be met in the year's operation when they are to fall due.

The agreement of 1937 has thus systematically avoided the expedient of seeking loans in case of deficit, an expedient that was prescribed by the agreement of 1921 and used quite extensively. The only expedient approved by the agreement of 1937 in case of deficit is to procure advances from the Treasury. These are short term notes since they must be repaid during the year following their issuance. In this manner, an effort has been made to prevent the accumulation of successive deficits which leads quickly to an accumulation of interest charges which cannot be met.

In case any given year shows a surplus instead of a deficit, the agreement provides that this surplus is to be used up to 80% to reimburse the State Treasury for the advances made from 1938 to 1943, the remainder is to be assigned to the purchase of new rolling stock and equipment. However, if this surplus is large enough, it is to be used also for the establishment of a reserve fund and, beyond that point, to the repayment of advances made by the State Treasury to the common sinking fund that was created by the Agreement of 1921.

127. GENERAL REPORT OF THE COMMITTEE OF INQUIRY ON PRODUCTION, DECEMBER 1937 [18]

The numerous causes of France's production lag and a group of proposals to remedy the deficiencies were the subject of a report rendered in December 1937 by a parliamentary committee of inquiry. A number of the recommendations were later adopted.

The [August 25, 1937] decree law (which appointed the Committee on Production) divided the task of the investigating committee among thirteen sub-committees, devoted to the different branches of production, with a central committee entrusted with the liaison among the sub-committees and the coordination of their work.

The technical sub-committees, composed of representatives from the ministries concerned and of delegates from employers' and workers' organizations, worked out questionnaires which were sent to Chambers of Agriculture, to Chambers of Commerce, and to trade organizations. They called in representatives of the employers' and workers' organizations, together with the official agents involved, received their testimonies, and studied the answers to the questionnaires. . . .

. . . . .

[18] France, Assemblée Nationale, *Journal Officiel de la République Française*, vol. 69, No. 291, December 16, 1937, pp. 13738-13744.

The Committee was often hampered in its work by the lack of economic statistics. Some employers' organizations had to admit that they did not possess the required statistics and information. This was also frequently true of trade unions. In the government agencies only out-of-date or incomplete records are to be found. . . .

. . . . .

I. NATIONAL EQUIPMENT

The present economic situation in France does not confront us, on the whole, with a problem of re-equipment. Industry has fairly modern equipment and has been able to meet . . . a demand greater than in 1937. . . .

. . . . .

[But] some branches of economic activity suffer either from an insufficient use of the existing equipment—as in the case of our ports— or from the need for certain innovations and improvements—as in the case of agriculture, coal mining, iron foundries and steel mills, some gas plants, the silk industry, the manufacture of linen, dry goods, the merchant marine and the fisheries, boat building, machine construction, printing, and certain branches of the food industry such as the chocolate factories. . . .

. . . . .

It has been pointed out that there are great delays in the delivery of raw materials, machinery, and equipment. . . . It is therefore important to take all possible steps in order to speed up deliveries of this sort. . . .

. . . . .

II. CREDIT

The financial situation, at present, is such as to preclude the possibility of requiring the State to extend credit facilities save in exceptional cases; on the other hand, the general problem of credit appears to be linked to the entire economic, social, and political situation of the country, upon which is dependent the return of exported capital and, more generally, the use for productive investment of the capital remaining in France.

. . . . .

III. TRADE ORGANIZATION AND TECHNIQUE

A. Trade Organization.

Even though much progress has been achieved in the course of the last few years, there is still much to be done in the field of trade organization.

1) Some trades try to organize a discipline of their own. Thus, trade codes are being prepared for printing and book selling and for the fishing industry.

Merchants are asking also that they be protected from competition with people whose past is not above reproach and from unethical practices. . . .

2) In some branches of our economic activity, such as agriculture, trade unions have not been sufficiently developed. . . .

3) Trade unions and syndicates do not always prove sufficient. It is sometimes necessary to go farther and to form economic ententes. . . .

Some such ententes would need a measure of control so as to avoid being instrumental in depriving the consumers of the benefits of economic and technical progress and being used to the disadvantage of domestic consumers.

When, on the contrary, an entente has as its sole purpose the promotion of better industrial and commercial techniques, a greater measure of rationalization and standardization in industry, and the organization of research and testing laboratories, such an entente can only be helpful to national production and deserves encouragement.

. . . . .

IV. LABOR

A. Labor Supply.

Generally speaking, there is no labor shortage.

Yet, in spite of the serious unemployment situation, industries find it very difficult to procure the necessary skilled workers. . . . This situation hurts production and in turn aggravates unemployment to the extent that each skilled worker, once put to work, needs the assistance of several unskilled workers and laborers. Immediate measures are required for the recruiting, and prolonged efforts must be made for the training, of skilled workers.

1) It is necessary to reorganize the employment agencies. . . .

2) The unemployment census by trade and specialization undertaken by the Under-Secretary of State for Labor will provide satistical data which will permit a rational utilization of labor.

3) It is important to prepare a detailed census of the labor requirements in the various industries and trades. . . .

4) Skilled workers employed as common laborers must be sent back to their specialties.

5) But skilled workers cannot be recruited nor kept unless substantial advantages are offered them. In this respect, wage scales should take greater account of the degree of skill of the workers.

B. Apprenticeship.

The training of apprentices and of skilled workers has not been given sufficient attention. . . .

C. Productivity of Labor.

It does not seem possible to draw any general conclusions from the observations that have been submitted to the Committee concerning the productivity of labor. . . .

. . . . .

E. Collective Bargaining.

The custom is developing more and more of having the questions concerning labor adjusted by collective bargaining. The possibility of having such bargaining made obligatory by a ministerial decree has favored this development.

But there have been complaints from employers and workers alike, against the delays caused by this procedure. Aside from the difficulties that are inherent in putting into effect any new legislation, the application of the law of June 24, 1936, is hampered by the insufficient personnel in the Ministry of Labor.

V. LABOR REGULATION

A. The 40-Hour Week.

The enforcement of the 40-hour week has created a situation in the whole field of French production which requires a series of adjustments all the more difficult because the reduction in the work-week coincided with the definite pick-up in business that followed the economic depression, and with the increased requirements for National Defense.

. . . . .

B. Adjustments in the Application of the 40-Hour Week.

The Committee . . . recommends . . . the following ways and means which . . . should render its application easier. . . .

1) Some decrees provide that industries of a seasonal character may offset, up to a maximum of one hundred hours of work per year, the time lost during the dull season. The seasonal character of such industries must be the subject of a ruling by the Minister of Labor. . . .

The decrees lack in precision and should be more clearly defined. . . .

2) Aside from the seasonal industries proper, many industries in the course of a year go through important variations in the demand for their products. Although such variations do not assume regularity, the same principle of offsetting the time lost during the dull season should apply here.

3) The Committee has already pointed out that a great many industries suffer from a lack of skilled labor. . . .

Consequently there should be prepared for each industry, by the Minister of Labor, after consultation with employers' and workers' representatives, a list of jobs requiring skilled labor.

For those jobs only, a credit of supplementary hours, up to a maximum of 75 hours per year and 3 hours per week, should be given to the enterprises which could prove that they were not able to find competent workers to fill these jobs.

4) . . . a certain number of industries upon whose activity an important part of our economic life is dependent already are producing up to their maximum capacity, at least under the conditions in which their work is at present organized. This is the case for various industries producing, or helping to produce, machinery and equipment, especially mechanical and electrical equipment.

This situation calls for special attention. The reduction in the hours of work requires, in many industries, additional machinery and equipment, which is not always available, except by resorting to importation from abroad. It is evident that this state of affairs is contrary to the interests of French economic prosperity and is one of the causes of the adverse balance of trade. . . .

In order to meet this situation, the Committee believes that, during the year 1938, further exceptions to the 40-hour law should be made in favor of the industries of this group. . . .

5) The attention of the Committee has been called to some decrees under the 40-hour law which, in certain instances, have limited to 40 hours not only the work-week of the personnel but also the period of utilization of the equipment and machinery.

Such limitation in the use of equipment and machinery has nothing to do with the principle of the 40-hour week, but only with the means devised for shifts. This involves considerable extra expense for the industries to which it applies, because it cuts down by one-sixth the period of time in which machinery and equipment, generally expensive, can be used. . . .

[The Committee] believes that the authorization for shifts should be given by decision of the Minister of Labor, after consultation with the employers' and workers' representatives. . . .

6) The Committee has investigated with special attention the difficulties encountered in the fulfillment of orders for war materials. It has sought to find ways to avoid, in the future, the delays that have occurred in deliveries of such materials. . . .

7) Lastly, the Committee points out the difficulties that arise, for certain branches of production or for certain regions, from the discrepancies between the regulations applied to industries or trades whose activities are necessarily interrelated.

. . . . .

VI. MARKETS

The search for markets must be especially active in the industries for which the supply exceeds the demand; but all industries should attempt to extend their markets even though they may have more orders than they can fill, for experience proves that the opening of new markets is generally a slow process. . . .

A. The Domestic Market.

. . . . .

Industry should endeavor to stimulate consumption by lowering its cost of production and, in turn, retail prices by a persistent effort to maintain high standards of quality, to improve its products, and to conform to the taste and needs of the consumer. Industry could, in many cases, take better advantage of the demands of the domestic market and this without any further tariff restriction. Especially should it attempt to supply those goods which are not now being made in France and which have to be imported in large quantities.

. . . . .

The various public agencies, being great purchasers of industrial products, can exert such influence on industry as to lead it to a more efficient organization. Public agencies can, most of all, distribute their orders so as to offset as much as possible the variation in the demand of private consumers. They may also introduce more standardization in the kind of industrial products they purchase.

B. Foreign Markets.

1) Under normal conditions, the first step in keeping or in opening foreign markets is that French exporters be in a position to offer to their customers products of good quality at stable prices and to make delivery without undue delay. All the recommendations of this report have for their object the stimulation of French production so that it will have products to offer to foreign markets without excessive delays. The recommendations also look upon a stable cost of production as an essential factor of economic expansion.

2) Aside from these fundamental points, the Committee believes that no effort should be spared in order to improve France's foreign trade, to expand her markets, and to direct our agricultural and industrial products toward foreign markets. . . .

It is also necessary to have a more rational organization of the export trade. This depends upon the initiative of producers and on the strength of their ententes: control of quality, adoption of standards for agricultural products and for manufactured goods, supervised advertising and selling. . . .

3) With regard to our colonies, protectorates, and mandates, there is a rational policy which can be helpful both to the natives and to the French. The Committee feels that it must insist that such a policy be followed by all departments of our government, with a sense of cooperation and continuity which will assure its complete success. . . .

4) The government's task is also one of control. It should make sure that agriculturalists, industrialists, and merchants make an effort to adjust themselves to the requirements of our economic life. The state can do this all the more efficiently because these people are asking for protective tariffs, diplomatic interventions, financial aid or moral encouragement. . . .

VII. TAXATION

Without undertaking a critical examination of the taxes that now bear upon production, the heavy burden of which hardly needs to be stressed, the Committee believes it opportune to point out some general rules which cannot be ignored without grave danger for national economic life and certain general reforms which are urgently needed.

1) It appeared to the Committee, . . . that in some cases the legitimate desire to improve the tax system has resulted in multiplying the changes in regulations and in modifying excessively, in too short a time, the basis and rates of the taxes. . . .

2) Sometimes, also, the taxes have struck operations that were already completed; such retroactive taxation . . . has a disastrous and unjust effect . . . which has interfered in turn with business recovery.

3) From a comparative study of the various branches of production it is clear that a complete revision of the *patente* (license to do business) is urgently needed. . . .

4) Machinery purchases and equipment improvement are often hampered by some fiscal methods of valuation and amortization.

5) There are also taxes which are so low that it is not worth while to collect them; this is the case for certain *octrois* (town dues).

. . . . .

CONCLUSION

Having come to the end of its investigation on the general conditions of production and manufacture in France, the Committee wishes to emphasize the magnitude of the effort required to raise the level of production to its indispensable minimum.

While production in neighboring countries has reached the 1929 level (Belgium, Italy, Netherlands) or even gone beyond it (by 19 per cent in Germany, by 25 per cent in England, by 45 per cent in Sweden), French production is 25 per cent below its 1929 level.

In comparison with this same year, public expenditures, either in the ordinary or in the extraordinary budget, have become much larger. They have increased from 75 billion francs to more than 100 billions, while at the same time the hourly wage for industrial workers has been considerably increased since 1929.

In order to meet this situation, which coincides with a substantial decrease in the national income, a considerable increase in French production is imperative.

Such increase can only be obtained by a systematic effort, making full use of the means recommended by this Committee in the preceding chapters. This effort should be aimed primarily at speeding up deliveries, at reducing imports, and at producing a surplus for export. . . .

Everyone is expected to cooperate in this common task so that, in spite of its magnitude and of the amount of energy required, prosperity may return.

128. THE CONSTITUTIONAL LAWS OF FRANCE [19]

The unwillingness of the Bourbon Count of Chambord, after the fall of the Second Empire, to accept the tricolor along with the throne of France, and his insistence upon divine-right monarchy and the white flag of his ancestors, made it necessary for the National Assembly to adopt at least a provisional constitution while awaiting his demise, which latter would make legitimate the claim to the throne of his nearest relative, the more liberal Count of Paris. Hence the instrument adopted in 1875 was really only a series of "Constitutional Laws." It would appear, however, that the inclusion—albeit by a majority of one—of a method for electing future presidents was a virtual recognition of the permanence of the republic. At any rate, these laws, with amendments, continued to serve the constitutional needs of the Third Republic.

CONSTITUTIONAL LAWS [20]

I.

CONSTITUTIONAL LAW ON THE ORGANIZATION OF THE PUBLIC POWERS
(February 25, 1875)

ARTICLE 1.

The legislative power shall be exercised by two assemblies: the Chamber of Deputies and the Senate.

The Chamber of Deputies shall be elected by universal suffrage, under the conditions determined by the electoral law.[21]

The composition, the method of election, and the powers of the Senate shall be regulated by a special law.[22]

ARTICLE 2.

The President of the Republic is chosen by an absolute majority of votes of the Senate and Chamber of Deputies united in National Assembly.

---

[19] Irish Free State, Constitution Committee, *Select Constitutions of the World. Prepared for Presentation to Dáil Eireann by Order of the Irish Provisional Government 1922*, Stationery Office, Dublin, 1922, pp. 397-403.

[20] *Note.* Where an Article or part of an Article has been repealed or substantially amended by subsequent legislation, or has become obsolete by efflux of time, it is printed in italic type. Minor amendments and later laws on the same subject are referred to in the footnotes.

[21] See laws of November 30, 1875, June 16, 1885, and July 12, 1919.

[22] See constitutional law of February 24, 1875, and laws of August 2, 1875, and December 9, 1884.

He shall be elected for seven years. He shall be eligible for re-election.

ARTICLE 3.

The President of the Republic shall have the initiative of laws concurrently with the members of the two Chambers. He shall promulgate the laws when they have been voted by the two Chambers; he shall look after and secure their execution.

He shall have the right of pardon; amnesty may only be granted by law.

He shall dispose of the armed forces.

He shall appoint to all civil and military positions.

He shall preside over state functions; envoys and ambassadors of foreign powers shall be accredited to him.

Every act of the President of the Republic must be counter-signed by a minister.

ARTICLE 4.

As vacancies occur on and after the promulgation of the present law, the President of the Republic shall appoint, in the Council of Ministers, the Councillors of State in ordinary service.

The Councillors of State thus chosen may be dismissed only by decree rendered in the Council of Ministers.

The Councillors of State chosen by virtue of the law of May 24, 1872, shall not, before the expiration of their powers, be dismissed except in the manner provided by that law. After the dissolution of the National Assembly, they may be dismissed only by resolution of the Senate.[23]

ARTICLE 5.

The President of the Republic may, with the assent of the Senate, dissolve the Chamber of Deputies before the legal expiration of its term.

In that case the electoral colleges are summoned for new elections within three months.[24]

ARTICLE 6.

The Ministers shall be collectively responsible to the Chambers for the general policy of the government, and individually for their personal acts.

[23] By the law of May 24, 1872, Councillors of State were elected by the National Assembly for a term of nine years. This clause therefore ceased to have any application after 1881.

[24] Amended by Article 1 of the constitutional law of August 14, 1884. *Ed. note: See p. 460.*

The President of the Republic shall be responsible only in case of high treason.[25]

ARTICLE 7.

In case of vacancy by death or for any other reason, the two Chambers assembled together shall proceed at once to the election of a new President.

In the meantime the Council of Ministers shall be invested with the executive power.[26]

ARTICLE 8.

The Chambers shall have the right by separate resolutions, taken in each by an absolute majority of votes, either upon their own initiative or upon the request of the President of the Republic, to declare that occasion has arisen for a revision of the constitutional laws.

After each of the two Chambers shall have come to this decision, they shall meet together in National Assembly to proceed with the revision.

The acts effecting revision of the constitutional laws in whole or in part, shall be passed by an absolute majority of the members composing the National Assembly.[27]

During the continuance, however, of the powers conferred by the law of November 20, 1873, upon Marshal MacMahon, this revision shall take place only upon the initiative of the President of the Republic.

ARTICLE 9.

The seat of the executive power and of the two Chambers is at Versailles.[28]

II.

CONSTITUTIONAL LAW ON THE ORGANIZATION OF THE SENATE [29]
(February 24, 1875)

. . . . .

ARTICLE 8.

The Senate shall have, concurrently with the Chamber of Deputies,

---

[25] See Article 12 of the constitutional law of July 16, 1875. *Ed. note: See p. 459.*

[26] See Article 3 of the constitutional law of July 16, 1875. *Ed. note: See p. 458.*

[27] Two paragraphs were added to this Article by Article 2 of the constitutional law of August 14, 1884. *Ed. note: See p. 461.*

[28] Repealed by constitutional law of June 21, 1879. See law of July 22, 1879. *Ed. note: See p. 460 and v. 32.*

[29] Articles 1 to 7 of this law were deprived of their constitutional character by the constitutional law of August 14, 1884, and were repealed by the law of December 9, 1884, which enacted provisions in substitution for them.

the power to initiate and to pass laws. Finance laws, however, shall first be introduced in and passed by the Chamber of Deputies.

ARTICLE 9.

The Senate may be constituted a Court of Justice to try either the President of the Republic or the Ministers and to take cognizance of attacks made upon the safety of the State.

. . . . .

III.

CONSTITUTIONAL LAW ON THE RELATIONS OF THE PUBLIC POWERS
(July 16, 1875)

ARTICLE 1.

The Senate and the Chamber of Deputies shall assemble each year on the second Tuesday in January, unless convened earlier by the President of the Republic.

The two Chambers shall continue in session at least five months each year. The sessions of the two Chambers shall begin and end at the same time.

On the Sunday following the opening of the session, public prayers shall be addressed to God in the churches and temples, to invoke His aid in the labours of the Chambers.[30]

ARTICLE 2.

The President of the Republic pronounces the closing of the session. He may convene the Chambers in extraordinary session. He shall convene them if, during the recess, an absolute majority of the members of each Chamber request it.

The President may adjourn the Chambers. The adjournment, however, shall not exceed one month, nor take place more than twice in the same session.

ARTICLE 3.

One month at least before the legal expiration of the powers of the President of the Republic, the Chambers shall be called together in National Assembly to proceed to the election of a new President.

In default of a summons, this meeting shall take place, as of right, the fifteenth day before the expiration of the term of the President.

[30] This third paragraph was repealed by the constitutional law of August 14, 1884. *Ed. note: See p. 461.*

In case of the death or resignation of the President of the Republic, the two Chambers shall assemble immediately, as of right.

In case the Chamber of Deputies, in consequence of Article 5 of the law of February 25, 1875, is dissolved at the time when the presidency of the Republic becomes vacant, the electoral colleges shall be convened at once, and the Senate shall assemble as of right.

ARTICLE 4.

Every meeting of either of the two Chambers which shall be held at a time when the other is not in session is illegal and void, except in the case provided for in the preceding article, and when the Senate meets as a court of justice; in the latter case, judicial functions alone shall be exercised.

ARTICLE 5.

The sittings of the Senate and the Chamber of Deputies shall be public.

Nevertheless either Chamber may meet in secret session, upon the request of a fixed number of its members, determined by its rules.

It shall then decide by absolute majority whether the sittings shall be resumed in public upon the same subject.

ARTICLE 6.

The President of the Republic communicates with the Chambers by messages, which shall be read from the tribune by a Minister.

The Ministers shall have entrance to both Chambers, and shall be heard when they request it. They may be assisted, for the discussion of a specific bill, by commissioners named by decree of the President of the Republic.

ARTICLE 7.

The President of the Republic shall promulgate the laws within the month following the transmission to the Government of the law as finally passed. He shall promulgate, within three days, laws the promulgation of which shall have been declared urgent by an express vote of each Chamber.

Within the time fixed for promulgation the President of the Republic may, by a message with reasons assigned, request of the two Chambers a new discussion, which cannot be refused.

ARTICLE 8.

The President of the Republic shall negotiate and ratify treaties. He shall acquaint the Chambers of them as soon as the interests and safety of the State permit.

Treaties of peace and of commerce, treaties which involve the finances of the State, those relating to the person and property of French citizens in foreign countries, shall be ratified only after having been voted by the two Chambers. No cession, exchange, or annexation of territory shall take place except by virtue of a law.

ARTICLE 9.

The President of the Republic shall not declare war without the previous consent of the two Chambers.

ARTICLE 10.

Each Chamber shall be the judge of the eligibility of its members, and of the regularity of their election; it alone may receive their resignation.

ARTICLE 11.

The *Bureau*[31] of each Chamber shall be elected each year for the duration of the entire session and of every extraordinary session which may be held before the regular session of the following year.

When the two Chambers meet together as a National Assembly, their *Bureau* shall be composed of the President, Vice-Presidents, and Secretaries of the Senate.

ARTICLE 12.

The President of the Republic may be impeached by the Chamber of Deputies only, and may be tried only by the Senate.

The Ministers may be impeached by the Chamber of Deputies for offences committed in the performance of their duties. In this case they shall be tried by the Senate.

The Senate may be constituted into a court of justice by a decree of the President of the Republic, issued in the Council of Ministers, to try all persons accused of attempts upon the safety of the State.

---

[31] The bureau of the Senate consists of a president, four vice-presidents, eight secretaries, and three questors; the bureau of the Chamber of Deputies has the same composition. "The questors have the business management of the Chamber in their hands. They look after the funds of the Chamber, paying the Deputies and employees and supervising other expenditures; they have charge of the archives, the library, and the buildings generally." . . .

If proceedings should have been begun in the regular courts, the decree convening the Senate may be issued at any time before the granting of a discharge.

A law shall determine the method of procedure for the accusation, trial, and judgment.

ARTICLE 13.

No member of either Chamber shall be prosecuted or held responsible on account of any opinions expressed or votes cast by him in the performance of his duties.

ARTICLE 14.

No member of either Chamber shall, during the session, be prosecuted or arrested for any offence or misdemeanour, except upon the authority of the Chamber of which he is a member, unless he be taken in the very act.

The detention or prosecution of a member of either Chamber shall be suspended for the session, and for the entire term of the Chamber, if the Chamber requires it.

REVISORY CONSTITUTIONAL LAWS

IV.

CONSTITUTIONAL LAW REVISING ARTICLE 9 OF THE CONSTITUTIONAL
LAW OF FEBRUARY 25, 1875
(June 21, 1879)

Article 9 [32] of the constitutional law of February 25, 1875, is repealed.

V.

CONSTITUTIONAL LAW PARTIALLY REVISING THE
CONSTITUTIONAL LAWS
(August 14, 1884)

ARTICLE 1.

Paragraph 2 of Article 5 of the Constitutional law of February 25, 1875, on the organization of the Public Powers,[33] is amended as follows:

"In that case the electoral colleges shall meet for new elections within two months and the Chamber within the ten days following the close of the elections."

---

[32] This article fixed the seat of government at Versailles. [*Ed. note: See p. 456.*] The seat of government was removed from Versailles to Paris by a law of July 22, 1879.
[33] See p. 455.—*Ed.*

Article 2.

To paragraph 3 of Article 8 of the same law of February 25, 1875,[34] is added the following:

"The republican form of government shall not be made the subject of a proposed revision.

"Members of families that have reigned in France are ineligible to the Presidency of the Republic."

Article 3.

Articles 1 to 7 of the constitutional law of February 24, 1875, on the Organization of the Senate, shall no longer have a constitutional character.[35]

Article 4.

Paragraph 3 of Article 1 of the constitutional law of July 16, 1875, on the Relations of the Public Powers, is repealed.[36]

129. THE FRENCH ELECTORAL LAW OF JULY 21, 1927 *(Extracts)* [37]

The French system of electing national deputies has several times been altered under the Third Republic. From 1875 to 1885 the single-member district system was in use. From 1885 until 1889 each department was regarded as a single constituency entitled to choose a number of deputies proportionate to its population. Single-member districts were restored from 1889 to 1919, but in the latter year a complicated system of proportional representation was introduced, again with the departments as the electoral districts. In 1927, by the law quoted below, the single-member district system was once more revived.

Article 1.

The members of the Chamber of Deputies are elected on the single-member district basis (*au scrutin uninominal*).

---

[34] See p. 456.—*Ed.*
[35] These articles were repealed by the law of December 9, 1884.
[36] See p. 457.—*Ed.*
[37] France, Assemblée Nationale, *Journal Officiel de la République Française*, vol. 59, No. 169, July 22, 1927, p. 7547.

ARTICLE 2.

The number of deputies is fixed for the 14th legislature at 612,[38] in accordance with the table annexed to the present law which delimits the electoral districts on a basis of population.

ARTICLE 3.

No one is elected on the first ballot (*au premier tour de scrutin*) unless he has received:

1° An absolute majority of the votes cast;

2° A number of votes equal to one-fourth of the number of registered voters.

On the second ballot, a plurality suffices.

In case of a tie vote, the eldest candidate is elected.

ARTICLE 4.

The second balloting shall be held on the Sunday following the day on which the results of the first ballot are proclaimed.

ARTICLE 5.

The ballots for each electoral district shall be counted in public at the department seat not later than the Wednesday following the balloting.

This is to be done by a commission composed of the president of the civil court, as president, and of the four members of the general council, not candidates, who have served the longest; in case of a tie in length of service, the eldest shall be designated. . . .

The operation of counting shall be certified by an official report.

· · · · ·

ARTICLE 9.

Two sample ballots for each candidate and, if requested, a circular . . . or any other communication relating exclusively to the election shall be sent to each voter, in a sealed, franked envelope. . . .

· · · · ·

---

[38] This number was later increased to 618.—*Ed.*

卍 卍 卍

130. DOUMERGUE'S PLANS FOR PARLIAMENTARY REFORM [39]

The government of Gaston Doumergue, appointed in February 1934 as explained in the note preceding Document No. 120, presented (September 1934) to parliament its plans for strengthening the government in a way that would ensure internal order and foreign security. Doumergue's views, quoted below from one of his speeches, were unacceptable to the deputies, who maintained that the cabinet must remain subordinate to parliament, not parliament to the cabinet.

You know that there is no lack of reformers. Their efforts, their projects are often interesting. I have read many of them with attention and even with profit. But they are voluble, they sometimes embrace too many things, and they generally assume that *la table est rase.* It isn't: far from it. There are realities which one cannot suppress with the stroke of a pen nor with a decree. . . .

I shall try to suggest reforms, taking full account of these realities, and put the most pressing ones first.

What we need most in our system, especially in the present circumstances, is to have a government with authority. Now it has scarcely any. Some of you may be tempted to reply to me that under a parliamentary and democratic régime no government *can* have authority. That is not my opinion. I am attached to this régime. I know its inconveniences, but also its advantages. I love liberty. We have very close to us, on the other side of the Channel, a very great and noble country which is our friend. It has long been under a parliamentary régime. Its governments, controlled by one side or the other, have great authority. Do you know why? Their head is invested with the powers of a head. He is called the prime minister, and he is that in fact.

This head and his government, upon assuming power, are assured of a long existence. Thence their authority. They are simultaneously assured of a budget in good time, and one which includes only the credits and expenditures which they have asked for. They have, finally, the assurance of support from a well-disciplined staff of functionaries and civil servants loyal to their duties and among whom insurrection against the state is not lightly tolerated.

[39] G. Doumergue, *Discours à la nation française,* Denoël et Steele, Paris, 1934, pp. 102-112. (Speech of September 24, 1934.) Reprinted by permission of Les Éditions Denoël.

I add that in Great Britain there really *is* a separation of powers and that the judiciary is divorced from politics, which is the only way to have completely impartial justice.

Such a system I intend to organize among ourselves. The matter is urgent.

In France, the head of the government, called President of the Council, is only a fiction. He has no special authority. The constitution ignores him, does not even mention him, which is a wrong. In law and in fact, he is a minister like the others, a situation which does not confer upon him authority sufficient to be the arbiter among his colleagues.

In our country, governments are not assured of long life. They have no homogeneous majority behind them because there are too many parties. They can be upset for the sake of a "yes" or a "no," without possibility of disagreeable consequence for those who overthrow them just for the fun of the massacre.

. . . . .

Governments in France seldom have their annual budgets voted in good time. They often function for months under the bothersome system of the twelfths. Moreover, the budgets contain expenditure items not proposed by the governments because they did not regard them as necessary. This is not calculated to augment their authority. On the contrary, it tends to lessen it.

In France, finally, there is a group of civil servants who aspire to be more and more independent of the state. They rebel and go on strike.

Are there any remedies for all this? Certainly! I would not have described the evils to you if there were no remedies.

Let us give the governments the authority which they so badly need by assigning to the head, through the insertion of a few words in the constitution, the quality of prime minister which he ought to have.

Then let us empower him, in case of disagreement between the government and the majority of the Chamber, to appeal to the country at once without having to resort to formalities and red tape. The people will thus be able to decide, because it is sovereign. A slight modification of the constitution would suffice to bring this about, except in certain clearly specified cases where the prior authorization of the Senate— which has rendered such great services to the Republic—would be necessary.

Rest assured that ministerial crises will become rare when the fear of immediate dissolution restrains the impatient and often unjustifiable ambitions which—rather than profound disagreements over ideas and principles—are generally at the root of these crises.

Let us also insert in the constitution a clause empowering the government alone to propose expenditures and denying this initiative to the members of either house.

To this change let us add another, permitting governments to extend by decree for a twelvemonth the current year's budget whenever that for the new year has not been voted within a reasonable time.

Finally, to assure the good, uninterrupted functioning of public services, which neither the state nor its individuals can do without, let us transform the statute on officials into a constitutional law. This is an absolute necessity.

Officials are privileged citizens. They are assured of emoluments and pensions. Life for other citizens is filled with discomforts and the possibilities of complete ruin. They are all exposed to the danger of having not a sou on which to live. The security which gives officials food and shelter to the end of their lives ought to be counterbalanced by the obligation to accept certain disciplines from which citizens who are not officials are exempt.

131. ANDRÉ TARDIEU'S PLANS FOR STATE REFORM, 1934 [40]

André Tardieu was another prominent French politician who came to recommend a constitutional revision to confer wider powers on the executive branch of the government. His own difficult experiences as premier made him feel keenly the need for curbing the carefree manner in which the Chamber of Deputies sometimes overthrew ministries. The average life of French ministries from 1875 to 1939 was about eight months.

The elective system in its present form is not equal to the task either of the administration of finances, the direction of public opinion, or the conduct of foreign affairs, and it may be swept away in some moment of panic.

Great changes are necessary to save it.

We need a lasting remedy. With a parliament which tends naturally, in accordance with historical law, to become a caste, and, like

[40] A. Tardieu, *La Réforme de l'état,* Ernest Flammarion, Paris, 1934, pp. 12-13, 14-15, 127-128, 129-131. Reprinted by permission of the publishers.

all castes, to become exclusive, . . . an organic reform is needed which
will reëstablish an equilibrium of power. The assemblies and the country
must revise the state of their relations.

The necessary liquidation.—Will some one object that our régime
of unlimited tolerance, our régime, à la Tolstoy, of non-resistance to
evil, corresponds to the traditions of individualism which have dominated the intellectual and economic revolutions from which the modern
age has sprung?

I will merely repeat what I have said above about the evolution of
régimes which do not improve as they go along and which die if one
does not reform them. We are the forced liquidators of the abuses with
which liberalism and materialism stamped the last century.

. . . . .

The difficulty is manifested in the first place through an intolerable
expansion of the legislative power at the expense of the executive—and
this at a time when, on the Left as well as on the Right, there is proclaimed the need for a strong government. It is further demonstrated
by the total subordination of the legislative power to the demands of
electoral oligarchies which submerge the general interest in a sea of
particular interests.

The executive, opposing the assemblies and functionaries, represents
only instability. The real power is no longer the minister, who leaves
at the end of a month. The real power is the rapporteur of the budget
who often succeeds himself under one legislature after another. The
Ministry of Public Works, to cite only it, has had thirteen heads in
seven years; but its budget has had only one rapporteur.

The legislature, devised by our grandfathers to control and check
expenditures, has become their accelerator—because it depends for its
election on the beneficiaries of its outlays. Thus it has happened that in
fewer than twenty years the number of officials has increased by nearly
200,000, and thus personnel charges have come to represent an enormous
share of the total budgetary charges.

. . . . .

No Frenchman would tolerate in his business or at his hearth this
régime of disorder, of privilege and instability, where everyone commands and no one is held responsible. But all Frenchmen support it
where the state is concerned.

To purify this régime, of what value would it be to find fault with those elements which compose it? Actually it would be necessary to blame everybody, a task before which the timid recoil.

When the public manifests its discontent, minor reforms are promised—administrative reform, for example, which the Chambers, without knowing what it is, unanimously applaud as soon as it is proposed.

But who does not see that, with the state—of which the administration is but the executive agency—remaining what it is, it is useless to pretend to improve the second [the executive] without altering the first [the state].

The headless body.—In our state it is authority which is lacking. This truth is proclaimed by the Left. It is proclaimed by the Right. It is murmured by the Centre. There must be no body without a head; no group without a leader.

Who then, in France, *is* the leader? It is not the President of the Republic. . . .

It is not the President of the Council, betrayed leader of a cabinet whose composition was dictated by the parliamentary groups and whose death knell is sounded by the autocratic Chambers immediately upon the reading of the ministerial declaration.

Nor is it the ministers, slaves of parliamentary or bureaucratic domination.

It is not even . . . the general body of officials intent upon consolidating their tenure. . . .

France is a body without a head. The body is unaware that the head is missing.

. . . . .

The essential remedies.—Admitting the principle of legal revision, the restoration of the separation of powers ought to be the first objective of this revision. The absence of such separation in France, and hence the bankruptcy of material and moral authority, is the result of the subordination of the executive to the legislature and the electorate, both in turn controlled by the oligarchies.

Through this double enslavement, power has passed where there is no, where there can be no, responsibility.

. . . . .

Through a re-separation of powers, the rights of the citizens would be restored.

To this end, among many measures, I have suggested two which typify the kind of revision needed.

Reëstablish the equilibrium between the executive and legislative branches of the government by giving the premier, in compensation for the power which the legislature has of turning him out, the right, to be shared by him with the Senate, to dissolve the lower house. Therein the Chamber of Deputies would find a strong motive for using the ministries less harshly.

Abolish the instrument of oppression [budgetary rapporteurs] which places in the hands of the begging oligarchies the right conferred upon the deputies to propose expenditures . . . : the representatives will then . . . come into the free exercise of their mandate.

. . . . .

I have proposed two other reforms, which . . . would make of universal suffrage . . . a living reality.

The first consists in giving women the same political rights as men.

The second consists in calling on this electoral body—enlarged in accordance with equity and the dictates of human dignity—to vote not only on names but also on ideas.

Woman suffrage and the referendum are the two reforms, neither of which can be denounced as an adventure because they are in force throughout the greater part of the civilized world. . . .

132. THE PROGRAM OF THE *CROIX DE FEU* [41]

France's leading fascist, for a time, appeared to be Colonel François de la Rocque, founder of the Croix de Feu. *The Fiery Cross movement grew to sufficiently large proportions so that the Blum Government dissolved the association by decree on June 18, 1936. La Rocque thereupon reorganized his society as the* Parti Social Français, *but its influence seemed to lessen in the ensuing years. The Fiery Cross program, like numerous "fascist" appeals, contained many mystical elements.*

The Plan of Action

What is to be understood by the term "plan of action," if not the

---

[41] F. de la Rocque, *The Fiery Cross, The Call to Public Service in France,* Lovat Dickson, London, 1936, pp. 23-25, 31-32, 78-79, 128-129, 131, 160, 161, 214-215. Reprinted by permission through the agency of William Aspenwall Bradley.

inventory, as it were, of all those combined efforts it is possible and desirable at any given moment to concentrate upon the achievement of some higher aim which has been formulated once and for all. That higher aim . . . I shall . . . describe . . . as the rehabilitation and preservation of France as a political, geographical, spiritual and traditional unit. All questions of government, or of the constitution, must be kept rigorously in their place as the *means* and instruments by which to obtain our objective and hold fast thereto. When that has once been accepted, the main motive forces decided upon as necessary to the achievement of that objective must dictate the activities of those charged with attaining it. Thereafter it will sweep them along and dominate their whole beings. . . .

[These forces are] the mystic consciousness of France, of a France that lives on and continuously marches forward. An awakening of the individual and collective conscience of the people in a free and fostered following of its deepest forces within the protective, co-ordinating and interrelated framework of a national discipline, rejuvenated and authoritarian. The elimination of irresponsible, underhand and self-seeking interests which, as parasitism and state interference, corrupt our public existence and bar the way to any revaluation of existing values. The harmonious adjustment of social and scientific progress to those basic factors which no civilization can ignore save at the cost of returning to the barbarism of prehistoric times, namely Work, the Family, and the Fatherland.

In taking these fundamental truths as my guide, how was I to envisage the preparation and utilization of the magnificent instrument represented by the organization of the Fiery Cross? My first care, I decided, must be to organize a parent cell impregnated with this mystic consciousness, this discipline, this patriotic and profoundly human devotion. Then its evolution, its growth must be protected, safe from the virus of the politicians that is so destructive to human energy, so favourable to disintegration. *Its real, its positive independence must be guarded from every outside influence to ensure its constant subordination to the commandments bequeathed us by our fifteen hundred thousand* [war] *dead.*

. . . . .

Our "Mystery"

For it is true that a mystic aim inspires us. The tragedy of France has its roots in that wave of materialism in which ex-Service and post-war men dissociated themselves from each other and drew apart in mutual conflict. Men of the Fiery Cross and National Volunteers [composed of sons of war veterans], together we stemmed the floods of greed, the rivalries of different claimants. And still we guarded pure our links with all the martyrs of the agony of France and thus we caused the national mystic consciousness to gush anew, rich in vitality, heroism, self-sacrifice: vital as in the days of Joan of Arc, of Fontenay, Valmy, Montmirail and Verdun.

Men of the Fiery Cross, my one-time comrades of the front-line trenches, and you, men of the later generations who are their Volunteers, behold your mission! To communicate the Faith to those who seek a sign to vanquish their fears, their doubts! On all hands, the eager hearts of France rise up and seek each other. Your part must be to gather them together in the gleaming furrow that trails behind you.

. . . . .

"Votism"

[By "votism"] I mean the far too widespread misconception that the people's verdict, whether the vote be limited or universal, subserves some higher end. "Good election results" are desired as though they meant salvation, and a seat in parliament seems the end of all earthly ambitions. It is the secret yearning, the spring-board to all honours. The word "votism" will keep on recurring in this book like a "leit-motiv." The state of mind to which it corresponds explains the sterility of this indifferent age. The activities it inspires increase the sum total of wasted energies and create innumerable false leaders. They undermine public opinion and a general scepticism soon takes their place. Agitation, *tartuffism*, and the exploitation of individual enthusiasms to gain votes, are all encouraged thereby. . . . Once the municipal or legislative seat has been won the betrayal begins, whether involuntary or premeditated, as demanded by, or in accordance with, party dictates or personal ambitions. "Votism" for many has become a sort of lay religion, the crown of a career, an Alladin's lamp, a refuge from the crisis, a paid profession, or a trinket gratifying to the vanity. Its base machinations have developed into a technique, and its vulgar disputes and degrading contests even employ the noble terminology of our agonies in the trenches. . . .

. . . . . .

Racism?

How, under such conditions, could we fall into the error of fostering a "racist" exclusiveness? It is impossible to see by what standards it could be applied. . . . The French race is a magnificent synthesis, disciplined, balanced, and possessing its own culture. It forms a whole. No linguistic researches, no analysis of heredity can prevail against that fact. No question of geographic origin or religious faith could have any relevance thereto. The quality, the devotion of its citizens as Frenchmen, is all that matters, so it be honest, tested and confirmed.

. . . . .

To sum up, "racism" is the exclusive appanage of such nations as have remained primitive and united in one moral purpose for invasion or revenge. "Racism" is a manifestation or weapon of war.

. . . . .

The French state does not need to be either "totalitarian" or "collectivist," absolutist or liberal. But it must be in a position to wield a stern authority indispensable to the execution of its task. It needs time, without which nothing can be built. The power that emanates from it, radiant, sturdy, can alone initiate that living fruitful process that leads to decentralization. . . .

. . . . .

The Nation

The French nation forms a whole, one and indivisible. Race antagonisms do not exist upon its love-worthy soil. No minority claim for independence raises its head among its offspring. Its frontiers embrace whole populations of foreign origin, who, oblivious of their language and ethnical sources, have learnt to toil in her cause, suffer for her and yet merge wholly into her. Such efforts to win self-government as strive from time to time to assert themselves, are never anything but trifling, childish, or revolutionary intrigues against civilization itself. Where regionalist aspirations manifest themselves, it is only because the better exploitation of their riches for the benefit of the whole nation is sought.

. . . . .

Who then can prevail against our patriotic faith, our incorruptible poverty, our enthusiastic discipline, the worship of our Dead and our passionate offering to those that now come after us?

133. REFORM VIEWS OF A FRENCH LABOR LEADER [42]

As leader of the French association of trade unions—the Confédération Générale du Travail—*Léon Jouhaux exercised considerable influence in the national life. He, too, advocated plans for the reform of France's political and economic structure. He was especially interested in bringing about a "planned economy" and the nationalization of the key industries.*

The plan [of economic reform] of the C.G.T. is first of all a program for struggle against the [current] crisis. It is addressed to all those who, in one way or another, are its victims and seek its end by a substantial remodelling of the economic system and the suppression of the privileges of capitalistic feudalism.

Such preciseness [of definition] is indispensable. It must be recognized that if our program has secured widest adherence, this has not all been given in the same spirit.

To some, the plan appears as one step along the way towards the greatest of changes; to others, it represents the maximum of change to which they will resign themselves and then only because of the exceptional gravity of the moment.

These divergencies are only normal; to wish that everyone accept the plan in the same spirit would be an illusion.

The problem posed today is how to make the "minimum" of some coincide with the "maximum" of the others in order to unite all in a bloc whose power will assure the common victory.

. . . . . .

Everyone's spirit is weighed down by the burden of the [present] crisis. We search anxiously for a solution. There is an instinctive revulsion against purely negative solutions and an ironic skepticism regarding those propositions which, thanks to their extremism, could be accepted only by a very restricted circle of individuals already convinced.

At bottom this is the reason why—doubtless thanks less to its technical spirit than to the *idées-forces* which it announces—the plan of the C.G.T. has had so wide a radiation and has constituted a force of considerable attraction.

---

[42] L. Jouhaux (with the collaboration of M. Harmel and J. Duret), *La C.G.T., ce qu'elle est, ce qu'elle veut,* 26 ed., Gallimard, Paris, 1937, pp. 174-184. Reprinted by permission of the publishers.

It matters little enough today that these initial divergencies still exist in part and that there still are censorious persons who cannot rally to the idea of a "planned economy." The essential thing is that often leading ideas formulated by the workers' movement are today accepted in the camp of the democrats: the need for an active struggle against the crisis by fulfilling the demands of the masses, the necessity for nationalization of credit and the key industries to reach this point, and the need for forming a compact bloc of the majority of the nation against the oligarchies.

. . . . . .

We have shown above that the decadence of the capitalist system does not *ipso facto* result in its inevitable replacement by a socialist system nor the substitution of new institutions more satisfactory than the old ones.

. . . . . .

It becomes clearer and clearer that without the nationalization of credit and the key industries—those control levers of the entire economic life of a modern nation—without a radical transformation of the motive powers, one cannot dream of constructing a "planned economy" nor reëstablish the equilibrium between production and consumption, nor succeed in the battle against the crisis.

. . . . . .

. . . The nationalization of banks and the key industries would make such a breach in the capitalist system that [the latter's] masters would never be able to close it and the struggle for the liberation of labor would enter a new phase. The nationalized portions would command the whole of the economic life of the country and would direct it in the interests of the laboring masses.

. . . . .

The prodigious development of modern techniques should permit all men to lead happy and dignified lives; it is merely a matter of abandoning an obsolete and unjust social system; all men, without distinction, would benefit thereby. Why restrict oneself by effecting partial reforms, incapable of curing the evils from which society is suffering, and which turn aside attention from an objective so easy to reach?

The thought is doubtless generous; the conception is singularly superficial: it is too beautiful a dream to believe that all that is necessary is to open wide the doors to production in order that resolute attacks may be made upon the problem of the division, the distribution of abundant wealth. . . .

134. THE MAGINOT LINE [43]

The following selection offers an interesting description of the famous French defences to the east, named after their chief proponent, André Maginot.

The Maginot Line, defending France's eastern frontiers, is the pre-eminent combination of passive obstacle and active defense. This French fortification hardly rises above the ground. The soldiers who christened it "the crust of the East" found the fitting expressive image. . . .

According to figures given this writer by engineer officers who superintended the work, 12,000,000 cubic meters of earth were dug out on the Maginot Line between 1929 and 1936; 1,500,000 cubic meters of concrete were cast; 50,000 tons of steel plates were set in position; galleries were hollowed out which in a straight line would cover the distance from Paris to Liège; 15,000 workmen were engaged on the construction; seven billions of francs were spent. Today new works have been begun to extend the "crust" facing the Jura and to fortify the north. On the "crust" itself, as I was able to see, work never ceases; its defense is incessantly reinforced.

Great precautions are taken by the builders to assure the maximum of resistance for this "crust." The towers of the underground workings, which weigh some 120 tons, are monolithic, and no shell can penetrate their concrete walls. . . .

Defense against gas is assured by a special process; electric machinery maintains in the interior an atmospheric pressure slightly higher than the exterior pressure. In order to prevent all communication with the gas-poisoned outer air, and also in order to do away with all loop-holes, the guns in the three turrets pivot on a ball mounted in the armor plate.

---

[43] R. Leurquin in *The New York Times,* September 4, 1938. Reprinted by permission of Mr. Leurquin.

The gunners lay their guns as sailors do in the turret of a warship without seeing anything, simply by following the indications on a dial controlled by an artillery officer, who is in a hermetically sealed armored chamber. The artillery officers see the outside world through panoramic telescopes built into the armor plate. . . .

The telephone lines . . . are buried five meters deep in concrete slabs. For each line there are at least two alternative lines on different circuits. This subterranean network ends in telephone exchanges installed fifty meters deep.

Thus protected, the soldiers of the "crust" can resist the fiercest bombardments. But that is not enough; in war it is necessary to strike—that is to say, there must be active defense.

The active role is played by the armament which the concrete protects.

Behind their cuspated embrasures the men of the Maginot Line can cover the frontier zone with a sheet of fire. . . . Each casemate is a volcano ready to spit flames in front, behind and on all sides at close as well as at long range.

All this zone of invisible death is further protected by look-out posts, alarm-signals, periscopes, sound-locating posts, barrages of infra-red rays. All over the region there are spying eyes, listening ears and weapons ready by day and night. . . . It is like 300 kilometers of haunted country.

. . . . .

The strength of the "crust of the East" lies in the diversity of its works; the variety of dimensions and of camouflage keeps the visitor in a state of complete astonishment. Between Metz and Besançon I visited more than thirty casemates and did not find two of them the same. Some were sunk in the earth, others crouched under railway embankments, others hung on the sides of precipices. I even found a casemate emerging from a swamp.

So much for the small links in the chain. But there are still the big forts. . . . They are nothing less than buried barracks with kilometers of passages lit by electricity and provided with metaled tracks; they have hot water laid on, electric ventilators and cookhouses. Whole hills have been hollowed out and concreted. Every measure has been taken, including victualing, to make them habitable for months on end.

The line is permanently occupied by what French soldiers ironically call "écrevisses de rempart." These "shellfish of the forts" . . . are distributed in squads of twelve men each over the first line of armored casemates, charged with the duty of holding them for the three days necessary to get the whole of the covering force in position. In peace time these men live the wartime life of the trenches: fifteen days in the line, fifteen days of rest.

The men have to keep watch, in rotation, day and night, in the alarm-post which projects above the surface of the ground as the periscope of a submarine sticks out of the sea. . . .

. . . . .

Apart from the hours on guard, the "shellfish" . . . work ceaselessly with pickax and shovel. They are forever digging, camouflaging, stiffening the network of barbed wire and tending the "asparagus" beds.

"Asparagus" are steel rails driven into the ground with their points upward. Their purpose is to arrest the progress of tanks. These rails are set at a slope and at different heights, so that the tank see-saws as it scales them. And, while the rails are tearing off the monsters' caterpillar tracks, the anti-tank guns, at ground level, will fire direct into their stomachs. If the tanks should escape this preliminary massacre, they would fall upon a second line, the "asparagus farci" (savory asparagus), where each rail has a detonator on top which would explode a charge capable of gutting the assailant.

In the World War, the shelter rarely deserved its name. For it a shelter has been substituted in the "crust of the East," which fulfills the formula of Marshal Pétain: "The minimum of danger, the maximum of comfort." Throughout the line the shelter is distinct from the casemate and is as far away from it as possible. . . .

Thus one fort sunk in the side of a hill has its shelter dug into the opposite side, to which it is connected by an underground passage 200 meters long. If, in an attack, one of the casemates should be forced, there are, as in a battleship, impervious partitions intended to hold the inrush of a wave—in this case of invaders. The galleries are divided up by movable metal-sheeted doors and interior gun chambers, which permit the fort to be defended section by section.

The men of the main line live near the forts, in portable villages of collapsible houses which fold up like concertinas. On the alarm being given everything is taken down and the men plunge underground. The longest time taken to occupy the large forts is sixty minutes.

. . . France is on guard in the Maginot Line; surprise is impossible.

135. THE ROME (LAVAL-MUSSOLINI) AGREEMENTS, JANUARY 7, 1935

In January 1935, before the League of Nations had had time to consider the request of Ethiopia for arbitration in its dispute with Italy over the Ualual (Walwal) incident of December 1934, Pierre Laval of France negotiated the Rome Agreements with Benito Mussolini. The agreements related to the general policies of the two powers in Europe, the expressed desirability of continuing to uphold the independence of Austria, certain African boundary rectifications in Italy's favor, the right of Italy to purchase some stock in the French-controlled Jibuti-Addis Ababa railway, and the rights of Italian residents in Tunisia. Although the French parliament failed to ratify the agreements, Italy was permitted to occupy some of the territories ceded to her in the agreements and to purchase a small block of shares in the railway. Then, in December 1938, Italy renounced the agreements as the opening move in a renewed campaign for the acquisition of Tunisia. Some Fascists also voiced demands—as they had done periodically since the World War—for Corsica, Savoy, and Nice.

a. DECLARATION OF FRIENDSHIP AND COLLABORATION, JANUARY 7, 1935 [44]

The Foreign Minister of the French Republic and the Head of the Italian Government,

Taking into consideration that the conventions of this day's date have assured the settlement of the principal questions which the former accords left pending between the States, and notably all questions relative to the application of Article 13 of the Treaty of London of April 26, 1915;[45]

Taking into consideration that any litigious questions which may arise in future between their Governments will be resolved either by means of diplomatic discussions or by the procedures established by the Covenant of the League of Nations, the Statute of the Permanent Court of International Justice, or the pact of general arbitration;

---

[44] *L'Europe Nouvelle Documentaire, No. 9, Supplement au No. 890 de l'Europe Nouvelle*, Paris, March 2, 1935, p. V.

[45] Under the terms of this treaty Italy agreed to join the Allies in the war against the Central Powers in return for territorial and financial concessions. Article 13 provided that "In the event of France and Great Britian increasing their colonial terrritories in Africa at the expense of Germany, those two Powers agree in principle that Italy may claim some equitable compensation, particularly as regards the settlement in her favour of the questions relative to the frontiers of the Italian colonies of Eritrea, Somaliland and Libya and the neighbouring colonies belonging to France and Great Britain."—*Ed.*

Declare the determination of their Governments to develop the traditional friendship which unites the two nations and to collaborate, in a spirit of mutual confidence, for the maintenance of the general peace.

In view of this collaboration they will proceed together to all consultations which circumstances may make necessary.

Done in duplicate, at Rome, January 7, 1935.

(*Signed*) PIERRE LAVAL.
MUSSOLINI.

b. SPECIAL PROTOCOL REGARDING TUNISIAN QUESTIONS, JANUARY 7, 1935 [46]

The two Governments are in agreement on the following points:

1. The convention contemplated by Article 1 of this day's treaty relating to the regulation of French and Italian interests in Africa[47] will be based on the maintenance until March 28, 1945, of the conventions actually in force.[48] The return to municipal law shall occur progressively from March 28, 1945.

2. In the matter of nationality, this convention will provide that individuals born in Tunisia of Italian parents before March 28, 1945, will be of Italian nationality; individuals born in Tunisia between March 28, 1945, and March 27, 1965, will be of Italian nationality but will be allowed, in the year following the attainment of their majority, to opt in favor of French nationality; they will be allowed, with the assistance of their legal guardians, to make this choice from the age of 16; after March 28, 1965, all individuals born in Tunisia of Italian parents will be of French nationality.

3. Regarding the royal Italian schools in Tunisia, the convention will provide for their maintenance until March 28, 1955, after which date they will become private schools subject to French Tunisian school legislation. . . .

4. Italians who, prior to March 28, 1945, will have been admitted to

---

[46] Transl. from French text in Royal Institute of Foreign Affairs, *Documents on International Affairs, 1935,* 2 vols., Oxford University Press, London, 1936, vol. I, pp. 21-22.

[47] Article 1 of this treaty read: "The position and rights of Italians and Italian colonial subjects in Tunisia and of Tunisians in Italy will be regulated by a special convention the bases of which are fixed in a special protocol of this day's date and which the High Contracting Parties bind themselves to negotiate with the least possible delay, in such manner that it shall enter into force on the same date as the present treaty." The remaining articles of this treaty rectified the boundaries of Libya and Eritrea in Italy's favor and recognized Italian sovereignty over the island of Doumeirah at the entrance to the Red Sea. By another agreement Italy was to be given participation in the French-owned Jibuti-Addis Ababa railway through the right to purchase a block of shares.—*Ed.*

[48] The reference was to the conventions of March 28, 1896, on the rights of Italians in Tunisia.—*Ed.*

the exercise of the liberal professions in Tunisia, notably those of law, medicine, pharmacy, mid-wifery, and architecture, are to be assured that, whatever the régime eventually established through the application of Article 1, they may continue in the exercise of such professions for the duration of their lives.

136. THE DEVELOPMENT OF FRENCH IMPERIAL RELATIONS [49]

In a determined effort to establish closer relations between France and her empire, the French Government arranged the first French Imperial Economic Conference which met in Paris from December 1934 to April 1935. The gathering proposed some interesting measures to further the cause of "a self-sufficing empire."

In December of 1934 . . . the first French Imperial [Economic] Conference met, and sat until April 13, 1935.

The result was the organization of forces to carry, by legislation and propaganda, an intensified fifteen-year program to perfect the mechanism now operating. The structural plan evolved was based on setting up a comprehensive Commission of Production to gather reports on every colonial product exportable to France and on every home article salable in the colonies, developing such production, or in case of need, diverting it to other markets. Second, a Commission of General Economy traced the limits and the methods of financial maintenance of colonial production, and urged business undertakings between metropolitan and colonial production specialists. Third, a Commission of Colonial Development prepared a program of expenditure of 11 milliards 200 million francs on improvements to be completed in fifteen years in two instalments. Fourth, a Financial Commission undertook to solve two essential problems, the administration of the colonial budgets and the organization of credit for the contemplated "Fifteen Year Plan." This Commission accepted the idea of a "Colonial Fund" proposed by the Commission of Development. Fifth, the Commission of Social Providence evolved a sanitary and demographic program calling for an expenditure of one milliard 350 million francs.

---

[49] H. I. Priestley, *France Overseas. A Study of Modern Imperialism,* D. Appleton-Century Company, New York, 1938, pp. 428-435. Reprinted by permission of the author and of the American Historical Association, holders of the copyright.

In the words of Albert Sarraut, the meeting had the purpose of preparing for the unity of *La France Totale;* of fusing into an economic imperial whole all the inequalities, competitions, and variant economies of the motherland and her colonies. No longer content with mere "self-supporting" colonies, it sought to establish an ordered and coherent structure of imperial economy independent as far as might be of the vicissitudes of international commerce. The Conference was to have frequent sessions in a *Maison de la France d'Outre-Mer* to be erected in Paris for the purposes of colonial administration.

The work of the General Commission of Production was divided among four sub-committees, the first of which had investigated the list of goods exportable to the colonies, tried to determine the actual state of this business, and find ways of improving and increasing it. It discovered a need to deflect more French goods into the colonies. . . . The second sub-committee, on mining production, studied means of increasing colonial production of coal, petroleum, copper, and other subsoil products, now imported in large quantities from foreign fields. It urged a general mineralogical survey by a central coördinating body. . . . The third sub-committee, on overseas agricultural production, made an inventory of colonial Mediterranean and tropical crops, studied means of improving their quality and quantity, and their adaptation to home and foreign markets. . . .

This sub-committee suggested (1) adjustment, by agreements or administrative acts, of the various crops produced at home and in the colonies, so as to fit them to the needs and economic possibilities of the empire; (2) permanent liaison between producers and consumers so as to control production, organize propaganda, and harmonize diverse interests; (3) protective tariffs for colonial products . . . ; (4) improvement of methods of production and of display of goods . . . ; (5) cutting costs of production, transport, middlemen's profits, and taxes . . . ; (6) suppression of frauds, and defense of the interests of overseas producers in commercial agreements with foreign countries.

The fourth sub-committee, on agriculture, studied actual methods of production, means of improving them, and a general program of improving conditions of life and work, so as to make the colonists at once better producers and consumers. More European colonists must be found; . . . Production must be turned toward polyculture; better food and better medical attention must be stressed. . . .

The second Commission, that of General Economy, studied means of harmonizing economic processes hitherto either too assimilative or

too autonomous, stopping contradictions of policy, and amplifying the
common effort. . . .

. . . . . .

The Economic Commission also suggested creation of new organs,
and renovation of some of the old ones, for carrying out the plans
suggested. . . .

In its choice of . . . "self-sufficiency" measures the Economic Commission preferred those having the least repercussion and costing the
least. It preferred priorities over quotas, and the latter to customs
duties; the government itself would have to choose which of the recommendations must be acted upon first. . . .

For a permanent program the Commission recommended that the
empire be made independent of certain imports, such as of cotton; . . .

The Commission [of Colonial Development], which studied the
equipment of the overseas possessions and means of financing its extension, gave first importance to public works to promote industrial
and commercial activity. . . . The Commission also gave earnest
consideration to the work of protective sanitation. . . .

The plan adopted . . . was the creation of a Fonds National pour
l'Outillage Public de la France d'Outre-Mer, largely inspired by the
English "Colonial Development Act of 1929." For this purpose, (1)
every territory was subjected to a survey of the equipment already
existing, to discover omissions in each as needed for political or economic purpose. (2) Only those projects were espoused in which
participation of the homeland was justified . . . (3) Provision was
made for a minimum fifteen-year program, and a (4) general synthesis followed the setting up of the particular programs, which in turn
were classified in order of urgency, and then divided into two instalments, the first for a seven-year, and the second for a following eight-
year period. The first called for expenditure of five milliards. (5) To
these two the Commission added a third, to include the railway from
the Mediterranean to the Niger and the Douala-Tchad railway. (6) The
proposals of the Commission covering the Fonds National deal with
only the first of these categories.

. . . . . .

The General Financial Commission was divided into two parts,
Public Credit and Private Credit. Four important reports were presented, one on Public Finances, one on Private Credit on Long and

Medium Term, and a third on Money and Exchange, and Private Short Term Credits; the fourth was on Agricultural Credits. The conclusions reached were that without modifying the autonomous financial colonial régimes set up by the law of 1900, some revision of the financial relations of the colonies with France was necessary, as was suggested by the limited financial capacity of the colonies, and also by the ideal of equity.

. . . . .

The Commission [of Social Providence] worked on problems of medical assistance and medicine, hygiene and social prophylaxis, and labor, demography, and peoplement. It was able to reach practical conclusions on principles of organization and action for each colony, with variations adapted to their diverse milieux and the social condition of the populations.

. . . The whole project of [Social Providence] calls for application of one milliard and 350 million francs, the latter sum for North Africa. . . .

Thus the second greatest colonial Power, on the eve of momentous changes, and in the face of crushing domestic problems, proposed to intensify its effort overseas on the basis of perfecting the self-sufficing empire. The whole program calls for action by parlement (*sic*) as occasion may offer. It is, then, an aspiration rather than a reality, and secondary to current political dangers. . . .

137. THE FRENCH CHARACTER [50]

George Meredith once spoke of the French as "the most mixed of any European nation." Whatever the degree of accuracy of this statement, the French character is certainly intensely interesting. The following description was written by a French economist of Protestant, Alsatian background.

According to the Chinese it is right and proper to steal from the state in order to support an aged parent. At heart the French share this opinion, for according to the dictates of their conscience the family certainly comes before the state, and their obligations to the community

---

[50] A. Siegfried, *France, A Study in Nationality,* Yale University Press, New Haven, 1930, pp. 18-22. Reprinted by permission of the publishers.

seem far off and unreal. The emphasis they place on the home is simply
a form of intersexual egotism, while the molecule which forms the
family provides a social cement of incomparable solidity. In the last
analysis the nation loses nothing for in this family pride, no longer
individualistic, lies a latent altruism. In a critical period, the state
has always had completely at its disposal great reserves which however
had not been accumulated in response to civic virtue.

As the essence of the French nation is social rather than political, an
outsider will often mistake a rowdy parliamentary session for a serious
national crisis. In a way, France resembles China, where life does not
follow any political plan but is attracted to a center of gravity lying far
deeper and therefore more stable. We are the despair of the political
moralists of the best tradition, for we never mean to borrow our pos-
terity from our political institutions. As the penetrating and delightful
Robert de Jouvenel observes, "France is a happy land where the soil
is rich, workmen are ingenious, and wealth widely distributed. Politics
are the concern only of those who have a bent that way but are not
the condition of their life."

We must now consider the conception of wealth which arises from
this. It is peculiar to France, and as the War has not altered it, it affords
an interesting anachronism. In France riches are not regarded as public
property as they are in England but are, on the contrary, entirely a
private matter. A Frenchman does not place his money at the disposal
of the community, and if by chance it falls into the hands of the state
it is quite against his will. At the back of his mind is always the thought
that his savings are not for the benefit of others but for himself or at
any rate his heirs. The French do not give generously to charity. One
does not hear of a magnificent donation to universities or social institutions, as in England or America. The use of wealth with us is less considered as a social duty, according to the feudal tradition, than under
the aspect of the right which we have to keep it and defend it, according
to the *bourgeois* ethics. This idea, hard and clear as one may glean it
from the writings of Balzac, gives the nation a foundation of astonishing solidity. No matter what an ass a man may make of himself
politically, as an individual he will stand firmly on his feet, so that being
perfectly self-possessed he may indulge in any foolishness he likes in
the realm of ideals. We are too inclined to look for the typical Frenchman among the people who frequent the Paris salons, or among the
southerners, so eloquent or astute. Actually we are more likely to find
him in the great central section of the country, amongst the brown-

haired brachycephalic *bougnats* in the province of Auvergne. How thickset and awkward they are, and how indefatigable when it comes to gathering in the shekels!

Could the spirit of citizenship ever hope to flourish in such an atmosphere? Hardly, I think, if we take the Anglo-Saxon meaning, which is that morals and personal interests work closely together toward the same material ends, for obviously this aspect of citizenship is not French. This is perhaps because we have drifted away from Protestant ideals, for as soon as we cross the Swiss frontier it reappears.

We have our own type of citizenship however. Ask a Frenchman for his money to save his country, and perhaps he will not give it to you, in fact at the very moment when he shows himself ready to sacrifice his life. But appeal to him if you are defending, not a political platform of interests, but ideals like liberty, equality, or the Republic, and you will find yourself surrounded by hundreds and thousands of enthusiastic supporters. Anyone who has been in personal contact with our electorate knows also that it can be swayed by sentiment quite as easily as by its own interests. Such a conception of citizenship is limited no doubt, since it comes from a party spirit which expands and rises above itself, but it is real. It gave us the revolutionary citizen of 1792 and the *quarante-huitard,* the *bon républicain* of Gambetta, the militant supporters of the Left and possibly of the Right, the militant syndicalists, and it may be many of our communists. . . .

This list of qualities and faults—it is not easy to say which are qualities and which are faults—is exceedingly perplexing to the foreigner, who, when he attempts to judge us, frequently goes sadly astray. He considers us frivolous, while in reality we are serious methodical workers; he finds us changeable, although we stick to our opinions through thick and thin; he thinks that we are tricky, but high professional conscience is as common here as anywhere; actually we are more *bourgeois* than he is himself, as conservative and well-balanced, but he insists that we are revolutionary; he fears we are decadent, but the race is socially sound and biologically indestructible.

Instinctively one turns to China for a simile: "There is a striking likeness between the Chinese and ourselves," writes Paul Morand, "the same passion for economy by making things last by repairing them endlessly, the same genius for cooking, the same caution and old-world courtesy; an inveterate but passive hatred of foreigners, conservatism tempered by social gales, lack of public spirit, and the same indestructible vitality of old people who have passed the age of illness.

Should not we think that all ancient civilizations have much in common?"

In fact these traits essentially belong to the old world civilization of craftsmen and peasants to which I referred earlier, but they have been molded by social life and disciplined by an administration which has been fully aware of the importance of its task. One quickly notices the qualities which are lacking: the sense of what credit and big business is, a collective banking and industrial tradition as distinct from the individual worth of business directors, in fact, a national economic doctrine and the equivalent of Manchester and the City of London. We have, of course, many centers of industry that are rich in genius and tradition, but geographically they are strictly localized, and any coöperation between our captains of industry is quite recent. France, when all is said, remains a nation of scattered organizations.

138. THE SPIRIT OF MODERN FRANCE [51]

One reason why French politics often seem so hopelessly complicated to foreigners is that they are unaware of the existence of what some observers have aptly called "the two Frances." Helen Hill has analyzed the situation with brevity and clarity.

France prides itself on being very old, on being not only the first born among modern nations but the heir of the ancient world, the transmitter to the west of Mediterranean civilization. That assumption conditions the main lines of France's action. It accounts, on the one hand, for the truly Roman catholicity with which it receives into its empire— empire of ideas, empire of temporal rule—the races and nations of mankind. It accounts, on the other, for its inclination to consider those outside that empire—empire of ideas, empire of temporal rule—as barbarians. The Mediterranean world was surrounded by the darkness of the unknown; the savage energies which thrust out of that darkness had either to be incorporated in the Roman system or repulsed. The French world is the heir of Rome: the recurrent French sense of menace from without springs from a conviction that whatever cannot be incorporated must be repulsed if civilization is to continue. . . .

[51] H. Hill, *The Spirit of Modern France* (*World Affairs Pamphlets,* No. 5), Foreign Policy Association, New York, 1934, pp. 5-17. Reprinted by permission of the publishers.

France's sense of being the destined transmitter of a civilization which once summed up the whole known world, and of having effected that transmission through a long memory of successfully warded attack —attack of ideas, attack of armed force—have clarified in the French mind the meaning of civilization. Civilization is defined primarily in terms of humanism, of the values and abilities by which man differentiates himself from the rest of the universe. The Frenchman is quite clear that natural life is less than civilization. It is only as man gives meaning to life that he removes it from the repetitive cycle of un-evaluated natural process.

This point of view appears very definitely in the French attitude toward nature. Nature in the raw is turbulent, meaningless, menacing. A cleared space, an ordered growth, an intelligible symmetry—and nature may be admitted within the pale of civilization. Until harmonized by man, nature belongs to barbarism. The carefully tended French forests are a present-day example of the "harmonizing" of nature; the formal garden of the eighteenth century was perhaps its most extreme form. When the *Marseillaise* rouses its singers to patriotic emotion, the *patrie* invoked is not the raw land of natural France, nor yet a vague general idea of a country. It is *nos sillons,* the furrows marked by plows, the land used by men. It is not for nothing that, in the course of the Germans' retreat across the north of France, the act of farmyard destruction of which they were most often indignantly accused was the cutting of the carefully pleached fruit trees along the village walls. They had hacked at the roots of a patiently civilized nature.

• • • • • • •

It is impossible to realize how confusing the American state of flux appeared, and still appears to the Frenchman, without taking account of the part played in his life by his concept of his *situation*. The English word "situation" conveys only a minimum of the contents of its French equivalent, because Anglo-Saxon pragmatism lacks the clarity of French logic. The Anglo-Saxon expects continual change, and welcomes the prospect. He consequently looks on any very careful weighing of the factors in an existing situation as more or less a waste of time. To a person who is primarily a doer, an integral plan, a global view, is a matter of somewhat secondary interest. To a person who is primarily a thinker, such a plan and such a view are of paramount importance. A Frenchman would be lost without his concept of his personal *situation*—which is repeated, on an enlarged scale, in his concept of every other *situation* up to and including the *situation* of his country as expressed in the diplomacy of the Quai d'Orsay. It includes a ruthlessly clear estimate of all his assets and liabilities, temporal and spiritual, a strict accounting of ways and means by which the former can be gradually augmented and the latter gradually retired, and a prospectus of a general plan towards whose consummation his every action should be directed. It is his indispensable guide.

The sense of a common *situation* is the cement which has held the French family together while in the rest of the Western world private life has disintegrated into nothingness. Both the intense reality of French private life and the breadth of its economic and social ramifications must be remembered in estimating the position of women in France: though public opinion limits woman's sphere to private life— the democratic Republic has been chary of giving women the vote for fear of strengthening the secular power of the Church—the activities included in that life, and its importance in the life of the nation, make it a far less limited sphere than not-quite-parallel conditions in other countries lead outsiders sometimes to assume. The French are indeed a nation of individuals, but of individuals grouped around family *foyers,* where, in economic and social privacy, a collective *situation* of mutual advantage is carefully worked out.

This private process is the mainspring of French public life. In other countries the usual economic unit is the corporation. In France, it is the family. The Frenchman prefers to handle his own funds. Where he cannot use all of his capital himself he prefers, to quasi-private handling, the full publicity of the state. The political loans of doubtful economic security habitually made by the French government have inspired in other governments an envious wonder that funds should be forthcoming to be thus precariously spent. The fact is that elsewhere the private corporation handles that kind of risk, while in France there is practically nothing between the sock and the state. Rather than open the strong-box of his economic privacy to the administration of other individuals, the Frenchman is willing to find an occasional uncuttable coupon among his government bonds.

. . . . . .

The ancient world made logic the key of the intellect, and of all the heritage received from the past that is the gift the French have most carefully guarded. The French are rational. . . .

Today, no matter to what French institution one turns, the operation of that principle is apparent. Logical clarity is the genius of the French language. The story is told in Geneva of a commission meeting in which the discussion was going more and more at cross purposes. Finally someone suggested that each delegate put the point which he wished to make into French. In the process of doing so, the points of divergence which had remained obscure in the loose constructions of English and German were brought into such sharp relief that they could be intelligently, rather than emotionally, dealt with.

Logical clarity is equally characteristic of all French legal concepts. The contrast between the Anglo-Saxon and the French mentality cannot be more clearly demonstrated than by a comparison of the proposals for world law made by their respective representatives at Geneva since the war. The Anglo-Saxons have acted in accordance with their habit of keeping arrangements flexible, of compromising differences, of making definite commitments only on central issues. The French have proposed measures calculated to codify all possible contingencies in a single legal instrument. To the Anglo-Saxons, safety has appeared to lie in a peace machinery developed as emergencies arise; to the French, safety has appeared to reside in a peace machinery worked out in advance of specific cases. The Geneva Protocol of 1924 epitomizes the French approach.[52]

• • • • •

The French Revolution irrevocably divided the internal politics of France; since that time there have been twin Frances, mortal enemies. The residual bitterness of the American Civil War is still a measurable political factor, yet in America the geographic solidarity of the two sides has been an incomparably softening influence. The French Revolution was a Civil War in which, over large areas, the lines were drawn on a social rather than a geographic basis; when it was over, no softening distance mitigated the bitterness of the ex-combatants. As the completeness of the democratic victory, with the passage of time and the coming of reaction, became less complete, two Frances emerged to confront each other—authoritarian France, founded on the institutional trinity of Monarchy, army and church, in later years particularly the church, and democratic France, founded on the ideological trinity of liberty, equality and fraternity between individual citizens. All through the nineteenth century these two were locked in an uncertain struggle for

---

[52] For the text of this protocol, see Document No. 53.—*Ed.*

supremacy, with now one the victor, now the other. Since the Revolution, each has been four times dominant. The Third Republic has now lasted some sixty years, but its stability has more than once been highly doubtful. Certain recurrent issues have never exhausted their dynamite; a generation ago the Dreyfus case touched off a charge no less powerful than that of the Dred Scott decision; today the Stavisky affair[53] is giving republican institutions a similar shock.

The ceaseless struggle between authoritarian and democratic France is the reality which renders French politics explicable. Three factors go to make it up—the political, the economic, the religious; and closely connected with all of them, since the French system of representation in this respect parallels the American, is that of geographic location.

The centralization of French life in Paris is all too apt to blind the foreigner to the diversity of provincial France, and to the way that diversity affects French politics.

Take the map of France as a study in political geography. Straight across the country, south of the Loire, lies the France of democracy. The French Revolution swept all before it in the south; Toulouse has never ceased to be the capital of radicalism. The Breton peninsula of the west also has changed but little since the bloody days of La Vendée; it is a country of Celtic extremes, where the black conservatism of church and château lowers over the red fringe of the fishing fleet. In the northeast is Alsace-Lorraine and the vulnerable frontier, the scene of past wars, present fortifications, future anxieties, where a strong government is held to be the best one. In the north-center is Paris, which exerts on these very diverse elements the unifying influence of a political capital.

Take the map of France as a study in economic geography. The south and east is the home of the French peasant proprietor, of most of the four and a half million Frenchmen with holdings of less than fifteen acres, of the million more with holdings of less than seventy-five. In the west are the large landed estates, little changed through a century. Eighty-five per cent of the industrial wealth of France lies in the north-north-east; the major part of the iron and steel industry is within a short gunshot of the frontier. In the cities—Paris, Lyons, Marseilles—are entrenched the class-conscious workers. . . .

Take the map of France as a study in religious geography. Thirty-six of the forty million French are adherents of the Roman Catholic

---

[53] See Document No. 120.—*Ed.*

Church, but in studying the political aspect of their religion it is important to discriminate between those who are Catholics by conviction and those who are Catholics by convention. There are some twelve million Catholics by conviction, the intensity of whose religious life causes them to be classified as *catholiques pratiquants*. There are twice as many others whose conventional Catholicism is directly comparable to the conventional Protestantism of the United States. They call the priest for weddings and funerals; they throng the churches for the principal services of Christmas and Easter Day; and when a campaign contains a religious issue, they vote with a passion that exceeds their faith. The famous Frenchman who said *"Je suis athée, mais naturellement, je suis catholique"* adequately summarizes the nature of their conformity. A church so constituted tends to become a temporal institution. It is the nominal Catholics who supply the voting strength of the church as a temporal power, who form the cohorts of authority: the geography of their consolidation, during the years just preceding the Dreyfus case, can be traced by locating the towns which were successive scenes of the ceremony of the Sacré Coeur. . . .

. . . . .

These three maps, superimposed on each other, give a rough picture of sectional politics. They can be further symbolized by portraits of the leaders they have produced. Poincaré, the son of Lorraine, of land where the flag is all-important, whose ministry of 1923 gave him the name of Poincaré-la-Ruhr, whose ministry of 1926 gave him the name of Poincaré-la-France; product of the frontier of the nation, called to office when the political needle pointed to danger abroad. Briand, the Celt from Brittany, who found a practical political value in the dream of a Europe beyond France; the only man who dared to take the rostrum at Geneva for extemporaneous speech, the only important figure of post-war France to have died with his word on his times unsaid; product of the west, called to office during periods of international calm. Tardieu, congenial ally of the big business whose base is close to the frontier, the efficient director, the industrial nationalist who sees eye to eye with the *Comité des Forges;* product of Paris, called to office in periods of dominance of the economic Right, aspirant to a Right dictatorship. Herriot, mayor of Lyons, center of organized labor surrounded by democratic France; product of the southeast, called to office when power passes to the hands of the economic as well as the political Left.

CHAPTER 7

ITALY

139. ITALY IN 1920 [1]

The rise of Fascism in Italy was attributable, in large measure, to the confusion and turbulence that prevailed in the early post-war years. The following description of the economic situation at the end of 1920 was written by two British officials whose testimony may be regarded as reasonably disinterested and reliable.

I. GENERAL ECONOMIC POSITION.

Exhaustion, disorganisation and impoverishment are disasters which the war has brought on almost all the combatant nations, and on Italy in a special degree because she was at the outset less well equipped to bear the strain. But the chief obstacle to her recovery is labour unrest.

A special danger arises from the fact that the labour movement in Italy is in the hands of the Communists. There are indications, however, that the constitutional parties, with whom the remedy lies and who have been hitherto apathetic, are beginning to organise themselves for resistance.

If to the settlement of the labour question can be added the efficient administration of the carefully considered legislative programme which has been framed to meet the emergency, the future will be clear. . . .

. . . . .

IV. INDUSTRY AND PRODUCTION.

General Conditions.

The Banks are inclined to restrict credit and have been doing so for some months past. . . . The Banks are reluctant to accept industrial

---

[1] Great Britain, Department of Overseas Trade, *General Report on the Commercial, Industrial and Economic Situation of Italy, in December, 1920* (By Sir E. C. Cure, Commercial Counsellor, and J. H. Henderson, Commercial Secretary to His Majesty's Embassy in Rome), His Majesty's Stationery Office, London, 1921, pp. 4, 18-22.

securities as collateral for loans and require three or four times the normal amount of cover. The observation however applies in varying degrees to different parts of Italy, and the situation appears to be easier in Sicily and Tuscany than in the North and the Naples district. . . .

The General Confederation of Industry recently instituted an enquiry into national production, and published a report in which it was stated that the metallurgical industry had declined with regard to the period of the war, but exceeded the pre-war level. The output of certain products, such as sheet-iron, was very small. . . . Production in the cotton industry had declined about 20 per cent. from the pre-war level. The enquiry revealed a universal reduction of working days and hours of work, especially noticeable in the metallurgical and engineering trades, due either to unauthorised absences or to waste of time in strikes and meetings. . . .

Labour.

The report of the Confederation confirms the conclusion, patent to every observer, that the labouring question lies at the root of the difficulty. A feature of the present year has been the unending series of strikes, large and small, in all branches of industry and in the public services. It is not easy to estimate the extent to which the strikes are economic and merely part of the general movement for a readjustment of the conditions of living and to what extent they are political, or to say how far the extremist leaders will be able to induce the people to follow them. . . . Almost all are agreed that the country will survive the crisis, but no one can be certain how it is to be accomplished. . . .

One factor in the situation is a want of confidence on the part of the employed, who refuse to work because they believe that they are being exploited, even although many would accept a system under which the rights of capital were recognised, provided that they were satisfied that it was being equitably administered. It is to be hoped that this difficulty will in part be removed by the introduction of the method of *Controllo operaio* put forward in the course of the recent Metal Workers' dispute, and conceded in principle by the final agreement. *Controllo operaio,* strictly speaking, connotes a right of audit and investigation by the workmen rather than a share in the management. Direct negotiations between employers and employed regarding the details of the scheme were commenced, but have broken down on account of a demand by the workmen to extend the meaning of the word, and in particular to make it include a right on their part to have a voice in the engagement and dismissal of employees.

Another factor is the existence in Italy of a strong and well organised body of extreme revolutionaries whose avowed aim is the destruction of the existing social order, who try to thwart every attempt at an equitable solution, and with whom compromise is impossible. How strong they are it is difficult to say, because the force of public opinion, by which alone they can be opposed, has so far shown itself weak and apathetic. There are, however, signs of reaction, of which the most noteworthy is the result of the recent local government elections. . . . the Socialist party . . . have not done so well as in the parliamentary elections of 1919. . . . Further, there are symptoms of disunion within the party itself, and of a growing disinclination to allow its policy to be dictated by extremists who take their orders from Moscow.

Government Policy in Industrial Disputes.

Signor Giolitti's [the premier's] policy has been to refrain from direct interference. One result of this has been the perpetration of a number of illegal acts, such as the occupation of the factories in the Metal Workers' dispute, and the growth of a spirit of lawlessness which has permeated certain classes of the community. This policy has been adversely criticised by some, but Signor Giolitti himself has defended it on the ground that it was the only alternative to more serious disturbance, and that, at a moment when established institutions are on their trial, a certain licence must be allowed in order that the parties to the conflict may measure their strength and decide their differences on equal terms. Whatever view is taken, however, one result has been to create an impression that private property cannot count on the protection of the law. . . .

The Land Question.

Agriculture, Italy's greatest industry, . . . has not escaped its share of labour trouble, a fact which in part explains why imported agricultural produce is at present the heaviest item in national expenditure.

The land problem differs in the various regions. In Sicily and the South of Italy the movement has been for the resumption by the community of "common land" appropriated in the past, for the division of the large estates and large farms, and for the compulsory occupation of uncultivated land. The Government, unable to oppose the movement, and to a certain degree sympathising with it, has issued a series of decrees regularising the procedure for settling small holders on the land, on proof that this will result in an increase of production. . . .

* * * * *

So far the results of the movement, considered by themselves and apart from the methods by which they have been obtained, do not perhaps go further than a reasonable readjustment of the relations between the proprietor and the tiller of the soil, and to the extent to which they tend to promote small holdings, they encourage the rise of a class whose interests are essentially conservative and anti-communistic.

140. SOME EARLY FASCIST SPEECHES OF MUSSOLINI [2]

Considerable interest attaches to the things that Benito Mussolini said when he first organized the fasci di combattimento *at Milan in 1919. Herewith are reproduced extracts from his speech delivered at the first Fascist meeting.*

SPEECH DELIVERED AT MILAN, 23RD MARCH 1919, AT THE
FIRST FASCISTA MEETING.

* * * * *

First of all, a few words about the proceedings. Without too much formality or pedantry, I will read you three declarations which seem to me worthy of being discussed and voted upon. Then in the afternoon we will resume the discussion of the declaration of our programme. I tell you at once that we cannot go into detail. Wishing to act, we must take salient facts as they exist.

The first declaration is as follows:

The Meeting of 23rd March first salutes with reverence and remembrance the sons of Italy who have fallen for the cause of the greatness of the country and the liberty of the world, the maimed and disabled, and all the fighters and ex-prisoners who fulfilled their duty, and declares itself

---

[2] *Mussolini as Revealed in His Political Speeches (November 1914-August 1923).* *Selected, Translated and Edited by Barone Bernardo Quaranta di San Severino,* J. M. Dent and Sons, Ltd., London and Toronto, 1923, pp. 87-90, 92-102. Reprinted by permission of E. P. Dutton & Co., Inc., publishers in the United States.

ready to uphold strongly the vindication of rights, both material and moral, advocated by the "Association of Fighters."

. . . . .

The National Vindications.   Second declaration:

The Meeting of the 23rd March declares that it will oppose Imperialism in other peoples which would be prejudicial to Italy, and any eventual Imperialism in Italy which would be prejudicial to other nations, and accepts the fundamental principle of the League of Nations, which presupposes the geographical integrity of every nation. This, as far as Italy is concerned, must be realised on the Alps and the Adriatic with the annexation of Fiume and Dalmatia.

We have forty million inhabitants and an area of 287,000 square kilometres, divided by the Apennines, which reduce still further the availability of the land capable of cultivation. In ten or twenty years' time we shall be sixty millions, and we have a bare million and a half square kilometres of land in the way of colonies, which to a great extent is barren, and to which we certainly can never send the surplus of our people. . . .

In view of the Elections.   Third declaration:

The Meeting of the 23rd March pledges the Fascisti to prevent by every means in their power the candidature of neutralists of any party.

. . . . .

SPEECH DELIVERED AT MILAN, 22ND JULY 1919,
AT THE LICEO BECCARIA.

I think that it will depend upon the sincerity and loyalty with which we join in this meeting whether it will become an historical event, or a little fact of everyday life destined to pass without leaving a trace.

. . . . .

What are we looking for, . . . we who are together represented in the Committee of Intesa e Azione (Understanding and Action) which was formed at the time of the movement against the high cost of living? We are looking for the least common denominator for this understanding and action. Shall we find it? Yes! We come from different schools; we have different temperaments, and temperaments divide men more widely than ideas; we belong to an individualist people; but all this does not prevent something else bringing us together and binding us both in these present contingencies and in that which has to do with the action of tomorrow.

The Basis of Unity. There can be a thousand shades of ideas among us, but upon one important point we are all agreed, and that is in regarding the Socialist manifestation as a bluff, a comedy, a speculation and blackmail. Also we are all agreed in making a differentiation between the Socialist Party and the mass of the workmen. The Socialist Party has usurped up to yesterday the name of being a pure revolutionary organisation, of being the protector and the exclusive, genuine representation of the working masses. That is all nonsense and must be cleared up. . . .

* * * * *

The Italian Situation. We agree upon a third point, in connection with existing circumstances, that is in maintaining that our national situation is critical, though far from being desperate. Briefly, it is this. From the 1st July we have been defaulting debtors of England. Since the 31st July other financial arrangements with the United States must be faced. To save the situation a loan of one milliard dollars (seven to eight milliard lire) must be arranged. The railways have a coal supply for only fifteen more days. There are enough provisions for another twenty days, that is to say until the end of the month. . . .

* * * * *

Reactionaries and vice versa. For me revolution is not an attack of St. Vitus' dance or an unexpected fit of epilepsy. It must have force, aims, and above all, method. In 1913, when the Socialist Party was already rotten, it was I who put into circulation the words which made the pulses of the big men of Italian Socialism beat: "This proletariat is in need of a bath of blood," I said. It has had it, and it lasted for three years. "This proletariat is in need of a day of history." And it has had a thousand.

It was necessary then to shake up the masses, because they had fallen into a state of weakness and insensibility. To-day this situation exists no longer. . . .

* * * * *

The Compass. At the same time, as regards reaction and revolution,

I have a compass in my pocket which guides me. All that which tends towards making the Italian people great finds me favourable, and—*vice versa*—all that which tends towards lowering, brutalising and impoverishing them finds me opposed.

Now Socialism comes in the second category. . . .

. . . . .

The Revision of the Treaty of Versailles. The Peace of Versailles is not a sufficient motive for the courted collaboration [with Italian Socialists]. Things must be made clear. The Socialists talk of annulling the peace; we simply wish to revise it. We do not condemn wholesale a peace which a German, and not one of the most insignificant, Edward Bernstein,[3] has called nine parts just. The revision of peace must not mean condemnation of the war. . . .

. . . . .

. . . Rather than seek or beg for useless co-operation, let us outline a programme of our own understanding and action. . . . I think that it is possible to create a strong economic organisation in Italy based upon these principles:

1. Absolute independence from all parties, groups and sets.
2. Federation and autonomy.
3. Abolition, as far as possible, of all paid officials.
4. No steps to be taken without having consulted regularly by means of a referendum, the masses interested.

The means of obtaining this end may be altered according to time and place. The organisation will promote at times co-operation, and at times war between the classes and the expropriation of class. It will not always be for co-operation, but neither will it always be in favour of class preservation; and when it expropriates, it will not be to make all poor, but to make all rich. . . .

. . . . . .

The revolution which we desired and obtained in 1915 will be ours again by the victorious peace in its conclusive phase, and it will be called, "Well-being," "Liberty" and, above all, "Italy." (Loud applause.)

---

[3] Bernstein was a prominent figure in the "Revisionist" movement toward the Right in the German Social Democratic Party.—*Ed.*

141. BENITO MUSSOLINI ON FASCISM [4]

Benito Mussolini himself has spoken and written much on Fascism as a doctrine, the following being one of his most forceful expositions.

In the Fascist conception of history, man is man only by virtue of the spiritual process to which he contributes as a member of the family, the social group, the nation, and in function of history to which all nations bring their contribution. Hence the great value of tradition in records, in language, in customs, in the rules of social life. Outside history man is a nonentity. Fascism is therefore opposed to all individualistic abstractions based on eighteenth century materialism; and it is opposed to all Jacobinistic utopias and innovations. It does not believe in the possibility of "happiness" on earth as conceived by the economistic literature of the XVIIIth century, and it therefore rejects the teleological notion that at some future time the human family will secure a final settlement of all its difficulties. This notion runs counter to experience which teaches that life is in continual flux and in process of evolution. In politics Fascism aims at realism; in practice it desires to deal only with those problems which are the spontaneous product of historic conditions and which find or suggest their own solutions. . . .

Anti-individualistic, the Fascist conception of life stresses the importance of the State and accepts the individual only in so far as his interests coincide with those of the State, which stands for the conscience and the universal will of man as a historic entity. It is opposed to classical liberalism which arose as a reaction to absolutism and exhausted its historical function when the State became the expression of the conscience and will of the people. Liberalism denied the State in the name of the individual; Fascism reasserts the rights of the State as expressing the real essence of the individual. . . . The Fascist conception of the State is all-embracing; outside of it no human or spiritual values can exist, much less have value. Thus understood, Fascism is totalitarian, and the Fascist State—a synthesis and a unit inclusive of all values—interprets, develops, and potentiates the whole life of a people.

. . . . .

. . . It is not the nation which generates the State; that is an anti-

---

[4] B. Mussolini, *The Doctrine of Fascism*, Vallecchi, Florence, 1936, pp. 11-45. The Italian Library of Information in New York was very helpful in making readily available some of the materials in this chapter.

quated naturalistic concept which afforded a basis for XIXth century publicity in favour of national governments. Rather is it the State which creates the nation, conferring volition and therefore real life on a people made aware of their moral unity.

. . . . .

The Fascist State, as a higher and more powerful expression of personality, is a force, but a spiritual one. It sums up all the manifestations of the moral and intellectual life of man. Its functions cannot therefore be limited to those of enforcing order and keeping the peace, as the liberal doctrine had it. It is no mere mechanical device for defining the sphere within which the individual may duly exercise his supposed rights. The Fascist State is an inwardly accepted standard and rule of conduct, a discipline of the whole person; it permeates the will no less than the intellect. It stands for a principle which becomes the central motive of man as a member of civilised society, sinking deep down into his personality; it dwells in the heart of the man of action and of the thinker, of the artist and of the man of science: soul of the soul.

. . . . .

Fascism is now clearly defined not only as a régime but as a doctrine. This means that Fascism, exercising its critical faculties on itself and on others, has studied from its own special standpoint and judged by its own standards all the problems affecting the material and intellectual interest now causing such grave anxiety to the nations of the world, and is ready to deal with them by its own policies.

First of all, as regards the future development of mankind,—and quite apart from all present political considerations—Fascism does not, generally speaking, believe in the possibility or utility of perpetual peace. It therefore discards pacifism as a cloak for cowardly supine renunciation in contra-distinction to self-sacrifice. War alone keys up all human energies to their maximum tension and sets [the] seal of nobility on those peoples who have the courage to face it. All other tests are substitutes which never place a man face to face with himself before the alternative of life or death. Therefore all doctrines which postulate peace at all costs are incompatible with Fascism. Equally foreign to the spirit of Fascism, even if accepted as useful in meeting special political situations—are all internationalistic or League superstructures which, as history shows, crumble to the ground whenever the heart of nations is deeply stirred by sentimental, idealistic or practical considerations. . . .

The demographic policy of the régime is the consequence of these premises. The Fascist loves his neighbour, but the word "neighbour" does not stand for some vague and unseizable conception. Love of one's neighbour does not exclude necessary educational severity; still less does it exclude differentiation and rank. Fascism will have nothing to do with universal embraces; as a member of the community of nations, it looks other peoples straight in the eyes; it is vigilant and on its guard; it follows others in all their manifestations and notes any changes in their interests; and it does not allow itself to be deceived by mutable and fallacious appearances.

Such a conception of life makes Fascism the resolute negation of the doctrine underlying so-called scientific and Marxian socialism, the doctrine of historic materialism which would explain the history of mankind in terms of the class struggle and by changes in the processes and instruments of production, to the exclusion of all else.

That the vicissitudes of economic life—discoveries of raw materials, new technical processes, scientific inventions—have their importance, no one denies; but that they suffice to explain human history is absurd. Fascism believes now and always in sanctity and heroism, that is to say in acts in which no economic motive—remote or immediate—is at work. Having denied historic materialism, which sees in men mere puppets on the surface of history, appearing and disappearing on the crest of the waves while in the depths the real directing forces move and work, Fascism also denies the immutable and irreparable character of the class struggle which is the natural outcome of this economic conception of history; above all it denies that the class struggle is the preponderating agent in social transformations. Having thus struck a blow at socialism in the two main points of its doctrine all that remains of it is the sentimental aspiration—old as humanity itself—toward social relations in which the sufferings and sorrows of the humbler folk will be alleviated. But here again Fascism rejects the economic interpretation of felicity as something to be secured socialistically, almost automatically, at a given stage of economic evolution when all will be assured a maximum of material comfort. Fascism denies the materialistic conception of happiness as a possibility, and abandons it to the economists of the mid-eighteenth century. This means that Fascism denies the equation: wellbeing = happiness, which sees in men mere animals. . . .

After socialism, Fascism aims its guns at the whole block of democratic ideologies, and rejects both their premises and their practical applications and implements. Fascism denies that numbers, as such, can be the determining factors in human society; it denies the right of numbers to govern by means of periodical consultations; it asserts the irremediable and fertile and beneficent inequality of men who cannot be levelled by any such mechanical and extrinsic device as universal suffrage. Democratic régimes may be described as those under which the people are, from time to time, deluded into the belief that they exercise sovereignty, while all the time real sovereignty resides in and is exercised by other and sometimes irresponsible and secret forces. . . .

. . . . .

A party holding "totalitarian" rule over a nation, is a new departure in history. There are no points of reference nor of comparison. From beneath the ruins of liberal, socialist, and democratic doctrines, Fascism extracts those elements which are still vital. It preserves what may be described as "the acquired facts" of history; it rejects all else. That is to say, it rejects the idea of a doctrine suited to all times and to all people. Granted that the XIXth century was the century of socialism, liberalism, democracy, this does not mean that the XXth century must also be the century of socialism, liberalism, democracy. Political doctrines pass; nations remain. We are free to believe that this is the century of authority, a century tending to the "right," a Fascist century. If the XIXth century was the century of the individual (liberalism implies individualism) we are free to believe that this is the "collective" century, and therefore the century of the State. . . .

. . . . .

The Fascist State organises the nation but it leaves the individual adequate elbow room. It has curtailed useless or harmful liberties while preserving those which are essential. In such matters the individual cannot be the judge, but the State only.

The Fascist State is not indifferent to religious phenomena in general nor does it maintain an attitude of indifference to Roman Catholicism, the special, positive religion of Italians. The State possesses a moral code rather than theology. . . . Fascism respects the God of ascetics, saints, and heroes, and it also respects God as conceived by the ingenuous and primitive heart of the people, the God to whom their prayers are raised.

The Fascist State expresses the will to exercise power and to command. Here the Roman tradition is embodied in a conception of strength. Imperial power, as understood by the Fascist doctrine, is not only territorial, or military, or commercial; it is also spiritual and ethical. An imperial nation, that is to say a nation which directly or indirectly is a leader of others, can exist without the need of conquering a single square mile of territory. Fascism sees in the imperialistic spirit—i.e. in the tendency of nations to expand—a manifestation of their vitality. In the opposite tendency, which would limit their interests to the fatherland, it sees a symptom of decadence. People who rise or revive are imperialistic; renunciation is characteristic of dying peoples. The Fascist doctrine is that best suited to the tendencies and feelings of a people which, like the Italian, after lying fallow during centuries of foreign servitude, is now reasserting itself in the world.

142. STATUTE OF THE NATIONAL FASCIST PARTY, NOVEMBER 12, 1932 *(Extracts)* [5]

The National Fascist Party was officially constituted in Rome on November 6, 1921. The latest revision of its statute occurred in 1932. The hierarchical organization of the party was devised by Mussolini.

NATURE OF THE PARTY

ARTICLE 1.

The National Fascist Party is a civil militia, under the orders of the DUCE, in the service of the Fascist State.

ARTICLE 2.

The National Fascist Party is composed of *Fasci di Combattimento,* which are grouped, in each province, into a Federation of *Fasci di Combattimento.*

The Secretary of a Federation of *Fasci di Combattimento,* whenever he considers it necessary, is authorized to organise the *Fasci di Combattimento* into regional groups or sub-sections, each directed by a Leader and by a Board of five members, to one of whom will be entrusted administrative functions.

A *Fascio di Combattimento* cannot be formed or dissolved without the authority of the Secretary of the National Fascist Party.

---

[5] B. Mussolini, *Fascism, Doctrine and Institutions,* Ardita, Rome, 1935, pp. 198-217.

In every provincial capital shall be established a University Fascist Group.

Attached to each *Fascio di Combattimento* shall be formed a *Fascio Giovanile di Combattimento* and a women's Fascio. The latter shall in its turn establish a group of girl Fascists.

Attached to the Federation of *Fasci di Combattimento* shall be established the provincial associations of Schools, of Public Employment, of Railways, of Posts and Telegraphs, of Employees in State Industrial Concerns, and the Section of District Doctors belonging to the Association of Public Employment.

ARTICLE 3.

The Black Shirt is the Fascist uniform and must be worn only on prescribed occasions.

The Fascist must wear the badge of the National Fascist Party.

. . . . .

ORGANS AND HIERARCHY

ARTICLE 5.

The National Fascist Party through its collegiate organs and its officers carries out its activities under the guidance of the DUCE and in accordance with the directions traced by the Grand Council.

The hierarchy are:

1) The Secretary of the National Fascist Party.

2) The members of the National Directorate of the National Fascist Party—the President of the Association of the Families of the Fascist Fallen and of Fascists Wounded or Disabled for the National Cause.

3) The Federal Secretary and the Federal Commander of the *Fasci Giovanili di Combattimento*—the Vice-Secretary of the University Fascist Groups.

4) The members of the Federal Directorates—the Secretaries of the University Fascist Groups—the Seconds-in-Command of the *Fasci Giovanili di Combattimento*—the Regional Inspectors—the Administrators of the Association of the Families of the Fascist Fallen and of Fascists Wounded and Disabled for the National Cause—the provincial Administrators of the Women's *Fasci*.

5) The Secretaries of the *Fasci di Combattimento*—the members of the Directorate of the *Fasci di Combattimento*—the members of the

Directorate of the University Fascist Groups—the Commanders of the
Fasci Giovanili di Combattimento—the Administrators of the Sub-
Sections—the Administrators of the Fascist University Nucleus—the
Secretaries of the Women's *Fasci.*

The Collegiate organs are:

1) The National Directorate of the National Fascist Party.

2) The National Council of the National Fascist Party.

3) The Directorate of the Federations of *Fasci di Combattimento*
(Federal Directorate).

4) The Directorate of the *Fasci di Combattimento.*

5) The Board of the Regional Groups.

6) The Directorate of the University Fascist Groups.

7) The Board of the Sub-Sections.

A Fascist who was present at the foundation of the *Fasci di Combattimento* (Piazza San Sepolcro, Milan, 23rd March 1919) shall have
precedence over other Fascists of his category.

ARTICLE 6.

Positions of authority, commands or other offices must be entrusted
to Black Shirts who have fought for or assisted the Revolution or to
Fascists who have risen from the Junior Organisations.

THE CENTRE

ARTICLE 7.

The National Directorate of the National Fascist Party, presided over
by the Secretary of the National Fascist Party, consists of two Vice-
Secretaries, an Administrative Secretary and six members.

The DUCE proposes to the King the nomination and dismissal of
the Secretary of the National Fascist Party. The Secretary of the National Fascist Party is a member of the Fascist Grand Council and is
also its Secretary; he can be summoned to take part in the sessions of
the Council of Ministers; he is a member of the Supreme Council of
Defence, of the Superior Council of National Education, of the Administrative Council of the National Fascist Institute of Culture, of the
National Council of Corporations and of the Central Corporative Committee; he is the President of the National Union of Italian Reserve
Officers, of the Administrative Commission of National Employment
Bureaux, Vice-President of the Central Board of University Activities,

Secretary of the University Fascist Groups and Commander of the
Fasci Giovanili di Combattimento.

The Secretary of the National Fascist Party, basing himself on the
general instructions of the Grand Council of Fascism (set up by the
law of December 9, 1928—VII, No. 2693) the supreme body issued
from the Revolution, which co-ordinates and integrates all the activities
of the régime, imparts instructions for the work to be carried out by
the dependent organisations, reserving to himself the fullest control. . . .

. . . . .

ARTICLE 9.

The National Council is composed of the Federal Secretaries and
is presided over by the Secretary of the National Fascist Party who
summons it with the previous authorisation of the DUCE.

It examines the activity of the National Fascist Party, and receives
general instructions for execution.

ARTICLE 10.

The DUCE summons to the General Meeting (*Gran Rapporto*) the
members of the Grand Council of Fascism, the National Directorate
of the National Fascist Party, the National Council of the National
Fascist Party and the Federal Directors.

IN THE PROVINCES

ARTICLE 11.

Federal Secretaries are appointed and removed by the DUCE, on the
proposal of the Secretary of the National Fascist Party.

They carry out the orders of the Secretary of the National Fascist
Party.

They promote and control the activities of the *Fasci di Combattimento*
of the province and exercise a political control over all the institutions
and organisations of the régime.

They keep in touch with Senators and Deputies and with the Com-
mandant of the Militia.

They preside over the Intersyndical Committee and the Joint Administrative Commission of the Provincial Employment Bureaux.

They are members of the Board of University Activities in cities
where Universities or Higher Educational Institutes are established.

They preside over the Relief Organisations and the provincial *Dopolavoro*.

They promote and regulate sport in the subordinate organisations.

They convene the Federal Directorate at least once a month, and at least once a year summon the Secretaries of the *Fasci di Combattimento* and with them examine and illustrate the problems confronting the *Fasci di Combattimento* and the political, moral and economic problems of the province. . . .

· · · · ·

THE FASCIST LEVY

ARTICLE 14.

The Fascist Levy takes place on April 21st, Labour Day.

The Fascist Levy consists in the promotion of Balilla to the ranks of the *Avanguardisti* and of *Avanguardisti* to the ranks of the Young Fascists, as well as of the latter to the National Fascist Party and the Fascist Militia.

The arrangements for the Levy are agreed upon by the Secretary of the National Fascist Party, the Under-Secretary of State for the Education and Physical Training of the Young, the President of the National Balilla Organisation and the Chief of Staff of the Fascist Militia.

The Young Fascists who enter the National Fascist Party take the oath before the Political Secretary of the *Fasci di Combattimento* in the following form:

"In the name of God and of Italy I swear to carry out without discussion the orders of the Duce and to serve the Cause of the Fascist Revolution with all my might and if necessary with my life."

DISCIPLINE

ARTICLE 15.

In the National Directorate of the National Fascist Party is instituted the Court of Discipline, presided over by a Vice-Secretary and composed of two full members, two supplementary members chosen from the National Directorate and a Secretary, appointed from time to time by the Secretary of the National Fascist Party.

Only such cases will be deferred to the Court as the Secretary of the National Fascist Party considers call for special examination.

The findings of the Court of Discipline will be submitted to the Secretary of the National Fascist Party for his decisions.

ARTICLE 16.

In every Federation of *Fasci di Combattimento* is instituted a Federal Disciplinary Commission presided over by the Federal Vice-Secretary and composed of five full members and two supplementary members and a secretary drawn from outside the Federal Directorate.

These appointments are made by the Federal Secretary. . . .

. . . . .

ADMINISTRATION

ARTICLE 26.

The Administrative Secretary of the National Fascist Party administers the property of the National Fascist Party and is responsible therefor. . . .

The Administrative Secretary of the National Fascist Party is in charge of the employment and supervision of personnel. . . .

. . . . .

MEMBERSHIP CARDS

ARTICLE 30.

The membership card of the National Fascist Party is issued gratuitously by the Political Secretary of the *Fasci di Combattimento* to:

  a) Disabled War Veterans;
  b) Disabled Fascists;
  c) Families of Fallen Fascists;
  d) Members who are fathers of families
       of seven or more children.

ARTICLE 31.

The Fascist Year begins on October 29th.[6]

-----

[6] On October 29, 1922, King Victor Emmanuel III asked Mussolini to form a cabinet. —*Ed.*

உ உ உ

143. LAWS ON THE GRAND COUNCIL OF FASCISM *(Extracts)* [7]

At the apex of the hierarchical Fascist party organization was placed the Fascist Grand Council, itself headed by Mussolini as Il Duce—the Leader. Its position and powers were defined by law.

Article 1.

The Grand Council of Fascism is the supreme organ which co-ordinates and integrates all the activities of the Régime issued from the Revolution of October 1922. The Council has deliberative functions in cases established by law, but may give its advice upon all other political, economic and social questions of national interest, when called upon to do so by the Head of the Government.

Article 2.

The Head of the Government . . . is by right President of the Grand Council of Fascism. The meetings of the Grand Council of Fascism are called by the Head of the Government whenever he may deem it necessary.

Article 3.

The General Secretary of the National Fascist Party is Secretary of the Grand Council. . . .

Article 4.

Members of the Grand Council of Fascism for an indefinite period [life] are the quadrumvirate of the March on Rome. [8]

Article 5.

Ex officio members of the Grand Council of Fascism for the whole duration of office are:

1. The President of the Senate and the President of the Chamber of Deputies.

2. The Ministers Secretaries of State for Foreign Affairs, Interior,

---

[7] Royal Decree-Law of December 9, 1928 (No. 2693), as modified by that of December 14, 1929 (No. 2099), in B. Mussolini, *Fascism, Doctrine and Institutions,* Ardita, Rome, 1935, pp. 194-197; original texts in *Gazzetta Ufficiale del Regno d'Italia,* Ministry of Grace and Justice, Rome, December 11, 1928, No. 287, and December 16, 1929, No. 292, respectively.

[8] This quadrumvirate comprised Italo Balbo, Michele Bianchi, Emilio de Bono, and Count C. M. de Vecchi di Val Cismon.—*Ed.*

Justice, Finance, National Education, Agriculture and Forestry, and Corporations.

3. The President of the Royal Academy of Italy.

4. The Secretary and the two Vice-Secretaries of the National Fascist Party.

5. The Commandant-General of the Voluntary Militia for National Security.

6. The President of the Special Tribunal for the Defence of the State.

7. The Presidents of the National Fascist Confederations and of the National Confederations of the Fascist Syndicates of Industry and Agriculture.

ARTICLE 6.

The appointment of the members of the Grand Council of Fascism is made by Royal Decree, upon the proposal of the Head of the Government. The same procedure is used to revoke the members.

. . . . .

ARTICLE 10.

The members of the Grand Council receive no remuneration. The State incurs no expense for the Grand Council. The meetings of the Grand Council are secret. Its mode of procedure is fixed by internal regulations which the Grand Council approves.

ARTICLE 11.

The Grand Council deliberates upon:

(a) the list of deputies designated as per . . . the . . . Electoral Law;[9]

(b) the statutes, resolutions and political activity of the National Fascist Party;

(c) the appointment and dismissal of the Secretary, Vice-Secretaries, Administrative Secretary and other members of the Directorate of the Fascist Party.

ARTICLE 12.

The advice of the Grand Council shall be requested upon all questions bearing upon the Constitution, which are the following:

(a) the succession to the Throne, attributions and prerogatives of the Crown;

---

[9] For the text of this electoral law, see Document No. 147.—*Ed.*

(*b*) the composition and functions of the Grand Council, the Senate and the Chamber of Deputies;

(*c*) the attributions and prerogatives of the Head of the Government . . . ;

(*d*) the right of the Executive to issue rules having the force of law;

(*e*) the syndical and corporate organisation;

(*f*) relations between the State and the Holy See;

(*g*) international treaties, when they entail modifications of the territory of the State and the Colonies. . . .

ARTICLE 13.

The Grand Council, on the proposal of the Head of the Government, draws up and keeps posted up to date a list of names to be submitted to the Crown, in case of vacancy for the position of Head of the Government.

. . . . .

144. THE SOCIALIST DEPUTY MATTEOTTI ON THE FASCISTS, 1924 [10]

The chief opposition group to the Fascists in parliament after the elections of April 1924 was the Socialist Party, one of whose leaders was an able young deputy named Giacomo Matteotti. In an anonymously published book he enumerated a series of Fascist outrages and threatened to expose as corrupt several of Mussolini's intimates. Soon thereafter he disappeared, his body being found in a wood a few weeks later. Not long after Matteotti's death, his book was published in Great Britain under the name of The Fascisti Exposed; *it is from this volume that the excerpts below are quoted.*

The Fascist Government justifies its armed conquest of political power, its use of violence and the risk it incurred of igniting civil war, by the plea of the urgent necessity of restoring the authority of law and the State, and of rescuing the country from economic and financial conditions approaching utter ruin.

---

[10] G. Matteotti, *The Fascisti Exposed; A Year of Fascist Domination,* Independent Labour Party Publication Department, London, 1924, pp. 1, 84-85. Reprinted by permission of the publishers.

The statistical and historical data and documents compiled in this book are a demonstration of the very contrary of this. They show that never as in this last year, during which Fascism has been in power, has the law been so thrust aside in favour of arbitrary action, the State so subjugated by a faction, or the nation so split up into two classes, a dominating and a subject class. The country's economic and financial condition has, on the whole, continued to show the improvement and the slow recovery from the devastation of the war, which had already begun in the preceding years; but had begun thanks to the energies of the people, not the excesses and extravagances of Fascist domination. As to this latter, one thing is demonstrably true: that the profits of the speculators and the capitalists have increased in proportion as the reward of labour and the small resources of the middle classes have diminished, while these two latter classes have lost all freedom and all that is of worth in citizenship.

·　·　·　·　·

PART IV.
—AND THE CHRONICLE OF DEEDS
May, 1923 [11]

Genoa.—At Marassi-Guezzi Fascists strike workmen found in public bars, fire revolver and rifle shots, and set fire to the Friendly Society's premises.

Leonessa.—Fascists command the Marshal of Carabineers to arrest four workers who had sung the "Red Flag."

Rome.—The placarding of manifestoes and of announcements of meetings is prohibited. Workers ordered to resume work on pain of dismissal.

·　·　·　·　·

Arzignano (Vicenza).—The manufacturer Pelizzari ordered by Fascists to dismiss immediately twelve workers who had celebrated May-day.

·　·　·　·　·

Jesi.—The local silk works ordered to close down because the work-women had celebrated May-day.

---

[11] The Report gives the chronicle of thirteen months' atrocities. The record of two typical months, May and November of last year (1923), is given in the following pages. —*Trans.*

Milan.—Chamber of Labour entered during the night and an attempt made to set it on fire.

. . . . .

Naples.—The Chamber of Labour laid waste.

. . . . .

Parma.—The Deputy Picelli insulted and threatened; the worker Maluberto Enrico, a war hero, decorated with one bronze and two silver medals, beaten; Campanini Pietro, a war invalid, seriously wounded.

. . . . .

145. THE LAW OF APRIL 3, 1926, ON COLLECTIVE LABOR RELATIONS *(Extracts)* [12]

The doctrine of syndicalism, one form of which advocated the substitution of government by economic groups for political government, had attracted numerous Italian workers in the pre-war days. After the war, many of these syndicalists, who firmly believed in the right of private property, united with the Fascist groups in fighting the radical workers and peasants. Under the leadership of Edmondo Rossoni they now formed Fascist syndicates and advocated a change in the parliamentary system so as to give representation to organized economic interests rather than to geographic-political units. When, by 1926, these syndicates had attracted a membership of 2,400,000, Premier Mussolini determined to control them. The instrumentality for the exercise of such control was found in a law of April 3, 1926, on collective labor relations. This act abolished collective bargaining and forbade strikes and lock-outs, substituting for them collective labor contracts enforced by special labor courts.

CHAPTER I

ON THE LEGAL RECOGNITION OF SYNDICATES AND ON COLLECTIVE LABOUR CONTRACTS

ARTICLE 1.

Associations of employers and of workers, both intellectual and manual, may obtain legal recognition when they can prove that they comply with the following requirements:

---

[12] Law of April 3, 1926 (No. 563), in B. Mussolini, *Fascism, Doctrine and Institutions,* Ardita, Rome, 1935, pp. 75-90; original text in *Gazzetta Ufficiale del Regno d'Italia,* Ministry of Grace and Justice, Rome, April 14, 1926, No. 87.

1) in the case of associations of employers, that the employers who have voluntarily registered as members employ not less than one-tenth of the workers in the service of the concerns of the kind for which the association has been formed, existing in the district in which it operates; and in the case of associations of workers that the workers who have voluntarily registered as members number not less than one-tenth of those of the class for which the association has been formed, existing in the district in which it operates;

2) that besides the protection of the economic and moral interests of its members the association proposes to promote, and does actually promote, the assistance, instruction, and moral and patriotic education of its members;

3) that the director of the association affords guarantees of ability, morality, and sound national loyalty.

Article 2.

When the conditions prescribed in the previous article exist, legal recognition can be given to associations of persons independently exercising an art, trade or profession.

Existing and legally recognised orders, colleges and associations of persons exercising the liberal professions will continue to be regulated by existing laws and regulations. Nevertheless, such laws and regulations may be amended, with a view to coordinating them with the provisions of this Act, by Royal Decree, after consultation with the Council of Ministers.

The statutes of incorporated associations of artists and persons exercising the liberal professions, existing prior to the promulgation of this Act, shall also be revised to bring them into harmony herewith.

Article 3.

The associations referred to in the preceding article consist of employers only or of workers only.

Associations of employers and of workers can be brought together by means of central liaison organs having superior officers common to both associations, but the separate representation of employers and of workers must be provided for, and when such associations include several classes of workers there must be separate representation for each of them.

. . . . .

ARTICLE 5.

The legally recognised associations are incorporated bodies legally representing the whole body of employers, workers, employees, artists, and professional men of the class for which they are formed, whether they be registered members thereof or not, within the territorial circumscription in which they operate.

The legally recognised associations are entitled to levy annual dues on all employers, workers, employees, artists, and professional men whom they represent, whether they be registered members or not, for an amount not to exceed, in the case of employers, one day's pay for each worker employed, and in the case of workers, employees, artists, and professional men, one day's pay. . . .

Only the regularly registered members participate in the activities of the associations and in the election or other form of appointment of its officers.

Only legally recognised associations can appoint representatives of employers or workers to sit on all councils or other bodies on which such representation is provided by law.

ARTICLE 6.

The associations may be communal, district, provincial, regional, inter-regional, or national.

Recognition may also be granted, under the provisions of this Act, to federations or unions of several associations, and to confederations of several federations. . . .

Legal recognition can only be granted to one association for each class of employers, workers, artists, or professional men. Similarly, legal recognition can only be given to one federation or confederation of employers or workers or artists or professional men. . . .

In no case can associations be recognised which, without the preliminary consent of the Government, have contracted any ties of discipline with or dependence on associations of an international character.

. . . .

ARTICLE 8.

. . . Communal, district, and provincial associations are subject to the supervision of the Prefect and are under the trusteeship of the (Provincial Assembly). . . . Regional, inter-regional and national associations are subject to the supervision and control of the competent Minister. . . .

· · · · ·

ARTICLE 10.

Collective labour contracts drawn up by the legally recognised associations of employers, workers, artists, and professional men, are valid in respect of all employers, workers, artists, and professional men belonging to the category to which said contracts refer. . . .

A copy of the collective contract . . . must be deposited with the local prefecture and published in the sheet of announcement of the Province in the case of communal, district, or provincial associations, and must be deposited with the Ministry of Economics and published in the *Gazzetta Ufficiale* of the Kingdom in the case of regional, inter-regional or national associations. . . .

ARTICLE 11.

The provisions of this Act on the legal recognition of syndical associations are not applicable to associations of persons in the employ of the State, the Provinces, the Communes, or public charity institutions, for whom provisions will be made by separate measures.

Such associations of officers, non-commissioned officers, and soldiers of the army, navy and air forces, and of other armed bodies of the State, Provinces and Communes, and associations of magistrates of the judicial and administrative orders, and of officials, employees, and dependents of the Ministries of the Interior, Foreign Affairs, and Colonies are, therefore, forbidden under penalty of dismissal, loss of rank, and removal from office, and other disciplinary measures to be set forth in the regulations according to the several cases.[13]

ARTICLE 12.

Associations of employers, workers, artists and professional men which are not legally recognised, continue to exist as *de facto* associations, regulated by existing laws, with the exception of those referred to in the second paragraph of the preceding article.

The provisions of the Royal Decree of January 24, 1924, No. 64, are applicable to them.

---

[13] A Royal Decree of March 17, 1927, added officials, employees, and dependents of the Ministry of Corporations to this list, and the persons attached to the Royal Household and the Attorney-General's office were placed in a similar category by a Royal Decree of January 13, 1930, and a law of April 13, 1933, respectively.—*Ed.*

CHAPTER II
OF LABOUR COURTS
ARTICLE 13.

All disputes arising as to the regulation of collective contracts, or of other existing regulations, or the request for new conditions of labour, come within the jurisdiction of the Courts of Appeal acting as Labour Courts. Before delivering judgment the President of the Court must attempt conciliation.

Disputes referred to in the above provisions may be settled by arbitration, in accordance with the provisions of Article 8 *et seq*. of the Civil Code.

No modification is made in the qualifications of the Board of Arbitrators and of the Provincial Arbitration Commissions for employers of private business concerns, as determined by the Act of 15th June 1893, No. 295, and by the Royal Decree of December 2, 1923, No. 2686.

Appeals against the decisions of such Boards and Commissions and of other jurisdictional bodies on individual labour contracts, in so far as they are subject to appeal under existing legislation, devolve upon the Courts of Appeal acting as Labour Courts.

ARTICLE 14.

To enable the Courts of Appeal to act as Labour Courts, a special section is established for each of the sixteen Courts of Appeal consisting of three magistrates, one as president of the section and the others as councillors of the Court of Appeal, to whom are associated on each occasion two experts on problems of production and labour, selected by the First President in accordance with the rules set forth in the next article. . . .

ARTICLE 15.

Each Court of Appeal shall draw up a panel of experts on problems of production and labour, classified by groups and sub-groups, according to the several kinds of business activities carried on within the jurisdiction of the court. This panel shall be revised every two years. . . .

Each year the first President shall designate for each group and sub-group the members of the panel who shall be called on to act as expert advisers in cases concerning the industries which form the group or sub-group. Persons directly or indirectly concerned in the disputes can never act as members of the judicial board.

ARTICLE 16.

The Court of Appeal, acting as a Labour Court for the enforcement of existing agreements, delivers judgment under the provisions of the law on interpretation and execution of contracts, in accordance with equity, conciliating the interests of the employers with those of the workers and safeguarding in all cases the superior interests of production.

When new conditions of labour are drawn up the period for which they will be valid must always be determined, said period, as a rule, to be that established by custom in the case of agreements freely entered into.

The decisions of the Court acting as a Labour Court are given after hearing the oral conclusions of the Public Prosecutor.

The decisions of the Court of Appeal acting as a Labour Court can be appealed against in the Court of Cassation on the grounds set forth in Art. 517 of the Code of Civil Procedure. . . .

ARTICLE 17.

Only associations which are legally recognized may take action in disputes arising out of collective labour agreements and such action must be taken against legally recognized associations, when they exist; otherwise against a trustee specially appointed by the President of the Court of Appeal. In the latter case voluntary intervention in the case of private individuals is admitted. . . .

CHAPTER III
OF LOCK-OUTS AND STRIKES

ARTICLE 18.

Lock-outs and strikes are forbidden.

Employers who, without justifiable motive, and for the sole purpose of obtaining from their dependents changes in existing labour agreements, suspend work in their factories, establishments, concerns, or offices, render themselves liable to a fine of not less than ten thousand and not to exceed one hundred thousand lire.

Three or more employees or workers who, by preconcerted agreement, leave their work or perform it in such wise as to interfere with its continuity or regularity, with a view to obtaining from their employers different labour conditions, render themselves liable to a fine of not less than one hundred and not to exceed one thousand lire. The provisions of articles 298 *et seq.* of the Code of Penal Procedure are applicable to the case.

When the persons guilty of the offences foreseen under the above paragraphs are more, the leaders, promoters, and organizers are liable to detention for not less than one year and not to exceed two years, besides the fine provided for under said paragraphs.

ARTICLE 19.

Persons in the employ of the State and of other public bodies or bodies performing essential public services who, in the number of three or more, by preconcerted agreement, leave their work or perform it in a manner likely to interfere with its continuity or regularity, render themselves liable to imprisonment for a period of not less than one month and not to exceed six months. The provisions of article 298 *et seq.* of the Code of Civil Procedure are applicable to the process. The leaders, promoters, and organizers are liable to imprisonment for a period of not less than six months and not to exceed two years, and to interdiction from public office for not less than three years.

Persons carrying on public services or services essential to the public who, without justifiable motives, suspend work in their establishments, concerns, or offices, are liable to imprisonment for a period of not less than six months and not to exceed one year, and to a fine of from five thousand to one hundred thousand lire, besides temporary interdiction from public office.

When the action referred to in this article causes danger to personal safety the penalty incurred is that of imprisonment for a period of not less than one year. Should such action be the cause of death to one or more persons the penalty incurred is that of imprisonment for a period of not less than three years.

ARTICLE 20.

Persons in the employ of the State and of other public bodies, persons carrying on public services and services essential to the public, and their dependents, who in the event of strikes or lock-outs fail to do all in their power to secure the regular working or the resumption of a public service essential to the public, are liable to detention for a period of not less than one month and not exceeding six months.

ARTICLE 21.

When the stoppage of work by employers or the act of leaving work or performing it irregularly by workers aims at coercing the will or influencing the decisions of a department or organ of the State, Provinces, or Communes, or of a Government official, the leaders, promoters and organizers render themselves liable to imprisonment for a period of not less than three and not to exceed seven years and to perpetual interdiction from public office, and the other persons concerned in such offence are liable to imprisonment for a period of not less than one and not to exceed three years and to temporary interdiction from public office.

ARTICLE 22.

Without prejudice to the enforcement of the provisions of the common law on civil liabilities for breach of contract, and on execution of the sentence delivered by the Court, employers and workers who refuse to conform to the sentences delivered by the Labour Court render themselves liable to detention for a period of not less than one month and not to exceed one year and to a fine of not less than one hundred and not to exceed five thousand lire.

The directors of legally recognised associations who refuse to carry out the sentence delivered by the Labour Court render themselves liable to detention for a period of not less than six months and not to exceed two years and to a fine of not less than two thousand and not to exceed ten thousand lire, besides dismissal from office. . . .

ARTICLE 23.

All provisions which run counter to this Act are repealed. . . .

146. THE FASCIST CHARTER OF LABOR, APRIL 21, 1927 [14]

Since the improvement of labor conditions under the operation of the law on collective labor relations (See Document 145) was slower than had been anticipated, the labor leader, Edmondo Rossoni, urged the issuance of a "Charter of Labor." Such a document was promulgated on April 21, 1927, the supposed anniversary of the founding of Rome.

[14] *Labour Charter. Introduction and Comment by Arnaldo Mussolini,* Istituto Poligrafico dello Stato Libreria, Rome, 1933, pp. 11-27. (A few alterations in wording have been made for the sake of clarity.)

I

The Italian Nation is an organism endowed with a purpose, a life, and means of action transcending those of the individuals composing it. It is a moral, political and economic unit which finds its integral realisation in the Fascist State.

II

Work in all its various forms—intellectual, technical or manual—is a social duty. On these grounds, and on these grounds alone, it is brought under the supervision of the State.

From the national standpoint the whole of production represents a single process; it has one and a single object, namely the well-being of those engaged in production and the development of national power.

III

There is complete freedom of professional or syndical organisation. But syndicates legally recognised and subject to State control alone have the right to represent legally the whole category for which they are constituted; to protect their interests in their relations with the State or other professional associations; to stipulate collective labour contracts binding on all members of the particular category; to impose dues and to exercise on their account public functions delegated to them.

IV

The concrete expression of the solidarity existing between the various factors of production is represented by the collective labour contract which conciliates the opposing interests of employers of labour and of workers, subordinating them to the higher interests of production.

V

The Labour Court is the organ by means of which the State intervenes in order to settle labour disputes, whether arising from the application of contracts or other existing rules or from the formulation of new labour conditions.

VI

Legally recognised professional associations ensure legal equality between employers and workers, keep a strict control over production and labour and promote the improvement of both.

The Corporations constitute the unitary organisation of the forces of production and integrally represent their interests.

By virtue of this integral representation, and in view of the fact that the interests of production are the interests of the Nation, the law recognises the Corporations as State organisations.

VII

The Corporative State considers that in the sphere of production private enterprise is the most effective and useful instrument in the interests of the Nation.

In view of the fact that the private organisation of production is a function of national concern, the organiser of the enterprise is responsible to the State for the direction given to production. Collaboration between the forces of production gives rise to reciprocal rights and duties. The worker, whether technician, clerk or labourer, is an active collaborator in the economic enterprise, the responsibility for the direction of which rests with the employer.

VIII

Professional associations of employers are required to promote by all possible means a continued increase in the quantity of production and a reduction of costs. The representative organs of persons exercising liberal professions or arts and associations of civil servants must encourage arts, science and letters, with a view to improving production and to achieving the moral objects of the corporative system.

IX

State intervention in economic production arises only when private initiative is lacking or is inadequate or when political interests of the State are involved. This intervention may take the form of control, assistance or direct management.

X

Judicial action cannot be invoked in collective labour controversies unless the guild organ has first attempted conciliation.

Professional associations have the right in individual disputes concerning the interpretation and application of collective labour contracts to employ their good offices for the purpose of conciliation.

Jurisdiction over such disputes is placed in the ordinary Courts assisted by assessors appointed by the professional association concerned.

COLLECTIVE LABOUR CONTRACTS AND THEIR GUARANTEES

XI

Professional associations are required to regulate by means of collective contracts the labour relations existing between the categories of employers of labour and of workers represented by them.

Collective labour contracts are concluded between first grade associations under the direction and control of the central organisations except in the event of the exercise of the power of substitution by the higher grade association in the cases specified in the laws and statutes.

All collective labour contracts must, under pain of nullity, contain precise rules on such matters as disciplinary relations, trial periods, the amount and payment of remuneration and hours of work.

XII

The action of the syndicate, the conciliatory efforts of the Corporations and the decisions of the Labour Courts shall guarantee that wages shall correspond to the normal demands of life, to the possibilities of production and the output of labour.

Wages shall be determined entirely without reference to any general rules by agreement between the parties to the collective system.

XIII

The consequences of crises in production and of monetary phenomena should be shared equally by all the different factors of production.[15]

The data furnished by public administrations, by the Central Statistical Office and by the legally recognised professional associations with respect to conditions of production and of work, the situation on the money market and the variations in the standard of life of workers shall, after having been co-ordinated and elaborated by the Ministry of Corporations, supply the standard for reconciling the interests of the various categories and of the various classes among each other and with the higher interests of production.

XIV

When the contract concerns piece-work and the payments due thereunder are made at intervals of more than fifteen days, adequate weekly or fortnightly sums on account are due.

Night work, with the exception of ordinary regular night shifts, must be paid at a higher rate than day work.

---

[15] This sentence does not appear in the later versions of the charter.—*Ed.*

In cases where the work is paid at piece-rate, the rate must be such that a diligent workman, of a normal working capacity, will be able to earn a minimum amount over and above the basic wage.

XV

The worker has the right to a weekly day of rest which shall fall on Sunday.

Collective contracts shall apply this principle while taking account of legal conditions in force, of the technical necessities of the enterprise and, within the limits of these necessities, shall see that civil and religious holidays are observed according to local traditions. The working time-table must be scrupulously and zealously observed by the worker.

XVI

Workers in enterprises of continuous activity shall, after the expiry of a year of uninterrupted service, have the right to an annual period of rest with pay.

XVII

In enterprises of continuous activity the worker has the right, in the event of a cessation of labour relations on account of discharge without any fault on his part, to an indemnity proportional to his years of service. Similar indemnity is also due in the event of the death of a worker.

XVIII

In enterprises of continuous activity the transfer of the enterprise into other hands shall not put an end to the contract of labour, and the workers employed shall have the same rights with regard to the new employer. Similarly, illness on the part of the worker, provided it does not exceed a certain period, shall not put an end to the contract of labour. Call to military service or to services in the National Militia shall not be grounds of discharge.

XIX

Breaches of discipline or the performance of acts which disturb the normal working of the enterprise on the part of the workers, shall be punished according to the gravity of the offence, by fine, suspension from work, or in certain cases of gravity, by immediate discharge without indemnity.

The cases when the employer can impose fines, suspension from work or immediate discharge without payment of indemnity, shall be specified.

XX

A worker on taking up a new post must go through a period of trial during which both parties have a right to the cancellation of the contract merely by payment of the wage or salary in respect of the time during which the worker was actually employed.

XXI

The privileges and control of the collective labour contract extend also to domestic workers. Special rules shall be issued by the State in order to ensure the control and hygiene of domestic labour.

LABOUR EMPLOYMENT BUREAUS

XXII

The State alone can ascertain and control the phenomenon of employment and unemployment of workers, which is a complex of the conditions of production and work.

XXIII

Labour Employment Bureaus founded on a mutual basis are subjected to the control of the Corporations. Employers have the obligation to employ workers whose names are on the register of the said Bureaus and have the right of choice among the names of those who are members of the Party and the Fascist syndicates according to their seniority on the Register.

XXIV

The professional associations of employers are required to exercise a process of selection among the workers with the object of achieving continuous improvement in their technical capacity and moral education.

XXV

The Corporative bodies shall ensure the observance of the laws on the prevention of accidents and the discipline of work on the part of individuals belonging to the federated associations.

INSURANCE, ASSISTANCE, EDUCATION AND INSTRUCTION

XXVI

Insurance is a further expression of the principle of collaboration, and the employer and the worker should both bear a proportional share of its burden. The State, through the medium of Corporations and professional associations, shall see to the coordination and unity, as far as possible, of the system and institutes of insurance.

XXVII

The Fascist State proposes:

1. the perfecting of accident insurance;
2. the improvement and extension of maternity assistance;
3. insurance against industrial diseases and tuberculosis as a step towards insurance against all forms of sickness; [16]
4. the perfecting of insurance against involuntary unemployment;
5. the adoption of special forms of endowment insurance for young workers.

XXVIII

The workers' associations are required to act as guardians of those they represent in administrative and judicial suits arising out of accident and social insurance.

Collective labour contracts shall establish, when this is technically possible, Mutual Sickness Funds, with contributions furnished by employers and workers, to be administered by representatives of both bodies, under the supervision of the Corporative organs.

XXIX

To assist the individuals it represents, whether members or non-members, is a privilege and a duty of the professional associations. The associations must exercise directly by their own organs the functions of assistance and may not delegate them to other bodies or institutes except for purposes of a general nature transcending the interests of single categories of producers.

XXX

The education and instruction, especially the professional instruction, of the individuals they represent is one of the principal duties of professional associations. These associations are required to work side by side with the National Leisure Time Institution *(Dopolavoro)* and other educational institutions.

---

[16] For a later tuberculosis insurance law, see Document No. 153.—*Ed.*

147. THE ELECTORAL LAW OF 1928 *(Extracts)* [17]

Through an electoral law of May 1928 Italy became the first great western state with a national legislature representing economic divisions. Only two elections were held under this law, in March 1929 and March 1934, and on both occasions the Fascist list received an overwhelming majority of the votes cast. The chamber elected in 1934 was soon called the "Suicide Chamber" because it was expected to vote its own final dissolution. This actually came to pass, on December 14, 1938, when the lower house voted itself out of existence. The Fascist Grand Council meanwhile (October 7, 1938) had decreed the organization of a new Chamber of Fasces and Corporations, whose membership was to be appointed chiefly by the government and the party. The Italian Senate, as an honorary body, was little affected by these changes.

. . . . .

ARTICLE 2.

All [male] citizens may be electors who are twenty-one years of age, or eighteen years provided they are married or widowers with children, and have attained these respective ages not later than May 31st of the year in which the revision of the electoral lists takes place. They must furthermore meet one of the following requirements:

a) Payment of dues to a syndicate . . . except when the voter is an administrator or member of an organisation or concern paying syndical dues. . . . In the case of holders of stock in limited and unlimited companies, only registered shares which have been in . . . possession for at least one year confer the right to vote;

b) Payment of at least 100 lire per annum of direct taxes to the State, province or commune, unless the voter has been for at least a year the owner or beneficiary of registered bonds of the public debt or of registered bonds of provincial or communal loans yielding an income of 500 lire annually;

c) Receipt of a stipend, salary or pension, or other emolument of continuous character, provided in the budget of the State, province or

---

[17] Royal Decree of September 2, 1928 (No. 1993), approving the text of the electoral law of May 17, 1928, in B. Mussolini, *Fascism, Doctrine and Institutions*, Ardita, Rome, 1935, pp. 182-194; original text in Supplement to *Gazzetta Ufficiale del Regno d'Italia*, Ministry of Grace and Justice, Rome, September 8, 1928, No. 210.

commune, or any other body which is subject by law to the supervision of the State, province or commune;

d) Membership of the Catholic clergy, secular or regular, or minister of another religion the exercise of which is admitted in the State.

. . . . .

ARTICLE 44.

The number of deputies for the Kingdom shall be 400.[18]
The Kingdom shall form a single national constituency.

. . . . .

ARTICLE 46.

The election of the deputies shall take place through:

1) the designation of candidates by the organisations mentioned in Articles 47 and 51;

2) the nomination of candidates by the Fascist Grand Council;

3) approval by the electoral body.

ARTICLE 47.

The right to designate candidates belongs first to the National Confederations of legally-recognised syndicates. . . .

The organisations mentioned above shall designate a total number of candidates which is double the number of deputies to be elected [800].

The distribution of this number among the various confederations is made in the table annexed to the present Law.

The candidates shall be designated, for each confederation, by its general or national council regularly elected and convoked in accordance with the Statutes.

The meetings called for the selection of candidates shall be held in Rome. The persons who receive the largest number of votes at these meetings shall be designated as candidates. . . .

. . . . .

ARTICLE 51.

Candidates may also be designated by legally-recognised *enti morale* [incorporated bodies] and by *de facto* associations having national im-

---

[18] This represented a reduction of 160 from the former total.—*Ed.*

portance and pursuing ends of culture, education, assistance and propaganda.[19]

The right of such *enti morale* and associations to designate candidates is recognised by Royal Decree if approval is expressed by a committee of five senators and five deputies named by their respective assemblies. The decree granting this right is subject to revision every three years.

The above-mentioned organisations may propose a total number of candidates equal to one-half of the deputies to be elected [200]. The distribution of this number among the various recognised organisations and the manner of selecting the candidates is set forth in the decree conferring the right to propose candidates. . . .

ARTICLE 52.

. . . The Secretariat of the Fascist Grand Council, on receiving the names of the proposed candidates, shall form a single list of candidates in alphabetical order, indicating beside each name the organisation proposing him. . . .

The Fascist Grand Council shall nominate a list of candidates, choosing freely from the list of those designated and even elsewhere if necessary, in order to include persons who have achieved fame in the sciences, letters, arts and politics, and in the defence services, who do not figure in the list of candidates.

A report on the deliberations of the Grand Council shall be drawn up under the direction of the Secretary of the Grand Council itself.

The list of nominated deputies, bearing the emblem of the "Lictors' Fasces," on the model prescribed for the emblem of the State, shall be published free of cost in the *Gazzetta Ufficiale* and posted in all the communes of the Kingdom under the direction of the Minister of the Interior.

ARTICLE 53.

The elections for the approval of the list of deputies nominated shall take place on the third Sunday following the publication of the list. . . .

The vote shall be cast on ballot papers bearing the sign of the "Lictors' Fasces" and the formula: "Do you approve the list of deputies nominated by the Fascist Grand Council?"

The vote shall be expressed beneath this formula by the word "Yes" or "No."   . . . . .

---

[19] The reference is to such *enti morale* as the Dopolavoro, for a description of which see Document No. 151.—*Ed.*

ARTICLE 88.

Should the list of deputies nominated not be approved, the Court of Appeal of Rome, by a decree, shall order new elections with competing lists of candidates, and shall set the date of the elections not sooner than 30 and not later than 45 days from the date of the decree. . . .

At the second election all associations and organisations having 5000 voting members who are regularly registered in the electoral lists may present lists of candidates. . . .

ARTICLE 89.

The lists containing the surnames and names of the candidates shall not contain a number of candidates exceeding three-fourths of the deputies to be elected. . . .

. . . . .

ARTICLE 100.

The Court of Appeal in Rome, acting as a national electoral office, . . . shall count the [popular] votes obtained by each list and proclaim the result of the ballot.

All the candidates of the list which has received the plurality of votes cast are declared elected.

Places reserved for minority representations shall be distributed among the other lists in proportion to the number of votes cast for each. . . .

. . . . .

TABLE OF CANDIDATES

Number of candidates that each National Confederation of legally-recognised syndical associations may propose for each hundred candidates presented by the Confederations:[20]

1. National Confederation of Agriculturists, 12;
2. National Confederation of Employees and Workers in Agriculture, 12;
3. National Confederation of Industrialists, 10;
4. National Confederation of Employees and Workers in Industry, 10;
5. National Confederation of Merchants, 6;

---

[20] Since the confederations together proposed 800 candidates, each individual confederation was given the right to propose eight times as many names as the number designated in the accompanying table.—*Ed.*

6. National Confederation of Employees and Workers in Commerce, 6;
7. National Confederation of Persons Conducting Air and Sea Transport Services, 5;
8. National Confederation of Employees and Workers in Air and Sea Transport Services, 5;
9. National Confederation of Persons Conducting Transport Services by Land, Lakes and Rivers, 4;
10. National Confederation of Employees and Workers in Transport Services by Land, Lakes and Rivers, 4;
11. National Confederation of Credit and Insurance, 3;
12. National Confederation of Employees of Credit and Insurance, 3;
13. National Confederation of Professionals and Artists, 20.

148. THE LAW ON CORPORATIONS, FEBRUARY 5, 1934 (Extracts) [21]

The law of April 3, 1926, on collective labor relations contemplated the co-ordination of the activities of the syndicates through the creation of special "corporations." For several years the status of these corporations remained vague and confused, and even the inauguration of a National Council of Corporations in April 1930 to "adjust disputes among the various groups in the interest of national production" did only little to clarify the situation. Finally, in February 1934, a law on corporations was passed which, with the supplementary decrees referred to in Document No. 149, completed the establishment of the corporate state in Italy.

ARTICLE 1.

Corporations . . . are instituted by decree of the Head of the Government, upon proposal of the Minister for Corporations and after consulting the Central Corporative Committee.

ARTICLE 2.

Corporations are presided over by a Minister or by an Under-Secretary of State, or by the Secretary of the Fascist Party, to be appointed

[21] Law of February 5, 1934 (No. 163), in B. Mussolini, *The Corporate State.* Vallecchi, Florence, 1936, pp. 107-110; original text in *Gazzetta Ufficiale del Regno d'Italia,* Ministry of Grace and Justice, Rome, February 20, 1934.

by decree of the Head of the Government, who is the chairman of the National Council of Corporations.

ARTICLE 3.

The decree instituting a Corporation states the number of members to be included in the Board, and how many of them should be designated by each of the Associations affiliated to the Corporation.

The members designated shall be approved by decree of the Head of the Government, upon proposal of the Minister for Corporations.

· · · · ·

ARTICLE 6.

The Head of the Government by his decree, upon proposal of the Minister for Corporations, after consulting the Central Corporative Committee, is empowered to constitute Corporative Committees for the regulation of economic activity concerning specified products. . . .

· · · · ·

ARTICLE 10.

The Corporation is empowered to fix tariffs for labour and professional services and prices for the sale of goods to the public at special terms.

ARTICLE 11.

Regulations, agreements and salary scales referred to in the foregoing articles, are subject to the approval of the General Assembly of the National Council of Corporations, and become compulsory when published by decree of the Head of the Government, and included as such in the official collection of laws and decrees of the Kingdom.

The infringement of these regulations, agreements and salary scales is punished according to rules applying to Collective Labour Contracts.

· · · · ·

ARTICLE 13.

Conciliation in collective labour disputes is attempted by the Corporation through a Board of Conciliation composed of members of the Corporation itself. In each separate case the members of this Board are selected by the President of the Corporation, with due regard to the nature and object of the controversy.

· · · · ·

149. THE 22 CORPORATIONS AND THEIR COUNCILS, ESTABLISHED IN 1934 [22]

*By three sets of decrees of May and June 1934, Premier Mussolini estab-
lished twenty-two corporations embracing the fields of agriculture, industry
and commerce, and services. In each case the membership of the corporation council was specified. The corporations were empowered to advise the
government, arbitrate disputes between employers and employees, and plan
and regulate production, distribution, and prices.*

Eight Decrees of the Head of the Government on May 29, 1934,
established eight corporations embracing argiculture, namely: 1. The
Corporation of Cereals; 2. The Corporation of Fruit, Vegetables, and
Flowers; 3. The Corporation of Viticulture and Wine; 4. The Corporation of Edible Oils; 5. The Corporation of Sugar-beets and Sugar;
6. The Corporation of Livestock and Fisheries; 7. The Corporation of
Lumber; and 8. The Corporation of Textiles.

Eight Decrees of the Head of the Government on June 9, 1934, es-
tablished eight corporations embracing industry and commerce, namely:
9. The Corporation of Building Construction; 10. The Corporation of
Metals and Engineering; 11. The Corporation of Clothing Trades;
12. The Corporation of Glassware and Pottery; 13. The Corporation of
Chemical Trades; 14. The Corporation of Paper and Printing; 15. The
Corporation of Extractive Industries (Mining and Quarrying); and 16.
The Corporation of Water, Gas, and Electricity.

Six Decrees of the Head of the Government on June 23, 1934, established six corporations embracing services, namely: 17. The Corporation of the Arts and Professions, comprising the four sections of the
legal, medical, and technical professions and the arts; 18. The Corporation of Internal Communications, comprising the four sections of
rail- and tramways and inland navigation, motor transport, traffic
auxiliaries, and communication by telephone, radio, and cable; 19. The
Corporation of Sea and Air Transport; 20. The Corporation of Hos-
pitality, comprising restaurants, hotels, and travel; 21. The Corporation
of Credit and Insurance; and 22. The Corporation of Amusements.

The composition of the corporation councils is illustrated by the following examples:

---

[22] Italy, Ministry of Grace and Justice, *Gazzetta Ufficiale del Regno d'Italia,* June 5,
1934 (No. 131); June 19, 1934 (No. 143); July 5, 1934 (No. 156).

Corporation of Cereals.—The Council consists of a President and 36 members as follows:

3 representatives of the National Fascist Party;

7 employers and 7 workers representing cereal growers;

1 employer and 1 worker representing the threshing industries;

3 employers and 3 workers representing milling, rice-dressing, edible pastes and confectionery;

1 employer and 1 worker representing the baking industries;

3 employers and 3 workers representing commerce in cereals and cereal products;

1 representative of cooperative societies of consumers;

1 representative of agricultural experts;

1 representative of small industries (artisans).

The total number of employers includes 3 representatives of persons managing agricultural, industrial and commercial concerns.

. . . . .

Corporation of Textiles.—The Council of the Corporation consists of a President and 58 members as follows:

3 representatives of the National Fascist Party;

3 employers and 3 workers representing cotton industries;

1 employer and 1 worker representing silk-worm breeding;

2 employers and 2 workers representing the production of wool;

2 employers and 2 workers representing wool industries;

1 employer and 1 worker representing silk-cocoon raising;

1 employer and 1 worker representing silk-throwing and reeling;

2 employers and 2 workers representing rayon;

2 employers and 2 workers representing the weaving of silk and rayon;

2 employers and 2 workers representing the cultivation of flax and hemp;

1 employer and 1 worker representing the jute industry;

2 employers and 2 workers representing the dyeing and printing of fabrics;

2 employers and 2 workers representing sundry textile industries;

3 employers and 3 workers representing commerce in cotton, wool, silk, rayon and other textiles, including the retail trade;

1 representative of agricultural experts;

1 representative of chemical experts;

1 representative of industrial experts;

1 representative of artists;
2 representatives of the small arts and crafts (artisans);
1 representative of cooperative dyeing plants.

The total number of employers includes 3 representatives of persons managing agricultural, industrial and commercial concerns.

. . . . .

Corporation of the Arts and Professions.—The Council of the Corporation consists of a President and 40 members as follows:

3 representatives of the National Fascist Party;	2 agricultural experts;
	1 surveyor;
	1 industrial expert;
3 barristers and attorneys;	1 chemist;
1 doctor in economics;	2 authors and writers;
1 notary;	2 artists (fine arts);
1 solicitor;	1 journalist;
1 commercial assessor;	1 musician;
1 accountant;	1 representative of private schools;
2 physicians;	1 representative of private teach-
1 pharmacist;	ers;
1 veterinary;	4 representatives of the small arts
1 trained nurse;	and crafts (artisans);
1 midwife;	2 representatives of dealers in an-
2 engineers;	cient and modern art.
2 architects;	

. . . . .

150. THE LAW CREATING THE BALILLA AND AVANGUARDISTI ORGANIZATIONS, 1926 *(Extracts)* [23]

With its emphasis on military preparedness and its belief in the importance of youth training, the Fascist State early provided for the organization of uniformed societies for children and youths. The name Balilla *was taken from the nickname of a Genoese boy, Giovanni Battista Perasso, who in 1746 performed deeds of heroism in a campaign against the Austrians.* Avanguardisti *means members of the Advance Guard.*

[23] Law of April 3, 1926 (No. 2247), in B. Mussolini, *Fascism, Doctrine and Institutions,* Ardita, Rome, 1935, pp. 264-269; original text in *Gazzetta Ufficiale del Regno d'Italia,* Ministry of Grace and Justice, Rome, January 11, 1927, No. 7.

Article 1.

An *Ente Morale* [incorporated body] is founded in Rome under the name of *Opera Nazionale Balilla,* for the moral and physical training of the young.

This institution is placed under the control of the Head of the Government, Prime Minister.[24]

Article 2.

Children of either sex are entitled to assistance provided for in the present law, until the age of eighteen, save in the cases of those who, in virtue of Article 7, are entitled to assistance until the completion of their studies.

Article 3.

The institution achieves its ends through the organisations of the *Balilla* and *Avanguardisti.*

The organisation of *Avanguardisti* shall more especially attend to the training of the young in preparation for military service.[25]

Article 4.

Children from the age of eight to fourteen belong to the organisation of the *Balilla,* children from fourteen to eighteen to the organisation of the *Avanguardisti.*[26]

Article 5.

The organisations of the *Balilla* and *Avanguardisti* are dependent on the National Balilla Institution.

Article 6.

With regard to military service, young men who have belonged to the corps of *Avanguardisti* for a term of four years and have received a certificate of competence upon leaving the corps, may benefit by privileges granted by existing laws to young men who have followed courses of pre-military training, . . .

---

[24] A law of November 14, 1929 (No. 1992), placed the institution under the control of the Minister for National Education.—*Ed.*

[25] A royal decree of June 14, 1928 (No. 1551), created "corps of *Avanguardisti* and *Balilla* sailors."—*Ed.*

[26] A proclamation of October 1934 created the Wolf Balilla for children from six to eight.—*Ed.*

ARTICLE 7.

In order to complete the activity carried out by the corps of *Balilla* and *Avanguardisti,* the National Balilla Institution is empowered to:

1) found institutions for the assistance of youth, or promote their foundation;

2) subsidise institutions not provided with sufficient funds, if their object be similar to that of the National Balilla Institution;

3) promote the reform of the Statute and regulations of institutions empowered to award scholarships, so that examinations for the award be made compulsory and that, in cases of equal merit, preference be given to children and youths belonging to the corps of *Balilla* and *Avanguardisti.*

ARTICLE 8.

Laws already providing for government control over public and private institutions or associations, whose object is to promote instruction, moral and physical training, professional and artistic training, moral and spiritual education of the young, remain unchanged, but the National Balilla Institution may require the qualified authorities to take measures that the activity of these bodies conform to the objects of the present law.

.   .   .   .   .

ARTICLE 10.

The National Balilla Institution is governed by a Central Council composed of a president,[27] a vice-president and twenty-three councillors, appointed by Royal Decree upon proposal of the Head of the Government, Prime Minister. . . .

.   .   .   .   .

ARTICLE 12.

A provincial Committee may be formed in each Province, composed of a president and ten councillors. . . .

.   .   .   .   .

ARTICLE 14.

A Communal Committee may be formed in each Commune. . . .

---

[27] A law of November 14, 1929 (No. 1992), made the Under Secretary of State for Physical and Moral Training of the Young ex-officio president of the National Balilla Institution.—*Ed.*

ARTICLE 15.

The offices of members of the Central Council, of the Executive Board, of the councils of directors, and of Provincial and Communal Committees are unpaid.

· · · · ·

151. THE LAW ESTABLISHING THE DOPOLAVORO, 1925 *(Extracts)* [28]

The Dopolavoro *or "After Work" society was established in 1925 to provide physical and cultural recreational facilities for, and to conduct Fascist propaganda among, Italian workers and their families. The privileges of membership were considerable, and in 1937 the society had 21,685 local branches with 3,180,000 members.*

ARTICLE 1.

The *Opera Nazionale Dopolavoro* is established in Rome, having for its aims and objects:

a) the healthful and profitable occupation of the worker's leisure hours, through institutions for developing the worker's physical, intellectual and moral capacity;

b) to promote the development of these institutions by furnishing them with the necessary support, and raising them to the standard of *Enti Morale* (incorporated bodies);

c) the grouping together of all such associations, in order to equip them materially and for purposes of propaganda, as well as in view of other common aims and interests;

d) to make known by publications and other means the advantages of these institutions, and such provisions as are made to raise the standard of the working classes;

e) the award of certificates of merit to members who have proved themselves particularly deserving, or who have shown notable proficiency and activity in working for the aims and objects of the organisation.

ARTICLE 2.

The *Opera Nazionale Dopolavoro* has juridical personality and may

---

[28] Royal Decree-Law of May 1, 1925 (No. 582), in B. Mussolini, *Fascism, Doctrine and Institutions,* Ardita, Rome, 1935, pp. 245-250; original text in *Gazzetta Ufficiale del Regno d'Italia,* Ministry of Grace and Justice, Rome, May 14, 1925, No. 112.

receive and administer subsidies, gifts, legacies and donations of all kinds and monetary values, may purchase and possess property and perform all other juridical acts necessary for the attainment of its own ends.

ARTICLE 3.

The patrimony of the *Opera Nazionale Dopolavoro* is provided by:

a) a contribution of Lire 1,000,000 from the Ministry of National Economy;

b) contributions from public administrations;

c) gifts, legacies and subsidies from public and private concerns and private persons;

d) members' subscriptions;

e) interest on invested capital.

ARTICLE 4.

In conformity with the rules set by the statute, provided for in Article 13, the following can be recognised members of the *Opera Nazionale Dopolavoro:* institutions of the *Dopolavoro* which exist as *Enti Morale,* associations and private persons who, with grants or periodic subscriptions, contribute towards the activities of the *Opera Nazionale Dopolavoro.*

. . . . .

ARTICLE 12.

The *Opera Nazionale Dopolavoro* is under the control of the Ministry of National Economy. . . .

A budget of the *Opera Nazionale Dopolavoro* and a report on its activities will be presented annually to Parliament. . . .

. . . .

152. THE LAW ON COMPULSORY OLD-AGE AND DISABILITY INSURANCE *(Extracts)* [29]

The law on compulsory old-age and disability insurance was among the first items on the social-legislative program of the Italian Fascists.

[29] Royal Decree of December 30, 1923 (No. 3184), in B. Mussolini, *Fascism, Doctrine and Institutions,* Ardita, Rome, 1935, pp. 277-284; original text in *Gazzetta Ufficiale del Regno d'Italia,* Ministry of Grace and Justice, Rome, February 16, 1924, No. 40.

Article 1.

Insurance against disablement and old age is made compulsory for persons of both sexes over the age of fifteen and under the age of sixty-five who are employed in the following capacities:

1. Workers, shop-boys, apprentices, servants, assistants, clerks, foremen and in general all persons employed in the industries, in trade, agriculture, including fishing and venary industries, public services, liberal professions, those who work at home by order (this implies people who do work for third persons in a place other than the third person's shop, and not under his direct supervision).

2. Servants and the like who are permanently employed in household services.

Foreigners working in Italy in any of the categories described above are compelled to become insured according to the rules set out in the present Decree; however they are not allowed to be entered on the quota of the State unless there be a special agreement with their own country allowing the same facilities for Italians residing there.

Article 2.

Insurance, according to the rules set out in the present Decree, is not compulsory:

1. for employees whose monthly wage exceeds Lire 800;

2. for persons employed on board Italian ships, if they contribute to the Seamen's Fund;

3. for persons belonging to the Civil Service, to the State Railways, employed in the Royal Household, or in Provincial and Communal Administrations, as well as in public charitable institutions.

Article 3.

The main object of the insurance is to provide a pension for old age or disablement. Minor purposes are:

1. the payment to the family of a monthly allowance in the case of decease of the persons insured;

2. prevention of and treatment for disablement.

Article 4.

Funds for the purposes specified in Article 3 are collected through contributions of insured persons, of employers and of the State.

Contributions are in proportion to wages as follows:

For persons earning a daily wage, the following sum shall be paid each fortnight in equal measure by employer and employee:

up to Lire 2 per day............Lire	0.50	per fortnight
from Lire 2 to Lire 4........... "	1.00	" "
" " 4 " " 6........... "	1.50	" "
" " 6 " " 8........... "	2.00	" "
" " 8 through Lire 10..... "	2.50	" "
over " 10.................... "	3.00	" "

ARTICLE 5.

Contributions are collected by means of fortnightly stamps, to be affixed to special cards with which each person insured should be provided.

Employers are responsible not only for their share of the contribution but for that of the employee as well, and shall in fact hold it back from the wage; all other forms of agreement between employer and employee in this respect are invalid.

Employers who hold back a larger share of the wage than is due for insurance fees by the employee are liable to a fine up to Lire 500.

If insurance is omitted, or if contributions are paid in smaller measure than is due, employers shall not only pay all their own share of contributions overdue, but shall also pay the share of employees as well as a fine ranging from Lire 100 to Lire 5000.

. . . . .

ARTICLE 7.

Pensions may be paid to persons insured in the following cases:

1. at the age of 65, when the person insured has paid in at least 240 fortnightly contributions;

2. at any age when the person is disabled, if a minimum of 120 fortnightly contributions have already been paid in.

Workers of all classes are considered disabled when their earning capacity is reduced to under one third of the normal earning capacity of persons doing the same work in the same place.

If the worker's conditions improve, and his earning capacity increases, the pension may be allowed to cease.

If disablement is due to an accident, and the person is insured against accidents, the pension paid according to the present Decree shall be reduced in such measure that, when added to the indemnity received for the accident, the yearly income should not exceed the former yearly wage earned by the person in question.

*   *   *   *   *

ARTICLE 10.

In cases where it is possible to recover from disablement through special treatment, the National Social Insurance Fund may invite the insured to undergo the treatment, all expenses entailed being charged up to the National Insurance Fund.

ARTICLE 11.

Pensions accruing under the provisions of this Decree cannot be seized or surrendered, unless this be in payment of hospital fees owed by the insured.

ARTICLE 12.

Persons insured who have reached the age of sixty and have paid in at least 240 fortnightly contributions, may be pensioned off, even if they are still in fit condition to work.

In such cases pensions are reduced in the following measure:

37 per cent if the insured is in the 61st year of age
32 "   "   "   "   "   "   "   " 62nd "   "   "
26 "   "   "   "   "   "   "   " 63rd "   "   "
19 "   "   "   "   "   "   "   " 64th "   "   "
10 "   "   "   "   "   "   "   " 65th "   "   "

Persons who continue to work after their 65th year of age shall pay their insurance dues unchanged, the same rule applying to their employers. After their 65th year of age they shall receive a further pension, as due to persons for whom insurance is voluntary.

ARTICLE 13.

The organisation through which insurance against old age disablement is made is the National Social Insurance Fund, formerly the Workmen's Old-Age Fund, which carries out its activities by means of local institutions called Institutions for Social Providence.

*   *   *   *   *

ARTICLE 29.

Italian citizens belonging to any of the classes of workers specified in Article 1 may increase their pension through extra contributions.

The following may also create a fund for old-age pension through voluntary contributions:

1. independent workers, including small land-owners, traders, industrialists, etc. provided taxation levied upon them by the State does not exceed Lire 500 per year;

2. married women who are not employed and whose husbands belong to one of the classes of workers specified above; women attending to household duties for relatives other than their husbands may also become insured, provided the members of their family be insured as specified above, and that they themselves have no other income upon which they pay government tax over and above Lire 60 per year;

3. those who have passed out of the class of workers for whom insurance is compulsory.

· · · · ·

ARTICLE 33.

Appropriations of the State budget to create a fund for the National Insurance Fund shall be 50 million lire per year for six years, to be paid over in two installments per year.

· · · ·

153. THE LAW ON COMPULSORY INSURANCE AGAINST
TUBERCULOSIS (Extracts) [30]

The Labor Charter (See Document No. 146) set as one of several aims of the government the provision of compulsory insurance against tuberculosis. A law of 1927 met this obligation.

ARTICLE 1.

Insurance against tuberculosis is compulsory for persons of both sexes who are also insured against old age and disablement, as per Ar-

[30] Decree-Law of October 27, 1927 (No. 2055), in B. Mussolini, *Fascism, Doctrine and Institutions*, Ardita, Rome, 1935, pp. 288-291; original text in *Gazzetta Ufficiale del Regno d'Italia*, Ministry of Grace and Justice, Rome, November 16, 1927, No. 265.

ticle 1 of the Royal Decree of December 30, 1923, No. 3184 [See Document No. 152].

Exceptions specified in Article 2 of the aforementioned Decree concerning insurance against old age and disablement, apply to the present Decree.

ARTICLE 2.

The Ministry for the Interior remains in charge of public health services for the prevention of tuberculosis, whereas the main object of the insurance against tuberculosis is to provide for the treatment in hospitals or homes of the persons insured and of their families.

Treatment is given:

a) in special homes and hospitals for tubercular patients, or in convalescent homes;

b) in hospitals for tubercular patients which are furnished with isolation wards, when the Provincial Board of Public Health considers the case serious enough for isolation.

Members of the family of the insured who are entitled to receive relief in virtue of the insurance policy are: the wife of the insured, the disabled husband of a woman who is insured, the legitimate or illegitimate children of the insured, the brothers and sisters of the insured when under the age of 15. Illegitimate children placed in custody by one of the parents enjoy the same rights as legitimate children.

Assistance is given to persons insured provided they have paid in a minimum of 12 fortnightly contributions in the course of two years preceding the illness for which they claim treatment through the insurance.

ARTICLE 3.

Funds for the purposes specified in the preceding article are collected through the contributions of the persons insured and of their employers.

Contributions are in proportion to wages reckoned upon a daily basis, and shall be paid in equal measure by employer and employee, as follows:

Class 1. Wages up to Lire 8 per day . . . . . . Lire 0.50 per fortnight
Class 2. Wages over Lire 8 per day . . . . . . Lire 1.00 per fortnight.

. . . . .

ARTICLE 5.

Insured persons who support any of the members of their family specified in Article 2 of the present Decree, shall receive a daily subsidy if they are removed to hospital. The subsidy shall be in proportion to contributions as follows:

> *Class 1.*   Lire 4.00 per day
> *Class 2.*   Lire 6.00 per day.

. . . . .

ARTICLE 8.

The National Social Insurance Fund, by agreement with the Provincial Committee for the Prevention of Tuberculosis and with the approval of the Minister for the Interior, may order the construction of homes and hospitals specified in Paragraph *a*) of Article 2 and may advance the capital required for such enterprise. The National Social Insurance Fund may recover this capital from contributions paid in for insurance against tuberculosis.

ARTICLE 9.

The management of homes and hospitals built by the National Social Insurance Fund may be given over to concerns which are already experienced in such work, by agreement with the Provincial Committee for Prevention of Tuberculosis.

ARTICLE 10.

Special offices to deal with compulsory insurance against tuberculosis shall be organised within the seat of the National Social Insurance Fund.

. . . . .

154. THE LAW ON ITALIAN LAND-RECLAMATION POLICY *(Extracts)* [31]

Fascist Italy has demonstrated great energy in the matter of land-reclamation projects, especially in the Campagna and the Pontine Marshes, and in much-needed schemes of reforestation. A law of February 13, 1933, clearly established the responsibility of the state and of private individuals in the matter.

[31] Royal Decree-Law of February 13, 1933 (No. 215), in Italy, Ministry of Grace and Justice, *Gazzetta Ufficiale del Regno d'Italia,* April 4, 1933, No. 79.

Article 1.

Integral land reclamation is provided for in the public interest, by means of reclamation works and land improvements. . . .

Article 2.

Land-reclamation circumscriptions belong to two categories. The first category comprises those of exceptional importance—especially for purposes of land-settlement—which require works entailing very heavy expenditures on the part of the owners concerned; the second category comprises all others.

Within the aforesaid circumscriptions, the State undertakes, in so far as they are required for the general purposes of the reclamation scheme:

a) works of reforestation and the reconstruction of deteriorated woods; the rectification of the mountain sector of water courses . . . ;

b) the reclamation of lakes and ponds, marshes and swamp-lands, and lands on which natural drainage is deficient;

c) the consolidation of cliffs and the planting of trees for wind-screens;

d) works for supplying drinking water to the rural population;

e) protective works against injury by water, and for the supply and utilisation of water for agricultural purposes;

f) the erection of electric-power conversion boxes and the installation of fixed or movable wires for the distribution of electric power, available for agricultural purposes . . . ;

g) roads, buildings, and other works of a collective interest . . . ;

h) the consolidation of several lots, even if these belong to separate owners, into suitable farm units.

The owners are responsible for and are required to carry out all other works considered necessary to the purposes of the reclamation plan.

. . . . .

Article 8.

The Ministry of Agriculture and Forests determines which categories of the works for which the owners are responsible . . . are entitled to a grant from the Treasury or a contribution toward interest charges payable on the loans. . . .

. . . . .

ARTICLE 11.

The distribution of the quota of expenditures among the landowners is made, in its final form, on the basis of the advantages accruing to each as a result of the reclamation works for which the Government is responsible . . . ; and provisionally, on the basis of approximate and presumptive data on the advantages obtainable. . . .

. . . . .

ARTICLE 34.

If in the land-reclamation circumscriptions there are zones with a considerable number of small lots belonging for the most part to separate owners, the consortium to which the concession for the reclamation works is granted, may, with a view to converting the said lands into suitable farm units, and if essential for the purposes of the reclamation, draft a plan for the rearrangement of the zone so as to provide, by consolidation of the several lots, suitable farm units to be assigned to those owners who offer the highest prices. . . .

. . . . .

ARTICLE 59.

Land-reclamation consortia are juridical persons, acting within the limits set for their activities by the law and by their articles of association. . . .

. . . . .

155. THE BATTLE OF WHEAT [32]

In an effort to reduce Italy's dependence on wheat and other grain imports, that is, to render her more nearly self-sufficient, the government launched an energetic campaign to increase the domestic production of the staples. The most spectacular aspect of the campaign was the "Battle of Wheat," well described in the selection below.

. . . nearly one-sixth of the cultivated area [of Italy] is under wheat. Wheat is the most important and most widespread of Italian crops.

[32] C. Longobardi, *Land-Reclamation in Italy. Rural Revival in the Building of a Nation*, P. S. King and Son, London, 1936, pp. 36-51. Reprinted by permission of the publishers.

It is cultivated throughout the country; on fertile and on poor soil, on humid and on dry, from the sea level up to high mountain elevations. . . .

Italy is a country of farmers, each of whom likes to grow his own wheat. Amid the variety and multiplicity of crops, wheat has a place on every farm. In its simplicity it is a complex crop, for it requires rotations and cattle. Therefore the proclamation of the wheat campaign meant the concentration of the attention of all concerned on a concrete symbol which stands for agriculture as a whole, not excluding animal husbandry.

. . . To speak in abstract or generic terms would have been too vague, and Mussolini's psychological insight led him to train his guns on one single product, wheat, a product dear to all, the symbol of the family, the land, civilization, progress, life, the staple food, the pivot of Italian agriculture, and the visible sign of its nobility.

Of wheat converted into bread Mussolini has said:

Italians!—Love bread—Heart of the home—Fragrance of the board—Joy of the hearth.
Respect bread—Sweat of the brow—Pride of the worker—Poetry of sacrifice.
Honour bread—Glory of the fields—Fragrance of the earth—Festival of life.
Do not waste bread—Wealth of the Motherland—God's sweetest gift—The holiest reward of human toil.

When the farmer sees his social function recognized in the wheat he grows, and when for the sake of that wheat he brings to the highest degree of perfection the tillage of the soil, the use of fertilizers, the adoption of new breeds of seed, his systems of rotation, his livestock, his use of machinery, and his recourse to the economic and social institutions at his service, then the whole of agriculture benefits by the latest improvements and the use of the new means now at the service of the farm is intensified.

The Wheat Campaign was opened on 4th July 1925, by a decree-law, No. 1181, establishing a permanent wheat committee. Presided over by Mussolini the Committee was charged to study and submit to the Government proposals for increasing the wheat output of the country, and it drew up concrete suggestions which were embodied in legislation enacted in that same month of July 1925. These measures, and the others which followed, have provided the rules regulating the Campaign, and can be summarized as follows:

(*a*) the foundation of organs to direct the Campaign (Permanent

Grain Committee), carry on the propaganda work (Provincial Commissions for wheat propaganda), increase the efficiency and importance
of the agricultural extension service (Travelling Chairs of Agriculture) . . . and the agricultural experiment stations;

(*b*) encouragement of special seed-breeding and mechanical seed
selection, repression of fraud in the preparation and sale of farm requisites and farm products, compulsory construction of scientific fertilizer-
tanks on the farm; encouragement of certain farm improvements and
provision of irrigation systems;

(*c*) an import duty on wheat and a fixed percentage of home-grown
wheat to be used by millers;

(*d*) exemption from custom's duty and sales tax on petrol required
for farm tractors; awards to encourage the breaking up of fallow lands,
motor-ploughing and electric tillage;

(*e*) provision of farm credit, with a special view to avoiding the
hasty sale of the crop immediately after the harvest, so as to prevent
price-slumps due to the concentration of sales over too brief a period;

(*f*) provincial and national prize competitions to encourage the
intensive cultivation of cereal crops.

The Wheat Campaign has four chief objects: (1) to emphasize the
social functions of farmers in the life of the country; (2) to improve
their conditions; (3) to reduce the unduly heavy adverse balance of
trade; (4) to secure for the country a certain degree of self-sufficiency
as regards its food supplies.

. . . . . .

In July 1925, Mussolini, presiding over the opening of the Permanent
Wheat Committee, outlined its policies as follows:

1.—It is not strictly necessary to increase the area under wheat in Italy.
Land must not be taken from other crops which may be more profitable
and which are anyhow necessary to national economic life. Any increase
of the area under wheat should therefore be avoided. It is the unanimous
opinion that the number of hectares sown to this crop in 1924, can be made
sufficient.

2.—It is, however, necessary to increase the average yield of wheat per
hectare. An average increase, even if modest, gives very marked global
results.

Starting from these principles, the work of the Permanent Wheat Committee must deal:

1—with the problem of seed selection.

2—with the problem of fertilizers and of technical improvements in general.

3—with the problem of prices.

The first of these problems presented two aspects:

(*a*) that of breeding new and superior types of wheat, resistent to the major ills from which Italian wheat crops suffer, to wit, criptogamic diseases, lodging, and shrinkage. To resist the latter, wheat should ripen early so as to escape unfavourable weather during the final period of growth, when in a few days, sometimes in a few hours, sudden scorching heats are liable to hasten the ripening process, thus impoverishing the kernel of the grain and not infrequently halving the yield.

(*b*) the other aspect was the need that the new varieties of seed should possess qualities enabling wheat growing to be placed on a profitable business basis by large investments of working capital in the different phases of wheat farming. For this purpose they should ensure early crops and very high yields, two requisites essential to profitable wheat growing.

* * * * * *

Italy can now avail herself of several selected breeds of wheat suited to her very varied environmental conditions and needs. . . .

The use of selected, and more especially of early ripening varieties, has spread rapidly since 1926; in 1931 it was estimated that they accounted for 46 per cent of the entire wheat crop of the country; in 1932 the percentage had risen to 54.9 per cent. A study published by the Central Statistical Institute shows that the area sown to selected wheat in 1933 accounted for 57.1 per cent of the total area under wheat, and that their use was further extended in 1934, accounting for 61.7 per cent of the total, the maxima being obtained in North and Central Italy with 93.3 per cent and 76.3 per cent respectively, and the minima in South Italy and the Islands with 44.0 per cent and 23.5 per cent respectively. The early ripening varieties have even made it possible to secure two crops: wheat followed by rice, wheat followed by maize, etc. on the same field during the same year.

If we turn to improvements in cultivation we find that not only has there been an increase in the use of fertilizers and machinery, but that the soil is now tilled with much greater care, and much more attention paid to the cultivation of wheat during the growing season.

* * * * *

. . . the Campaign has secured the desired increase in the yield per unit of area. It is the general opinion that the returns for the 1934 harvest illustrate more than any other the efficacy of the campaign, for without it the yield for the country as a whole would have been one of the lowest on record, mainly on account of the injury caused by excessive rains in the autumn and winter. When this volume was already under press the following data for the 1935 wheat crop became available: area 5,027,000 ha.; production 7,714,500 metric tons; yield 1.53 metric tons per ha.

The following particulars published by the *Corriere della Sera* on the crops obtained at the gates of Milan have lost none of their value as a description of some of the technical details of the Wheat Campaign, although they refer to the harvest of 1933.

In 1931 when the harvest of the whole country yielded 6.7 million metric tons of wheat, the yields obtained with early ripening varieties rose to as much as 6, 6.5, and 6.8 metric tons per hectare, results then considered quite exceptional but which were exceeded in 1932 by yields rising to 7.2, 7.3, and even 7.4 metric tons per hectare, and this not on experiment fields, but over farms covering several hectares. In 1933 the *Corriere della Sera* records a yield of 8.83 metric tons per hectare.

. . . . .

With its yield of 8.1 million metric tons the 1933 harvest suffices to meet the needs of the home market, leaving a margin of safety for poor crop years and for increased consumption, and marks the victory of the wheat campaign, as Mussolini pointed out to the meeting of the Permanent Wheat Committee on 21st November 1933. Taking the results thus secured as a basis, the Duce was able to indicate as follows the further developments of the programme for the Campaign, which are reflected in the new rules drawn up for the national prize competition [33] for the Wheat Victory. In this connection he said:

As the competition is to point to the logical development of the activities of the Wheat Campaign, it should recall—and it will do so even in its name —that the Wheat Campaign aims at encouraging progress with a view to

---

[33] In connection with the 1934 harvest, 1,136,000 lire were distributed in awards on the 25th November 1934 to the winners of the provincial prize competitions, and 864,000 lire were distributed in Rome on the 2nd December to the winners of the national prize competition. Thus a total sum of 2 million lire has been paid out in awards to prize-winners in this competition in which some 15,000 persons took part.

improving the cultural-economic system and the farming technique of the leading crops, on the basis of practical experience and scientific experimentation now being exhaustively made in the several typical zones of the country. Starting with the crop-year 1934-35, the national prize competition for the Wheat Victory will therefore make way for the "National Prize Competition for Wheat and Farming," which will aim at securing such co-ordinated objectives as that of obtaining, along with further progress in the yield of wheat per unit, the increase of forage crops and the improvement of animal husbandry, surface drainage and the reconditioning of lands; the increase of market-gardening and fruit crops. The competition is therefore of a comprehensive character and its rules will have to be carefully studied and will ensure further progress for Italian agriculture along the path of technical progress and economy in production costs.

* * * * *

The facts we have set forth in this chapter clearly show the connection between integral land-reclamation and the Wheat Campaign. Indeed, the two undertakings complete each other. Land-reclamation makes new rural areas available for utilization along progressive lines; the Wheat Campaign raises to the utmost the value of the crops, thus coming to the assistance of that agricultural progress which is not only the purpose of integral land-reclamation but is also the means which makes it possible to confer on it an integral character.

156. THE WORK OF THE MINISTRY FOR THE PRESS AND PROPAGANDA [34]

Possibly because of the success attained by the Ministry for Public Enlightenment and Propaganda established under the able headship of Dr. Joseph Goebbels in Nazi Germany (See Document No. 196), Premier Mussolini decided to create a similar organization in Italy. Hence, to inform the people of the official interpretation of domestic and foreign affairs and simultaneously to exercise a more efficient censorship over domestic and foreign publications, an Italian Ministry for the Press and Propaganda was organized in 1934 by Count Nobile Galeazzo Ciano, son-in-law of Il Duce.

[34] *Speech Delivered in the Senate on May 22nd, 1936 by H. E. Galeazzo Ciano, Minister for the Press and Propaganda,* Società Editrice di Novissima, Rome, 1936, pp. 1-31.

Gentlemen,

The Ministry for the Press and Propaganda, upon whose budget I
have the honour to report, developed around a nucleus provided by the
Press Office of the Head of the Government, which had been instituted
immediately after the triumph of our Revolution. It was obvious from
the start that this Press Office was . . . a definitely political organ,
whose task it was to direct, coordinate and potentiate Italian journalism
in order that it might be worthy of its mission. . . . Thus it was that
the Press ceased to be a private business undertaking and became an
instrument of civilisation at the service of the country; a formidable
means for the education of the Fascist People who, after receiving the
fundamental elements of culture in the schools, could now find scope
for their moral, intellectual and political development in their daily
readings.

It was obvious, therefore, that having assigned such an important
role to the press, the State was also compelled to intervene, either
directly or by means of special organs, whenever control or an impelling
influence were required.

. . . . .

In view of these . . . developments, that particular organ of the
State which I have just described, took on such size and importance
as to require an initial transformation into an Undersecretariat of State
and eventually, when its scope expanded farther afield, into a full-
fledged Ministry.

This is the first time that the Budget of the new organisation is submitted to the consideration of this Assembly, . . . and I assume that
there may be some interest and utility in making a rapid survey of the
various sections comprised by the Ministry and of the activities which
are being pursued by them.

The Department of the Italian Press and the Department of the
Foreign Press which come first by the chronological order of their
institution, carry out their activity in obviously different spheres, but
in complete harmony with one another.

The Department of the Italian Press, besides its principal task of
directing the trend of all daily and periodical publications, is also entrusted with the duty of supervising all journalistic and other literary
activities in order that the existing rules and by-laws be fully complied
with.

The control exerted by this Department is by no means confined to a negative action, such as prohibiting the publication of certain items of news or the handling of certain problems. On the contrary, all matters which are of interest to the press, are promptly pointed out by the Ministry to the competent authorities, and in other cases to the newspapers themselves in order that the latter may give them the vast repercussion they deserve.

. . . . .

Once journalism had been shaped in this mould, it followed that the use of the profession had to be regulated likewise. In the past, journalism was often the profession of those who had no other. This has ceased to be so, the syndicates having taken the matter firmly in hand and issued proper rules. In our Regime journalists are placed on the same moral and material plane as persons engaged in any other profession. . . .

. . . . .

Books, too, receive our very special attention. Former laws on the control over literature were somewhat vague. From the holes of the loosely-woven net there escaped and were circulated certain publications which proved undesirable for a number of reasons.

In virtue of a circular issued by the Head of the Government on April 3, 1934 and of a subsequent decree promulgated on October 24, 1935 this legislation has been modified, the Ministry for the Press and Propaganda having been empowered to revise all publications, and to perform this task on new and revolutionary principles. Let it be stressed that there is no shortsighted or mean censorship which confines the freedom of the artist or limits the work of the scientist. Every wholesome expression of the mind is welcomed, respected and circulated. But if unqualified contraband were being smuggled under cover of art, or if ideas which prove offensive to the national, religious and social ethics of Fascism were disseminated under cover of science, the Ministry would become intransigent and publications of the foregoing nature be suppressed without mercy.

. . . . .

As regards the Foreign Press our activity is confined to assisting foreign correspondents in Rome and other centers in freely carrying out their activity by keeping them in touch with the editorial staffs of their papers through our diplomatic representatives. Press Attachés have been recently appointed for this purpose. Specialized officials of the Ministry for the Press, like other technical experts, will be qualified to keep in touch with the journalistic world in countries to whose governments they are accredited.

Their duties will not be confined to the reading of the local papers, since, by following the daily movement of the press, they shall perform a certain amount of wholesome propaganda, with the object of disseminating the knowledge of our creative and political work, and of our spiritual, cultural and scientific activities. The Press Attaché will help to carry Italian thought, art and culture throughout the world adequately presented in the light of our millenary traditions and of the living reality of our strenuous present.

. . . . .

The development of broadcasting is of special interest at the present time. That is, no doubt, the most formidable instrument at the service of international propaganda. . . .

In this field Italy made a late start as compared to other countries, but thanks to the work accomplished in 1934 and 1935, the technical and political equipment of our broadcasting system has risen to a rank which places it at least on a level with that of radio organisations of countries which were formerly at the vanguard of all others.

In due course I shall deal with the artistic aspect of broadcasting, but I first wish to dwell upon the journalistic and political side of the matter. Thanks to our excellent wireless equipment, we can address the world in 18 languages, among them being: Albanian, Bulgarian, Arab, German, Hungarian, English, Croatian, French, Greek, Spanish, Portuguese, Esperanto, Hebrew, etc. Our news bulletins are listened to with the keenest interest everywhere. No less than 59,084 letters received from radio listeners last year bear witness to this statement, and each one has been answered. Whosoever applied for information or explanation on some point was given it. 24,008 requests for publications and data on Fascism were met by the shipment of 124,546 publications and pamphlets.

A new feature was introduced in broadcasting by the institution of courses of lessons in the Italian language, with the distribution of free papers on grammar especially prepared for students in Germany, Great Britain, France, Spain, Hungary, Greece and Roumania. The total number of students following these courses exceeds 35,000, and thou-

We are by no means convinced of the commonly accepted fact that
the cinema has killed the stage, indeed we maintain that the latter has
some very real and deep-rooted reasons to subsist, and we have therefore
organised an office known as the Stage Inspector's Department, whose
duty it is to reorganise and supervise theatricals of every kind including
musical activities.

· · · · ·

Once the various forms of propaganda had been brought together
into a single organisation, we began to realize the utility of placing all
matters connected with Tourist Travel under the same guidance.
Propaganda is connected with Travel for two outstanding reasons: one,
because the action pursued by us, as by all countries, in order to attract
international travel is nothing short of propaganda, and two, because
no form of propaganda is more effective than to make the foreign visitor an eye-witness to the well disciplined and active life of Fascist Italy.

The Tourist Travel Department have studied the economic aspect of
the problem as well as its political side with great care. . . .

· · · · ·

In this period of glory in which we have the fortune to live, may the
Minister for the Press and Propaganda be, and increasingly become, the
centre which collects and radiates the forces of the great revival which
derives its name from the Duce.

157. THE LATERAN ACCORD, FEBRUARY 11, 1929 *(Extracts)* [35]

The signing of the Lateran Accord on February 11, 1929, between Italy
and the Papacy, marked the end of a "conflict of conscience" that dated
from 1870, when Italian troops entered Papal Rome and Pope Pius IX
retired to the Vatican, calling himself "the prisoner of a usurping power."
The accord which settled this "Roman Question" consisted of three docu-
ments: a political treaty, a financial convention, and a concordat. Ratifica-
tions were exchanged in Rome on June 7, 1929, and soon thereafter Pope
Pius XI emerged from the Vatican as head of the new state of Vatican City.

[35] *L'Europe Nouvelle,* June 29, 1929; translation from Royal Institute of International
Affairs, *Documents on International Affairs 1929,* Oxford University Press, London,
1930, pp. 216-241. Reprinted by permission of the Royal Institute of International
Affairs and the publishers.

1. POLITICAL TREATY

In the name of the Most Holy Trinity.

Whereas the Holy See and Italy have recognized the desirability of eliminating every reason for dissension existing between them and arriving at a final settlement of their reciprocal relations which shall be consistent with justice and with the dignity of both High Contracting Parties, and which by permanently assuring to the Holy See a position *de facto* and *de jure* which shall guarantee absolute independence for the fulfilment of its exalted mission in the world, permits the Holy See to consider as finally and irrevocably settled the Roman Question which arose in 1870 by the annexation of Rome to the Kingdom of Italy, under the Dynasty of the House of Savoy;

And whereas it was obligatory, for the purpose of assuring the absolute and visible independence of the Holy See, likewise to guarantee its indisputable sovereignty in international matters, it has been found necessary to create under special conditions the Vatican City, recognizing the full ownership, exclusive and absolute dominion and sovereign jurisdiction of the Holy See over that City;

His Holiness the Supreme Pontiff Pius XI and His Majesty Victor Emmanuel III, King of Italy, have agreed to conclude a Treaty, appointing for that purpose two Plenipotentiaries, being on behalf of His Holiness, His Secretary of State, viz. His Most Reverend Eminence the Lord Cardinal Pietro Gasparri, and on behalf of His Majesty, His Excellency the Cav. Benito Mussolini, Prime Minister and Head of the Government; who, having exchanged their respective full powers, which were found to be in due and proper form, have hereby agreed to the following articles:

Article 1.

Italy recognizes and reaffirms the principle established in the first Article of the Italian Constitution dated March 4, 1848, according to which the Catholic Apostolic Roman religion is the only State religion.

Article 2.

Italy recognizes the sovereignty of the Holy See in international matters as an inherent attribute in conformity with its traditions and the requirements of its mission to the world.

Article 3.

Italy recognizes the full ownership, exclusive dominion, and sovereign authority and jurisdiction of the Holy See over the Vatican as at present constituted, together with all its appurtenances and endowments, thus creating the Vatican City, for the special purposes and under the conditions hereinafter referred to.

The boundaries of the said City are set forth in the map called Annex I of the present Treaty, of which it forms an integral part.

It is furthermore agreed that, although forming part of the Vatican City, St. Peter's Square shall continue to be normally open to the public and shall be subject to supervision by the Italian police authorities, which powers shall cease to operate at the foot of the steps leading to the Basilica, although the latter shall continue to be used for public worship. The said authorities shall, therefore, abstain from mounting the steps and entering the said Basilica, unless and except they are requested to do so by the proper authorities.

Should the Holy See consider it necessary, for the purpose of special ceremonies, temporarily to prohibit the public from free access to St. Peter's Square, the Italian authorities shall (unless specially requested to do otherwise) withdraw to beyond the outer lines of Bernini's Colonnade and the extension thereof.

Article 4.

The sovereignty and exclusive jurisdiction over the Vatican City, which Italy recognizes as appertaining to the Holy See, forbid any intervention therein on the part of the Italian Government, or that any authority other than that of the Holy See shall be there acknowledged.

. . . . .

Article 8.

Considering the person of the Supreme Pontiff to be sacred and inviolable, Italy declares any attempt against His person or any incitement to commit such attempt to be punishable by the same penalties as all similar attempts and incitements to commit the same against the person of the King.

All offences or public insults committed within Italian territory against the person of the Supreme Pontiff, whether by means of speeches, acts, or writings, shall be punished in the same manner as offences and insults against the person of the King.

. . . . .

ARTICLE 11.

All central bodies of the Catholic Church shall be exempt from any interference on the part of the Italian State (save and except as provided by Italian law in regard to the acquisition of property made by *corpi morali* [recognized public bodies], and with regard to the conversion of real estate).

ARTICLE 12.

Italy recognizes the right of the Holy See to passive and active Legation, according to the general rules of International Law. Officials accredited by foreign Governments to the Holy See shall continue to enjoy, within the Kingdom of Italy, all the prerogatives of immunity enjoyed by diplomatic agents under International Law, and their headquarters may continue to be within Italian territory whilst enjoying the immunity due to them under International Law, even in the event of their State not having diplomatic relations with Italy.

It is understood that Italy undertakes in all cases to allow the freedom of correspondence for all States, including belligerents, to and from the Holy See, as well as free access to the Apostolic See by Bishops from all over the world. . . .

ARTICLE 13.

Italy recognizes the full ownership of the Holy See over the Patriarchal Basilicas of St. John Lateran, Sta. Maria Maggiore, and St. Paul, with their annexed buildings.

The State transfers to the Holy See the free management and administration of the said Basilica of St. Paul and its dependent Monastery, also paying over to the Holy See all monies representing the sums set aside annually for that church in the budget of the Ministry of Education.

It is also understood that the Holy See shall remain the absolute owner of the edifice of S. Callisto, adjoining Sta. Maria in Trastevere.

ARTICLE 14.

Italy recognizes the full ownership by the Holy See of the Papal Palace of Castel Gandolfo, . . . and Italy also undertakes to hand over, within six months after the coming into force of the present Treaty, the Villa Barberini in Castel Gandolfo, . . .

. . . . .

ARTICLE 24.

In regard to the sovereignty appertaining to it also in international matters, the Holy See declares that it desires to take, and shall take, no part in any temporal rivalries between other States, nor in any international congresses called to settle such matters, save and except in the event of such parties making a mutual appeal to the pacific mission of the Holy See, the latter reserving in any event the right of exercising its moral and spiritual power.

The Vatican City shall, therefore, be invariably and in every event considered as neutral and inviolable territory.

. . . . .

ARTICLE 27.

Within four months after the signature thereof, the present Treaty shall be submitted for ratification by the Supreme Pontiff and the King of Italy, and shall enter into force as soon as ratifications are exchanged.

Dated in Rome this 11th day of February, 1929.

(*Signed*) PIETRO Cardinal GASPARRI.

BENITO MUSSOLINI.

2. FINANCIAL CONVENTION

Whereas the Holy See and Italy, following upon the stipulations of the Treaty by means of which the Roman Question has been finally settled, consider it to be requisite and necessary that their financial relations be regulated by a separate Convention which shall, however, form an integral part of such Treaty:

And whereas the Supreme Pontiff—considering from a lofty point of view the great prejudice suffered by the Apostolic See by reason of the loss of the Patrimony of St. Peter, represented by the former Papal States and the property belonging to ecclesiastical bodies, and, on the other hand, the ever-increasing demands made upon the Church, even in the city of Rome alone; and moreover considering the financial position of the State and the economic conditions of the Italian people (especially after the War)—has seen fit to limit the request for indemnity to what is strictly necessary, by asking for a sum, payable partly in cash and partly in Consolidated Stock, the value of which is much less than that which the State should have disbursed to the Holy See, even under the obligation assumed by the Law of May 13, 1871, alone: [36]

And whereas the Italian State, approving the paternal sentiments of the Supreme Pontiff, considers compliance with the request for payment of such sum to be its bounden duty:

The High Contracting Parties, represented by the same Plenipotentiaries, have agreed as follows:—

ARTICLE 1.

Italy undertakes to pay to the Holy See, upon exchange of the ratifications of the Treaty, the sum of 750,000,000 Italian *lire,* and to hand over simultaneously to the Holy See aforesaid such a sum in Italian 5% Consolidated Bearer Bonds, with coupon payable on June 30 of the current year attached, as shall represent the nominal value of 1,000,000,-000 Italian *lire.* [37]

ARTICLE 2.

The Holy See agrees to the above conditions in final settlement of its financial relations with Italy arising out of the events of 1870.

. . . . .

3. THE CONCORDAT

In the name of the Most Holy Trinity.

. . . . .

ARTICLE 1.

For the purposes of Article 1 of the Treaty, Italy assures to the Catholic Church the free exercise of spiritual power and the free and public exercise of its worship, as well as jurisdiction in ecclesiastical matters, in accordance with the provisions laid down in the present Concordat, where requisite and necessary, and grants to ecclesiastics for the spiritual ministry the privilege of defence by their own authorities.

In consideration of the sacred character of the Eternal City, the Episcopal See of the Supreme Pontiff, centre of the Catholic world, and goal of pilgrimage, the Italian Government will be careful to keep Rome free from anything which should be inconsistent with such character.

---

[36] The reference is to the Law of Papal Guarantees which, among other things, guaranteed to the popes, by way of compensation for their territorial and fiscal losses through the Italian occupation of Rome, an annual income of about $645,000. Pope Pius IX and his successors refused to accept the law and hence also rejected the payments.—*Ed.*

[37] Representing, at the time, $39,375,000 and $52,500,000, respectively.—*Ed.*

ARTICLE 2.

The Holy See shall communicate and correspond freely with its Bishops, with its Clergy, and with the whole Catholic world, without any interference on the part of the Italian Government. Similarly, Bishops shall be entitled to communicate and correspond freely with their Clergy and with all the faithful. . . .

The ecclesiastical authorities shall be at liberty, without any interference on the part of the civil authorities, to cause collections to be made both inside and outside churches, or in the buildings belonging to them.

ARTICLE 3.

. . . Clerics ordained *in sacris,* and members of religious Orders who have taken vows, shall be exempted from military service, save in the case of general mobilization. In that eventuality, priests will be drafted to the armed forces of the State, but shall continue to wear the habit, in order that they may exercise their sacred office amongst the troops, . . .

ARTICLE 4.

Ecclesiastics and members of religious Orders are exempted from jury service.

· · · · ·

ARTICLE 7.

No magistrate or other authority shall be entitled to request ecclesiastics for information regarding persons or events known to them by reason of their sacred office.

· · · · ·

ARTICLE 16.

The High Contracting Parties shall, by means of Mixed Commissions, proceed with the revision of the geographical delimitation of Dioceses, in order that it may, if possible, correspond to that of the provinces.

It is understood that . . . no part of the territory under the sovereignty of the Kingdom of Italy shall be under a Bishop whose See may be in territory under the sovereignty of another state; . . .

· · · · ·

Article 19.

The Holy See shall appoint Archbishops and Bishops. Before nominating an Archbishop or a Diocesan Bishop, or a Coadjutor *cum jure successionis,* the Holy See shall communicate the name of such candidate to the Italian Government, in order to be assured that the latter has no objections of a political nature to this nomination.

The steps necessary in this connexion shall be taken with all possible speed and secrecy, so that the name of the person chosen may not become known until his final nomination.

Article 20.

Previous to taking possession of their Sees, Bishops shall swear allegiance to the Head of the State, using the following form of oath, viz:

"Before God and on His Holy Gospels, I promise and swear allegiance to the Italian State, in such a manner as is proper to a Bishop.

"I promise and swear to respect, and to cause to be respected by my clergy, the King of Italy and the Italian Government, as constituted by the laws of the State.

"I further promise and swear that I shall enter into no agreement, nor attend any council, which may be prejudicial to the interests of the Italian State or to public order, and that I shall lay a similar prohibition on my clergy.

"Being zealous for the good and the advantage of the Italian State, I shall do my utmost to prevent any evil which might threaten it."

. . . . .

Article 29.

The laws of the Italian State concerning ecclesiastical matters shall be revised, in order that they may be reformed and completed and brought into harmony with the principles which inspired the Treaty concluded with the Holy See and the present Concordat. . . .

. . . . .

Article 34.

Being desirous of restoring to the institution of marriage, which is the basis of the family, that dignity which is in keeping with the Catholic traditions of the Italian people, the Italian State recognizes the sacrament of marriage as legal for civil purposes, when administered according to Canon Law. . . .

. . . . .

Article 36.

The teaching of Christian doctrine, in the form admitted by Catholic tradition, is considered by Italy to be the basis and the apex of public education. For this reason, Italy agrees that religious education, which is now given in the public elementary schools, be in future extended to and developed in secondary schools, according to a programme to be settled between the Holy See and the State.

Such instruction shall be imparted by means of teachers and professors who are priests or members of religious Orders approved by the ecclesiastical authorities, and, in an auxiliary manner, by lay teachers and professors who shall for that purpose be provided with a certificate of qualification issued by the Ordinary of the Diocese. Should this certificate be revoked by the Ordinary, the teacher concerned shall be immediately deprived of the right to teach. Only books and text-books approved by the ecclesiastical authorities shall be used for such religious instruction in the public schools.

Article 37.

In order to render possible the religious instruction and assistance of youths entrusted to their care, the heads of Government associations for physical training, and for instruction preceding military training, of the Avanguardisti and Balilla, shall arrange their time-tables in such a manner as not to prevent the carrying out of their religious duties on Sundays and days of obligation. The heads of State schools shall make similar arrangements, in the event of meetings of their pupils on such days.

. . . . . .

Article 39.

All Universities, greater or lesser Seminaries (diocesan, inter-diocesan or regional), Academies, Colleges, and other Catholic institutions for training and education of ecclesiastics, shall continue to be solely dependent on the Holy See, without any intervention on the part of the educational authorities of the Kingdom.

. . . . .

ARTICLE 43.

The Italian State recognizes the organizations connected with the "Azione Cattolica Italiana" [Catholic Action], in so far as these shall (as provided by the Holy See) carry on their activities outside any political party, and under the immediate direction of the hierarchy of the Church, for the diffusion and practice of Catholic principles.

The Holy See takes the opportunity afforded by the present Concordat to renew its veto with regard to any Italian ecclesiastics and members of religious Orders joining, or working in, any political party.

ARTICLE 44.

Should any divergence arise in future with regard to the interpretation of the present Concordat, the Holy See and Italy shall arrive at an amicable settlement by mutual accord.

ARTICLE 45.

. . . A commission composed of persons delegated by both High Contracting Parties shall be appointed immediately after the execution of the present Concordat, for the carrying out of the provisions thereof.

Rome, this 11th day of February, 1929.

(*Signed*) PIETRO Cardinal GASPARRI.

BENITO MUSSOLINI.

158. POPE PIUS XI ON THE RECONSTRUCTION OF THE SOCIAL ORDER, 1931 [38]

Not long after the ratification of the Lateran Accord, it became evident that some differences of opinion still existed between the pope and the government of Italy, particularly where the division of their respective spheres of influence in matters of economic and social import was concerned. On May 25, 1931, Pope Pius XI issued an encyclical called Quadragesimo Anno, *because it was published on the fortieth anniversary of Leo XIII's encyclical on labor,* Rerum Novarum. *Many Fascists were displeased with the new encyclical because in it the pope protested not merely against the new social order as created by the Bolsheviks, but also against some aspects of life in a totalitarian state such as Italy.*

---

[38] *Four Great Encyclicals,* The Paulist Press, New York, 1931, Addenda, pp. 27-30, 32-35, 37-38. Reprinted by permission of the publishers.

QUADRAGESIMO ANNO
ENCYCLICAL LETTER OF HIS HOLINESS PIUS XI
BY DIVINE PROVIDENCE
POPE

To Our Venerable Brethren: The Patriarchs, Primates, Archbishops, Bishops and Other Ordinaries, in Peace and Communion with the Apostolic See, and to All the Faithful of the Catholic World on Reconstructing the Social Order and Perfecting It Conformably to the Precepts of the Gospels, in Commemoration of the Fortieth Anniversary of the Encyclical "Rerum Novarum."

. . . . .

HARMONY BETWEEN RANKS IN SOCIETY

Now this is the primary duty of the state and of all good citizens: to abolish conflict between classes with divergent interests, and thus foster and promote harmony between the various ranks of society.

The aim of social legislation must therefore be the reestablishment of vocational groups. Society today still remains in a strained and therefore unstable and uncertain state, being founded on classes with contradictory interests and hence opposed to each other, and consequently prone to enmity and strife. Labor, indeed, as has been well said by Our Predecessor [Leo XIII] in his Encyclical, is not a mere chattel, since the human dignity of the workingman must be recognized in it, and consequently it cannot be bought and sold like any piece of merchandise. None the less the demand and supply of labor divides men on the labor market into two classes, as into two camps, and the bargaining between these parties transforms this labor market into an arena where the two armies are engaged in combat. To this grave disorder which is leading society to ruin a remedy must evidently be applied as speedily as possible. But there cannot be question of any perfect cure, except this opposition be done away with, and well-ordered members of the social body come into being anew, vocational groups namely, binding men together not according to the position they occupy in the labor market, but according to the diverse functions which they exercise in society. For as nature induces those who dwell in close proximity to unite into municipalities, so those who practice the same trade or profession, economic or otherwise, combine into vocational groups. These groups, in a true sense autonomous, are considered by man to be, if not essential to civil society, at least its natural and spontaneous development.

. . . . .

It is hardly necessary to note that what Leo XIII taught concerning the form of political government can, in due measure, be applied also to vocational groups. Here, too, men may choose whatever form they please, provided that both justice and the common good be taken into account.

Just as the citizens of the same municipality are wont to form associations with diverse aims, which various individuals are free to join or not, similarly, those who are engaged in the same trade or profession will form free associations among themselves, for purposes connected with their occupations. . . . Not only is man free to institute these unions which are of a private character, but he has the right to adopt such organization and such rules as may best conduce to the attainment of their respective objects. The same liberty must be claimed for the founding of associations which extend beyond the limits of a single trade. . . .

THE RESTORATION OF THE TRUE GUIDING PRINCIPLE OF ECONOMICS

Still another aim must be kept in view. Just as the unity of human society cannot be built upon class warfare, so the proper ordering of economic affairs cannot be left to free competition alone. From this source have proceeded in the past all the errors of the "Individualistic" school. This school, ignorant or forgetful of the social and moral aspects of economic matters, teaches that the state should refrain in theory and practice from interfering therein, because these possess in free competition and open markets a principle of self-direction better able to control them than any created intellect. Free competition, however, though within certain limits just and productive of good results, cannot be the ruling principle of the economic world. This has been abundantly proved by the consequences that have followed from the free rein given to these dangerous individualistic ideals. It is therefore very necessary that economic affairs be once more subjected to and governed by a true and effective guiding principle. Still less can this function be exercised by the economic supremacy which within recent times has taken the place of free competition; for this a headstrong and vehement power, which, if it is to prove beneficial to mankind, needs to be curbed strongly and ruled with prudence. It cannot, however, be curbed and governed by itself. More lofty and noble principles must therefore be sought in order to control this supremacy sternly and uncompromisingly: to wit, social justice and social charity.

To that end all the institutions of public and social life must be imbued with the spirit of justice, and this justice must above all be truly operative. It must build up a juridical and social order able to pervade all economic activity. Social charity should be, as it were, the soul of this order and the duty of the state will be to protect and defend it effectively. This task it will perform the more readily if it free itself from those burdens which, as We have already declared, are not properly its own.

Further, it would be well if the various nations in common counsel and endeavor strove to promote a healthy economic cooperation by prudent pacts and institutions, since in economic matters they are largely dependent one upon the other, and need one another's help.

. . . . .

Within recent times, as all are aware, a special syndical and corporative organization has been inaugurated which, in view of the subject of the present Encyclical, demands of Us some mention and opportune comment.

The state here grants legal recognition to the syndicate or union, and thereby confers on it some of the features of a monopoly, for in virtue of this recognition, it alone can represent respectively workingmen and employers, and it alone can conclude labor contracts and labor agreements. Affiliation to the syndicate is optional for everyone; but in this sense only can the syndical organization be said to be free, since the contribution to the union and other special taxes are obligatory for all who belong to a given branch, whether workingmen or employers, and the labor-contracts drawn up by the legal syndicate are likewise obligatory. It is true that it has been authoritatively declared that the legal syndicate does not exclude the existence of unrecognized trade associations.

The corporations are composed of representatives of the unions of workingmen and employers of the same trade or profession, and as true and genuine organs and institutions of the state, they direct and coordinate the activities of the unions in all matters of common interest.

STRIKES AND LOCK-OUTS ARE FORBIDDEN

If the contending parties cannot come to an agreement, public authority intervenes.

Little reflection is required to perceive the advantage of the institution thus summarily described; peaceful collaboration of the classes, repression of Socialist organizations and efforts, the moderating influence of a special ministry.

But in order to overlook nothing in a matter of such importance, and in the light of the general principles stated above, as well as of that which We are now about to formulate, We feel bound to add that to Our knowledge there are some who fear that the state is substituting itself in the place of private initiative, instead of limiting itself to necessary and sufficient help and assistance. It is feared that the new syndical and corporative institution possesses an exclusively bureaucratic and political character, and that, notwithstanding the general advantages referred to above, it risks serving particular political aims rather than contributing to the initiation of a better social order.

We believe that to attain this last named lofty purpose for the true and permanent advantage of the commonwealth, there is need before and above all else of the blessing of God, and, in the second place, of the cooperation of all men of good will. . . .

. . . . .

DOMINATION HAS FOLLOWED FROM FREE COMPETITION

. . . it is patent that in our days not alone is wealth accumulated, but immense power and despotic economic domination is concentrated in the hands of a few, and that those few are frequently found not the owners, but only the trustees and directors of invested funds, who administer them at their good pleasure.

. . . . .

This concentration of power has led to a threefold struggle for domination. First, there is the struggle for dictatorship in the economic sphere itself; then, the fierce battle to acquire control of the state, so that its resources and authority may be abused in the economic struggles. Finally, the clash between states themselves.

This latter arises from two causes:—Because the nations apply their power and political influence, regardless of circumstances, to promote the economic advantages of their citizens; and because, vice versa, economic forces and economic domination are used to decide political controversies between peoples.

DISASTROUS CONSEQUENCES

You assuredly know, Venerable Brethren and Beloved Children, and you lament the ultimate consequences of this Individualistic spirit in economic affairs. Free competition is dead, economic dictatorship has taken its place.

Unbridled ambition for domination has succeeded the desire for gain; the whole economic life has become hard, cruel and relentless in a ghastly measure. Furthermore, the intermingling and scandalous confusing of the duties and offices of civil authority and of economics have produced crying evils and have gone so far as to degrade the majesty of the state. The state which should be the supreme arbiter, ruling in kingly fashion far above all party contention, intent only upon justice and the common good, has become instead a slave, bound over to the service of human passion and greed. As regards the relations of peoples among themselves, a double stream has issued forth from this one fountainhead: on the one hand, economic nationalism or even economic imperialism; on the other, a not less noxious and detestable internationalism or international imperialism in financial affairs, which holds that where a man's fortune is, there is his country.

· · · · ·

CHANGES IN SOCIALISM

Since the days of Leo XIII, Socialism too, the great enemy with which his battles were waged, has undergone profound changes, no less than economics. At that time Socialism could fairly be termed a single system, which defended certain definite and mutually coherent doctrines. Nowadays it has in the main become divided into two opposing and often bitterly hostile camps, neither of which, however, has abandoned the principle peculiar to Socialism, namely, opposition to the Christian Faith.

THE MORE VIOLENT SECTION, COMMUNISM

One section of Socialism has . . . degenerated into Communism. Communism teaches and pursues a twofold aim: Merciless class warfare and complete abolition of private ownership; and this it does, not in secret and by hidden methods, but openly, frankly, and by every means, even the most violent. To obtain these ends, Communists shrink from nothing and fear nothing; and when they have attained power it is unbelievable, indeed it seems portentous, how cruel and inhuman they show themselves to be. . . .

· · · · ·

MORE MODERATE SECTION

The other section, which has retained the name of Socialism, is much less radical in its views. Not only does it condemn recourse to physical force; it even mitigates and moderates to some extent class warfare and the abolition of private property. It does not reject them entirely. It would seem as if Socialism were afraid of its own principles and of the conclusions drawn therefrom by the Communists, and in consequence were drifting towards the truth which Christian tradition has always held in respect; for it cannot be denied that its programs often strikingly approach the just demands of Christian social reformers.

* * * * *

CATHOLIC AND SOCIALIST ARE CONTRADICTORY TERMS

If, like all errors, Socialism contains a certain element of truth (and this the Sovereign Pontiffs have never denied), it is nevertheless founded upon a doctrine of human society peculiarly its own, which is opposed to true Christianity. "Religious Socialism," "Christian Socialism" are expressions implying a contradition in terms. No one can be at the same time a sincere Catholic and a true Socialist.

* * * * *

159. DECREE ON THE SURNAMES OF FAMILIES IN THE FORMER SOUTH TIROL, 1926 [39]

With the acquisition of the South Tirol after the World War, Italy also acquired a minority problem, for the area was inhabited by a quarter-million Germans. At the time of transfer the natives had been assured that their language and cultural institutions would be respected, but the Fascists were determined to "make Italians" of them. Among the decrees most objectionable to the Tirolese was one of January 10, 1926, which ordered the "restoration" of the supposed Italian forms of the natives' surnames.

ARTICLE 1.

The families of the province of Trento which bear an original Italian or Latin surname translated into other languages or deformed by for-

---

[39] Royal Decree-Law of January 10, 1926 (No. 17), in Italy, *Gazzetta Ufficiale del Regno d'Italia*, Ministry of Grace and Justice, Rome, January 15, 1926, No. 11.

eign orthography or by the addition of foreign suffixes will reassume their original surnames in their original forms.

Similarly restored to their Italian forms shall be surnames of toponomical origin, derived from places, where these names have been translated into other languages or deformed by foreign orthography, and likewise titles of nobility translated or reduced to foreign forms.

The restitution of the Italian forms will be announced by decree of the prefect of the province who will notify the parties concerned. . . .

He who, after the announced restitution, continues to make use of the surname or title of nobility in its foreign form, is punishable by a fine of from 500 to 5000 lire.

ARTICLE 2.

Besides the cases mentioned in the preceding article, foreign surnames of foreign origin may be converted to Italian forms by decree of the prefect upon the request of the persons concerned. . . .

ARTICLE 3.

By Royal Decree the dispositions of Articles 1 and 2 may, in whole or in part, be extended to other provinces of the Kingdom. . . .

160. PACT OF FRIENDSHIP AND SECURITY BETWEEN ALBANIA AND ITALY (TREATY OF TIRANA), NOVEMBER 27, 1926 [40]

Prevented by President Wilson from getting a mandate over Albania at the Paris Peace Conference, Italy found other means of extending her influence over her small neighbor across the Straits of Otranto. One of the first steps in the establishment of a protective relationship was the signing of the Treaty of Tirana on November 27, 1926. An accompanying letter, deposited with the League Secretariat, stated that Italy had the right to intervene in Albanian affairs only when requested to do so by the Tirana Government. The treaty was registered with the League on February 8, 1927. It was renewed in 1930.

Albania and Italy, with the object of strengthening the ties of mutual friendship and security, having regard to their geographical position, and in order to promote the consolidation of peace,

---

[40] League of Nations, *Treaty Series 1927*, vol. LX, pp. 19-20.

Actuated by the desire to maintain the political, legal, and territorial *status quo* of Albania, within the scope of the treaties to which they both are Signatories and by the Covenant of the League of Nations,

Have agreed to conclude the present pact of Friendship and Security, And have for that purpose appointed as their Plenipotentiaries:

. . . . .

Who having examined their full powers, found to be in good and due form, have agreed on the following provisions:

ARTICLE 1.

Albania and Italy recognise that any disturbance threatening the political, legal and territorial *status quo* of Albania is contrary to their common political interests.

ARTICLE 2.

In order to safeguard the above-mentioned interests, the High Contracting Parties undertake to afford each other mutual support and cordial co-operation; they also undertake not to conclude with other Powers any political or military agreements prejudicial to the interests of the other Party, including those defined *(anche definiti)* in the present Pact.

ARTICLE 3.

The High Contracting Parties undertake to submit to special conciliation and arbitration procedure any questions which may give rise to dispute between them, and which it may not have been possible to settle by ordinary diplomatic procedure. The details of this procedure of pacific settlement shall form the subject of a special Convention to be concluded as soon as possible.

ARTICLE 4.

The present Pact shall remain in force for five years, and it may be denounced or renewed one year before its expiration.

ARTICLE 5.

The present Pact shall be ratified and subsequently registered with the League of Nations. The ratifications shall be exchanged at Rome.

Done at Tirana, November 27, 1926.

(*Signed*) H. VRIONI.

POMPEO ALOISI.

161. PROCLAMATIONS ISSUED BY THE PRESIDENT OF THE
UNITED STATES DURING THE ITALO-ETHIOPIAN
DISPUTE, OCTOBER 5, 1935 [41]

*On October 5, 1935, two days before the League declared Italy to be the
aggressor in the conflict with Ethiopia, President Franklin D. Roosevelt of
the United States exercised his powers to proclaim the fact of war, to forbid
the export of arms to either party in the dispute, and to warn American
civilians not to travel on the vessels of either belligerent.*

a. A PROCLAMATION

WHEREAS Section 1 of a Joint Resolution of Congress, entitled
"JOINT RESOLUTION providing for the prohibition of the export
of arms, ammunition, and implements of war to belligerent countries;
the prohibition of the transportation of arms, ammunition, and implements of war by vessels of the United States for the use of belligerent
states; for the registration and licensing of persons engaged in the business of manufacturing, exporting, or importing arms, ammunition or
implements of war; and restricting travel by American citizens on
belligerent ships during war," approved August 31, 1935, provides in
part as follows:

"That upon the outbreak or during the progress of war between, or
among, two or more foreign states, the President shall proclaim such
fact, and it shall thereafter be unlawful to export arms, ammunition,
or implements of war from any place in the United States, or possessions
of the United States, to any port of such belligerent states, or to any
neutral port for transshipment to, or for the use of, a belligerent
country."

AND WHEREAS it is further provided by Section 1 of the said joint
resolution that—

"The President, by proclamation, shall definitely enumerate the arms,
ammunition, or implements of war, the export of which is prohibited
by this Act."

AND WHEREAS it is further provided by Section 1 of the said
joint resolution that—

"Whoever in violation of any of the provisions of this section, shall
export, or attempt to export, or cause to be exported, arms, ammunition,

[41] *The Statutes at Large of the United States of America from January 1935 to June
1936,* vol. XLIX, pt. 2, Government Printing Office, Washington, 1936, pp. 3474-3477.

or implements of war from the United States, or any of its possessions, shall be fined not more than $10,000 or imprisoned not more than five years, or both, and the property, vessel, or vehicle containing the same shall be subject to the provisions of sections 1 to 8, inclusive, title 6, chapter 30, of the act approved June 15, 1917. (40 Stat. 223-225; U. S. C. title 22, secs. 238-245)"

NOW, THEREFORE, I, FRANKLIN D. ROOSEVELT, President of the United States of America, acting under and by virtue of the authority conferred on me by the said joint resolution of Congress, do hereby proclaim that a state of war unhappily exists between Ethiopia and the Kingdom of Italy; and I do hereby admonish all citizens of the United States or any of its possessions and all persons residing or being within the territory or jurisdiction of the United States or its possessions to abstain from every violation of the provisions of the joint resolution above set forth, hereby made effective and applicable to the export of arms, ammunition, or implements of war from any place in the United States or its possessions to Ethiopia or to the Kingdom of Italy, or to any Italian possession, or to any neutral port for transshipment to, or for the use of, Ethiopia or the Kingdom of Italy.

And I do hereby declare and proclaim that the articles listed below shall be considered arms, ammunition, and implements of war for the purposes of section 1 of the said joint resolution of Congress;

Category I

(1) Rifles and carbines using ammunition in excess of cal. 26.5, and their barrels;

(2) Machine guns, automatic rifles, and machine pistols of all calibers, and their barrels;

(3) Guns, howitzers, and mortars of all calibers, their mountings and barrels;

(4) Ammunition for the arms enumerated under (1) and (2) above, i.e., high-power steel-jacketed ammunition in excess of cal. 26.5; filled and unfilled projectiles and propellants with a web thickness of .015 inches or greater for the projectiles of the arms enumerated under (3) above;

(5) Grenades, bombs, torpedoes, and mines, filled or unfilled, and apparatus for their use or discharge;

(6) Tanks, military armored vehicles, and armored trains.

Category II

Vessels of war of all kinds, including aircraft carriers and submarines.

Category III

(1) Aircraft, assembled or dismantled, both heavier and lighter than air, which are designed, adapted, and intended for aerial combat by the use of machine guns or of artillery or for the carrying and dropping of bombs or which are equipped with, or which by reason of design or construction are prepared for, any of the appliances referred to in paragraph (2) below;

(2) Aerial gun mounts and frames, bomb racks, torpedo carriers, and bomb or torpedo release mechanisms.

Category IV

Revolvers and automatic pistols of a weight in excess of 1 pound 6 ounces (630 grams), using ammunition in excess of cal. 26.5, and ammunition therefor.

Category V

(1) Aircraft, assembled or dismantled, both heavier and lighter than air, other than those included in category III;

(2) Propellers or air screws, fuselages, hulls, tail units, and under carriage units;

(3) Aircraft engines.

Category VI

(1) Livens projectors and flame throwers;

(2) Mustard gas, lewisite, ethyldichlorarsine, and methyldichlorarsine.

And I do hereby enjoin upon all officers of the United States, charged with the execution of the laws thereof, the utmost diligence in preventing violations of the said joint resolution, and this my proclamation issued thereunder, and in bringing to trial and punishment any offenders against the same.

And I do hereby delegate to the Secretary of State the power of prescribing regulations for the enforcement of section 1 of the said joint resolution of August 31, 1935, as made effective by this my proclamation issued thereunder.

IN WITNESS WHEREOF, I have hereunto set my hand and caused the seal of the United States to be affixed.

DONE at the city of Washington this fifth day of October, in the year of our Lord nineteen hundred and thirty-five, and of the Independence of the United States of America the one hundred and sixtieth.

FRANKLIN D. ROOSEVELT

By the President:
CORDELL HULL
Secretary of State.

b. A PROCLAMATION

WHEREAS Section 6 of the Joint Resolution of Congress, approved August 31, 1935 (Public Resolution No. 67—74th Congress), provides that

"Whenever, during any war in which the United States is neutral, the President shall find that the maintenance of peace between the United States and foreign nations, or the protection of the lives of citizens of the United States, or the protection of the commercial interests of the United States and its citizens, or the security of the United States requires that the American citizens should refrain from traveling as passengers on the vessels of any belligerent nation, he shall so proclaim, and thereafter no citizen of the United States shall travel on any vessel of any belligerent nation except at his own risk, unless in accordance with such rules and regulations as the President shall prescribe: *Provided, however,* That the provisions of this section shall not apply to a citizen traveling on the vessel of a belligerent whose voyage was begun in advance of the date of the President's proclamation, and who had no opportunity to discontinue his voyage after that date: *And provided further,* That they shall not apply under ninety days after the date of the President's proclamation to a citizen returning from a foreign country to the United States or to any of its possessions. When, in the President's judgment, the conditions which have caused him to issue his proclamation have ceased to exist, he shall revoke his proclamation and the provisions of this section shall thereupon cease to apply."

AND WHEREAS war now unhappily exists between Ethiopia and the Kingdom of Italy; and

WHEREAS I find that the protection of the lives of citizens of the United States requires that American citizens should refrain from traveling as passengers on the vessels of either of the belligerent nations;

NOW, THEREFORE, I, FRANKLIN D. ROOSEVELT, President of the United States of America, acting under and by virtue of the authority vested in me by the said Joint Resolution of Congress, do hereby admonish all citizens of the United States to abstain from traveling on any vessel of either of the belligerent nations contrary to the provisions of the said Joint Resolution; and

I do hereby give notice that any citizen of the United States who may travel on such a vessel, contrary to the provisions of the said Joint Resolution, will do so at his own risk.

IN WITNESS WHEREOF, I have hereunto set my hand and caused the seal of the United States to be affixed.

DONE at the city of Washington this fifth day of October, in the year of our Lord nineteen hundred and thirty-five, and of the Independence of the United States of America the one hundred and sixtieth.

FRANKLIN D. ROOSEVELT

By the President:
CORDELL HULL
Secretary of State.

162. THE DECLARATION OF ITALY AS AN AGGRESSOR BY THE LEAGUE COUNCIL, OCTOBER 7, 1935 [42]

On October 7, 1935, the League Council, except for Italy who was a party to the dispute, approved the report of a Committee of Six (Chile, Denmark, France, Great Britain, Portugal, and Rumania) which declared that Italy had resorted to war (against Ethiopia) in disregard of her obligations under the Covenant. Thus, for the first time in the history of the League of Nations, that body specifically designated the aggressor in an armed conflict.

REPORT OF THE COUNCIL COMMITTEE, OCTOBER 7, 1935

I

1. At its meeting on October 5, the Council, after hearing the statements of the representatives of Italy and Ethiopia and taking cognizance of the grave facts laid before it, set up a Committee of the Council "to

---

[42] League of Nations, *Official Journal*, November 1935, pp. 1223-1226.

study the situation and report to the Council so as to enable it to take decisions with full knowledge of the matters involved."

2. In order to study this situation, brought about by events subsequent to October 2, it was the Committee's duty to specify these events and to determine their character in relation to the obligations of the Covenant.

The Committee accordingly considered whether there had been a resort to war in disregard of Articles 12, 13, or 15 of the Covenant.[43] . . .

. . . . .

III

After an examination of the facts stated above, the Committee have come to the conclusion that the Italian Government has resorted to war in disregard of its covenants under Article 12 of the Covenant of the League of Nations.

. . . . .

THE PRESIDENT [Council President Ruiz Guiñazú of Argentina].—In the name of the members of the Council, I am obliged to repeat the declaration which I made from the chair at the private meeting. It is as follows:

The report of the Committee which is before the Council describes facts from official sources and draws attention to the provisions of the Covenant.

To-day, October 7, five days after the opening of hostilities, the establishment of the existence of a state of war, in relation to the obligations of the Covenant, compels the members of the Council to face their responsibilities. This obligation does not in any way prejudice the rights of the parties to make known their observations subsequently at another meeting of the Council. However anxious the members of the Council may be courteously to take account of the convenience of one of their colleagues, they cannot allow that anxiety to take precedence over a primary duty.

I take note of the protest made by the representative of Italy, and, in the name of the Council, I declare, as its President and as its mandatory—with, therefore, the unanimous consent of my colleagues other than the parties—that the members of the Council will be called upon

---

[43] See Document No. 14.—*Ed.*

at to-day's meeting to state their views as to the conclusions of the Council Committee, and that the Council will hear the representative of Italy, should he so desire, at another meeting.

We will proceed by roll-call to the consultation of the members of the Council and of the two parties.

I will begin by consulting the members of the Council other than the parties.

The members of the Council other than the parties, consulted by roll-call, declared themselves in agreement with the conclusions of the report.

THE PRESIDENT.—I will now consult the parties.

BARON ALOISI [Italy].—While making every reservation as to the procedure which is now being followed, I state, for all useful purposes, that I do not approve the conclusion of the report.

I also reserve my right to submit, at a later meeting, any observations I may have to offer on the document before us.

M. TECLÉ-HAWARIATE [Ethiopia].—I accept the report.

THE PRESIDENT.—I take note that fourteen members of the League of Nations represented on the Council consider that we are in presence of a war begun in disregard of the obligations of Article 12 of the Covenant.

Accordingly, the report of the Council Committee and the minutes of the present meeting will be sent to all the members of the League of Nations. . . .

The Council has now to assume its duty of co-ordination in regard to the measures to be taken. . . .

163. THE EFFECT OF SANCTIONS UPON ITALIAN TRADE, 1935-1936 [44]

Under League auspices there was compiled an interesting table to illustrate in figures the effect of the sanctions upon Italian trade. These sanctions, imposed under Article 16 of the League Covenant, went into effect on November 18, 1935 (marked in Italy by the flying of flags), and were withdrawn on July 15, 1936. They did not apply to oil.

[44] League of Nations, *Document No. A. 81. 1935-36*, VII, p. 17.

TABLE TO ILLUSTRATE THE EFFECT OF SANCTIONS UPON ITALIAN TRADE, NOVEMBER
1935-APRIL 1936, AS COMPARED WITH THE PERIOD NOVEMBER 1934-APRIL 1935.

	Number of countries for which statistics are available	Percentage of Italian exports to these countries in 1932-3 as compared with the total Italian exports	Imports from Italy and Italian colonies (in millions of former United States gold dollars)		Percentage of imports from these countries to Italy in 1932-3 as compared with the total Italian imports	Exports to Italy and Italian colonies (in millions of former United States gold dollars)		Net imports of gold from Italy (in millions of former United States gold dollars)
			1934	1935		1934	1935	1935
Nov.	69	96.5	21,884	26,050	95	31,910	32,085	22,044
Dec.	68	96.5	21,942	17,482	95	30,479	21,945	8,477
			1935	1936		1935	1936	1936
Jan.	67	96	19,470	10,168	94.5	26,793	15,292	27,211
Feb.	62	95.5	19,694	8,657	93.5	27,757	16,799	16,318
Mar.	38	86	17,979	9,315	86	26,326	15,589	12,771
Apr.	22	60	12,185	5,061	56.5	15,580	8,296	4,129

164. HOW THE SANCTIONS AGAINST ITALY WERE APPLIED [45]

*It was widely contended that the application of sanctions against Italy in
1935-1936 was not a real test of the potential value of sanctions. This view
was ably defended in an article by M. J. Bonn of the London School of
Economics, formerly of Berlin University.*

The League's policy was never complete. Not only were certain
war materials, such as oil, left untouched, but shipping, the tourist trade
and emigrants' remittances were not interfered with. The Italian attitude was simple and clear. "We shall stand all sanctions which do not
seriously hamper us; if they do more than inconvenience us, we shall
fight." The League had the choice either of accepting this challenge
and imposing such sanctions as would make war hopeless for Italy; or
of acknowledging that the independence of Abyssinia was not worth
a world war. Quite possibly such a war would never have come; but
this cannot be known for certain. It cannot be said that sanctions failed.
For pressure which has not been exercised cannot be said to have
failed. Nor is it proven that the exercise of pressure must have led to

[45] M. J. Bonn, "How Sanctions Failed," in *Foreign Affairs,* January 1937, pp. 359-361.
Reprinted by permission of the Council of Foreign Relations.

war, nor that it must under all circumstances lead to war. If a realistic and rational policy was expected from the Italian Government, war against the League would scarcely have been the appropriate method for winning the war in Abyssinia. If, on the other hand, its policy was due to irrational motives, . . . overwhelming military pressure should have been in evidence from the beginning.

To brand Italy as the aggressor at a meeting of the League for having broken a solemn Covenant, and to implore this moral offender at the same time to remain within the League, whose statutes he had violated deliberately, was so incongruous that moral failure was inevitable even if material failure had not taken place. There might be reasons for maintaining diplomatic relations with Italy—they exist with non-members of the League, regardless of the moral principle which their governments represent. But to let Italy remain a member of the League Council, entitled to all its privileges, while at the same time breaking its fundamental law, was a mockery which Italy could not but look upon as an encouragement to go to the limit.

Sanctions inconvenienced Italy considerably: her imports of essential foodstuffs and raw materials declined from $48,500,000 for the period from December 1934 to March 1935 to $26,000,000 for the corresponding period of the next year. However, their pressure might have increased in severity. The exhaustion of the gold supply and the foreign exchange obtainable by the disposal of foreign securities might have brought about real scarcity. But in the meantime stocks on hand, the practice of economies, the development of substitutes, and the purchase of goods with gold, foreign securities, emigrants' remittances and tourists' disbursements kept the country going without too severe a strain. The fear of increasing pressure nevertheless existed; . . .

With the improvement in world trade, the total volume of trade of some countries did not suffer much as a result of the imposition of sanctions. Exports from the United Kingdom to all countries except Italy rose from $118,000,000 in December 1935 to $124,000,000 in March 1936; exports to Italy declined from around $3,000,000 before the embargo to a paltry hundred thousand; thus the loss in Italian markets was made good elsewhere. Other countries, however, were less fortunate. Italian imports from France fell from $1,700,000 in March 1935 to $350,000 in March 1936; France's other exports declined in the same period from $50,000,000 to $49,000,000. Rumania's total monthly trade, March 1935 to March 1936, declined from $5,200,000 to $4,800,000, and her trade with Italy from $830,000 to $219,000.[46]

Arrangements were devised for the mutual support of states, in accordance with which damages resulting from the application of the most favored nation clause, from scarcity due to the absence of Italian goods or to the loss of Italian markets, were to be offset by particular concessions from other sanctionist countries. The proposal for creating a mutual support fund was not accepted. But measures were taken for the shifting of some goods and for the granting of some compensation quota. As an unequal incidence of losses was inevitable, a certain amount of recrimination between various nations followed. This may account for the decline of pressure which the March statistics seem to reveal.

Evidently it was very difficult for League members to have a uniform economic policy against a recalcitrant state, while their normal economic relations with each other were antagonistic. Collective security in the political field cannot be achieved when aggressive anarchy prevails in economic affairs.

Dissatisfaction was naturally expressed by interested groups which lost trade. Hitherto, foreign wars had offered excellent opportunities for making good profits; sanctions not only prevented such profits, but were bound to inflict losses on certain industries. Some of these losses may have been imaginary; it was easy enough to sell goods to the Italian Government; it might not have been quite so easy to collect for them. Sanctions made safe such trade as remained, by restricting its amount and by putting it on a cash basis. Unfortunately the sanctionist governments refused to pay compensation for loss of trade to their nationals; and indeed the settling of claims of that nature would have been anything but easy. But there is no reason why the burden of economic warfare should be borne by a particular group of people—why, for example, British coal-owners should suffer loss while British oil interests make profits. Had the principle been accepted from the beginning that the nation—not certain groups—should bear the cost of economic warfare, opposition would have been reduced considerably. Moreover, the aggressor should have been told that he would be expected to make good the damage he had done to trade. The payment

---

[46] German exports to Italy rose from a minimum of $3,300,000 (February 1935) to $6,000,000 (December 1935); they declined by March 1936 to about $3,600,000. The minimum of the United States (December 1934) was not quite $3,000,000; it rose to $4,700,000 (December 1935) and remained above $4,000,000 in February and March after declining to $3,200,000 in January. Austria's minimum was $636,000 (January 1935), and her maximum was $1,700,000 (March 1936).

of a war indemnity is frequently an immoral imposition; too often the victor constitutes himself into a kind of court and assesses damages to himself. But the members of the League, the rules of which had been broken by an aggressor who was a fellow member, would have been entitled to claim compensation.

Though sanctions were not as efficient as they might have been made, they were the only weapon the League held against Italy. To let it slip before the conclusion of peace between the League and the nation which had violated its Covenant was evident proof of the fact that those in positions of responsibility either did not know how to handle the economic weapon, or did not dare to use it properly, or both.

165. ASSUMPTION OF THE IMPERIAL TITLE BY THE KING OF ITALY, MAY 9, 1936 [47]

King Victor Emmanuel III of Italy assumed the title Emperor of Ethiopia on May 9, 1936, four days after Italian troops entered Addis Ababa, the capital from which Emperor Haile Selassie had recently fled.

Victor Emmanuel III, by the Grace of God and by the Will of the Nation, King of Italy.

In consideration of Article 5 of the Fundamental Statute of the Kingdom; in consideration of Article 3, No. 2, of the law of January 31, 1926, in the fourth year of Fascism, No. 100; in consideration of the law of December 9, 1928, in the seventh year of Fascism, No. 2693; having recognized the urgency and absolute necessity of passing this provision; the Grand Council of Fascism having considered it; the Council of Ministers having heard it; on proposal of the Head of the Government, the Prime Minister Secretary of State;

We have decreed and we now decree:

ARTICLE I.

The territory and peoples which belong to the Empire of Ethiopia are hereby placed under the full and complete sovereignty of the Kingdom of Italy.

The title of Emperor of Ethiopia is assumed for himself and for his successors by the King of Italy.

[47] Royal Decree-Law of May 9, 1936 (No. 754), in *Gazzetta Ufficiale del Regno d'Italia,* Ministry of Grace and Justice, Rome, May 9, 1936, No. 108.

ARTICLE II.

Ethiopia is ruled and represented by a Governor-General who has the title of Viceroy and on whom are dependent also the Governors of Eritrea and Somaliland.

All the civil and military authorities of the territory placed under his jurisdiction are dependent upon the Governor-General, Viceroy of Ethiopia.

The Governor-General, Viceroy of Ethiopia, is nominated by Royal Decree on proposal of the Head of the Government, the Prime Minister Secretary of State, and the Minister Secretary of State for the Colonies.

ARTICLE III.

Regulations for Ethiopia will be provided by Royal Decree, to be issued on the proposal of the Head of the Government, the Prime Minister Secretary of State, and the Minister Secretary of State for the Colonies.

ARTICLE IV.

The present Decree, which becomes effective on the day of its date, will be presented to Parliament for conversion into law. The Head of the Government, Prime Minister Secretary of State, on his proposal, is authorized to present the draft law.

We order the present Decree stamped with the seal of the State and inserted in the official collection of laws and decrees of the Kingdom of Italy,[48] making its observation and enforcement obligatory.

Done at Rome, 9th May 1936—Year XIV.

VICTOR EMMANUEL.

MUSSOLINI.

166. THE ADVOCACY OF "RACISM" BY A GROUP OF ITALIAN PROFESSORS, JULY 14, 1938 [49]

On July 14, 1938, a group of Italian university professors published in the Giornale d'Italia *a report, prepared for the Ministry of Popular Culture, which outlined the "scientific bases" for an "Aryan" racial policy in Italy. The ten propositions of this report, summarized below, became the platform on which an Italian anti-Semitic campaign was built. The number of Jews*

---

[48] This collection is called *Raccolta Ufficiale delle Leggi e dei Decreti del Regno d'Italia,* Rome, Provveditorato Generale dello Stato Libreria, annual.—*Ed.*

[49] *The New York Times,* July 15, 1938. Reprinted by permission.

*in Italy was placed by the authorities at seventy thousand. Prior to 1938
Premier Mussolini had displayed no signs of anti-Semitism.*

The anonymous university professors' report consists of ten propositions given here in abstract:

First, human races are a reality that cannot be overlooked. To say
that human races exist is not the same as saying that there are inferior
and superior human races, but only that there are different human
races.

Second, not only do major systematic groups exist, which are commonly called races and are individualized by only a few common
characteristics, but there are also minor systematic groups, such as
Nordics, Mediterraneans, Dinarics, etc., individualized by a greater
number of common characteristics. These groups, from a biological
point of view, represent the true races whose existence is an evident
reality.

Third, the conception of race is purely biological and is based on
considerations other than those of peoples and nations, which are
founded on historical, linguistic and religious considerations. At the
basis, however, of the differences between various peoples and various
nations stand differences of race. The various peoples have been made
up in very ancient times of various proportions of different races,
whether one race has complete mastery over others or whether all races
have fused harmoniously together or whether various races co-exist un-
assimilated.

Fourth, the present Italian population in its majority is of Aryan
origin and its civilization is Aryan. This population with Aryan civilization has lived on the Italian Peninsula for several thousand years
and very little is left of the pre-Aryan peoples' civilization.

Fifth, it is a legend that large masses of people settled in Italy in
historical times. Since the Lombard invasion, no influx has occurred
capable of influencing the racial make-up of the Italian nation. The
overwhelming majority of the 44,000,000 Italians of today, therefore,
have descended from families that have lived in Italy for at least a
thousand years.

Sixth, a pure Italian race now exists. This statement is based, not
on confusion between the biological conception of race and the historical and linguistic conception of peoples and nations, but on the
pure kinship of blood that unites Italians of today with the generations that for thousands of years have inhabited Italy.

Seventh, it is time the Italians frankly adopted a racial policy. All that Fascism has done in Italy has a racial foundation. In Premier Benito Mussolini's speeches there have been frequent references to conceptions of race.

The question of racialism must be treated in Italy from a purely biological point of view without philosophical or religious intentions. The Italian racial conception must be essentially Italian and Aryan Nordic in trend. This does not mean that German racial theories should be introduced in Italy as they are or that an Italian is the same as a Scandinavian.

It is merely intended to point out to Italians a physical and, above all, a psychological model of the human race, which, owing to its purely European characteristics, is clearly differentiated from all non-European races, and which means to elevate the Italian to an ideal of superior consciousness of himself and of greater responsibility.

Eighth, it is necessary to draw a clear distinction between European Mediterraneans (Occidentals) on the one side and Orientals and Africans on the other. Those theories are dangerous which uphold the African origin of some European peoples and include in a common Mediterranean race also the Semitic and Hamitic populations, establishing absolutely inadmissibile ideological relations and sympathies.

Ninth, Jews do not belong to the Italian race. Nothing generally has remained of the Semites who landed on Italian soil in the course of the centuries. Even the Arab occupation of Sicily left nothing except the memory of some names, and, in any case, the process of assimilation has always been very rapid in Italy.

Jews represent only the part of the population that has never been assimilated in Italy because it is made up of non-European racial elements differing absolutely from the racial elements that have given origin to Italians.

Tenth, the physical and psychological characteristics of Italians must not be altered in any way. Union between different races is admissible only within the ambit of European races, and in this case one cannot talk of hybridism in the true sense of the term, seeing that these races belong to a common stock and differ only in certain characteristics, while they are similar in many others.

An Italian's purely European character is altered by the admixture of blood of any extra-European race that carries with it a civilization different from the many-thousand-year-old civilization of Aryans.

CHAPTER 8

SPAIN

167. THE "RULE OF THE MASSES" IN SPAIN [1]

The following thoughtful contribution on the "historical invertebration" of Spain was written by José Ortega y Gasset, Madrid-born scion of a newspaper-owning family. Ortega studied in Germany, became a magazine editor and a professor of philosophy at Madrid University, and was elected a deputy to the first Republican Cortes. Sick at heart over the events of the Spanish Civil War, he went to France to live.

RULE OF THE MASSES

A nation is a human mass which is organized and given structure by a minority of chosen individuals. Whatever our political creed, we must recognize this truth. It belongs to a stratum of historical reality much deeper than that concerned merely with political problems. The legal form which a nation may adopt can be as democratic or even as communistic as you choose; but its living and extra-legal constitution will always consist in the dynamic influence of a minority acting on a mass.

This is a natural law, and as important in the biology of social bodies as is the law of densities in physics. When solid bodies of differing density are thrown into a liquid, they stay suspended at a height which corresponds to their densities. In the same way, the members of every human group act according to the differing vital densities they possess. You can see it in the simplest form of society—a conversation. When six men come together, they fall into two parts, one of which leads the conversation while the other follows. When this does not happen, it is because the second group resists being led by the first, and conversation is thereupon rendered impossible. In a nation, when the mass refuses to be a mass—that is to say, when it refuses to follow the directing

[1] J. Ortega y Gasset, *Invertebrate Spain*, W. W. Norton & Company, Inc., New York, 1937, pp. 62-68, 86-87. Reprinted by permission of the publishers.

minority—the nation goes to pieces, society is dismembered, and social chaos results. The people as a people are disarticulated and become invertebrate.

In Spain we are now living in the midst of an extreme case of this historical invertebration.

* * * * *

Every page of this rapid survey is intended to correct that myopia which sees social and historical phenomena as political phenomena, and the ailments of a national body as political disorders. It is true that the political manifestations form the show window, the outside skin of the social organism, and as such are the first to meet the eye. And it is also true that there are certain national ailments which are mere political disturbances—eruptions or infections of the social skin. But when the only thing that is sick in a country is its political life, then the illness is not really serious. The social body will sooner or later recover from such passing ailment.

In Spain, unfortunately, this situation is reversed. The illness is not confined to the country's political life. It is society itself which is sick. It is the head and the heart of almost every Spaniard which is ailing.

And what is this illness? There is much talk of "public immorality," or lack of justice in the courts, graft among officials, systematic stealing in businesses which have to do with the government. Press and Parliament call the attention of citizens to these crimes as the cause of our progressive decomposition. I do not doubt that we are suffering from a severe case of public immorality, but at the same time I think that a people which had nothing worse could survive and might even flourish.

• • • • •

Unfortunately, Spain's illness is a much graver thing than mere public immorality. It is worse to be an illness than merely to have one. That a society suffers from immorality is bad, but that a society is not a society is much worse. This is our condition. Our Spanish society is disintegrating because the force that made it a society is infected at the root.

The first of all social acts is the organization of a human mass into those who lead and those who are led. This supposes in some a certain capacity to lead; in others, a certain ability to let themselves be led. Without a minority to act on a collective mass, and a mass which knows how to accept the influence of the minority, there is no society, or there will very shortly be none.

In Spain today we have given ourselves over to the rule of the masses. People who are politically nearsighted do not believe this, because they see no street riots and no assaults on the banks and ministries. But street revolutions of that kind are merely the political mask worn by the proletariat.

I am talking about a much more fundamental kind of rule than a mere disturbance in a public square. It is more profound, more widely diffused, more omnipresent; it belongs not to one class but to all of them, and especially to the masses in those groups which have the greatest potentiality of power—the middle and the upper class.

I referred above to the strange phenomenon that, even among the parties of the extreme Right, it is not the leaders who lead the masses, but the masses who force their leaders to adopt this attitude or that. During the Great War the young Maurists refused to accept the international policy that Maura proposed, and tried to force on their chief the kind that rattled around in their empty and inconsequential heads. The same thing happened with the Carlists, who put their leader out and forced him to seek refuge in a place of safety. Defense Juntas are just another example of this state of moral perversion in which the masses turn against the select minority. In the mess halls and the guard rooms men believe, in good faith—and this good faith is the clearest evidence of the gravity of the disease—that they know more about politics than is known by men who have spent many years in the study and practice of public affairs.

This spiritual insubordination shows itself more clearly as we move away from the zone of politics. The public which goes to spectacles and to concerts thinks itself superior to dramatist, composer, and critic alike, and delights in upsetting them. Our public is moved by the suspicion that anyone who pretends to know about anything would best be removed. The same thing happens among the aristocracy. It is not the ladies best dowered with wit and elegance whose tastes and manners inspire the rest, but the most bourgeois, dull and dowdy who crush their betters under the weight of their stupidity. Wherever you choose to look you see the depressing spectacle of the worst—who form the majority—rising feverishly against the best.

Spain drags itself along invertebrate, not only in its political life, but—and this goes deeper and is more fundamental—in its own social living together. None of the mechanisms which integrate the machinery of public life can function this way. One institution breaks down today, another tomorrow, until complete historic collapse will overtake us.

Then there will be no way out. As long as the mass denies its own biological mission—which is to follow the best of our people—it will neither listen to nor accept their opinions, and only the opinions of the mass itself, which are inchoate, erroneous, and childish, will triumph.

When the mass of the nation degenerates to that point, reasoning and prediction are useless. It is sick, and its illness makes it impervious to all reason. It does not want to listen, it does not want to be influenced. The more you try to teach it, the more completely will its ears be sealed against you, and the greater will be the violence with which it will trample on those who try to preach to it. And it will not be cured until it suffers in its own flesh the results of its straying. This is what has always happened.

Periods of decadence are those in which the directing minority of a people—their aristocracy—have lost the very qualities of excellence which raised them to the rank of leaders. Against this corrupt and ineffective aristocracy the masses rebel, and justly. But then they begin to argue from the particular to the general, and try to make of their rebellion a rule of life. Instead of replacing the decadent aristocracy with another group of leaders who are more virtuous they try to do away with the whole aristocratic pattern. They come to believe that social existence is possible without a directing minority; even worse, they construct political and historical theories which offer as the ideal a society devoid of leaders. As such a thing is impossible, the nation goes faster and faster along its trajectory of decadence. Things get worse every day. The masses in the different social groups—the bourgeois one day, the military another, the proletariat the third—try one panacea and then another to bring about good government. Finally their own failure, brought about by their own experiments, makes them suspect, with all the force of a discovery, that matters are more complicated than they seem, and consequently that they are not the ones who are called upon to handle them.

Along with political failure they suffer the results of disorganization in their own private lives. Public security is endangered; private economy is weakened; everything becomes anguished and desperate; there is nowhere to turn for aid.

. . . . .

There are peoples who stay forever in the village stage of evolution. They may occupy enormous areas, but their spirit is always that of the rustic. . . .

That our race has never been able to rise above its ruralism is the curse of Spain. But that, not having done so, we should, dazzled by the possession of a few pseudo-modern cities, pretend to be a normal nation, is much worse. Every profound reform of our collective organism must start with the realization that we are a "fellah" people, a mass of country humanity, and that, in attempting any reorganization, we must turn our attention to problems of the land.

The great misfortune of Spanish history has been the lack of eminent minorities and the undisturbed predominance of the masses. From now on a new imperative must govern our spirits and order our wills —the imperative of selection.

There is no other means of racial purification and improvement than this eternal instrument—a will which operates selectively. With it as a chisel, we must create a new type of Spaniard.

168. CATALONIAN PETITION FOR AUTONOMY, NOVEMBER 25, 1918
(Extracts) [2]

Though modern Spain appeared as a united country on the map after 1492, its people had little unity of language, thought, or traditions. The obstructive geography of the country and centuries of frontier existence occasioned by the wars against the Moors, gave rise to a strong provincialism that manifested itself, from time to time, in troublesome separatist movements. The widespread propaganda on the subject of self-determination during the World War encouraged particularly the Catalonians, especially in the industrial province of Barcelona, to hope at least for autonomy. In November 1918 a group of Catalonian parliamentary delegates presented the following petition to the Spanish Premier.

Your Excellency.

When a problem is of vital importance for a people, when it is not merely a question of parties or classes but the expression of necessities deep-rooted in the national soul, it appears repeatedly throughout historical epochs and bursts forth afresh if, during a period of decadence and prostration, it may have been momentarily clouded in the collective conscience.

[2] From Catalonia, *Petició d'Autonomia presentada al Govern d'Espanya per la Mancomunitat de Catalunya,* Gener, Barcelona, 1919, pp. 7-8, 12-17, 21-22; text in English.

Such is our problem, Your Excellency, not an artificial creation of literary men and politicians, the effect of a passing exaltation nor of ephimerous (*sic*) currents that appear and again disappear in the course of time—as has often been said—but an expression of the most fervent and unanimous will of Catalonia, the deep, firm, but clear, voice of Catalonia's Spirit which, dating far back in History, grows to a roar as the liberties of this noble country are gradually being restricted or suppressed.

. . . . .

FUNDAMENTAL PRINCIPLES
FIRST. THE TERRITORY OF CATALONIA

A) *Its constitution.*

The Territory of Catalonia shall be understood to consist of what is now the provinces of Barcelona, Gerona, Lérida y Tarragona.

B) *The possibility of increase.*

There may be added to the Territory of Catalonia wholly or in part other Spanish provinces under the following conditions:

a) That the petition be made, at least, by two-thirds of the Municipal Councils of the Territory in question and that it be approved by means of a referendum of the electors of such territory.

b) That it be approved by the Regional Parliament of Catalonia.

c) That the territories in question are not separated from those of Catalonia by others which form no part of Catalonia.

d) The agreement of aggregation may be simple or conditional.

SECOND. THE REGIONAL GOVERNMENT OF CATALONIA

A) *Its organization.*

The Regional Government of Catalonia shall consist of the following elements:

a) A Parliament consisting of two Chambers: one elected by universal direct suffrage and the other by the vote of the Councillors of all the Municipal Councils.

b) An Executive responsible to the said Parliament.

B) *Its faculties.*

The Regional Government consisting of the aforesaid elements shall enjoy full sovereignty regarding the home affairs of Catalonia with the following exceptions respecting which the sovereignty of the State shall subsist in all its entirety and without any limitation whatsoever.

a) The international relations and the diplomatic and consular representation.

b) The Army, Navy and fortifications of the Coast and Frontiers and all matters referring to the national defence.

c) The conditions attaching to Spanish nationality and the exercise of individual rights established under the first title of the Constitution.

d) The ruling Customs tariffs, dues and treaties of Commerce.

e) The flag of merchant ships and all rights and benefits that the Spanish flag may grant.

f) Railways and canals of general interest.

g) Penal and Mercantile Legislation in which is included the regulations regarding industrial and intellectual property.

h) Weights and measures, the monetary system and the conditions for issue of paper money.

i) The regulation of the postal and telegrafic (*sic*) service.

j) The efficacy of public documents, sentences and official communications.

k) Social legislation.

The regulation and concession of hydraulic exploitations is reserved to the Central Power in the following cases:

a) If the waters in any part of their course do not pass through Catalan territory and

b) If the object of the exploitation is to transport power out of the Catalan territory.

All the property of the State included in the articles 339 and 340 of the Civil Code, situated in Catalonia and not affecting the services reserved to the Central Power, shall be transferred to Regional Authorities as shall also the State's Rights arising from acts of sovereignty exercised in the territory of Catalonia which have no reference to the functions and matters reserved to the Central Power.

All documents relating to the services and functions reserved to the Central Power shall be delivered up.

So long as the Regional Parliament does not legislate about those matters submitted to its sovereignty the laws that now apply to such matters will continue to be valid in Catalonia only with the modification that the Authorities and Tribunals of Catalonia will administer such laws in place of the Authorities and Tribunals of the State.

With the same exception all the regulations dictated by the Government of the State will be valid in the Territory of Catalonia so long as they be not modified or substituted by the Regional Government.

C) *The guarantees.*

Regarding all the matters not reserved to the Central Power, the Sovereignty of the Regional Parliament and Executive shall have no other limits than those expressly stated in the Statutes of Constitution. To settle conflicts that may arise between the Authorities and Government of the State and those of the Regional Power a joint tribunal shall be appointed which beside the faculty of deciding questions of jurisdiction shall declare as to the nullity and inefficacy of any legislative or Government measure whether coming from the State or Regional Power which may invade the sphere assigned respectively to the Sovereignty of one or the other.

THIRD. FINANCIAL MEANS

The preparation and execution of the estimate of income shall appertain exclusively to the Regional Power in so far as this may refer to the autonomous Government of Catalonia. . . .

The product of such taxes as are based on the faculties reserved to the Central Power shall also appertain to the State.

In case the incomes appertaining to the State should prove insufficient for the expenses of such services, Catalonia will contribute in due proportion to the payment of the deficit in the same way as the State proceeds to liquidate the same. So that there may never be any confusion between the two Treasuries for the purposes of the foregoing paragraph an absolute separation of the expenses and receipts of a general character and those particular to the regions shall be established in the general State Budget showing those that are employed for the purpose of those services that in Catalonia are reserved for the Regional Authorities.

In presenting these fundamental principles the Council declares that it is not its intention to draw up a draft of a Law of Autonomy, the honour of such an initiative appertaining to the Government. Only the general outlines have been sketched which it considers should form the basis of the future Constitution to be granted to the Catalan people.

In this solemn moment of Universal History, [with] the triumph throughout the world of the collective right of peoples to dispose freely of themselves and to be governed by institutions which have received their assent, the Catalans address the Spanish Government and people to declare their will to rule the life of Catalonia autonomically. If the

Government listens to our petition and succeeds [in] dealing justly therewith, we are sure that . . . the fraternal unity binding together the peoples of the peninsula and the nations of the whole world will be strengthened and more enduring.

God Save Your Excellency.

Barcelona, 25th November, 1918.—*The President of the Permanent Council of the "Mancomunidad" of Catalonia,* J. Puig I Cadafalch.— *The Councellors (sic),* Joan Vallès I Pujals—Agustí Riera—Josep Ulled —Josep Mestres—Josep M. a Espana—Anselm Guasch—Martí Inglès— Fransesc Bartrina—Juan Pich I Pon—Miguel Junyent—August Pi I Sunyer—Salvador Albert—Josep Zulueta—Juli Fournier—Josep Matheu —Francesc Cambó—Joan Ventosa I Calvell—Felip Rodés—Narcís Batlle.

169. THE BACKGROUND OF DICTATORSHIP [3]

On September 13, 1923, Captain-General Miguel Primo de Rivera, military governor of Barcelona, executed a coup d'état, suspended the constitution of 1876, and set himself up as military dictator of Spain, assisted by a directorate containing, besides himself, eight generals and an admiral. The factors underlying this establishment of a dictatorship were varied and complex, so that it has seemed worth while to quote here from two interesting— and differing—explanations of the event. The first was written by Sir George Young, a former British diplomat, the other by Frank A. Manuel, an American of leftist sympathies.

A.

. . . At first sight, the Spanish Monarchy emerged from [the World War] greatly strengthened by the success of the King in maintaining a profitable neutrality and in restoring Spain to her pride of place among the Powers. But, none the less, the Great War had nearly everywhere in Europe, and as much as anywhere in Spain, created a proletarian pressure for reconstruction beyond the power of any parliamentary party system, least of all that of Spain. This pressure for

[3] *A.* From G. Young, *The New Spain,* Methuen & Company, Ltd., London, 1933, pp. 78-83. Reprinted by permission of the author and publishers. *B.* From F. A. Manuel, *The Politics of Modern Spain,* McGraw-Hill Book Company, Inc., New York, 1938, pp. 38-47. Reprinted by permission of the publishers.

both radical and regional reconstruction soon became a menace of social revolution, and the only means of preventing it seemed to be a continuance of repression and a commencement of reconstruction by the Crown and by the Cuerpos Armados.[4]

Meantime, as so often happens, the course of national history left this main channel, though the Cuerpos Armados were still the main current. The loss of the Empire overseas [in 1898] had led to a national renascence, and that again to a revival of imperialism. And the obvious, indeed the only, object of such imperialism was Morocco. The British for their own purposes had reserved extensive rights for Spain in Morocco, that were imperilled by the steady expansion of the French African Empire. Moreover, Morocco was a geographic and economic hinterland of Spain, a strategic outpost and a dependancy that could be militarily administered. It offered congenial employment for officers from Cuba or the Philippines and Conquistadorial enterprises for Big Business. Wealthy public men like Count Romanones, and clerical capitalists like the Jesuits, were soon involved in the interests that called for a conquest of Western Morocco. But though public opinion could be more easily propaganded for a crusade against the ancient foe, the Moors, than against Germans or Americans, it remained tolerant of the Morocco campaign only in so far as it did not cost much in men or money. The Cortes, willing to have the Army occupied out of Spain, but well aware of its deficiencies, had established a compact with the military authorities in Morocco which allowed them a free hand provided they did not risk serious operations. But this defensive-offensive did not suit the officers left in Spain, who saw in unoccupied Spanish Morocco profitable employment and easy promotion in the conquest of the Berbers and Riffi.

We are not concerned with the Spanish conquest of Morocco that had begun in 1912, or with the conduct of the Morocco campaign except in its consequences for the Crown and Constitution of Spain. They were crucial. The King favoured active prosecution, as the campaign was compromising the credit of Spain in more ways than one. When incompetent organization and incapable officers caused distress and presaged disaster, so far from dis-associating himself from the enterprise he tried personally to meet the deficiencies. At heavy cost to his private

---

[4] Of this phrase, Young says (p. 37): "It is under some such designation . . . that Spaniards themselves refer to the Regular Forces, the Civil Guard and Carabineers which are constabulary, and the new Republican Guardias de Asalto and Municipal Police which are civil."—*Ed.*

purse the King and Queen supplied sun helmets, clothing and medical comforts. It was well-meant, but it was a mistake. For political interests jealous of his position succeeded in preventing the publicity his patriotism deserved, while the generous gesture associated him with a political system that was imposing useless sacrifices on his subjects and unnecessary sufferings on his soldiers. At last the mounting cost (700 million pesetas a year) and growing criticism convinced the King that the campaign must be pressed to a conclusion. So, following his procedure of direct communication with military commanders, he entered into personal and private correspondence with both Generals, Berenguer and Silvestre, respectively commanding at Tetuan and Melilla. After this and possibly on account of this, major operations were undertaken on both the Western and Eastern fronts. The former were not unsuccessful; but the latter ended in the disaster of Anual, the death of Silvestre and of 10,000 Spaniards, and the destruction of the whole force (1921). This massacre of young conscripts by a savage and secular enemy within sight of Spain made a far deeper impression than being manœuvered in 1898 out of remote colonies by a first-class Power of far superior resources. There followed mutinies at the Malaga base when reinforcements were ordered to embark, and *motins* in Catalonia when recruits and reserves were called up. Spain demanded a scapegoat and Alfonso was the goat.

Thus began the question of "responsibilities" which did more than anything else to undermine the Monarchy. The Radical and Socialist parties and Press clamoured for an enquiry that was expected to expose the King; the Conservative and Liberal politicians called for one that should inculpate the military commanders. The military, finding that a white-washing enquiry by General Picasso was insufficient as a lightning conductor, put in action the Supreme Military Council of Justice who dismissed General Berenguer. He was immediately given a Court appointment by the King; a solatium that may or may not have been a silencer. The Cortes thereupon set up a parliamentary Commission of Enquiry (July 1922). All of which led to nothing definite, but kept alive an agitation that was rapidly becoming anti-monarchical.

In this situation the King's support of a dictatorship has been attributed to his anxiety to avoid an exposure of his responsibility for Anual. This personal advantage may have influenced him, but there were also powerful inducements of public interest. For the general condition of affairs was such that Lenin and his followers seemed for once to be justified in anticipating that a European State was about to follow the Russian example. The general elections of 1919 and 1920 had been as much "made" and meaningless as ever. The assassination of the Conservative Premier, Dato (March 1921), gave a red danger signal against further drifting. The successful resistance of Clericalism to a measure of religious toleration was retaliated by the murder of a Cardinal. The persistant refusal of social reform had created a class conflict that was exploited by syndical Anarchists in a murder campaign that for two years killed off bankers and business men at a rate of one per working day. In 1922-1923 over five hundred employers were shot, poisoned or made away with; one hundred and sixty in Barcelona alone and twenty-two in two nights. The Catalans, repeatedly disappointed of a restoration of their autonomy, had begun to go separatist. The cities, disgusted with the futilities of the party system, had begun to go Communist or Syndical Anarchist. The Officers' Juntas, against which Sanchez Guerra had taken strong action, were in ferment. Therewith the defence of the *status quo* was *usque ad triarios*. There was ample justification for a public servant, such as Alfonso considered himself, taking the field for reform—as he did.

. . . . .

It was the Captain-General of Catalonia, General Primo de Rivera, who presented himself as the "iron surgeon," who by the simple operation of a *coup d'état* should cure all the ills that Spain was heir to. He had got into trouble in 1917 and again in 1921 for advocating the evacuation of Morocco and the exchange of Ceuta for Gibraltar. For the first offence he had lost his command, for the second his seat in the Senate. But having inherited a grandeeship as Marquis de Estella, having earned the gratitude of centralists, clericalists and capitalists by his repression of crime in Catalonia, having the gift of the gab, and being a fanatic in the faith of all Generals that government is giving orders, Primo de Rivera was well qualified to become as he soon did *secundo do Mussolini.*

B.

For years after the Restoration of 1874 the *haute bourgeoisie* of Spain still vacillated between grand hopes of dominating the state and a secret dread of the unleashed elements of the proletariat, should a temporary upheaval allow revolutionary principles to be freely paraded. The Bolshevik Revolution of 1917, however, taught the Spanish middle class a graphic lesson. The pretensions of a few great Russian industrialists had brought them Kerensky, and Kerensky had opened the door for Lenin. Spain's bourgeoisie would be wiser; it would be contented with less profit, less grandeur, and fewer offices in the state. It would maintain intact the idols of the old regime, preserve the clerics and the warriors, and intimidate the masses; in return, its personal security would be assured in a turbulent world where the specter of communism had taken on flesh and blood. Even after the introduction of hydro-electric power plants, the Spanish middle class remained a modern appendage to a semifeudal system, for thus it hoped to save itself from all the ills to which capitalism was heir. "A living dog is better than a dead lion."

Having appeared late in the capitalist epoch, the Spanish bourgeoisie of the twentieth century could not mature into a successful revolutionary class in its own right; at the first symptoms of social and political disorder it might be relied upon to support staunchly the "feudals." Although the industrialization of the World War period had again held forth the prospect of a society in which the feudal landlords and spiritual mentors would occupy a subordinate position, the factory owners resisted the temptation. Terrified by the workers, they felt that Spain was far safer for them under the aegis of a minister of God— even though there was no God.

For the working classes of Spain the World War had brought new relationships and novel conditions of existence. Communication between cities and the countryside had been somewhat improved. There was a marked movement of population from agricultural districts to larger towns; provincial capitals reported far greater increases in the number of inhabitants than did country areas. The normal attraction of the higher wages which accompany industrial revolutions was fast building up new urban centers. Moreover, during this same period, the events of world politics were so striking that new ideas seeped through to the lower strata of Spanish society.

· · · · · ·

As soon as news of the Russian Revolution spread over the peninsula, the workers in Spain became sanguine about the possibilities of a similar victory in their own land. Throughout 1917 the anarchists were constantly gaining in power and were sorely harassing the Barcelona industrialists. Then even their rivals, the Socialists of the General Union of Workers, ventured to become militant. On August 10, 1917, revolutionary strikes whose aim was the proclamation of a republic broke out in Barcelona, Madrid, Bilbao, Valencia, and Oviedo. Barricades were raised. Several hundred victims within a few days was the toll of the abortive revolutionary attempt. During this crisis the throne of Alfonso XIII was preserved by a loyal army which did not hesitate to use its machine guns. And in the years which followed the alliance of the monarch and the military came to play an ever more dominant role in Spanish history. . . . . .

. . . During the War of Independence and the subsequent Civil Wars, *pronunciamientos,* and *coups d'état* Spain had come to suffer from a hypertrophy of her military bodies. So many young people had been drawn into the armed profession that during the rare intervals of peace which Spain enjoyed in the nineteenth century most of the soldiers could not be absorbed in other occupations. Thus the ranks of the military establishments swelled beyond the normal necessities of the land. The military came to be accepted by tradition as an integral part of the state organism and the administrative bureaucracy. It was no longer a body primarily devoted to national defense or even national conquest. Its duty was to preserve the government in power, and hence, by a loose interpretation of this mission, to alter a regime when it no longer harmonized with the army's desires. . . . . .

The army in an incompletely industrialized country like Spain could not pretend to continue the conquistadorial traditions of its past into the twentieth century or to compete for world dominion with imperialist powers accoutred with massive mechanical weapons. In lieu of foreign wars, it turned its mind to the internal problems of the regime. As a field of exercise it had a narrow strip of territory in Morocco, where its generals could win medals for valor while suffering defeats in skirmishes with the wild tribesmen. At home the military had earned the gratitude of the upper classes because only the violence of the soldiers had in 1917 preserved the existing social system from revolutionary overthrow. . . . . .

. . . Spanish generals fancied themselves as modern counterparts of Pizarro and Cortez, as conquerors unfortunately handicapped by the petty restrictions of capitalist civilization. And in reward for their suppression of the workers the army *juntas* were actually granted controlling power in the state. The Bourbon monarch himself subordinated attributes of divinity and sovereignty to his most prized title, which in his mind best expressed his true nature—that of first soldier in the kingdom. Though the leading conservative politicians in the Cortes were not always docile in the face of the extravagances of the military, the army could not be insulted with impunity. A Law of Jurisdictions dragged before a military tribunal any civilian who dared to cast improper reflections upon the army or its personnel. The integrity of the army was as indisputable as the dogmas of the Faith.

The army was not mechanized and its inefficiency was notorious. Since it had not been afforded the experiences which perfected other European war machines in the years 1914-1918, the long-drawn-out Moroccan campaigns were checkered with defeats. . . .

Alfonso XIII contributed his share in the movement to discredit the politicians in the Cortes, when he fostered discontent among would-be leaders of the two major parties, Conservatives and Liberals, whose orderly alternation in office had previously lent a semblance of stability to the regime. By sponsoring enough splinter groups the smooth working of the constitutional system, such as it was, would be destroyed. Since parliamentary majorities could be formed only by fortuitous combinations which were easily dissolved, no minister survived long enough to gain public confidence. Nothing nurtured antidemocratic sentiments more than the frequent recurrence of feverish ministerial crises. After 38 cabinets had passed in and out of office during a single reign, the people would welcome a dictator to displace the bungling ministers. There are indications that the King himself preferred the prevailing system of fast political change and its concomitant bewilderment, in the midst of which he could reassert his royal prerogatives in seventeenth century formulae.

. . . . .

The conservative parliamentarians, sensing danger to their hegemony, had prepared a document on the whole Moroccan adventure, the Picasso Report. This was their attempt to humble—not to destroy—the growing power of the military. Evidence which was about to be presented before the Cortes in September, 1923, would have revealed the complicity of Alfonso himself in the disaster of Annual (1921). According

to the documents, destroyed by Primo de Rivera as soon as he came
into office but since gathered verbally from various members of the
investigating commission, Alfonso had interfered with the regular
processes of government. The warrior-king had privately goaded General Silvestre on to launch a grand offensive movement against the
Riff without the consent of the minister of war, even without the
knowledge of General Berenguer, the commanding officer in Morocco.
When Silvestre's foolhardy gesture at Annual resulted in the most
overwhelming defeat of a European army at the hands of natives since
the Italian disaster at Adowa, a peculiar telegram from Alfonso was
discovered among the effects of the General, who had probably committed suicide. It read: "Ole hombre—I'm waiting." This is the cry
which the populace shouts at a bullfight in order to inspire the toreador
to perform his most daring movements. The directness of this royal
intervention was so bold that the parliamentarians were determined
at least to chastise Alfonso for his extension of the manners of the arena
to military affairs involving the lives of thousands of Spaniards.

The commission of inquiry hardly realized the serious implications
of its charges and their possible consequences. Fatuous parliamentarians, they had been carried too far by the zest of their own debating,
and they were about to disgrace their King-Father and his army, to
reveal scandals which would provide material for the anarchist agitators.
In their zeal to vindicate themselves they were proferring official documents to frantic mothers who had been asking why and for whom their
sons were being sent against the wild tribesmen of Morocco. Women
had laid themselves across railway tracks in Barcelona in crazed attempts to stop the departure of the transport trains. What might they
do if the facts about the massacre of Annual were published? Should
too many details of official corruption come to light, the whole social
structure might crash. Sanctity would be torn from the church and
nobility from the army. What could the money-lenders and war contractors expect as a saving grace?

The King-Father of a constitutional regime was not strong enough
to survive the crisis. He needed a guardian angel or a major-domo or
a dictator—and General Primo de Rivera came forward, pushed by
a small army clique. On September 13, 1923, Alfonso submitted to the
pronunciamiento of Primo de Rivera, the governor-general of Barcelona, and made him chief of a military directorate. The Cortes never
met to hear the Picasso Report. The army in its own right, with the sup-

port of the King and the sanction of the church, "saved face" by driving the politicians from their debating society. The middle classes acquiesced, because after half a century of socialist and anarchist agitation they were frightened.

. . . Primo de Rivera had made an old-fashioned *coup d'état,* as befitted the status of Spain's economy. In 1926 the journalist Ramón Martínez de la Riva asked the dictator for some anecdote about the origin of the movement which led to power. The general laughed and exclaimed: "Hombre, the whole movement was anecdotal."

170. EXTRACT FROM AN OFFICIAL SUMMARY OF PRIMO DE RIVERA'S ACHIEVEMENTS, 1929 [5]

Miguel Primo de Rivera found to his discomfort that it was one thing to set up a dictatorship and another to pursue policies that would satisfy most elements among a strongly discontented people. Finally, on January 28, 1930, after more than six years of difficult rule, he resigned, dying in Paris a few weeks later. While his enemies pointed out that the general had disregarded constitutionalism, had failed to end corruption in public life, had done little to improve the economic and financial position of the monarchy, and had permitted Spain to sink lower in the eyes of the world, Rivera himself had summarized his achievements in a special statement to the press on March 5, 1929.

If the present administration had not counted with the enormous amount of public opinion which supports it, it would already have succumbed to the obstinate campaign of attacks from outside the country and inhibitions and silences within. But it is a rare Spaniard indeed who by this time has not in some way felt the beneficent consequences of being well governed. Peace in Morocco and within the country, personal safety, reduction of the term of military service, subsidies to large families, the creation of thousands of schools and some institutes, protection to agriculture, higher wages, social legislation, old age pensions and adequate establishments for the correction of delin-

---

[5] Official statement to the press, March 5, 1929, as translated in Foreign Policy Association, *Information Service,* September 4, 1929, p. 226. Reprinted by permission of the Foreign Policy Association.

quents, many and good roads, irrigation works, sanitariums, hospitals, dispensaries, sewerage, water supplies, dozens of bridges, modern armaments, powerful navy units, small increases in the income of the lower clergy and dependent classes (widows and orphans of government employees, soldiers, etc.), appropriate establishments for our representatives abroad, treaties of commerce and of peace and arbitration—all these constitute an achievement which only a stupid people could fail to appreciate. . . .

171. ALFONSO'S SUSPENSION OF HIS OWN ROYAL POWERS, APRIL 14, 1931 [6]

The Spanish municipal elections of April 12, 1931, resulted in an overwhelming republican victory. Premier Admiral Juan Aznar, a loyal monarchist, thereupon resigned (April 13), and Niceto Alcalá Zamora, who had led a premature republican outbreak in the previous December, now, on behalf of a republican junta, threatened armed revolution unless the king abdicated. On April 14, then, King Alfonso XIII took ship at Cartagena, having left behind a document in which he suspended the exercise of his royal powers. Though this was not an actual abdication, Zamora at once proclaimed a republic with himself as provisional president.

The elections held on Sunday [April 12] have revealed to me that I no longer hold the love of my people, but my conscience tells me that this attitude will not be permanent, because I have always striven to serve Spain with all my devotion, to the public interest, even in the most critical times. A King may make mistakes and without doubt I have done so on occasion, but I know that our country has always shown herself generous towards the faults of others committed without malice.

I am King of all Spaniards and I am a Spaniard. I could find ample means to maintain my Royal Prerogatives in effective resistance to those who assail them. But I prefer to stand resolutely aside rather than provoke a conflict which might array my fellow-countrymen against one another in civil and fratricidal strife.

I renounce no single one of my rights which, rather than being

---

[6] *The Times* (London), April 16, 1931.

mine, are an accumulated legacy of history for the guardianship of which I shall one day have to render strict account.

I shall await the true will and full expression of the collective conscience and, until the nation speaks, I deliberately suspend my exercise of the Royal power and am leaving Spain, thus acknowledging that she is the sole mistress of her destinies. Also I now believe that I am fulfilling the duty which the love of my country dictates. I pray God that all other Spaniards may feel and fulfill this duty as sincerely as I do.

172. THE SPANISH CONSTITUTION OF DECEMBER 9, 1931 *(Extracts)* [7]

The first national election since 1923 was held in Spain on June 28, 1931. Twenty-five parties had nominated candidates for a constituent cortes which was to assemble on July 14. The voters (men only) gave a majority of the 470 seats to moderate republicans and socialists, only fourteen of the candidates ever having had any previous parliamentary experience. Among the most important tasks of the assembly was the drafting of a constitution. Such a document was finally proclaimed on December 9, 1931.

SPAIN, IN THE EXERCISE OF ITS SOVEREIGNTY AND REPRESENTED BY THE CONSTITUENT CORTES, DECREES AND SANCTIONS THE PRESENT CONSTITUTION:

ARTICLE 1.

Spain is a democratic Republic of workers of every class, organised under a system of liberty and justice.

The powers of all its authorities emanate from the people.

The Republic constitutes an integral State which is compatible with the autonomy of the municipalities and the Regions.

The flag of the Spanish Republic is red, yellow and purple.

ARTICLE 2.

All Spaniards are equal before the law.

ARTICLE 3.

The Spanish State has no official religion.

[7] Great Britain, Foreign Office, *British and Foreign State Papers 1931*, vol. CXXXIV, His Majesty's Stationery Office, London, 1936, pp. 1141-1166. Reprinted by permission of the Controller of His Britannic Majesty's Stationery Office.

ARTICLE 4.

Castilian is the official language of the Republic.

Every Spaniard is obliged to know it and has the right to use it, without prejudice to the rights that the laws of the State may concede to the languages of the provinces or the Regions.

Unless special laws shall so order, no one may be required to learn or use any regional language.

. . . . .

ARTICLE 6.

Spain renounces war as an instrument of national policy.

. . .

ARTICLE 8.

The Spanish State within the irreducible limits of its present territory, shall be composed of municipalities combined into provinces, and of Regions which shall be constituted under a system of autonomy.

The sovereign territories of North Africa shall be organised under an autonomous system in direct relationship with the central power.

ARTICLE 9.

All municipalities of the Republic shall be autonomous in matters within their competence and shall elect their municipal councils by universal, equal, direct and secret suffrage, except when acting under a system of open councils. The mayors shall always be appointed by the direct election of the people or by the municipal council.

. . .

ARTICLE 11.

If one or several adjoining provinces with common historical, cultural and economic characteristics agree to organise themselves into an autonomous Region for the purpose of forming a politico-administrative nucleus within the Spanish State, they shall submit their statute in conformity with the terms of Article 12.

In this statute a petition may be made for the powers, either wholly or in part, laid down in articles 15, 16 and 18 of this Constitution; without prejudice, in the latter case, to the securing, by petition, of all or

part of the remainder by the same process established in this fundamental code.

The condition of being adjacent is not requisite for insular territories
inter se.

Upon approval of the statute it shall be the basic law of the politico-
administrative organisation of the autonomous Region, and the Spanish
State shall recognise it and protect it as an integral part of its juridical
order.

ARTICLE 12.

The following conditions are required for approval of the statute of
an autonomous Region:—

(*a*) That it be proposed by the majority of its municipal councils
or, at least, by the councils of those municipalities which comprise two-
thirds of the electoral census [registered voters] of the Region;

(*b*) That it be acceded to, by the procedure specified in the electoral
law, by at least two-thirds of the electors registered in the census of
the Region. Should the plebiscite give a negative result, the proposition
for autonomy may not be renewed until after the lapse of five years;

(*c*) That it receive the approval of the Cortes.

Regional statutes shall be approved by the Congress [Cortes] provided that they are in conformity with this part and do not in any case
contain provisions contrary to the Constitution or the organic laws of
the State in matters not capable of delegation to regional authority,
without prejudice to the faculty ascribed to the Cortes by articles 15
and 16.

ARTICLE 13.

In no case shall the federation of autonomous Regions be permitted.

ARTICLE 14.

Legislation and direct execution in connexion with the following
matters lie within the exclusive competence of the Spanish State:—

(1) Acquisition and loss of nationality and regulation of constitutional rights and duties;

(2) Relations between the churches and the State; and the régime
governing religious bodies;

(3) Diplomatic and consular representation and, in general, representation of the State abroad; declaration of war; treaties of peace;
colonial and protectorate régimes; and every class of international
relations;

(4) Defence of public order in conflicts of supra-regional or extra-regional character;

(5) Maritime fisheries;

(6) National debt;

(7) Army, navy and national defence;

(8) Customs tariffs, commercial treaties, custom houses and the free circulation of merchandise;

(9) Registration of merchant ships, their rights and privileges and lighting of the coasts;

(10) Extradition proceedings;

(11) Jurisdiction of the Supreme Court, with the exception of the attributes accorded to autonomous regional authorities;

(12) Monetary system, fiduciary issue and the regulation of banking in general;

(13) General communication systems, air lines, posts, telegraphs, submarine cables and wireless communication;

(14) Hydraulic improvements and electric installations, either when the waters discharge themselves outside an autonomous Region or the energy produced is exported therefrom;

(15) Sanitary defence in so far as it affects extra-regional interests;

(16) Frontier police, emigration, immigration and aliens;

(17) General finances of the State;

(18) Control of the manufacture of and traffic in arms.

Article 15.

Legislation in the following matters is an attribute of the Spanish State, but its execution may be delegated to autonomous Regions within the scope of their political competence, if so decided by the Cortes:

(1) Legislation on penal, social and commercial matters and judicial proceedings; and matters relating to civil legislation, the form of matrimony, the compilation of registers and mortgages, the bases of contractual obligations and the regulation of personal, real and formal statutes, in order to co-ordinate the application and adjust the conflicts between the different civil legislations of Spain;

The execution of social laws shall be supervised by the Government of the Republic, in order to guarantee their strict fulfilment and that of international treaties in connexion therewith. . . .

(12) Socialisation of natural resources and economic enterprises, the

ownership and powers of the State and the Regions being defined by legislation. . . .

ARTICLE 16.

In matters not comprised in the two foregoing articles, the right of exclusive legislation and direct execution thereof may be delegated to the autonomous Regions, in conformity with the terms of their respective statutes as approved by the Cortes.

. . . . .

ARTICLE 21.

The law of the Spanish State takes precedence over that of the autonomous Regions in all matters not placed under their exclusive jurisdiction in their respective statutes.

. . . . . .

ARTICLE 25.

No juridical privilege may be based upon birth, relationship, political ideals or religious belief.

The State does not recognise distinctions and titles of nobility.

ARTICLE 26.

All religious confessions shall be regarded as associations subject to special law.

The State, Regions, provinces and municipalities shall not maintain, favour or aid economically churches or religious associations and institutions.

A special law shall provide for the total elimination, within the maximum period of 2 years, of the clerical budget appropriation.

Such religious Orders shall be dissolved as impose by their statutes, besides the three canonical vows, a special vow of obedience to an authority other than the legitimate authority of the State. Their properties shall be nationalised and allocated to beneficent and educational purposes.

The other religious Orders shall be subjected to a special law passed by this Constituent Cortes and based on the following principles:

(1) Dissolution of such Orders whose activities constitute a menace to the safety of the State;

(2) Registration in a special register kept by the Ministry of Justice of those which are to continue in existence;

(3) Incapacity to acquire and retain, for themselves or through intermediaries, other properties than those which, upon proof thereof, are designed for their dwellings or for the direct fulfilment of their particular objects;

(4) Prohibition of the exercise of industry, commerce or education;

(5) Submission to all the taxation laws of the country;

(6) Obligation to render to the State annual reports on the use made of their properties in connexion with the objects of the association.

The properties of religious Orders may be nationalised.

ARTICLE 27.

Liberty of conscience and the right to profess and practise freely any religion are guaranteed in Spanish territory, on condition of due respect to the exigencies of public morality. . . .

. . . .

ARTICLE 36.

Citizens of both sexes over 23 years of age shall possess the same electoral rights in conformity with the provisions of law.

ARTICLE 40.

All Spaniards, without distinction of sex, are admissible to public posts and offices according to their merit and capacity, except for such disabilities as the law may specify.

ARTICLE 43.

The family is under the special protection of the State. Matrimony is based on equality of rights for both sexes, and may be dissolved by mutual consent or upon the petition of either of the spouses, with allegation, in such case, of just cause. . . .

ARTICLE 44.

All the resources of the country, whosoever may be their owner, are subordinated to the interests of national economy, and are for the maintenance of public charges in accordance with the Constitution and the laws.

Property of all kinds may be made the object of enforced expropriation for purposes of social utility upon adequate indemnification being paid, unless it be otherwise provided by a law approved by an absolute majority of the members of the Cortes.

On the same conditions property may be socialised.

Public services and such exploitations as concern the general interests may be nationalised in cases where social necessities so demand.

The State may intervene legally in the exploitation and co-ordination of industries and enterprises when the rationalisation of production and the interests of national economy require such action.

In no case shall the penalty of confiscation of property be imposed.

ARTICLE 45.

All the artistic and historical riches of the country, whosoever may be their owners, constitute the cultural treasure of the nation and shall be under the protection of the State. . . .

ARTICLE 46.

Work, in its various forms, is a social obligation and shall enjoy the protection of the laws.

The Republic shall assure to every worker the conditions necessary for a fitting existence. Its social legislation shall regulate: cases of insurance for illness, accident, unemployment, old age, invalidity and death; the labour of women and young persons, and especially the protection of maternity; the working day and the minimum and family salary rate; annual holidays with pay; conditions of Spanish workers abroad; co-operative institutions; the economic and legal relationship of factors entering into production; the participation of workers in the direction, administration and benefits of enterprises; and everything connected with the protection of workers.

ARTICLE 47.

The Republic shall protect peasants and to this end shall legislate, among other matters, concerning the non-sequestrable family patrimony exempt from any kind of taxation, agricultural credits, indemnification for loss of crops, co-operative associations for production and consumption, insurance funds, practical schools of agriculture, experimental farms, irrigation works and rural communication routes.

The Republic shall protect fishermen in a similar manner.

ARTICLE 48.

Cultural service is an essential function of the State and shall be rendered by means of educational institutions together with the system of unified schools.

Primary instruction shall be gratuitous and compulsory.

Masters, teachers and professors are public officials. The liberty of the teacher is recognised and guaranteed. . . .

Instruction shall be lay in character and shall make work the basis of its methods and activities. It shall be inspired by ideals of human solidarity.

Churches are accorded the right, subject to State inspection, to teach their respective doctrines in their own establishments.

. . . .

ARTICLE 50.

The autonomous Regions may organise instruction in their respective languages, in accordance with the powers granted to them in their statutes. The study of the Castilian language is obligatory, and this language shall also be used as the medium of instruction in all centres of primary and secondary instruction in the autonomous Regions. . . .

. . . .

ARTICLE 86.

The President of the Council and the Ministers constitute the Government.

. . . .

ARTICLE 91.

Members of the Council are responsible to Congress as a body for the policy of the Government, and individually for their own ministerial acts.

. . . .

ARTICLE 94.

Justice shall be administered in the name of the State.

The Republic shall assure gratuitous justice to poor litigants.

Judges are independent in their offices. They are subject only to the law.

. . . . .

Done at the Palace of the Constituent Cortes on the 9th December, 1931.

173. THE LAW OF 1933 RESPECTING RELIGIOUS BODIES *(Extracts)* [8]

The same cortes which had adopted the republican constitution continued to sit as a regular parliament until after the elections of November-December 1933. In execution of articles 26 and 27 of the constitution, this assembly passed a drastic church law which was signed by President Zamora on June 2, 1933.

ARTICLE 1.

The present law relating to religious bodies and associations, issued in execution of articles 26 and 27 of the constitution of the Spanish Republic, will govern this matter throughout Spanish territory, and any further measure on the subject, whether by decree or by regulation, shall conform strictly to this law.

ARTICLE 2.

In accordance with the constitution, liberty of conscience, the practice of religious activities and abstention therefrom are guaranteed in Spain.

Without prejudice to the provisions of articles 70 and 87 of the constitution, no privilege or restriction of rights may be based on a person's religious condition or beliefs.

ARTICLE 3.

The State has no official religion. All religious bodies may hold their services freely within their churches. For religious worship outside churches special Government permission is required in every case.

---

[8] Great Britain, Foreign Office, *British and Foreign State Papers 1933*, vol. CXXXVI, His Majesty's Stationery Office, London, 1938, pp. 822-830; original text in Spain, *Colección Legislativa de España*, April-June 1933, Ser. 1, Pt. 1, pp. 463 *ff*. Reprinted by permission of the Controller of His Britannic Majesty's Stationery Office.

Religious meetings and demonstrations, wherever they may be held, may not have a political character.

The signs, notices, announcements or emblems on buildings destined for worship will be subject to general police rules.

. . . . .

ARTICLE 7.

Religious bodies shall appoint freely all ministers, administrators and incumbents of ecclesiastical posts and functions, who must be Spaniards.

Notwithstanding the provision contained in the foregoing paragraph, the State reserves the right not to recognize in their functions persons appointed in virtue of the foregoing provision, when the appointments devolve on persons who might be dangerous to the order or security of the State.

. . . . .

ARTICLE 9.

Any alteration in the territorial boundaries of the Catholic Church must be brought to the knowledge of the Government before it is carried into effect.

Other religious bodies shall be obliged to communicate to the Government the boundaries which they propose to establish, or have established, in Spain, as well as the alterations thereof, in accordance with the terms of the foregoing paragraph.

ARTICLE 10.

In accordance with the provisions of article 26 of the constitution, the State, the Regions, the provinces and the municipalities may not support, favor or assist economically churches or religious bodies and institutions.

ARTICLE 11.

The following compose national public property: churches of all kinds with attached buildings; episcopal palaces and rectories, with or without adjoining gardens; seminaries, monasteries and other buildings destined to the service of the Catholic religion or of its ministers. The same shall apply to the furniture, ornaments, images, pictures, vessels, jewels, cloths and other objects of this nature placed in such buildings and destined expressly and permanently to Catholic worship, to its embellishment or to needs connected with it.

The objects mentioned in the foregoing paragraph and the rights connected with them are under the protection of the State as the juridical personification of the nation to whom they belong, and they are subject to the provisions of the following articles.

ARTICLE 12.

The objects and rights referred to in the foregoing article will continue to be destined to the same religious purpose of Catholic worship, and to this end will remain in the possession of the Catholic Church for preservation, administration and use, according to their nature and purpose. The Church may not dispose of them and shall only employ them for the purpose to which they are assigned.

The State alone, for justified reasons of public necessity, and by virtue of a special law, may dispose of such property for purposes other than those specified in the foregoing paragraph.

The buildings attached to churches, episcopal palaces and rectories, with or without adjoining gardens, seminaries and other buildings destined for the use of ministers of the Catholic faith, will be subject to the taxation inherent in the use of the same.

ARTICLE 13.

Pending the enactment of the special law contemplated, the objects referred to in the foregoing articles shall be inalienable and imprescriptible, and no rights may be created in regard to them other than those compatible with their purpose and condition.

· · · · ·

ARTICLE 19.

Property acquired by the Catholic Church after the promulgation of the present law, and that of other religious bodies, will have the character of private property, within the limitations of the present article.

The Catholic Church, its institutions and entities, as well as the other religious bodies, are recognised as having power to acquire and possess movable property of any kind.

They may also acquire, by any title, immovable estate and real rights, but may only retain them up to the amount necessary for religious service. Estates exceeding such requirements will be alienated and the proceeds invested in Spanish State bonds.

In like manner must be alienated, and the proceeds invested in the same way, movable property producing interest or income, or sharing in profit of industrial or mercantile concerns.

By means of a law the State may restrict the acquistion by religious bodies of any kind of property in excess of the normal requirements of religious services.

Article 20.

The Churches may found and direct establishments destined for the teachings of their respective doctrines and the preparation of their ministers.

State inspection will ensure that within these establishments no doctrines are taught which threaten the security of the Republic.

Article 21.

All private charitable institutions and trusts of which the management, direction or administration belongs to religious authorities, corporations, institutions or juridical persons, are obliged, if they were not previously obliged, to send within the period of one year an inventory of all their property, securities and objects, as well as to render an annual account to the Ministry of the Interior of the state of their property and the management of their finances even though by their charter they may have been exempted from rendering such account. . . .

. . . . .

Artcle 23.

The religious orders and congregations allowed in Spain in accordance with article 26 of the constitution may not engage in any political activities whatsoever.

The infringement of this provision, should such activities constitute a danger to the security of the State, will justify the closing by the Government, as a preventive measure, of all or some of the establishments belonging to the religious society which might be accused. The Cortes will decide, according to circumstances, as to the definitive closing of the establishment or the dissolution of the religious institution.

Article 24.

Religious orders and congregations are subject to the present law and to the general legislation.

For their legal existence inscription in the public register is essential, in accordance with the provisions of the following article.

Article 25.

For the purposes of this inscription orders and congregations shall present to the competent special registry at the Ministry of Justice within a maximum period of 3 months:—

(a) Two copies of their statutes, stating the form of management, both as regards canonical provinces or assimilated monastic groupings, and houses, or residences or other local entities.

(b) A certificate as to the objects to which the religious institution concerned is dedicated and the house or residence for the inscription of which application is made.

(c) A certificate issued by the property registry stating what buildings are occupied by the community; these must be owned by Spaniards and may not be encumbered or transferred in favour of foreigners.

(d) A statement of all the real property, securities and precious objects owned by them directly or through an intermediary.

(e) The Christian names and surnames of the provincial and local superiors, who must be of Spanish nationality.

(f) A return of the Christian names and surnames and condition of their members, stating which hold administrative or representative posts. At least two thirds of the members of an order or congregation must be of Spanish nationality.

(g) A return of the property brought to the community by each of its members.

The Ministry of Justice shall be informed within 60 days of any alterations in the above returns.

. . . . .

Article 29.

Religious orders and congregations may not engage in commerce, industry or agricultural exploitation on their own account or through an intermediary.

ARTICLE 30.

Religious orders and congregations may not devote themselves to teaching.

Such teaching as may be organized for the preparation of their own members shall not be understood as included in this prohibition.

State inspection will guard against the creation or maintenance by religious orders and congregations, either directly or by taking advantage of a third lay party, of private teaching establishments.

ARTICLE 31.

Before the admission of any person to an order or congregation, the amount and nature of the property brought or transferred for administration shall be authentically recorded.

The state will assist any member of an order or congregation who wishes to retire therefrom, notwithstanding the vow or promise made to the contrary. The order or congregation will be obliged to restore to such person any property brought or transfered to the order or congregation after deduction of the property exhausted by use.

The two following are the sole transitory or additional provisions for the execution of the present law:—

(a) The Government shall fix the time-limit, which may not exceed one year from the publication of the present law, during which religious orders and congregations engaged in typical industries or having introduced innovations which imply a source of wealth, must cease from such activities.

(b) Teaching by religious orders and congregations will cease on the 1st October next, with the exception of primary education, which will cease on the 31st December next. The Government will adopt the measures necessary for the substitution of both grades of teaching within the time-limits mentioned.

Wherefore I order, &c.

NICETO ALCALÁ-ZAMORA Y TORRES
ALVARO DE ALBORNOZ Y LIMINIANA,
Minister for Justice.

Madrid, June 2, 1933.

꘠ ꘠ ꘠

174. THE EDUCATIONAL PROGRAM OF THE SPANISH REPUBLIC [9]

The educational aims of the Spanish Republic were set forth at length in a speech delivered at Bronxville, New York, on April 7, 1937, by Dr. Fernando de los Rios, "Ambassador of Spain. Former Minister of Education. Former Minister of Justice. Former President of the University of Madrid." Although the talk was given during the civil-war period, the portions quoted, at least, would seem to be reasonably free from elements of propaganda.

We thought that it was urgently necessary to put all the resources and the efforts of the State at the service of the education of the people. That is why, when, at the end of 1931, the Spanish Republic entrusted me with the responsibilities of the Ministry of Education, I put into this cause all the enthusiasm and the devotion of a man for whom popular education had been for many decades the most cherished dream of his life. I shall attempt to sketch . . . the work that was carried out during the two years in which I was the head of the Department of Education. I shall divide my outline into three sections, namely: popular, elementary education; secondary education; and higher, specialized education.

What was the scope of our program of popular education?

1st: the creation of elementary schools
2nd: the organization of state-maintained school-lunch-rooms
3rd: the education of adults, liquidating illiteracy
4th: the artistic education of the people.

When the Republic was established, Spain needed no less than 40,000 new schools. There were cities, like Madrid itself, where thousands and thousands of children were lacking the opportunities of getting the most elementary education. One month before the new institutions were inauguarated, the mothers of Madrid were standing in queues at the doorsteps of the schools, fearing that overcrowding might lessen the chances of securing admission for their children. . . . Thus, our first and most urgent task was that of opening new schools, and within the period of two years, 10,500 new institutions were founded in both urban and rural Spain.

---

[9] Spanish Embassy, Washington, D. C., Bureau of Information, *Excerpts from a Speech Delivered . . . on April 7, 1937, by Professor Fernando de los Rios, Ambassador of Spain. Former Minister of Education.*

Nevertheless, the children of the small villages,—the children of the agricultural regions, where life is so shockingly miserable—found it impossible to attend these schools, because their parents had to send them to take care of the flocks, or to pick olives in the fields (which, by the way, they did not own), so that they might earn a few cents to help keep life going in their poverty-stricken homes. How were we going to rescue these children, and bring them under the influence of the school? The only way of accomplishing that was to organize the "cantinas" (school-lunch-rooms) and the "roperos" (clothing store-rooms) in the schools; that is to say, to give them food and clothing, so that the parents might release them from their work. To this effect the Republic increased its budget for "cantinas" and "roperos" an 800%. As a result of this, there was such a run of children to the rural schools that it was practically impossible at the beginning, due to the lack of buildings, to accommodate them all.

This situation compelled me to introduce a bill in Parliament proposing a loan of 400,000,000 pesetas, for the exclusive use of school construction. Parliament granted me that money, and in 8 years we planned to build a minimum of 20,000 new buildings. This was begun on a great scale in 1932.

· · · · ·

My next project was to make similar provisions for adult education—that is to say, I wanted to organize all over the country community suppers at the schools, for the peasants, during the course of which they could be taught to read and write. This plan did not materialize, because the time factor did not enable me to carry out the idea systematically as first conceived. The education of the adult was accomplished, however, through another method, namely, the *"Pedagogical Missions,"* the *theatre,* and the *traveling museum.*

· · · · ·

The Spanish Republic attacked with enormous enthusiasm this enterprise. The Pedagogical Mission was composed of a group of true missionaries of culture: boys and girls, teachers of both sexes, university students, and youngsters from the work-shops, who would go, with the traveling theatre or library, the radio, the movie, etc., to the village, to spend a few days with the peasants, putting within their reach some of the cultural facilities which they were lacking. Sometimes young medical students and nurses would also teach the peasant mother how to take care of her children, how to keep them clean, to prevent infectious diseases, etc. Students in agriculture would teach those peasants who owned some land how to cultivate it more efficiently, how to prevent or check tree diseases, how to take care of the domestic animals, etc. Thus, we were trying to enrich not only the intellectual world of the peasant, but also to improve the economic means at his command.

. . . .

All this required, however, an essential supplement. This was found in the "Escuelas de Trabajo" (Schools of Workers), the aim of which was to convert the untrained workers into skilled workers. Through establishment of horticultural and agricultural schools we found an effective medium for changing the ignorant peasant into a farmer knowing the economic possibilities of his land.

This necessitated a special type of teacher, and with this purpose in mind we reformed the curriculum of the Normal School in such a way that a completed program of secondary education universal in character, was a prerequisite for the specialized courses for those teachers who were to teach workers. Furthermore, we organized the institution of the "Pedagogium" in the provinces—that is to say, intensive courses for the teachers themselves. Under this system the teachers took turns in giving demonstration lessons before the Provincial Congress of Teachers, which were followed by discussions on the ways and means of improving the teachers' technique.

We also fostered field-trips from one province to another, and during the Summer we used such palaces as that [at] Rio Frio, in the state of Segovia, for summer-schools. Here thousands of children lived in the invigorating air of the mountains, or else we would send thousands of children to the sea-shore for the same healthful purpose. We took great pains to do away with the over-academic atmosphere in the secondary schools; instead of a university in miniature we made of it an integrated educational institution, in which the emphasis was less on indoctrination and more on the give-and-take relationship between teacher and student, and, above all, on the development of a spirit of social responsibility in both teacher and student.

A cultural work of this kind, however, is incomplete if it has no repercussion on the institutions of higher learning, such as universities, research bodies, museums, etc. With this last purpose in mind, we founded on a similar basis, in 1932, in Granada and Madrid, the "Centros de Investigacion," the "Centro de Estudios Historicos," and the "Seccion de Monumentos Hispanicos," to bring to light unexamined

documents of historical importance, of medieval Spain, and to reinter-
pret on their basis those which had been already uncovered. We also
founded the "Museo Iberico" in Soria, the "Museo de Epigrafia Greco-
romana" in Tarragona, and the "Museo de Estatuaria Policromada," in
Valladolid. We also founded centers of research in economics, physical
science, international politics, etc., to which large sums were allotted in
the Federal budget. There never was before in Spain a greater interest
for cultural problems than that witnessed between 1931-1932.

Finally, we conceived the project, which fortunately I was able to put
into effect, of creating the International University of Santander. In the
magnificent "Palacio de la Magdalena," in the midst of a forest, near
the shores of the Mar Cantabrico,—a palace which was formerly used
as a summer resort by the Spanish kings—, thousands of students and
professors from all over Europe and America gathered between July
and September of each year, to discuss and analyze cultural problems
of international character. In this way we were helping to develop an
international consciousness in the realms of the arts and the sciences,
and we were putting the University youth of the world in direct contact
with each other, making them work together on problems of a universally human nature. The work accomplished so far by the International
University of Santander is, in my opinion, something which will have
a lasting influence.

This is in brief the educational program brought into effect by the
Spanish Republic during the last 6 years, especially in 1931-1933 and
1936.

175. THE FUNDAMENTAL LAW OF CATALONIA, 1933 (Extracts) [10]

*In response to the persistent demands of the Catalonians (See Document
No. 168), the Spanish Cortes on September 9, 1932, passed a Catalonian
Statute of Autonomy. Under the terms of this act, a Catalonian Parliament
met on December 6, 1932, the first such instance since 1705. On May 26,
1933, President Francesc Macia of Catalonia signed the fundamental law
passed by this parliament. Late in 1934 the Madrid Government, headed by
Alejandro Lerroux, suspended the autonomy statute.*

[10] Great Britain, Foreign Office, *British and Foreign State Papers 1933,* vol. CXXXVI,
His Majesty's Stationery Office, London, 1938, pp. 168-180; original text in Castilian and
Catalan in Catalonia, *Butlletí Oficial de la Generalitat de Catalunya,* No. 45, May 27,
1933. Reprinted by permission of the Controller of His Britannic Majesty's Stationery
Office.

The people of Catalonia, on recovering their political personality and constituting themselves into an autonomous Power, lay down by the authority of their Parliament the following fundamental law.

. . . . .

ARTICLE 1.

Power in Catalonia emanates from the people, who exercise it through the organisms of the *Generalitat.*

ARTICLE 2.

The capital of Catalonia is Barcelona.

ARTICLE 3.

The language of Catalonia is Catalan.

ARTICLE 4.

The flag of Catalonia is the traditional one of four red bars on a yellow field.

. . . . .

ARTICLE 7.

The following shall have the political status of Catalonians:—

(1) Persons who are natural-born Catalonians and have not acquired domicile outside of Catalonia.

(2) Persons who, being Spaniards, have acquired administrative domicile in Catalonia. The political status of Catalonians does not involve the application of the civil law in force in Catalonia, which matter will be regulated by the provisions of the laws governing this subject.

A woman may, by the fact of marriage with a Catalonian, acquire forthwith the political status of her husband. . . .

. . . . .

ARTICLE 9.

The exercise of the right of ownership must be inspired by social interest. The *Generalitat* protects and confirms it, so far as it conduces to this end, and the powers granted by the statute to Catalonia will be applied with this object in view. All the natural riches of the country are subordinate to the interests of the general economic structure.

Parliament may intervene, by means of legislation, in the exploitation and co-ordination of industries and private undertakings, provided that this course be enjoined by the rationalization of production and in the collective interest of Catalonian economy.

. . . . .

ARTICLE 11.

Primary education will be obligatory, free and Catalan in language and spirit. It will be inspired by the ideals of work, liberty, social justice and the solidarity of humanity, and it will be carried out by educational institutions, interrelated by a system of unified schools. In all its grades it will be secular.

The *Generalitat* will facilitate access to all grades of education to better qualified pupils who lack means.

Academic freedom is recognized and guaranteed.

The *Generalitat* will protect the existence and the work of private institutions and foundations of learning which, in compliance with legal regulations, contribute to the spread of education and the intellectual development of the Catalonian people.

ARTICLE 12.

Work in all its forms is a social duty. The *Generalitat* will protect it within the limits of its competence.

. . . . .

ARTICLE 14.

Social assistance is a duty of the *Generalitat*. The *Generalitat* will provide for assistance in cases of maternity, infancy, old age, infirmity and invalidity in collaboration with the social insurance system, with the object of providing workers with means to meet the contingencies to which life is subject.

The *Generalitat* will control benevolent institutions of a private character.

. . . . .

ARTICLE 17.

The *Generalitat* is the judicial organism of Catalonian autonomy.

It is composed of the Parliament, the President and the Executive Council or Government. . . .

ARTICLE 18.

The power of making and repealing laws appertains to Parliament, constituted of Deputies elected by the people by means of universal, direct, equal and secret suffrage.

Elections will be effected by lists and for extensive areas.

ARTICLE 19.

Citizens over 23 years of age are eligible for the post of deputy, without distinction of sex or civil status, if they possess the political status of Catalonians and fulfil the requirements which will be laid down by the electoral law.

. . . . .

ARTICLE 24.

The parliamentary mandate lasts 5 years, counting from the date of elections. . . . . .

ARTICLE 39.

The President of the *Generalitat* is elected by Parliament. If no absolute majority of the votes of sitting deputies is obtained at the first voting, a fresh election will take place, and the person who obtains a majority of votes of the deputies who take part in the voting will be elected. If no candidate obtains this majority, a fresh election will take place, in which the candidates are limited to the two who obtained the greatest number of votes in the previous election. Whichever obtains the greater number of votes will be elected.

The President will normally leave office when a new Parliament is constituted, to which he will submit his resignation.

. . . . .

ARTICLE 41.

The President lays down the general outlines of the policy of the Government and directs its execution. He is responsible to Parliament, and in case of losing its confidence he must resign.

. . . . .

ARTICLE 43.

Ecclesiastics, ministers of any religious confession, members of religious orders and military on the active list shall not be eligible for the office of President.

. . . . .

ARTICLE 50.

The Executive Council or Government is composed of the President of the Commonwealth and the Councillors.

. . . . .

ARTICLE 53.

The Government must resign whenever Parliament refuses its confidence. . . . . This rule will apply also to the Councillors individually.

. . . . .

ARTICLE 69.

Judges and magistrates may not be superannuated, dismissed, suspended from their duties or transferred from the positions they occupy except in conformity with the law.

. . . . .

FINAL PROVISION.

The present domestic statute will enter into force on the day of its publication in the *Butlletí Oficial de la Generalitat*.

Wherefore I order all citizens of Catalonia to aid in complying with this law, and all tribunals and authorities to enforce compliance.

Barcelona, the 26th May, 1933.

FRANCESC MACIA

CARLOS PI I SUNYER
  Councillor Delegate.

176. RESULTS OF THE PARLIAMENTARY ELECTIONS OF FEBRUARY 16, 1936 [11]

In the Spanish elections of February 16, 1936, the voters were faced with a choice between a leftist and a right-center coalition. As a result of the

[11] Spain, Cortes Constituyentes Biblioteca, *Boletín de Información Bibliográfica y Parlamentaria de España y del Extranjero,* vol. I, No. 6, November-December 1933, Madrid, 1933, p. 1069, and vol. I, No. 1, January-February 1936, Madrid, 1936, pp. 121-148. The groupings of parties given here are based on those in Foreign Policy Association, *Reports,* January 1, 1937, p. 254.

ballotting, and the distribution of votes, the Popular Front, though it re-
ceived only a plurality, captured 258 of the 473 seats in the chamber. Al-
though all radical groups had supported the Popular Front candidates,
there were no socialists, communists, or syndicalists in the cabinet which
now was formed by Manuel Azaña.

A.

TABLES SHOWING THE NUMBER OF DEPUTIES RETURNED IN THE SPANISH
ELECTIONS OF DECEMBER 1933 AND FEBRUARY 1936

i. Group Results, 1933 and 1936

	1933	1936	Change
Radical Parties......................	60	110	+ 50
Left-Wing Liberal Parties.............	32	148	+116
	92	258[12]	+166
Center Parties........................	173	62	−111
Right Parties.........................	196	152	− 44
	369	214	−155
	461[13]	472[13]	

ii. Results for Leading Individual Parties, 1933 and 1936

	1933	1936	Change
Radical Parties			
Communist (Bolívar; Ibarruri)[14]...............	1	14	+13
Socialist (Caballero).........................	59	89	+30
Left-Wing Liberal Parties			
Catalonian Republican (Companys)...........	17	21	+ 4
Left Republican (Azaña).....................	11	82	+71
Center Parties			
Radical (Lerroux)...........................	101	8	−93
Agrarian (Velasco)..........................	31	13	−18
Right Parties			
Agrarian People's (Gil Robles)................	115	98	−17
Catalonian League (Cambó).................	26	11	−15
Monarchists................................	36	23	−13

[12] These deputies represented the so-called Popular Front.—*Ed.*
[13] The total number of deputies was fixed at 473; there were vacant or disputed seats
at the time of the count.—*Ed.*
[14] The names in parentheses are those of the leaders or most prominent members.—*Ed.*

B.

POPULAR VOTES, 1936

Popular Front Parties 4,206,156
Center Parties 681,047
Right Parties 3,783,601

177. ITALIAN FIGHTERS IN SPAIN [15]

During 1937 the supporters of the Madrid Government in the civil war routed a Franco force on the Guadalajara front northeast of Madrid. A leading part in this fight was taken by Italian "volunteers" who had come to assist Franco, but they were beaten at Brihuega, where numerous important documents fell into the hands of the "Loyalists." The Madrid Government published this information as indicated in the samples below.

A. NOTE FROM THE SPANISH GOVERNMENT TO THE SECRETARY-GENERAL OF THE LEAGUE OF NATIONS.

[*Translation from the Spanish.*]   Valencia, March 13th, 1937.

The statements of the Italian officers and men taken prisoner during the last few days in the Guadalajara sector confirm beyond possibility of denial the presence of regular military units of the Italian army sent to fight on Spanish soil in flagrant violation of the provisions of Article 10 of the Covenant, whereby "the Members of the League undertake to respect and preserve as against external aggression the territorial integrity and existing political independence of all Members of the League."

From these statements made in the presence of the Spanish authorities, it appears that, on February 6th and the following days, numbers of Italian regular troops, equipped, armed and supplied, landed at Cadiz from the Italian steamer *Sicilia* and other ships. They were concentrated in the port of Santa Maria and subsequently conveyed to the Guadalajara front to take part in the present offensive. This is being conducted by four divisions of the Italian army—the first, second and third divisions of Blackshirts, the last being commanded by General Nuvoloni, whose headquarters are at Brihuega, and the first Littoria

---

[15] Spanish White Book, *The Italian Invasion of Spain. Official Documents and Papers Seized from Italian Units in Action at Guadalajara,* Spanish Embassy, Washington, 1937, pp. 8-10, 23-25.

division, commanded by General Bergonzoli, with headquarters at Almadrones. The commander-in-chief of this army corps is General Mangini, whose headquarters are at Algora. The attacking forces are completed by two special brigades, one of German and Italian regular troops and the other of German regular troops and four motorised companies of "carabinieri." . . . The above is a summary of the statements made by Antonio Luciano, major on the active list of the Italian regular army, commanding the machine-guns of the first Littoria division; Achille Sacchi, lieutenant on the active list of the Italian regular army, of the third Blackshirt division; Giuseppe Moretti, of the first company of batallion 835; Andrea Cappone, of the mortar platoon of mortar battalion 835; Francesco Lodo, rifleman of battalion 835; Giuseppe Rossotto, of the second company of battalion 624, etc.

These facts, besides constituting an attack upon the "territorial integrity and political independence" of Spain, represent a series of consummated acts which reproduce under aggravated circumstances the situations incompatible with international law created in recent times by the totalitarian States and amount to a resort to war without previous declaration—a dangerous proceeding denounced by the representative of Spain in the September Assembly.

The Government of the Republic, being of the opinion that, ever since the foundation of the League of Nations, there has been on the continent of Europe no more scandalous violation of the obligations imposed by the Covenant, and in the same spirit of loyalty to the great institution to which it belongs that led it in December to ask for the extraordinary meeting of the Council to denounce a situation "affecting international relations which threatens to disturb international peace," now brings to Your Excellency's notice the facts stated above and requests you to communicate them urgently to all States Members.

(*Signed*) Julio Alvarez del Vayo.

His Excellency M. Joseph Avenol,
Secretary-General of the League of Nations, Geneva.

B. IDENTICAL NOTE FROM THE SPANISH GOVERNMENT TO THE GOVERNMENTS OF FRANCE, THE UNITED KINGDOM AND THE UNION OF SOVIET SOCIALIST REPUBLICS.

[*Translation from the Spanish.*]   Valencia, March 29th, 1937.

During the recent action at Guadalajara, the Republican forces seized the orders of the Italian Headquarters Command directing the military operations in that sector and the service documents of the Italian divisions fighting on the side of the rebels.

These documents reveal, in a form which leaves no room for doubt, the nature of the Italian armed intervention in Spain denounced to the League of Nations on November 27th, 1936, and again referred to by the Government of the Republic in its communication to the Secretary-General of March 13th, 1937, and its Notes to the Powers of the same date.

The existence of an Italian army of occupation fighting against the legitimate Government of Spain not only constitutes a violation of international law and plainly conflicts with the Council resolution of December 12th, 1936, affirming that "every State is under an obligation to refrain from intervening in the internal affairs of another state," but represents the most flagrant infringement so far committed of the non-intervention policy and the international obligations resulting from the Declaration of Non-Intervention of August last.

By this procedure, Italy has helped to prolong the war in Spain, has infringed Article 10 of the League Covenant and has acted as a real belligerent Power.

The following conclusions emerge from an examination of the documents accompanying the present Note:

1. The existence on Spanish territory of complete units of the Italian army whose personnel, material, organs of liaison and command are Italian.

2. The Italian military units are behaving in the sectors assigned to them exactly as a veritable army of occupation.

3. The Italian Government has established on Spanish territory its own services for its military units.

4. The most outstanding personages of the regime are taking an active part in the operations of the Italian forces in Spain and are directing and encouraging them.

5. All this is equivalent to an invasion of Spain by Italy, with the result that the confidence which should be engendered by solemn agreements is being seriously undermined and that the security of Western Europe and the cause of peace in general are being gravely endangered.

The Government of the Republic regards the evidence in its possession, attached to the present Note, as sufficient basis for the foregoing conclusions, and has the honour to communicate it to the Government of France (the United Kingdom, the Union of Soviet Socialist Republics), without waiting for the whole of the material collected to be sorted out.   (*Signed*) Julio Alvarez del Vayo.

C. COMMAND OF THE FIRST BRIGADE OF (ITALIAN) VOLUNTEERS.

Order of the day No. 1.

[*In manuscript:*] Serial No. 51.   Seville, January 1st, 1937/XV.
  24.1.37/XV.

VOLUNTEERS!

I am to-day taking command. I greet you; I know and think highly of you; I feel sure that I can rely—now and at all times—on you all, officers, N.C.O.s, corporals and Blackshirts, to carry out any task, no matter how difficult, to fight fiercely and to conquer.

We, the Volunteers of the 1st Brigade, have asked to come to Spain to fight for the triumph of the Fascist Idea.

It is our duty to carry out our engagement and the hard task we have undertaken. We shall triumph because this is our determination as Italian soldiers and Fascists.

Firmly united by the same ideal and a common duty, and inspired by a vigorous and warlike spirit, we, the Volunteers of the 1st Brigade, will uphold the honour of our Imperial and Fascist Italy, and will conquer in the sacred name of Rome and under the propitious sign of the "Fascio Littorio."

Let us prepare ourselves passionately, gravely, and with an active joy for the ordeals that await us, and we shall conquer.

It is the will of God—this is the watchword of the Brigade, which expresses and defines the nature of our undertaking, because we, the Volunteers, are true "Crusaders" of the Fascist Idea, which, as a result of our inevitable victory, will triumph throughout Spain, inspiring the enemies with the human and divine Truth inherent in our Idea.

VOLUNTEERS OF THE 1ST BRIGADE!

Lift up your hearts, your bayonets, and the Black Flames!

Let us remember at all times that we represent our great, powerful and beloved country and the fighting strength of Fascist Italy. Remember that we must conquer, and we shall conquer at all costs! "IT IS THE WILL OF GOD!"

Who is going to win? WE ARE!

The Brigadier-General:

(*Signed*) ARNALDI.

Countersigned:

Lieut-Col. Chief of Staff:

(R. NASI).

[*Autograph signature.*]

N.B.—The present order to be read by company commanders to their respective units, in armed formation, and afterwards to be commented on.

178. INTERNATIONAL ACTION TO RESTRAIN PIRACY IN THE MEDITERRANEAN DURING THE SPANISH CIVIL WAR, 1937

While a special "non-intervention committee" was discussing various aspects of foreign help to one side or the other in the Spanish civil war, there began a series of submarine attacks on neutral merchant vessels in the Mediterranean. The ships apparently were all carrying cargoes for the "Loyalist" Government, and the attacks occurred simultaneously at widely separated points in the Mediterranean. In September 1937 the Soviet Government openly accused Italian submarines of having torpedoed two Soviet freighters. Eventually this "piracy" led Great Britain and France to call a conference of powers to meet at Nyon near Geneva on September 10. The German and Italian governments refused to send delegates because Moscow did, but on September 14, 1937, the representatives of nine Mediterranean and Black sea powers signed the Nyon Agreement providing for an international patrol of ships and planes, chiefly British and French. Eventually Italy also joined the "piracy patrol" and soon the submarine attacks ceased.

A. THE NYON ARRANGEMENT, SEPTEMBER 14, 1937 [16]

Whereas arising out of the Spanish conflict attacks have been repeatedly committed in the Mediterranean by submarines against merchant ships not belonging to either of the conflicting Spanish parties; and

Whereas these attacks are violations of the rules of international law referred to in Part IV of the Treaty of London of April 22nd, 1930 [Document No. 58], with regard to the sinking of merchant ships and

---

[16] League of Nations, *Treaty Series 1937-1938,* vol. CLXXXI, pp. 137-140.

constitute acts contrary to the most elementary dictates of humanity, which should be justly treated as acts of piracy; and

Whereas without in any way admitting the right of either party to the conflict in Spain to exercise belligerent rights or to interfere with merchant ships on the high seas even if the laws of warfare at sea are observed and without prejudice to the right of any Participating Power to take such action as may be proper to protect its merchant shipping from any kind of interference on the high seas or to the possibility of further collective measures being agreed upon subsequently, it is necessary in the first place to agree upon certain special collective measures against piratical acts by submarines:

In view whereof the undersigned, being authorised to this effect by their respective Governments, have met in conference at Nyon between the 9th and the 14th September 1937, and have agreed upon the following provisions which shall enter immediately into force:

I. The Participating Powers will instruct their naval forces to take the action indicated in paragraphs II and III below with a view to the protection of all merchant ships not belonging to either of the conflicting Spanish parties.

II. Any submarine which attacks such a ship in a manner contrary to the rules of international law referred to in the International Treaty for the Limitation and Reduction of Naval Armaments signed in London on April 22nd, 1930, and confirmed in the Protocol signed in London on November 6th, 1936, shall be counter-attacked and, if possible, destroyed.

III. The instruction mentioned in the preceding paragraph shall extend to any submarine encountered in the vicinity of a position where a ship not belonging to either of the conflicting Spanish parties has recently been attacked in violation of the rules referred to in the preceding paragraph in circumstances which give valid grounds for the belief that the submarine was guilty of the attack.

IV. In order to facilitate the putting into force of the above arrangements in a practical manner, the Participating Powers have agreed upon the following arrangements:

[Here follow the patrol zone delimitations, with the heaviest assignments going to the British and French fleets.]

* * * * *

Done at Nyon this fourteenth day of September nineteen hundred and thirty-seven, in a single copy, in the English and French languages, both texts being equally authentic, and which will be deposited in the archives of the Secretariat of the League of Nations.

[Here follow the signatures of the representatives of the United Kingdom of Great Britain and Northern Ireland, Bulgaria, Egypt, France, Greece, Rumania, Turkey, the Union of Soviet Socialist Republics, and Yugoslavia.]

B. AGREEMENT SUPPLEMENTARY TO THE NYON ARRANGEMENT, GENEVA, SEPTEMBER 17, 1937 [17]

Whereas under the Arrangement signed at Nyon on the 14th September, 1937, whereby certain collective measures were agreed upon relating to piratical acts by submarines in the Mediterranean, the Participating Powers reserved the possibility of taking further collective measures; and

Whereas it is now considered expedient that such measures should be taken against similar acts by surface vessels and aircraft;

In view whereof, the undersigned, being authorised to this effect by their respective Governments, have met in conference at Geneva on the seventeenth day of September and have agreed upon the following provisions which shall enter immediately into force:

I. The present Arrangement is supplementary to the Nyon Arrangement and shall be regarded as an integral part thereof.

II. The present Agreement applies to any attack by a surface vessel or an aircraft upon any merchant vessel in the Mediterranean not belonging to either of the conflicting Spanish parties, when such attack is accompanied by a violation of the humanitarian principles embodied in the rules of international law with regard to warfare at sea, which are referred to in Part IV of the Treaty of London of April 22nd, 1930, and confirmed in the Protocol signed in London on November 6th, 1936.

III. Any surface war vessel, engaged in the protection of merchant shipping in conformity with the Nyon Arrangement, which witnesses an attack of the kind referred to in the preceding paragraph shall:

(*a*) If the attack is committed by an aircraft, open fire on the aircraft;

(*b*) If the attack is committed by a surface vessel, intervene

---

[17] League of Nations, *Treaty Series 1937-1938*, vol. CLXXXI, pp. 151-152.

to resist it within the limits of its powers, summoning assistance if such is available and necessary.

In territorial waters each of the Participating Powers concerned will give instructions as to the action to be taken by its own war vessels in the spirit of the present Agreement.

Done at Geneva this seventeenth day of September 1937, in the English and French languages, both texts being equally authentic, in a single copy, which will be deposited in the archives of the Secretariat of the League of Nations.

[Here follow the same signatures as to the Nyon Arrangement above.]

179. A SPANISH RIGHTIST EXPOSITION [18]

Among the leading opponents of leftist republican Spain was José Maria Gil Robles, a lawyer and assistant editor of the leading clerical paper, El Debate. *He advocated a form of Catholic Fascism and was one of the organizers of the Agrarian People's Party, which upheld the preservation of landed property, defended Catholicism, and opposed all forms of separatism. When the Spanish Civil War broke out on July 17, 1936, Gil Robles supported the "Insurgent" side, though he soon came to play a much less prominent part than had been generally anticipated. Nonetheless, his views on the future of Spain coincided with those of many of the rightist leaders.*

THE SPANISH REPUBLIC AND THE FUTURE

It is logical that, once the determining factors of the national Spanish movement have been summarily examined, people should ask themselves what form of government will be established in Spain once the war is over.

In the opinion of some, our nation will necessarily organize itself along Fascist or National Socialist lines, like Italy or Germany. Others believe that Spain will return to a parliamentary constitutional system, slightly different from that established in 1931.

In dispassionately examining this most delicate question, I ought not to proceed either like one initiated into the problems of Spain who is lifting, as far as is humanly possible, the veil of the future, nor like the

---

[18] J. M. Gil Robles, *Spain in Chains*, The America Press, New York, 1937, pp. 17-24. Reprinted by permission of the publishers.

leader of a political party expounding the synthesis of his desires. I should limit myself to stating the most likely hypotheses, in an impartial review of the integrating factors in the Nationalist movement.

Basically, the forces which support the action of the Spanish army are four. Enumerated in order of their antiquity in public life, these forces are: Tradicionalistas (Requetés), Acción Popular, Renovación Española, and Falange Española.

The Tradicionalistas (Traditionalists) are a legitimist monarchial organization which opposes morganatic democracy and upholds the historical characteristics of the various regions.

Acción Popular (Popular Action) is a party which was organized to contend in the field of democracy. It professes the doctrine that forms of Government are accidental, aims at giving an organic structure to Spanish society, and upholds a broad program of social justice.

Renovación Española (Spanish Renovation) is a separated sector of Popular Action, with scant numerical strength, with special appeal to the upper classes, and in full progress toward organic and authoritative principles, upholds the Monarchy in the person of Alfonso XIII.

Lastly, Falange Española (Spanish Phalanx) is a group whose principles and methods of action are inspired by the modern totalitarian schools. Its social program is extraordinarily advanced, but it proposes no definite solution to the problem of the form of government to be established.

Initiator of the movement and hub of its future development is the army, which is really independent of any of the political parties that support it.

From this group of factors, representing almost all shades of public opinion in Nationalist Spain, may be deduced what is reasonably likely to be its type of government, in the immediate and distant future.

It is logical to expect that when the war comes to an end, with the indisputable victory of the army, there will be a provisional period of military dictatorship.

The demobilizing of the fighting forces, the disarming of the last Marxist groups, the applying of sanctions for public crimes committed by the Reds, the urgent repairing of the more serious elements in the immense material damage caused by international Communism in our country, the unifying of all efforts in a work of collective sacrifice to initiate the task of national reconstruction—all this will require, at first, the formation of a government entirely or preponderantly military. During its rule, the various sectors of Nationalist political opinion will be able to unite and to lay the foundations of the State's future structure.

This provisional military period should not last too long, since the task of government does not normally belong to the army, and the prolongation of a government of this sort beyond the limits of necessity would blight the blossoming of civic virtues indispensable to the stability of a nation's political institutions.

Granted the limited duration of a military government, what will be the final organization of Spanish public life?

Many superficial individuals, judging merely by appearances, assert that Spain will be organized purely and simply as a Fascist government. The propaganda of Moscow has possessed itself of this idea. Holding Fascism before the eyes of the people as a system of tyrannical government, it tries to consolidate the mass of opinion in democratic countries against any tendency that may be suspected of sympathy with Fascism.

Yet, without even remotely admitting the unjust and derogatory meaning that Communist propaganda attaches to the term Fascism, no one in good faith can possibly maintain the theory that Spain will set up a government of this type. For the present, one must not forget that Mussolini himself has declared on many occasions that Fascism is a typically Italian product suited to the needs and characteristics of Italy and impossible of application in other countries. In agreement with this fundamental statement is that of General Franco, the Chief of the Spanish State, who affirms, on his part, that the present movement in Spain is not of the Fascist order.

If we succeed in maintaining a middle course among doctrinal tenets favored by the political groups which support the Nationalist movement in Spain and the aspirations most commonly felt by the great mass of Rightist opinion, we shall easily succeed in establishing the following basic assertions concerning a possible political regime in Spain.

1. *Strengthening of authority:* In Latin countries, Parliamentarianism—we are forced to recognize the fact—has not been able to harmonize human liberty with the principle of authority (not despotism) indispensable to the preservation and progress of society.

The strict dependence which governments are obliged to maintain with regard to Parliament and the subordination in which Parliament, in its turn, must hold with regard to a public opinion at once fickle, vehement, and without solid civic formation, has given rise to the growing instability of governments and the relaxing of the basic means of authority. While public opinion was polarized around two great alternative parties—using England for its model—governments enjoyed at least relative stability, and the executive power, somewhat more detached from the legislative, could accomplish its mission with relative efficacy. Still more when the increasing break-up of parties and the dependence of governments upon Parliament (firmly established by the post-war democratic constitutions) reduced the executive power to a docile instrument in the hands of the people's representatives, the State lost the principal means of command at the precise moment when the violent clash of social classes was creating a situation of latent civil war, always ready to manifest itself in anarchic riots and bloody outbursts.

Thence came the unanimous desire of Latin peoples for a strong central power, withdrawn as far as possible from the flux of fickle public opinion, and capable of imposing itself upon selfish class or regional party-interests, in order to unite them in seeking the supreme collective good.

Spain, which has so keenly experienced of late the effects of the weakness in which the central power was left by a vicious Parliament incompatible with her psychology and her history, feels more than any other country the need of a strong authority. Upon this first characteristic of her future government all sectors of Nationalist Spain are agreed.

2. *Organic concept of democracy:* In my opinion, those who propose the great juridical problem of the modern world in terms of a simplified dilemma—democracy or anti-democracy—are fundamentally mistaken.

In the foreword of the Spanish translation of a book by Tardieu, I wrote two years ago that the problem of the present day was not one of achieving but of organizing democracy.

Democracy is a very broad concept, which supposes simply participation by the people in the problems of State government. From this point of view, democracy is a definite achievement of modern peoples. This democracy, so broadly conceived, can suffer partial eclipse; but in point of fact it represents a common basis for contemporary nations.

As against this broad and comprehensive concept which germinates from the principles of true political science, what actually happens is that the idea of democracy tends to convert itself into a monopoly of those who can conceive of no democracy other than inorganic, based upon the individual as the only fundamental political reality, and expressed through universal suffrage. Those who aspire to retain this monopoly feel that whatever is not inorganic universal suffrage is not democracy.

Many thinkers and writers, from the Catholic school of civil law to the modern integral corporativists, such as Bottai, Manoïlesco or Spann, passing for positivists of the type of Léon Duguit, have maintained that political society is integrated not merely by individuals but by societies or inferior personalities, some perfect and others imperfect, some complete and others incomplete (family, city, region, profession), through which the individual develops the entirety of his spiritual and material activities.

To incorporate the individual in the State by means of these units, to give organic structure to the will of the people, is the most effective means of guaranteeing true democracy, which is not just a blind rule by mathematical reckoning (*de la mitad mas una*) of atomized wills.

Nationalist Spain desires just this organic structure, through which Spaniards themselves shall be the masters of their country's destinies.

3. *Disappearance of class struggle:* The great solvent principle of modern societies is the materialist interpretation of history, whence is derived the postulate of class struggle, which rends nations in a continuous civil strife. To eliminate this corrosive principle is the most urgent need of the epoch in which we live.

The process begun in Spain in the year 1931 is not, as one might at first glance suppose, a political overthrow; but, rather, a true social evolution. Of all the solvent forces favored by the Republic, only the Marxist organizations knew where they were going. For the Leftist burghers, the laic and democratic Republic was an end. For the Socialists and Communists it was only a means. The Republic laid bare the fierce class struggle which for years had been silently palpitating. With the new political order, the shock assumed the tragic features of the present war. It would not be strange, therefore, if, when the war is over, the destruction of the deadly germs of materialistic and inhuman Marxism were to be the common ambition of Nationalist Spain.

The sorrowful experience of these years has convinced the Spanish Rightists that class struggle will not disappear solely through the energetic intervention of a strong political power. If the evil be not attacked at its root, during a period of apparent peace, it will bud forth with a degree of strength proportionate to the degree of energy which has been expended in the attempt to destroy it by material compulsion.

This does not mean that the action of authority is not effective, but

that compulsion alone is not sufficient. Class struggle will not diminish
so long as minds are not pacified, and this supreme task of pacification
can only be accomplished by a drawing together of classes through the
realization of a broad and rational plan of social justice which, without
attempting impracticable levelings in conflict with the original inequalities of men and incompatible with the structure of society itself, shall
bind all men in a supreme collective interest.

For this reason the idea of combating class struggle through the
joint action of a strong central power and of a social justice imbued
with the Christian spirit is firmly fixed in the minds of the immense
majority of those who support the Spanish Nationalist movement.

4. *National unity and regional variety:* The Constitution of 1931,
inspired by the disruptive principles which led to the present tragedy,
made possible in Spain a system of regional autonomies which in actual
fact exceeded the limits of federalism, and went to the criminal extremes of a practical disruption of national unity.

The present movement initiated by the army is characterized, as is
logical, by a vigorous reaction against this anti-national tendency and
the expression of the contrary—namely, the sacred and intangible unity
of the country. On this point there will be not the slightest possibility
of concessions to the dissembled separatism of Catalonians and Basques.

But unity does not mean uniformity. The Spanish districts have
extremely varied physiognomies, which, without prejudice to supreme
national unity, form regional personalities recognized by all the Rightist
forces. The spontaneity with which military leaders of the movement
have realized from the first this indisputable reality of Spanish life, is
the best guarantee that the principle of a fruitful diversity in the bosom
of supreme national unity shall be one of the most solid foundations
of the Spanish State's future organization. The outlines of this organization have already begun to be traced, even in the midst of the passionate tension produced by the acute present phase of the war.

Such, in my opinion, are the central points of agreement in the
various currents which nourish the wholesome stream of Nationalist
opinion in my country. They are the property of no party, and they
are the property of all. I feel certain that, through inevitable experiments and corrections, Spain will find the fertile channel through which
shall flow the waters, today impetuous, tomorrow tranquil, of her longing for stability and work. To find it, Spain will not need to resort
to foreign models, so difficult of adaptation to her acknowledged personality. In her tradition, in her history, in the immortal teaching of

her writers she will find the necessary material for the building up of her new State, which of necessity shall possess the characteristics of being genuinely Christian and profoundly human.

As upon Spain has devolved the honor of being the soldier and martyr of Christian civilization, so likewise upon her shall devolve the task of demonstrating to the world how it is possible to merge the intangible efforts of human personality with the authoritative requirements of a modern State, which must direct all national energies through the conquest of common ideals.

180. DECLARATION OF "WAR AIMS" OF THE LOYALIST GOVERNMENT, APRIL 30, 1938 [19]

In May 1937 the "Loyalist" Government came under the headship of Juan Negrín, a right-wing socialist and former finance minister. He introduced a number of changes, in a conservative direction, permitting limited church services and forbidding military officers to engage in political activity. In a speech of April 30, 1938, he outlined his government's aims in the civil war.

The Government of National Union, which has the confidence of all parties and trade union organizations of Loyalist Spain and which represents and has the support of all those Spanish citizens subject to the constitutional authority of the Government, solemnly declares for the knowledge of its compatriots and for the information of the world that its aims in carrying on the war are:

1. To assure the absolute independence and complete integrity of Spain. A Spain completely free from all foreign interference, whatever may be its nature and origin, with its peninsular and island territory as well as its possessions intact, protected against any attempt at partition, alienation, or mortgage, and conserving the Protectorate Zones assigned to Spain by international conventions as long as these conventions are not modified with Spain's participation and assent.

Conscious of the duties which accompany her tradition and her history Spain will extend towards the other countries of her language the bonds which are imposed by a common origin and the feeling of universality which has always characterised our people.

---

[19] *The Thirteen Points for Which Spain Is Fighting. Declaration of Doctor* [Juan] *Negrín, the Prime Minister, on April 30, 1938,* Ediciones Españolas, Barcelona, 1938, pp. 7-19.

2. Liberation of our territory from the foreign military forces which have invaded it as well as from those elements who have come to Spain after July 1936 with the pretext of technical collaboration and who are intervening and trying to dominate for their own benefit the legal and economic life of Spain.

3. A people's Republic represented by an energetic State based on principles of pure democracy which exercises its actions by means of a Government empowered with full authority conferred on it by the vote of citizens and universal suffrage. A State which is the symbol of firm executive power, dependent at all times on the directions and wishes of the Spanish people.

4. The legal and social structure of the Republic will be the result of the will of the nation freely expressed by means of a plebiscite which will take place as soon as the war is over and which will be carried out with full guarantees and with no restrictions or limitations in order to ensure those participating against any possible reprisal.

5. Respect for the liberties of the various regions without prejudice to the unity of Spain. Protection and encouragement of the development of the personality and characteristics of the various peoples forming Spain. This is imposed by a right and a historic fact which, far from meaning a dissolution of the nation, constitutes the best manner of uniting the elements which form it.

6. The Spanish State will guarantee full rights to citizens in civil and social life, freedom of conscience, and will assure the free exercise of religious belief and practice.

7. The State will guarantee property legally and legitimately acquired, within the limits imposed by the supreme interest of the nation, and also the protection of the producer. Without harming individual initiative, it will prevent accumulation of wealth from leading to the exploitation of citizens and from infringing on the rights of the people as a whole which it could do only by decreasing the State's control in the social and economic field. With this aim in view the State will encourage the development of small property, will guarantee a livelihood for each family and will stimulate every measure leading to the economic, moral and racial improvement of the producing classes.

The property and legitimate interests of those foreigners who have not aided the rebellion will be respected and inquiries will be opened regarding compensation which may be due to them owing to damage involuntarily caused during the course of the war. For the study of such damage the Government has already set up the Foreign Claims Commission.

8. Thorough agrarian reform which will liquidate the old semi-feudal aristocratic property. This property, lacking in all human national and patriotic feeling, has always been the greatest obstacle in the development of the great possibilities of the country. The basing of the new Spain on a broad and solid democracy of the peasants who shall be the owners of the land on which they work.

9. The State will guarantee the rights of the worker by means of advanced social legislation in accordance with the specific needs of Spanish life and economy.

10. The cultural [,] physical and moral improvement of the race will be the prime and basic concern of the State.

11. The Spanish Army at the service of the nation itself will be free from all hegemony of tendency or party, and the people will see in it the sure instrument for the defence of their liberties and their independence.

12. The Spanish State reaffirms the constitutional doctrine of renouncing war as an instrument of national policy. Spain, faithful to pacts and treaties, will support the policy symbolised in the League of Nations which will continue being the key-note of its policy. The Spanish State reaffirms and maintains its rights and, as a Mediterranean power, demands a place in [the] concert of nations. It is always disposed to collaborate in bringing about collective security and in the defence of peace in general.

In order to contribute to this policy in an efficacious manner Spain will develop and intensify all its possibilities of defence.

13. A broad amnesty for all those Spaniards who wish to cooperate in the immense task of the reconstruction and elevation of Spain. After a cruel struggle, such as that which is staining our land with blood, in which the old virtues of heroism and idealism of the race have been reborn, he who does not repress and suffocate all idea of vengeance and reprisal will be a traitor to the destinies of our country. This must be done for the sake of collective work and sacrifice which we are under the obligation to make in order to save the future of Spain and of all her sons.

卍 卍 卍

CHAPTER 9

GREAT GERMANY

181. THE "STAB-IN-THE-BACK"

From the very beginning of the German defeat in the World War, German nationalists have maintained that the disaster was brought on mainly by a cowardly "stab-in-the-back" delivered by traitors at home. This question was made the subject of an inquiry by a Reichstag commission, from whose report the following quotations were taken. General von Kuhl, whose report is first summarized, was attached as military expert to the sub-committee on the causes of the German collapse in 1918; the comment on von Kuhl's report was made by Albrecht Philipp, chairman of the sub-committee and a Reichstag deputy representing the German National People's Party.

A. SUMMARY OF THE REPORT BY GENERAL HERMANN VON KUHL [1]

The expression "stab-in-the-back" (*"Dolchstoss"*) in the oft-used sense, as if the country had attacked the victorious army in the rear and as if the war had been lost for this reason alone, is not accurate. We succumbed for many reasons.

It is certain, however, that a pacifistic, international, anti-military, and revolutionary undermining of the army took place which contributed in no small measure to the harm done and the disintegration of the army. It originated at home, but the blame does not attach to the entire population, which in the four and a half years of war endured superhuman sufferings; it attaches only to the agitators and corrupters of the people and of the army who for political reasons strove to poison the bravely-fighting forces.

The effects of this pernicious activity became especially apparent when, after the failure of our offensive in the summer of 1918, the war seemed hopelessly lost. But the subversive work had long before been

---

[1] Germany, Reichstag, *Untersuchungsausschuss über die Weltkriegsverantwortlichkeit. Vierter Unterausschuss, Die Ursachen des deutschen Zusammenbruches im Jahre 1918. Vierte Reihe im Werk des Untersuchungsausschusses,* Deutsche Verlagsgesellschaft für Politik und Geschichte m. b. H., Berlin, 12 vol. in 15, 1925-1929, vol. VI, p. 39.

systematically begun. One should therefore speak, not of a stab in the back, but of a *poisoning of the army*.

The expression "stab-in-the-back" may, however, be applied to the sudden and devastating effects of the *revolution* itself. It literally attacked the army from the rear, disorganized the lines of communication, prevented the forwarding of supplies, and destroyed all order and discipline as if at a blow. It made all further fighting impossible and compelled the acceptance of any armistice terms. The revolution was not the result of the collapse of the offensive, although this substantially furthered its outbreak and its effects. On the contrary, the revolution was prepared long beforehand.

The revolution further gave rise to the danger of the complete dissolution of the army during the retreat and thus of a monstrous catastrophe. This danger was averted only with the greatest difficulty.

B. THE STATEMENT OF CHAIRMAN ALBRECHT PHILIPP ON KUHL'S REPORT [2]

In view of the many interpretations of the expression "stab-in-the-back," it is better not to use this term for the influences which, coming from home, weakened the army's will to fight. That such influences were present in large number cannot be denied. Heavy blame doubtless lies with those circles which fostered the efforts to disintegrate or poison the armed forces. But the available factual material does not suffice to prove that these circles alone were to blame. Von Kuhl declares quite correctly: "We succumbed for many reasons." All those revolutionary efforts can be blamed, not for the circumstance that we had to evacuate the West and thus give up the prospects of winning the war, but for the way in which the end of the war overwhelmed Germany. The expression "stab-in-the-back" is absolutely correct as a criticism of the revolution as a single event, but it can be applied only with limitations to the motive powers of the development which prepared the ground for the German Revolution.

182. APPEAL OF THE COUNCIL OF COMMISSARS TO THE GERMAN NATION, NOVEMBER 12, 1918 *(Extracts)* [3]

On November 9, 1918, Chancellor Prince Maximilian of Baden placed the government of Germany into the hands of Friedrich Ebert, who became joint chairman with Hugo Haase of a Council of People's Commissars com-

---

[2] Germany, Reichstag, *op. cit.,* vol. IV, p. 15.

[3] Germany, *Reichsgesetzblatt,* Reichsdruckerei, Berlin, 1918, Jahrg. 1918, vol. I, No. 153, Law 6528, pp. 1303-1304.

*posed of three Social Democrats and three Independent Socialists. Having
promised the prince to maintain order and issue an early call for a constituent assembly, the commissars now appealed to the people to behave quietly,
regard human life as sacred, and protect private property.*

TO THE GERMAN NATION!

The government that grew out of the revolution, whose political
leadership is purely socialistic, sets itself the task of realizing the socialistic program. It immediately proclaims with the force of law the
following:

1. The state of siege is lifted.
2. There is no restriction on the right of meeting and assembly, not
   even for officials and state employees.
3. There is no censorship. The theatre censorship is lifted.
4. The expression of opinions orally or in writing is free.
5. Religious freedom is granted. No one may be compelled to perform a religious act.
6. An amnesty is declared for all political crimes. Pending suits for
   political crimes are dropped.

. . . . .

9. The regulations protecting labor which were abrogated at the beginning of the war are hereby restored to force.

Additional social-political regulations will be proclaimed shortly. The
maximum eight-hour day will be enforced by January 1, 1919, at the
latest. The government will do everything to provide sufficient employment opportunities. A decree for the support of the unemployed has
already been completed. It distributes the burden among the Reich, the
states, and the counties. . . . . .

The government will maintain the regular means of production and
protect private property against attacks by private individuals, as well
as [protect] the freedom and security of persons.

Henceforth all elections for public bodies are to be held on a basis
of equal, secret, direct, and universal suffrage, with proportional representation, for all men and women who are at least twenty years old.

. . . . .

[*Signed*]
EBERT   HAASE   SCHEIDEMANN   LANDSBERG   DITTMANN   BARTH

183. THE SPARTACIST MANIFESTO OF JANUARY 6, 1919 [4]

The communists, called Spartacists after the pseudonym of their leader, Karl Liebknecht, were as much opposed to the establishment of a liberal or socialist republic as they had been to the empire. Hence they decided to oust the government before the elections scheduled for January 19, 1919, could be held. The manifesto quoted below was calculated to incite the workers of Berlin against the council of commissars, but, though a huge crowd gathered in the center of Berlin on January 6, 1919, the radical leaders failed to appear with instructions and the movement collapsed. On January 15 Liebknecht was killed on the way to prison.

Comrades! Workers!

The Ebert-Scheidemann Government has rendered itself impossible. It is hereby declared deposed by the undersigned Revolutionary Committee, the representative of the revolutionary socialist workers and soldiers (Independent Social Democratic Party and Communist Party).

The undersigned Revolutionary Committee has provisionally assumed the conduct of the business of government.

Comrades! Workers!

Support the measures of the Revolutionary Committee.

Berlin, January 6, 1919.

The Revolutionary Committee

[GEORGE] LEDEBOUR   [KARL] LIEBKNECHT   [PAUL] SCHOLZE

184. THE WEIMAR CONSTITUTION *(Extracts)* [5]

The Weimar Assembly, chosen by the vote of all men and women over nineteen, and controlled by a coalition of Social Democrats, Centrists, and Democrats, adopted a republican constitution on July 31, 1919. President Friedrich Ebert signed the document, which contained 181 articles, on August 11. It is noteworthy that under Articles 25, 48, and 50 the president was empowered, with the co-operation of the chancellor, to exercise dictatorial rule in time of emergency.

---

[4] Quoted in F. Stampfer, *Die vierzehn Jahre der ersten deutschen Republik,* Verlagsanstalt "Graphia," Karlsbad, 1936, p. 85.

[5] Germany, *Reichsgesetzblatt,* Verlag des Gesetzsammlungsamts, Berlin, 1919, Jahrg. 1919, vol. I, Nr. 152, pp. 1383-1418.

ARTICLE 1.

The German Reich is a Republic. . . .

ARTICLE 2.

The Reich territory consists of the territory of the German States. Other territories may be absorbed into the Reich by law, if their populations, on the basis of self-determination, so desire.

. . . . .

ARTICLE 25.

The Reich President may dissolve the Reichstag, but only once for any one cause.

A new election will take place not later than the sixtieth day following the dissolution.

. . . . .

ARTICLE 43.

The term of office of the Reich President is seven years. Reëlection is permissible.

Before the expiration of the term, the Reich President, upon motion of the Reichstag, may be recalled by a popular vote. The decision of the Reichstag requires a two-thirds majority. Through such decision the Reich President is prevented from any further exercise of the office. The rejection of the recall motion by the popular referendum counts as a new election and results in the dissolution of the Reichstag. . . .

. . . . .

ARTICLE 48.

. . . The Reich President may, in the event that the public order and security are seriously disturbed or endangered, take the measures necessary for their restoration, intervening, if necessary, with the aid of the armed forces. For this purpose he may temporarily abrogate, wholly or in part, the fundamental principles laid down in Articles 114, 115, 117, 118, 123, 124, and 153. [These articles form the Bill of Rights of the constitution.]

The Reich President must, without delay, inform the Reichstag of all measures taken in accordance with . . . this Article. These measures must be rescinded upon the demand of the Reichstag. . . .

. . . . .

ARTICLE 50.

All orders and decrees of the Reich President, including those relating to the armed forces, must, in order to be valid, be countersigned by the Reich Chancellor or the competent Reich Minister. Through the countersignature the responsibility is assumed.

. . . . .

ARTICLE 54.

The Reich Chancellor and the Reich Ministers require the confidence of the Reichstag for the administration of their offices. Each one of them must resign when the Reichstag, by means of an express resolution, withdraws its confidence.

. . . . .

ARTICLE 60.

A Reichsrat is formed to give the German States representation in the law-making and administration of the Reich.

. . . . .

ARTICLE 63.

The States are represented in the Reichsrat by members of their governments. . . .

. . . . .

ARTICLE 73.

A law of the Reichstag must be submitted to popular referendum before its proclamation, if the Reich President, within one month of its passage, so decides. . . .

. . . . .

ARTICLE 80.

Colonial matters are the exclusive affair of the Reich.

. . . . .

ARTICLE 109.

All Germans are equal before the law.

Men and women have the same fundamental civil rights and duties. . . .

. . . . .

ARTICLE 130.

All officials are servants of the totality, not of any one party. . . .

. . . . .

ARTICLE 148.

All schools must strive to inculcate morality, civic-mindedness, and occupational skill in the spirit of the German nationality and international conciliation. . . .

. . . . .

ARTICLE 165.

. . . Statutory bodies representative of workmen and employees are to be created for the protection of their social and economic interests, namely, local workers' councils, district workers' councils, organized so as to correspond with industrial areas, and a National Workers' Council.

The district workers' councils and the National Workers' Council are to join with representatives of employers and other interested sections of the community to form district economic councils and a National Economic Council for the accomplishment of the economic tasks in general and to collaborate in the execution of the socialization laws in particular. . . .

Bills relating to matters of social and economic policy, before being introduced into the Reichstag, shall be submitted by the cabinet to the National Economic Council for an expression of its opinion. The National Economic Council itself has the right to initiate such bills. If the cabinet does not agree with any such bill it is nevertheless bound to introduce it into the Reichstag, with an explanation of its own standpoint. The National Economic Council may delegate one of its members to appear before the Reichstag in support of the bill. . . .

. . . . .

185-188. POST-WAR GERMAN AUSTRIA, 1918-1919

185. THE FOOD SITUATION IN POST-WAR GERMAN AUSTRIA [6]

The terrible food-shortage in post-war Austria was well described in an official report of the State Bureau for Public Nourishment.

[6] Austria, *Mitteilungen des Staatsamtes für Volksernährung über die Verhandlungen mit den alliierten Hauptmächten über die Lebensmittelversorgung der Republik Österreich in der Zeit vom Dezember 1918 bis Anfang Oktober 1919,* Österreichische Staatsdruckerei, Vienna, 1920, pp. 7-8.

The food situation, already difficult before the great political up-heavals of the end of October 1918, had become considerably more unfavorable for German Austria through the revolution and the eco-nomic separation from Hungary and the other succession states. Austria was suddenly separated, as if by a blow, from her former sources of supply. Vienna, a city of millions, for which it had been found impos-sible even during the War to secure large reserve supplies, was now almost completely without resources. Even the rural areas were in dis-tress. Lower and Upper Austria, the only two provinces which pro-duce sizable grain crops, were naturally unable to assure permanently Vienna's supply, despite the grant of premiums for grain deliveries and other advantages extended to the farmers. Besides, the administration, understandably, functioned rather inefficiently during the first weeks of the overturn, at which time the provisioning of the retreating army also caused grave concern; moreover, the contact between the Vienna Government and the provinces was frequently interrupted. The Hun-garian and Czechoslovak boundaries were closed. At first, flour ship-ments from Germany, which had been promised to our delegates sent to Berlin toward the end of October [1918], helped over our most press-ing needs. Despite largely curtailed bread and flour rations and the most strenuous efforts calculated to round up a sufficiency of these com-modities in our own country, the supply of flour and bread in Vienna and in almost all the German-Austrian lands was assured for only a very limited period, and absolute uncertainty remained as to how the population of German Austria was to be supplied with flour beginning with the new year. There was absolutely no prospect for a regular or permanent supply of potatoes, since the Bohemian, Moravian, and Gali-cian potato reserves could no longer be transported on account of frost even if the Czech and Polish Governments had opened their closed borders. Vienna was without potatoes. The meat supply could only be maintained at a starvation level; the fat, egg, and milk supplies were altogether inadequate.

In the National Assembly session of December 4, 1918, the secretary of state for food supplies (*der Staatssekretär für Volksernährung*) re-ported the desperate food situation and indicated that its salvation could be effected only with the help of the Allied Powers.

Steps had been taken immediately after the revolution to obtain help from them. Relying on Article 5 of the Armistice Conditions (Naval Conditions), whereby, despite the continuance of the blockade, a com-mission, to be appointed by the United States and the Allied Governments, could grant exceptions to the blockade, the then ministry of foreign affairs, through the good offices of neutral states, on November 5, 1918, immediately after the conclusion of the armistice, requested the governments of the Entente to set up such a commission in a place where we could get in touch with it in order to obtain a permit for a number of our idle ships to make overseas trips to bring us wheat, fat, and meat.

The new German-Austrian Foreign Office, immediately after its organization, on November 9, 1918, approached Washington, through the good offices of Switzerland, with the request to send us food as soon as possible and to notify us if and from what source we might expect first help.

The American Government thereupon gave notice through its legations in Stockholm and Bern on November 11, 1918, that President Wilson would consider our call for help and intended to send Food Administrator Hoover to Europe. On November 24, 1918, our legation in Bern was notified by the Swiss Political Department that the President of the United States and the representatives of the Allied Governments had unanimously resolved to do everything possible to provide the Central Powers with food and to take steps to organize this relief action in the same systematic way that had been done previously for Belgium. . . .

186. THE PLIGHT OF POST-WAR VIENNA [7]

Bad as was the situation of all Austria in the immediate post-war period, the plight of Vienna was undoubtedly worse. The position of the city's unfortunate inhabitants was graphically described by the Inter-Allied Commission on Relief of German Austria.

Vienna, with its two-and-a-quarter million inhabitants, from being the capital of an Empire has become the chief town of a State which outside it numbers less than six million inhabitants; it is an enormous

---

[7] Inter-Allied Commission on Relief of German Austria, *Interim Report, by British Delegate* [Sir William Beveridge], *Paris, January 17, 1919,* Paris, 1919, pp. 10-11, 20-21, as quoted in N. Almond and R. H. Lutz, eds., *The Treaty of St. Germain: A Documentary History of Its Territorial and Political Clauses,* Stanford University Press, Stanford University, 1935, pp. 91-93. Reprinted by permission of the Stanford University Press.

head on the body of a dwarf. The territory of German Austria, moreover, even apart from questions of size, is singularly little qualified to support a large capital; it contains only relatively small industrial districts (chiefly in Styria and the neighbourhood of Vienna); even of the rural areas large portions are mountainous and relatively unproductive (Tirol, Vorarlberg, Salzburg, &c.). The part of Austria now claimed by the Czechs, while it contains only about one-third of the total population of Austria, accounts for 90 per cent. of the coal production, 80 per cent. of the iron and steel, 90 per cent. of the cotton, 95 per cent. of the sugar, and practically all the wool and ceramic trades.

The principal industry of Vienna was the manufacture of clothing and ornaments. Its importance lay in its position as a centre of government, culture, finance, commerce, and transport. For none of these services to be rendered by Vienna is there at present any demand. It is not clear to what extent the world will have a use for Vienna in the future. Even assuming that the Associated Governments are prepared directly or indirectly to grant a loan to German Austria (which appears no less necessary as a means of enabling it to start trade with its neighbours than as a means of obtaining imported food), it is quite an open question whether any adequate security for the loan is available, either under the heading of present properties or under that of prospective earnings. German Austria is a bankrupt with no assurance of ever being able to earn money again.

At any rate the most hopeful outlook for Vienna (and so for its creditors) lies in restoring its importance as a transport and trading centre; this in turn probably depends upon restoring as much as possible of the previous economic unity of Austria-Hungary, despite its political dismemberment. A movement for an "Economic Confederation of the Danube," which would also be for German Austria a movement away from Germany, may thus be both financially and politically desirable from the point of view of the principal Allies; whether the feeling between the different States that must compose the confederation is such as to allow of its being realised in any reasonable period of time is another question.

Meanwhile a tendency for still further dismemberment is showing itself in the shape of movements in the Vorarlberg, the Tirol, and other parts of German Austria to set up separate Governments and to cut themselves free from the incubus of Vienna. . . .

CONCLUSION AND RECOMMENDATION

The cessation of war without the restoration of peace in Austria-Hungary, combined with its political dismemberment, has produced a state of general economic paralysis. It seems difficult to avoid the conclusion that, in order to prevent a collapse of the social order comparable to what has occurred in Russia, the Allies must practically, if not formally, treat the war with all parts of Austria as finished, and must give positive help in reconstruction there. The reason for this is not that the Hungarians or German Austrians deserve special consideration, or have a claim to avoid suffering as Northern France and Belgium suffered. The real grounds are twofold: (i) The war is in fact so completely finished, as far as these countries are concerned, and they are so completely smashed, that war-time standards of inhumanity are no longer applicable. (ii) The further spread of disorder in Europe is a danger to the Allied countries themselves.

A third ground was advanced by representative men, both in German Austria and in Hungary. In each case they stated that if they were left alone and on unfriendly terms with their immediate neighbours (Czecho-Slovakia, Jugo-Slavia, Roumania)—since it was impossible for them to stand alone with their reduced territories and economic impoverishment—they would be bound to fall into close relations with Germany, which would thus get a material accession of strength. If, on the other hand, German Austria and Hungary could enter on reasonable terms into a close economic relation with their neighbouring States—an "Economic Confederation of the Danube"—the whole might form a group of connected States too clearly differentiated in character ever to join Germany as a whole, yet with sufficient internal cohesion to prevent any one member of the group breaking off to join Germany alone. A permanent equipoise would be produced in the south to German power in the north.

This argument touches the fringe of very large and much-debated questions, and I only give it for what it is worth. In the mouths of most of these who used it it was certainly not a threat, but an expression of their own desires. The making, in effect if not in form, of an earlier economic peace in the whole of Austro-Hungary (*sic*), and thus leaving Germany alone to the last, would be a simple continuance of the strategy which terminated the war, by a succession of armistices at different dates. . . .

187. THE CONTEMPLATED UNION OF AUSTRIA WITH GERMANY [8]

The desire of both the German and the Austrian authorities for the political union of their states was clearly demonstrated in the early legislation of both governments. The Allies, however, forbade this Anschluss, *and its consummation was delayed until March 1938, when Adolf Hitler energetically liquidated the problem (See Document No. 206).*

A. LAW OF NOVEMBER 12, 1918, OF THE PROVISIONAL GOVERNMENT (VIENNA)

ARTICLE 1.

German Austria is a democratic Republic. . . .

ARTICLE 2.

German Austria is a constituent part of the German Republic. Special laws shall regulate the participation of German Austria in the law-making and administration of the German Republic. . . .

B. LAW OF MARCH 12, 1919, OF THE CONSTITUENT ASSEMBLY (VIENNA)

ARTICLE 1.

The Constituent Assembly repeats, confirms, and solemnly ratifies as follows the Resolution concerning the political and administrative form of German Austria laid down by the Provisional Government in its laws of November 12, 1918:

1. German Austria is a democratic Republic. . . .
2. German Austria is a constituent part of the German Republic.

C. ARTICLE 61 OF THE CONSTITUTION OF THE GERMAN REPUBLIC, AUGUST 11, 1919

German Austria shall receive, after its union with the German Reich, the right of participation in the Reichsrat with a number of votes proportionate to its population. Until then the representatives of German Austria shall have an advisory capacity.

---

[8] Austria, *Staatsgesetzblatt für den Staat Deutschösterreich,* Vienna, Deutschösterreichische Staatsdruckerei, 1918, 1919, *Jahrgang 1918, 1. Stück, Gesetz Nr. 5, Jahrg. 1919, 54. Stü., Nr. 174;* Germany, *Reichsgesetzblatt,* Jahrg. 1919, Verlag des Gesetzsammlungsamts, Berlin, 1919, vol. I, Nr. 152, p. 1934.

188. THE AUSTRIAN PEASANT [9]

This selection on the Austrian peasant is included because it offers such a helpful word picture of an important but little-known subject in the history of Central Europe.

The world of the peasant is a world apart into which few strangers have ever really penetrated.

It is perfectly true to say of him, as his detractors invariably do with their first breath, that he is absolutely, obstinately, mulishly, incurably conservative. It is true, moreover, to add that this conservatism is largely due to both ignorance and stupidity, and that both are partly of his own making. The reason is not far to seek. His life is an incredibly hard one. From dawn to dusk he wrings a scanty living in the sweat of his brow from stubborn and ungrateful fields. In this harsh and precipitous land, on these small and scattered properties, the work is far harder, the hours far longer than on a large well-organised estate. Each member of his small staff must be Jack of all trades, ready to attend to the horses and cattle, the sowing, ploughing and harvesting, the carting and marketing, the repairs and housework. The grown man has few hours of freedom, the woman and child none of those leisured years which we [the British] accord them as of right. The peasant woman is one of the most hardly-used creatures in the world. To an almost ceaseless drudgery on the farm she adds the toil of bearing and bringing up children, both of which processes she is consequently apt to perform hurriedly and carelessly, with disastrous results. As for the child, nominally his education up to the age of fourteen is compulsory. Actually, the peasant boycotts this law, and generally contrives to get the child to work at the farm by the time he is twelve years old. For him, theory and book-learning are things to be eschewed, even opposed actively. Manual labour of the narrowest kind, the nose to the plough, alone produces tangible results, and this alone does he hold useful. Thus, by his own action, he perpetuates the backwardness, spiritual and economic, of his class.

---

[9] C. A. Macartney, *The Social Revolution in Austria,* Cambridge University Press, Cambridge, 1926, pp. 176-180, 197-198. Reprinted by permission of the publishers.

Outside of the routine of his farm, he has only two main interests . . . : they are his religion and his drink.

The Catholic Church in Austria is intimately connected with the
peasant's life in a way not easy for an Englishman to picture. Perhaps
wisely, it has made no attempt to imitate the ideal of a "resident
country gentleman in every parish." The local priest stands on a lower
pedestal above his flock than the English parson. He is less immune
from the common frailties of the flesh, but the nearer for that to their
lives. Like his creed as a whole, he is warmer, more human, more
tolerant of backsliding. He is most often himself a peasant's son, not
differing greatly from his congregation in birth, education or even
morals. But he is able to tap a natural supply of religious feeling,
welling up alike in his soul and in theirs, and, on the whole, he exerts
the great influence which this gives him well according to his lights.

The peasant has little knowledge of the wide world, of his fellow-
men, or even of the State, except as an oppressive force which takes
the produce of his labour for taxes, or calls his son away from the
plough to serve in the army. But he is continually face to face with
God. God placed him where he is. God's bounty sent the harvest,
God's act let down the hail and snow. The often incalculable moods
of nature, on which his existence depends, are the decrees of God.
Religion, his relation to God, colours all his life.

Indeed, his religion knows very little of abstruse theology, is very
full of superstition, very nearly akin to nature-worship. The peasant's
prayers do not differ greatly, except in the matter of proper names,
from those which his dim forbears offered up to the tutelary deities
of wood and stream, summer and winter. Old thoughts linger on and
old customs. In the lighting of fires and the drawing of waters, the
ploughing and harvesting, he follows with awe the custom of his
pagan ancestors; and the only change is that his propitious and unpro-
pitious days have put on new dresses and appear now as the Eve of
St. John, or the feast of the Conception.

This very blending with the earth and with old tradition makes his
religion a very living thing. Not only the church in every little village
bears witness to it, but the countless tiny shrines at the wayside, at
the cross-roads, on the edge of the field. As he passes them, he crosses
himself and mutters a prayer; and on Sundays and his numerous
holidays he leads down his family and household to worship in the
nearest church.

These reunions during and after Mass are not only the spiritual occasions in his life but also almost the only opportunities for social intercourse. . . . Outside the villages large enough to run a "Verein," musical, religious, or political, social life is confined to the church or the village inn.

The absence of competition is a treasured advantage of the Church. Only Socialism seriously challenges its supremacy, and is therefore anathema to it. The mentality of the peasant of the old style is peculiarly acceptable to the Church. Submissiveness to authority, contentment with one's lot, are virtues fragrant in God's nostrils, a pleasant contrast to the stinking unrest, Socialism, atheism, which the life of the great cities engenders. The ideal of the Church is a healthy peasantry, decently prosperous, but not necessarily endowed either with great riches or with great brains. . . . The priest is not afraid to denounce Socialism from the altar as a combination of Satan, to threaten its followers in the confessional with the pains of hell-fire. . . .

He [the peasant] is hard and quarrelsome, and the holiday evenings often end in a general scrap. His vices spring to a large extent from the besetting sin of drunkenness, a great evil in Austria, which the Church as a whole has done scandalously little to combat, and has often even fostered in her character of large proprietor of vineyards, breweries and distilleries. Individual priests make brave efforts, but the Socialists, who have made temperance one point of their programme, have a right to claim great credit for it. . . .

. . . Mountainous little Austria is not a country where farming on a big scale is practicable at all. If the world arrangements are ever really so adjusted that farming is done on the most economic lines, and the produce distributed internationally, only a part of Austria's present country population will be able to produce for the market at all. The small farms of the outlying mountain districts will remain outside the scheme of things, and their present occupiers, who, as far as they can exist at all, must do so mostly by supplying their own requirements, will remain a class outside organised society, neither capitalists nor exploited, an Absolute Value. To a large extent they are already in this position, and the question arises whether their existence, already threatened by its hardships and economic difficulties, with the consequent rural depopulation, be worth preserving. The question is less economic than spiritual; in the old days, military. Socialism, on the whole, answers no. The Church emphatically yes. And weighing in the balances much good and much evil, one is bound also to answer yes. The stock of the mountains is, after all, hardy and virile, capable of producing great things, given more wisdom and more consideration to those who are in authority over it. Even as an untouched reserve of strength, or a reservoir to reinforce and purify the adulterated blood of towns and factories, it is a factor which no State can lightly dare to do without. A State which has lost its independent peasantry is perilously near the verge of degeneration.

189. THE FOREIGN POLICY OF GUSTAV STRESEMANN [10]

Gustav Stresemann was among the ablest statesmen of post-war Europe. Born in 1878 in Berlin, the son of a beer merchant, he studied at Berlin and Leipzig, devoting himself especially to philosophy, political science, and economics. Skilful as an organizer and devoted to his country and to the interests of big business, he first entered the Reichstag in 1907 as a National Liberal, ten years later becoming the head of his party. After the war he continued to favor monarchy but was willing to support the republic in the interests of peace, unity, and business revival. Chancellor for a few months in 1923, he was foreign minister continuously from 1923 until his death in 1929. As chief advocate in Germany of the policy of reconciliation and fulfilment, he topped his career with the ratification of the Locarno Pact and the admission of Germany into the League in 1926. In the speech quoted below he explained the difficulties surrounding the negotiations at Locarno.

The publicity given to our negotiations at Locarno was in certain regards unfortunate. We had decided that our negotiations should be absolutely confidential, which was sensible; no worse nonsense has been talked lately than that about the abolition of secret diplomacy. Every merchant who has some new scheme in view for the coming year does not proclaim it in an announcement in a Berlin newspaper, so that any competitor may see what is coming and take measures accordingly. We perhaps rather overdid the art of secret diplomacy. In the art of saying nothing in our *communiqués,* we really had no rivals. But the Press representatives had to telegraph a thousand lines

[10] Speech of December 14, 1925, on the Locarno Pact to the Central Association of Provincial Organizations, from E. Sutton, ed. and tr., *Gustav Stresemann. His Diaries, Letters, and Papers,* 2 vols., New York, 1935-1937, vol. II, pp. 215-229. By permission of The Macmillan Company, publishers.

a day, and they naturally telegraphed a great deal of nonsense. . . .
There were stories of marvellous trips on Lago Maggiore in a boat
that was picturesquely named the *Orange Blossom,* and the German
citizen thought to himself that we were having a very good time
indeed. The fact was that on this marvellous trip we spent more than
five hours in the cabin; the first two and a half hours were occupied
in a discussion of Article 16 of the League Covenant, and the remaining two and a half hours were taken up with the French guarantee
regarding the Eastern European treaties. I have never been so tired
and done up as I was on that occasion. And the discussions were so
acrimonious that I wished the minutes of them could have been published afterwards. . . . I fancy that most of the attacks upon us would
be silenced if the minutes of the meeting were published at which we
discussed German disarmament, and in the face of Briand, Chamberlain, and Vandervelde, rejected the charge of War Guilt. I tell you
that you are not to conceive matters as though, under the sunshine of
Locarno, we had stumbled into a fresh alliance of friendship. . . .

Now let me speak of two groups of questions that were especially
prominent at Locarno. The first was the question of Alsace-Lorraine
and Eupen-Malmédy. In Articles 1 and 2 of the treaty is stated what
the Powers are to renounce. They are to renounce war, force, and
invasion. It was laid down in the preamble of the draft—for the draft
was altered three times . . . that the intention of these treaties is the
maintenance of the *status quo* in the West. This clause was struck
out at the suggestion of the German Delegation, and replaced by the
words "maintenance of peace." Our resistance was the fundamental
idea of the whole transaction. The worst of it is that, out of respect
for what was confidential, we cannot give the proper balance to the
situation; it would then become clear that there was no question of
a moral renunciation, but merely a recognition of the fact, which every
sensible person would admit, that it would to-day be madness to play
with the idea of a war with France.

The second question that came into consideration as regards the
West was that of Eupen-Malmédy. Vandervelde's organ, *Le Peuple,*
stated about a fortnight ago that if Germany would help Belgium
over the stabilization of the franc by the recognition of the mark
agreement, Belgium might take into consideration the institution of

a new plebiscite in Eupen-Malmédy to decide whether it wanted to belong to Germany or Belgium. I may perhaps remark at this point that this statement did not surprise me, but I cannot understand how those who are aware that such matters are at issue should bring themselves to say that Germany had recognized the frontiers in the West as permanent. If the organ of the Belgian Foreign Minister announces in a public newspaper a possible negotiation over the return of Eupen-Malmédy, as indeed a Catholic newspaper had already done, in order to prepare public opinion in Belgium for the eventuality, I may perhaps draw the conclusion that Vandervelde does not regard the Treaty of Locarno as a permanent settlement of frontiers, but is entirely in agreement with our view that a peaceful understanding regarding an alteration of the frontier is not affected by the Treaty.

The next group of questions was the future of the frontiers in the East. Herr Beneš and Herr Skrzynski, the Czech and Polish Foreign Ministers, both wanted to co-operate in the treaty of Locarno, and both put forward a draft arbitration treaty for their respective States. Herr Beneš' first proposal was rejected by us without discussion, *a limine,* upon which it became apparent that Herr Beneš had made a mistake; he had intended another, which was available, and thereupon put up for discussion. But this second treaty was not discussed either. Two questions were at issue in connection with the Eastern treaties. They wanted what is called in the English phrase a "non-aggression pact," that is to say a pact by which we bound ourselves to abstain from any attack. This obligation we undertook in the West, but we refused it in the East. Membership of the League does not exclude the possibility of war. I should be very glad if many of those who talk about the League would read through the clauses of the League Covenant, which are extraordinarily interesting in regard to what they do, and do not, say. The League leaves war as a potentiality, if agreement cannot be reached in political matters. The attempt to force us into line was made in the Briand Note of June 16th. In that document we were required to agree to unconditional arbitration treaties; which meant that we were to decide all questions, including frontier questions, solely by arbitration, to the exclusion of any other method. If you look at the Briand Note of June 16th you will find it therein stated that the German proposals are inadequate; that Germany consents to recognize a decision by arbitration for juridical questions, but not where matters of national existence are concerned;

this could not be accepted since in that case the Eastern frontiers would not be recognized. No unconditional arbitration treaties were concluded, but the German system of arbitration treaties was accepted at Locarno. . . . Germany refused to discuss the recognition of frontiers, or the renunciation of war, and was only prepared to consider questions quite distinct from these. . . .

Then came the attempt of the former Allies to force us in this direction. The attempt failed. . . . Herr Beneš, an astute politician, not having got his way, acted as though he had, smiled all over his face and looked cheerful. Herr Skrzynski could not hide his agitation. When you read that the Polish Minister left the room first after the documents had been initialled, I could wish you had been there to see him do it; you would then ask yourselves whether Poland regarded Locarno as a Polish success. . . . But I am not a little shocked to observe, on looking over the Polish Press as a whole—I have had the appropriate extracts before me—that with the exception of two official newspapers, the entire Polish Press has attacked the Treaty of Locarno, and described it as a preliminary to the fourth partition of Poland. Then on our side I see efforts being made to manufacture arguments which are to lead the Poles to think that their frontiers are in fact guaranteed.

· · · · ·

As touching Eastern European questions, where the principle of national self-determination has been so grievously violated, I have no notions of decisions to be reached by war. What I have in mind is that when conditions arise which indicate that European peace or the economic consolidation of Europe is threatened by developments in the East, and when it is realized that this entire non-consolidation of Europe appears to have its origin in impossible frontier-lines in the East, that Germany might succeed with her claims, if she had previously effected a political understanding with all the world Powers who would have to decide the matter, and established a common economic interest with her opponents. That, in my opinion, is the only practicable policy. That we should not recognize the frontier in the East, I made clear, to the disgust of the Polish Government, in a public speech before the Foreign Committee of the Reichstag, when I stated that in my opinion no German Government, from the German Nationals to the Communists, would ever recognize this frontier. And I shall never shrink from repeating this declaration.

I see the importance in another connection of this security for peace between ourselves and France. It is true that these are all matters that lie in the future; a nation must not adopt the attitude of a child that writes a list of its wants on Christmas Eve, which contains everything that the child will need for the next fifteen years. The parents would not be in a position to give it all this. In foreign politics I often have the feeling that I am being confronted with such a list, and that it is forgotten that history advances merely step by step, and Nature not by leaps and bounds. But what stands in the way of a strengthening of Germany? What stands in the way of a recovery of German soil, or a junction with Austria? What stands in our way is the eternal anxiety that if this 60-million nation becomes a 70-million nation, we are threatened by France, and we cannot so far endanger our vital political interests. The moment the incessant threat of war on our western frontier ceases to exist, this argument is no longer valid. As a consequence our prospects in this connection are entirely favourable.

I am indeed under no illusion that in other respects the Treaty of Locarno contains dangers in itself. A State that is very little pleased with it is Italy. It is openly said on the Italian side that the Treaty creates two kinds of frontiers in Europe, a first-class frontier, and a second-class frontier, and it is interesting to observe that Italy tried to introduce the Brenner line into the discussion. The attempt was made in Paris, London, and Locarno. I have also been directly approached in Berlin. I said to the person who first spoke to me on the matter: I am obliged to you for your statement that the Brenner line must also be discussed, for I assume from this that there is no longer any obstacle in the way of the union of German Austria with the German Reich. If this were the case, I could negotiate regarding the Brenner line; hitherto I had assumed that it was an Austrian frontier. But since a statement as to the first point was not available, I had to decline any statement on the second point and say that the matter could not be considered open for discussion. But quarters that were formerly not disinclined to this union are now sceptical and aggressive, and take the view that if it is no longer an enfeebled Austria that stands behind the Irredenta of Tirol, but the German nation, that Irredenta becomes far more dangerous for Italy. As a consequence you may see that the attitude on this point has undoubtedly grown stiffer. You may also see a policy in operation that I regard as extremely short-sighted. Apart from

all the sympathetic reactions that it must evoke in us, it is the most
short-sighted policy that one could conceive; this sort of proceeding will
never force a stiff-necked peasant race to their knees, as Mussolini
thinks; just as I conceive that his kind of policy is merely transient,
and not one that promises to endure.

.   .   .   .   .

One word about the ratification of the Treaty and the League of
Nations. As regards the latter, it may be asked whether it is better for
Germany to remain outside or to join it. The League was in its origin
directed against us. Its proceedings were hostile to us. It is responsible
for the verdict that, in the Upper Silesian question, transferred to
Poland cities in which 92 per cent of the inhabitants had voted for
Germany. We had, from our own point of view, no cause to be very
sympathetic to the League. But in the present state of affairs I do
not ask whether people are sympathetic to me or not, I ask whether
a thing is to my advantage, or otherwise. Now I look at the situation in the following way. Everything that most deeply affects the
German people, all the unsolved problems arising out of the World
War, can there be most suitably brought forward. All the awkward
questions, which we cannot after all leave alone, may be dealt with by
that assembly. We asked at Locarno that Disarmament should be introduced into the programme of the League. This was done. Yesterday
we received the invitation to take part in the conference, and it would
be faint-hearted to believe that nothing will be achieved. . . . And if I
myself have no army and cannot equip it, I must demand that the
others should disarm, so that we may meet on reasonable terms.

The most important question is that of minorities. On this point the
Covenant of the League was altered before we joined that body, whence
I assume that the other Members were nervous of our collaboration.
But this alteration does not prevent us from interceding in favour of
minorities. There exists a committee of three to deal with minority
questions. Kindred nations may not belong to it—in other words, Germany; for we are akin to so many nations. But this committee of three
may not take any decision unless the Council of the League agrees;
and as the Council may only take unanimous decisions, the veto of our
representative will be enough to make a decision against a German
minority ineffective and to bring it before the League. Moreover every
Power represented on the Council has the right to remove any question

that it regards as important in principle from the competence of the committee of three and bring it direct before the League Council. If I were to represent Germany at Geneva I would make it my business to bring every question before the Council, so that these gentlemen might see the result of altering the Covenant.

. . . . .

Thus I see in the entire movement of affairs a step forward, not as the result of any affection for us from outside, but as a consequence of this whole inner complex that I have described. In this I see the only possible policy that will get us forward. I do not know whether it will lead us wholly to success; for in these days of world revolution, whoever presumes to say what will happen in the next year is to be envied for his imagination. I frankly declare that it is to-day not possible to lay out a programme of policy, because in certain circumstances events dash onward like a torrent, and in others, barely trickle forward at all. I do not resent criticism; it is always of some service, and it has often made me think. But every criticism must have a positive sense. . . . I believe that it is always better to live under a foreign policy with ideas, even when they are sometimes wrong, than under a foreign policy that is merely passive instead of trying to set a course. And for my part I think that in one thing at least we have succeeded—in making a little progress towards a better future for Germany.

190. THE PROGRAM OF THE NATIONAL SOCIALIST GERMAN WORKERS' PARTY [11]

The official program of the National Socialist German Workers' Party was drawn up on February 24, 1920, by Gottfried Feder, an engineer who had been one of the original half-dozen colleagues of Adolf Hitler and who later became, for some years, economic adviser to the party. The program was first proclaimed on February 25, 1920, in the Festsaal *of the Munich* Hofbräuhaus.

The programme of the German Workers' Party is limited as to period. The leaders have no intention, once the aims announced in it

---

[11] G. Feder, *Hitler's Official Programme and Its Fundamental Ideas,* tr. from the 5th (1934) German ed., George Allen and Unwin, Ltd., London, 1934, pp. 38-43. Reprinted by permission of the publishers.

have been achieved, of setting up fresh ones, in order to ensure the continued existence of the Party by the artificially increased discontent of the masses.

1. We demand the union of all Germans, on the basis of the right of the self-determination of peoples, to form a Great Germany.

2. We demand equality of rights for the German People in its dealings with other nations, and abolition of the Peace Treaties of Versailles and St. Germain.

3. We demand land and territory (colonies) for the nourishment of our people and for settling our superfluous population.

4. None but members of the nation may be citizens of the State. None but those of German blood, whatever their creed, may be members of the nation. No Jew, therefore, may be a member of the nation.

5. Anyone who is not a citizen of the State may live in Germany only as a guest and must be regarded as being subject to the Alien laws.

6. The right of voting on the leadership and legislation is to be enjoyed by the citizens of the State alone. We demand therefore that all official appointments, of whatever kind, whether in the Reich, the provinces, or the smaller communities, shall be granted to citizens of the State alone.

We oppose the corrupt Parliamentary custom of the State of filling posts merely with a view to party considerations, and without reference to character or capacity.

7. We demand that the State shall make it its first duty to promote the industry and livelihood of the citizens of the State. If it is not possible to nourish the entire population of the State, foreign nationals (non-citizens of the State) must be excluded from the Reich.

8. All further non-German immigration must be prevented. We demand that all non-Germans who entered Germany subsequently to August 2, 1914, shall be required forthwith to depart from the Reich.

9. All citizens of the State shall possess equal rights and duties.

10. It must be the first duty of every citizen of the State to perform mental or physical work. The activities of the individual must not clash with the interests of the whole, but must proceed within the framework of the community and must be for the general good.

We demand therefore:

11. Abolition of incomes unearned by work.

Abolition of the Thraldom of Interest

12. In view of the enormous sacrifice of life and property demanded

of a nation by every war, personal enrichment through war must be regarded as a crime against the nation. We demand therefore the ruthless confiscation of all war profits.

13. We demand the nationalization of all businesses which have (hitherto) been amalgamated (into Trusts).

14. We demand that there shall be profit-sharing in the large industries.

15. We demand a generous development of provision for old age.

16. We demand the creation and maintenance of a healthy middle class, immediate communalization of wholesale warehouses, and their lease at a low rate to small traders, and that the most careful consideration shall be shown to all small purveyors to the State, provinces, or smaller communities.

17. We demand a land-reform suitable to our national requirements, the passing of a law for the confiscation without compensation of land for communal purposes, the abolition of interest on mortgages, and prohibition of all speculation in land.[12]

18. We demand ruthless war upon all those whose activities are injurious to the common interest. Common criminals against the nation, usurers, profiteers, etc., must be punished with death, whatever their creed or race.

19. We demand that the Roman law, which serves the materialistic world order, shall be replaced by a German common law.

20. With the aim of opening to every capable and industrious German the possibility of higher education and consequent advancement to leading positions, the State must consider a thorough re-construction of our national system of education. The curricula of all educational establishments must be brought into line with the requirements of practical life. Directly the mind begins to develop the schools must aim at teaching the pupil to understand the State idea (State sociology). We demand the education of specially gifted children of poor parents, whatever their class or occupation, at the expense of the State.

21. The State must apply itself to raising the standard of health in

---

[12] On April 13, 1928, Adolf Hitler made the following declaration: "It is necessary to reply to the false interpretation on the part of our opponents of Point 17 of the Programme of the N. S. D. A. P. Since the N. S. D. A. P. admits the principle of private property, it is obvious that the expression 'confiscation without compensation' refers merely to the creation of possible legal means of confiscating, when necessary, land illegally acquired, or not administered in accordance with the national welfare. It is therefore directed in the first instance against the Jewish companies which speculate in land. Munich, April 13th, 1928. (*Signed*) Adolf Hitler."

the nation by protecting mothers and infants, prohibiting child labour, and increasing bodily efficiency by legally obligatory gymnastics and sports, and by extensive support of clubs engaged in the physical training of the young.

22. We demand the abolition of mercenary troops and the formation of a national army.

23. We demand legal warfare against conscious political lies and their dissemination in the Press. In order to facilitate the creation of a German national Press we demand:

(*a*) That all editors of and contributors to newspapers employing the German language must be members of the nation;

(*b*) That special permission from the State shall be necessary before non-German newspapers may appear. These need not necessarily be printed in the German language;

(*c*) That non-Germans shall be prohibited by law from participating financially in or influencing German newspapers, and that the penalty for contravention of the law shall be suppression of any such newspaper, and immediate deportation of the non-German involved.

It must be forbidden to publish newspapers which do not conduce to the national welfare. We demand the legal prosecution of all tendencies in art and literature of a kind likely to disintegrate our life as a nation, and the suppression of institutions which militate against the above-mentioned requirements.

24. We demand liberty for all religious denominations in the State, so far as they are not a danger to it and do not militate against the morality and moral sense of the German race.

The Party as such stands for positive Christianity, but does not bind itself in the matter of creed to any particular confession. It combats the Jewish-materialistic spirit *within* and *without* us, and is convinced that our nation can achieve permanent health from within only on the principle:

The Common Interest before Self Interest

25. That all foregoing requirements may be realized we demand the creation of a strong central power of the Reich with unconditional authority of the politically central Parliament over the entire Reich and its organization in general.

We demand the formation of Diets and vocational Chambers for the purpose of carrying out the general laws promulgated by the Reich in the various States of the Confederation.

The leaders of the Party swear to proceed regardless of consequences—if necessary at the sacrifice of their lives—towards the fulfillment of the foregoing Points.

Munich, February 24, 1920.

191. THE HORST WESSEL SONG [13]

The anthem of the Nazi Party was written by and named for Horst Wessel, a Berlin youth who had early joined the movement and who, having met a violent death, was labeled a martyr and eventually raised to the level of a national hero. (Translation of song given on the next page.)

1.

Die Fahne hoch! Die Reihen dicht geschlossen!
S. A. marschiert mit ruhig festem Schritt.
Kam'raden, die Rotfront und Reaktion erschossen,
Marschier'n im Geist in unseren Reihen mit.

2.

Die Strasse frei den braunen Bataillonen!
Die Strasse frei dem Sturmabteilungsmann!
Es schau'n aufs Hakenkreuz voll Hoffnung schon Millionen,
Der Tag für Freiheit und für Brot bricht an.

3.

Zum letzten Mal wird Sturmalarm geblasen!
Zum Kampfe steh'n wir alle schon bereit.
Bald flattern Hitlerfahnen über allen Strassen,
Die Knechtschaft dauert nur noch kurze Zeit!

4.

Die Fahne hoch! Die Reihen dicht geschlossen!
S. A. marschiert mit ruhig festem Schritt.
Kam'raden, die Rotfront und Reaktion erschossen,
Marschier'n im Geist in unseren Reihen mit.

---

[13] Courtesy of German Consulate-General in New York; translated by Annina Periam Danton.

1.

Aloft the banner! Close the firm ranks serried!
S. A. goes marching on with steadfast stride.
Comrades, by Red Front and Reaction slain, lie buried,
Yet march along in spirit by our side.

2.

Make clear the highway for the Brown Battalions!
For the Storm Trooper make the highway clear!
The Swastika is full of hope for gazing millions,
The day for freedom and for bread is here.

3.

One final blast the trumpet now is blowing!
Ready for combat all prepared we stand.
Soon Hitler's banners o'er all highways will be flowing,
The end of German slav'ry is at hand!

4.

Aloft the banner! Close the firm ranks serried!
S. A. goes marching on with steadfast stride.
Comrades, by Red Front and Reaction slain, lie buried,
Yet march along in spirit by our side.

192. PAUL VON HINDENBURG'S POLITICAL TESTAMENT, MAY 11, 1934 [14]

President Paul von Hindenburg died on August 2, 1934, three months before his eighty-eighth birthday. Thirteen days later the Nazi Government published his last will and testament, dated May 11, 1934.

In 1919 I wrote in my message to the German people:
"We were at the end! Like Siegfried under the cunning javelin throw of the enraged Hagen, so our exhausted front collapsed; in vain had it attempted to drink new life from the drying well of native strength. Thenceforth it was our task to rescue the remaining strength of our

---

[14] F. Endres, ed., *Hindenburg. Briefe-Reden-Berichte,* Wilhelm Langewiesche-Brandt, Munich, 1934, pp. 188-192. Reprinted by permission of the publishers.

army for the later reconstruction of the fatherland. The present was lost. Thus there remained only hope in the future. On to work!

"I understand the idea of escape from the world which took possession of many officers in view of the collapse of all that was dear and precious to them. The yearning 'not to want to know any more' of a world in which seething passions have altered beyond recognition the true qualities of our people is humanly understandable, and yet—I must speak out frankly, just as I think: Comrades of the once so grand, proud German army! Can you speak of despairing? Think of the men who more than a hundred years ago created for us an intrinsically new fatherland. Their religion was faith in themselves and in the sacredness of their cause. They created the new fatherland, basing it not upon a doctrinal madness *(Doktrinwut)* foreign to our nature, but building it up on the basis of the free development of the individual within the framework and obligation of the common weal! This same path will again be trodden by Germany, as soon as she is able to tread once more.

"I have the firm conviction that now, as in those times, the tie with our great, rich past will be preserved and, where it has been broken, restored. The old German spirit will again assert itself, even though perhaps only after thorough purification in the furnace of suffering and passion. Our opponents knew the strength of this spirit; they admired and hated it in times of peace, they were astonished at and feared it on the battlefields of the great war. They tried to make our strength comprehensible to their peoples with the empty word 'Organization.' The spirit which created for itself this covering and lived and functioned within it, they passed over in silence. But with and in this spirit we will courageously rebuild.

"Germany, focal point of so many of the inexhaustible values of civilization and culture, will not go under as long as it retains its faith in its great historical world mission. I have the sure confidence that the strength and depth of thought of the best in our fatherland will succeed in blending new ideas with the valued treasures of former times and from the combination coin lasting values, to the welfare of our fatherland.

"That is the unshakable conviction with which I left the bloody field of the battle of the nations. I have seen the heroic agony of my fatherland and I will never, never believe that it was its throes of death.

"For the present a storm-whipped flood of wild political passions and resounding phrases has buried our entire former state conception, apparently destroying all sacred traditions. But this flood will run off. Then, from the eternally agitated sea of human life, there will again emerge that rock to which the hopes of our fathers clung and on which, almost half a century ago, through our strength, we confidently founded the future of our fatherland—the German Empire! Once the national idea, the national consciousness has again been raised, then, out of the great war—on which no people can look back with more legitimate pride and clearer conscience than can our own, as long as it was faithful,—as well as out of the bitter earnest of the present days, morally precious fruits will ripen for us. The blood of all those who died in the belief in Germany's greatness will then not have flowed in vain.

"In this certainty I lay down my pen and rely firmly on thee—thou youth of Germany!"

These words I wrote in darkest hour and in the presumed conviction that I was standing at the end of a life devoted to service to the fatherland. But fate decreed otherwise concerning me. In the spring of 1925 a new chapter in my life was opened. Once more I was to co-operate in the destiny of my people. Only my firm confidence in Germany's inexhaustible wellsprings gave me the courage to accept the first and second elections to the national presidency.

This firm belief also gave me the inner strength unswervingly to carry on my difficult office. The last part of my life was also the most difficult for me. Many have failed to understand me in these troublous times and have not comprehended that my only care was to restore the mutilated and discouraged German people to a self-confident unity.

I began and conducted my office in the consciousness that, in both domestic and foreign politics, a preliminary period of renunciation was essential. From the Easter message of 1925—in which I exhorted the nation to the fear of God and social justice, to internal peace and political cleanness—onwards, I have not tired to foster the internal unity of the people and the self-examination of its best qualities. Withal, I was conscious that the constitution and form of government which the nation provided for itself in an hour of great need and inner weakness was unsuited to the true needs and attributes of our people. The time had to come when this recognition would become general. Hence it appeared as duty to me to guide the country through the valley of external oppression and humiliation and internal distress and self-laceration without jeopardizing its existence, until this hour struck.

The symbol of and firm support for this construction had to be the protector of the state, the Reichswehr. On it, as a firm foundation, there had to rest the old Prussian virtues of self-evident devotion to duty, of simplicity, of comradeship.

The German Reichswehr, after the collapse, cultivated in model form the continuance of the high tradition of the old army.

Always and at all times the army must remain an instrument of the highest administrative authority, an instrument which, untouched by any internal political developments, strives to do full justice to its high obligation of defending the country.

When I shall have returned to my comrades above, with whom I fought on so many battlefields for the greatness and honor of the nation, then I shall call out to the young generation:

"Prove yourselves worthy of your ancestors and never forget that, if you want to secure the peace and welfare of your homeland, you must be prepared to sacrifice even the utmost for this peace and the honor of the country. Never forget that your deeds, too, will some day be tradition."

To all the men who have built up and extended the Reichswehr are due the thanks of the Field-Marshal of the World War and their later supreme commander.

In foreign politics the German people has had to travel the road to Calvary. A frightful treaty weighed heavily upon it and threatened, in its mounting consequences, to bring our nation to collapse. For long the surrounding world failed to understand that Germany had to live, not merely for her own sake but, as the standard bearer of occidental culture, for the sake of Europe as well.

The ties which bound us therefore had to be loosened gradually, without arousing an overwhelming resistance. If some of my old comrades did not at the time understand the necessity of this way, then history will judge more righteously how bitter, yet how essential for the sake of maintaining German life, many an act of state signed by me really was. In harmony with the growing internal recovery and strengthening of the German people it was possible, on the basis of its own national honor and dignity, to strive for, eventually achieve, a progressive and—God willing—blessed collaboration on the problems facing all Europe.

I thank Providence that it permitted me, in the evening of my life, to witness the hour of renewed strength. I thank all those who, in selfless love of fatherland, collaborated in the reconstruction of Germany.

My Chancellor Adolf Hitler and his movement have taken a decisive step of historical importance toward the great goal of leading the German people above all professional and class distinctions to internal unity. I know that much remains to be done and I desire with all my heart that behind the act of national exaltation and popular coöperation there may stand the act of reconciliation which embraces the entire German fatherland.

I depart from my German people in the full hope that that which I longed for in 1919 and which in slow fruition led to [the events of] January 30, 1933, may mature to the complete realization and fulfilment of the historic mission of our people.

In this firm belief in the future of the fatherland I can close my eyes in peace.   von Hindenburg.

193. THE LAW TO COMBAT THE CRISIS OF PEOPLE AND STATE, MARCH 24, 1933 [15]

On March 23, 1933, a new Reichstag, elected a few days after the Reichstag building was almost destroyed by a fire that appeared to be of incendiary origin, voted by 441 to 94 to endow the Hitler Government (which had come into office on the previous January 30) with dictatorial powers for four years. This Enabling Act became the legal base for all future political acts of the National Socialists.

The Reichstag has enacted the following law which, with the consent of the Reichsrat, and in view of the determination that the requirements for laws changing the constitution have been complied with, is hereby promulgated:

Article 1.

National laws can be enacted by the national cabinet as well as in accordance with the procedure established in the constitution. . . .

Article 2.

The national laws enacted by the national cabinet may deviate from the constitution insofar as they do not affect the position of the Reich-

---

[15] Germany, *Reichsgesetzblatt,* 1933, vol. I, No. 25, March 24, 1933, p. 141.

stag and the Reichsrat as such. The powers of the Reich President remain untouched.

ARTICLE 3.

The national laws enacted by the national cabinet are prepared by the chancellor and proclaimed in the *Reichsgesetzblatt*. They take effect, unless otherwise specified, upon the day following their publication. . . .

ARTICLE 4.

Treaties of the Reich with foreign states which relate to matters of national legislation do not require the consent of the bodies participating in legislation. The national cabinet issues the necessary provisions for the execution of these treaties.

ARTICLE 5.

This law becomes effective on the day of its publication. It becomes invalid on April 1, 1937; it further becomes invalid if the present national cabinet is replaced by another.

194. THE LAW FOR THE RESTORATION OF THE CIVIL SERVICE, APRIL 7, 1933 *(Extracts)* [16]

The Civil-Service Act of April 7, 1933, was the instrumentality whereby the Nazi Government brought about the dismissal from service of all officials and honorary officials who were "non-Aryan" or whose previous political activity had been motivated by a false spirit. Certain exceptions were recognized by this law, but they were gradually repealed by later acts and decrees or by practice.

1

(1) For the restoration of a national civil service and the simplification of the administration, officials may be discharged from office according to the following regulations, even when the suppositions required by existing law are not present.

(2) Officials in the sense of this law are direct and indirect officials of the Reich, direct and indirect officials of the states, and officials of the communities and districts (*Gemeindeverbände*), officials of public law corporations, as well as establishments and businesses of equal

[16] Germany, *Reichsgesetzblatt*, 1933, vol. I, No. 34, April 7, 1933, pp. 175-177.

status. . . . The regulations are also to be applied to social insurance employees who have the rights and duties of officials.

(3) Officials in the sense of this law also include those who are in temporary retirement.

(4) The Reichsbank and the German State Railways are empowered to make corresponding arrangements.

2

(1) Officials who have entered the service since November 9, 1918, without possessing the prescribed or customary training or other qualifications for their career, are to be dismissed from the service. For the span of three months after their dismissal, they will be paid the salaries which they have hitherto received.

(2) They have no claim to an allowance for waiting (*Wartegeld*), to a pension, or to pensions for their heirs, nor to the continued use of the office-designation, the title, the uniform, or the office insignia.

(3) In cases of distress, especially when the officials support destitute relatives, an annuity, withdrawable at any time, amounting up to one-third of the existing basic salary of the positions last held by them, can be granted to them; reinsurance under the provisions of the national insurance law is not possible.

(4) The regulations of paragraphs 2 and 3 are to find corresponding application to persons designated in paragraph 1, who were pensioned before this law became effective.

3

(1) Officials who are not of Aryan descent, are to be retired (Articles 8ff.); where honorary officials are concerned they are to be discharged from office.

(2) Paragraph 1 does not apply to officials who have been in the service since August 1, 1914, or who fought in the World War at the front for the German Reich or its allies, or whose fathers or sons fell in the World War. The minister of the interior in ageement with the competent minister or the highest state authorities may permit further exceptions in the case of officials who are in foreign countries.

4

Officials who on the basis of their previous political activity do not offer security that they will at all times exert themselves for the national state without reservations, may be dismissed. For three months after the dismissal they will be paid their former salaries. From then on they receive three-quarters of their pensions (Article 8) and corresponding maintenance for their survivors.

5

(1) Every official must submit to a transfer to an office of the same or an equally-valued career, also to one of lesser rank and scheduled salary—with a refund of the prescribed moving expenses—if the needs of the service so demand. When the official is transferred to a position of lesser rank and scheduled salary, the official retains the title and the salary of the office which he formerly held.

(2) The official may, within a month, demand that in place of a transfer to an office of lesser rank and scheduled income (Par. 1), he be pensioned.

6

For the simplification of the administration, officials may be pensioned even when they are still fit for service. When officials are retired for this reason, their positions may not be filled again.

7

(1) Dismissals from office, transfers to other offices, and retirement cases are announced with finality by the highest national or state authorities without legal recourse.

(2) The dispositions according to Articles 2 to 6 must be made by September 30, 1933, at the latest. The time-limit may be shortened in agreement with the minister of the interior if the highest competent national or state authorities declare that within their administrative sphere the provisions of this law have been carried out.

8

Officials retired or dismissed according to Articles 3 and 4 will not receive pensions if they have not completed at least ten years' service; this applies also in those cases in which, according to prevailing regulations of national and state law, a pension is granted even after a shorter period of service.

· · · · ·

14

(1) It is permissible to institute legal proceedings, even after their retirement or dismissal, against officials who, on the basis of this law, have been retired or dismissed for infractions perpetrated during their

term of office, with the aim of depriving them of their pensions, the pensions for their survivors, the office-designations, titles, uniforms, and service emblems. The institution of such proceedings must occur by December 31, 1933, at the latest. . . .

. . . . . .

195. FIRST DECREE FOR THE EXECUTION OF THE LAW FOR THE RESTORATION OF THE CIVIL SERVICE, APRIL 11, 1933
(Extracts) [17]

Since the Nazi Government proposed to exclude "non-Aryans" from most aspects of the national life, it became necessary to define this class. A decree of April 11, 1933, accomplished the object.

. . . . .

2

(1) All those count as non-Aryans who are descended from non-Aryan, particularly Jewish, parents or grandparents. It suffices if one parent or one grandparent is non-Aryan. This is especially to be accepted if one parent or one grandparent professed the Jewish religion.

. . . . .

196. DECREE CONCERNING THE TASKS OF THE MINISTRY FOR PUBLIC ENLIGHTENMENT AND PROPAGANDA, JUNE 30, 1933 [18]

One of the reasons for the general success of the Nazis in Germany was undoubtedly their skilful use of propaganda methods. Indeed, Adolf Hitler's book, Mein Kampf, is an excellent text on the subject of popular enlightenment. In accordance with the Führer's principles, therefore, a decree of June 30, 1933, defined the tasks of a Ministry for Public Enlightenment and Propaganda. Dr. Paul Joseph Goebbels was placed at the head of the ministry. As chief, moreover, of the Reich Culture Chamber (Reichskulturkammer), Dr. Goebbels was entrusted with the task of "co-ordinating" all aspects of Germany's cultural life.

---

[17] Germany, *Reichsgesetzblatt*, 1933, vol. I, No. 37, April 11, 1933, p. 195.
[18] *Ibid.*, No. 75, July 5, 1933, p. 499.

Based on the decree of the Reich President of March 13, 1933, . . .
I [Hitler] decree, in agreement with the minister of foreign affairs,
the minister of the interior, the minister of economics, the minister for
food and agriculture, the minister of posts, the minister of communications, and the minister for public enlightenment and propaganda, the
following:

The minister for public enlightenment and propaganda is competent
to deal with all measures of spiritual influence upon the nation, publicity
for the state, culture, and business, instruction of the public within and
without the nation concerning the above, and the administration of all
arrangements which serve all these purposes.

Consequently the following are transferred to the jurisdiction of the
minister for public enlightenment and propaganda:

1. From the jurisdiction of the foreign office: Intelligence reports
and publicity in foreign countries, art, art exhibits, film and sport matters in foreign countries.

2. From the jurisdiction of the ministry of the interior:

General domestic political enlightenment,

The Hochschule für Politik,

Establishment and celebration of national holidays and state cele-
brations, with the participation of the minister of the interior,

The Press (with the Institute of Journalism),

The Radio,

The National Anthem,

The Deutsche Bücherei in Leipzig,

Art (but not including the Art-Historical Institute in Florence,
copyright for works of literature and art, the index of the valuable national works of art, the German-Austrian treaty on the
exportation of art, protection of art objects and monuments, protection and care of the landscape and natural monuments, game
and forest preserves, the preservation of buildings of especial
historical significance, the preservation of national monuments,
the Association of German Societies for Folklore, the national
honor-monument),

Music cultivation (including philharmonic orchestras),

Theatrical affairs,

The Cinema,

Combating of trash and obscenity.

3. From the jurisdictions of the ministry of economics and the ministry for food and agriculture:

Business publicity for expositions, fairs, and other advertising matters.

4. From the jurisdictions of the ministry of posts and the ministry of communications:

Travel publicity.

All radio matters which in the past were dealt with by the ministry of posts are transferred from its jurisdiction insofar as they do not pertain to the technical administration outside the National Radio Corporation and the radio corporations' buildings. In matters of technical administration the minister for public enlightenment and propaganda is to participate insofar as is necessary for the execution of his own duties, especially in the determination of conditions for loans to radio-plants and the regulations of their dues. In particular, the representation of the Reich in the National Radio Corporation and in the radio corporations is transferred completely to the minister for public enlightenment and proganda.

In the designated fields the minister for public enlightenment and propaganda is at the head of all matters, including legislation. For participation by the remaining national ministers, the general regulations apply.

197. THE LAW CONCERNING THE FORMATION OF NEW PARTIES, JULY 14, 1933 [19]

Soon after the Nazi Party came to power in Germany, the other political parties were either abolished or else dissolved themselves. The Catholic Center Party delayed its own dissolution until July 5, 1933, and then a law of July 14 confirmed the fact that the Nazi Party was "the only" political party in Germany.

1

The National Socialist German Workers' Party is the only political party in Germany.

[19] Germany, *Reichsgesetzblatt*, vol. I, No. 81, July 15, 1933, p. 479.

2

Whoever undertakes to maintain the organization of another political party or to form a new political party is to be punished with confinement in a penitentiary up to 3 years or imprisonment in a jail from 6 months to 3 years unless the act is punishable by a higher penalty under other provisions.

198. THE LAW TO PREVENT THE PERPETUATION OF HERITABLE DISEASES, JULY 14, 1933 (Extracts) [20]

It was a corollary of the Nazi doctrine of German racial supremacy that the nation must produce the greatest possible number of healthy, "Aryan" children. Hence early marriages and large families were encouraged. But, by the same token, the state frowned upon reproduction by individuals who had heritable diseases or were chronic alcoholics or congenitally feebleminded. Consequently a law was passed on July 14, 1933, effective from the following January 1, providing for the sterilization, in certain circumstances, of such individuals.

1

(1) Whoever suffers from a heritable disease may be made unfruitful (sterilized) through surgical means if, in the experience of medical science, it may, with great likelihood, be expected that his descendants will suffer from serious heritable physical or mental defects.

(2) Whoever suffers from one of the following ailments is considered to be heritably diseased within the meaning of this law:

1. congenital feeble-mindedness
2. schizophrenia
3. manic-depression
4. congenital epilepsy
5. heritable St. Vitus's dance (Huntington's Chorea)
6. hereditary blindness
7. hereditary deafness
8. serious heritable malformations.

(3) Further, anyone suffering from chronic alcoholism may also be made unfruitful.

---

[20] Germany, *Reichsgesetzblatt*, 1933, vol. I, No. 86, July 25, 1933, pp. 529-531.

2

(1) Entitled to request [sterilization], is he who is to be made unfruitful. If he should be incapacitated or under guardianship because of feeble-mindedness or not yet 18 years of age, then his legal representative is empowered to make the motion. In the other cases of limited capacity the request must be consented to by the legal representative. If the person is of age and has a nurse, the consent of the latter is necessary.

(2) The request is to be accompanied by a certificate from a physician accredited by the German Reich stating that the one to be sterilized has been enlightened regarding the nature and consequences of sterilization.

(3) The request for sterilization is subject to recall.

3

Sterilization may also be recommended by
1. the official physician,
2. the official in charge of the institution in the case of inmates of a hospital, sanitarium, or prison.

4

The request is to be presented in writing to, or put into writing by the business office of, the Health-Inheritance Court (*Erbgesundheitsgericht*). The facts underlying the request are to be certified to by a medical document or in some other way authenticated. The business office of the court must notify the official physician.

. . . . .

7

(1) The proceedings before the Health-Inheritance Courts are secret.

. . . . .

10

. . . (3) The Supreme Health-Inheritance Court has final jurisdiction.

11

(1) The surgical operation necessary for sterilization may be performed only in a hospital and by a physician accredited by the German Reich. . . .   .

18

This law becomes effective January 1, 1934.

199. THE HEREDITARY FARMS LAW, SEPTEMBER 29, 1933 (Extracts) [21]

It was the view of Dr. Richard Walther Darré, Minister of Agriculture in the Hitler Cabinet, that Germany's future leaders must come from a hereditary, "Aryan," small-landholding nobility. To create such a "farmer aristocracy" or "yeoman aristocracy," the government, on September 29, 1933, passed a Hereditary Farms Law, applying, generally, to farms ranging in size from about 2 hectares to 125 hectares (from about 5 to about 310 acres).

The national government desires to preserve the peasantry, through the surety of the ancient German mode of inheritance, as the blood source (Blutquelle) of the German people.

The farms shall be protected against excessive debt and division during the process of inheritance, so that they may remain permanently as heritages of the clan in the hands of free peasants.

Efforts shall be made to bring about a healthful partition of the large landed estates, inasmuch as the existence of a large number of prosperous small and medium-sized farms distributed as regularly as possible over the entire country offers the best guarantee for keeping people and state vigorous.

The national government has therefore decided upon the following law. The fundamental thoughts of the law are:

Land and forestry property of a minimum size of one soil subsistence (Ackernahrung) and a maximum of 125 hectares [308.8 acres] constitutes a Hereditary Farm, if it belongs to a person competent to be a peasant.

The owner of a Hereditary Farm is called peasant (Bauer).

Only he can be a peasant who is a German citizen, of German or kindred blood, and who is honorable.

The Hereditary Farm passes undivided to the heir-apparent.

The claims of the joint heirs are limited to the remaining property of the peasant. Descendants not classed as heirs-apparent receive a vocational training and establishment commensurate with the capabilities of the farm; should they fall into want through no fault of their own, then they are entitled to find sanctuary at home. . . .

The Hereditary Farm is inherently inalienable and unattachable.

[21] Germany, *Reichsgesetzblatt*, 1933, vol. I, No. 108, September 30, 1933, pp. 685-692.

. . . . .

Article 2.

. . . (2) That amount of land is to be regarded as a soil subsistence (*Ackernahrung*), which is necessary to nourish and clothe a family independently of market conditions and the general economy and to maintain the economic life of the farm.

. . . . .

Article 11.

. . . (2) The owner or possessor of other land or forestry properties is called husbandman (*Landwirt*).

. . . . .

Article 15.

(1) The peasant must be honorable. He must be capable of administering his farm in orderly fashion. . . .

(2) Should the suppositions of Paragraph 1 fall away or should the peasant fail to live up to his obligations, assuming that these could be met under a proper administration of affairs, then the Inheritance Court (*Anerbengericht*), on motion of the State Peasant Leader, may transfer the administration and usufruct of the estate permanently or temporarily to the spouse of the peasant or to him who, in the event of the peasant's death, would succeed him as heir-apparent. . . .

Article 16.

If the peasant loses his peasant status he may no longer call himself *Bauer*. . . .

. . . . .

Article 20.

The following are designated heirs in the order named:

1. The sons of the testator (*Erblasser*); the sons and grandsons take the place of a deceased son;
2. The father of the testator;
3. The brothers of the testator; the sons and grandsons take the place of a deceased brother;
4. The daughters of the testator; the sons and grandsons take the place of a deceased daughter;

5. The sisters of the testator; the sons and grandsons take the place of a deceased sister;

6. The female descendants of the testator and their descendants insofar as they do not already come under no. 4. He who is closer to the male line of the testator excludes him who is more remote. In all other cases the male line has preference.

ARTICLE 21.

. . . (3) Within each category of heirs, local custom determines whether the right of the eldest or the youngest shall prevail. Where there is no definite custom, the right of the youngest prevails. In case of doubt regarding the existence or character of custom, the Inheritance Court shall decide, upon motion of one of the parties concerned.

. . . . .

ARTICLE 31.

The surviving spouse of the testator may, insofar as self-support out of available funds may be impossible, demand from the heir lifelong support on the farm in the customary circumstances.

. . . . .

ARTICLE 55.

The heir is exempt from the inheritance tax or the agrarian property tax upon the transference of the Hereditary Farm.

. . . . .

200. THE LAW TO REGULATE NATIONAL LABOR, JANUARY 20, 1934 [22]

Laws to regulate afresh the relations between capital and labor in the Third Reich became effective in the spring of 1934. Rejecting the idea of an inevitable capital-labor conflict, this legislation upheld the principles of leadership and the placing of the common before the individual welfare. The following summary of the lengthy act of January 20, 1934, was prepared by the International Labor Office in Geneva.

[22] International Labour Office, *Industrial and Labour Information*, vol. 49, No. 8, International Labour Office, Geneva, 1934, pp. 245-250; original in Germany, *Reichsgesetzblatt*, 1934, vol. I, No. 7, January 23, 1934, pp. 45-56.

. . . . .

Leader of the Undertaking and Trust Council.

The Act provides that within each undertaking the employer, as head or "Leader" *(Führer)* of the undertaking, and his salaried and wage-earning employees as his "Followers" *(Gefolgschaft)* shall work together to promote the objects of the undertaking and the common welfare of people and State. The head of the undertaking is responsible towards his staff for all decisions affecting the business, and must seek to promote the welfare of his employees, who in turn must serve him with the loyalty on which the works community is founded.

The employer, or in the case of incorporated persons or groups of persons, his lawful representative, may delegate a person holding a responsible post in the management of the undertaking to act for him, and must do so when he does not himself conduct the business. For the purposes of the Act the term "undertaking" also includes the management. The Act does not, however, apply to the crews of craft engaged in maritime, inland and air navigation, or to wage-earning and salaried employees in the public services.

In undertakings normally employing not less than twenty persons, the head of the undertaking will be assisted by counsellors chosen from among the staff, who will act in an advisory capacity and form, with the head of the undertaking and under his leadership, the "Trust Council" of the undertaking. It is the duty of the Council to promote mutual trust within the works community and to discuss any measures for the improvement of work, the establishment and maintenance of general conditions of employment, and in particular of rules of employment, the maintenance and improvement of safety conditions in the undertaking, the promotion among all members of the undertaking of a spirit of solidarity both among themselves and with the undertaking, and the welfare of all members of the community. The Council must also try to settle all disputes arising within the undertaking and must be consulted prior to the infliction of any fines provided for in the rules of employment. The Council may delegate particular duties to its individual members.

In order to be eligible to serve on the Council an employee must be not less than twenty-five years of age and must have had at least one year's service in the business or undertaking concerned and at least two years' service in the same or an allied occupation or industry. He must be in full possession of his civil rights, must be a member of the German Labour Front, and must offer evidence of exemplary human qualities and every assurance that in all circumstances he will unreservedly support the interests of the national State. The head of the undertaking, in agreement with the Chief of the organisation for establishing National-Socialist "cells" in business undertakings, must draw up a list of the councillors and their substitutes in March of every year.

The staff of the undertaking is required to elect the Council from this list by secret ballot. If no Council is formed in this manner, the Labour Trustee has power to appoint the requisite number of councillors.

The Council must be convened as required by the head of the undertaking and must in any case be convened if a meeting is demanded by at least half the members. The duties of its members are honorary and may not be rewarded by payment, but the regular wage must be paid on account of any working time spent by members in performance of their duties. Any necessary expenditure must be borne by the management, which must also place at the disposal of the Council all facilities and institutions necessary for the conduct of its business and the orderly discharge of its duties. The Labour Trustee may cancel the appointment of any member of the Council on account of his practical or personal unsuitability.

The council may by a majority decision appeal directly in writing to the Labour Trustee against any decision taken by the head of the undertaking in respect of general conditions of employment, and in particular of the rules of employment, which does not appear to be justified by the social or economic conditions of the undertaking. The enforcement of the decision contested is not stayed by the lodging of an appeal. The Labour Trustee has power to rescind the decision and himself issue the necessary regulations.

Labour Trustees.

A Labour Trustee will be appointed for every large industrial area. It will be the duty of this officer to promote the maintenance of industrial peace, and in pursuance of this object:

(1) To supervise the constitution and procedure of the Trust Council and give a decision in any case of dispute;

(2) To appoint and dismiss members of the Council in cases specified in the Act;

(3) To invesigate, on appeal by a majority of the Trust Council, decisions of the leader of the undertaking concerning the establishment of general conditions of employment, and in particular, of the rules of employment, and, if necessary, himself to take the necessary action;

(4) In the event of extensive dismissals, to undertake the duties hitherto devolving upon the Commissioner for dismissals under the Decree concerning the closing down of undertakings;

(5) To supervise the application of the provisions concerning rules of employment;

(6) To supervise the principles and provisions of collective rules and their application;

(7) To co-operate in enforcing the jurisdiction of the Social Honour Courts (see below);

(8) To keep the German Government regularly informed as to the development of social conditions in such manner as the Federal Minister of Labour and the Federal Minister of Economy may require.

The Federal Minister of Labour and the Federal Minister of Economy may allot to the Labour Trustee further duties under the Act.

The Decree concerning the closing down of undertakings is repealed. It is provided, however, that the Labour Trustee must be notified beforehand of any extensive dismissals contemplated, and that these may not take effect until a time-limit of four weeks has expired. This time-limit may be extended by the Labour Trustee to not more than two months. As under the provisions of the repealed Decree, the Labour Trustee may authorise the working of short time until the expiry of this period.

Deputy Labour Trustees may be appointed by the Federal Minister of Labour as required by the extent and special economic conditions of the industrial area concerned; to them the Federal Minister of Labour or the Labour Trustee may delegate all or part of the latter's functions in respect of a certain district or a certain branch of industry or of specified duties.

Any person who deliberately and persistently disregards general regulations issued in writing by the Labour Trustee in the execution of his duties is liable to a fine, which in especially serious cases may be replaced or supplemented by imprisonment. Proceedings in such cases may be opened only on the application of the Labour Trustee.

The Labour Trustee may appoint an expert board of advisers recruited from the various branches of industry within his jurisdiction, for consultation on general questions or matters of principle connected with his duties. In special cases, and more particularly prior to issuing collective rules, the Labour Trustee may also appoint a special committee of experts.

Rules of Employment and Collective Rules.

Rules of employment for the staff must be drawn up in writing by the head of every undertaking normally employing at least twenty persons. These rules must cover the following conditions of employment:

(1) Beginning and end of normal daily hours of work and breaks;

(2) Date and manner of payment of wages and salaries;

(3) Principles for the calculation of piece or job work, where these systems are in force;

(4) Provisions concerning the nature, amount and collection of fines, where these are provided for;

(5) Reasons justifying summary dismissal without notice (apart from those laid down by law);

(6) Application of the sums due as compensation for unlawful breach of the relationship between employer and employee, in so far as this is payable under law, rules of employment, or contract of employment.

In addition to the above requirements of the Act, the rules of employment may also lay down provisions governing the rates of remuneration and other conditions of employment, and also further regulations respecting the conduct of the undertaking, the behaviour of the employees in the undertaking and the prevention of accidents.

Where the rules of employment fix the remuneration due to wage-earning and salaried employees, minimum rates must be fixed, which nevertheless must leave scope for the remuneration of individual employees according to the quality of their services. In general also provision must be made for the possibility of appropriately rewarding special services. The provisions contained in the rules of employment are legally binding on the employer as minimum rates for his employees. The Labour Trustee, after consulting a committee of experts, may lay down guiding principles for the establishment of rules of employment and of individual contracts of employment. If it is urgently necessary for the protection of the employees of a given group of undertakings included within the district of the Labour Trustee that minimum standard conditions of employment should be established, the Labour Trustee, after consulting the committee of experts, may issue collective rules in writing, the terms of which are binding as minimum standards for the employments which they cover. Any provisions of rules of employment which conflict with these standards are void. The Labour Trustee may expressly withdraw any disputes arising out of the relations between employees and apprentices and their employers from the jurisdiction of the civil courts by stipulating that they shall be decided by an arbitration court.

The Labour Trustee may similarly issue collective rules to regulate the relations of home-workers with the employers whose orders they carry out. The Federal Minister of Labour or the Labour Trustee may deal in the same way with other home-workers, middlemen and independent workers of similar standing who are not economically independent.

Social Honour Court.

Each member of a works community is responsible for the conscientious performance of the duties entailed by his position in that community. His conduct must be such as to deserve the consideration attaching to his position, and in particular he must be constantly mindful of his duty to devote his energies wholeheartedly to the services of the undertaking and to subordinate himself to the general good.

Any person who flagrantly disregards the social duties arising out of his membership of a works community will be charged before an Honour Court with offending against social honour. These duties will be deemed to have been disregarded by the following persons:

(1) Industrialists, heads of undertakings or other persons in supervisory positions who maliciously abuse their authority in the undertaking to exploit the labour of the employees or offend against their honour;

(2) Employees who endanger industrial peace in the undertaking by maliciously fostering discontent among their fellows, and in particular those who as members of the Trust Council deliberately exercise unjustifiable interference in the management or continually and maliciously try to undermine the corporate spirit of the undertaking;

(3) Members of the works community who repeatedly address frivolous and baseless complaints and appeals to the Labour Trustee or who persistently contravene his written instructions;

(4) Members of the Trust Council guilty of the unauthorised publication of confidential information concerning industrial or business secrets obtained in performance of their duties and of the confidential nature of which they were informed.

Public servants and soldiers are exempted from the jurisdiction of the Honour Courts.

The penalties which may be inflicted by the Honour Courts are: warning, reprimand, fine up to 10,000 marks, disqualification to act as leader of an undertaking or member of a Trust Council, removal to a different place of employment.

The procedure of the Honour Courts is mainly governed by the provisions of the code of penal procedure applicable to penal proceedings within the jurisdiction of the regional courts, but without the co-operation of the official legal services.

Cases relating to offences against social honour will be decided, on application by the Labour Trustee, by an Honour Court to be set up in each Labour Trustee's district. Each of these courts will consist of a chairman, who must be a public magistrate, and one leader of an undertaking and one member of a Trust Council as assessors. The leader of the undertaking and the member of the Trust Council are appointed by the chairman of the court from lists nominated by the German Labour Front.

Complaints concerning offences against social honour must be submitted to the Labour Trustee, who will investigate their substance.

If the chairman of the court, who may himself undertake further enquiries, considers that the Trustee's complaint is well founded, he may inflict a penalty in the form of a warning, reprimand, or fine of not more than 100 marks. Appeal against his decision may be lodged by the accused person or by the Labour Trustee. If the chairman does not decide the case himself, proceedings will be opened before the Honour Court, the Trustee being authorised to attend the principal proceedings and to submit proposals.

Appeal against decisions of the Honour Court may be made to the Federal Court of Honour, consisting of two higher officials of the magistrature, one leader of an undertaking, and one member of a Trust Council.

Protection against Dismissal.

Any wage-earning or salaried employee dismissed after at least one year's service from an undertaking normally employing at least ten workers may appeal to the Labour Court against his dismissal if the latter is unduly harsh and is not justified by the conditions of the undertaking. No such appeal may be made, however, if the dismissal was in accordance with law or with collective rules. The appeal must be accompanied by a certificate from the Trust Council stating that the matter has already been discussed in the Council without effect.

If the Court decides that the dismissal should be cancelled it must also fix the compensation due from the employer in the event of his refusal to comply with the judgment, and the employer must then state whether he prefers to reinstate the worker or to pay the compensation.

The amount of the compensation is fixed proportionately to the length of service, but may not exceed four-twelfths of the last annual earnings of the person concerned. . . .

Final and Transitional Provisions.

Except for certain provisions, the Act will come into force on 1 May, 1934. . . .

. . . Leaders and employees of the legal advice centres set up by the German Labour Front, and the official lawyers authorised by the German Labour Front to represent a party in a particular case, will in future have full powers of representation in cases before the Labour Courts.

The Federal Minister of Labour has power to issue further regulations to administer and supplement the Act.

Lastly, it is provided that collective agreements in force at 1 December 1933 or which come into force after that date shall remain operative until 30 April 1934, failing their revision or suspension before that date by the Labour Trustee.

201. THE LAW CONCERNING THE HEAD OF THE GERMAN REICH, AUGUST 1, 1934 [23]

On the night preceding the death of President Paul von Hindenburg— that is, on August 1, 1934—the German Cabinet adopted a decree providing for the union of the offices of president and chancellor from the moment of the aged marshal's death. From August 2, therefore, Adolf Hitler stood alone as Führer and Chancellor of the Third Reich.

[23] Germany, *Reichsgesetzblatt*, 1934, vol. I, No. 89, August 2, 1934, p. 747.

1

The office of Reich President is united with that of chancellor. Hence the authority hitherto exercised by the Reich President passes to the leader and chancellor, Adolf Hitler. He appoints his deputy.

2

This law becomes effective from the moment of the death of President von Hindenburg.

202. THE REICH LABOR SERVICE LAW, JUNE 26, 1935 *(Extracts)* [24]

A law of June 26, 1935, established compulsory labor service for most young "Aryan" Germans of both sexes.

The Reich Government has decided upon the following law which is hereby promulgated:

Article 1.

(1) The Reich Labor Service is a service of honor to the German people.

(2) All young Germans of both sexes are required to serve their nation in the Reich Labor Service.

(3) The Reich Labor Service is to educate German youth in the spirit of National Socialism in order that it may acquire a true national community spirit *(Volksgemeinschaft)*, a true conception of labor, and, above all, a proper respect for manual labor.

(4) The Reich Labor Service is to carry out public welfare projects.

Article 2.

(1) The Reich Labor Service is under the jurisdiction of the Reich Minister of the Interior. Subordinate to him, the Reich Labor Leader exercises supreme authority over the Reich Labor Service.

(2) The Reich Labor Leader is at the head of the Reich administration of the Labor Service; he determines the organization, regulates the distribution of work, and directs training and education.

---

[24] Germany, *Reichsgesetzblatt*, 1935, vol. I, No. 64, June 27, 1935, pp. 769-771.

Article 3.

(1) The Führer and Reich Chancellor determines the number of people to be called annually for service and sets the service period.

(2) Obligation for service begins, at the earliest, with the completion of the eighteenth year and ends, at the latest, with the completion of the twenty-fifth year.

(3) Those subject to compulsory service will, as a rule, be called for Reich Labor Service in the calendar year in which they complete their nineteenth year. Voluntary enlistment in the Reich Labor Service at an earlier age is possible. . . .

Article 4.

Those subject to compulsory service are drafted by the recruiting officers of the Reich Labor Service.

Article 5.

(1) The following are excluded from the Labor Service:
    a) Those who have been punished with penal servitude;
    b) Those who are not in possession of the rights of citizenship;
    c) Those subject to the measures for security and improvement according to Article 42a of the Criminal Code;
    d) Those expelled from the National Socialist Labor Party because of dishonorable activities;
    e) Those punished by court for treasonable activity.

(2) The Reich Minister of the Interior may make exceptions to (c) and (e) of Paragraph 1.

(3) Those subject to compulsory service in the Reich Labor Service, who were deprived of eligibility to hold public office, may be called for service only after the expiration of the period of sentence.

Article 6.

(1) No persons shall be recruited for the Labor Service who are completely unfit for the Reich Labor Service.

(2) Those subject to the Labor Service who live abroad or who desire to go abroad for an extended period may be relieved of the duty of labor service for a period up to two years, in exceptional cases permanently, but at the longest for the period of the stay abroad.

ARTICLE 7.

(1) No one shall be allowed to serve in the Reich Labor Service who is of non-Aryan descent or who is married to a person of non-Aryan descent. . . .

(2) Non-Aryans who by Article 15, Paragraph 2 of the Army Law have been declared worthy of military service may also be allowed to serve in the Reich Labor Service. They cannot, however, become officers in the Reich Labor Service.

ARTICLE 8.

Those subject to service may gain a postponement up to two years; in the event of pressing occupational reasons, up to five years.

ARTICLE 9.

The provisions for the Labor Service duties of the female youth remain subject to special legal regulations.

ARTICLE 10.

(1) Members of the Reich Labor Service are:
  a) the permanent staff,
  b) those recruited for the Labor Service,
  c) volunteers in the Labor Service. . . .

ARTICLE 11.

(1) The permanent staff consists of the regular leaders and officials as well as the candidates for these posts. The regular leaders and officials are active professionally in the Reich Labor Service.

(2) A candidate for leader must, before his elevation to regular troop leadership, engage in writing to serve continuously for at least ten years and give proof of his Aryan descent; he must also have completed his active service in the army.

(3) Regular leaders and officials are retired upon attainment of specified age limits.

(4) Officials from other departments who are transferred to the Reich Labor Service retain all the salary rights which they had up to then acquired.

(5) The Führer and Reich Chancellor appoints and dismisses all members of the Reich Labor Service from the rank of Work Leader upwards. All other members of the permanent staff are appointed and

dismissed by the Reich Minister of the Interior on recommendation of the Reich Labor Leader. He may yield these powers to the Reich Labor Leader.

. . . . .

ARTICLE 16.

(1) Those subject to the compulsory Labor Service and volunteers may be dismissed from the Reich Labor Service ahead of time

    a) upon application, if, after they have been called, a reason for postponement in accordance with Article 8 is forthcoming,

    b) if they no longer possess the necessary physical and mental powers for the exercise of their duties.

(2) Advance dismissal of compulsory and voluntary members of the Labor Service is obligatory if reasons barring membership in the Reich Labor Service as indicated in Articles 5 and 7 are subsequently established.

. . . . .

ARTICLE 18.

Members of the Reich Labor Service must get permission to marry.

. . . . .

ARTICLE 25.

(1) The Führer and Reich Chancellor, or any agency empowered by him, may permit retiring members of the Reich Labor Service to wear the uniform of the Reich Labor Service, subject to recall.

(2) This right will, as a rule, be granted only after honorable service of at least ten years' duration.

. . . . .

ARTICLE 27.

This law goes into effect on the day of its proclamation.

The Reich Minister of the Interior is empowered to determine a later date on which individual provisions of this law are to take effect.

卐 卐 卐

203. DECREE ON THE TERMS OF SERVICE IN AND THE STRENGTH OF THE REICH LABOR SERVICE AND THE LABOR SERVICE FOR THE FEMALE YOUTH, SEPTEMBER 6, 1936 [25]

A decree of September 6, 1936, later extended and amended, established the terms of service in and the numerical strength of the Reich Labor Service for boys and girls.

ARTICLE 1.

The term of service in the Reich Labor Service for all those subject to military service is half a year.

ARTICLE 2.

The strength of the Reich Labor Service is to be raised to 230,000 men (including permanent staff) between October 1936 and the beginning of October 1937, 275,000 men (including permanent staff) in the period to the beginning of October 1938, [and] 300,000 men (including permanent staff) in the period to the beginning of October 1939.

ARTICLE 3.

(1) The Labor Service for the female youth, temporarily based on voluntary enlistments, is to be further developed according to plan.

(2) The strength of the Labor Service for the female youth is to be raised to 25,000 Labor Maids *(Arbeitsmaiden)* in the period from April 1937 to March 1938.

204. THE LAW FOR THE PROTECTION OF GERMAN BLOOD AND GERMAN HONOR, SEPTEMBER 15, 1935 [26]

On September 15, 1935, the Nazi Government promulgated the so-called Nürnberg Laws which, among other restrictions, forbade marital and extra-marital relations between Jews and citizens of "German or kindred blood."

Imbued with the knowledge that the purity of German blood is the prerequisite for the continuance of the German nation and animated

---

[25] Germany, *Reichsgesetzblatt,* 1936, vol. I, No. 85, September 28, 1936, p. 747.
[26] *Ibid.,* 1935, vol. I, No. 100, September 15, 1935, pp. 1146-1147.

with the unbending will to ensure the German nation for all the future, the Reichstag unanimously resolved upon this law, which is herewith proclaimed:

1

(1) Marriages between Jews and citizens of German or kindred blood are prohibited.

(2) Annulment proceedings can be brought only by the Public Prosecutor.

2

Extramarital relations between Jews and citizens of German or kindred blood are prohibited.

3

Jews may not employ in their households female citizens of German or kindred blood who are under 45 years of age.

4

(1) Jews are forbidden to hoist the Reich and national flag and to display the Reich colors.

(2) They may, on the other hand, display the Jewish colors. The exercise of this right is under state protection.

5

(1) Whoever acts contrary to the prohibition of Article 1 is liable to penal servitude.

(2) The man who acts contrary to the prohibition of Article 2 is punishable by jail or penitentiary sentence.

(3) Whoever acts contrary to the provisions of Articles 3 and 4 is punishable with a jail sentence up to one year and a money fine or with either of these penalties.

---

205. PROCLAMATION OF THE FOUR-YEAR PLAN AT THE EIGHTH PARTY CONGRESS, NÜRNBERG, SEPTEMBER 9, 1936 (Extracts) [27]

From September 9, 1936, German economic life came to be dominated by the demands of a Four-Year Plan for national self-sufficiency announced by the Führer at the Eighth Party Congress at Nürnberg. The execution of

[27] *Frankfurter Zeitung,* September 10, 1936, pp. 1-2. Read by Adolf Wagner for Adolf Hitler.

the plan was entrusted to General Hermann Wilhelm Göring. During 1937 and 1938 it became increasingly evident that the economic ideas of Göring conflicted with the more conservative views of Dr. Hjalmar Schacht, minister of economics and president of the Reichsbank. Probably because of this difference, Schacht resigned from the economics ministry on November 15, 1937, effective from the next January 15, and was removed from the presidency of the Reichsbank by Hitler in January 1939. In both offices Schacht was replaced by Dr. Walther Funk, long a friend and economic adviser of the chancellor.

. . . I [Hitler] therefore today present the following as the new Four-Year Plan: In four years Germany must be wholly independent of foreign areas in respect of those materials which can in any way be produced through German ability, through our chemistry and machine industry as well as through our mining industry!

The re-creation of this great German raw-material industry will also gainfully employ those masses released by the completion of the rearmament. . . .

. . . The execution [of the plan] will take place with National Socialist energy and vigor. But independently thereof, Germany can not forego the solution of its colonial demands. The right to live of the German people is as great as the [corresponding] rights of other nations. . . .

. . . The realization of this plan therefore becomes merely a question of our energy and determination. As National Socialists we never have known the word "impossible" and hence we do not in future want to take it up as an enrichment of our vocabulary. . . .

206. THE LAW ON THE REUNION OF AUSTRIA WITH THE GERMAN REICH, MARCH 13, 1938 *(Extracts)* [28]

On March 12, 1938, while the civil war in Spain continued to rage, while France was torn by internal dissension, while Italian soldiers were busy in Spain, Ethiopia, and Lybia, while Great Britain was adopting a foreign policy friendlier to Berlin, and on the day before an Anschluss plebiscite ordained by Chancellor Kurt von Schuschnigg was to have been held in

---

[28] Austria, *Bundesgesetzblatt für den Bundesstaat Österreich*, Österreichische Staatsdruckerei, Vienna, Jahrg. 1938, St. 25, Nr. 75.

Austria, German troops occupied the little republic—birthplace in its earlier imperial form of Adolf Hitler—to the accompanying cheers of a majority of its inhabitants. The fact of the absorption was legalized by a brief law of March 13, 1938.

ARTICLE 1.

Austria is a state of the German Reich.

ARTICLE 2.

On Sunday, April 10, 1938, there will be a free, secret plebiscite of all German men and women of Austria over 20 years of age on the reunion with the German Reich.

ARTICLE 3.

A majority of the votes cast determines the plebiscite.

. . . . .

ARTICLE 5.

(1) This federal, constitutional law is effective on the day of its proclamation.

. . . . .

207. DECREE ON THE INTRODUCTION OF THE FOUR-YEAR PLAN IN THE STATE OF AUSTRIA, MARCH 19, 1938 [29]

Within a week after the absorption of Austria into the Reich, the Four-Year Plan (See Document No. 205) was applied to the new province (Land).

. . . . .

The Reich Minister of Economics is empowered, within his jurisdiction in the spheres of raw-material and currency economy, to take all necessary measures required for the preparation of the Four-Year Plan in the State of Austria.

---

[29] Germany, *Reichsgesetzblatt*, 1938, vol. I, No. 30, March 19, 1938, p. 262.

208. DECREE ON THE BALLOT FOR THE PLEBISCITE AND GREAT-GERMAN REICHSTAG ELECTIONS, APRIL 10, 1938 [30]

A plebiscite on the "reunion" of Austria with Germany and elections for the new Great-German Reichstag were held simultaneously on April 10, 1938. The "reunion" and the Führer's list of candidates were accepted by an affirmative vote of 99.07 per cent in a total valid vote that represented 99.59 per cent of the qualified electorate of Great Germany.

BALLOT

Do you agree to the reunion of Austria with the German Reich carried out on March 13 and do you vote for the [Reichstag] list of our Leader, Adolf Hitler?

209. THE DECREE ON JEWISH-OWNED PROPERTY, APRIL 26, 1938
(Extracts) [31]

A decree of April 26, 1938, required all Jews in Germany who possessed property worth more than 5000 marks to report their belongings to the state. Article 7 of the decree appeared to tie up the measure with the Four-Year Plan.

ARTICLE 1.

Every Jew . . . shall report and evaluate in accord with the following instructions his entire domestic and foreign property and estate on the day when this decree goes into force. Jews of foreign citizenship shall report and evaluate only their domestic property.

The duty to report holds likewise for the non-Jewish marital partner of a Jew.

Every reporting person's property must be given separately.

ARTICLE 2.

. . . Property does not include movable objects used by the indi-

---

[30] Austria, *Gesetzblatt für das Land Österreich,* Österreichische Staatsdruckerei, Vienna, 1938, St. 16, Nr. 49.

[31] *The New York Times,* April 29, 1938; decree issued by Field Marshal Göring.

vidual or house furnishings as far as the latter are not classed as luxury objects.

ARTICLE 3.

. . . No report is necessary when the total worth of the property to be reported does not exceed 5000 marks.

ARTICLE 4.

. . . The report is to be presented on an official form by June 30, 1938, to the administrative office responsible at the place of residence of the reporting individual. When such a report is not possible by this date the responsible office can extend the period. In such case, however, an estimate is to be presented by June 30, 1938, together with a statement of the hindering grounds.

ARTICLE 5.

The reporting individual must report, after this decree goes into force, to the responsible office every change of said individual's total property as far as it exceeds a proper standard of living or normal business transactions. . . .

. . . . .

ARTICLE 7.

The Commissar for the Four-Year Plan is empowered to take such necessary measures as may be necessary to guarantee the use of the reported property in accord with the necessities of German economy.

ARTICLE 8.

Whoever with purpose or through carelessness does not fulfill his duty to report and evaluate . . . or who does not fulfill it correctly or promptly or who acts contrary to the measures under Article 7 will be punished with imprisonment and a fine or one of the two said punishments. . . . A delinquent is likewise punishable when the crime was committed abroad. An effort to commit such a crime is equally punishable.

Besides the punishment provided above, confiscation of the property can also be imposed as far as said property was involved in a punishable action. When no definite individual can be prosecuted, confiscation alone can be imposed when the prerequisites for confiscation are demonstrated.

210. DISTRIBUTION OF ANTI-SEMITIC SENTIMENT IN A GROUP OF GERMAN NATIONAL SOCIALISTS [32]

In a useful study based on the life histories of six hundred German Nazis, Professor Theodore Abel enumerated certain interesting conclusions. One of these, concerning the distribution of anti-Semitic sentiment, is herewith reproduced.

Anti-Semitic sentiments are most frequently recorded in the life-histories of the older generation (forty years and over). Thus 50 per cent of this generation, against 26 per cent of the younger men (twenty to forty) expressed antagonism against the Jews. Anti-Semitism also is more frequent in towns and cities than in rural districts (40 against 23 per cent) and more frequent among the middle and upper classes than among workers (47 against 29 per cent). Correspondingly, the number of anti-Semites is higher among those occupied in government service, clerical jobs, professions and trade than among those engaged in industry and agriculture (48 against 29 per cent). Finally, anti-Semitism is less frequent among those who had only a public school education than among those who went to high school and attended a university (32 against 46 per cent).

211-213. THE NAZI PUTSCH IN AUSTRIA, JULY 25, 1934

211. THE DEATH OF CHANCELLOR DOLLFUSS [33]

Chancellor Engelbert Dollfuss, who strove to resist German Nazi penetration of Austria by building up a concrete alternative in the form of a Catholic, anti-socialist, authoritarian, Austrian movement, fell victim to a Nazi Putsch of July 25, 1934, in Vienna. The official Austrian version of his death is herewith reproduced.

The rebels entered the Chancellery at 12:53 and in a very short time had succeeded in disarming and arresting the military guard, to-

[32] T. Abel, *Why Hitler Came into Power. An Answer Based on the Original Life Stories of Six Hundred of His Followers*, Prentice-Hall, Inc., New York, 1938, p. 164n. Reprinted by permission of the publishers.

[33] Austria, Bundeskommissariat für Heimatdienst, *The Death of Dollfuss. An Official History of the Revolt of July, 1934, in Austria*, transl. by Johann Messinger, Denis Archer, London, 1935, pp. 126-133. Reprinted by permission of the publishers.

gether with those police and detectives who were on duty. They arrived in the midst of the changing of the guard, when the two officers were going through the usual formalities. Suddenly eight terrorists rushed into the guard-room with drawn revolvers. The two second-lieutenants had not even loaded their revolvers and were unable to offer any resistance, and in the same way the rifles of the sentries themselves were empty. Before anyone was able to take the situation in— once again it must be emphasized that the leaders of the rebels were in the uniform of army officers—the whole guard was captured.

That the rifles were unloaded is explained by the fact that the Chancellery Guard is merely a guard of honour and has only to provide two sentries for the entrance in Ballhaus Square—a guard of honour which, in accordance with regulations, carry unloaded weapons. There was no difficulty in overpowering the police officials and detectives, owing to the fact that they were distributed in the maze of corridors and passages and were very considerably outnumbered by armed and determined insurgents. Furthermore the rebels were in possession of detailed scale-maps of the building that had been prepared months previously.

While one group was overpowering the guard a second section made for the Chancellor's suite. At the moment of their entry into the building Dr. Dollfuss was in his study. But by this time, accompanied by Herr Fey and Karwinsky, he had gone into the Pillar Hall to find out what was the matter. Herr Fey and several others attempted to bolt the door between the Pillar Hall and an antechamber, but met a considerable number of the rebels who were, moreover, armed with revolvers and rifles. The officials and staff in attendance in the Pillar Hall were captured and forced to sit round the conference table.

Just before the insurgents entered the Pillar Hall Karwinsky decided to take Dr. Dollfuss upstairs, and thence to safety. Shouting: "Come up to the third floor, Chancellor, you will be safe there," he took Dr. Dollfuss by the arm and hurried him to the Pillar Hall, hoping to reach the back-stairs through rooms in the rear.

The commissionaire, named Hedvicek, however, had determined to take Dr. Dollfuss through the office of the Presidential Chancellery, through the State Archives and thence into the street, and with this purpose grasped the Chancellor's arm. The latter shook off Karwinsky and hurried back with Hedvicek in the direction of his study. At that moment a group of Nazis burst into the Pillar Hall led by Holzweber.

Immediately adjoining the Chancellor's study in the direction of Ball-haus Square is the Corner Room, and next to this is the Congress Hall with a balcony looking on to the Square. The commissionaire, Hed-vicek, had just reached the door connecting the Corner Room with the Congress Hall, and was about to open it, when some of the rebels rushed inside through a door opening on to the staircase.

One of the rebels, Otto Planetta, walked up to the Chancellor and without a word fired two shots at him. Both hit Dr. Dollfuss. The latter put his hands to his head and, turning half round, fell to the floor. He murmured "help!" twice, but the Nazis took no notice. At the point of a revolver Hedvicek was made to hold his hands above his head and to turn round facing the wall. About ten minutes later he was taken into the Pillar Hall and kept under guard. Karwinsky in the meantime had been captured in the adjoining secretarial room, soon after he left the Chancellor, and was later taken into the Pillar Hall. . . .

From these remarks it is evident that the Chancellor received his fatal wounds a few minutes after one o'clock. There is no conclusive evidence as to the subsequent events for the next three-quarters of an hour in the Corner Room where Dr. Dollfuss lay dying; it can be almost certainly assumed, however, that the rebels made the Chancellor believe that an armed revolt of the Army and of the executive forces had taken place, and Rintelen [Austrian Minister to Italy and reputedly the choice of the Nazis to be Dollfuss' successor] had formed a new Government; in other words it is extremely probable that the essence of the wireless announcement and the reports given out in various parts of the Chancellery were repeated to him.

At 1:45 Superintendent Johann Greifeneder and Rudolf Messinger, who had been arrested by the rebels, were allowed to attend to Dr. Dollfuss, who by this time had fallen into a stupor. After a little while the two police officers succeeded in bringing him round. He inquired after the other ministers and asked to speak to Dr. Schuschnigg. A little later one of the rebel leaders appeared, and the Chancellor re-peated his request to see Herr Schuschnigg. He was told that the Minister was not in the building. Several times Dr. Dollfuss asked to be allowed to see a priest and a doctor, or to be taken to [a] hospital. None of these requests were fulfilled.

Some time later, the exact hour cannot be ascertained, the Nazi, Holzweber, who was generally referred to as Captain Friedrich, brought Herr Fey, under heavy guard, to see the Chancellor. Up to that time neither Fey nor any of those in the Pillar Hall had been given any definite information as to the fate of Dr. Dollfuss. Now, to his horror, Herr Fey found the Chancellor gravely wounded. The latter was lying on a small couch covered with a piece of draping. On the two wounds in his neck a pad of cotton wool had been laid, on his head and on his forehead was a wet dressing.

The conversation which followed between the Chancellor and Herr Fey was extremely difficult. The former could only whisper, and Fey was forced to bend down right over him to catch what he was saying. The essence of their talk is given by Herr Fey from memory:

"The Chancellor complained that he could not move. Then he thanked me for my past co-operation with him and asked that care should be taken of his family. If this should prove impossible he asked that Signor Mussolini should be requested to look after them. Then he inquired about the other Ministers, particularly about Dr. Schuschnigg, whom he wished to be his deputy. Next he asked that further bloodshed should be avoided, and I did my best to console him and promised that everything would be done according to his wishes. In the meantime the escort was ordering us to finish the conversation, and told the Chancellor, somewhat brusquely, to say what he had to quickly. Dr. Dollfuss repeated that all he wished was to avoid further bloodshed, and that he wanted Dr. Rintelen to make peace. I was anxious to hear more and asked that a doctor should be called in to attend the Chancellor, but at that point I was taken away.

"The attitude of the Nazis gave me the impression that they had brought influence to bear on Dr. Dollfuss before I saw him and that that was why he referred to Dr. Rintelen."

The two Nazis, Josef Fleischer and Franz Felber, who were present during the conversation, stated that Dr. Dollfuss declared that Rintelen should be appointed Chancellor. But Herr Fey is emphatic that the accession of Rintelen to the Chancellorship was not mentioned, and that Dr. Dollfuss only pronounced his name in connection with making peace. The two police officers, Greifeneder and Messinger, who were in attendance upon the Chancellor throughout, declare that they heard nothing connecting Rintelen's name with the Chancellorship, and add that they were close by the Chancellor's side the whole time.

Whatever the last political utterances of the Chancellor may have been, it is quite certain that he could not have been clear in his mind as to the situation. In his last hour he was most probably under the impression that the Army and the police had risen against him and against his Cabinet. As he lay dying he was made to believe that his life-work had collapsed.

After the conversation with Herr Fey the police officers, Greifeneder and Messinger, remained with the Chancellor, attending to him in his last moments. Dr. Dollfuss gradually grew weaker, and thanked them, saying: "My boys, you are very good to me. Why aren't the others like you?

"I only longed for peace. We have never taken the offensive, we have always had to defend ourselves. May the Lord forgive them."

His last dying words were a message of love to his wife and children.

It was probably about 3:45 when Dr. Dollfuss, Austria's great Chancellor, died. For nearly two and three-quarter hours he lay suffering, and during the whole of that time his murderers refused to allow him a priest or a doctor.

This persistent refusal of the services of a priest was particularly brutal, as the rebels must have been only too well aware of the Chancellor's deep religious feeling. The fact that medical attendance was denied him is conclusive proof that his assassination was part of their plan, for had the fatal wounds been the accidental result of some impetuous Nazi action it is probable that the rebels would, at least, have made some effort to save his life. . . .

It has been suggested that the officials of the Chancellery should have attempted to cover the person of Dr. Dollfuss with their own bodies, but in point of fact they had no opportunity to protect him. Dr. Dollfuss left the Pillar Hall at a moment of great confusion, and his only companion was the commissionaire, Hedvicek. These two went to the Corner Room. None of those left in the Pillar Hall knew where he was. A few minutes later the rebels burst into the Pillar Hall, and at the same moment the Chancellor was shot in the Corner Room.

212. THE ATTACK ON THE RAVAG BROADCASTING STATION [34]

The initial overt step in the attempted Nazi Putsch in Vienna on July 25, 1934, was an attack on the government radio broadcasting station. The following is the official Austrian version of the attack.

[34] Austria, Bundeskommissariat für Heimatdienst, *The Death of Dollfuss. An Official History of the Revolt of July, 1934, in Austria,* transl. by Johann Messinger, Denis Archer, London, 1935, pp. 151-154. Reprinted by permission of the publishers.

The object of the attack by the rebels on the Broadcasting House of the Austrian Radio Company was to obtain control of the wireless news service and thereby mislead both the authorities and the public by spreading false reports on the resignation of the Dollfuss Cabinet and the success of the revolt. In some parts of Austria the wireless report was the signal for insurrection.

The energetic and rapid action of the Federal Police, however, was responsible for the failure of this part of the rising, so that the Nazis were unable to influence the public by means of the wireless as had been their intention.

The attack on the Ravag building in Johannes Street was made by the S. S. Standarte No. 89, according to plans that had been prepared.

One group of terrorists assembled near the Café Kolowrat in the "Ring," and approached the building by way of Seilerstaette. Another section arrived from the Kaerntner Street. Each man was armed with a Steyr revolver, and 100 rounds.

As, some days previously, an attempt had been made by Nazis, secreted in one of the broadcasting rooms, to blow up a studio, certain precautionary measures had been taken. The entrance was guarded by a policeman and a member of the Schutzcorps, and every visitor was obliged to prove his identity.

Shortly after 12:30 p.m. two policemen arrived and informed the Police Inspector on duty, named Fluch, that they had been detailed to stand by at the Ravag. Fluch told them that they were merely to assist the member of the Schutzcorps who was on duty.

At about 1 p.m. several separate groups of young men in plain clothes approached the building. One of them managed to obtain entry by saying that he had an appointment with the Manager, Dr. Nuechtern. The very next moment the men who had been approaching from the "Ring" rushed the entrance, overpowered the Schutzcorps guard and threatened the two above-mentioned police, who at once surrendered their arms without resistance. The Inspector of Police Fluch, who had been standing on the other side of the street, rushed to the door, but collapsed, fatally wounded. The door was at once closed and barricaded.

During the short space of time in which these events took place, the second group, which had approached the Broadcasting Station from Kaerntner Street, rushed through the entrance of the adjacent elementary school, and thence to the gymnasium in the courtyard, where workmen were doing some redecorating. The Nazis forced their way past the men by threatening them with their revolvers, crossed the courtyard and broke into the Ravag building through the windows on the ground floor.

Inside the building they proceeded according to programme. The doors were barricaded and guarded; one group broke into the broadcasting rooms, drove the employees and artists into one corner and forced the engineer, Dr. Lothaller, to connect up the building with the Bisamberg transmitter. The announcer, Herr Ehrenberg, was then forced to give out the following statement: "The Dollfuss Government has resigned. Dr. Rintelen has taken over control of the Government." Another group occupied the telephone exchange of the building and forced the girl on duty to cut off all communications.

The officials of the Ravag on the upper floors had taken refuge in various rooms and barricaded themselves against intruders.

The existence of a second switchboard and a separate broadcasting station in Schelling Street was apparently not known to the insurgents, and the managers, imprisoned in the building, were able to maintain communcation with the outside world, and to order the immediate disconnection of the Bisamberg transmitter from the Broadcasting Station, Johannes Street.

Within a few minutes the Ravag building was surrounded by Federal police. It proved impossible to force the main entrance. The police then attempted to enter the rooms of the Ravag through the windows of the housekeeper's flat. To do this, however, they found they had to cross a small backyard which was under the fire of the terrorists. A detachment of police then managed to get through the nearby building at No. 4 Johannes Street into the Gymnastic Hall, where they came under heavy fire, and Superintendent Kaufmann was fatally shot. At this point Superintendent Ferdinand Schweiger gave orders to barricade the doors of the houses in Anna Street, and thence forced his way into the courtyard of the Ravag building, only narrowly escaping the fire of the rebels from the broadcasting room. He then called out the Flying Squad of the Federal Police. In the meantime police who approached over the roofs of the neighbouring buildings were fired at by the Nazis.

Finally it was found necessary to employ hand-grenades. After the explosion of the first, the police stormed the first courtyard but were driven back by fire from the broadcasting room, and were again obliged to use bombs. After the third explosion fire broke out in the broadcasting room, necessitating the intervention of the fire brigade. A number of the rebels fled in the meantime to the top floors, but at last surrendered to the police.

The Nazis displayed an intimate knowledge of all the strategical positions of defence in the building, and took full advantage of them. This may explain how fifteen men were able to hold the building through an hour and three-quarters of continuous fighting.

The ringleader of the Nazis was killed. On the side of the police the two superintendents, already mentioned, Fluch and Kaufmann, were killed, Schutzcorpsman Kauf was wounded in the thigh. The chauffeur of the Ravag was seriously wounded when the rebels entered the building, and died before the end of the fight. An actor, Herr Ferstl, completely lost his head, and, in a fit of madness, jumped into the worst of the firing and was instantly killed by a bullet.

Thirteen of the fifteen insurgents, all of whom belonged to the S. S. Standarte No. 89, were arrested. One Nazi was able to make his escape during the confusion owing to the difficulty of distinguishing between the rebels and radio employees or visitors to the building. The two policemen who had played an ambiguous part in the first assault on the building surrendered after the hand-grenade attack.

The subsequent investigations and the trial before the military court in Vienna on August 14th and 18th proved beyond doubt the connection between the attack on the Ravag Broadcasting Station and the other revolutionary events of the day.

213. SCHUSCHNIGG ON THE FIRST ANNIVERSARY OF DOLLFUSS' DEATH *(Extract)* [35]

The successor of Dollfuss as Austrian Chancellor was Kurt von Schuschnigg, who strove to continue his late friend's policies. Because he forcefully resisted Nazi activities and favored an early Habsburg restoration, he was regarded as a traitor by the Germans who, after the absorption of Austria into the Reich, placed him in confinement. The following paragraph from a memorial speech of July 1935 is revealing of his character.

[35] *The New Austria,* Österreichischer Bundesverlag, Vienna, 1937, p. 2.

The path we are following is clearly mapped out and unalterable. We are not seeking the via triumphalis, we are even prepared—if it has to be and Providence wills it—to travel some way up Mount Calvary. However, we shall always keep to the Dollfuss-road, of which we know that it leads us to social justice and social peace, to national Unity embodied in the solidarity of the Corporations in a free Austria.

214. THE FRANCO-GERMAN AGREEMENT ON THE CESSION OF THE FRENCH STATE'S RIGHTS OF OWNERSHIP OVER PROPERTY IN THE SAAR TERRITORY, FEBRUARY 18, 1935 (Extracts) [36]

The Treaty of Versailles placed responsibility for the government of the Saar Basin upon the League, but France was given full ownership of all coal mines and mining accessories. At the end of fifteen years, there was to be a plebiscite of all men and women over twenty who lived in the Saar at the time the treaty was signed, to assist the League in determining whether the territory should remain under League control, go to France, or be returned to Germany. In the last case, Germany would repurchase from France control of the mines, etc., at a price to be determined by a French, a German, and a neutral (League-appointed) expert. In 1934, by agreement, the plebiscite date was set on January 13, 1935. It was also provided that if the decision favored Germany, the latter would pay France a total of 900,-000,000 francs in settlement of all Saar claims. About ninety per cent of the votes cast favored the return of the Saar to Germany; a formal transfer accordingly took place on March 1, 1935. The following extracts relate to the property and ownership agreement entered into between France and Germany.

The French Government and the German Government,

In view of the provisions of paragraphs 36 and 38 of the Annex to Articles 45 to 50 of the Treaty of Versailles:

In view of Parts III and V of the Franco-German Agreement of Rome, dated December 3, 1934;

In view of the resolution of the Council of the League of Nations dated January 17, 1935:

Have agreed on the following provisions as regards the conditions of

[36] League of Nations, *Official Journal*, 1935, pp. 470-476.

France's cession to Germany of her rights of ownership over the mines, railways, and other immovable property situated in the Saar Territory.

· · · · ·

ARTICLE 2.

1. The property and rights transferred are enumerated in an inventory which has already been transmitted to the German Government and which will be regarded as annexed to the present agreement. The inventory is a list with a summary description enabling the installations to be identified; their nature, state or value may not be the subject of any dispute on questions of detail, nor may any aggregate estimate be made which would involve a settlement of accounts between the two parties. Any errors or omissions observed in the inventory or in the Land Register will form the subject of correction, to which the French State undertakes to lend its assistance as far as necessary, without thereby taking upon itself any pecuniary burden or any fresh obligation towards its successor or third parties. . . .

ARTICLE 3.

1. The taking-over of the mines is fixed for midnight on the night of February 28/March 1, 1935, when the responsibility for operation and the management and profits or charges thereof will pass to the German Reich.

2. The French State remains a creditor for the value of the products dispatched with waybills or similar documents (records of meters, &c.) before March 1, 1935, rents and leases relating to the period previous to March 1, 1935, compensation due for damage caused before that date at the mines, and various deliveries made by the mines.

3. On the other hand, the French State is a debtor for wages and salaries earned at that date, taxes, charges, rents, &c., relating to the previous period, the cost of equipment arriving before March 1, 1935, at its storehouses, damage caused, and, in particular, any surface damages noted, as laid down in the Agreement of December 3, 1934.

4. Legal disputes and, in particular, surface damages shall be dealt with by the agents of the French liquidation service working on the spot in co-operation with the German Mine Services.

5. The French Government and the German Government are, however, prepared to consider a lump-sum settlement based on the follow-

ing principles as soon as more accurate data regarding the matter are available:

(a) Damage caused to the railways, tramways, and roads to be estimated within the framework of the existing agreements by a commission consisting of four arbitrators, each party appointing two, and a Referee who shall be neither French nor German and who shall be appointed, in the absence of an agreement between the arbitrators, by the President of the Bank for International Settlements;

(b) The damage caused to property of other kinds (houses, &c.) and notified before March 1, 1935, to be divided by the Arbitration Commission between the French Administration and the German Administration in such a manner as to ensure the correct interpretation of the term "noted" appearing in the Agreement of December 3, 1934; payment for the damage thus charged to the French Administration to be estimated inclusively after a brief expert opinion has been given by the parties or by the Arbitration Commission;

(c) Outstanding lawsuits to be estimated under the same conditions.

The German Administration shall debit the French Administration with the lump sums thus fixed for these three categories of disputes and shall ensure their liquidation in lieu of the French Administration, which shall be relieved of all obligations.

ARTICLE 4.

1. The services of the French personnel shall terminate at midnight on the night of February 28/March 1, 1935. In order, however, to help the new owners to take over the services and to complete current transactions for which it assumes responsibility, such as the payment of wages on the due dates, &c., the Administration of the State mines shall retain the services of the necessary personnel and provide for their remuneration for a short period to be determined in each case.

2. The Administration of the State mines shall endeavour to release, within periods compatible with the service and with the position of its French personnel, the service dwellings occupied by the latter. In the present state of affairs, except for cases of *force majeure,* it proposes to release 250 dwellings for March 15, 1935, and 200 more for April 15, while, as regards the remainder, the French Administration will do all in its power to expedite their release and does not intend to retain any of the dwellings after April 30, 1935.

In order to ensure the proper execution of this plan, the German

Government will, for its part, take no steps to prevent French removal firms called into the Saar, after the local resources have been exhausted, from entering the territory and working there with their men.

3. The French personnel which have not yet left on April 1, 1935, shall be regarded, from the fiscal point of view, as already domiciled outside Germany. In general, the personnel remaining in the service dwellings after March 1, 1935, will continue to enjoy normal advantages in kind. The instruction given to the children of such personnel in the college and French school of Saarbruck will come to an end on April 1, 1935.

ARTICLE 5.

1. The allocation of the archives will take place in the following manner:

The French Mines Administration will transmit to the German Administration:

Archives previous to 1930 which are still in existence;

Files of the personnel remaining in service;

Files of surface damages;

Files of purchases, sales or leases of buildings;

Files of lawsuits which have been concluded;

Copies of current commercial contracts taken over by the German Administration, together with the commission notes, transport contracts, execution cards, order notes, tariffs, lists of customers and supplies.

On the other hand, the French Administration will retain the commercial accountancy documents and cash vouchers necessary, in accordance with the rules of French public accountancy, to furnish evidence of its administration, the documents relating to the personnel leaving the service of the Mines, and the files of legal disputes which it undertakes to liquidate.

2. The two Administrations shall send each other copies of the documents in the files which they retain, in so far as this is necessary for dealing with current matters or matters in course of liquidation.

ARTICLE 6.

1. On the conclusion of the operation referred to in Article 4, paragraph 1, a part of the French personnel not exceeding thirty persons shall remain on the spot as agents of the French liquidation service in order to deal with questions still remaining to be settled, and, in particular, the questions referred to in Article 3, paragraph 4. The German

Administration shall place at the disposal of these agents, for their work, suitable offices and means of transport, and shall give them the necessary facilities for studying and settling disputes. . . .

3. The activity of these agents shall come to an end either by the conclusion of the lump-sum settlement provided for in Article 3, paragraph 5, or, on the expiry of their work, by agreement between the two Administrations.

ARTICLE 7.

1. France transfers to Germany all her rights over the railways situated in the Saar.

2. All claims of the French State against the Reich in respect of the railways shall be deemed to be settled.

3. The transfer of rights shall take place at midnight on the night of February 28/March 1, 1935.

4. The provisions of the present article shall also apply to the settlement of the claims made by France in respect of the construction in the Saar of Customs stations on the old frontier between the Saar and the rest of Germany.

ARTICLE 12.

1. Receipts accruing as from March 1, 1935, shall be payable to Germany and, similarly, liabilities arising as from the same date shall be assumed by Germany. Unrecovered claims dating from before March 1, 1935, shall accrue to the Alsace-Lorraine Railways Administration, and, similarly, liabilities arising before March 1, 1935, shall devolve on the Alsace-Lorraine Railways Administration. . . .

ARTICLE 13.

The personnel of German nationality employed on the railway lines shall be taken over by the German Government. The French Government shall withdraw the personnel of French nationality. The payment of pensions to officials already in retirement, to disabled and injured workmen and to their surviving dependants, shall devolve on the State of which the beneficiary is a national on March 1, 1935. The French Government shall pay the German Government an amount equal to the payments made by German personnel to French pension funds and old age and invalidity insurance funds.

. . . . .

ARTICLE 17.

Details of the transfer and transitional arrangements shall be settled between the Railway Administrations concerned.

ARTICLE 18.

1. Referring to the provisions of Part V of the Agreement of December 3, 1934, the German Government declares that it is its intention to endeavour to cause the return to the Saar, for exchange into Reichsmarks under the conditions laid down in that Agreement, of the notes of the Bank of France and other foreign means of payment which may have been exported by Saar inhabitants in order to evade the exchange of currencies, to whatever use they may have been put and wherever the exchange value has been deposited.

2. The notes of the Bank of France and the other foreign means of payment recovered in this manner up to October 1, 1935, shall be paid to the Bank of France in order that they may be used in accordance with the terms of the above-mentioned Agreement.

3. The transactions connected with the return of currency may be carried out by transfer in order to simplify their material execution.

. . . . .

ARTICLE 36.

The present Agreement, approved this day by the League of Nations in accordance with the procedure provided for by the Council resolution of January 17, 1935, shall be ratified. The exchange of the instruments of ratification shall take place in Rome as early as possible. The Agreement shall enter into force on the day on which the instruments of ratification are exchanged. If, however, by February 27, the ratifications have been secured although the instruments thereof have not yet arrived in Rome, the Embassies of the two countries shall draw up a formal record of this fact and the Agreement shall enter into force on February 28.

In faith whereof the undersigned plenipotentiaries, duly authorized, have signed the present Agreement.

Done in duplicate at Naples, February 18, 1935.

卍 卍 卍

215. THE MUNICH AGREEMENT REGARDING CZECHOSLOVAKIA, SEPTEMBER 29, 1938 [37]

The danger that the German-Czechoslovak dispute over Sudetenland and other German portions of Czechoslovakia might lead to war, was removed through a "last-minute" conference among the premiers of Great Britain, France, Germany, and Italy. The resulting Munich Agreement kept the peace by according to Germany without war, though at a somewhat slower rate than had at first been demanded, virtually all the items that the Führer had asked for.

A. PERSONAL MESSAGE SENT BY THE PRIME MINISTER [NEVILLE CHAMBERLAIN] TO THE REICHSCHANCELLOR ON SEPTEMBER 28, 1938

After reading your letter I feel certain that you can get all essentials without war and without delay.

I am ready to come to Berlin myself at once to discuss arrangements for transfer with you and representatives of Czech Government, together with representatives of France and Italy if you desire.

I feel convinced we could reach agreement in a week. However much you distrust Prague Government's intentions, you cannot doubt power of British and French Governments to see that promises are carried out fairly and fully and forthwith. As you know I have stated publicly that we are prepared to undertake that they shall be so carried out.

I cannot believe that you will take responsibility of starting a world war which may end civilisation for the sake of a few days' delay in settling this long-standing problem.

B. AGREEMENT CONCLUDED AT MUNICH ON SEPTEMBER 29, 1938

Germany, the United Kingdom, France and Italy, taking into consideration the agreement, which has been already reached in principle for the cession to Germany of the Sudeten German territory, have agreed on the following terms and conditions governing the said cession and the measures consequent thereon, and by this agreement they each hold themselves responsible for the steps necessary to secure its fulfilment:—

---

[37] *Further Documents Respecting Czechoslovakia, Including the Agreement Concluded at Munich on September 29, 1938. Presented by the Secretary of State for Foreign Affairs to Parliament by Command of His Majesty,* Misc. No. 8 (1938), Cmd. 5848, His Majesty's Stationery Office, London, 1938, pp. 2, 3-6.

1. The evacuation will begin on the 1st October.

2. The United Kingdom, France and Italy agree that the evacuation of the territory shall be completed by the 10th October, without any existing installations having been destroyed and that the Czechoslovak Government will be held responsible for carrying out the evacuation without damage to the said installations.

3. The conditions governing the evacuation will be laid down in detail by an international commission composed of representatives of Germany, the United Kingdom, France, Italy and Czechoslovakia.

4. The occupation by stages of the predominantly German territory by German troops will begin on the 1st October. The four territories marked on the attached map will be occupied by German troops in the following order: the territory marked No. I on the 1st and 2nd of October, the territory marked No. II on the 2nd and 3rd of October, the territory marked No. III on the 3rd, 4th and 5th of October, the territory marked No. IV on the 6th and 7th of October. The remaining territory of preponderantly German character will be ascertained by the aforesaid international commission forthwith and be occupied by German troops by the 10th of October.

5. The international commission referred to in paragraph 3 will determine the territories in which a plebiscite is to be held. These territories will be occupied by international bodies until the plebiscite has been completed. The same commission will fix the conditions in which the plebiscite is to be held, taking as a basis the conditions of the Saar plebiscite. The commission will also fix a date, not later than the end of November, on which the plebiscite will be held.

6. The final determination of the frontiers will be carried out by the international commission. This commission will also be entitled to recommend to the four Powers, Germany, the United Kingdom, France and Italy, in certain exceptional cases minor modifications in the strictly ethnographical determination of the zones which are to be transferred without plebiscite.

7. There will be a right of option into and out of the transferred territories, the option to be exercised within six months from the date of this agreement. A German-Czechoslovak commission shall determine the details of the option, consider ways of facilitating the transfer of population and settle questions of principle arising out of the said transfer.

8. The Czechoslovak Government will within a period of four weeks

from the date of this agreement release from their military and police forces any Sudeten Germans who may wish to be released, and the Czechoslovak Government will within the same period release Sudeten German prisoners who are serving terms of imprisonment for political offences.

ADOLF HITLER.
NEVILLE CHAMBERLAIN.
ÉDOUARD DALADIER.
BENITO MUSSOLINI.

Munich,
September 29, 1938.

Annex to the Agreement.

His Majesty's Government in the United Kingdom and the French Government have entered into the above agreement on the basis that they stand by the offer, contained in paragraph 6 of the Anglo-French proposals of the 19th September [Cmd. 5847] relating to an international guarantee of the new boundaries of the Czechoslovak State against unprovoked aggression.

When the question of the Polish and Hungarian minorities in Czechoslovakia has been settled, Germany and Italy for their part will give a guarantee to Czechoslovakia.

ADOLF HITLER.
NEVILLE CHAMBERLAIN.
ÉDOUARD DALADIER.
BENITO MUSSOLINI.

Munich,
September 29, 1938.

Declaration.

The Heads of the Governments of the four Powers declare that the problems of the Polish and Hungarian minorities in Czechoslovakia, if not settled within three months by agreement between the respective Governments, shall form the subject of another meeting of the Heads of the Governments of the four Powers here present.

ADOLF HITLER.
NEVILLE CHAMBERLAIN.
ÉDOUARD DALADIER.
BENITO MUSSOLINI.

Munich,
September 29, 1938.

Supplementary Declaration.

All questions which may arise out of the transfer of the territory shall be considered as coming within the terms of reference to the international commission.

ADOLF HITLER.
NEVILLE CHAMBERLAIN.
ÉDOUARD DALADIER.
BENITO MUSSOLINI.

Munich,
September 29, 1938.

Composition of the International Commission.

The four Heads of Government here present agree that the international commission provided for in the agreement signed by them to-day, shall consist of the Secretary of State in the German Foreign Office, the British, French and Italian Ambassadors accredited in Berlin, and a representative to be nominated by the Government of Czechoslovakia.

ADOLF HITLER.
NEVILLE CHAMBERLAIN.
ÉDOUARD DALADIER.
BENITO MUSSOLINI.

Munich,
September 29, 1938.

216. THE CONCORDAT BETWEEN GERMANY AND THE HOLY SEE, JULY 20, 1933 *(Extracts)* [38]

When Adolf Hitler became chancellor in 1933 relations between German Catholics and the Vatican were governed by three separate concordats— with Prussia, Bavaria, and Baden. Since this situation was out of harmony with the general co-ordinating policies of the Nazis, Vice-Chancellor Franz von Papen was sent to Rome to negotiate a single concordat for all Germany. Such a document was signed on July 20, 1933.

His Holiness the Sovereign Pontiff Pius XI and the President of the German Reich, in their reciprocal desire to consolidate and develop the

---

[38] *Text of the Concordat between the Holy See and Germany,* National Catholic Welfare Conference News Service, Washington, 1933, pp. 1-6. (Mimeographed.) Reprinted by permission of the N.C.W.C.

amicable relations existing between the Holy See and the German Reich, and wishing to regulate the relations between the Catholic Church and the State throughout the territory of the German Reich in a manner that is stable and satisfactory for the two parties, have resolved to conclude a solemn convention which completes the Concordat concluded with individual German States and assures to the others a uniform treatment for the solution of questions to which it pertains. . . .

Article 1.

The German Reich guarantees the freedom of the profession and the public exercise of the Catholic Religion. It recognizes the right of the Catholic Church, within the limits of the general laws in force, to regulate and to administer freely her own affairs and to proclaim, in the field of her competence, laws and ordinances binding upon her members.

Article 2.

The Concordats concluded with Bavaria (1924), Prussia (1929) and Baden (1932) remain in force and the rights and liberties of the Catholic Church which they recognize remain unchanged in the territory of these respective States. For the other States the dispositions contained in the present Concordat are binding integrally. They are obligatory also for the said three States with respect to matters not regulated in their respective Concordats, or which complete the dispositions already established. In the future the conclusion of Concordats with individual States shall be effected only in accord with the Government of the Reich.

. . . . .

Article 4.

The Holy See shall enjoy the full liberty of communicating and corresponding with the bishops, the clergy and with all those who belong to the Catholic Church in Germany. The same shall be valid for the bishops and other diocesan authorities in their communications with the faithful with respect to everything pertaining to their pastoral ministry.

The instructions, ordinances, pastoral letters, official diocesan bulletins and all other acts regarding the spiritual government of the faithful and emanating from ecclesiastical authorities in the field of their competence shall be published freely and brought to the knowledge of the faithful in the forms used heretofore.

ARTICLE 5.

In the exercise of their sacerdotal activity, ecclesiastics shall enjoy the protection of the State in the same manner as the employes of the State. Offenses to their persons and to their quality as ecclesiastics, as well as interference in the exercise of their ministry, shall be punished under the terms of the general laws of the State, and protection on the part of the civil authorities when necessary is guaranteed.

ARTICLE 9.

Ecclesiastics shall not be required by magistrates or other authorities to give information on things or affairs which have been entrusted to them in the exercise of the care of souls and which for that reason fall under the secrecy of their spiritual office.

ARTICLE 14.

The Catholic Church, in principle, has the right to confer freely all the ecclesiastical offices and benefices, without the assistance of the State or the municipality, with the exception of the cases provided for in the accords established in the Concordats to which reference is made in Article 2. . . .

In addition, there shall be agreement on the following points:

1. Catholic priests who fill, in Germany, an ecclesiastical charge or who exercise an activity in the care of souls or in education must:

(a) Be German citizens;

(b) Have obtained a diploma which entitles them to attend a German higher institution of learning;

(c) Have at least finished three years of philosophical and theological studies either in a German university of the State or in a German ecclesiastical academy, or in a Pontifical university of Rome.

2. Before releasing Bulls of nomination of archbishops, bishops or coadjutors *cum jure successionis,* or any *praelatus nullius,* the name of the person chosen shall be made known to the Reichsstathalter of the respective State so as to assure that there are no objections to him of a general political character. . . .

ARTICLE 16.

The bishops, before taking possession of their dioceses, shall place in the hands of the Reichsstathalter of the particular State, or else into the hands of the President of the Reich, an oath of allegiance according to the following formula: "Before God and on the Holy Gospels, I swear and promise, as is proper to a bishop, allegiance to the German Reich and to the State of. . . . I swear and promise to respect and cause to be respected by my clergy the Government established according to the constitutional laws of the State. Concerning myself, in dutiful solicitude for the welfare and interest of the German State, I will try, in the exercise of the holy ministry entrusted to me, to ward off all harm that might threaten it."

. . . . . .

ARTICLE 19.

The Faculties of Catholic Theology in the Universities of the State shall be preserved. . . .

ARTICLE 20.

Except for other accords in force, the Church has the right to erect, for the training of the clergy, schools of philosophy and theology which depend exclusively on ecclesiastical authority, provided no State subsidy is claimed.

The erection, the direction and management of seminaries and ecclesiastical boarding schools shall be the concern of the ecclesiastical authorities alone, within the limits of the general laws in force.

ARTICLE 21.

The teaching of the Catholic religion in the elementary, vocational, secondary and superior schools shall be a regular subject and shall be given in conformity with the principles of the Catholic Church. . . .

ARTICLE 22.

The designation of teachers of religion shall be governed by mutual agreement between the Bishops and the Government of the particular State.

Teachers whom the Bishops shall have declared, because of their beliefs or moral conduct, to be unsuitable for giving religious instruction shall not be employed for this instruction so long as the obstacle remains.

ARTICLE 23.

The preservation and new erection of Catholic confessional schools shall remain guaranteed. In all the communities where parents, or those who hold the place of parents, propose it, elementary Catholic schools shall be conducted if it shall appear that, taking into account the number of pupils and the local conditions of school organization, it is possible to operate the school according to the terms of the regulations of the State.

. . . . . .

ARTICLE 27.

To the German Army shall be conceded special services for Catholic officers, functionaries and soldiers belonging to the Army and their respective families.

The direction of the spiritual assistance to the Army belongs to the Military Bishop. His ecclesiastical nomination shall be made by the Holy See, after the latter has been in communication with the Government of the Reich in order to name a suitable person. . . .

. . . . .

ARTICLE 29.

Catholics resident in the German Reich and belonging to non-German ethnical minorities, in everything that concerns the use of their mother tongue in services, in religious instruction and in ecclesiastical associations shall have a treatment no less favorable than that which corresponds to the legal and factual status of citizens who originally were German-speaking, within the territory of the corresponding foreign State.

. . . . . .

ARTICLE 31.

Catholic organizations and associations which have exclusively religious, cultural and charitable aims, and which as such depend upon ecclesiastical authority, shall be protected in their institutions and in their activity. . . .

Wherever youth organizations—for sports or other purposes—exist and are supported by the Reich or the particular State, care shall be taken to make it possible for members to fulfill their religious duties on Sundays and Holy Days and to remove any obligation to do anything incompatible with their convictions and with their religious or moral duties.

Article 32.

By reason of the present particular circumstances of Germany and in consideration of the guaranties created by the dispositions of the present Concordat, legislation which safeguards the rights and liberties of the Catholic Church in the Reich and in the States, the Holy See shall enact dispositions excluding ecclesiastics and religious from membership in political parties and from activity in this respect.

· · · · ·

Article 34.

The present Concordat, the German and Italian texts of which shall have equal force, shall be ratified and the instruments of the ratifications shall be exchanged as soon as possible. It shall enter into effect the day of the exchange of the said instruments.

· · · · ·

FINAL PROTOCOL

At the moment of proceeding to the signing of the Concordat today concluded between the Holy See and the German Reich, the undersigned, duly authorized plenipotentiaries, have reached an agreement on the following points which shall be an integral part of the said Concordat.

To Article 3.

The Apostolic Nuncio to the German Reich is, in conformity with the notes exchanged between the Apostolic Nunciature at Berlin and the Minister of Foreign Affairs, under date of March 11 and 27, 1930, the dean of the diplomatic corps accredited there.

· · · · ·

To Article 29.

The Government of the Reich having shown its readiness to accept this favorable disposition for the non-German minorities, the Holy See declares that, in confirmation of the principles always defended concerning the right to the mother tongue in the ministry of souls, in religious instruction and in the life of Catholic organizations, on the occasion of the concluding of future concordatory conventions with other states, it will endeavor to have inserted a like disposition for the protection of the rights of German minorities.

. . . . .

To Article 32.

It is understood that the Government of the Reich shall take like dispositions concerning political activity in parties with respect to non-Catholic confessions.

The obligation imposed on German priests and religious, under the execution of Article 32, does not signify a limitation of any sort upon public teaching and explaining (which is their duty) of dogmatic and moral doctrine and of principles of the Church.

At Vatican City, on July 20, 1933.

(*Signed*) Eugenio Cardinal Pacelli.
Franz von Papen.

217. THE POPE ON THE CONDITION OF THE CHURCH IN GERMANY, 1937 *(Extracts)* [39]

Not long after the signing of the concordat between Vatican City and Berlin, friction developed over the question of its interpretation. The Reich accused the Catholic clergy and lay brothers of mixing in politics and violating the currency laws, and the Church accused the Nazis of violating its rights with respect to education and objected to the sterilization law (See Document No. 198) and the attacks on the Old Testament. In 1937 Pope Pius XI was moved by the course of events to issue a special encyclical dealing with the condition of the Catholic Church in Germany.

1. With deep anxiety and increasing dismay, We have for some time past beheld the sufferings of the Church, and the steadily growing oppression of those men and women who, loyally professing their faith in thought and deed, have remained true to her amidst the people of

[39] *Encyclical Letter of His Holiness, Pope Pius XI (Vatican Press Translation), Issued March 14, 1937,* National Catholic Welfare Conference, Washington, 1937, pp. 1-35. Reprinted by permission of the N.C.W.C.

that land to which St. Boniface once brought the light and glad tidings of Christ and the Kingdom of God.

. . . . .

3. In the summer of 1933, Venerable Brethren [the archbishops and bishops of Germany], We accepted the offer made by the Government of the Reich to institute negotiations for a Concordat in connection with a proposal of the previous year, and to the satisfaction of you all brought them to a conclusion with a solemn agreement. In this We were guided by the solicitude incumbent upon Us to safeguard the freedom of the Church in the exercise of her apostolic ministry in Germany and the salvation of the souls entrusted to her, and at the same time by the sincere wish of rendering an essential service to the progress and prosperity of the German people.

5. If the tree of peace which We planted with pure intention in German soil has not borne the fruit We desired in the interests of your people, no one in the wide world who has eyes to see and ears to hear can say today that the fault lies with the Church and her Head. The lessons of the past year make it clear where the responsibility lies. They disclose machinations that from the beginning had no other aim than a war of extermination. In the furrows where We labored to plant the seeds of sincere peace, others were sowing—like the enemy in Holy Scripture—the tares of distrust, of discord, hatred, calumny, of secret and open enmity against Christ and His Church, an enmity in principle, fed from a thousand springs and working with every means at its disposal. With them and only with them, as well as with their open and silent supporters, lies the responsibility that now, instead of the rainbow of peace, the storm-clouds of destructive religious conflicts are visible on the German horizon.

6. We have not tired, Venerable Brethren, of portraying to the responsible guides of the destinies of your country the consequences that necessarily follow if such trends are left unhindered and much more if they are viewed with favor. . . . Everyone in whose mind there is left the least perception of truth, in whose heart there is a trace of feeling for justice, will then have to admit that in these grievous and eventful years after the signing of the Concordat, in every word and in every action of Ours, We have stood faithful to the terms of the agree-

ment. But with amazement and deep aversion he will be obliged to admit that to change the meaning of the agreement, to empty the agreement of all its significance, and finally more or less openly to violate the agreement, has been made the unwritten law of conduct by the other party.

7. The moderation We have shown in spite of everything was neither dictated by considerations of human expediency nor motivated by unseemly weakness, but simply by the desire that We might not perchance tear up valuable wheat with the tares; . . . Even today, when the open campaign waged against the denominational school guaranteed by the Concordat, when the nullification of the freedom of the vote for Catholics who should have the right to decide in the matter of education, shows the dreadful seriousness of the situation in a most important field of the Church's life and the unparalleled torment of conscience of believing Christians, Our pastoral care for the salvation of souls counsels Us not to leave unheeded even the slight prospects of return to a loyal adherence to a responsible agreement. In compliance with the prayers of the Most Reverend Episcopate, We shall not weary in the future also of pleading the cause of outraged right with the rulers of your people. . . .

. . . . . .

9. Take care, Venerable Brethren, that first of all belief in God, the primary and irreplaceable foundation of all religion, be preserved true and unadulterated in German lands. He is not a believer in God who uses the word of God rhetorically but he who associates with the sacred word the true and worthy idea of God.

. . . . .

11. He who replaces a personal God with a weird impersonal Fate supposedly according to ancient pre-Christian German concepts denies the wisdom and providence of God, that "reacheth from end to end mightily and ordereth all things sweetly" and directs everything for the best. Such a one cannot claim to be numbered among those who believe in God.

12. He who takes the race, or the people, or the State, or the form of Government, the bearers of the power of the State or other fundamental elements of human society—which in the temporal order of things have an essential and honorable place—out of the system of their

earthly valuation, and makes them the ultimate norm of all, even of religious, values, and deifies them with an idolatrous worship, perverts and falsifies the order of things created and commanded by God. . . .

. . . . .

14. This God has given His commandments in His capacity as Sovereign. They apply regardless of time and space, country or race. As God's sun shines on all that bear human countenance, so does His law know no privileges or exceptions. The rulers and the ruled, crowned and uncrowned, high and low, rich and poor, all alike are subject to His law. . . . Only superficial minds can lapse into the heresy of speaking of a national God, of a national religion; only such can make the mad attempt of trying to confine within the boundaries of a single people, within the narrow blood stream of a single race, God the Creator of the world, the King and Lawgiver of all peoples before whose greatness all peoples are small as a drop of a bucket.

. . . . .

16. We thank you, Venerable Brethren, your priests and all the faithful, who have done and continue to do their duty in defending the sovereign rights of God against the aggressive neo-paganism that unfortunately in many instances is favored in influential quarters. Our thanks are doubly sincere and coupled with admiration and approval of those who in the exercise of their duty were found worthy of making earthly sacrifices for God's sake and of enduring earthly suffering.

. . . . .

18. . . . The sacred books of the Old Testament are all God's Word, an organic part of His revelation. . . . As is inevitable in the case of books of history and law, they are the reflections in many particulars of human imperfection, weakness and sin. Side by side with infinitely much that is high and noble, they relate the dissipation and worldliness that occurred time and again among the covenanted people who bore the revelation and promise of God.

19. . . . Only blindness and pride can close their eyes to the treasures of instruction for salvation, that are in the Old Testament. He who wants to see Biblical history and the wisdom of the Old Testament banished from the Church and school, blasphemes the Word of God, blasphemes the Almighty's plan of salvation, makes the narrow and

limited mind of man judge over the divine plan of history. He denies belief in the real Christ, Who appeared in the flesh, Who took his human nature from that people which was to nail Him to the cross. He stands uncomprehendingly before the world-drama of the Son of God Who opposed to the felony of his crucifiers the Divine high-priestly action of the Redeemer's death and thus brought the Old Testament to its fulfilment and completion in the New, by which it is superseded.

20. The climax of revelation reached in the Gospel of Jesus Christ is definite, is obligatory for ever. This revelation knows no addition from the hand of man, above all, knows no substitution and no replacement by arbitrary "revelations" that certain speakers of the present day wish to derive from the myth of blood and race. . . .

23. . . . When zeal for reform did not spring from the pure source of personal singleness of heart, but was the expression and outbreak of passionate frenzy, it caused confusion instead of bringing light, tore down instead of building up; and not seldom was the point of departure for errors more disastrous than were the evils that it was the intention or the pretended intention to correct. . . .

24. In your districts, Venerable Brethren, voices are raised in ever louder chorus urging men on to leave the Church. Among the spokesmen there are many who, by reason of their official position, seek to create the impression that leaving the Church, and the disloyalty to Christ the King which it entails, is a particularly convincing and meritorious form of profession of loyalty to the present State. With cloaked and with manifest methods of coercion, by intimidation, by holding out the prospect of economic, professional, civic and other advantages, the loyalty of Catholics and especially of certain classes of Catholic officials to their faith is put under a pressure that is as unlawful as it is unworthy of human beings. All our fatherly sympathy and deepest condolence We offer to those who pay so high a price for their fidelity to Christ and the Church. . . .

27. Revelation, in the Christian sense, is the word of God to man. To use the same word for the "whispered inspirations" of blood and race, for the manifestations of the history of a people, is confusing

in any case. Such false coinage does not deserve to be received into
the vocabulary of a believing Christian.

. . . . .

29. Immortality in the Christian sense is the continuance of the life
of a man after temporal death, as a personal individual, to be rewarded
or punished eternally. To designate with the word immortality the
collective continued enjoyment of life in association with the continued existence of one's people on earth for an undetermined length
of time in the future, is to pervert and falsify one of the principal truths
of the Christian faith and strike at the foundations of every religious
philosophy that demands a moral ordering of the world. If they do
not want to be Christians, at least they should forego enriching the
vocabulary of their unbelief from the Christian treasure of ideas.

. . . . . .

33. . . . Grace in the proper and Christian sense of the word embraces . . . the supernatural manifestations of divine love, the loving
kindness and working of God, whereby He raises men to that inward
participation of life with Himself, that is called in the New Testament
sonship of God. . . . The repudiation of this supernatural elevation
of grace on account of the supposedly peculiar German type of being,
is an error and an open challenge to a fundamental truth of Christianity. . . .

37. Conscientious parents, aware of their duty in the matter of
education, have a primary and original right to determine the education
of the children given to them by God in the spirit of the true faith and
in agreement with its principles and ordinances. Laws or other regulations concerning schools that disregard the rights of parents guaranteed
to them by the natural law, or by threat and violence nullify those
rights, contradict the natural law and are utterly and essentially immoral.

38. The Church, the guardian and exponent of the divine natural
law, cannot do otherwise than declare that the registrations which have
just taken place in circumstances of notorious coercion are the result
of violence and void of all legality.

42. No one has intention of obstructing the youth of Germany on the road that is meant to bring them to the realization of true popular union, to the fostering of the love of freedom, to steadfast loyalty to the fatherland. What We do object to, and what We must object to, is the intentionally and systematically fomented opposition which is set up between these educational purposes and those of religion. Therefore we call out to youth: Sing your songs of freedom, but do not forget the freedom of the sons of God while singing them. . . . He who sings the song of loyalty to his earthly country must not, in disloyalty to God, to his church, to his eternal country, become a deserter and a traitor. You are told a great deal about heroic greatness, in designed and false contrast to the humility and patience of the Gospel. Why is silence kept about the heroism of moral struggle? Why is it not told you that the preservation of baptismal innocence represents an heroic action which should be assured of the appreciation it deserves in the religious and moral sphere? . . . You are told a great deal of the exercises of sport. Undertaken with discretion, the cult of physical fitness is a benefit for youth. But now so much time is devoted to it, in many cases, that no account is taken of the harmonious development of mind and body, of what is due to family life, of the commandment to keep holy the Lord's day. With a disregard bordering on indifference, the sacredness and peace that are in the best tradition of the German Sunday are taken from it. With confidence We expect from Catholic youth that, in the difficult circumstances of obligatory State organization, they will insist unflinchingly on their right to keep Sunday in a Christian manner, that in the cult of physical fitness they will not forget the interests of their immortal souls; . . .

43. We address a special word of recognition, encouragement and exhortation to the priests of Germany, on whom, in subordination to their Bishops, there rests the task of showing the flock of Christ in a trying time and under difficult circumstances, the right paths, by precept and example, by daily sacrifice and apostolic patience. . . . The trials and sorrows through which your people have passed since the war have left their mark on its soul. They have left behind conflicts and bitterness that can be healed only slowly, that can be overcome only in the spirit of unselfish and active charity. . . . This comprehending and merciful charity towards the erring, and even towards the contemptuous, does not mean and cannot mean, that you renounce in any way the proclaiming of, the insisting on, and the courageous defense

of the truth and its free and unhindered application to the realities about you. . . .

. . . . .

51. He Who searches the heart and reins is Our witness, that We have no more heartfelt wish than the restoration of a true peace between Church and State in Germany. But if, through no fault of Ours, there shall not be peace, the Church of God will defend her rights and liberty in the Name of the Almighty, Whose arm even today is not shortened. . . .

. . . . .

Given at the Vatican, on Passion Sunday, March 14th, 1937.

Pius PP. XI.

218. THE COLONIAL QUESTION IN A HITLER-YOUTH HANDBOOK [40]

As a matter of general interest there is quoted below a discussion of the colonial question translated by Professor Harwood L. Childs from a Handbook for Schooling the Hitler Youth *published by the Central Publishing House of the National Socialist Party. The account is not altogether accurate.*

The German colonies likewise are to be looked upon as spheres of German cultural influence. They experienced their first development under German administration, were opened up and explored by Germans, and have thereby received a German imprint.

The German Reich began to acquire colonies very late. There are two reasons for this. In the first place the Spanish Hapsburgs sat on the throne of Germany at the time of great colonial expansion. They not only set for themselves the task of conquering a world empire "in which the sun never set" but they also wished to establish Catholicism as the sole religion in this world empire. The task of acquiring the world empire itself was assigned to the Spanish motherland, while the Germans were supposed to fight to win Europe back to Catholicism. And so the German Reich was entangled in bloody, religious wars, while Spain, Portugal, England and France won for themselves an enor-

---

[40] H. L. Childs, tr., *The Nazi Primer*, Harper and Brothers, New York, 1938, pp. 163-171. Reprinted by permission of the publishers.

mous colonial empire. As a result of this division of labor the German Reich got the raw end of the deal. Another reason is to be found in the fact that the German Reich first, during the second half of the last century, attained that cohesive unity which is necessary for a successful colonizing enterprise. All attempts, therefore, undertaken before this time were destined to fail.

In the year 1528 the Welser had acquired the land of Venezuela as a family fief from Emperor Charles V. They tried to build it up as a German colony. Nevertheless this attempt had to be given up by 1555 after the German leader had been murdered.

Later the Great Elector attempted once again to set foot in Africa. In 1683 he conquered the territory along the Gold Coast and in 1687 along the Cape of Arguin. But the attempt to establish permanent colonies here did not succeed this time either. Although the natives remained true to Brandenburg the African occupation had to be given up again in 1718.

It was the united German Reich under its great Chancellor Bismarck which finally succeeded in actually acquiring colonial possessions. Although the so called representatives of the people at that time even opposed the possession of colonies, Bismarck finally brought about the acquisition of colonies, bearing in mind the colonial urge of our people. How greatly the German people longed for colonial activity is shown by the fact that all our colonies were originally private business undertakings of German trading companies.

In this way the Bremen merchant, Adolf Lüderitz, by treaty with the ruling house of the Hottentots acquired in 1883 the Bight of Angra, which is called Lüderitz-Bight after him today. In the following year he purchased additional stretches of land along the coast, about 150 kilometers in width, from the Orange River up as far as the Hottentot Bay. On April 24, 1884 Bismarck placed the territory under the protection of the German Reich. The first German colony was thereby established. Further treaties with the natives enlarged the colony to its present size. In January 1904 the Herero uprising broke out and in the fall of the same year the Hottentots revolted. At the end of 1906 peace was reestablished. Following this satisfactory state of affairs German South-West Africa quickly blossomed forth. Great irrigation projects, ranches, mines and flourishing little towns spread out over all the land. Before the War 13,500 Germans lived in German South-West Africa, which is twice the size of the Reich.

In July 1884 the well known German African explorer, Dr. Nachtigal, was commissioned to raise the German flag in Togoland and the Cameroons. After considerable trouble with England Bismarck forced the London Colonial Conference in August 1884 to recognize the three aforementioned African colonies. As a result of colonial negotiations with France the Cameroons were enlarged in 1911 to their present dimensions.

German East Africa goes back to the pioneer work of Dr. Karl Peters, a true son of Lower Saxony. At 27 years of age he went to East Africa and by treaties with the chief tribes acquired, in 1884, four large tracts of land. The German East African Company which he founded received an imperial letter of protection from Bismarck on February 27, 1885. Some years later there followed the final determination of the boundaries of German East Africa through the German-English agreement of April 1, 1890. All the land between the Indian Ocean and the three great internal seas of Africa, the Victoria, Tanganjika and the Niassa Sea, was recognized as a German protectorate. The former rulers of this land, the Arabs, staged a bloody uprising in 1888 which was put down by Hermann Wissmann. In 1905 an uprising of the negroes in the hinterland of Kilwa broke out, which was quickly suppressed however. Climatic conditions in German East Africa are favorable and permit Europeans to settle there. Soon large plantations sprang up from which coffee, hemp, cotton, oil seeds, and spices were harvested. Before the War 4701 Germans lived in East Africa.

The German South Sea possessions were acquired during these same decades. Adolf von Hausemann had extensive interests in New Guinea and brought about the acquisition of this territory by the German Reich in 1884. The acquisition of Karolina, Mariana, Palau Island and Samoa followed in 1899.

The German colonies were built up by great sacrifices on the part of the Reich. After profiting from the first experiences the colonies blossomed forth mightily and soon demonstrated that they were profitable. Their soil was not only moistened with the sweat of German planters and laborers, but watered with the blood of German soldiers. In spite of that the German people were denied the right to colonies at Versailles. The lie regarding colonies, which is refuted by the German successes and by the natives themselves, was intended merely to veil and to excuse the robbery. German East Africa fell to England; German South-West Africa to the Union of South Africa. France received the Cameroons and Togoland was divided up between England and France. New Guinea was given to the Federation of Australia and the remaining South Sea possessions were assigned to Japan. To be sure these countries received only the power of "Mandatories" over the colonies, so that legally the possibility exists of restoring them to the owner. The German Reich will at all events never cease to demand the restoration of its colonies.

CHAPTER 10

THE SOVIET UNION

219. ORDER NO. 1 OF THE PETROGRAD SOVIET, MARCH 14, 1917 [1]

One of the important elements in the weakening of the military resistance of Russia to the Central Powers was "Order Number One" of the Petrograd Soviet (Council) of Workers' and Soldiers' Deputies which had invited all factory and army units to send delegates to its meetings. Observance of the order meant disregard of essential military discipline.

ORDER NUMBER ONE

March 1 (14), 1917.

To the garrison of the Petrograd District. To all the soldiers of the Guard, army, artillery and fleet for immediate and precise execution, and to the workers of Petrograd for information.

The Soviet of Workers' and Soldiers' Deputies has decided:

1. In all companies, battalions, regiments, depots, batteries, squadrons and separate branches of military service of every kind and on warships immediately choose committees from the elected representatives of the soldiers and sailors of the above mentioned military units.

2. In all military units which have still not elected their representatives in the Soviet of Workers' Deputies elect one representative to a company, who should appear with written credentials in the building of the State Duma at ten o'clock on the morning of March 2.

3. In all its political demonstrations a military unit is subordinated to the Soviet of Workers' and Soldiers' Deputies and its committees.

4. The orders of the military commission of the State Duma are to be fulfilled only in those cases which do not contradict the orders and decisions of the Soviet of Workers' and Soldiers' Deputies.

---

[1] Translated from *Revolutsia 1917 goda. Khronika sobytii (The Revolution of 1917. Chronicle of Events)*, 6 vols., Moscow, 1923-1930, vol. I, pp. 186-187, in W. H. Chamberlin, *The Russian Revolution 1917-1921*, 2 vols., New York, 1935, vol. I, pp. 429-430. Reprinted by permission of The Macmillan Company, publishers.

5. Arms of all kinds, as rifles, machine-guns, armored automobiles and others must be at the disposition and under the control of the company and battalion committees and are not in any case to be given out to officers, even upon their command.

6. In the ranks and in fulfilling service duties soldiers must observe the strictest military discipline; but outside of service, in their political, civil and private life soldiers cannot be discriminated against as regards those rights which all citizens enjoy.

Standing at attention and compulsory saluting outside of service are especially abolished.

7. In the same way the addressing of officers with titles: Your Excellency, Your Honor, etc., is abolished and is replaced by the forms of address: Mr. General, Mr. Colonel, etc.

Rude treatment of soldiers of all ranks, and especially addressing them as "thou," is forbidden; and soldiers are bound to bring to the attention of the company committees any violation of this rule and any misunderstandings between officers and soldiers.

This order is to be read in all companies, battalions, regiments, marine units, batteries and other front and rear military units.

PETROGRAD SOVIET OF WORKERS' AND SOLDIERS' DEPUTIES.

220. LENIN ON THE NEED FOR AN ARMED UPRISING, OCTOBER 21, 1917 [2]

Shortly before the actual Bolshevik coup d'état occurred, Vladimir Ilyich Ulyanov, alias Lenin, exhorted his followers by letter to realize the need for an armed uprising, which he called a "special" kind of political struggle.

ADVICE FROM AN OUTSIDER [3]

I am writing these lines on October 21, and I have little hope that they will be in the hands of the Petrograd comrades before the 22nd. It is possible that they will arrive too late, for the Congress of the Northern

---

[2] V. I. Lenin, *Collected Works* XXI: *Toward the Seizure of Power*, Bk. II, International Publishers, New York, 1932, pp. 97-99. Reprinted by permission of the publishers.

[3] Being forced to live in hiding, and unable to be personally present at the Bolshevik meetings and conferences, Lenin had to depend on correspondence as the means of contact with the Central Committee.—*Ed.* [This footnote was written by the editor of the Lenin volume, namely, Alexander Trachtenberg.]

Soviets has been fixed for October 23. However, I shall try to give my "advice from an outsider," in case the anticipated action of the workers and soldiers of Petrograd and vicinity will take place soon, but has not yet taken place.

That all power must pass to the Soviets is clear. It must also be beyond dispute for every Bolshevik that the revolutionary-proletarian (or Bolshevik, which is now the same thing) power is guaranteed the greatest sympathy and the most loyal support of all the toilers and exploited of all the world in general, in the belligerent countries in particular, and above all among the Russian peasantry. It is not worth while to dwell on these truths that are too well known and have long since been proven.

We must dwell on that which is not quite clear to all the workers, namely, that the passing of power to the Soviets means at present in reality an armed uprising. This would seem self-evident, but not every one has been and is giving earnest thought to this. To renounce an armed uprising at present would mean to renounce the chief slogan of Bolshevism ("All Power to the Soviets") and all revolutionary-proletarian internationalism generally.

Armed uprising, however, is a *special* kind of political struggle, subject to special laws, to which we must give our serious attention. Karl Marx expressed this truth in a remarkably striking manner when he wrote that the armed *"uprising, like war, is an art."*

As the chief rules applicable to this art Marx advanced the following:

1. Never *play* at uprising, but once it is begun, remember firmly that you have to *go to the very end*.

2. It is necessary to gather *a great preponderance of forces* in a decisive place at a decisive moment, else the enemy, being in a position of better preparation and organisation, will annihilate the insurgents.

3. Once the uprising has been begun, one must act with the greatest decisiveness, one must take the offensive, absolutely, and under all circumstances. "Defence is the death of an armed uprising."

4. One must strive to take the enemy by surprise, to take advantage of a moment when his troops are scattered.

5. One must try *daily* for at least small successes (one may even say hourly, when it is a question of one city), thus maintaining under all circumstances a *"moral superiority."*

Marx summarised the lessons of all revolutions concerning the armed uprising in the words of the greatest master of revolutionary tactics in history, Danton: "Audacity, more audacity, and still more audacity."

Applied to Russia and to October, 1917, this means a simultaneous offensive, as sudden and swift as possible, on Petrograd, by all means, from inside *and* from outside, from the workers' section *and* from Finland, Reval, and Cronstadt, an offensive by the *whole* fleet, the accumulation of a *gigantic preponderance of forces* over the fifteen to twenty thousand (perhaps even more) of our "bourgeois guard" (military cadets), our "Vendée troops" (a part of the Cossacks), etc.

Combine our three main forces: the fleet, the workers, and the army units, so as surely to occupy and hold, *no matter what the cost:* (a) the telephone exchange; (b) the main telegraph office; (c) the railroad stations; and above all (d) the bridges.

Pick the most resolute elements (our "shock" elements and the *young workers;* and also the best sailors) into small detachments, to occupy all the most important points, and to *participate* everywhere, in all the important operations, for instance:

Surrounding Petrograd and cutting it off, taking it by a combined attack by the fleet, the workers, and the army—this is a task which demands *art* and *triple daring.*

Forming detachments from the best workers with rifles and bombs, to advance and surround the "centres of the enemy" (the military schools, and telegraph and telephone centres, etc.); their watchword must be: *Let all die, but do not allow the enemy to pass.*

Let us hope that in case the action is decided upon the leaders will successfully apply the great teachings of Danton and Marx.

The success of both the Russian and the world revolution depends upon two or three days of struggle.

AN OUTSIDER.

Written October 21, 1917.
First published in Pravda, *No. 250, November 7, 1920.*

221. THE SOVIET DECREE ON PEACE, NOVEMBER 8, 1917 [4]

On November 8, 1917, the day following their seizure of power, the Bolshevik leaders proposed an immediate general peace "without annexations and without indemnities" and on a basis of self-determination for all peoples. The Allies, however, apparently expecting that the Russian people

[4] Translated from the *Collection of Legislative Acts*, No. 1, Article 2, in W. H. Chamberlin, *The Russian Revolution 1917-1921*, 2 vols., New York, 1935, vol. I, pp. 472-474. Reprinted by permission of The Macmillan Company, publishers.

would repudiate the Bolshevik Revolution, paid no heed and, in fact, refused
to recognize the Soviet Government. Thereupon, on December 15, 1917,
the latter concluded a separate armistice with the Central Powers.

The Workers' and Peasants' Government, created by the Revolution
of October 24-25 (November 6-7) and supported by the Soviets of
Workers', Soldiers' and Peasants' Deputies, proposes to all combatant
peoples and to their governments to begin immediate negotiations for
an honest democratic peace.

The Government regards as an honest or democratic peace, which is
yearned for by the overwhelming majority of the workers and the
toiling classes of all the fighting countries, who are exhausted, tormented
and tortured by the War, which the Russian workers and peasants
demanded most definitely and insistently after the overthrow of the
Tsarist monarchy,—an immediate peace without annexations (*i.e.*,
without the seizure of foreign land, without the forcible taking over
of foreign nationalities) and without contributions.

Such a peace the Government of Russia proposes to all the fighting
peoples to conclude immediately, expressing its readiness to take without the least delay immediately all the decisive steps, up to the final
confirmation of all the conditions of such a peace by the authorized
assemblies of peoples' representatives of all countries and all nations.

As annexation or seizure of alien lands the Government under-
stands, in conformity with the conception of justice, of democracy in
general and of the toiling classes in particular, any addition to a large
or strong state of a small or weak nationality, without the precisely,
clearly and voluntarily expressed agreement and desire of this nationality, irrespective of when this forcible annexation took place, and also
irrespective of how advanced or how backward is the nation which is
violently annexed or violently held within the frontiers of another state.
Irrespective, finally, of whether this nation lives in Europe or in far-
away transoceanic countries.

If any nation is kept within the frontiers of another state by violence,
if it is not granted the right, despite its expressed desire,—regardless
of whether this desire is expressed in the press, in people's meetings, in
the decisions of parties or in riots and uprisings against national oppression,—to vote freely, with the troops of the annexationist or stronger
nation withdrawn, to decide without the least compulsion the question

of the form of its state existence, then the holding of such a nation is annexation, *i.e.,* seizure and violence.

To continue this war in order to decide how to divide between strong and rich nations the weak nationalities which they have seized, the Government considers the greatest crime against humanity; and it solemnly avows its decision immediately to sign conditions of peace which will stop this War on the terms which have been outlined, equally just for all nationalities, without exception.

Along with this the Government states that it does not regard the above mentioned conditions of peace as ultimative, *i.e.,* it is willing to consider any other conditions of peace, insisting only that these be presented as quickly as possible by one of the fighting countries, and on the fullest clarity, on the absolute exclusion of any ambiguity and secrecy in proposing conditions of peace.

The Government abolishes secret diplomacy, announcing its firm intention to carry on all negotiations quite openly before the whole people, proceeding immediately to the full publication of the secret treaties, ratified or concluded by the Government of landlords and capitalists betweeen February and October 25, 1917. All the contents of these secret treaties, inasmuch as they are directed, as usually happened, toward the obtaining of advantages and privileges for Russian landlords and capitalists, toward the maintenance or the increase of Great Russian annexations, the Government declares unconditionally and immediately annulled.

Turning with its proposal to the Governments and peoples of all countries to begin immediately open negotiations for the conclusion of peace, the Government expresses its readiness to carry on these negotiations by means of written communications, by telegraph, by means of negotiations between representatives of different countries or at a conference of such representatives. To facilitate such negotiations the Government will nominate its plenipotentiary representative in neutral countries.

The Government proposes to all Governments and peoples of all combatant countries immediately to conclude an armistice, considering it desirable that this armistice should be concluded for a period of not less than three months, in the course of which time it would be quite possible both to complete negotiations for peace with the participation of representatives of all nationalities or nations which have been drawn into the War or have been forced to participate in it and to convoke authoritative assemblies of peoples' representatives of all countries for the final confirmation of the peace conditions.

Turning with these proposals of peace to the Governments and the peoples of all the combatant countries, the Provisional Workers' and Peasants' Government of Russia also appeals especially to the class-conscious workers of the three leading nations of humanity and the largest states which are participating in the war, England, France and Germany. The workers of these countries rendered the greatest services to the cause of progress and socialism, and the great examples of the Chartist Movement in England, a number of revolutions of world significance, carried out by the French proletariat, finally the heroic struggle against the Exceptional Law in Germany and the long, stubborn, disciplined work of creating mass proletarian organizations in Germany (which was a model for the workers of the whole world),—all these examples of proletarian heroism and historic creation serve us as a guaranty that the workers of the above mentioned countries understand the problems which now fall on them, of liberating humanity from the horrors of war and its consequences, that these workers by their decisive and devotedly energetic activity will help us to bring successfully to its end the cause of peace and, along with this, the cause of freeing the toiling and exploited masses of the population from slavery and exploitation of every kind.

President of the Soviet of Peoples' Commissars,
VLADIMIR ULIANOV-LENIN.

222. THE DECREE REPUDIATING STATE DEBTS, FEBRUARY 10, 1918 [5]

Among the most far-reaching early acts of the Soviet authorities was the repudiation, on February 10, 1918, of all foreign and domestic state loans.

1. All state loans made by the governments of the Russian landowners and bourgeoisie . . . are hereby annulled (abolished) as from December 1917. The December coupons of these loans are not subject to payment.

[5] Translated from *Sbornik dekretov i postanovlenii po narodnomu khoziaistvu, 25 oktiabria 1917 g.-25 oktiabria 1918 g.,* Moscow, 1918, p. 875, in J. Bunyan and H. H. Fisher, eds., *The Bolshevik Revolution 1917-1918. Documents and Materials,* Stanford University Press, Stanford University, 1934, pp. 602-603. Reprinted by permission of the Stanford University Press.

2. Guaranties given by the said governments on loans made by different enterprises and institutions are likewise annulled.

3. All foreign loans without exception are unconditionally annulled.

4. Short term notes and State Treasury bonds retain their value. Interest on them will not be paid, but the bonds themselves are to circulate as legal tender.

5. Citizens of small means who hold certificates of not more than 10,000 rubles (nominal value) of annulled internal state loans are to receive in exchange certificates of the new loan of the Russian Socialist Federated Soviet Republic up to but not exceeding 10,000 rubles. There will be a special announcement of the terms of the loan.

6. Deposits made in the state savings banks and interest on them are not disturbed. All bonds of the annulled loans belonging to savings banks are transferred to the debit books of the Russian Federated Soviet Republic.

7. Co-operatives, municipalities, and other democratic and public service institutions which own bonds of the annulled loans will be indemnified in accordance with the rules to be determined by the Supreme Council of National Economy in co-operation with representatives of the above institutions, provided it can be proved that the bonds were acquired prior to the publication of the present decree.

Note: Local organs of the Supreme Council of National Economy shall determine whether the institutions presenting a claim are of a democratic or public service character.

8. The general liquidation of the state loans is in the hands of the Supreme Council of National Economy.

9. All detailed matters of liquidation are handled by the State Bank, which is to proceed at once to register all state bonds in the hands of different owners and other interest-bearing securities, irrespective of whether or not they are subject to annulment.

10. The local Soviets of Workers', Soldiers', and Peasants' Deputies, in agreement with the local councils of national economy, are to form commissions to determine what citizens fall within the category of [those having] small means.

The commissions have the right to annul completely unearned savings, even if the sum does not exceed 5,000 rubles.

YA. SVERDLOV
*Chairman of the All-Russian Central
Executive Committee.*

223. THE FIRST (BAKU) CONGRESS OF THE PEOPLES OF THE EAST, 1920 [6]

In an attempt to extend their influence over the Orient and simultaneously to harass the western colonial powers, especially Great Britain, the Bolsheviks called together at Baku a great "Congress of the Peoples of the East," vividly described in the following selection. Optimistically called the "First" such congress by its sponsors, it also proved to be the last.

Bolshevik propaganda in the East took concrete form in a unique assembly convened in Baku during September, 1920. Zinoviev and Radek, President and Secretary of the Comintern, and Bela Kun [7] came from Moscow to inspire this "Congress of the Peoples of the East." It was an odd gathering, a museum of Oriental costumes, a Babel of tongues, a confusion of ideas and aims. Hindus, Turks, Bokharans, Uzbecks, Ingushi, Persians, Chechentzi, Turkomans, Jews, Armenians, Bashkirs, Kalmucks, Ukrainians, Russians, Tadjiks, Georgians—1,891 delegates belonging to thirty-seven nationalities were present. A battery of interpreters shouted from the platform.

. . . . .

Soviet supporters pointed to the freedom and cultural autonomy granted to the Tartars, the Bashkirs, the Kirghizi and all other nationalities in Russia. Other peoples, they urged, must strive towards a similar goal.

The Comintern's policy had been outlined by Zinoviev on the evening of September 1. It was past midnight when his address drew to a dramatic close. "The Communist International," he announced, "turns to-day to the peoples of the East and says to them: 'Brothers, we summon you to a Holy War first of all against British Imperialism.'" "Jehad, Jehad," [8] the delegates thundered. Every man in the hall jumped to his feet. Studded daggers were drawn, Damascan swords unsheathed, revolvers brought out of their holsters and lifted on high while their owners yelled "We swear," "We swear."

[6] Based on the *Stenographic Record of the Congress at Baku of the Peoples of the East*, Moscow, 1920, in L. Fischer, *The Soviets in World Affairs*, 2 vols., Jonathan Cape, London, 1930, vol. I, pp. 283-284. Reprinted by permission of the publishers.

[7] Bela Kun was an ex-journalist and politician who had been active head of the Hungarian Soviet Republic from March 20 to August 1, 1919.—*Ed.*

[8] Jehad means Holy War.—*Ed.*

Despite this oath of arms, the Holy War was conceived as a non-military offensive directed by the Council of Propaganda and Action created by the Congress to match the Council of Action of the British trade unions. "The infantry of the East would reinforce the cavalry of the West."

The Eastern nations which concerned the Congress above all were Turkey, Persia, Afghanistan, and India. In these, England's rôle was most important. England was most despised. Therefore British Imperialism stood in the foreground of the assembly's attention, while France received only secondary consideration.

This meeting went down into history as the *"First* Congress of the Peoples of the East." It established a permanent organization on the assumption that annual or periodical gatherings would follow. But the first congress remained the only congress. The establishment of normal diplomatic relations between the Governments of Eastern countries and the Government of Russia began to take precedence over the relations between the revoluntionary movements in Eastern countries and the revolutionary movement of Russia. . . .

224. THE TREATY OF FEDERATION OF THE U.S.S.R., 1922 *(Extracts)* [9]

Between 1919 and 1921 Bolshevik sympathizers succeeded in gaining control, by force, of the governments of Great Russia, the Ukraine, White Russia, and Transcaucasia (the states of Azerbaijan, Armenia, and Georgia). Under Great Russian instigation, and owing especially to the activities of Joseph Visserionovich Dzhugashvili, alias Stalin, himself a Georgian, delegates from the four states met at Moscow and on December 30, 1922, signed a treaty of federation. The treaty became effective in July 1923 and the federation was called the Union of Soviet Socialist Republics.

The Russian Socialist Federal Soviet Republic, the Ukrainian Socialist Soviet Republic, the White Russian Socialist Soviet Republic and the Transcaucasian Socialist Federal Soviet Republic hereby conclude the present treaty regarding their union into one united State, the Union of Soviet Socialist Republics, on the following basis:

1. To the competence of the Union of Soviet Socialist Republics, as exercised by its supreme organs, there appertain:—

---

[9] Great Britain, Foreign Office, *British and Foreign State Papers 1932*, vol. CXXXV, His Majesty's Stationery Office, London, 1937, pp. 723-727. Reprinted by permission of the Controller of His Britannic Majesty's Stationery Office.

(a) The representation of the Union in international relationships.

(b) The alteration of the external boundaries of the Union.

(c) The conclusion of treaties regarding the reception into the Union of new Republics.

(d) The declaration of war and the conclusion of peace.

(e) The flotation of foreign State loans.

(f) The ratification of international treaties.

(g) The establishment of the regulations governing foreign and domestic trade.

(h) The establishment of the principles and the general scheme of the entire national economy of the Union, and the conclusion of concessionary agreements.

(i) The regulation of transport and posts and telegraphs.

(j) The organisation and direction of the armed forces of the Union.

(k) The ratification of the unified State budget of the Union, the establishment of currency and credit systems and of a system of taxation for the Union, the various Republics and the localities.

(l) The establishment of the general principles of land distribution and exploitation and of the exploitation of the mineral wealth, forests and waterways throughout the whole territory of the Union.

(m) General Union legislation on migration and settlement.

(n) The establishment of the principles of court structure and procedure, and also civil and criminal legislation for the Union.

(o) Fundamental labor legislation.

(p) The establishment of the general principles of national education.

(q) The adoption of general measures for the protection of national health.

(r) The establishment of systems of weights and measures.

(s) The organisation of general statistics.

(t) Fundamental legislation in the domain of Union citizenship with regard to the rights of foreigners.

(u) General amnesty legislation.

(v) The vetoing of decisions infringing the treaty of union passed by Congresses of Soviets, Central Executive Committees and Councils of People's Commissaries of the Republics of the Union.

. . . . .

6. The Congress of Soviets of the Union elects the Central Executive Committee, consisting of representatives of the united Republics, in proportion to the population of each, to the total number of 371 members.

7. Ordinary sessions of the Central Executive Committee of the Union shall be held three times a year; extraordinary sessions shall be convoked by order of the Presidium of the Central Executive Committee of the Union or upon the demand of the Council of People's Commissaries of the Union or of the Central Executive Committee of one of the constituent Republics.

8. The Congresses of Soviets and the sessions of the Central Executive Committee of the Union shall assemble in the capitals of the united Republics in the order fixed by the Presidium of the Central Executive Committee of the Union.

. . . . .

10. The Presidium of the Central Executive Committee of the Union shall consist of 19 members, from whom the Central Executive Committee shall appoint 4 Presidents, one for each of the united Republics.

. . . . .

12. For the purpose of ratifying revolutionary legislation within the territory of the Union, and of co-ordinating the efforts of the United Republics in their struggle against counter-revolution, there shall be established in the Central Executive Committee of the Union a Supreme Court with the functions of a court of supreme control, and in the Council of People's Commissaries of the Union an organ of the State Political Department, the president of which is a member of the Council of People's Commissaries of the Union in a consultive capacity.

13. The decrees and orders of the Council of People's Commissaries of the Union are binding on all the united Republics and shall be put into execution throughout the whole territory of the Union.

14. The decrees and orders of the Central Executive Committee and of the Council of People's Commissaries of the Union shall be published in the languages generally in use in the united Republics (Russian, Ukrainian, White Russian, Georgian, Armenian and Tartar).

15. The Central Executive Committees of the united Republics may lodge protests against the decrees and orders of the Council of People's Commissaries of the Union with the Presidium of the Central Executive Committee of the Union, but without suspending their execution.

. . . . .

17. The execution of orders of the People's Commissaries of the Union may be suspended by the Central Executive Committees of the united Republics, or the Presidia, only in exceptional circumstances,

when they are in clear conflict with the decrees of the Council of People's Commissaries or of the Central Executive Committee of the Union. The Central Executive Committee of the allied Republics or its Presidium, shall in such case immediately notify the Councils of People's Commissaries of the Union and the appropriate Commissary of the Union regarding the suspension of the orders.

. . . . .

20. The Republics which form part of the Union shall have their own budgets, which shall form integral parts of the general budget of the Union and shall be passed by the Central Executive Committee of the Union. The revenue and expenditure sides of the budgets of the Republics shall be drawn up by the Central Executive Committee of the Union. The statement of revenues and the amount of each, forming part of the budgets of the united Republics, shall be determined by the Central Executive Committee of the Union.

21. A single Union citizenship shall prevail for citizens of the united Republics.

22. The Union shall have its own flag, coat of arms and State Seal.

23. The capital of the Union shall be Moscow.

24. The United Republics shall modify their constitutions as necessitated by the present treaty.

25. The Congress of Soviets of the Union is alone competent to ratify, alter or add to the treaty of union.

26. Each of the united Republics retains the right of freely leaving the Union.

Moscow, December 30, 1922.

225. THE CONSTITUTION OF THE U.S.S.R., 1923, WITH AMENDMENTS OF 1925 AND 1927 *(Extracts)* [10]

The constitution of the U.S.S.R. became effective on July 6, 1923. Like the constitutions of the lesser members of the Union, it was patterned closely after that of the Russian Socialist Federated Soviet Republic (R.S.F.S.R., the former Great Russia), adopted by the fifth All-Russian Congress of Soviets on July 10, 1918. A new constitution for the U.S.S.R. was adopted in 1936 (See Document No. 239).

[10] Soviet Union, Information Bureau, *The Constitution of the Union of Soviet Socialist Republics,* Washington, 1929, pp. 8-27.

CHAPTER I.

COMPETENCE OF THE SUPREME ORGANS OF AUTHORITY OF THE U.S.S.R.

ARTICLE 1.

The Sovereignty of the Union of Soviet Socialist Republics, as exercised through the supreme governing departments, shall include:

a) The representation of the Union in international relations, the conduct of all diplomatic intercourse and the conclusion of political and other treaties with other foreign states;

b) The modification of the external frontiers of the Union and the regulation of questions dealing with the alteration of boundaries between the Constituent Republics;

c) The conclusion of treaties for the admission of new Republics into the Union;

d) The declaration of war and the conclusion of peace;

e) The contracting of foreign and domestic loans by the U.S.S.R., and the sanctioning of foreign and domestic loans of the Constituent Republics;

f) The ratification of international treaties;

g) Control of foreign trade, and establishment of a system of internal trade;

h) Establishment of the basic principles and of a general plan for the whole national economic system of the Union; determination of the branches of industry and of separate industrial undertakings which are of federal scope; and the conclusion of concession agreements, both of federal scope and in behalf of the various Constituent Republics;

i) The control of transport, posts and telegraphs;

j) The organization and control of the armed forces of the U.S.S.R.;

k) The approval of a single State budget for the U.S.S.R. comprising the budgets of the Constituent Republics; determination of the taxes and revenues applying to the whole U.S.S.R., as also of deductions therefrom and additions thereto for the budgets of the Constituent Republics; authorization of additional taxes and dues for the budgets of the Constituent Republics;

l) Establishment of a single currency and credit system;

m) Establishment of general principles governing the distribution and use of land, and the exploitation of mineral wealth, forests and waterways throughout the whole territory of the U.S.S.R.;

n) Federal legislation on migration from one Republic to another, and establishment of a colonization fund;

o) Establishment of basic principles for the composition and procedure of the courts and the civil and criminal legislation of the Union;

p) The establishment of fundamental labor laws;

q) Establishment of the general principles of public education;

r) Adoption of general measures for the protection of public health;

s) Establishment of a system of weights and measures;

t) The organization of federal statistics;

u) Fundamental legislation in the matter of citizenship of the
U.S.S.R. in relation to the rights of foreigners;

v) The rights of amnesty extending over the whole territory of the
Union;

w) The repeal of decisions adopted by the different Soviet Congresses
and Central Executive Committees of the several Constituent Republics
infringing upon the present Constitution;

x) Settlement of controversies arising between the Constitutent Republics;

ARTICLE 2.

The ratification and amendment of the fundamental principles of
the present Constitution shall be exclusively delegated to the Congress
of Soviets of the U.S.S.R.

CHAPTER II.

THE SOVEREIGNTY OF THE SEVERAL CONSTITUENT REPUBLICS AND FEDERAL CITIZENSHIP.

ARTICLE 3.

The sovereignty of the Constituent Republics is restricted only within
the limits stated in the present Constitution, and only in respect of
matters referred to the competence of the Union. Beyond these limits
each Constituent Republic exercises its state authority independently.
The U.S.S.R. protects the sovereign rights of the Constituent Republics.

ARTICLE 4.

Each of the Constituent Republics shall have the right of free withdrawal from the Union.

ARTICLE 5.

The Constituent Republics shall introduce alterations in their respective constitutions to bring them in conformity with the present Constitution.

ARTICLE 6.

The territory of the Constituent Republics shall not be altered without their consent. For the modification, limitation or repeal of Article 4 of the present Constitution the consent of all the Republics forming the U.S.S.R. is required.

ARTICLE 7.

A uniform citizenship of the U.S.S.R. is established for citizens of the Constituent Republics.

CHAPTER III.

CONGRESS OF SOVIETS OF THE UNION OF SOVIET SOCIALIST REPUBLICS.

ARTICLE 8.

The supreme authority of the U.S.S.R. shall be vested in the Congress of Soviets, and, during the intervals of sessions of the Congresses of Soviets, in the Central Executive Committee of the U.S.S.R., which shall consist of the Council of the Union and the Council of Nationalities.

ARTICLE 9.

The Congress of Soviets of the U.S.S.R. shall be composed of representatives of City Soviets and Soviets of urban settlements on the basis of 1 deputy for each 25,000 electors, and of representatives of Provincial and District Soviet Congresses on the basis of 1 deputy for each 125,000 inhabitants.

ARTICLE 10.

The representatives to the Congress of Soviets of the U.S.S.R. shall be elected at the Provincial and District Soviet Congresses. In those Republics which have no provincial or district units, the delegates shall be elected directly at the Congresses of Soviets of the respective Republics.

ARTICLE 11.

Ordinary Congresses of the Soviets of the U.S.S.R. shall be convened by the Central Executive Committee of the U.S.S.R. once in two years; extraordinary congresses shall be convened by the Central Executive Committee of the U.S.S.R. either on its own initiative, or on the demand of the Council of the Union, or Council of Nationalities, or of any two of the Constituent Republics.

ARTICLE 12.

Under extraordinary circumstances preventing the convening of the Congress of the Soviets of the U.S.S.R. at the appointed time, the Central Executive Committee of the U.S.S.R. shall have the right to postpone the convening of the Congress.

CHAPTER IV.

THE CENTRAL EXECUTIVE COMMITTEE OF THE UNION OF SOVIET SOCIALIST REPUBLICS.

ARTICLE 13.

The Central Executive Committee of the U.S.S.R. shall consist of the Council of the Union and the Council of Nationalities.

ARTICLE 14.

The Congress of Soviets of the U.S.S.R. shall elect the Council of the Union from among the representatives of the Constituent Republics counted in proportion to the population of each Republic, the number to be determined by the Congress of Soviets of the U.S.S.R.

ARTICLE 15.

The Council of Nationalities shall be formed of the representatives of the Constituent and Autonomous Soviet Socialist Republics on the basis of five representatives from each; and of the representatives of autonomous areas on the basis of one representative from each. The composition of the Council of Nationalities as a whole shall be subject to confirmation by the Congress of Soviets of the U.S.S.R.

ARTICLE 16.

The Council of the Union and the Council of Nationalities shall examine all decrees, codes and regulations submitted to them by the Presidium of the Central Executive Committee and the Council of People's Commissars of the U.S.S.R., by separate People's Commissariats of the Union, or by the Central Executive Committees of the Constituent Republics; as well as those proposed on the initiative of the Council of the Union and the Council of Nationalities.

ARTICLE 17.

The Central Executive Committee of the U.S.S.R. issues codes, decrees, regulations, and orders, combines the work of legislation and administration of the U.S.S.R., and determines the scope of activities of the Presidium of the Central Executive Committee and the Council of People's Commissars of the U.S.S.R.

ARTICLE 18.

All decrees and ordinances determining the general principles of the political and economic life of the U.S.S.R., and also those which introduce fundamental changes in the existing practice of the State organs of the U.S.S.R., must be submitted for the examination and ratification of the Central Executive Committee of the U.S.S.R.

ARTICLE 19.

All decrees, regulations and orders issued by the Central Executive Committee must be immediately carried out throughout the territory of the U.S.S.R.

ARTICLE 20.

The Central Executive Committee of the U.S.S.R. shall have the right to suspend or repeal decrees, regulations and ordinances of the Presidium of the Central Executive Committee of the U.S.S.R., of the Congresses of Soviets and of the Central Executive Committees of the Constituent Republics, and of other organs of authority within the territory of the U.S.S.R.

. . . . .

ARTICLE 22.

Legislative bills submitted for consideration by the Central Executive Committee of the U.S.S.R., shall become laws only after having been passed by both the Council of the Union and the Council of Nationalities; they are published in the name of the Central Executive Committee of the U.S.S.R.

ARTICLE 23.

In case of disagreement between the Council of the Union and the Council of Nationalities, the question at issue shall be referred to an Adjustment Commission appointed by these two organs.

ARTICLE 24.

If no agreement be reached in the Adjustment Commission, the question shall be referred to a joint session of the Council of the Union and of the Council of Nationalities, wherein, in the event that no majority vote of the Council of the Union or of the Council of Nationalities can be obtained, the question may be referred, on the demand of either of these bodies, for decision to either the regular or extraordinary Congress of Soviets of the U.S.S.R.

ARTICLE 25.

The Council of the Union and the Council of Nationalities each elects a Presidium of nine of its members to arrange its sessions and conduct the work of the latter.

ARTICLE 26.

In the intervals between sessions of the Central Executive Committee of the U.S.S.R. supreme authority is vested in the Presidium of the Central Executive Committee of the U.S.S.R., formed by the Central Executive Committee of the U.S.S.R., of twenty-seven members, amongst whom are included the whole of the Presidium of the Council of the Union and the Presidium of the Council of Nationalities.

For the purpose of constituting the Presidium of the Central Executive Committee of the U.S.S.R., and the Council of People's Commissars of the U.S.S.R., in accordance with Articles 26 and 37 of this Constitution, a joint session of the Council of the Union and of the Council of Nationalities is called. The voting at the joint session of the Council of the Union and of the Council of Nationalities is effected separately by the Council of the Union and by the Council of Nationalities.

ARTICLE 27.

The Central Executive Committee elects, in accordance with the number of Constituent Republics, the chairmen of the Central Executive Committee of the U.S.R.R., from among members of the Presidium of the Central Executive Committee of the U.S.S.R.

. . . . .

CHAPTER V.

THE PRESIDIUM OF THE CENTRAL EXECUTIVE COMMITTEE OF THE U.S.S.R.

ARTICLE 29.

The Presidium of the Central Executive Committee of the U.S.S.R. shall, during the intervals between the sessions of the Central Executive

Committee of the U.S.S.R., be the highest legislative, executive and administrative organ in the U.S.S.R.

. . . . .

ARTICLE 31.

The Presidium of the Central Executive Committee of the U.S.S.R. shall have the power to suspend or to repeal the decisions of the Council of People's Commissars and of the individual People's Commissariats of the U.S.S.R., and of the Central Executive Committees and the Councils of People's Commissars of the Constituent Republics.

ARTICLE 32.

The Presidium of the Central Executive Committee of the U.S.S.R. shall have the power to suspend the decisions of the Congresses of Soviets of the Constituent Republics, and subsequently thereto to submit such decisions for examination and ratification to the Central Executive Committee of the U.S.S.R.

. . . . .

CHAPTER VI.
THE COUNCIL OF PEOPLE'S COMMISSARS OF THE U.S.S.R.

ARTICLE 37.

The Council of People's Commissars of the U.S.S.R. shall be the executive and administrative organ of the Central Executive Committee of the U.S.S.R., and it shall be formed by the Central Executive Committee of the U.S.S.R., as follows:

Chairman of the Council of People's Commissars of the U.S.S.R.;
Vice-Chairmen;
People's Commissar for Foreign Affairs;
People's Commissar for Army and Navy;
People's Commissar for Foreign and Domestic Trade;
People's Commissar for Transport;
People's Commissar for Posts and Telegraphs;
People's Commissar for Workers' and Peasants' Inspection;
Chairman of the Supreme Council of National Economy;
People's Commissar for Labor;
People's Commissar for Finance;
Director of Central Statistical Board.

ARTICLE 38.

The Council of People's Commissars of the U.S.S.R., within the limits of the powers conferred upon it by the Central Executive Committee of the U.S.S.R., and by virtue of the Statute about the Council of People's Commissars, shall issue decrees and regulations which must be executed throughout the territory of the U.S.S.R.

• • • • •

ARTICLE 41.

Decrees and regulations of the Council of People's Commissars of the U.S.S.R. may be suspended and repealed by the Central Executive Committee of the U.S.S.R., and its Presidium.

• • • • •

CHAPTER VII.
THE SUPREME COURT OF THE U.S.S.R.

ARTICLE 43.

In order to maintain revolutionary legality throughout the territory of the U.S.S.R., there shall be created a Supreme Court, attached to the Central Executive Committee of the U.S.S.R., which shall have the power and jurisdiction:

a) To give the Supreme Courts of the Constituent Republics guiding interpretations on questions concerning general Federal legislation;

b) To examine and appeal to the Central Executive Committee of the U.S.S.R., on the motion of the Attorney General of the Supreme Court of the U.S.S.R., against resolutions, decisions and verdicts of the Supreme Courts of the Constituent Republics on the ground of their being in contradiction to the general legislation of the U.S.S.R., or in so far as they affect the interests of other Republics;

c) To give opinions at the request of the Central Executive Committee of the U.S.S.R. on the legality of any regulations made by the Constituent Republics from the point of view of the Constitution;

d) To adjudicate judiciable controversies between the Constituent Republics;

e) To try charges against high officials of the U.S.S.R. for offenses committed in the discharge of their duties.

ARTICLE 44.

The Supreme Court of the U.S.S.R. shall function through:

a) Plenary sessions of the Supreme Court of the U.S.S.R.;

b) Civil and Criminal Departments of the Supreme Court of the U.S.S.R.;

c) Military Division.

. . . . .

CHAPTER VIII.

THE PEOPLE'S COMMISSARIATS OF THE U.S.S.R.

ARTICLE 49.

For the direct conduct of the separate branches of State administration included in the sphere of the Council of People's Commissars of the U.S.S.R., ten People's Commissariats are set up, enumerated in Article 37 of the present Constitution, which shall act in accordance with the Statutes regarding People's Commissariats, confirmed by the Central Executive Committee of the U.S.S.R.

ARTICLE 50.

The People's Commissariats of the U.S.S.R. shall be divided into: (a) Federal People's Commissariats for the entire U.S.S.R., and (b) Joint People's Commissariats of the U.S.S.R.

ARTICLE 51.

The Federal People's Commissariats for the whole U.S.S.R. shall be the following:

Foreign Affairs;

Army and Navy;

Foreign and Domestic Trade;

Transport;

Posts and Telegraphs.

NOTE: In the matter of regulating domestic trade the People's Commissariat for Foreign and Domestic Trade of the U.S.S.R. enjoys the rights of a Joint People's Commissariat of the U.S.S.R.

ARTICLE 52.

The Joint People's Commissariats of the U.S.S.R. shall be the following:

Supreme Council of National Economy;

Labor;

Finances;

Workers' and Peasants' Inspection;

Central Statistical Board.

ARTICLE 53.

The Federal People's Commissariats of the whole U.S.S.R. shall have their plenipotentiary representatives in the Constituent Republics, who shall be directly subordinated to the Federal People's Commissariats.

ARTICLE 54.

The organs of the Joint People's Commissariats of the U.S.S.R., which fulfill their functions in the territory of the Constituent Republics shall be the People's Commissariats of the same name of these Republics.

ARTICLE 55.

At the head of the People's Commissariats of the U.S.S.R., stand the members of the Council of People's Commissariats—the People's Commissars of the U.S.S.R.

. . . . .

CHAPTER IX.

THE JOINT STATE POLITICAL DEPARTMENT OF THE U.S.S.R.

ARTICLE 61.

In order to combine the revolutionary efforts of the Constituent Republics in the fight against political and economic counter-revolution, espionage and banditism, a Joint State Political Department (O.G.P.U.) is created, attached to the Council of People's Commissars of the U.S.S.R., the chairman of the Department entering the Council of People's Commissars of the U.S.S.R., with the right of advisory vote.

ARTICLE 62.

The Joint State Political Department (O.G.P.U.) of the U.S.S.R. shall direct the activities of the local branches of the State Political Department (G.P.U.), through its representatives attached to the Councils of People's Commissars of the Constituent Republics, acting in accordance with a special statute ratified by legislative act.

ARTICLE 63.

The control of the legality of the acts of the Joint State Political Department of the U.S.S.R. shall be exercised by the Attorney General of the Supreme Court of the U.S.S.R., on the basis of a special decree made by the Central Executive Committee of the U.S.S.R.

CHAPTER X.

THE CONSTITUENT REPUBLICS.

ARTICLE 64.

Within the territory of each Constituent Republic the supreme organ of authority of the latter shall be the Congress of Soviets of the Republic, and during the intervals between congresses, its Central Executive Committee.

. . . . .

ARTICLE 69.

The right of amnesty, as well as the right of pardon and rehabilitation in regard to citizens condemned by the judicial or administrative organs of the Constituent Republics shall be the prerogative of the Central Executive Committees of these Republics.

CHAPTER XI.

THE EMBLEM, THE FLAG AND THE CAPITAL OF THE U.S.S.R.

ARTICLE 70.

The State emblem of the U.S.S.R. shall consist of a sickle and hammer mounted on a terrestrial globe illuminated by sunrays and surrounded by ears of grain; the ears are intertwined with ribbons, bearing the inscription, in the six languages mentioned in Article 34, "Proletarians of all countries, unite!" Above the emblem is a five-pointed star.

ARTICLE 71.

The flag of state of the U.S.S.R. shall be of red or scarlet cloth; in the upper corner at the staff are a golden sickle and hammer, surmounted by a five-pointed star with a golden border. Proportion of width to length is 1:2.

ARTICLE 72.

The capital city of the U.S.S.R. shall be the City of Moscow.

226. THE CONSTITUTION OF THE COMMUNIST PARTY, ADOPTED BY THE SEVENTEENTH PARTY CONGRESS, FEBRUARY 10, 1934 *(Extracts)* [11]

Actual power in the Soviet Union is exercised through the All-Union Communist Party. The seventeenth Party Congress on February 10, 1934, slightly revised the constitution accepted by the fourteenth Party Congress in December 1925.

The All-Union Communist Party (Bolsheviks), being a section of the Communist International, is the organized vanguard of the proletariat of the Union of Soviet Socialist Republics (USSR), the highest form of its class organization.

. . . . .

The Party is a unified militant organization held together by conscious, iron proletarian discipline. The Party is strong because of its coherence, unity of will and unity of action which are incompatible with any deviation from its program, with any violation of Party discipline or with factional groupings within the Party. The Party demands from all its members active and self-sacrificing work to carry out the program and rules of the Party, to fulfil all decisions of the Party and its organs, to ensure unity within the Party and the consolidation of the fraternal international relations among the toilers of the nationalities of the USSR as well as among the proletarians of the whole world.

I. PARTY MEMBERS AND THEIR DUTIES

1. A Party member is anyone who accepts the program of the Party, who works in one of its organizations, submits to its decisions and pays membership dues.

2. It is the duty of a Party member:

(*a*) To observe strict Party discipline, to take an active part in the political life of the Party and of the country, and to carry out in practice the policy of the Party and the decisions of the Party organs;

(*b*) To work untiringly to raise his ideological equipment, to master the principles of Marxism-Leninism, and the important political and

---

[11] As translated by S. N. Harper in W. E. Rappard et al., *Source Book on European Governments,* D. Van Nostrand Company, Inc., New York, 1937, pp. V34-V52. Courtesy of D. Van Nostrand Company, Inc.

organizational decisions of the Party and to explain these to the non-party masses;

(*c*) As a member of the ruling party in the Soviet state, to set an example in the observance of labor and state discipline, master the technique of his work, and continually raise his production and work qualifications.

3. Members are admitted to the Party only individually. New members are admitted from among the candidates who have gone through a specified period of candidateship (probation), who have graduated from a school of political training and who have mastered the program and the rules of the Party. Workers, collective farmers, Red Army men, students and employees who have proved their worth in their work in sympathizers' groups, in the Soviets, trade unions, Communist Union of Youth, co-operative organizations or delegates' meetings may be admitted to Party membership after the receipt of an informative statement of the organization where the applicant worked or is working.

The procedure in admitting Party members from among the candidates is as follows:

(*a*) Four categories are laid down: (1) Industrial workers with a production record of not less than five years; (2) industrial workers with a production record of less than five years, agricultural workers, Red Army men from among workers or collective farmers, and engineers and technicians working directly in shops or sectors; (3) collective farmers, members of handicraft or artisan co-operatives and elementary school teachers; (4) other employees.

(*b*) To be admitted to the Party, persons in the first category must submit three recommendations of Party members of five-years' Party standing; persons in the second category—five recommendations of Party members of five-years' Party standing and the recommendation of a representative of the political department of the machine-tractor station or of the district committee; persons in the fourth category—five recommendations of Party members of ten-years' Party standing.

Note: When members of the Communist Union of Youth falling under any category are admitted to the Party, the recommendation of the district committee of the All-Union Leninist Communist Union of Youth is treated as equivalent to the recommendations of two Party members.

(*c*) Former members of other parties are admitted in exceptional cases on the recommendation of five Party members, three of whom must be of ten-years' Party standing and two of pre-revolutionary Party standing, and only through an industrial primary organization; the admission of such a candidate must be endorsed by the Central Committee of the Party, irrespective of the social status of the applicant.

> *Note:* The Central Committee may delegate the right of final endorsement of former members of other parties to the respective regional Party committee or the Central Committee of the national Communist Parties.

(*d*) The verification of recommendations must precede admission and is the duty of the local Party committee.

(*e*) The question of admission to the Party is preliminarily considered by the primary Party organization, is decided by the general meeting of the organization and goes into effect on the endorsement: for the first and second categories—by the district or city committee; for the third and fourth categories—by the regional committee or the Central Committee of the respective national Communist Party.

(*f*) Young persons up to and including the age of twenty may join the Party only through the All-Union Leninist Communist Union of Youth.

4. Persons recommending applicants for admission are responsible for those they recommend. Those giving unsound recommendations are liable to Party penalties including expulsion from the Party.

. . . . .

7. Party members and candidates who have failed to pay their membership dues for three months without sufficient cause are regarded as having dropped out the Party and notice of this must be conveyed to the general membership meeting of the primary organization.

8. The question of the expulsion of any member from the Party is decided by the general meeting of the Party organization to which the member belongs and must be approved, for the first and second categories—by the regional committee, and for the third and fourth categories—by the district or city committee. The person in question is removed from Party work the day he is expelled by the general meeting of the Party organization or by the Party committee. Notice of expulsion of Party members must be published in the Party press, stating the reasons for the expulsion.

9. By periodic decisions of the Central Committee of the Party, purgings are held for the systematic cleansing of the Party of:

Class-alien and hostile elements;

Double-dealers who deceive the Party and who conceal their real views from it and who disrupt the policy of the Party;

Overt and covert violators of the iron discipline of the Party and of the State;

Degenerates who have coalesced with bourgeois elements;

Careerists, self-seekers and bureaucratized elements;

Morally degraded persons who by their improper conduct lower the dignity of the Party and besmirch the banner of the Party;

Passive elements who do not fulfill the duties of Party members and who have not mastered the program, the rules and the most important decisions of the Party.

II. CANDIDATES FOR PARTY MEMBERSHIP

10. All persons desirous of joining the Party must pass through a period of candidateship, the object of which is to give them an opportunity to become thoroughly acquainted with the program, the rules and the tactics of the Party and to test the personal qualities of the candidates.

11. The method of admission of candidates (division into categories, character of recommendations and their verification, the decision of the organization on the admission and the endorsement of the Party committee) is identical with that applying to Party members.

12. The period of candidateship is fixed: for the first category, at one year; for the second, third and fourth categories, at two years.

Note: Former members of other parties, irrespective of their social status, have to go through a three-year period of candidateship.

. . . . .

IV. THE ORGANIZATIONAL STRUCTURE OF THE PARTY

18. The guiding principle of the organizational structure of the Party is democratic centralism, which signifies:

(*a*) The application of the elective principle to all leading organs of the Party, from the highest to the lowest;

(*b*) The periodic accountability of the Party organs to their respective Party organizations;

(*c*) Strict Party discipline and subordination of the minority to the majority;

(*d*) The absolutely binding character of the decisions of the higher organs upon the lower organs and upon all Party members.

19. The Party is built on the basis of democratic centralism according to the territorial-productional principle: the organization serving a certain area is regarded as superior to any organization serving part of the same area; or an organization serving a whole branch of production or administration is regarded as superior to any organization serving part of the same branch.

· · · · ·

23. The scheme of the Party organization is as follows:

(*a*) USSR—All-Union Congress—Central Committee of the Party;

(*b*) Regions (*oblast* and *krai*), republics—regional Conferences, Congresses of the national Communist Parties—Regional Committees, Central Committes of the national Communist Parties;

(*c*) Cities, districts—city, district conferences—city, district committees;

(*d*) Factories, villages, collective farms, machine-tractor stations, Red Army units, offices—general meetings, primary Party organization conferences—primary Party committees (mill Party committee, factory Party committee, Red Army unit Party bureau, etc.).

· · · · ·

V. THE CENTRAL INSTITUTIONS OF THE PARTY

27. The supreme body of the Party is the Congress. Regular sessions are convened not less than once in three years. Special congresses are called by the Central Committee on its own initiative, or at the demand of not less than one-third of the total membership represented at the preceding Party Congress. Notice of the convocation of the Party Congress and of its agenda must be given not later than a month and a half before the Congress. Special Congresses must be convened within two months.

The Congress is regarded as valid if the delegates attending represent not less than half the total membership of the Party represented at the preceding regular congress.

The apportionment of representatives of the Party Congress is laid down by the Central Committee.

· · · · ·

29. The Congress:

(*a*) Hears and approves the reports of the Central Committee, of the Commission of Party Control, of the Central Auditing Commission and of other central organizations;

(*b*) Revises and amends the program and rules of the Party;

(*c*) Determines the tactical line of the Party on the principal questions of current policy;

(*d*) Elects a Central Committee, a Commission of Party Control, a Central Auditing Commission, and nominates the members of the Commission of Soviet Control to be submitted for approval to the Central Executive Committee and the Council of People's Commissars of the USSR.

. . . . .

32. The Central Committee organizes a Political Bureau for political work, an Organizational Bureau for the general guidance of the organizational work, and a Secretariat for current work of an organizational or executive nature.

33. The Central Committee, during the interval between congresses, guides the entire work of the Party, represents the Party in its relations with other parties, organizations and institutions, forms various Party institutions and guides their activities, appoints the editorial staffs of the central organs working under its control and confirms the appointment of the editors of the Party organs of large local organizations, organizes and manages enterprises of public importance, distributes the forces and resources of the Party and manages the central funds.

The Central Committee directs the work of the central Soviet and public organizations through the Party groups in them.

. . . . .

36. The Commission of Party Control:

(*a*) Controls the fulfillment of decisions of the Party and of the Central Committee of the Party;

(*b*) Brings proceedings against those who have violated Party discipline;

(*c*) Brings proceedings against those who have violated Party ethics.

. . . . .

VI. THE REGIONAL AND REPUBLIC ORGANIZATIONS OF THE PARTY

38. The highest organ of the regional or republic Party organizations is the Regional Party Conference or the Congress of the national Communist Party, and in the interval between them—the Regional Committee or the Central Committee of the national Communist Party. They are guided in their activities by the general decisions of the Communist Party of the Soviet Union and its leading organs.

39. Regular Regional Conferences or Congresses of the national Communist Parties are called once every year and a half by the respective Regional Committee or Central Committee of the national Communist Party, while special conferences or congresses are called by decision of the Regional Committee or the Central Committee of the national Communist Party, or at the demand of one third of the total membership of the organizations in the region or republic.

· · · · ·

VII. CITY AND DISTRICT (RURAL AND URBAN) PARTY ORGANIZATIONS

44. The City or District Party Conference is called by the City or District Committee at least once a year; a special conference—by decision of the City or District Committee or at the demand of one third of the total membership of the organizations in the city or district.

The City or District Conference hears and adopts the reports of the City or District Committee, of the Auditing Committee and all the other city or district institutions, elects the City or District Committee, the Auditing Committee and the delegates to the Regional Conference or Congress of the national Communist Party.

45. The secretary of the City Committee must be a Party member of ten-years' standing, and the secretary of the District Committee—of seven-years' standing. The secretaries of the City and District Committees are confirmed by the respective Regional Committees or the Central Committees of the national Communist Parties.

· · · · ·

VIII. PRIMARY PARTY ORGANIZATIONS

48. The primary Party organizations form the basis of the Party. Primary Party organizations are set up at mills, factories, Soviet farms and other economic enterprises, at collective farms, machine-tractor stations, Red Army units, in villages, offices, etc., if they have no less

than three Party members. At factories, collective farms, offices, etc., where there are less than three Party members, candidate or Party-Communist Union of Youth groups, headed by a Party organizer appointed by the District or City Committee or the political department, are established. The primary Party organizations are confirmed by the District or City Committees or by the corresponding political departments.

49. In large factories, offices, collective farms, etc., having a great number of Communists (from 100 to 3,000 or more members), shop, sector, department, etc., Party organizations may be formed within the general primary organization which comprises the whole enterprise, office, etc., as may be required in any particular case, subject to the approval of the District or City Committee or of the corresponding political department. Brigade, machine unit, etc., Party groups of the enterprise may in their turn be established within the shop, sector, and other organizations.

. . . . . .

IX. PARTY ORGANIZATIONS IN THE RED ARMY

52. The general guidance of Party work in the Red Army, in the Red Navy and Air Fleet is exercised by the Political Administration of the Workers' and Peasants' Red Army having the rights of a military department of the Central Committee of the Party. This Political Administration of the Revolutionary Military Council of the Republic exercises its guidance through the political departments appointed by it, through military commissars and through Party commissions elected at the corresponding Army Conferences.

The Party organizations of the Red Army, Navy and Air Fleet work on the basis of special instructions confirmed by the Central Committee of the Party.

53. The chiefs of political departments of territories, fleets and armies must be Party members of ten-years' standing, the chiefs of political departments of divisions and brigades—of six-years' standing.

. . . . .

X. PARTY GROUPS IN NON-PARTY ORGANIZATIONS

55. At all congresses, conferences and elective organs of non-Party Soviet, trade union, co-operative and other mass organizations in which

there are not less than three Party members, Party groups are organized whose task it is to consolidate the influence of the Party in every respect and to carry out its policy in the non-party environment, to strengthen the iron Party and Soviet discipline, to struggle against bureaucracy and to supervise the fulfillment of Party and Soviet directives.

The group elects a secretary for its current work.

. . . . .

XI. INTERNAL PARTY DEMOCRACY AND PARTY DISCIPLINE

57. The free and business-like discussion of questions of Party policy in individual organizations or in the Party as a whole is the inalienable right of every Party member derived from internal Party democracy. Only on the basis of internal Party democracy is it possible to develop Bolshevik self-criticism and to strengthen Party discipline, which must be conscious and not mechanical. But extensive discussion, especially discussion on an All-Union scale, of questions of Party policy must be so organized that it cannot lead to attempts by an insignificant minority to impose its will upon the vast majority of the Party, or to attempts to form factional groupings which break the unity of the Party, to attempts at a split which may shake the strength and endurance of dictatorship of the proletariat, to the delight of the enemies of the working class. Therefore a wide discussion on an All-Union scale can be regarded as necessary only if: (a) this necessity is recognized by at least several local Party organizations whose jurisdiction extends to a region or a republic; (b) if there is not a sufficiently solid majority in the Central Committee itself on very important questions of Party policy; (c) if in spite of the existence of a solid majority in the Central Committee which advocates a definite standpoint, the Central Committee still deems it necessary to test the correctness of its policy by means of a discussion in the Party. Only compliance with these conditions can safeguard the Party against an abuse of internal Party democracy by anti-Party elements; only under these conditions can internal Party democracy be counted on to be of profit to the cause and not to be used to the detriment of the Party and the working class.

58. The maintenance of Party unity, the relentless struggle against the slightest attempt at a factional fight or a split and the strictest Party and Soviet discipline are the foremost duties of all Party members

and of all Party organizations. In order to realize strict discipline within the Party and in all Soviet work, and attain the greatest possible unity with the elimination of all factionalism, the Central Committee of the Party has the right, in the case of a violation of discipline, or of a revival or development of factionalism, to inflict any Party penalty including expulsion from the Party, and in the case of members of the Central Committee—demotion to candidateship and as an extreme measure expulsion from the Party. The convocation of the plenum of the Central Committee, to which all alternate members of the Central Committee and all members of the Commission of Party Control are invited, must be a condition precedent for the application of such an extreme measure to any member of the Central Committee, alternate member of the Central Committee or member of the Commission of Party Control. If such a general meeting of the most responsible leaders of the Party by a two thirds' vote recognizes the necessity of demoting a member of the Central Committee or of the Commission of Party Control to a candidate or of expelling him from the Party, such measure must be immediately carried out.

· · · · ·

XII. PARTY FUNDS

61. The funds of the Party and of its organizations are made up of membership dues, of the revenue from Party enterprises and of other items of revenue.

62. The following are the established amounts of monthly membership dues payable by Party members and candidates:

Those who receive up to 100 rubles in wages pay 20 kopeks
Those who receive from 101-150 rubles in wages pay 60 kopeks
Those who receive from 151-200 rubles in wages pay 1.00 ruble
Those who receive from 201-250 rubles in wages pay 1.50 rubles
Those who recieve from 251-300 rubles in wages pay 2.00 rubles
Those who receive from 301-500 rubles in wages pay 2 per cent
   of their earnings
Those who receive more than 500 rubles in wages pay 3 per
   cent of their earnings

63. Upon admission as a candidate, an initiation fee is charged which amounts to two per cent of the wages received.

227. THE CREATION OF THE CHEKA, DECEMBER 20, 1917 [12]

The Bolsheviks eventually developed two powerful weapons in their war against foreign and domestic opposition. Foreign opposition was met and overcome by a disciplined, well-drilled "Red Army." Domestic opposition was crushed by a police organization known from its initials in Russian as the Cheka. The following description of the creation of the Cheka was written by Martin I. Latsis, a prominent member of that body. The Cheka was abolished in 1922 but its functions were transferred to the O.G.P.U. (See Document No. 228).

The All-Russian Extraordinary Commission was formed on December 20, 1917, when it had its first meeting and decided to call itself the Extraordinary Commission to Fight Counter-Revolution and Sabotage.

At this time the Soviet Government . . . was attacked on all sides. The "officials" . . . sabotaged in the hope of stopping the machinery of government; the cadets and the old army officers started one uprising after another with the intention of taking the power from the hands of the Soviets; Vikzhel [the Central Executive Committee of the All-Russian Union of Railwaymen] planned a railroad strike; the Mensheviks and the Socialist-Revolutionists of the Right employed all kinds of weapons in waging a continuous war against the Soviet Government; the profiteer took advantage of the difficult situation of the country to carry on his nefarious trade. . . . At the same time the German troops of occupation were advancing, threatening the capital. . . . Only strong measures could save the situation and such measures were taken by the Soviet of People's Commissars.

To fight the external foe there was organized a Red Guard, which later became the Red Army. To fight the internal foe it was necessary to create an organ . . . that would protect the rear of the Red Army and permit the peaceful development of the Soviet form of government. Such an organ was the Extraordinary Commission to Fight

Counter-Revolution and Sabotage. Later on its functions were enlarged to include negligence of duty, profiteering, and banditry.

The Commission itself (composed at that time of Dzerzhinsky, Ksenofontov, Averin, Sergo, Peterson, Peters, Evseev, and Trifonov) outlined its duties as follows: *To cut off at the roots all counter-revolution and sabotage in Russia; to hand over to the revolutionary court all who are guilty of such attempts; to work out measures for dealing with such cases; and to enforce these measures without mercy.* . . . It was necessary to make the foe feel that there was everywhere about him a seeing eye and a heavy hand ready to come down on him the moment he undertook anything against the Soviet Government. . . .

228. THE ACTIVITIES OF THE O.G.P.U. [13]

Upon the abolition of the Cheka (See Document No. 227.) in 1922, the tasks of spying out, suppressing, and punishing opposition groups was entrusted in the R.S.F.S.R. to a State Political Administration (G.P.U.) and then, after the formation of the Soviet Union, to a Unified State Political Administration or O.G.P.U. This body, too, was abolished, in July 1934, but its activities, as described in the accompanying excerpt, were taken over by a new commissariat for internal affairs.

The ninth All-Russian Congress of Soviets meeting in December 1921, passed among other matters a resolution abolishing the extraordinary commission, commonly known as the "Cheka." [See Document No. 227]. . . . With the coming of more normal times, it was decided to re-organize this fearful institution into the G.P.U. (State Political Administration).

Nominally, this new secret police differs from the old Cheka in that the G.P.U. is under constitutional control. A decree issued on February 8, 1922, abolished the Cheka and instituted a state political administration (G.P.U.) attached to the commissariat of the interior. Departments of the G.P.U. were instituted in the various political subdivisions of the Russian Federation and were under the jurisdiction of the central organ in Moscow. When the Union was formed in 1923, a general provision was made for the legal status of the G.P.U., which stipulated that, for

---

[13] B. W. Maxwell, *The Soviet State. A Study of Bolshevik Rule,* Steves & Wayburn, Topeka, 1934, pp. 246-249. Reprinted by permission of Dr. Maxwell.

the purpose of combining the revolutionary efforts of the constituent republics in the struggle with political and economic counter-revolution, etc., the O.G.P.U. was to be established in connection with the Council of People's Commissars of the U.S.S.R. The president of the organization was to be a member of the Council with a consulting voice. . . .

In practice, the authority which controls the work of this amazing political police is the Polit-bureau and the Central Executive Committee of the Party.

. . . The number of the G.P.U. is estimated at 100,000 uniformed men and many thousands in the secret service. Its jurisdiction is extended to all offenses which are considered subversive to the Soviet régime and include in detail counter-revolutionary activity, brigandage, espionage, contraband, crossing of borders without permission, and looting on railroads and waterways. It also assists . . . as a censoring board in the matter of publications appearing in the Soviet Union. The official organization finds numerous helpers in the ranks of the Communist Party and other elements of the population who serve as informers.

The G.P.U. may not only arrest but may exile and imprison accused persons without a judicial trial. It may also include in its action the extreme penalty of death, the latter, however, only with the approval of the Central Executive Committee. While no one is immune from the authority of the G.P.U., certain classes of people are endowed with special guarantees in regard to arrest. Members of the Union and All-Russian Central Executive Committees may not be arrested and confined and their premises searched by administrative or judicial orders without special sanction of the respective presidia of the committees. In extraordinary circumstances, the chairmen of the committees may give permission for such action, and report it to the appropriate presidia.

. . . The activity of the G.P.U. is concentrated on the anti-Soviet elements composed of the old aristocracy, the former intelligentsia, private traders, irreconcilable priests of the old church, some socialistic factions which refused to join the Bolsheviks, anarchists, and certain elements of the Communist Party formerly led by the exiled Trotsky.

In the nature of things the work of the G.P.U. is secret, and arrests are usually made late at night. The agents in plain clothes are generally accompanied by uniformed, armed soldiers. The arrests are made with authorized warrants. The agents of the G.P.U. are not beneath setting traps for suspected persons, which usually take the form of stationing operatives on the premises of suspected persons for some days. The G.P.U., whose leaders are tried Bolsheviks, have learned a lesson or two from the tsarist *Ochrana* and have improved on it.

In accordance with the decree of February 1922, the agents of G.P.U. are authorized to undertake arrests, searches, or seizures without special permission of higher authorities in cases of persons caught in the act or within forty-eight hours of having committed a crime. All other arrests, searches, and seizures are only permissible by special authorization of higher organs. The prisoner must be indicted not later than two weeks after arrest. At the expiration of two months after the day of arrest, the G.P.U. must either free the prisoner or ask special permission from the Central Executive Committee for a longer period of detention. This may be granted at the discretion of the Central Committee if circumstances in the case warrant such action; otherwise, the case must be transferred to the courts. The majority of violations in connection with speculation and dereliction of official duties and similar offenses, which were under the jurisdiction of the Cheka, are now transferred to the jurisdiction of revolutionary tribunals or regular courts.

. . . . .

Unfortunately the provisions as stated above are not adhered to in practice, and most political cases originating with arrests by the G.P.U. are dealt with administratively and not by regular judicial procedure. Economic cases, on the other hand, are turned over to the courts. The G.P.U. may also exile a person involved in offenses against the state. . . .

The organization in the various republics is similar to that of the central organ and is directed by the Union agency. A prosecutor appointed by the central executive committee of the respective republic is in charge of the activity in that state. The local G.P.U. may appeal any disagreement with the local prosecutor to the Union Central Executive Committee. All activity of the local units of the G.P.U. must be reported to the central headquarters in Moscow. The Central Executive Committee is the last resort in any change of sentence. . . .

In recent years there have been in Soviet publications complaints of the low educational qualifications of militsiamen [policemen]. There is also considerable criticism of the character of the police force. In some cities members of the police force had to be disciplined for drunkenness, failure to execute orders, desertion of their posts, discourteous treatment of the public, etc. There is considerable agitation for the increase of salaries and betterment of living conditions in order to attract superior types of men into the service, and in recent legislation passed in 1931 some of these demands have been met. However, with the exceptions of the activities of the G.P.U. as described above, all fair observers and students of Soviet Russia agree that the Soviet police is not more unreasonable than the police the world over. . . . There is one phase of Russian life, however, which cannot be duplicated in any other country unless it is in Italy or Germany, and that is the insistence on political orthodoxy, which is justified by Bolsheviks as an absolute necessity in a proletarian state, constantly plotted against by internal and external foes. The state in its fight for existence, they argue, must use all means to prtoect itself. . . .

229. "WAR COMMUNISM," 1918-1921 [14]

Owing partly to the exigencies of the military situation and partly to the unrestrained enthusiasm of some members of the revolutionary councils, the Bolsheviks attempted, from 1918 to 1921, to introduce a completely communistic system in the economic and social as well as political spheres. This process and the reasons for its failure were well described by William H. Chamberlin, former Russian correspondent of the Christian Science Monitor *and one of the ablest American reporters of the Soviet scene.*

The economic system which prevailed in Soviet Russia from 1918 until 1921 has gone into history under the name: war communism. And the name accurately reflects the double nature of the system, which was a compound of war emergency and socialist dogmatism.

. . . . .

The sugar industry was nationalized on May 2 [1918] and the petroleum industry on June 17. Soon after this, on June 28, a very important decree indicated that Soviet economic policy was set definitely in the direction of the complete expropriation of the private capitalists. This decree called for the nationalization of the largest undertakings in the mining, metallurgical, metal-working, textile, electro-technical, pottery, tanning and cement industries. It set in motion a huge process of

---

[14] From W. H. Chamberlin, *The Russian Revolution 1917-1921,* 2 vols., New York, 1935, vol. II, pp. 96-102, 105, 110. By permission of The Macmillan Company, publishers.

confiscation which continued until all the large factories in Soviet territory had been taken over by the state and reached its culminating point when a decree of November 29, 1920, declared nationalized all plants which employed more than ten workers, or more than five workers if motor power were employed. The Soviet census of 1920 showed that 37,000 undertakings were in the hands of the state; many of these were the smallest kind of workshops or enterprises where sometimes only a single worker was employed.

. . . A decree of November 21, 1918, abolished legal internal trade, making the Food Commissariat the sole institution authorized to supply the population with articles of consumption and giving it the right to confiscate all stocks of goods which might still be in private hands. A decree of March 20, 1919, abolished the autonomy which the coöperatives had formerly enjoyed and fused them with the huge apparatus of the Food Commissariat, bringing them under the strictest state control.

War communism as a system was characterized by six main principles, which were more and more rigorously and intensively applied as the system early in 1921 approached its final crisis, which led to the substitution of the entirely different New Economic Policy. The first of these was that the state through its central or local organs took over all means of production and reduced the sphere of private ownership to the narrowest possible limits. Not only factories, railroads and banks, but private houses of any size, large libraries, privately owned objects of value, such as gold and jewels, were confiscated and taken from their owners.

The second principle of war communism was state control over the labor of every citizen. Especially in the later phase of the system, which began early in 1920, . . . compulsory labor was applied on a very wide scale. Armies which had no further military occupation were kept as "labor armies" and set to such mass tasks as felling trees, building roads, loading and unloading freightcars. Different categories of workers were mobilized under threat of punishment and assigned to the places where they were most needed. The peasants were subjected to a number of compulsory labor duties, such as supplying teams for carting wood and clearing snow from the railroad tracks. A decree of February 5, 1920, established in more concrete and definite form the obligation, already written into the Soviet Constitution, of every Soviet citizen to work.

Typical of the numerous labor mobilizations of 1920 was an order to all women between the ages of eighteen and forty-five to sew underwear for the Red Army.

A third feature of the system was the effort of the state to produce everything in its own undertakings. With the nationalization even of the smaller workshops and the legal prohibition of private trade (which, incidentally, was continually disregarded and evaded) all production in the towns, on paper at least, was brought under state control. A logical extension of this system, decreed just on the eve of its final collapse, was the effort to control and direct from above the agricultural activities of millions of peasant households. . . .

. . . . . .

. . . sowing committees were set up in every province, county and township, for the purpose of supervising the work of the peasants and inducing or compelling them to plant as much as was required.

A fourth characteristic of the system was extreme centralization. There was an effort . . . to place the entire regulation of the economic life of a vast country, with a population of well over a hundred millions, in the hands of a few hastily improvised state bureaucratic organizations. Prominent among these was the Supreme Economic Council, created by a decree of December 15, 1917, which described as the function of the new body "the organization of national economic life and of state finances." Originally it was supposed to possess wide powers in various branches of economic life, another clause in the decree granting it the right of "confiscation, requisition, sequestration and compulsory trustification of different branches of industry and trade and of taking other measures in the field of production, distribution and state finances."

In actual functioning, however, the Supreme Economic Council became a specialized department for the management of industry. As constituted in 1918 it consisted of sixty-eight members, of whom ten were nominated by the Soviet Central Executive Committee, thirty by the industrial trade-unions, twenty by the local Supreme Economic Councils and the remainder by various Commissariats and by the Workers Coöperative Organization. Actual executive power rested in the hands of its presidium, which was made up of ten or twelve members. Typical of the activity of the presidium in taking away the property of individual owners is a partial record of its decisions in the month of November, 1918, which includes the following items:

"To nationalize thirteen paper factories. (November 14.)

"To nationalize all metals and metal products in wholesale warehouses in Russia. (November 19.)

"To nationalize all the cloth goods in Moscow. (November 5.)

"To nationalize the automobile factories, 'Russian Renaud,' 'Amo' and the factory of Lebedev. (November 26.)

"To nationalize all the property of the chemical-bacteriological laboratory of Professor M. N. Ostromislensky in Moscow. (November 16.)"

. . . . .

The management of the individual factories, after the original owners or directors had been driven away, passed through several stages of organization. In the first process of nationalization, in 1918, authority was usually vested in a collegium, or committee, of workers. The activity of such a collegium was usually characterized by much talk and little concrete action; and with the passing of time there was a tendency first to limit the numbers of the collegia and finally to pass over to a system of one-man management. A. I. Rykov, President of the Supreme Economic Council, declared in the autumn of 1920 that in the great majority of cases there was definite improvement as soon as full authority and responsibility were vested in a single manager. . . .

. . . . .

The fifth principle of war communism was that the state attempted to assume the functions not only of the sole producer, but of the sole distributor. The all-powerful Food Commissariat took from industry whatever it produced for distribution among the population and took from agriculture, mainly on the basis of forced levies, whatever could be extracted from the peasants and distributed it among the town population, which was placed on ration cards. The "class principle" was rigidly applied in the allotment of rations. The Moscow Soviet in September, 1918, divided the population into four categories. The first consisted of manual workers engaged in harmful trades; the second, of workers who were obliged to perform heavy physical labor; the third, of workers at light tasks, employees, housewives; the fourth, of professional men and women and persons living on income or without employment. Such food supplies as were available were doled out to these four categories in the ratio: 4;3;2;1. Inasmuch as even the favored class, the manual workers, received so little food in those years that great masses of them fled from the cities to the villages, the persons in the fourth category received practically nothing, and were likely to die of malnutrition or starvation unless they were able to barter some of their former possessions for extra supplies of food on the illegal free market, which existed all through these years, although it was subjected to periodic raids and confiscations.

. . . . .

The sixth outstanding feature of war communism was the attempt to abolish money altogether as a means of exchange, to go over to a system of natural economy, in which all transactions were carried out in kind. As in the case of the other features of the system, this attempt was not made all at once. The whole trend of Soviet policy, the complete concentration of production and distribution in the hands of the state, the substitution of requisitions for free purchases from the peasants, the tendency to pay a larger part of wages and salaries in allotments of food and clothing was in the direction of making money superfluous. Communist economists of that period, far from deploring the visible shrinkage in the value of Soviet currency, welcomed it as a step toward a new and higher economic stage. . . .

. . . . .

So the economic system which had grown up in Russia until the roar of cannon during the Kronstadt uprising and the ominous rumble of peasant insurrections in many parts of the country brought about a sharp change in the spring of 1921 was one in which the state aspired to the rôle of sole producer and sole distributor, in which labor under state direction and regimentation was compulsory, in which payments were in kind, in which both the need for and the use of money had largely disappeared. What were the practical results of this system?

. . . . .

The Communist economist and historian of war communism, L. Kritzman, after analyzing the economic collapse of the country, makes the frank and indisputable assertion: "Such a decline in the productive forces not of a little community, but of an enormous society of a hundred million people . . . is unprecedented in the history of humanity."

230. LENIN ON THE NEW ECONOMIC POLICY [15]

Among the reasons for Lenin's success must be counted his ability to recognize mistakes and his willingness to admit and correct them. Thus, at the tenth congress of the Communist Party, in March 1921, he explained that the attempt to establish pure communism at a stroke had failed and that it was necessary now to effect a retreat—a strategic retreat. He therefore advocated a New Economic Policy (NEP) involving "as much communism as the exigencies of the situation would permit, and no more." In effect, he proposed a form of "state capitalism" and a temporary compromise with small capitalists and with the farmers who had not yet become imbued with the Marxist spirit. The accompanying selection formed part of a speech delivered by Lenin in October 1921 before a group of persons whose duty it was to explain the new conditions to the people.

Partly under the influence of the military tasks with which we were . . . overwhelmed, and partly owing to the desperate position, as it seemed, of the Republic, we made the mistake [in 1918] of trying to bring about an immediate transition to Communist production and distribution. . . . [But] a not very long experience served to convince us that this structure was a mistake and in contradiction to what we had formerly written as to the transition from Capitalism to Socialism, and that if we did not pass through the period of Socialist accounting and control it would be impossible to pass even to the lowest stage of Communism.

. . . This is the essence of what was forgotten by us when we were compelled, at the height of the civil war, to take unavoidable steps in the matter of reconstruction. Our new economic policy consists essentially in this, that having suffered a heavy defeat in this policy, we have begun a strategic retreat. . . . There is no manner of doubt that we have suffered a defeat on the economic front, and as Communists we cannot permit a heavy defeat, so in full consciousness we turn to deal with the question of a new economic policy.

. . . . . .

[15] Speech delivered to the Congress of Local Organizations for Political Enlightenment in October 1921, in *The Labour Monthly,* vol. I, No. 6, The Labour Publishing Company, Ltd., London, December 15, 1921, pp. 506-510, 515-516. Reprinted by permission of the publishers.

. . . On the economic front, from the attempt to establish Communism up to the spring of 1921, we suffered a more serious defeat than any inflicted on us by Koltchak, Denikin, or Pilsudsky, a defeat indicating that the superstructure of our economic policy was not built on a firm foundation. . . .

- -

The new economic policy with its agricultural tax in place of requisitions denotes the re-establishment of Capitalism in a significant degree. To what degree—we do not yet know. Concessions to foreign capitalists . . . and leases to private capitalists represent a direct re-introduction of Capitalism and are radically connected with the new economic policy. . . .

- -

Our present struggle will have for its result either a victory for the capitalist, to whom we are opening the door, and even several doors, or a victory for the proletarian State power. . . .

- -

The whole question is as to who will forestall whom. Should the capitalists succeed in organising themselves first—they will drive out the Communists without more ado. . . . Will the proletarian State power prove itself capable, relying on the peasants, to hold Messieurs the capitalists in check, in order to direct Capitalism along the State path and to create a Capitalism subordinate to the State and serving it?

- -

Let us industrialize everything. Capitalists will be amongst us, foreign capitalists, concessionaires, and lease holders: they will wrest from us hundreds per cent. of profit, they will flourish around us. Let them flourish; we will learn from them how to carry on industry, and then we shall be able to construct our Communist Republic. From the point of view of learning quickly any kind of slacking is the greatest crime. It is necessary to adopt this apprenticeship, an apprenticeship burdensome, severe, sometimes even cruel, for there is no other way forward.

- -

In our uncultured state we cannot by a frontal attack achieve the destruction of Capitalism. At a different level of culture it would have been possible to accomplish the task more directly, and perhaps other countries will be able to do so when the time comes for the construction of their Communist Republics. But *we* cannot solve the problem by the direct method.

The State must learn to carry on trade so that industry can satisfy the peasants, so that the peasants by trade can satisfy their needs. It is necessary to put the matter so that every worker will devote his powers to strengthening the workers-peasants' State. Only then can a large-scale industry be created.

231. A SOVIET ESTIMATE OF THE ECONOMIC STRUCTURE OF THE U.S.S.R., 1927 [15]

Perhaps because of the example set by Lenin, the Communist Party in the Soviet Union from time to time took stock of the economic structure of the country and inscribed the debit as well as the credit side of the ledger. An interesting example of this procedure was cited by Stuart Chase in a co-operative work on Russia in the decade of the 1920's.

In conclusion I [Stuart Chase] should like to quote from a remarkable political document. It is the economic summary for the current year . . . issued by the Plenum of the Communist Party in September, 1927. . . . There are ten favorable items and ten unfavorable items as follows.

Favorable

1. The steady increase in industrial production. . . .

2. The outlay of over $500,000,000 in 1927 for new industrial capital, including electrification.

3. The increase in real wages during the first nine months of 1927, accompanied by an improvement in the productivity of labor.

4. The turning point of high retail prices was reached in January, 1927. Since then retail prices have begun slowly to fall.

5. The stability of grain prices paid to the farmer during the year, and the decline in retail prices for grain products.

---

[15] Summarized in S. Chase, R. Dunn, and R. G. Tugwell, eds., *Soviet Russia in the Second Decade. A Joint Survey by the Technical Staff of the First American Trade Union Delegation,* The John Day Company, New York, 1928, pp. 51-52. Reprinted by permission of the publishers.

6. The increase in land cultivated for technical crops—sugar beets, etc.

7. The growing importance in trade of the coöperatives and the government stores as contrasted with the private trader. . . .

8. The attainment of a favorable foreign trade balance.

9. A balanced federal budget.

10. The increasing purchasing power of the ruble; the increase in savings bank deposits on the part of the people at large.

Unfavorable

1. Considerable miscalculations in capital investment, particularly in respect to higher costs than were anticipated for new construction.

2. The slow progress made in restoring housing. . . .

3. The extremely slow rate at which industrial costs decline.

4. The high general level of prices for industrial goods despite all efforts, and the great discrepancy between wholesale and retail prices.

5. The difficulties in securing adequate raw materials.

6. A less than anticipated increase in the corn-growing area.

7. The fact that too much credit has been granted to large farmers, and to pseudo-agricultural coöperatives.

8. The slow increase in the facilities for railway transport.

9. The great disparity between the development of foreign trade and internal economy.

10. The large amount of unemployment particularly among unskilled workers and government trade employees, accompanied by a shortage of skilled workers.

232. THE FULFILMENT OF THE FIRST FIVE-YEAR PLAN [16]

While the New Economic Policy was in force, the government appointed numerous state bureaus to gather statistical information on every phase of economic and social life in the Soviet Union. With the aid of the data thus accumulated a State Planning Commission (Gosplan) prepared a complete economic and social forecast for the Union for the five-year period 1928-1933. Under the watchful eye of Joseph Stalin this Five-Year Plan (Piati-

---

[16] Union of Soviet Socialist Republics, *Report of the State Planning Commission of the Council of People's Commissars of the Union of Soviet Socialist Republics: Summary of the Fulfilment of the First Five-Year Plan for the Development of the National Economy of the U.S.S.R.,* State Planning Commission of the U.S.S.R., Moscow, 1933, pp. 34-37.

*letka) was placed in operation on October 1, 1928. In the circumstances
it was understandable that, in some cases, the production and distribution
schedules were left far behind, while in others the goal was not reached;
similarly, the level of costs and prices was often much higher in actuality
than on paper. Generally, however, the results were regarded as sufficiently satisfactory so that the plan was declared fulfilled on December 31,
1932, after four years and a quarter.*

The task set by the Five-Year Plan was successfully carried out in
four years.

In the first Five-Year Plan period, the socialist forms of economy
became the absolutely predominant forms in the U.S.S.R. The question
as to "who will win"—collective or private enterprise—has been settled,
not only for the towns, but also for the countryside. The foundation of
socialist economy has been laid. The U.S.S.R. has entered into the
period of socialism.

The Soviet Union has created its own industrial base for the reconstruction of industry, transport and agriculture. From the position of
a backward country, the U.S.S.R. has moved into the front rank of
the technically and economically highly developed countries. From an
agrarian country, it has been transformed into an industrial country,
and it has developed its machine building industry on a scale that will
secure the production of the decisive share of the equipment for Soviet
enterprises and by that, it has to an enormous degree increased the
technical and economic independence and defence capacity of the
country.

In spite of the assertions of the bourgeoisie and of its armour bearers,
the Mensheviks, that the proletariat, having destroyed the old world,
is incapable of building up a new socialist world, the working class of
the U.S.S.R. led by the Communist Party headed by Joseph V. Stalin,
transformed the Five-Year Plan into a real and tangible fact which
is incorporated in hundreds of thousands of industrial and agricultural
enterprises that have been created in the Five-Year Plan period, and
in the exceptionally significant achievements in the improvement of
the material conditions of the toilers in town and country.

The economic and political positions of the proletarian dictatorship
have been reinforced; the leading role of the working class has im-
measurably increased. The most dangerous enemy of the proletarian
revolution, the *kulaks,* has been routed. Owing to the fact that the bulk

of the peasantry have been transformed into collective farmers, the alliance with the peasantry has been reinforced on a firmer foundation.

The Soviet Government is the most firmly established government in the world.

The victory of socialism has decisively turned the intelligentsia to the side of the Soviet Government. The overwhelming majority of the intelligentsia have firmly taken up the position of the October Revolution. Tens of thousands of new proletarian specialists have poured into the ranks of the intelligentsia and have thus changed its social composition and political complexion.

The position of the proletarian dictatorship has become consolidated in the republics of the national minorities and districts that were formerly economically and culturally backward. The socialist geographic distribution of the productive forces of the country during the Five-Year Plan period has transformed these former colonies of tsarist Russia into important proletarian centres having strong native proletarian cadres.

The defence capacity of the country has been considerably strengthened. During the Five-Year Plan period, the U.S.S.R. has become a mighty country capable at any time of repelling any attempt at armed intervention.

Overcoming enormous difficulties connected with the necessity of simultaneously solving the problems of creating a heavy industry, of developing light industries, of reconstructing agriculture and of improving the material conditions of the toilers in town and country, the U.S.S.R. is successfully coping with all these problems and is presenting to mankind the socialist type of industrialization of the country.

The U.S.S.R. did not have long-term foreign loans to help it to solve all these problems; it solved them with its own resources, by the growth of internal accumulation, by drawing into productive labour the whole of the able-bodied population of the country and abolishing unemployment, and by abolishing the consumption of parasitic elements, by encouraging science and technique, by rousing a socialist attitude towards labour and by creating fundamentally different relations between town and country.

As a result of socialist industrialization and the victory of large-scale agriculture, the U.S.S.R. in the first Five-Year Plan period succeeded in removing the main disproportions in national economy, the lag of industry behind the requirements of national economy, the excessive lag of agriculture behind industry as a consequence of its small peasant character, and by that it has crossed the most difficult barrier of internal difficulties. This in its turn has created the possibility of removing, during the second Five-Year Plan period, certain partial disproportions which still remain (the lag of the output of the iron and steel industry and transport behind the general rate of increase of national economy, the complete abolition of the lag of agriculture).

The fulfilment of the Five-year Plan has revealed the enormous advantages of the young and not yet completely developed socialist system. Already in the process of the reconstruction of national economy, the U.S.S.R. secured a gigantic development of the productive forces during the first Five-Year Plan period which translated the theory that socialism is a higher form of social production than capitalism into the language of facts and figures.

The victory of the Five-Year Plan has irrefutably proved the historical correctness of the teachings of Marx and Lenin concerning the road of emancipation of the exploited and oppressed masses from the power of capital and concerning the building of a new and higher social system: socialism.

The gigantic achievements of the first Five-Year Plan made it possible to set, in the second Five-Year Plan, the task of finally abolishing the capitalist elements and of classes generally, and of transforming the whole of the working population of the country into conscious and active builders of classless socialist society; it has also permitted the raising of the great question of completing the technical reconstruction of the whole of the national economy of the Soviet Union, of bringing the U.S.S.R. to the first place in Europe in regard to technical development, and of finally securing the technical and economic independence of the U.S.S.R.

233. ACHIEVEMENTS OF THE FIRST, AND AIMS OF THE SECOND, FIVE-YEAR PLAN [17]

In its published outline of the Second Five-Year Plan (1933-1937), the State Planning Commission reviewed the general achievements of the first plan and set the aims for the second one. The second plan emphasized

---

[17] Union of Soviet Socialist Republics, State Planning Commission of the U.S.S.R., *The Second Five-Year Plan for the Development of the National Economy of the U.S.S.R. (1933-1937)*, International Publishers, New York, 1937, pp. 3-5, 24-25. Reprinted by permission of the publishers.

quality more than quantity and betrayed less of the "giant-mania" than had its predecessor. The new industries, moreover, were allocated to regions closer to the sources of raw materials and, incidentally, nearer the Ural Mountains, relatively safe from foreign attack. Finally, in an endeavor to raise the general standard of living, greater emphasis was placed on consumers' than producers' goods. This plan, too, on the whole, worked out to the satisfaction of the Bolsheviks.

Already during the First Five-Year Plan period, thanks to the heroic struggle of the working class, the foundation of socialist economy was laid, the last capitalist class—the kulaks (rich peasantry)—was routed and the basic masses of the peasantry—the collective farmers—became a firm support of the Soviet Government in the countryside. The U.S.S.R. finally established itself on the socialist road.

During the years covered by the First Five-Year Plan a large-scale, technically advanced industry was created in the U.S.S.R., and especially remarkable successes were achieved in the establishment of a modern heavy industry—the material base of socialism, the foundation of the reconstruction of the whole national economy and the condition for the accelerated development of light industry, the food industry and agriculture. Dozens of new branches of industry were organized; complex machine-tool construction, an automobile and tractor industry, harvester-combine construction, aircraft and aeroplane-motor construction, the manufacture of powerful turbines and generators, of special steels, ferro-alloys and aluminum, a modern chemical industry, a synthetic rubber industry, the manufacture of nitrates, artificial fibres, etc. The knit-goods, needle-trades, footwear, meat-packing, canning, paper and other industries were reconstructed on the basis of modern technique. Thousands of modern enterprises were built which elevated the whole national economy to a high plane of new technical culture, on a par with the best examples of capitalist technique.

Agriculture was radically reconstructed during the First Five-Year Plan period. The proletariat led by the Leninist Party convinced the millions of the peasantry of the superiority of collective production and created a new collective farm system in the countryside. The victories in the development of industry conditioned the gigantic successes achieved in switching agriculture to the track of machine-operated technique. The U.S.S.R. has become the country of the largest-scale agriculture in the world.

The great successes in the establishment of a new socialist labour discipline, the improvement in the skill of the workers and the considerable achievements in the organization of production have made it possible to score enormous victories in promoting labour productivity during the course of the technical reconstruction. In the rate of increase of labour productivity the U.S.S.R. outstripped all capitalist countries, even in comparison with the years of their greatest upsurge.

The proletariat, which has overcome the tremendous difficulties resulting from the realization of the First Five-Year Plan, achieved victories of historic importance in the matter of improving the position of the toilers in town and country. The superiority of the Soviet order, even at the stage of development attained, permitted of the complete elimination of unemployment, the introduction of the seven-hour working day and the abolition of destitution and pauperism in the countryside.

. . . . .

"The chief political task of the Second Five-Year Plan is the final abolition of the capitalist elements and of classes in general; fully to destroy the causes which gave rise to class distinction and exploitation; to overcome the survivals of capitalism in economic life and in the minds of people; to transform the whole working population of the country into conscious, active builders of classless, socialist society." *(Resolution of the Seventeenth Conference of the C.P.S.U.)*[18]

The final abolition of the remnants of the parasitic classes and the general growth of the national income which is placed entirely at the disposal of the toiler must ensure during the Second Five-Year Plan period a still more rapid improvement in the well-being of the worker and collective farm masses, a considerable growth of real wages, and a 2- to 3-fold rise in the level of consumption of the toilers.

The realization of these tasks is possible only on the basis of the broad technical reconstruction of the whole of national economy, of industry, of transportation, of agriculture. Therefore the completion of the reconstruction of the whole of national economy is the fundamental and decisive economic task of the Second Five-Year Plan period. Mastery of the new technique and of the manufacture of new products is necessarily the decisive condition for the completion of technical

[18] The 17th Congress of the Communist Party of the Soviet Union adopted this resolution unanimously on February 10, 1934.—*Ed.*

reconstruction in national economy during the Second Five-Year Plan period. "Fervour for *new construction*" must be supplemented during the Second Five-Year Plan period by "fervour for *mastering* the new factories and the new technique, for seriously increasing the productivity of labour, for seriously reducing cost of production." (Stalin.)

· · · · ·

The Seventeenth Congress of the C.P.S.U. places on record that the Second Five-Year Plan . . . ensures:

a) The abolition of capitalist elements and of classes in general, the final abolition of the private ownership of the means of production on the basis of the full completion of collectivization of peasant holdings and the inclusion of all artisans in co-operative organizations, the abolition of the multiplicity of socio-economic systems in the Soviet Union and the establishment of the socialist mode of production as the only mode of production, together with the transformation of the entire toiling population of the country into active, conscious builders of socialist society;

b) The completion, on the basis created during the First Five-Year Plan period, of technical reconstruction which is advancing along the road of the further rapid rise of industry producing means of production (heavy industry);

c) A more rapid improvement in the well-being of the worker and peasant masses together with a decided improvement in housing and municipal services in the U.S.S.R.;

d) The entrenchment of the economic and political positions of the proletarian dictatorship on the basis of the alliance between the working class and the peasantry for the final abolition of capitalist elements and of classes in general;

e) The further reinforcement of the defensive strength of the country.

The realization of these tasks, which leads to the forcing out of the last remnants of the capitalist elements from their old positions and dooms them to final extinction, cannot but call forth a sharpening of the class struggle, new attempts by the rich peasants to undermine the work of the collective farms, attempts at wrecking and sabotage of our industrial enterprises by anti-Soviet forces. On the other hand the realization of the tasks of the Second Five-Year Plan period, the five-

year period of a radical rise in the standard of living of the workers and
peasant masses on the basis of the completion of the technical reconstruction of the whole national economy, cannot but call forth the
enthusiasm of the toilers, a high tide of productional activity and a
growing aspiration among the broadest masses of the toilers—the
builders of socialism—to master the new technique.

234. DESCRIPTION OF A MODEL CONSTITUTION FOR COLLECTIVE FARMS [19]

*During the official celebration of the twentieth anniversary of the Bol-
shevik Revolution, in November 1937, the Soviet authorities proudly announced that 90 per cent of all peasant households had become collectivized.
The 245,000 collective farms, it was said, accounted for 98 per cent of the
area sown to grain. (Two million peasant households were still non-collectivized; they had to deliver higher grain quotas and pay higher agricultural taxes than their collectivized neighbors.) The constitutions of most of
these collectives were based on a model proposed in 1935 by the head of the
agricultural section of the Central Committee of the All-Union Communist
Party.*

In an address delivered at the second Congress of Collective Farm
Shock Workers, held in Moscow in February [1935], Y. A. Yakovlev,
head of the agricultural section of the Central Committee of the Communist Party of the Soviet Union, outlined the changes which had taken
place in collective farming since the first congress, held in 1932, and
submitted a proposed new model constitution for agricultural artels
(collectives). He pointed out that while the first congress had taken
place at a time when collective farms were faced with great difficulties,
the present assembly met at a time when agriculture could record
numerous successes. . . . On the basis of these developments, the government considered it necessary to revise the constitution of the artels,
originally drawn up in 1930, so as to give the benefits of the experience
of the most advanced collective farms to the entire system of collectivized agriculture. The changes were embodied in a model consti-

---

[19] *Economic Review of the Soviet Union*, vol. X, No. 3, Amtorg Trading Corporation,
Information Department, New York, April 1935, pp. 88-89. Reprinted by permission of
the publishers.

tution adopted by the Congress and ratified by the Council of People's Commissars and the Central Committee of the Communist Party on February 17 [1935].

As regards the question of the division and organization of the land, the basic principles are formulated as follows:

Artel land is state property, the property of the whole of the people, which, according to the laws of the Workers' and Peasants' State, is assigned to the artel for permanent utilization and is subject neither to purchase, sale nor lease.

The total land unit of the artel must not be reduced under any circumstances. The allotment of land from the land area of the artel to members of the artel leaving it is prohibited. Those who leave the artel may receive land only from the free state lands.

The lands of the artel are divided into fields in accordance with the agreed crop rotation.

In crop rotation fields, a section is permanently attached to every field tillage brigade for the whole term of the crop rotation.

The land to be allotted to collective farmers for their own use is to range from one-quarter hectare[20] to one hectare (exclusive of the land occupied by the dwelling), depending on the district. The dimensions will be determined by the People's Commissariat for Agriculture.

All the working cattle, agricultural equipment, seed reserves, fodder to the amount necessary for maintaining the socialized livestock, the buildings required for the work of the artel and all enterprises for processing of agricultural produce constitute socialized property of the collective. On the other hand, the dwelling house of the member of the artel, his personal livestock and poultry, and the buildings necessary for maintaining the livestock which is personally used by the collective farmer are not socialized and remain at his disposal.

The small agricultural implements required for work on the land around the member's house are also not collectivized. When necessary, the management must set aside a number of horses for the personal needs of the members of the artel.

To stimulate the development of stock farms, the constitution makes it obligatory for all artels to organize collective livestock farms and to develop within certain limits the secondary personal livestock of the members of the artels.

[20] A hectare=2.471 acres.—*Ed.*

Each household in collective farms in grain, cotton, beet, flax, hemp, potato and vegetable, tea and tobacco districts, may have at its own disposal a cow, up to two young large horned cattle, one or two pigs with offspring, up to 10 sheep and goats and an unlimited number of poultry and rabbits and up to 20 beehives.

In livestock districts where tilling is of small significance in the holdings (districts of settled herding) or of almost no significance whatever (districts of nomad herding), the People's Commissariat for Agriculture of the separate republics will establish higher norms of personal ownership of cattle in accordance with local conditions. In such cases the number of cows (aside from calves) may go up to 10, the number of sheep and goats up to 150, etc.

On the problem of whom to admit and whom to exclude from the artel and on what basis, Yakovlev pointed out that a certain amount of leniency on the part of the collective farms towards the individual peasants and reformed kulaks was now necessary. On January 1, 1935, he stated, there were 16.5 million peasant households in collectives, which left about five million households still outside—about 25 million persons in all. If individual peasants, within two years of making application for membership, have sold their horses and possess no seed, they can be accepted provided they agree to pay up the cost of the horses and seed within a period of six years. The old constitution did not permit this. Regarding the right of former kulaks or their children to enter the artels, here also the collectives could afford to show greater leniency. A number of these former kulaks had shown by hard and honest work during the past few years that they could be reformed. Such peasants should be permitted to enter the collective farms.

The proposal on expulsions from artels was as follows:

A member may be expelled from an artel only upon the decision of a general meeting of the members of the artel, at which not less than two-thirds of the total number of members of the artel are present. It is necessary to record in the protocol of the general assembly the number voting for expulsion.

In case a member of an artel appeals the decision on his expulsion to the district executive committee of the soviet, the question is finally decided by the presidium of the district executive committee of the soviet in the presence of the chairman of the administration of the artel and the plaintiff.

The constitution includes directives to the artels with regard to the introduction of various measures to improve the work of the collective farms. These include the extension of sowing with selected seed; the introduction of proper crop rotation and deep plowing; the expansion of tillage of fallow land; the use of mineral fertilizers, manure and other local fertilizers; inter-row cultivation of technical crops carried out in a careful manner; planting of forests; protection of irrigation structures; the introduction of auxiliary branches of agriculture—beekeeping, etc.

A series of measures was proposed for the improvement of the financial control and management of the artels. The constitution provides for election of auditing commissions to check up on finances and to institute a régime of economy. The rights and duties of the chairman of the artel and other officers are clearly specified, the calling of regular meetings is provided for, etc. Payment for work is based on the qualifications required for the particular job and the amount of work accomplished; piece work is the general rule. Brigade leaders are to keep careful check on the amount of work done by each member of their group; the administration of the artel is to post the list of the number of working days due each member of the collective two weeks before the general meeting confirming the distribution of income. For breaches of discipline, poor work, etc., punishments of reprimands and fines (not exceeding five work days) are provided.

Yakovlev's report also dealt with the increasing importance of the woman collective farmer. The number of women on artel administrations has grown from 85,000 to 165,000 in the two years since the first congress of collective farm shock workers. The number of women brigade leaders rose from 12,000 to 50,000, while the number of women chairmen of artels rose from 1,200 in 1931 to 7,000 in 1935; there are now [1935] 19,000 women managers of collective farm livestock sections as compared with 3,000 four years ago. This growing importance of the woman collective farmer had made necessary the inclusion of a clause in the constitution on the duty of the artel administration to draw women into production and social life of the artel, to promote capable and experienced women collective farmers to leading posts, freeing them as much as possible from domestic duties by forming crêches, kindergartens, etc. Pregnant women are to be given leaves of absence from work for a period of two months with half pay.

꙼ ꙼ ꙼

235. STALIN ON THE KULAKS AND ON CLASS WAR, 1925 [21]

The richer peasants in the Soviet Union, or those who held out against collectivization, were generally called kulaks. *In view of the manner in which this group is being "liquidated," it is interesting to note Joseph Stalin's personal opinion of the kulaks and of class war. The excerpt is from a speech delivered by Stalin at Sverdloff University on June 9, 1925. The talk consisted of replies to ten questions which had been submitted to Stalin, the one quoted below being the third.*

How is the fight against the kulaks to be waged successfully without kindling the class war? [The third question.]

The author of this question, so it seems to me, has tried to be too concise. His endeavour to abridge has led him to choose his words badly. What class war is here in question? If it refers to the class war in the countryside as a general phenomenon, then I would draw attention to the fact that the proletariat does not wage this war against the kulaks alone. The antagonisms between the proletariat and the peasantry as a whole—what have we here but a class struggle, though it is a class struggle of a peculiar and unusual kind? The proletariat and the peasantry are the two main classes of our present-day community. Between these two classes certain antagonisms exist which may, in the course of time, disappear, but which here and now are very much alive and give rise to conflicts between the two classes.

When we consider the relationship between town and countryside, between proletariat and peasantry, it seems to me that the class war in Russia is proceeding along three main lines.

(*a*) The struggle between the proletariat as a whole (represented by the State) and the peasantry in connexion with the fixing of maximum prices for industrial and agricultural products, in connexion with standardising taxation, and so forth.

(*b*) The struggle between the proletariat as a whole (represented by the State) and the rural bourgeoisie or kulaks in connexion with the reduction of prohibitive prices fixed by speculators for agricultural

[21] J. Stalin, *Leninism*, 2 vols., George Allen and Unwin, Ltd., London, 1928-1932, vol. I, pp. 308-314. Reprinted by permission of George Allen and Unwin, Ltd., and the International Publishers.

products, in connexion with the transference of the main burden of taxation onto the kulaks, etc.

(c) The struggle between the poor peasants, and more especially the farm labourers, and the kulaks.

We may consider these three aspects of the class struggle as three fronts differing in importance and in the nature of the issues that are being fought. Our attitude towards the various forms of the struggle along these fronts should, therefore, vary accordingly.

Let us examine the matter in greater detail.

First Front. In consequence of the mediocrity of our industrial development and the impossibility of raising loans wherewith to set it on a secure footing, the proletariat (represented by the State) has enacted a number of important measures for the defence of our industry against foreign competition, and with a view to expanding it in such a way as to advantage *(sic)* the whole of our national economy, including agriculture. These measures are: State monopoly of foreign trade, agricultural tax, State purchase and sale of agricultural produce, an all-embracing plan for the development of our national economy. The measures are based upon the idea of nationalisation of the chief branches of industry, transport and credit. The results from an application of these measures have been anticipated. They put a stop to the fall in the prices of industrial commodities, and to the rise in the excessively high price of agricultural produce. Nevertheless, it is obvious that the peasants, who have no option but to buy industrial commodities and to sell their agricultural products, will endeavour to buy cheap and to sell dear. In addition, the peasants would like to see the agricultural tax abolished, or, at least, to see it reduced to an absolute minimum.

Here we have a definite cause for a struggle between proletariat and peasantry.

Is the State in a position to renounce the above-mentioned measures? No, it is not. Such action on the part of the State at this juncture would ruin our industries, disrupt the proletariat as a class, change our country into an agrarian dependency of the industrially advanced lands, and frustrate the whole of the achievements of the revolution.

Is it to the interest of the peasantry as a whole that these measures should be abolished? Certainly not; for if these measures were abolished it would mean the triumph of the capitalist trend, which in its turn would mean the impoverishment of the majority of the peasants and the enrichment of a handful of wealthy persons, of capitalists. Who would venture to maintain that the peasantry desires its own impoverishment, that it desires to see our country turned into a colony, that it has not been keenly interested in the development of our economic system along socialist lines?

We here have a definite ground for an alliance between proletariat and peasantry.

Does this mean that our industrial institutions, relying on the State monopoly, are in a position to force up the prices of commodities to the disadvantage of the peasant masses and, in the long run, to the disadvantage of industry itself? No such thing! Industry would be the first victim of such a policy. It would then become impossible to transform our industry from the hothouse plant it was but yesterday into the healthy and flourishing concern it promises to be in the future. Hence our campaign in favour of a reduction of the prices of manufactured goods, and for raising the productivity of labour—which has had a fair measure of success.

· · · · ·

Second Front. Here the combatants are the proletariat (represented by the State) and the rural bourgeoisie or kulaks. The class struggle in this case assumes just as special a form as it did in the case of the fight on the *First Front.*

With a view to giving the agricultural tax a specifically income-tax character, the State has thrown the burden of it upon the shoulders of the kulaks. But the kulaks respond by trying to wriggle out of paying their contribution and by using all their influence in the villages with a view to shifting the burden on to the shoulders of the middle and poor peasants.

In its fight against soaring prices and in its endeavour to stabilise wages, the State is forced to take measures of an economic nature. These measures aim at fixing a just price for agricultural produce, a price which shall in every way meet the needs of the peasants. The kulaks respond by buying up the harvest of the middle and poor peasants, and by thus amassing huge reserves, which they store in their barns. They do not, forthwith, send these goods to market, for they know that the "corner" they thus establish will lead to an artificial rise in prices, and that large profits will accrue to the successful speculator. . . .

The class war on this front, with its special characteristics, and in a more or less veiled form, arises from such causes as I have enumerated.

At first sight it might seem that the policy of intensifying the class war on this front would be sound. This supposition is, however, quite false. Here, likewise, it is not to our interest to accentuate the class struggle. We can and must avoid provocation, and all the complications such provocation might entail.

We must put fresh life into the soviets, win over the middle peasants, and organise the poor peasants within the framework of the soviets. Thereby the main burden of taxation will be thrust on to the shoulders of the kulaks, and the broad masses of the peasantry will be relieved from the weight of taxation. Excellent results have already been achieved by the measures we have adopted to carry out these plans.

It is imperative that the State should have at its disposal a sufficient reserve of food, so as to be able to bring pressure to bear upon the market, to have the power of intervening when necessary, to keep prices at a level which is acceptable to the working masses, and thus to scotch the machinations of the rural speculators. Recently, as you know, tens of millions of poods[22] have been utilised for this purpose. Here, likewise, we have secured very gratifying results. Not only in such towns as Leningrad, Moscow, and Ivanovo-Voznesensk, and in such areas as the Donetz coalfield, were we able to keep down the price of grain, but in many other districts we forced the kulaks to capitulate and to put their corn reserves on the market.

Of course we cannot always arrange these matters as we should like. It is possible that, in certain cases, the kulaks will take the law into their own hands and themselves fan the flames of class war, will transform the struggle into something resembling an attack by brigands or an insurrectionary movement. In such an event the policy of kindling the class war would not be our policy but the kulaks' policy, it would be a counter-revolutionary policy. The sufferings entailed by the carrying out of such a policy (one, mark you, directed against the Soviet State) would fall upon the kulaks, who would have to pay dear for the step they had taken.

You will see that on this front, too, a deliberate kindling of the class struggle is out of the question, as far as we are concerned.

Third Front. The combatants on this front are the poor peasants (more especially the agricultural labourers) and the kulaks. The State

---

[22] A pood weighs about forty pounds.—*Ed.*

is not directly concerned. This front is not so extensive as the other two. But the class war is obvious and open here, whereas it is more or less veiled on the other fronts.

On the third front, there is direct exploitation of wage-labour or semi-wage-labour by the peasant proprietor. It would, therefore, be unsuitable if we embarked upon a policy of mitigating or of moderating the fight. What we have to do is to organise the poor peasants for the struggle against the kulaks, and ourselves to act as leaders in the fight.

But, you will ask, is not this "kindling the class war"? Not at all! When we speak of kindling the class war, we do not talk of the organisation and leadership of an unavoidable struggle, but, rather, of the artificial and deliberate stimulation of struggle where struggle is better avoided. Do we need to have recourse to artificial means now that we have the dictatorship of the proletariat, and now that the Party and the trade unions have absolute freedom of action? Of course not.

The policy of kindling the class war is, as we see, just as inept on this front as on the other two.

So much for the third question.

You will have no difficulty in realising that the question of the class struggle in the rural areas is not quite so simple as might appear at first sight.

236. FAMINE AS A POLITICAL WEAPON IN THE SOVIET UNION [23]

The ruthlessness of the campaign against non-collectivized kulaks reached a climax in the official use of famine as a political weapon in 1932-1933. The testimony is by William H. Chamberlin, already referred to (See introduction to Document No. 229) as one of the ablest former foreign correspondents in the Soviet Union.

The "liquidation of the kulaks as a class" in regions where collectivization was fairly complete was announced by Stalin as a policy and was legally authorized and carried into effect in the winter of 1929-1930. Under this system the kulak families were driven from their homes, with few possessions except the clothes on their backs, and were

---

[23] From W. H. Chamberlin, *Russia's Iron Age,* Boston, 1934, pp. 80-89. An Atlantic Monthly Press publication. Reprinted by permission of Little, Brown and Company.

either deported in freight cars to the northern forests and other places
of forced labor or obliged to live in dugouts and shanties on the out-
skirts of the village. . . .

Some relaxation of pressure on the peasantry took place in the spring
of 1930, when the authorities realized that an enormous destruction of
cattle had taken place as a result of the prevalent policy of forcing the
peasants to surrender all their animals to the possession of the collective
farm. . . .

. . . . .

But the worst of Russia's agrarian crisis was not over. As a result of
poor climatic conditions, the crop of 1931 was substantially inferior to
that of 1930. The state exactions from the peasantry, on the other hand,
were not relaxed, but intensified. In 1932, climatic conditions were
better; but the peasants, discouraged and in many cases already suffering
from undernourishment, showed little interest in reaping the crops
which, as they felt, would be taken away from them anyway. The stage
was set for a . . . catastrophe. The government had in reserve and was
prepared to employ the last and sharpest weapon in the armory of class
warfare: organized famine.

Rumors of wholesale starvation in the villages, especially in the southern and southeastern provinces of European Russia and in Central Asia,
began to filter into Moscow in the early spring. A clear intimation that
things were happening in the country districts which the Soviet censors
very definitely wished to conceal from the outside world was the unprecedented action of the authorities in forbidding several foreign correspondents to leave Moscow, and the establishment of a new ruling to
the effect that no foreign correspondent could travel in the countryside
without submitting a definite itinerary and obtaining permission to
make the trip from the Commissariat for Foreign Affairs.

No such permissions were granted until September, when the new
harvest was largely gathered in, the corpses had all been buried, the
trucks which, during late winter and early spring, made regular rounds
in Poltava, Kiev, and other centres of the famine region, picking up the
corpses of refugees from the country districts, had ceased to function,
and conditions were generally more normal. After the prohibition had
been lifted, I visited three widely separated districts of the Soviet Union
—Kropotkin, in the North Caucasus, and Poltava and Byelaya Tserkov,
in Ukraina. . . . On the basis of talks with peasants and figures sup-

plied not by peasants, who were often prone to exaggeration, but by local Soviet officials and collective-farm presidents, whose interest was rather to minimize what had taken place, I have no hesitation in saying that the southern and southeastern section of European Russia during the first six months of 1933 experienced a major famine, far more destructive than the local famines which occurred, mostly on the Volga, in exceptionally bad drought years under Tsarism, second in the number of its victims probably only to the famine of 1921-1922.

The first thing that struck me when I began to walk about in the Cossack villages in the neighborhood of Kropotkin was the extraordinary deterioration in the physical condition of what had once been an extremely fertile region. Enormous weeds, of striking height and toughness, filled up many of the gardens and could be seen waving in the fields of wheat, corn, and sunflower seeds. Gone were the wheaten loaves, the succulent slices of lamb that had been offered for sale everywhere when I visited the Kuban Valley in 1924. At that time every Cossack settlement had its large number of fierce, snapping dogs, trained to guard sheep and cattle; now there was an almost ghostly quiet; the bark of a dog was never heard. "The dogs all died or were eaten up during the famine," was the general explanation of their disappearance.

. . . . . .

. . . Hot dry winds had blighted some of the crops in 1932, and there had been a good deal of neglect in cultivation, as a result of apathy and discouragement. The huge weed crop choked out much of the grain, and in some cases a considerable part of the crop remained unharvested. Still it was the general testimony of the peasants that they could have pulled through if the local authorities had not swooped down with heavy requisitions. The last reserves of grain, which had been buried in the ground by the desperate peasants, were dug up and confiscated. A man named Sheboldaev, with a reputation for cruelty in "liquidating" kulaks in the lower Volga district, was made President of the North Caucasus, where the passive resistance was doubtless stiffer than in other sections of the country, because a considerable part of the population consisted of Cossacks, who had enjoyed a higher standard of living than the mass of the peasants before the Revolution and who had mostly fought on the side of the Whites during the civil war. Under Sheboldaev's orders whole communities, such as Poltavskaya, in the Western Kuban, were deported *en masse* to the frozen regions of the

north in the dead of winter. Other villages which did not fill out the
grain quotas that were demanded from them were "blockaded," in the
sense that no city products were allowed to reach them. Local officials
who protested against the pitiless repression were deposed, arrested,
in a few cases shot.

. . . .

Two noteworthy features of the famine were that far more men died
than women and far more *edinolichniki* (individual peasants) than
members of collective farms. . . . Of course not all who died passed
through the typical stages of death from outright hunger. . . . The
majority died of slight colds which they could not withstand in their
weakened condition; of typhus, the familiar accompaniment of famine;
of "exhaustion," to use the familiar euphemistic word in the death
reports. . . . The famine area, so far as I could observe and learn from
reliable information, included Ukraina, the North Caucasus, a number
of districts in the middle and lower Volga, and considerable sections
of remote Kazakstan, in Central Asia. . . .

. . . . .

Of the historic responsibility of the Soviet Government for the famine
of 1932-1933 there can be no reasonable doubt. In contrast to its policy
in 1921-1922, it stifled any appeal for foreign aid by denying the very
fact of the famine and by refusing to foreign journalists the right to
travel in the famine regions until it was all over. Famine was quite
deliberately employed as an instrument of national policy, as the last
means of breaking the resistance of the peasantry to the new system
where they are divorced from personal ownership of the land and
obliged to work on the conditions which the state may dictate to them
and deliver up whatever the state may demand from them.

"The collective farmers this year have passed through a good school.
For some this school was quite ruthless." In this cryptic understatement
President Kalinin summed up the situation in Ukraina and the North
Caucasus, from the Soviet standpoint. . . .

There can be no doubt that famine . . . was an effective means of
breaking any tendency on the part of the peasants to indulge in passive
resistance or "sabotage." There was general testimony that work in
the collective farms proceeded at a much faster pace in 1933 than in
preceding years, even when the collective-farm members were weakened
by hunger.

237. SOME DISTINGUISHING CHARACTERISTICS OF SOVIET BANKS [24]

The system of banking in the Soviet Union differs not merely from the system that formerly prevailed in Tsarist Russia, but from that in any of the "capitalist" powers. Dr. Arnold has well summarized these differences.

The new order eliminated a good many of the old institutions, and with them a number of the banking transactions that are peculiar to capitalist countries. For example, the speculative and investment activities in stocks and bonds, which used to create business for the old Russian banks, were entirely abolished. Under the old régime, business enterprises used to sell their securities or borrow against them from the banks, thus creating deposits, a feature which the new régime has eliminated. Dividends used to be paid and deposited in the banks by the recipients. Loans used to be granted against real-estate mortgages, but here again with the abolition of private property these transactions entirely disappeared and with them another section of bank loans and bank deposits. Furthermore, price control and government regulation of the markets eliminated large-scale speculative operations in commodities, together with all the banking transactions that used to arise therefrom.

There are also other and very important differences between Soviet banks and the old Russian banks, or, what is the same, between Soviet banks and banks in capitalist countries. Soviet banks are not only *economic* institutions, they are *socio-political* institutions as well. They are used by the state as a means for the preservation of the dictatorship of the proletariat and for the building of socialism. For example, the *kulaks* (well-to-do peasants) and some private traders or speculators may be better able to meet a loan at maturity and could pay more for its use than the poorest peasants, or some state enterprises or collective farms, but because the state considers it socially and politically desirable to extinguish the former and to strengthen the latter, bank loans are denied to the *kulaks* and private traders.

The *yield* from the investment of funds or from the extension of credit does not at all influence Soviet banks. The charges that they make *(interest* or *discount rates)* are calculated to enable them to meet

[24] A. Z. Arnold, *Banks, Credit, and Money in Soviet Russia,* Columbia University Press, New York, 1937, pp. 273-275. Reprinted by permission of the publishers.

losses without an impairment of their capital and provide for an expansion of their resources. The discount rate, as we have seen, is not the result of an interaction of the supply of credit and the demand for it. Nor does it serve as a regulator of the volume of credit. Regulation in the Soviet Union is sought through conscious planning and not through natural or automatic devices.

The banks not only help their clients to plan their business activities and particularly the expenditure of the loans, but also exercise control over them during the life of the loans. The loans are generally granted for specific purposes and must be so applied. The banks, therefore, attempt to guide and watch the application of the borrowed funds and to make sure that the borrower lives up to the plan which was presented by him when the request for credit was made and which was incorporated into the general credit plan.

Control over the borrowers was exercised during the years under review not only through the banks, but also through such agencies of the state as the *Workers' and Peasants' Inspection,* the *State Financial Control Board,* various auditing committees of the trusts and other economic units, and, finally, through public opinion.

Soviet banks have no choice in the matter of selecting "customers." Credit granting, as will presently be shown, is governed by plans. Nevertheless, a Soviet bank need not continue dealing with an enterprise which fails to honor its obligations. If a given enterprise is in deficit because it is young, inexperienced, and so forth, but its output is needed, the state or the local budget will take care of it. If an investigation shows that its losses are due to inefficient, dishonest, or disloyal managers, steps are taken to remove them. It takes time, of course, before the discovery is made, and this is one of the reasons why not all loans are paid at maturity and some are never paid.

But failure to maintain liquidity under the Soviet régime, it must be understood, is not fraught with the same danger as under the capitalist régime. Under the former, financial panics and runs are quite impossible inasmuch as the borrowers and depositors are state agencies which obey the work of the same master that the banks do. If an obligation cannot be met promptly the doors of the bank need not be shut, the client will be instructed to call at some other time.

But Soviet banks are not at all oblivious to the importance of meeting obligations when they are due. If they were, they would wreck the elaborate apparatus of national planning; for how could a given

enterprise furnish its quota of the planned output when the required
credit for it was not furnished on time? As a matter of fact they
attempt to estimate in advance the resources that will be at their disposal
within a given period and try not to create more obligations than can
be met. In other words, credit is planned in the Soviet Union. This
planning of credit is also one of the most important characteristics of
Soviet Banking.

238. THE STAKHANOV MOVEMENT [25]

*A young coal miner named Alexei Stakhanov in May 1935 discovered an
improved method for extracting coal. This fact was utilized by the government to launch a great publicity campaign for increased efficiency in production. Stakhanov became a national hero and the "Stakhanov movement"
was hailed as a special contribution of the socialist system—as explained
below by the chairman of the State Planning Commission of the U.S.S.R.
Actually, when Stakhanovism was applied to piece work, it bore a close
resemblance to the "speed up" system long in use in "capitalist" countries
and often denounced by Bolsheviks.*

As a result of the rapid progress made in the economic life of the
country and of the changes in the social composition of the population,
a new social consciousness is being formed, the survivals of capitalist
mentality are being outlived and a new, socialist attitude toward work
is being developed. The progress made in this sphere between 1933 and
1935 is immeasurable. The profound revolution in the minds of people,
in their attitude toward work, has received powerful expression in the
movement which in the autumn of 1935 sprang from the ranks of the
workers and produced exceptional results in raising labour productivity—the Stakhanov movement.

A plain miner, the Donetz Basin hewer, Alexei Stakhanov, in response to Stalin's speech of May 4, 1935, the keynote of which was
care for the human being and which marked a new stage in the
development of the U.S.S.R., proposed a new system of labour organi-

---

[25] Union of Soviet Socialist Republics, State Planning Commission of the U.S.S.R.,
*The Second Five-Year Plan for the Development of the National Economy of the U.S.S.R.
(1933-1937)*, International Publishers, New York, 1937, pp. xviii-xxi. (From *Foreword
to the English Edition by V. I. Mezhlauk, Chairman of the State Planning Commission
of the U.S.S.R.*) Reprinted by permission of the International Publishers.

zation for the extraction of coal. The very first day his method was applied he cut 102 tons of coal in one shift of six hours instead of the established rate of 7 tons. In a few days he doubled his own record.

Within a few weeks this movement to exceed the established rates of output, to increase the productivity of labour, had taken hold of the workers in the most varied trades and enterprises. Steel smelters, metal rollers, weavers, pneumatic pick-hammer operators, locomotive engineers, firemen, mechanics, turners and lathe operators began to revise their methods of work, to organise their production processes more rationally and to exceed all established rates of output. At a number of enterprises world records were scored. . . .

"The significance of the Stakhanov movement consists in the fact that it is a movement which is smashing the old standards of output because they are inadequate, which in a number of cases is surpassing the productivity of labour of the foremost capitalist countries and is thus creating the practical possibility of further consolidating socialism in our country, the possibility of converting our country into the most prosperous of all." (Stalin.)

. . . . .

The Stakhanov movement is a new and higher stage in socialist competition.

The Plenum of the Central Committee of the Communist Party of the Soviet Union, held in December 1935, pointed to the following features as summarizing the essence of the Stakhanov movement: the organization of labour in a new way, rationalization of technological processes, proper division of labour, exemption of skilled workers from preliminary work of secondary importance, better organization of the work place, rapid growth of labour productivity and a considerable increase in wages for workers and employees.

Resulting as it does from the victory of socialism in the U.S.S.R., the Stakhanov movement opens up "the practical possibility of the further consolidation of socialism," of a still more rapid increase in production, particularly articles of consumption, and of a constantly increasing well-being of the whole working population.

Stakhanov workers are workers who have mastered technique, who have smashed the established technical standards of output and get the utmost out of the machinery they operate; they are plain workers who, however, are able to supplement and correct the work of engineers and scientists. Stakhanov workers approach their work like real masters of the country who feel their responsibility to the whole people, who practice genuine socialist labour discipline. Stakhanov workers are workers who not only know how to turn out high-grade products but also how to organize work, to rationalize it and direct it along new lines. Stakhanov workers are workers who not only know how to plan their own work and the work of their brigades but who, thanks to the unprecedented productivity of their labour, make changes necessary in the plans of whole enterprises, branches of industry and even in the entire plan of national economy. A number of factories, mines and railroads, which for a long time failed to fulfill their plans, have begun regularly to overfulfill them. The Stakhanov movement has revealed vast latent potentialities of production, has demonstrated the possibility of materially increasing production without new capital investments.

The powerful Stakhanov movement in industry and transportation finds its counterpart in the radical change that has occurred in the minds of the collective-farm peasantry. The very act of joining a collective farm, of abandoning the age-old forms of individual husbandry, was the reflection of a most profound revolution in the minds of the peasant masses.

239. THE SOVIET CONSTITUTION OF 1936 *(Extracts)* [26]

The All-Union Congress of Soviets on December 5, 1936, adopted a new constitution to replace that of 1923 (See Document No. 225). Especially worthy of note were the articles protecting the rights of ownership and inheritance of small private properties (7 and 10), altering the original Bolshevik maxim of "From each according to his ability, to each according to his needs" to the newer "From each according to his ability, to each according to his toil" (12), extending equality of suffrage to peasants and proletarians (34), and providing for the secret ballot (140). The first general election under the new constitution was held on December 12, 1937. The returns indicated a complete victory for the list of Stalinist candidates— there being no other.

---

[26] Translated by C. A. Manning in Carnegie Endowment for International Peace, *International Conciliation*, No. 327, February 1937, pp. 143-163. A few changes have been made in the interest of smoother translation.—*Ed.*

CHAPTER I.

THE ORGANIZATION OF SOCIETY.

ARTICLE 1.

The Union of Soviet Socialist Republics is a socialist State of workers and peasants.

ARTICLE 2.

The political basis of the U.S.S.R. is formed by the councils (soviets) of toilers' deputies, which have developed and become strong as a result of the overthrow of the power of the landlords and capitalists and the winning of the dictatorship of the proletariat.

ARTICLE 3.

All power in the U.S.S.R. belongs to the toilers of city and village as represented by the councils of toilers' deputies.

ARTICLE 4.

The economic basis of the U.S.S.R. is formed by the socialist system of economy and the socialist ownership of implements and means of production, which have been firmly established as a result of the liquidation of the capitalistic system of economy, the abolition of private ownership of implements and means of production, and the destruction of the exploitation of man by man.

ARTICLE 5.

Socialist ownership in the U.S.S.R. has either the form of State ownership (the property of the whole people), or the form of cooperative-collective ownership (the property of individual collective farms, the property of cooperative associations).

ARTICLE 6.

The land, its deposits, waters, forests, mills, factories, shafts, mines, railroad, water and air transport, banks, means of communication, large agricultural undertakings organized by the State (State farms, machine-tractor stations, etc.) and also communal undertakings and the fundamental fund of dwellings in cities and industrial points, are State property, that is the property of the whole people.

ARTICLE 7.

Public undertakings in the collective farms and cooperative organizations with their livestock and implements, production effected by the collective farms and cooperative organizations, as well as their public structures are the public, socialist property of the collective farms and cooperative organizations.

Each collective farm household, aside from its basic income from the public collective farm economy, has for its own use a small piece of land attached to the homestead and as individual property the auxiliary economy on this attached piece, a dwelling house, productive livestock, poultry and minor agricultural implements—in accordance with the regulation of the agricultural artel.

ARTICLE 8.

The land occupied by collective farms is secured to them for use without payment and without time limit, that is, forever.

ARTICLE 9.

Along with the socialist system of economy, which is the prevailing form of economy in the U.S.S.R., there is permitted by law small private economy of individual peasants and handicraftsmen, based on their personal labor and excluding the exploitation of the labor of another person.

ARTICLE 10.

The right of personal property of citizens in the income from their toil and in their savings, in their dwelling house and auxiliary domestic economy, in articles of their domestic economy and use, in articles of personal use and comfort, as well as the right of inheritance of personal property of citizens—are protected by law.

ARTICLE 11.

The economic life of the U.S.S.R. is defined and directed by the State plan of national economy in the interests of the increase of the public wealth, the constant raising of the material and cultural level of the toilers, the strengthening of the independence of the U.S.S.R., and the strengthening of its defensive ability.

ARTICLE 12.

Toil in the U.S.S.R. is an obligation and a matter of honor of each citizen who is fit for toil, according to the principle: "He who does not work, does not eat."

In the U.S.S.R. there is being realized the principle of socialism: "From each according to his ability, to each according to his toil."

CHAPTER II.
THE ORGANIZATION OF THE STATE.

ARTICLE 13.

The Union of Soviet Socialist Republics is a federal State on the basis of the voluntary association of the Soviet Socialist Republics with equal rights:

the Russian Soviet Federated Socialist Republic,

the Ukrainian Soviet Socialist Republic,

the Byelorussian (White Russian) Soviet Socialist Republic,

the Azerbaidjan Soviet Socialist Republic,

the Gruzian (Georgian) Soviet Socialist Republic,

the Armenian Soviet Socialist Republic,

the Turkmen Soviet Socialist Republic,

the Uzbek Soviet Socialist Republic,

the Tadjik Soviet Socialist Republic,

the Kazakh Soviet Socialist Republic,

the Kirghiz Soviet Socialist Republic.

ARTICLE 14.

Within the jurisdiction of the Union of Soviet Socialist Republics as represented by its highest organs of power and organs of State administration belong:

a) the representation of the Union in international relations, the conclusion and ratification of treaties with other states;

b) questions of war and peace;

c) the acceptance of new republics into the organization of the U.S.S.R.;

d) control over the observance of the Constitution of the U.S.S.R. and the ensurance of conformity of the Constitutions of the Union republics with the Constitution of the U.S.S.R.;

e) the approval of changes of boundaries between Union republics;

f) the approval of the formation of new provinces and regions and also of new autonomous republics within Union republics;

g) the organization of the defense of the U.S.S.R. and also the direction of all the armed forces of the U.S.S.R.;

h) foreign trade on the basis of a State monopoly;

i) the protection of State security;

j) the establishment of the plans of national economy of the U.S.S.R.;

k) the approval of a single State budget of the U.S.S.R., and also of the taxes and revenues which serve to form the budgets of the Union, republics, and localities;

l) the administration of banks, industrial and agricultural establishments and enterprises, and also trading enterprises of All-Union significance;

m) the administration of transport and communications;

n) the direction of the monetary and credit system;

o) the organization of State insurance;

p) the contracting and granting of loans;

q) the establishment of basic principles for the use of land, and also the use of its deposits, as well as of forests and waters;

r) the establishment of basic principles in the field of education and public health;

s) the organization of a single system of national economic accounting;

t) the establishment of the bases of labor legislation;

u) legislation on the judicial structure and judicial procedure; criminal and civil codes;

v) laws on Union citizenship; laws on the rights of foreigners;

w) the issuing of All-Union acts of amnesty.

ARTICLE 15.

The sovereignty of the Union republics is restricted only within the limits set forth in Article 14 of the Constitution of the U.S.S.R. Outside of these limits, each Union republic embodies State power independently. The U.S.S.R. protects the sovereign rights of the Union republics.

ARTICLE 16.

Each Union republic has its own Constitution which takes into account the special features of the republic and is drawn up in full conformity with the Constitution of the U.S.S.R.

ARTICLE 17.

To each Union republic is preserved the right of free withdrawal from the U.S.S.R.

ARTICLE 18.

The territory of the Union republics cannot be altered without their consent.

ARTICLE 19.

The laws of the U.S.S.R. have the same force in the territories of all Union republics.

ARTICLE 20.

In case of a conflict of the law of a Union republic with the All-Union law, the All-Union law prevails.

ARTICLE 21.

For citizens of the U.S.S.R. there is one Union citizenship.
Every citizen of a Union republic is a citizen of the U.S.S.R.

. . . . . .

CHAPTER III.

THE HIGHEST ORGANS OF STATE POWER OF THE U.S.S.R.

ARTICLE 30.

The highest organ of State power of the U.S.S.R. is the Supreme Council of the U.S.S.R.

ARTICLE 31.

The Supreme Council of the U.S.S.R. exercises all rights granted to the Union of Soviet Socialist Republics, in accordance with Article 14 of the Constitution, in so far as they do not come, by virtue of the Constitution, within the competence of organs of the U.S.S.R. which are accountable to the Supreme Council of the U.S.S.R.: the Presidium of the Supreme Council of the U.S.S.R., the Council of People's Commissars of the U.S.S.R., and the People's Commissariats of the U.S.S.R.

ARTICLE 32.

The legislative power of the U.S.S.R. is exercised exclusively by the Supreme Council of the U.S.S.R.

ARTICLE 33.

The Supreme Council of the U.S.S.R. consists of two chambers: the Council of the Union and the Council of Nationalities.

ARTICLE 34.

The Council of the Union is elected by the citizens of the U.S.S.R. by electoral districts on the basis of one deputy for every 300,000 of population.

ARTICLE 35.

The Council of Nationalities is elected by the citizens of the U.S.S.R. by Union and autonomous republics, autonomous regions, and national districts on the basis of: 25 deputies from each Union republic, 11 deputies from each autonomous republic, 5 deputies from each autonomous region and one deputy from each national district.

ARTICLE 36.

The Supreme Council of the U.S.S.R. is chosen for a term of four years.

ARTICLE 37.

Both chambers of the Supreme Council of the U.S.S.R., the Council of the Union and the Council of Nationalities, have equal rights.

ARTICLE 38.

The Council of the Union and the Council of Nationalities possess in the same measure legislative initiative.

ARTICLE 39.

A law is considered approved, if it is accepted by both chambers of the Supreme Council of the U.S.S.R. by a simple majority of each.

. . . . .

ARTICLE 46.

Sessions of the Supreme Council of the U.S.S.R. are called by the Presidium of the Supreme Council of the U.S.S.R. twice a year.

Extraordinary sessions are called by the Presidium of the Supreme Council of the U.S.S.R. at its discretion or on the demand of one of the Union republics.

Article 47.

In case of disagreement between the Council of the Union and the Council of Nationalities, the question is referred for settlement to a conciliation commission, established on a parity basis. If the conciliation commission does not arrive at an agreement or if its decision does not satisfy one of the chambers, the question is considered a second time in the chambers. In the absence of an agreed decision of the two chambers, the Presidium of the Supreme Council of the U.S.S.R. dissolves the Supreme Council of the U.S.S.R. and sets new elections.

Article 48.

The Supreme Council of the U.S.S.R. chooses at a joint meeting of both chambers the Presidium of the Supreme Council of the U.S.S.R. which consists of: the chairman of the Presidium of the Supreme Council of the U.S.S.R., eleven vice-chairmen, the secretary of the Presidium, and 24 members of the Presidium.

The Presidium of the Supreme Council of the U.S.S.R. is accountable to the Supreme Council of the U.S.S.R. in all its activities.

Article 49.

The Presidium of the Supreme Council of the U.S.S.R.:

a) convenes sessions of the Supreme Council of the U.S.S.R.;

b) gives interpretations of the laws of the U.S.S.R. in force, issues decrees;

c) dissolves the Supreme Council of the U.S.S.R. on the basis of article 47 of the Constitution of the U.S.S.R., and sets new elections;

d) carries out an interrogation of the whole people (referendum) on its own initiative or on the demand of one of the Union republics;

e) annuls decisions and orders of the Council of People's Commissars of the U.S.S.R. and the Council of People's Commissars of the Union republics in case they do not conform to the law;

f) in the period between sessions of the Supreme Council of the U.S.S.R., relieves of their positions and appoints People's Commissars of the U.S.S.R. at the instance of the chairman of the Council of People's Commissars of the U.S.S.R., subject to subsequent confirmation by the Supreme Council of the U.S.S.R.;

g) awards decorations and bestows titles of honor of the U.S.S.R.;

h) exercises the right of pardon;

i) appoints and removes the high command of the armed forces of the U.S.S.R.;

j) in the period between sessions of the Supreme Council of the U.S.S.R., proclaims a state of war in case of armed attack upon the U.S.S.R. or in case of the necessity of carrying out international treaty obligations for mutual defense against aggression;

k) proclaims general or partial mobilization;

l) ratifies international treaties;

m) appoints and recalls plenipotentiary representatives of the U.S.S.R. in foreign States;

n) receives letters of credence and recall of diplomatic representatives of foreign States accredited to it.

. . . . .

ARTICLE 52.

A deputy of the Supreme Council of the U.S.S.R. cannot be called to judicial responsibility or be arrested without the consent of the Supreme Council of the U.S.S.R., and in the period when there is no session of the Supreme Council of the U.S.S.R.,—without the consent of the Presidium of the Supreme Council of the U.S.S.R.

. . . . .

CHAPTER IV.
THE HIGHEST ORGANS OF STATE POWER OF THE UNION REPUBLICS.

ARTICLE 57.

The highest organ of State power of the Union Republic is the Supreme Council of the Union republic.

ARTICLE 58.

The Supreme Council of the Union republic is elected by the citizens of the republic for a term of four years.

The ratios of representation are determined by the constitutions of the Union republics.

. . . . .

CHAPTER V.
THE ORGANS OF STATE ADMINISTRATION OF THE U.S.S.R.

ARTICLE 64.

The highest executive and administrative organ of the State power

of the Union of Soviet Socialist Republics is the Council of People's
Commissars of the U.S.S.R.

. . . . .

ARTICLE 68.

The Council of People's Commissars:

a) coordinates and directs the work of the All-Union and Union-
republic People's Commissariats of the U.S.S.R. and other economic
and cultural institutions under its jurisdiction;

b) adopts measures to carry out the plan of national economy, the
State budget, and the strengthening of the credit-monetary system;

c) adopts measures to maintain public order, defend the interests of
the State and guard the rights of citizens;

d) exercises general direction in the sphere of relations with foreign
States;

e) determines the yearly quotas of citizens subject to call for active
military service, directs the general organization of the armed forces of
the country;

f) forms, in case of necessity, special committees and central administrations in connection with the Council of People's Commissars
of the U.S.S.R. on matters of an economic, cultural, and defensive
character.

. . . . .

ARTICLE 70.

The Council of People's Commissars of the U.S.S.R. is formed by the
Supreme Council of the U.S.S.R. and consists of:

the Chairman of the Council of People's Commissars of the U.S.S.R.;
the Vice-Chairmen of the Council of People's Commissars of the
U.S.S.R.;
the Chairman of the State Planning Commission of the U.S.S.R.;
the Chairman of the Commission of Soviet Control;
the People's Commissars of the U.S.S.R.;
the Chairman of the Committee of Reserves (warehouses);
the Chairman of the Committee on the Arts;
the Chairman of the Committee on Higher Education.

. . . . .

ARTICLE 74.

The People's Commissariats of the U.S.S.R. are either All-Union or Union-republic.

ARTICLE 75.

The All-Union People's Commissariats administer the branch of State administration entrusted to them throughout the whole territory of the U.S.S.R. either directly or through organs appointed by them.

ARTICLE 76.

The Union-republic People's Commissariats administer the branch of State administration entrusted to them, as a rule, through identically named People's Commissariats of the Union republics and administer directly only a definite, limited number of enterprises on a list approved by the Presidium of the Supreme Council of the U.S.S.R.

ARTICLE 77.

To the All-Union People's Commissariats belong the People's Commissariats of:

Defense;   Communications;
Foreign affairs;   Water transport;
Foreign trade;   Heavy industry;
Railways;   Defense industry.

ARTICLE 78.

To the Union-republic People's Commissariats belong the People's Commissariats of:

Food industry;   Finance;
Light industry;   Internal trade;
Timber industry;   Internal affairs;
Agriculture;   Justice;
State grain and livestock farms; Public health.

CHAPTER VI.

ORGANS OF STATE ADMINISTRATION OF THE UNION REPUBLICS.

ARTICLE 79.

The highest executive and administrative organ of State power of a Union republic is the Council of People's Commissars of the Union republic.

. . . . . .

CHAPTER VIII.

THE LOCAL ORGANS OF STATE POWER.

ARTICLE 94.

The organs of State power in provinces, regions, autonomous regions, districts, rayons, cities, rural areas are the Councils of workers' deputies.

ARTICLE 95.

The Councils of workers' deputies of provinces, regions, autonomous regions, districts, rayons, cities, rural areas are chosen correspondingly by the toilers of each province, region, autonomous region, district, rayon, city, rural area, for a term of two years.

ARTICLE 96.

The ratios of representation of the Councils of workers' deputies are determined by the Constitution of the Union republics.

. . . . .

CHAPTER IX.

THE COURT AND THE STATE ATTORNEYS.

ARTICLE 102.

Justice in the U.S.S.R. is represented by the Supreme Court of the U.S.S.R., the Supreme Courts of the Union republics, provincial and regional courts, courts of autonomous republics and autonomous regions, district courts, special courts of the U.S.S.R., formed by the decision of the Supreme Council of the U.S.S.R., and People's Courts.

. . . . .

ARTICLE 104.

The Supreme Court of the U.S.S.R. is the highest judicial organ. To the Supreme Court of the U.S.S.R. is assigned supervision of the judicial activity of all judicial organs of the U.S.S.R. and Union republics.

. . . . .

CHAPTER X.

THE FUNDAMENTAL RIGHTS AND OBLIGATIONS OF CITIZENS.

ARTICLE 118.

Citizens of the U.S.S.R. have the right to toil, that is the right to receive guaranteed work with payment for their toil in accordance with its quantity and quality.

The right to toil is ensured by the socialist organization of national economy, by the unceasing growth of the productive forces of soviet society, the elimination of the possibility of economic crises, and the liquidation of unemployment.

ARTICLE 119.

Citizens of the U.S.S.R. have the right to rest.

The right to rest is ensured by the shortening of the working day for the overwhelming majority of workers to seven hours, the establishment of yearly leaves to workers and those in service with the maintenance of their labor pay, by reserving for the use of the toilers a wide network of sanatoria, houses of rest, and clubs.

ARTICLE 120.

Citizens of the U.S.S.R. have the right to material security in old age and also in case of illness and loss of capacity to toil.

This right is ensured by the wide development of social insurance of workers and those in service at the expense of the State, free medical help for toilers, the reserving for the use of the toilers of a wide network of health resorts.

ARTICLE 121.

Citizens of the U.S.S.R. have the right to education.

This right is ensured by universal, compulsory elementary education, by the fact that no pay is demanded for education, including higher education, by the system of State scholarships for the overwhelming majority of those studying in the higher schools, by the giving of instruction in schools in the native language, by the organization in mills, State farms, machine-tractor stations and collective farms of free industrial, technical and agronomic training for the toilers.

ARTICLE 122.

Women in the U.S.S.R. are offered equal rights with men in all fields of economic, State, cultural, and public-political life.

The possibility of exercising these rights of women is ensured by the granting to woman equal right with man to toil, payment for toil, rest, social insurance, and education, by State protection of the interests of mother and child, the granting to woman during pregnancy of leave with the continuation of maintenance, a wide network of maternity homes, nurseries, and kindergartens.

ARTICLE 123.

The equal rights of citizens of the U.S.S.R., independent of their nationality and race, in all fields of economic, State, cultural, and public-political life is an unalterable law.

Any direct or indirect limitation of rights, or conversely, any establishment of direct or indirect preferences of citizens dependent upon their racial and national membership, as well as all preaching of racial or national exclusiveness, or of hate and contempt, is punishable by law.

ARTICLE 124.

In the object of ensuring to the citizens freedom of conscience, the church of the U.S.S.R. is separated from the State and the school from the church. Freedom of service of religious cults and freedom of anti-religious propaganda is acknowledged for all citizens.

ARTICLE 125.

In accordance with the interests of the toilers and in the object of strengthening the socialist system, the citizens of the U.S.S.R. are guaranteed by law:

a) freedom of speech,
b) freedom of the press,
c) freedom of assemblies and meetings,
d) freedom of street processions and demonstrations.

These rights of citizens are secured by placing at the disposal of toilers and their organizations printing presses, supplies of paper, public buildings, streets, means of communication, and other material conditions necessary for their exercise.

ARTICLE 126.

In accordance with the interests of the toilers and with the object of the development of the organized self-expression and political activity of the popular masses, there is ensured to the citizens of the U.S.S.R. the right of union into public organizations, professional unions, cooperative organizations, organizations of youth, sport and defense organizations, cultural, technical and scientific societies, and the most active and conscious citizens from the ranks of the working class and other strata of toilers are united in the All-Union Communist Party (Bolsheviks) which is the vanguard of the toilers in their struggle for the strengthening and development of the socialist order and represents the directing kernel of all organizations of toilers, both public and State.

．．．．．

Article 129.

The U.S.S.R. offers the right of refuge to foreign citizens, persecuted for the defense of the interests of the toilers or scientific activity or for a struggle for national liberation.

．．．．．

Article 132.

Universal military obligation is a law.

Military service in the Workers' and Peasants' Red Army is an honorable obligation of citizens of the U.S.S.R.

．．．．．

CHAPTER XI.
THE ELECTORAL SYSTEM.

Article 134.

Elections of deputies to all the Councils of toilers' deputies: to the Supreme Council of the U.S.S.R., the Supreme Councils of the Union republics, provincial and regional Councils of toilers' deputies, Supreme Councils of autonomous republics, Councils of toilers' deputies of districts, rayons, cities, and rural areas are made by the electors on the basis of universal, equal and direct electoral right with secret ballot.

Article 135.

Elections of deputies are universal: all citizens of the U.S.S.R., who have reached the age of eighteen, independent of racial and national affiliations, confession of faith, educational rank, domicile, social origin, property status and past activity, have the right to take part in the election of deputies and to be elected, with the exception of the insane and persons condemned by a court to be deprived of electoral rights.

Article 136.

The elections of deputies are equal; every citizen has one vote; all citizens take part in the elections on the same basis.

．．．．．

ARTICLE 139.

Elections of deputies are direct; elections to all councils of toilers' deputies, beginning with the rural area and city Councils of toilers' deputies up to the Supreme Council of the U.S.S.R. are made by citizens directly by means of direct elections.

ARTICLE 140.

Voting at elections of deputies is secret.

ARTICLE 141.

Candidates at the elections are nominated by electoral districts.

The right of nomination of candidates is ensured to public organizations, professional unions, cooperatives, organizations of youth, cultural societies.

. . . . .

CHAPTER XIII.

THE METHOD OF CHANGING THE CONSTITUTION.

ARTICLE 146.

Change of the Constitution of the U.S.S.R. is made only on the decision of the Supreme Council of the U.S.S.R., accepted by a majority of not less than two-thirds of the votes in each of the chambers.

240. THE MOSCOW TRIALS, 1937 [27]

August 1936 and January 1937 witnessed in the Soviet Union the two most spectacular in a long series of trials of prominent Bolsheviks accused of conspiring against the safety of the state and the lives of Stalinist leaders. The public prosecutor charged the defendants with having formed ties, under the exiled Leon Trotsky's leadership, with agents of Nazi Germany and Imperial Japan. To the amazement of the spectators (including foreign correspondents) in the courtroom and of the world reading public, the accused pleaded guilty and seemed to vie with each other in denouncing their own and their colleagues' crimes. Of the seventeen defendants listed

---

[27] Union of Soviet Socialist Republics, People's Commissariat of Justice of the U.S.S.R., *Report of the Court Proceedings in the Case of the Anti-Soviet Trotskyite Centre, Heard before the Military Collegium of the Supreme Court of the U.S.S.R., Moscow, January 23–30, 1937*, People's Commissariat of Justice of the U.S.S.R., Moscow, 1937, pp. 4-8, 562-563.

at the beginning of this document thirteen were sentenced to be shot; four, including Radek and Sokolnikov, were given prison terms of from eight to ten years.

~~~~~~

Indictment

in the case of Y. L. Pyatakov, K. B. Radek, G. Y. Sokolnikov, L. P. Serebryakov, N. I. Muralov, Y. A. Livshitz, Y. N. Drobnis, M. S. Boguslavsky, I. A. Knyazev, S. A. Rataichak, B. O. Norkin, A. A. Shestov, M. S. Stroilov, Y. D. Turok, I. Y. Hrasche, G. E. Pushin, V. V. Arnold accused of treason against the country, espionage, acts of diversion, wrecking activities and the preparation of terrorist acts, *i.e.,* of crimes covered by Articles 58^{1a}, 58^8, 58^9 and 58^{11} of the Criminal Code of the R.S.F.S.R.

The investigation of the case of the united Trotskyite-Zinovievite terrorist centre, members of which were convicted by the Military Collegium of the Supreme Court of the U.S.S.R., on August 24, 1936, established that in addition to the above-mentioned centre, there existed a so-called reserve centre, formed on the direct instructions of L. D. Trotsky, for the eventuality of the criminal activities of the Trotskyite-Zinovievite *bloc* being exposed by the organs of the Soviet Government. The convicted members of the united Trotskyite-Zinovievite centre, Zinoviev, Kamenev and others, testified that the reserve centre consisted of Y. L. Pyatakov, K. B. Radek, G. Y. Sokolnikov and L. P. Serebryakov, all known for their past Trotskyite activities.

The preliminary investigation of the present case established that the so-called reserve centre was actually a parallel Trotskyite centre, organized and operating under the direct instructions of L. D. Trotsky, now in emigration.

The Trotskyite parallel centre developed its criminal activities most energetically after the dastardly murder of Sergei Mironovich Kirov, and the subsequent break-up of the united Trotskyite-Zinovievite centre.

The main task which the parallel centre set itself was the forcible overthrow of the Soviet Government with the object of changing the social and state system existing in the U.S.S.R. L. D. Trotsky, and on his instructions, the parallel Trotskyite centre, aimed at seizing power with the aid of foreign states with the object of restoring capitalist social relations in the U.S.S.R.

These treasonable designs against the Soviet Union were expounded by L. Trotsky in their most outspoken form in his letter of instructions to the parallel Trotskyite centre, received by the accused K. B. Radek in December 1935.

The accused Radek, during his examination on December 22, 1936, testified on this point as follows:

"It must be understood, Trotsky wrote, that without to a certain extent bringing the social structure of the U.S.S.R. in line with that of the capitalist states, the government of the *bloc* will not be able to maintain itself in power and to preserve peace. . . .

"The admission of German and Japanese capital for the exploitation of the U.S.S.R. will create important capitalist interests on Soviet territory. Those strata in the villages which have not outlived the capitalist psychology and are dissatisfied with the collective farms will gravitate towards them. The Germans and Japanese will demand that we relieve the atmosphere in the rural districts; we shall therefore have to make concessions and allow the dissolution of the collective farms or withdrawal from the collective farms."

And further:

"Pyatakov and I arrived at the conclusion that this directive sums up the work of the *bloc,* dots all the *i's* and crosses all the *t's* by bringing out very sharply the fact that under all circumstances the government of the Trotskyite Zinovievite *bloc* could only be the government of the restoration of capitalism."

The accused Pyatakov, in his turn, relating his conversation with L. Trotsky near Oslo in December 1935, testified that L. Trotsky, in demanding that the diversive, wrecking and terrorist activities of the Trotskyite organization in the U.S.S.R. be intensified, emphasized that as a result of an agreement with capitalist states, it was necessary, as he put it, to retreat to capitalism. According to the testimony of the accused Pyatakov, L. Trotsky said:

"This means, it will be necessary to retreat. This must be firmly understood. Retreat to capitalism. How far and to what degree, it is difficult to say now—this can be made concrete only after we come into power."

That the program of the parallel Trotskyite centre was a program of the restoration of capitalism in the U.S.S.R. was testified to by the accused G. Y. Sokolnikov during examination on November 30, 1936:

"This program provided for the renunciation of the policy of industrial-ization and collectivization, and, as a result of this renunciation, the revival in the villages, on the basis of small farming, of capitalism, which, combined with the capitalist elements in industry, would develop into capitalist restora-tion in the U.S.S.R.

". . . All the members of the centre were agreed in recognizing that in the existing circumstances there could be no other program, and that it was necessary to carry out precisely this program of the *bloc*."

Proceeding from this program, L. D. Trotsky and his accomplices in the parallel centre entered into negotiations with agents of foreign states with the object of overthrowing the Soviet government with the aid of armed intervention.

As a basis for these treasonable negotiations, L. D. Trotsky and the parallel centre put forward: the permission in the U.S.S.R. of the development of private capital, the dissolution of the collective farms, the liquidation of the state farms, the leasing of a number of Soviet enterprises as concessions to foreign capitalists, and the granting to such foreign states of other economic and political advantages including the surrender of a part of Soviet territory.

On this point, L. D. Trotsky, according to the statement of the accused K. Radek, wrote in his aforementioned letter to K. Radek:

"It would be absurd to think that we can come to power without securing the favourable attitude of the most important capitalist governments, par-ticularly of the most aggressive ones, such as the present governments of Germany and Japan. It is absolutely necessary to have contacts and an under-standing with these governments right now. . . ."

The investigation has established that L. D. Trotsky entered into negotiations with one of the leaders of the German National-Socialist Party with a view to waging a joint struggle against the Soviet Union.

As testified by the accused Pyatakov, L. Trotsky, in his conversation with the accused in December 1935, informed him that as a result of these negotiations he had concluded an agreement with the said leader of the National-Socialist Party on the following terms:

"1) to guarantee a generally favourable attitude towards the German government and the necessary collaboration with it in the most important questions of an international character;

"2) to agree to territorial concessions;

"3) to permit German industrialists, in the form of concessions (or some other forms), to exploit enterprises in the U.S.S.R. which are essential as complements to Germany economy (iron ore, manganese, oil, gold, timber, etc. were meant);

"4) to create in the U.S.S.R. favourable conditions for the activities of German private enterprises;

"5) in time of war to develop extensive diversive activities in enterprises of the war industry and at the front. These diversive activities are to be carried on under Trotsky's instructions, agreed upon with the German General Staff.

"These principles of the agreement, as Trotsky related, were finally elaborated and adopted during Trotsky's meeting with Hitler's deputy, Hess.

"Likewise, said Trotsky, he had well-established connections with the ——— government."

The nature of this agreement and the extent of the territorial concessions proposed were communicated by L. Trotsky in his letter to the accused Radek in December 1935.

In that letter, as testified by the accused K. Radek, L. Trotsky wrote the following:

". . . We shall inevitably have to make territorial concessions. . . . We shall have to yield the Maritime Province and Amur region to Japan, and the Ukraine to Germany.

"Germany needs raw materials, foodstuffs and markets. We shall have to permit her to take part in the exploitation of ore, manganese, gold, oil, apatites, and to undertake to supply her for a definite period with foodstuffs and fats at less than world prices.

"We shall have to yield the oil of Sakhalin to Japan and to guarantee to supply her with oil in case of war with America. We shall also have to permit her to exploit gold-fields. We shall have to agree to Germany's demand not to oppose her seizure of the Danube countries and the Balkans, and not to hinder Japan in the seizure of China. . . ."

*   *   *   *   *

Definition of the Charge

The investigating authorities consider it established:

1) that, on the instruction of L. D. Trotsky, there was organized in 1933 a parallel centre consisting of the following accused in the present case: Y. L. Pyatakov, K. B. Radek, G. Y. Sokolnikov, and L. P. Serebryakov, the object of which was to direct criminal anti-Soviet

espionage, diversive and terrorist activities for the purpose of undermining the military power of the U.S.S.R., accelerating an armed attack on the U.S.S.R., assisting foreign aggressors to seize territory of the U.S.S.R. and to dismember it and of overthrowing the Soviet Power and restoring capitalism and the rule of the bourgeoisie in the Soviet Union:

2) that, on the instructions of the aforesaid L. D. Trotsky, this centre, through the accused Sokolnikov and Radek, entered into communication with representatives of certain foreign states for the purpose of organizing a joint struggle against the Soviet Union, in connection with which the Trotskyite centre undertook, in the event of its coming into power, to grant these states a number of political and economic privileges and territorial concessions;

3) that, moreover, this centre, through its own members and other members of the criminal Trotskyite organization, systematically engaged in espionage on behalf of these states, supplying foreign intelligence services with secret information of the utmost state importance;

4) that, for the purpose of undermining the economic strength and defense capacity of the U.S.S.R., this centre organized and carried out a number of wrecking and diversive acts at certain enterprises and on the railways, which caused loss of human life and the destruction of valuable state property;

5) that this centre prepared a number of terrorist acts against the leaders of the Communist Party of the Soviet Union and of the Soviet government, and that attempts were made to carry out these acts;

6) that besides its leaders—the accused Y. L. Pyatakov, G. Y. Sokolnikov, K. B. Radek and L. P. Serebryakov—the following accused took an active part in the aforesaid criminal activities of this centre: Y. A. Livshitz, N. I. Muralov, Y. N. Drobnis, M. S. Boguslavsky, I. A. Knyazev, Y. D. Turok, S. A. Rataichak, B. O. Norkin, A. A. Shestov, M. S. Stroilov, I. Y. Hrasche, G. E. Pushin, and V. V. Arnold.

All the accused have pleaded guilty to all the charges preferred against them and stand convicted by the documents in the file, by the material evidence, and by testimony of witnesses.

. . . . .

[*Last words in court of one of the accused, A. A. Shestov*]: Citizen judges! For 13 years I was a member of one of the counter-revolutionary Trotskyite terrorist, disruptive and fascist organizations. For the last five years I was actively preparing and attempted to kill the leaders of the toiling people, the leaders of the working class and of those oppressed in the capitalist world. For the last five years I carried on actual destruction and disruptive work in the coal pits and mines of the Kuznetsk Basin. For the last five years I was a traitor, I was an agent of the most reactionary detachment of the world bourgeoise, an agent of German fascism.

What forced me, a former worker, the son of a working family, to belong to the organization of murderers, to the organization of traitors to the socialist fatherland? I will not conceal that from 1923 on, step by step, stage by stage, I climbed higher and higher and came close to the organizer of the fascist agents—Trotsky and to his closest lieutenants—Sedov, Smirnov and Pyatakov. My acquaintance with them, the rapprochement and especially the last meeting in 1931 and their attention to me, flattered me and I abandoned myself fully and wholeheartedly to counter-revolutionary terrorist and espionage activities. In 1923 I first betrayed the working class. In 1923 I first began to struggle against the Party headed by Stalin, who holds and carries the banner of Marx, Engels and Lenin in his strong, firm hands. In that struggle I employed every loathsome, every filthy and every destructive method. I stand before you utterly exposed. I told of everything that brought me to the dock. I did not surrender on the first day of my detention. For five weeks I denied everything, for five weeks they kept confronting me with one fact after another, with the photographs of my dastardly work and when I looked back I myself was appalled by what I had done.

A particle, still not killed, of working man's conscience, of the conscience of the toiling people, that I still retained, compelled me to tell the truth and I decided like a prodigal son to go to my class brothers and tell everything I knew and had done. There in Siberia, at the headquarters of the People's Commissariat of Internal Affairs, at the preliminary investigation, in cell number 23, I often quivered like an aspen leaf when facing my crimes, and it was this that gave me the calmness with which I told you of my criminal activities. I knew what I was headed for, I knew where I was going, and I knew what was in store for me if the organization I was leading were exposed. I am not asking for mercy. I do not want clemency. The proletarian Court must not and cannot spare my life. Here before you, in the face of the whole working people, in the face of those oppressed by capitalism in all countries, to the best of my ability I shot to pieces the ideology that held me captive for thirteen years. And now I have only one desire, to stand with the same calmness on the place of execution and with my blood to wash away the stain of a traitor to my country.

241. RELIGION IN THE SOVIET UNION [28]

The official Bolshevik view on religion and the attitude of the Russian people to the official anti-religious activities were well described by Dr. Julius F. Hecker. Dr. Hecker was born in St. Petersburg, studied in Russia and in the United States, received the degree of doctor of philosophy from Columbia University in New York, and returned to become Professor of Social Ethics in the Moscow Theological Academy.

Is there room in this type of civilization for religion, and, in particular, is there a place of honor for the Christian religion?

The Communist says, definitely, "No." The future, he believes, belongs to the materialist philosophy, according to which all things, visible or invisible, tangible or spiritual, including man, are an expression of cosmic energy or matter. Man cannot be separated from the planet upon which he lives; he must determine his own destiny; he cannot expect any help from gods or demons; he is his own God and is master or slave of nature. There are no other lives to come for him and therefore he must make the most of *this life* upon *this earth*. His means are science and cooperative toil and his goal is beauty and the good life, where there is no exploitation of wealth and no privileged class, but where all races live and work in cooperation with each other for the common good. Religion, he believes, is a reactionary phenomenon inherited from the period in the history of man when he was helpless in the struggle against nature and lived in an imaginary world of fear and baseless hopes. Historically, religion has been one of the chief weapons in the exploitation of classes and in the oppression of the poor, of which the Czarist régime is a most glaring example.

The Communist is a militant materialist and atheist. He not only demands a confession of atheism from the members of his party, but he most zealously preaches his atheism and materialistic philosophy to

---

[28] J. F. Hecker, *Religion under the Soviets,* Vanguard Press, New York, 1927, pp. 191-195. Reprinted by permission of the publishers.

non-party members and shapes the program for the education of the young in such a way as to prepare the new generation for a materialistic conception of life.

At the initiative of the party there has been founded a special propaganda society, "The Union of the Godless," which accepts non-party members and carries on intense anti-religious propaganda by methods very similar to those of religious organizations. They work with the aid of literature, special study classes, regular lectures and discussions, and so forth. The Society forms its locals wherever it can get hold of a group of followers, and particularly directs its efforts upon the factory workers and the peasant population. It also has special sections for work among the non-Christian religions and the sectarians.

The Union of the Godless gets the full support of the Communist party and is actually but one of its propaganda organizations. It publishes a weekly paper, an illustrated biweekly, and a monthly magazine, giving direction and help for the work of teachers and agitators of atheism.

Has its work been successful and is atheism popular among the masses and the members of the Communist party? According to the statements of the leaders of the atheist movement, their propaganda faces great difficulties, on the one hand because of the disinterestedness of the party members, who think they have done their duty if they "subscribe" to atheism and show no outward signs of affiliation to any religious cult, and on the other because of the protests of the population. Thus in the Ukraine the party found it politically inexpedient to continue the existence of the Union of the Godless and closed it, seeking different and more indirect ways to continue their propaganda.

The crude mockery of religion as depicted in the cartoons of the atheistic press, the *Comsomol* (Communist Youth) Christmas carnivals, and the frequent unfair attacks on the Church had, on the whole, a result opposite from that desired. Many indifferent elements, who until then were rather apathetic, sided with religion. All this was quickly recognized by the party, and at its Thirteenth Conference (1925) it introduced a new policy of religious propaganda. The resolution outlining this policy says:

"It is necessary definitely to cease any kind of effort to fight religious prejudice by administrative means, such as the closing of churches, mosques, synagogues, and prayer-houses. The anti-religious propaganda in the village must have exclusively the character of a materialistic interpretation of the conditions which the peasant is familiar with. To explain the origin of hail, rain, storm, drouth, the appearance of harmful insects, the character of the soil, the role of fertilizers, and so forth, is the best kind of anti-religious propaganda. The center of such propaganda ought to be the school and the cottage reading-room under the direction of party organizations.

"It is necessary to watch with particular care that the religious feelings of believers should not be hurt. A victory over these can be obtained only through a long period of years of persistent educational work. Such care is particularly necessary in the eastern republics and provinces.

"Particularly close attention must be paid to the sectarians, many of whom were subjected to most cruel persecution under Czarism, and among whom is observed great activity. It is necessary to direct them into the channels of Soviet activity by tactful approach, for among the sectarians there is a considerable economic-cultural element. In view of the great mass of sectarians, this work is of great significance. This problem must be solved in relation to local conditions."

As a result the character of the anti-religious propaganda changed greatly. There is less of the vulgar mockery and a more real, though of course strongly biased, interpretation of nature and the history of man. The anti-religious papers are now publishing articles in popular sciences, anthropology, history of religion, and biblical criticism. . . .

242. A SOVIET PLAN FOR GENERAL DISARMAMENT, 1928 [29]

In 1928 Maxim Litvinov startled the fifth session of the Preparatory Commission of the Disarmament Conference by presenting a plan for the complete and absolute disarmament of all powers, to be carried out in either one or four years. Only Germany and Turkey supported the Soviet views, the others apparently feeling with Great Britain that the motive behind the scheme was simply to enable the Bolsheviks the better to carry on their international propaganda. The accompanying document is a reproduction of the official memorandum explaining the Soviet proposals.

[29] Union of Soviet Socialist Republics, *The Soviet Union and Peace,* International Publishers, New York, 1929, pp. 162-167. See also League of Nations, *Document C. P. D. 117* and *Minutes of the Fifth Session of the Preparatory Commission, C. 165, M. 50, 1928, IX.* Reprinted by permisssion of the International Publishers.

[Official Text of the] Memorandum Explaining the [Soviet Union's]
Draft Convention for General, Complete and
Immediate Disarmament.

1. The Draft Convention on General, Complete and Immediate Disarmament is based on the destruction of the principal elements which form the military power of a country, that is to say, the organised armed forces on land, on sea and in the air, their material, and the industries connected with the production of armaments.

The Draft Convention further provides that, at the close of a year after its coming into force, the land, naval, and air forces of all countries shall be reduced to an establishment which would be useless for warfare, thus limiting the possibility of armed conflict, even before disarmament has been completed.

2. The Draft Convention merely sets forth the general principles of disarmament applicable to the armed forces of all countries, without going into the details of each, on the supposition that, when the essential principles have been adopted, all these details will be dealt with in a subsequent discussion of the whole question of disarmament.

Thus in any case there is no need to work out the technical details, this being a matter for a special body to be set up after the Convention has come into force.

3. Chapter I of the Draft Convention embodies the principles of disarmament so far as they relate to effectives.

For the first year, it provides for the discharge of half the total establishment of officers, officials, and other ranks, the closing down of military schools, Ministries of War, Marine and Military Aviation, military staffs, commands, institutions and establishments, and, at the same time, the destruction of mobilisation plans for the armed forces and rolls of trained reserves.

By these means, armies and fleets will be reduced to a condition in which they cannot easily be used for attacks by one country on another. What is left of them will be principally occupied in effecting disarmament as regards material, the destruction of which requires a certain amount of personnel for work of all kinds.

In this connection, questions concerning the organisation of armed forces for carrying out the first stage of disarmament are looked upon as domestic questions for each country.

As regards armies organised on the territorial system, with small cadres periodically supplemented by variable effectives, disarmament will be carried out on the same principle, namely, that at the end of the first year fifty per cent of the cadres and fifty per cent of the trained reserves included in the variable effectives will be discharged.

For the rest, Chapter I of the Draft Convention develops and explains in detail the proposals put forward by the U.S.S.R. delegation at the fourth session of the Preparatory Commission for the Disarmament Conference.

4. Chapter II contains the most important provisions regarding the destruction of material:

(a) This chapter again contemplates the principal aspect of disarmament during the first stage—the destruction of all reserve stores intended for mobilisation, of which the first to be destroyed should be those that might be employed against the civil population.

(b) After the first stage of disarmament, the army of each country will retain such arms and munitions as are strictly necessary for the establishment maintained during the succeeding years. Moreover, the proportion of technical war material will be limited by a special convention. The object of this limitation, as of all the measures contemplated in Chapter I, is to prevent the armaments maintained during those years from being used for purposes of war.

(c) By the destruction of material is meant its reduction to a condition in which it cannot possibly be used for purposes of war.

The technique of the destruction of material will be worked out later in all its details, on the principle that the utmost possible use should be made of material which has value for purposes of other than military production, and for the increased welfare of peoples.

(d) Article 15 of the Draft Convention provides that sporting guns of non-military pattern and revolvers for sporting purposes and for self-defence may be retained. In view of the general social situation, these measures are particularly necessary in countries where communications are undeveloped.

(e) As regards naval armaments, the Draft Convention provides in the first place for the destruction of capital ships, cruisers, aircraft-carriers, etc., all of which are mostly used in the pursuit of imperialistic aims. The classes of warship enumerated above are removed from the effective battle fleet by the immediate discharge of the entire ship's company, which will limit the possibility of using them; thereafter, all the ship's artillery equipment will be put out of action and then removed and destroyed (the first to be removed will be the indispensable parts of the guns, gunlaying apparatus, fire-control apparatus, mine-laying and torpedo-firing apparatus, etc.). When the material is rendered useless, the munitions, mines and torpedoes will at the same time be destroyed. It will thus become impossible to use these warships for war purposes without lengthy preparation.

The Draft Convention allows of the use of disarmed warships as merchant vessels when necessary alterations have been made.

By dismantling warships is meant their disarmament by the removal of their armour plating, the destruction of special apparatus such as turrets, gun platforms, control positions *(roofs de guerre),* aircraft platforms, war signalling apparatus, and any other special devices for war purposes.

(f) The disarmament of military air forces involves in the first place the destruction of heavy aircraft as engines of war. Taking into consideration the social importance of aircraft as a means of communication, the Draft Convention does not make the destruction of the material essential to disarmament, since some of the aircraft can be converted to social and economic uses; but as there is no great difficulty in fitting aircraft for bomb-dropping, and as this can be done very quickly, the number of aircraft in the civil fleet must admittedly be proportionate to the country's genuine needs, and this is provided for in Article 28 of the Draft Convention.

(g) Fortifications and bases must be destroyed, since they can be used as places of arms for purposes of attack.

(h) The question of the destruction of military industries is particularly complicated because a highly-developed industry conceals great potential forces for the production of armaments. Here, again, however, there are a number of essential elements by the destruction of which the manufacture of armaments can be made very difficult. These include drawings, measuring instruments, models, frames, machines, tools, and appliances specially designed for the manufacture of armaments. Further, the actual demilitarisation of military factories, their use for the manufacture of non-military products, the employment in other factories of plant that is not specifically military, and the destruction of everything necessary for mobilisation preparations, will make it a very complicated matter to use these factories for war purposes.

5. Chapter III deals with the organisation of protection and, in this connection, in order to prevent any possibility of using the various forces for military purposes, or as a foundation for disguised military forces, the establishment of the police forces or militia, gendarmerie and other kinds of guards must be kept strictly within its present limits throughout the period of four years provided for the completion of general disarmament. Subsequently, the establishment of the Customs and fiscal guards and local police will be fixed by a special Convention.

Police forces of every kind must be armed with modern weapons, of the simplest pattern, because, if a more complicated armament were retained, it might be easier for these formations to be used as armed forces in attacks by stronger upon weaker countries.

Naval policing is regarded not as a matter to be dealt with separately by each country, but as providing for the needs of a whole group of countries, so that it cannot be turned to imperialistic ends. Maritime police will only be provided with the armament strictly necessary for the performance of their duties.

6. Although complete and general disarmament is wholly conditional upon the goodwill of all countries, it seems necessary to make definite arrangements for its successive stages and for the maintenance of proportions, and to establish a special body to work out the technical details of disarmament and settle any disputes that may arise.

With this object, Chapter IV of the Draft Convention lays down the principles of the control which is based upon extensive reciprocity, full publicity, and participation in the work by those classes of the population which are most interested in the speedy completion of disarmament.

As there is at present in the world no authority whose decisions must be obeyed by all countries, this status might be conferred upon a Permanent International Commission of Control—which, of course, presupposes the goodwill and the consent of all countries. The composition of this Commission would be a guarantee of impartiality in its decisions and, as there would be a Committee of Experts attached to it, technical questions could be quickly settled.

7. Chapter V contains suggestions for the conclusion of supplementary conventions on various questions connected with disarmament, and indicates the procedure for ratifying conventions and settling any questions arising out of violations.

It is this group of questions that are the most complicated; but the

Draft Convention does not allow of any military pressure being brought to bear on anybody, because such measures are apt to give rise to serious international conflicts, and it is hoped that most countries are so genuinely anxious to effect complete and general disarmament that other means will always be found to compel any country seeking to violate the obligations it has assumed to discharge them faithfully.

243. RECOGNITION OF THE U.S.S.R. BY THE UNITED STATES, 1933 [30]

At the beginning of 1933 the United States was the only great power that still withheld recognition from the Soviet Union. By that time the governments of both countries felt inclined to resume diplomatic intercourse—the American Government in the hope that new Soviet orders might help American business, the Soviet for reasons of prestige and because of the critical Far Eastern situation. When, therefore, President Franklin D. Roosevelt invited Moscow to send representatives to Washington to discuss the possibility of a resumption of diplomatic relations, the response was a prompt acceptance. Maxim Litvinov came to the United States and, after ten days of negotiations, diplomatic relations between the two states were formally reopened through an exchange of letters dated November 16, 1933. The action made little appreciable difference in American business or life.

. . . There were 3 days of conference between officials of the State Department and Mr. Litvinoff, and there were vastly more important and pivotal conversations between Mr. Litvinoff and President Roosevelt at the White House. There were no stenographers present and no reports made. . . .

There was an agreement touching the matter of subversive propaganda. . . . The agreement is expressed in one of Mr. Litvinoff's notes to the President. . . . He described it as a "fixed policy" coincident with the establishment of diplomatic relations . . . that his government would scrupulously respect the indisputable right of the United States to order its own life within its own jurisdiction, in its own way, and would refrain from interference in any manner in the internal affairs of the United States, its territories or possessions. . . .

[30] United States, Department of State, *Press Release,* November 25, 1933, pp. 287-293.

There was an agreement touching the religious rights of our nationals in Russia. . . . [The President asked] complete assurance that our nationals in Russia shall enjoy religious freedom. . . .

In reply he received . . . from Mr. Litvinoff a comprehensive summary of existing laws assuring the religious freedom of foreigners within the Soviet territory. To the ample security these laws afford if fairly administered there is a single exception, and as to that he stipulated that as a part of the "fixed policy" persons shall not be refused admission because of their ecclesiastical status, the President having said in his note that he would expect that religious groups or congregations in Russia should have their spiritual needs ministered to by clergymen, priests, rabbis, or other ecclesiastical functionaries, being nationals of the United States, and that such persons shall not be denied admission because they are ecclesiastics. Assuming as we must that the agreement will be observed, it is not perceived how our nationals of any denomination and their spiritual leaders will be under any disadvantage. . . .

Another matter to which the President gave particular attention is the treatment of our nationals in the Soviet Union who may be accused of criminal offense. As to that Mr. Litvinoff agreed that immediately following the establishment of relations between the two countries a consular convention should be negotiated giving our nationals rights with reference to legal protection not less favorable than those enjoyed by citizens of the nation most favored in that respect, and that such rights should be extended to our nationals immediately upon the establishment of relations between the two countries. These rights include notice to American consular officers of arrests of our nationals and the right of such officers to visit those under arrest, as now provided in a compact between the Soviet Union and Germany. In his reply note the President said that he was prepared to negotiate a convention on this matter, and he added that—

"American diplomatic and consular officers in the Soviet Union will be zealous in guarding the rights of American nationals, particularly the right to a fair, public and speedy trial and the right to be represented by a counsel of their choice. We shall expect that the nearest American diplomatic or consular officer shall be notified immediately of any arrest or detention of an American national, and that he shall promptly be afforded the opportunity to communicate and converse with such national."

Still another matter, that of economic espionage . . . having received much notice in connection with the recent trial of certain English en-

gineers in the Soviet Union, . . . Mr. Litvinoff gave an explanation in writing which removes the danger of any American being punished for disseminating economic information not obtained by criminal methods and not within the category of information which the Government has impressed with the stamp of secrecy.

. . . The Soviet Government agrees to take no steps to enforce decisions of courts or to start new litigation about amounts admitted to be due from American nationals, or that might be found due it, as the successor of prior governments of Russia or otherwise, and assign all such amounts to the Government of the United States. . . . Beyond this it was agreed that the Soviet Government shall not make any claim in respect to judgments rendered . . . by American courts in relation to property rights . . . in which the Soviet or its nationals may have had or may claim to have an interest, and shall not make any claim with respect to acts done or settlement made by or with the Govern ment of the United States, or public officials in the United States, or nationals, relating to property, credits, or obligations of any governme of Russia or nationals thereof. And beyond all of this the Soviet G ernment agreed to waive any and all claims arising out of activitie military forces in Siberia subsequent to January 1, 1918, and to reg them as finally settled. . . . Finally, there was a joint statemen the President and Mr. Litvinoff saying:

"In addition to the agreements which we have signed today, there has taken place an exchange of views with regard to methods of settling all outstanding questions of indebtedness and claims that permits us to hope for a speedy and satisfactory solution of these questions which both of our Governments desire to have out of the way as soon as possible. . . ."

244. MANIFESTO OF THE SIXTH WORLD CONGRESS OF THE COMMUNIST INTERNATIONAL, SEPTEMBER 1, 1928 [31]

The following "manifesto" is quoted as an example of the style and tactics employed by the Third International to fulfil its avowed mission of bringing about a world proletarian revolution.

[31] *International Press Correspondence,* English edition, Vienna, vol. 8, No. 92, December 31, 1928, pp. 1769-1771.

To the Workers of the World! To all Workers and Peasants!
To all Oppressed Colonial Peoples! To the Soldiers and Sailors of the
Capitalist Armies and Navies!

Comrades, Fellow Workers!

The Sixth Congress of the Communist International, the representative of the revolutionary workers all over the world, of all nations, peoples and races, appeals to you from Moscow, the red capital of the new world, to prepare yourselves for a struggle against the ever more insolent forces of capitalism.

The master of the world, capital, which exploits the labour power of the workers in the most brutal fashion, which sucks out their strength, which turns the proletarian into a unit of capitalist technique, which wears out its proletarian slaves in the process of production, which places the most wonderful discoveries of science in the service of the golden calf, which introduces ever more complicated and splendid machines, which introduces to an ever increasing extent the conveyor and flings millions of workers on to the streets, which gives them stones instead of bread, capital is now marching into the struggle against the rights and freedom of the working class. It is pressing the standard of living of the workers down ever lower, raising the bloody sword of the white terror and preparing for a new world war under the cloak of lying and bombastic phrases of world peace.

Imperialism has once again placed the question of war upon the agenda. From day to day the competition between the great powers and their finance-capitalist cliques is sharpening. Their attacks upon the colonies are becoming ever more brutal, their attempts to encircle the tremendous body of the Union of Soviet Socialist Republics ever more determined.

· · · · ·

Despite all the contradictions and antagonisms which exist between the capitalist powers, and despite their deep and growing mutual hatred, they are preparing with Great Britain at their head for a war against the Soviet Union. They are systematically preparing for war. They are preparing for war with all the means at their disposal. Every hour is filled with war preparations. The attempts of a number of powers, from the powerful United States to pitiful Austria, the mutilated invalid in the ranks of the European nations, to blockade the Soviet Union financially, the breaking off of diplomatic relations with the Soviet Union by Great Britain, the conclusion of diplomatic and military alliances against the Soviet Union, the constant provocative threats of the republic of Marshal Pilsudski, this insolent militarist who has placed the so-called representation of the people into the category of prostitution [32] and who rattles with the sabre to the same degree as he licks the boots of the generals and ministers of Great Britain and France, the almost open work of the General Staffs of the Entente in the Baltic states and in Roumania, and finally the insolent provocations of Japanese imperialism—all these things must act as a warning to all honest workers, for all proletarians and all the oppressed all over the world who see in the Soviet Union their fatherland wrung from the hands of the capitalists and rich landowners by the hot blood of the sons of the working class.

· · · · ·

The history of humanity has never known anything so hypocritical and sanctimonious, so lying and disgusting as the present ideology of modern "pacifist" imperialism, whose foreign political tasks consist in the most criminal, most barbarous, most counter-revolutionary, most destructive form of warfare ever known. The more furious the armament race becomes, the more energetic become the official and unofficial agents of imperialism in their howls of "peace" and in the production of "peace pacts" and in the organization of conferences and discussions, in the elaboration of projects and proposals for "peace."

The "League of Nations," the product of Versailles, the most shameless robber treaty of the last decades, cloaks the warlike work of its members by working out projects for disarmament. The Soviet Union has exposed this game: the great friends of peace refused to disarm when their bluff was called.[33] The diplomatic comedy turned into a vulgar farce. The mask of peace fell to the ground and the brutal features of imperialism were revealed to the whole world.

· · · · ·

The Communist International appeals to all toilers, and in particular to the industrial workers, to take up the struggle for every inch of ground that has been won, to fight against the offensive of capitalism, to fight against the ruthless exploitation of capitalism, to fight against the enslavement of the proletariat, to fight against the policy of the imperialists and against imperialist war. The Communist International

---

[32] A reference to an uncomplimentary remark of Pilsudski's aimed at the deputies in the Polish Parliament.—*Ed.*

[33] The reference is to the cold reception accorded the Soviet disarmament proposals summarized in Document No. 242 above.—*Ed.*

appeals to all workers and to all oppressed peoples devotedly to defend the Chinese revolution, whose heroes and martyrs have fallen under the axe of the executioner. The Communist International appeals to all honest proletarians to form a wall of iron around the Soviet Union against which imperialism is raising the sword of war. The Communist International appeals for increased watchfulness and for a direct fight against the pacifist lies and pacifist deception. The Communist International appeals for a complete break with the bourgeoisie and for the unity of the ranks of the workers in a ruthless struggle against the class enemies of the proletariat.

Against the social democratic unity with the bourgeoisie—for the class unity of the proletarians!

Against social imperialism—for the heroic support of our brothers in the colonies!

Against the pacifist lies—for the devoted fight against the imperialist war!

Against reformism and fascism—for the proletarian revolution!

Long live the proletarian dictatorship in the Soviet Union!

Long live the proletarian world revolution!

Moscow, September 1, 1928.

SIXTH WORLD CONGRESS OF THE COMMUNIST INTERNATIONAL.

245. THE COMMUNIST INTERNATIONAL AND THE ADVOCACY OF THE UNITED FRONT, 1935

At the meeting of the Congress of the Third International in 1935, the communists decided that the fascist advance could best be stemmed through the co-operation of all labor groups, moderate as well as radical, in a united front. Except in Spain, and for a while in France, these overtures were not especially well received by the more moderate labor organizations. (See, for example, Document No. 93.)

A. REPORT BY COMRADE GEORGI DIMITROV (AUGUST 2, 1935) ON *THE OFFENSIVE OF FASCISM AND THE TASKS OF THE C. I. IN THE STRUGGLE FOR THE UNITY OF THE WORKING CLASS AGAINST FASCISM* [34]

Comrades, millions of workers and toilers of the capitalist countries

---

[34] *International Press Correspondence,* English edition, London, vol. 15, No. 37, August 20, 1935, p. 963.

ask the question: How can fascism be prevented from coming to power and how can fascism be overthrown after it has been victorious? To this the Communist International replies: The first thing that must be done, the thing with which to commence, is to form a united front to establish unity of action of the workers in every factory, in every district, in every region, in every country, all over the world. Unity of action of the proletariat on a national and international scale is the mighty weapon which renders the working class capable not only of successful defence but also of successful counter-offensive against fascism, against the class enemy.

Importance of the United Front

Is it not clear that joint action by the adherents of the parties and organisations of the two Internationals, the Communist and the Second International,[35] would facilitate the repulse of the masses to the fascist onslaught, and would enhance the political importance of the working class?

Joint action by the parties of both Internationals against fascism, however, would not be confined to influencing their present adherents, the Communists and Social-Democrats; it would also exert a powerful influence on the ranks of the Catholic, anarchist and unorganised workers, even on those who had temporarily become the victims of fascist demagogy.

Moreover, a powerful united front of the proletariat would exert tremendous influence on all other strata of the toiling people, on the peasantry, on the urban petty bourgeoisie, the intelligentsia. A united front would inspire the wavering groups with faith in the strength of the working class.

But even this is not all. The proletariat of the imperialist countries has possible allies not only in the toilers of its own countries but also in the oppressed nations of the colonies and semi-colonies. Inasmuch as the proletariat is split both nationally and internationally, inasmuch as one of its parts supports the policy of collaboration with the bourgeoisie, in particular its system of oppression in the colonies and semi-colonies, this alienates from the working class the oppressed peoples of the colonies and semi-colonies and weakens the world anti-imperialist front. Every step on the road to unity of action directed towards the support of the

---

[35] The Second International, with which at one time were affiliated most of the Socialist and Labor parties of the world, was established in 1889. Its activities received a check during the World War, but it was revived in 1919. It expressed hostility to the program and methods of the Third (Communist) International.—*Ed.*

struggle for the liberation of the colonial peoples on the part of the proletariat of the imperialist countries, denotes the transformation of the colonies and semi-colonies into one of the most important reserves of the world proletariat.

If finally we take into consideration that international unity of action by the proletariat relies on the steadily growing strength of a proletarian state, the land of socialism, the Soviet Union, we see what broad perspectives are revealed by the realisation of united action on the part of the proletariat on a national and international scale. The establishment of unity of action by all sections of the working class irrespective of their party or organisational affiliations is necessary even before the majority of the working class is united in the struggle for the overthrow of capitalism and the victory of the proletarian revolution.

· · · · · ·

What objections can the opponents of the united front have and how do they voice their objections?

Some say: "To the Communists the slogan of the united front is merely a manœuvre." But if it is a manœuvre, we reply, why don't you expose the "Communist manœuvre" by your honest participation in a united front? We declare frankly: "We want unity of action by the working class, so that the proletariat may grow strong in its struggle against the bourgeoisie in order that while defending to-day its current interests against attacking capital, against fascism, the proletariat may be in a position tomorrow to create the preliminary conditions for its final emancipation."

B. RESOLUTION OF THE CONGRESS (AUGUST 20, 1935) ON THE REPORT OF DIMITROV [36]

In the face of the towering menace of fascism to the working class and all the gains it has made, to all toilers and their elementary rights, to the peace and liberty of the peoples, the Seventh Congress of the Communist International declares that *at the present historical stage it is the main and immediate task of the international labour movement to establish the united fighting front of the working class.* For a successful struggle against the offensive of capital, against the reactionary measures of the bourgeoisie, against fascism, the bitterest enemy of the toilers, who, without distinction of political views, have been deprived of all

---

[36] *International Press Correspondence,* English edition, London, vol. 15, No. 46, September 19, 1935, p. 1178.

rights and liberties, it is imperative that unity of action be established between all sections of the working class, irrespective of what organisation they belong to, even before the majority of the working class unites on a common fighting platform for the overthrow of capitalism and the victory of the proletarian revolution. But it is precisely for this reason that this task makes it the duty of the Communist Parties to take into consideration the changed circumstances and to apply the united front tactics *in a new manner,* by seeking to reach agreements with the organisations of the toilers of various political trends for joint action on a factory, local, district, national and international scale.

卍 卍 卍

INDEX

INDEX